# Management of a Sales Force

**Alreck & Settle**
The Survey Research Handbook,
*2/E*

**Anderson, Hair & Bush**
Professional Sales Management,
*2/E*

**Arens**
Contemporary Advertising,
*7/E*

**Bearden, Ingram & LaForge**
Marketing: Principles & Perspectives,
*2/E*

**Belch & Belch**
Introduction to Advertising and Promotion: An Integrated Marketing Communications Approach,
*4/E*

**Berkowitz, Kerin, Hartley & Rudelius**
Marketing,
*5/E*

**Bernhardt & Kinnear**
Cases in Marketing Management,
*7/E*

**Bowersox & Closs**
Logistical Management,
*1/E*

**Bowersox & Cooper**
Strategic Marketing Channel Management,
*1/E*

**Boyd, Walker & Larreche**
Marketing Management: A Strategic Approach with a Global Orientation,
*3/E*

**Cateora & Graham**
International Marketing,
*10/E*

**Churchill, Ford & Walker**
Sales Force Management,
*5/E*

**Churchill & Peter**
Marketing,
*2/E*

**Cole & Mishler**
Consumer and Business Credit Management,
*11/E*

**Cravens**
Strategic Marketing,
*5/E*

**Cravens, Lamb & Crittenden**
Strategic Marketing Management Cases,
*6/E*

**Crawford**
New Products Management,
*5/E*

**Dillon, Madden & Firtle**
Essentials of Marketing Research,
*1/E*

**Dillon, Madden & Firtle**
Marketing Research in a Marketing Environment,
*3/E*

**Douglas & Craig**
Global Marketing Strategy,
*1/E*

**Dwyer & Tanner**
Business Marketing,
*1/E*

**Etzel, Walker & Stanton**
Marketing,
*11/E*

**Futrell**
ABC's of Relationship Selling,
*5/E*

**Futrell**
Fundamentals of Selling,
*6/E*

**Gretz, Drozdeck & Weisenhutter**
Professional Selling: A Consultative Approach,
*1/E*

**Guiltinan & Paul**
Cases in Marketing Management,
*1/E*

**Guiltinan, Paul & Madden**
Marketing Management Strategies and Programs,
*6/E*

**Hasty & Reardon**
Retail Management,
*1/E*

**Hawkins, Best & Coney**
Consumer Behavior: Building Marketing Strategy
*7/E*

**Hayes, Jenster & Aaby**
Business to Business Marketing,
*1/E*

**Johansson**
Global Marketing,
*1/E*

**Johnson, Kurtz & Scheuing**
Sales Management: Concepts, Practices & Cases,
*2/E*

**Kinnear & Taylor**
Marketing Research: An Applied Approach,
*5/E*

**Lambert & Stock**
Strategic Logistics
Management,
*3/E*

**Lambert, Stock, & Ellram**
Fundamentals of Logistics
Management,
*1/E*

**Lehmann & Winer**
Analysis for Marketing
Planning,
*4/E*

**Lehmann & Winer**
Product Management,
*2/E*

**Levy & Weitz**
Retailing Management,
*3/E*

**Levy & Weitz**
Essentials of Retailing,
*1/E*

**Loudon & Della Bitta**
Consumer Behavior: Concepts
& Applications,
*4/E*

**Mason, Mayer & Ezell**
Retailing,
*5/E*

**Mason & Perreault**
The Marketing Game!,
*2/E*

**McDonald**
Direct Marketing: An
Integrated Approach,
*1/E*

**Meloan & Graham**
International and Global
Marketing Concepts and Cases,
*2/E*

**Monroe**
Pricing,
*2/E*

**Moore & Pessemier**
Product Planning and
Management
*1/E*

**Oliver**
Satisfaction: A Behavioral
Perspective on the Consumer,
*1/E*

**Patton**
Sales Force: A Sales Management Simulation Game,
*1/E*

**Pelton, Strutton &
Lumpkin**
Marketing Channels: A
Relationship Management
Approach,
*1/E*

**Perreault & McCarthy**
Basic Marketing: A Global
Managerial Approach,
*13/E*

**Perreault & McCarthy**
Essentials of Marketing: A
Global Managerial Approach,
*7/E*

**Peter & Donnelly**
A Preface to Marketing
Management,
*7/E*

**Peter & Donnelly**
Marketing Management:
Knowledge and Skills,
*5/E*

**Peter & Olson**
Consumer Behavior and
Marketing Strategy,
*5/E*

**Peter & Olson**
Understanding Consumer
Behavior,
*1/E*

**Quelch**
Cases in Product
Management,
*1/E*

**Quelch, Dolan & Kosnik**
Marketing Management: Text
& Cases,
*1/E*

**Quelch, Kashani &
Vandermerwe**
European Cases in Marketing
Management,
*1/E*

**Rangan**
Business Marketing Strategy:
Cases, Concepts &
Applications,
*1/E*

**Rangan, Shapiro &
Moriarty**
Business Marketing Strategy:
Concepts & Applications,
*1/E*

**Rossiter & Percy**
Advertising Communications
and Promotion Management,
*2/E*

**Stanton, Spiro, & Buskirk**
Management of a Sales Force,
*10/E*

**Sudman & Blair**
Marketing Research: A
Problem-Solving Approach,
*1/E*

**Ulrich & Eppinger**
Product Design and
Development,
*1/E*

**Walker, Boyd & Larreche**
Marketing Strategy: Planning
and Implementation,
*3/E*

**Weitz, Castleberry &
Tanner**
Selling: Building
Partnerships,
*3/E*

**Zeithaml & Bitner**
Services Marketing,
*1/E*

**TENTH EDITION**

# Management of a Sales Force

**William J. Stanton**
University of Colorado

**Rosann Spiro**
Indiana University

Boston   Burr Ridge, IL   Dubuque, IA   Madison, WI   New York  San Francisco   St. Louis
Bangkok   Bogotá   Caracas   Lisbon   London   Madrid
Mexico City   Milan   New Delhi   Seoul   Singapore   Sydney   Taipei   Toronto

*Irwin/McGraw-Hill*

A Division of The **McGraw·Hill** Companies

MANAGEMENT OF A SALES FORCE

Copyright © 1999 by The McGraw-Hill Companies, Inc. All rights reserved. Previous editions © 1959, 1964, 1969, 1974, 1978, 1983, 1987, 1991, and 1995, by Richard D. Irwin, a Times Mirror Higher Education Group, Inc. company. Printed in the United States of America. Except as permitted under the United States Copyright Act of 1976, no part of this publication may be reproduced or distributed in any form or by any means, or stored in a data base or retrieval system, without the prior written permission of the publisher.

This book is printed on acid-free paper.

1 2 3 4 5 6 7 8 9 0 DOC/DOC 9 3 2 1 0 9 8

ISBN 0-256-21896-X

Vice president/Editor-in-chief: *Michael W. Junior*
Publisher: *Gary Burke*
Sponsoring editor: *Karen Westover*
Editorial assistant: *Katharine Norwood*
Senior marketing manager: *Colleen J. Suljic*
Project manager: *Paula M. Buschman*
Production supervisor: *Scott M. Hamilton*
Art director: *Francis Owens*
Photo research coordinator: *Sharon Miller*
Photo freelancer: *Michelle Oberhoffer*
Supplement coordinator: *Carol Loreth*
Compositor: *Carlisle Communications, Ltd.*
Typeface: *10 / 12 Century Schoolbook*
Printer: *R.R. Donnelley & Sons Company*

**Library of Congress Cataloging-in-Publication Data**

Stanton, William J.
   Management of a sales force / William J. Stanton, Rosann Spiro,
  --10th ed.
     p.  cm.
   Includes bibliographical references and index.
   ISBN 0-256-21896-X
   1. Sales management. I. Spiro, Rosann L. II.
  Hobart, 1927-  .  III. Title.
  HF5438.4.S78 1998
  658.8′1—dc21               98-40414

http://www.mhhe.com

To: Imma and Rockney.

# About the Authors

**WILLIAM J. STANTON** is Professor Emeritus of Marketing at the University of Colorado in Boulder. He earned his M.B.A. and Ph.D. degrees at Northwestern University. For 35 years, Bill worked extensively with both undergraduate and graduate students at Colorado, developing teaching/learning materials and curricular programs.

As an extension of his teaching interests, he has worked in business and has taught in management development programs for sales and marketing executives. For many years he taught in management development programs sponsored by Sales and Marketing Executives—International, including the Field Sales Management Institute (for middle-level sales executives) and the Graduate School of Sales and Marketing Management (for top-level sales and marketing executives).

Bill also designed, coordinated, and taught in the first management development programs sponsored by Advanced Management Research for sales executives. He has served as a consultant for business organizations and has engaged in research projects for the federal government.

Bill has lectured at universities in Europe, Asia, Mexico, and New Zealand and has written various journal articles and monographs. One of his other books, a widely used principles of marketing text, has been translated into Spanish, Portuguese, Italian, and Indonesian; and separate editions have been adapted (with co-authors) especially for students in Canada, Australia, and Italy.

In a survey of marketing educators, Bill Stanton was voted one of the top seven leaders in marketing thought. He is listed in *Who's Who in America* and *Who's Who in the World.* In his "spare" time, Bill thoroughly enjoys jogging, downhill skiing, gardening, and traveling.

**ROSANN L. SPIRO** is a Professor of Marketing at the Kelley School of Business, Indiana University in Bloomington, Indiana, where she teaches Sales Management, Business-to-Business Marketing, International Marketing, and Managerial Research in Marketing. After receiving her undergraduate degree in Economics and an M.B.A. in Marketing from Indiana, she joined the Shell Oil Company as a Senior Analyst/Statistician in the Economics and Planning Department. She then moved on to the more exciting area of sales: as the first woman to become a Shell Oil sales representative, she sold a wide variety of products to major industrial accounts.

In 1973, when the national oil crisis caused a shortage of products to sell, Rosann returned to school, earning a Ph.D. degree in Marketing from the University of Georgia. She then taught at the University of Tennessee and subsequently moved to Indiana University. She also spent a year at the University of Arhus in Denmark as a Visiting Professor of Marketing. She has lectured at universities and institutes in western, central, and eastern Europe as well as South Africa. Rosann is a well-known author whose work in marketing has appeared in numerous national and international publications. She won the Outstanding Article of the Year in the *Journal of Personal Selling & Sales Management* in 1996, 1986, and 1981. She is on the editorial review boards of the *Journal of Marketing,* the *Journal of Personal Selling & Sales Management,* and *Marketing Management.*

Currently Rosann is the Vice President of the World Marketing Association and the Vice President of Global Relations for the American Marketing Association. She has also served as President of the World Marketing Association and as Chairperson of the Board of the American Marketing Association as well as Vice President of the Education Division and as a member of the Advisory Board for the Business Marketing Division of AMA. Currently she serves on an advisory board to the U.S. Census Bureau. She is a frequent consultant to businesses and participates in national and international management development programs.

Outside of work Rosann enjoys her family, jogging, tennis, skiing, sailing, and reading.

# Preface

## ▦ THIS BOOK—GEARED FOR THE TWENTY-FIRST CENTURY

The new edition of *Management of a Sales Force* is coming out at a time when we are entering a new century. The market environment in the new century will be dramatically different. The age and ethnic mixes of the population of the United States are changing considerably; the population is getting older and less white. By the beginning of the first decade of the twenty-first century, one-third of the American population will be part of a minority group. People's values are changing as we show more concern for our social and physical environments and our overall quality of life. Along with these changes, we now expect that leaders in government, business, and other institutions adhere to higher standards of ethical and social responsibility than in the past. In this next century, most businesses will be internationally oriented, buying from and/or selling to the global markets. Today the U.S. market has reached the saturation point for many consumer and industrial products; but new markets such as eastern Europe and China have opened up. European, Asian, and U.S. trade agreements have made it easier for companies to sell products and services in Europe, Asia, Central and South America, and Canada. Growth for many American companies in the twenty-first century will come from the Asian, European, and South and Central American markets. At the same time, competition in the United States from foreign competitors has greatly intensified.

New developments in communication and information technology are changing our everyday lives and our business practices. In the next decade, most salespeople will use some type of computer technology to assist them in serving their customers, and most sales managers will use computer technology to assist them in managing their salespeople. Customers too will be using new technologies, such as the Internet, to assist them in gathering product information and in making purchase decisions. The customers of the twenty-first century will demand higher quality and greater levels of service.

As a result of these economic and competitive pressures and the social and cultural changes, companies are being forced to become more market oriented—more responsive to the customer. The role of the sales force will expand greatly. The salesperson of the twenty-first century will be a professional who is as much a marketing consultant as a salesperson. These new salespeople will engage in consultative relationships with their customers. They will be expected to solve customer problems, not just sell products. Their focus will be on building long-term relationships with their customers. In many cases, companies will respond to their customers' needs by using *selling teams,* rather than a single salesperson.

As the nature of personal selling changes, so will the role of the sales manager. Tomorrow's sales managers will be viewed as *team leaders* rather than *bosses.* They will empower and collaborate with their salespeople rather than control and dominate them. Managers in the twenty-first century will be asked to manage multiple sales channels, such as telemarketing and electronic marketing as well as field salespeople. They will also assume a greater responsibility for directing and coordinating the marketing efforts of their firms.

Your career success will depend greatly on your ability to adapt to the environmental challenges and changes that will occur in the coming decade. The contents of this book can be valuable to you because you will use the knowledge contained in your sales course fairly immediately. Within a very few years many of you may well be some type of sales force manager, perhaps at a district level. Even as salespeople, you may be called upon to use material covered in this book. The year following your graduation, you may come back to your alma mater as a member of your firm's employee recruiting team. Or you may be called upon for suggestions regarding a proposed compensation, expense, or quota plan. We wrote this book to help make the transition from college to a professional selling career easier for you.

## WHAT'S NEW IN THIS EDITION

The tenth edition has been substantially revised to reflect the changing social and economic conditions that will present major challenges to sales force managers during the 2000s. Of the many new features in this edition, probably the most noticeable is the emphasis placed on **relationship selling** and particularly the use of **selling teams** to develop stronger relationships with customers. Many of the chapters have a highlighted box which discusses the principles within the chapter as they relate to managing selling teams. Some of the specific topics include:

- Keys to successful team selling.
- Organizational options for team selling.
- Recruiting for team selling.
- Hiring for the team.
- Training for team selling skills.

- Motivation for team selling.
- Compensating teams.
- Team leadership.
- Team selling and morale.

In this edition, we have also added a chapter on **personal selling.** This chapter focuses on the steps in the sales process, noting the differences between the techniques used in traditional transactional selling and those used in more complex relationship selling situations.

The cases have always been a strength of this book. Out of 54 cases, the 10th edition contains 16 new cases. All of these cases involve sales management problems faced by real companies. Five of these are longer, **integrative cases,** which have been placed in an appendix at the end of the book. The accompanying case-by-chapter grid indicates the chapters for which cases are most appropriate.

Many new figures, boxed materials, and other graphics have been added to make the book more readable and understandable. **Key terms** and **experiential exercises** have been added to the end of each chapter. Many new company examples illustrate the principles discussed in the text and many chapters contain new topics which reflect changing market conditions and new management practices. Some of these include:

- The concept of **relationship marketing** is discussed in greater depth in Chapters 1 and 2. For example, Chapter 2 includes a highlighted discussion on how to practice relationship marketing.
- An extensive discussion of **national account management** has been added as well as expanded coverage of **organizational options for international sales** (to Chapter 4).
- The latest trends in recruiting and selection are discussed including the use of **electronic databases** for recruiting and **performance-based interviews** in selection processes.
- The chapter on training now includes new sections on **relationship building skills, team selling skills, business skills,** and **computer-assisted selling skills.** There is also a new discussion of the **reinforcement of training** and a revised section on **training assessment** which reflects the trend toward **customization of training.**
- A discussion of **charisma** as it relates to leadership has been added (Chapter 12), and the concepts of **esprit de corps** and **corporate culture** have been added to the discussion of sales force morale (Chapter 13).
- In the discussion of forecasting, all of the examples have been updated, using 1997 data.

## ◼ STRUCTURE OF THIS BOOK

Those who are familiar with the earlier editions will find that we have retained the features that have made this text an outstanding teaching and learning resource. The writing style continues to make the book clear and interesting to read. The section-heading structure makes for easier reading and outlining. We still have the excellent end-of-chapter discussion questions. Most of these questions are thought-provoking and involve the application of text material, rather than being answerable "right out of the book." The issue-oriented cases provide an opportunity for problem solving and decision making, rather than being simply a vehicle for long-winded discussion of a company's action.

We have also retained the basic scope and organization that have made this book the market leader in the sales management field for over 20 years. With respect to its *scope, this book still is concerned specifically with the management of an outside sales force and its activities.* Because outside salespeople—those who go to the customers—are distinguished here from over-the-counter salespeople to whom the customers come, the book deals largely with the management of sales forces of manufacturers and wholesaling middlemen. Thus the scope of this book does *not* include any significant treatment of the broader fields of marketing management.

The tenth edition continues the *real-world approach* that has successfully characterized previous editions. Students who learn from this book can talk to sales executives in the business world, and sales executives appreciate the material in this book. In fact, this book has been used in many executive development programs for sales managers.

The text is divided into five main parts:

1. **Introduction to sales force management.** The three chapters in this section set the scene for the rest of the book. Chapter 1 covers the nature, scope, and importance of personal selling and sales force management. This opening chapter also sets forth our basic managerial philosophy, which permeates the entire book. We believe that staffing—the selection of personnel at any level in organization—is the *most* important function of administrators. In Chapter 2 we discuss strategic planning and the role of sales force planning as it relates to marketing planning and total-company planning. Chapter 3 presents the steps in the personal selling process.

2. **Organizing, staffing, and training a sales force.** Part II (Chapters 4 to 8) covers the first steps in operating a sales force. The major types of sales organizational structures and additional strategic organizational alternatives are treated in Chapter 4. The task of selecting salespeople is discussed in some detail over the next two chapters. A separate chapter (7) is devoted to the key tasks of actually hiring the selected sales reps and socially assimilating them

into the sales force. The development of a sales training program is the topic of Chapter 8.

3. **Directing sales force operations.** In this part (Chapters 9 to 13) we continue our discussion of operating a sales force. We start with the conceptual and practical aspects of sales force motivation. One chapter is devoted to compensating a sales force, followed by a chapter on sales force expenses and transportation. We conclude Part III with coverage of leadership and supervision of a sales force and a chapter on sales force morale.

4. **Sales planning.** This section (Chapters 14 to 16) begins with an explanation of why we place sales planning after sales operations in the book. Part IV covers sales planning activities, starting with estimating market demand and sales forecasting. Then we discuss the design and coverage of sales territories, and we conclude with the subject of sales budgets and quotas.

5. **Evaluating sales performance.** The final stage in the management process of planning–implementation–evaluation is covered in Part V (Chapters 17 to 20). This part includes a sales volume analysis of an organization's total sales performance, a marketing cost and profitability analysis, and an evaluation of the performance of individual salespeople. The final chapter is a macroevaluation of sales force management in which we discuss ethical and legal responsibilities facing sales managers.

Following the text are two appendixes:

**Appendix A: Integrative cases.** This appendix includes five lengthy integrative cases which may be used in conjunction with several different chapters. Included at the beginning of the appendix is a grid that suggests which chapters the integrative cases supplement.

**Appendix B: Careers in sales management.** This appendix discusses the opportunities and challenges of a career in sales management. It describes typical career paths and the everyday life of a sales executive. It also describes what it takes to be a successful sales manager.

## TEACHING SUPPLEMENTS

An extensive *Instructor's Teaching Supplement* has been prepared to accompany the tenth edition of *Management of a Sales Force*. The teaching supplement includes:

- Case notes.
- Answers to end-of-chapter questions.
- Suggestions for experiential exercises, including exercises that utilize the Internet.

- Suggestions for role-playing exercises.
- Managerial decision problems appropriate for spreadsheet analysis and suggested answers.
- Transparency masters, which are also available on powerpoint.
- An extensive, revised test bank of objective true–false and multiple-choice questions.
- Computest—A computerized version of the test bank is available upon request to all adopters. Computest allows the instructor to tailor and edit the exam questions to meet specific class needs.

*Videotapes* available with *Management of a Sales Force* depict selling and sales management situations. The *Sales Force–Sales Management Simulation* developed by Wesley Patton is also available as a teaching supplement.

## ACKNOWLEDGMENTS

Many people contributed directly to the improvements in this edition. Several of the cases were prepared by other professors and students, and in each instance their authorship is identified with the case. The concept of the Majestic Plastics Company problems and the first set of these incidents used in earlier editions were originally developed by Phillip McVey when he was at the University of Nebraska–Lincoln. George R. Cook of the Xerox Corporation contributed several ideas, as well as supplying the Xerox company forms that nicely illustrate several concepts in the sales force selection chapters. Dick Canada, a former Sales Training Manager for Xerox and currently Chairperson of Dartnell Corporation, contributed ideas for the training chapter and wrote one of the training cases. We also are grateful to William D. Perreault Jr. (University of North Carolina at Chapel Hill) for his participation in preparing the spreadsheet problems.

Through the years, many sales executives, present and past colleagues, and other professors have contributed greatly to this book. Many of these debts are acknowledged in footnotes and other references throughout the text. Perhaps, however, our greatest debt is to our students who have used this text. Their suggestions, constructive criticisms—and yes, sometimes even their complaints—have led to many changes and improvements in the book. To all these people we are deeply grateful.

We would also like to extend our sincere thanks to all those people who offered valuable critiques and thoughtful recommendations in the reviewing process of the revision. Their efforts have helped to create a strong and effective tenth edition of *Management of a Sales Force*. We would especially like to thank the following people:

Avery Abernethy—Auburn University
Ramon Avila—Ball State University

Andrew Brogowicz—Western Michigan University
Ned Cooney—University of Colorado at Boulder
Mort Ettinger—Salem State College
David Good—Central Missouri State University
Darrell Goudge—University of Central Oklahoma
Alicia Gresham—Stephen F. Austin State University
Thomas Leigh—University of Georgia
Victor Massad—University of North Texas
Ronald E. Michaels—University of Central Florida
Lori Millet—Bay State College
Greg Rich—Bowling Green State University
Robert Roe—University of Wyoming
Winston Stahlecker—Western Texas A & M
Eugene Teeple—University of Central Florida
Nick Williamson—University of North Carolina–Greensboro

Finally, we would also like to thank Brenda Crohn, whose skills made the original WordPerfect manuscript really look . . . perfect. Finally, we would like to recognize, with grateful appreciation, the creative efforts of the people at McGraw-Hill. We especially want to thank Karen Westover, our sponsoring editor, who kept us going through two mergers, Irwin and McGraw-Hill as well as her own marriage. We also appreciate the efforts of Katharine Norwood, editorial assistant, and those of Paula Buschman, our project manager, for working with us in a patient, gracious, and most helpful manner.

William J. Stanton
Rosann L. Spiro

# CONTENTS

# PART II

## ORGANIZING, STAFFING AND TRAINING A SALES FORCE 79

# PART III
## DIRECTING SALES FORCE OPERATIONS 250

## PART IV
## SALES PLANNING  388

# PART V
# EVALUATING SALES PERFORMANCE 479

# Management of a Sales Force

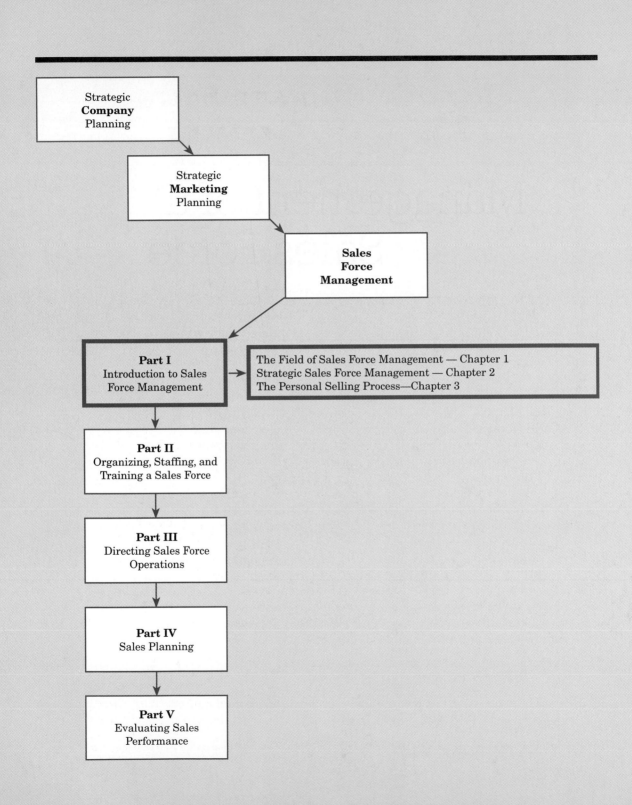

Strategic **Company** Planning

Strategic **Marketing** Planning

**Sales Force Management**

**Part I**
Introduction to Sales Force Management

The Field of Sales Force Management — Chapter 1
Strategic Sales Force Management — Chapter 2
The Personal Selling Process—Chapter 3

**Part II**
Organizing, Staffing, and Training a Sales Force

**Part III**
Directing Sales Force Operations

**Part IV**
Sales Planning

**Part V**
Evaluating Sales Performance

# PART 1

# INTRODUCTION TO SALES FORCE MANAGEMENT

For firms with an outside sales force, the activities involved in personal selling typically include more people and cost more money than any other phase of the firm's marketing program. Moreover, the success experienced by the salespeople usually is a major factor in determining the success enjoyed by the firm. Consequently, sales force management—the topic of this book—is a very important part of a company's total management effort.

Part I of this book, consisting of three chapters, introduces the field of sales force management. Chapter 1 starts with a statement of the scope and focus of this book. We then discuss the nature of personal selling—the wide variety of sales jobs and how they differ from other jobs. Next, we talk about sales managers—their role as administrators and how their job is distinctive. The chapter ends with a set of challenges which will be faced by sales managers in the 21st century.

Before sales managers can make strategic decisions about their sales forces, they first should understand how the marketing system works in their companies. Chapter 2 deals with these relationships, starting with a marketing system and its environment. Objectives, strategies, and tactics then are discussed in relation to strategic planning and tactical operations. To conclude, we consider relationships in strategic planning at companywide, marketing, and sales force levels, and discuss the latest strategic trends in sales management. Chapter 3 details the eight steps of the sales process and highlights the differences between the simple, one-time sale and more complex sales.

## ■ PLAN OF THIS BOOK

The management process in any organization consists basically of three stages, as shown in Figure 1: planning a program, implementing it, and

■ **FIGURE 1**              **The management process**

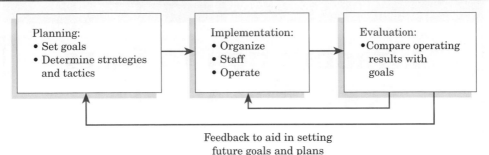

Feedback to aid in setting
future goals and plans

evaluating its results. The **planning** stage includes setting goals and deciding how to reach them. **Implementation** includes organizing and staffing the organization and directing the actual operations of the organization. The **evaluation** stage is a good example of the interrelated, continuing nature of the management process. That is, evaluation is both a look back and a look ahead. Looking back, management compares the operating results with the plans and goals. Looking ahead, this evaluation is used as an aid in future strategic planning.

This book follows the management process as it relates to the strategic management of an outside sales force. The particular model we use to structure this book is shown in Figure 2. Note that sales force management must be placed within the context of marketing strategy and overall company strategy. As you read through the model, you may wonder why sales planning comes so late in the book. If planning is the first stage in the management process, then why doesn't the section on sales planning appear after Chapter 2? Why does planning *follow,* instead of precede, Parts II and III on sales organization, staffing, and operations?

There is no question but that logically sales planning should follow Chapter 2. But *pedagogically*—that is, from a teaching and learning point of view—we believe it is better to cover sales force staffing and operations before getting into sales planning. We believe that will make this course and this book far more interesting to you—the student. The topics in staffing and operating typically generate student interest and embody the challenge and dynamism that is modern sales force management. To start early in the course with sales planning, including demand forecasting and budgeting and territorial design, might suggest that sales management is all statistics and accounting.

There is another basic reason for stressing the importance of staffing and operations—the implementation stage of the management process. Most middle-level and lower-level sales executives spend the bulk of their time on staffing and operational matters, not on the planning or evaluation stages of the management process. Also, the cost of staffing and operating a sales force is by far the largest single marketing cost in most firms.

■ **FIGURE 2**          **The plan of this book**

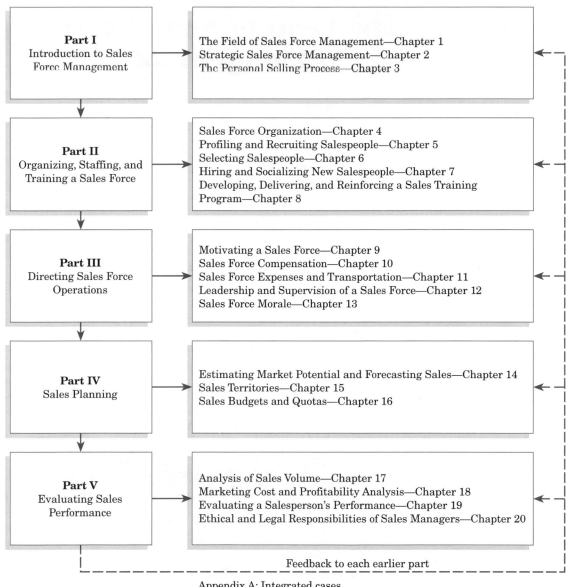

| Part I<br>Introduction to Sales<br>Force Management | The Field of Sales Force Management—Chapter 1<br>Strategic Sales Force Management—Chapter 2<br>The Personal Selling Process—Chapter 3 |
| Part II<br>Organizing, Staffing, and<br>Training a Sales Force | Sales Force Organization—Chapter 4<br>Profiling and Recruiting Salespeople—Chapter 5<br>Selecting Salespeople—Chapter 6<br>Hiring and Socializing New Salespeople—Chapter 7<br>Developing, Delivering, and Reinforcing a Sales Training<br>Program—Chapter 8 |
| Part III<br>Directing Sales Force<br>Operations | Motivating a Sales Force—Chapter 9<br>Sales Force Compensation—Chapter 10<br>Sales Force Expenses and Transportation—Chapter 11<br>Leadership and Supervision of a Sales Force—Chapter 12<br>Sales Force Morale—Chapter 13 |
| Part IV<br>Sales Planning | Estimating Market Potential and Forecasting Sales—Chapter 14<br>Sales Territories—Chapter 15<br>Sales Budgets and Quotas—Chapter 16 |
| Part V<br>Evaluating Sales<br>Performance | Analysis of Sales Volume—Chapter 17<br>Marketing Cost and Profitability Analysis—Chapter 18<br>Evaluating a Salesperson's Performance—Chapter 19<br>Ethical and Legal Responsibilities of Sales Managers—Chapter 20 |

Feedback to each earlier part

Appendix A: Integrated cases
Appendix B: Careers in Sales Management

# CHAPTER 1

# The Field of Sales Force Management

The best executive is the one who has enough sense to pick good people to do what he wants done and self-restraint enough to keep from meddling with them while they do it.

**Theodore Roosevelt**

As we move into the 21st century, the world of professional selling is changing dramatically. Much of this change is driven by shifts in the way customers, particularly business customers, buy products. Customers are more sophisticated and more demanding than in the past. They no longer focus on just buying products; rather they are more interested in finding solutions to their business problems. They expect suppliers and salespeople to help them find solutions to their problems.

Additionally, although the number of competitors in most product categories has grown tremendously, companies are using fewer sources of supply. In the past most companies had a large supplier base, often pitting one company against another to drive prices down. Today customers form strategic partnerships with a smaller set of suppliers that can work together to provide greater value to the end customer. For example, in recent years, Xerox cut the number of its suppliers by 90 percent, from 5,000 to 500; Motorola cut its suppliers by 70 percent; and General Motors cut its suppliers by 45 percent.[1]

Along with using fewer sources of supply, business customers are increasingly purchasing some products from foreign producers. As fewer sources of supply are used and foreign companies enter domestic markets, the competition among suppliers has intensified greatly. Adding to these competitive pressures is the rapid transfer of technology, which enables competitors to copy each other's products much more quickly than in the past. As a result, competing products are not as distinctive from one another as they used to be.

With less product differentiation and greater customer and competitive pressures, the selling task will become increasingly difficult and complex. Large accounts will require more sophisticated selling. Smaller, less profitable accounts will often be served through low-cost channels of distribution and communication, such as telemarketing, direct marketing, and electronic marketing. The sales force must be able to identify and develop relationships with the high profit potential accounts. *Successful companies will distin-*

---

### Changes in Purchasing Patterns in the 21st Century

■ Finding solutions rather than products     ■ Forming strategic partnerships with suppliers
■ Narrowing sources of supply               ■ Using more foreign sources of supply

---

*guish themselves by the relationships they develop with their customers.* This means that managing the sales force will become more important to the ultimate success of most companies. *Sales management is primarily responsible for what happens when the salesperson or selling team meets the customer.*

Along with changes in their approach to customers, salespeople will change themselves. They will have more in-depth customer knowledge and more sophisticated selling and service skills. As a result, salespeople will be higher paid, more highly trained, and more skilled professionals.

The success that sales executives enjoy as they enter the 21st century will depend largely on their ability to enable, support, and assist salespeople in developing profitable relationships with their customers. To introduce the dynamic field of sales force management, we start this chapter by explaining the scope and focus of the book.

## ■ SCOPE AND FOCUS OF THIS BOOK

This is a book about sales management—also called sales force management. *We define sales management as the management of the personal-selling component of an organization's marketing program.* The central focus of the book is the design of sales management strategies and tactics that will help an organization achieve its marketing goals.

Specifically, this book deals with the management of a sales force that calls on prospective customers. This contrasts with situations in which customers come to the salespeople—called across-the-counter selling. This book deals almost entirely with the management of what is known as an **outside sales force.** Such a sales force makes in-person sales calls, usually at the customer's place of business or home. Managing an outside sales force presents a unique set of problems, since most of the salespeople are geographically outside the organization's offices.

Most outside sales forces belong to producers and wholesaling middlemen who sell to business users rather than to household consumers. However, our definition of an outside sales force also includes (1) producers who sell directly to household consumers (e.g., insurance companies such as Prudential or Metropolitan Life and in-home sellers such as Avon Products); (2) retail salespeople (such as aluminum siding dealers) who go to prospective customers; and (3) outside sales forces for nonprofit organizations (e.g., fund raisers, college athletic recruiters, religious missionaries, and workers for political candidates). See Figure 1-1.

■ **FIGURE 1-1**

Scope of
personal
selling

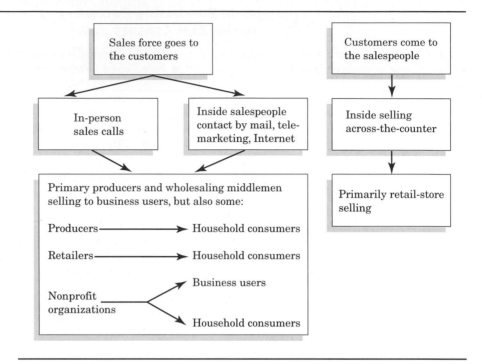

Today many firms are using a sales force that goes to the customers, but not with in-person sales calls. Instead, salespeople are "going to the customers" by means of telephone, computer, cable television, and facsimile (fax) machines. In effect, some outside selling is becoming electronic, and the terms **telemarketing** and **electronic marketing** have been coined to describe such communications systems. Many firms have used telephone selling for decades, and sales reps have for years contacted some customers periodically by mail or telephone. What is new about telemarketing and electronic marketing is the innovative use of telecommunications equipment to aid in the going-to-the-customer selling effort.

## ■ THE NATURE OF PERSONAL SELLING

We just said that sales management is the management of the personal selling effort in an organization. So let's begin by looking at some aspects of personal selling to see what it is that sales managers manage.

### Personal Selling and the Marketing Mix

The term **marketing mix** describes the combination of four ingredients that constitute the core of a company's marketing system. When these four—product, price, distribution, and promotion—are effectively blended, they form a marketing program that provides want-satisfying goods and services to the company's market.

Promotional activities form a separate submix that we call the **promotional mix,** or the **communications mix,** in the company's marketing program. The major elements in the promotional mix are the company's advertising, sales promotion, and personal selling effort. Publicity and public relations are also part of the promotional activities, but typically they are less widely used than the first three elements. In the American economy, personal selling is the most important of the big three elements in terms of people employed, dollars spent, or sales generated.

## Relationship Marketing and the Role of Personal Selling

In the face of intense competition, companies today are trying to improve their performance in every dimension of their operations. As a result, companies expect more from their suppliers. Salespeople who represent these suppliers are expected to make a contribution to their customers' success. To do this, salespeople must understand their customers' needs and be able to discover and/or help customers solve their problems.

At the same time, companies are finding it harder to develop or sustain product-based competitive advantages. Most product-based advantages are soon copied by competitors. Thus companies must focus on strengthening the value-added components of their offerings. **Value-added components** are those which augment the product itself, such as information and service.

To understand customer needs and to provide customers with value-added solutions to their problems, salespeople must develop close, long-term relationships with their customers. These relationships are built on *cooperation, trust, commitment,* and *sharing information.* The process by which a firm builds long-term relationships with customers for the purpose of creating mutual competitive advantages is called **relationship marketing,** or **relationship selling.** Salespeople who are engaged in relationship selling concentrate their efforts on developing trust in a few carefully selected accounts over an extended period of time, rather than calling on a larger number of accounts. Relationship selling is distinctive from the traditional **transaction selling,** whereby salespeople focus on the immediate one-time sale of the product. These differences are presented below:[2]

| **Transaction-Oriented** | **Relationship-Oriented** |
| --- | --- |
| Get new accounts | Retain existing accounts |
| Get the order | Become the preferred supplier |
| Cut the price to get the sale | Price for profit |
| Manage all accounts to maximize short-term sales | Manage each account for long-term profit |
| Sell to anyone | Concentrate on high profit potential accounts |

## The Nature of Sales Jobs

Sales jobs encompass a wide variety of activities and responsibilities. Most sales jobs are quite different from one another, and sales jobs generally are different from nonselling jobs. Further, most sales jobs today are quite different from those of the past. Before we discuss each of these differences, we interject a note on pertinent terminology. The term *sales rep* will be used frequently throughout this book as a short form of *sales representative*. *Sales rep* is commonly used in business and parallels such titles as *factory rep* or *manufacturer's rep*. We shall treat the term *sales rep* as synonymous with *salesperson, saleswoman,* or *salesman*.

### Wide Variety of Sales Jobs

No two selling jobs are alike. The types of jobs and the requirements needed to fill them cover a wide spectrum. The job of a Pepsi-Cola driver–salesperson who calls in routine fashion on a group of retail stores is in another world from that of the IBM client manager who heads up a team of product specialists dedicated to serving the information needs of a specific industry. Similarly, a salesperson for Avon Products selling door-to-door has a job only remotely related to that of a Cessna airplane rep selling executive-type aircraft to large firms.

One useful way to classify the different types of sales jobs is to look at them on the basis of the amount of problem solving and selling required, from the simple to the complex. One such classification is as follows:

1. **Driver–salesperson.** A position in which the salesperson primarily delivers the product—for example, soft drinks, milk, or fuel oil. The selling responsibilities are secondary; few of these people originate sales.

2. **Inside order-taker.** A position in which the salesperson is primarily an *inside* order-taker—for example, the retail clerk standing behind a counter. The customers come to the salespeople. Most of them have already decided to buy; salespeople may help customers decide which of several products will work best for them. They may also suggest complimentary products.

3. **Outside order-taker.** A position in which the salesperson is primarily an *outside* order-taker, going to the customer in the field. Examples include a packing house, soap, or spice salesperson who calls on retail food stores. Both selling and problem solving are left to executives higher in the organization, while the primary responsibility of the reps is to ensure that their products are getting as much shelf space and promotional attention as possible.

4. **Missionary salesperson.** A sales job intended to build goodwill, perform promotional activities, and provide information and other services for the customers. A missionary sales rep is not expected or permitted to solicit an order. An example of this position is a missionary

salesperson for a distiller or a detail sales rep for a pharmaceutical manufacturer.

5. **Sales engineer.** A position in which an engineer provides technical advice or assistance with regard to the products and their application to the customer's process. Sales engineers may be part of the sales team brought in to assess customer needs before the sale or after the sale to help solve customer problems; they are not expected to *sell* the product.

6. **Consultive salesperson, tangible goods.** A position that involves the consultive selling of tangible goods such as pharmaceuticals, airplanes, food products, or oil-well drilling equipment. This sales job often is difficult because salespeople must thoroughly understand their customers' business. In order to sell their products, salespeople must be able to understand customer problems and provide solutions through the integration of their products with customer needs.

7. **Consultive salesperson, services and other intangibles.** A position that calls for selling intangibles such as services, ideas, or social causes, such as insurance, information services, or the United Way. This position also requires that salespeople understand their customers' needs. Intangibles are usually difficult to sell because you can't see, touch, taste, or smell them. In order to sell them, salespeople must be able to demonstrate how these services or ideas will contribute to the customers' profit or well-being.

The preceding seven types of sales jobs may be regrouped into three categories—**sales facilitation, sales support,** and **sales development**—depending on the activities that the reps perform (see Figure 1-2). People holding sales jobs in the first three of the categories essentially are order-takers. Their work is fairly routine. They facilitate sales to consumer or to business accounts which have already been established by taking orders and/or by delivering the product.

People in categories 4 and 5 are sales-support personnel. Their activities generally *support the actual selling* done by the reps in the other categories. Support personnel are engaged in building goodwill, performing sales promotional activities, and working with customers' salespeople in a training and educational capacity. The support people who are technical-product specialists—sales engineers—work with customers to assist with technical problems. These reps may help adapt a customer's system to the seller's products or help the seller design new products to fill the customer's particular needs.

The final two of the seven groups are the sales developers. They are the ones who do the *creative, developmental selling* to existing or new accounts. These are the most difficult types of sales jobs. They require considerable patience, perseverance, and persuasiveness, as well as product knowledge and an understanding of the customers' needs.

■ **FIGURE 1-2**

**Types of sales jobs**

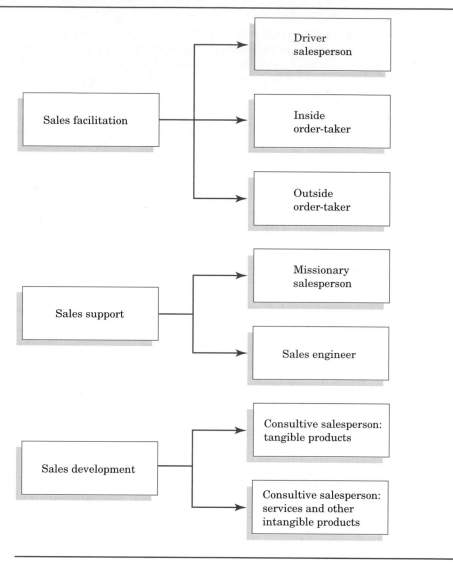

## Wide Variety of Companies, Products, and Customers

Salespeople have different responsibilities because they work for different types of companies, selling different types of products to different types of customers. For example, salespeople for Quaker Oats, Ford Motor Co., Eli Lilly, Nike, Coca-Cola, or Mary Kay sell consumer products to manufacturers, wholesalers, retailers, or the final consumer. These reps may be maintenance salespeople who mainly take orders, developmental salespeople who get orders by helping solve customer problems, and/or support salespeople. They are expected to *sell* by providing product information and promotional assistance, solving problems, and sometimes delivering merchandise.

Salespeople from Du Pont, Alcoa, Inland Steel, Textron, Georgia Pacific, IBM, Xerox, Merck, and Airborne Express generally sell industrial and business products to manufacturers, wholesalers, and institutions, such as universities, hospitals, or government agencies. These reps are usually developmental salespeople and sales support personnel who *sell* by providing product information and technical assistance and by solving customer problems. It should be noted that many companies, such as Eli Lilly and Ford Motor Co., employ more than one type of salesperson because they sell to more than one type of customer.

## Sales Jobs Differ from Other Jobs

Why is it useful to study management of a sales force separately from the management of other classes of business personnel? Why are there no courses in the management of accountants or finance personnel? The answer is that a sales job is so different from other jobs and so important to a company's financial well-being. Figure 1-3 provides an overview of the activities for which a salesperson may be responsible. Not all reps perform all of these activities. Which activities they perform depends on the types of products they sell and the types of customers to whom they sell. Now let's take a closer look at some of the key differentiating features of a sales job.

- *The sales force is largely responsible for implementing a firm's marketing strategies in the field.* Moreover, the sales reps generate the revenues that are managed by the financial people and used by the production people.

- *Salespeople are among the few employees authorized to spend company funds.* They are responsible for spending company money for entertainment, rooms, food, transportation, and other business expenses. Their effectiveness in discharging this responsibility significantly influences marketing costs and profits.

- *Salespeople represent their company to customers and to society in general.* Opinions of the firm and its products are formed on the basis of impressions made by these people in their work and outside activities. The public ordinarily does not judge a company by its factory or office workers.

- *Salespeople represent the customer to their companies.* As noted earlier in the chapter, salespeople are primarily responsible for transmitting information on customer needs and problems back to the various departments in their own firms.

■ **FIGURE 1-3**     **Selected activities of salespeople**

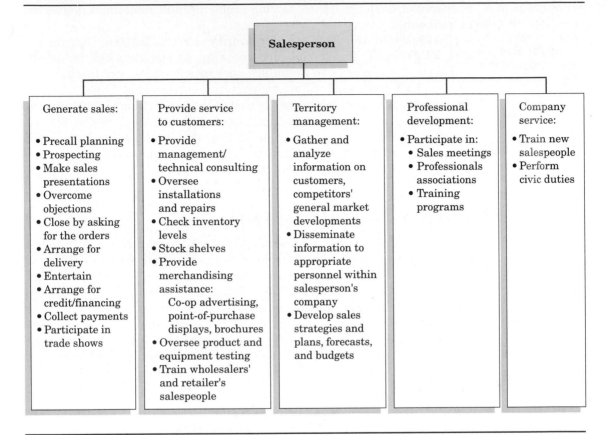

Salesperson

| Generate sales: | Provide service to customers: | Territory management: | Professional development: | Company service: |
|---|---|---|---|---|
| • Precall planning<br>• Prospecting<br>• Make sales presentations<br>• Overcome objections<br>• Close by asking for the orders<br>• Arrange for delivery<br>• Entertain<br>• Arrange for credit/financing<br>• Collect payments<br>• Participate in trade shows | • Provide management/ technical consulting<br>• Oversee installations and repairs<br>• Check inventory levels<br>• Stock shelves<br>• Provide merchandising assistance:<br>  Co-op advertising, point-of-purchase displays, brochures<br>• Oversee product and equipment testing<br>• Train wholesalers' and retailer's salespeople | • Gather and analyze information on customers, competitors' general market developments<br>• Disseminate information to appropriate personnel within salesperson's company<br>• Develop sales strategies and plans, forecasts, and budgets | • Participate in:<br>  • Sales meetings<br>  • Professionals associations<br>  • Training programs | • Train new salespeople<br>• Perform civic duties |

■ *Sales reps operate with little or no direct supervision and require a high degree of motivation.* For success in selling, a sales rep must work hard physically and mentally, be creative and persistent, and show considerable initiative. Salespeople are frequently required to develop innovative solutions to difficult problems. Sales reps do not get the sale every time. They must be able to handle the negative feelings that come with "losing the sale."

■ *A salesperson needs more tact and social intelligence than other employees on the same level in the organization.* Many sales jobs require the rep to socialize with customers, who frequently are upper-level people in their companies. Considerable social intelligence may also be needed in dealing with difficult buyers.

■ *Sales jobs frequently require considerable travel and time away from home and family.* This places an additional physical and mental burden on salespeople who already face a lot of pressure and demands.

**This sales manager is in a meeting with the marketing manager and the design engineer.**

© Index Stock Photos

## New Dimensions of Personal Selling— The Professional Salesperson

Personal selling today is quite different from what it was years ago. The cigar-smoking, back-slapping, joke-telling salesman (and virtually all outside sales reps were men in those days) is generally gone from the scene. Moreover, his talents and methods are usually not effective in today's business environment.

Instead, a new type of sales representative has emerged—a professional salesperson who is also a marketing consultant. This new breed works to relay consumer wants back to the firm so that appropriate products may be developed. They engage in a *total* consultative, nonmanipulative selling job and are expected to solve customers' problems, not just take orders. For example, Medtronics, a leader in the design and manufacture of high-tech surgical devices, sells to surgeons. These doctors often want the sales rep to be in the operating room during surgery to advise them in the best use of the product.[3] An AT&T client manager brings together a team of technical advisers, each from a different area of specialty, to find the best solutions for their customers' needs.[4] These are examples of relationship selling, described earlier in the chapter, where salespeople succeed by enhancing their customers' performance.

The new-style reps also serve as *territorial profit managers*. They have more autonomy and more responsibility for making decisions which affect their customers and their own territory profitability. Many decisions which in the past would have been made by the sales manager are today made by the salesperson. Salespeople are *empowered* to act in the best interests of their firms. They are also responsible for feeding marketing intelligence back to the firm, and they may participate in recruiting, sales planning in their territories, and other managerial activities. To a large extent, salespeople have been empowered by making use of technology to increase the quality of contact and service provided to their customers, by allowing them to tap into huge data banks of information. IBM, for example, has provided their reps software which gives them total access to complete cost information so that they can determine the profitability of every transaction.[5]

Whose sales forces best reflect this new professionalism? *Sales & Marketing Management* conducts an annual survey among sales executives to determine America's best sales forces. Results for 1996 are shown in Figure 1-4.

# THE NATURE OF SALES MANAGEMENT

During the early stages in the evolution of marketing management, sales management was narrow in scope. The major activities were recruiting and selecting a sales force, and then training, supervising, and motivating these people. Today personal selling and sales management have much broader dimensions. Many sales executives are responsible for strategic planning, forecasting, budgeting, territory design, and sales and cost analyses, as well as the more traditional activities. Sales managers must see that all of these tasks are integrated. Figure 1-5 illustrates how each of the sales management activities is linked with the others. If one of these activities is performed poorly, it will have a ripple effect on the others. For example, if the wrong people are hired, efforts to train and motivate them will almost always result in failure.

Furthermore, it is the sales manager's responsibility to see that all of the activities which support the sale of products and services, such as pro-

---

■ **FIGURE 1-4**

**America's best sales forces***

| | |
|---|---|
| 1. Hewlett-Packard | 7. Xerox |
| 2. Northwestern Mutual | 8. Microsoft |
| 3. IBM | 9. Motorola |
| 4. Walt Disney | 10. Saturn |
| 5. Federal Express | 11. Intel |
| 6. Coca-Cola | 12. Procter & Gamble |

*One hundred sales experts, including sales executives, renowned authors, and professors, rank companies on the basis of sales performance and the best reputation for customer and employee satisfaction.
Source: *Sales & Marketing Management,* November 1996, pp. 38–70.

**Sales
management
responsibilities**

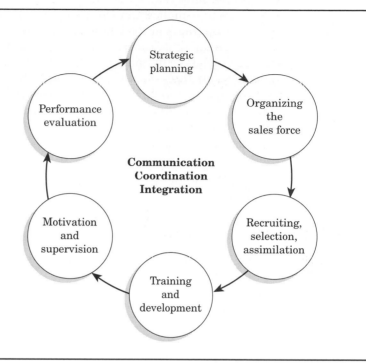

duction, advertising, and distribution, are coordinated with the efforts of
the sales department.

## Primary Responsibility of a Sales Manager

*The primary responsibility of a sales manager is to staff the organization
with the right people.* This is the basic philosophy of this book regarding
managing people. The most important job that any manager has is to select
the right person for a given job. If the right people have been hired, even bad
plans may be successful. But more important, the right people will not make
many bad plans. Well-selected people can minimize managerial problems.

Good selection is particularly important in sales management because marketing is an art of implementation. The success of most marketing plans rests not so much with the plan as with how well it is carried
out—how well the advertising is done, how well the sales force does its job,
and how well the product is made.

## Role and Skills of a Sales Manager

As the role of the salesperson has changed, so has that of the sales manager. With high-quality, empowered sales forces, sales managers are likely
to provide support and resources more frequently than one-on-one coaching. They focus on internal coordination of the sales efforts so that their

salespeople can spend more time with their customers. Increasingly, they will be asked to manage multiple sales channels—field salespeople as well as telemarketing and electronic marketing.

The demanding, controlling, volume-oriented sales manager is a dying breed. Today, the most successful sales managers are seen as *team leaders* rather than *bosses*. They still direct and advise people, but they do so through collaboration and empowerment rather than control and domination. To be successful in the 21st century, sales managers, like salespeople, will need to adapt their strategies, styles, and attitudes. Some of the critical changes are:[6]

- Developing a more detailed understanding of customers' business.
- Treating salespeople as equals and working in partnership with them to achieve profitability and customer satisfaction.
- Applying flexible motivational tools to a hybrid sales force of tele-sellers, direct marketers, and field salespeople.
- Keeping up-to-date on the latest technologies affecting buyer–seller relationships.
- Working closely with other internal departments as a member of the corporate team seeking to achieve customer satisfaction.
- Continually seeking ways to exceed customer expectations and bring added value to the buyer–seller relationship.
- Creating a flexible learning and adapting environment.

In terms of abilities, "people skills" are more important than analytical and evaluative skills. The ability to develop team-oriented relationships is particularly important. Today's sales manager must be sensitive to individual needs and skills, caring more about communicating and coaching than monitoring and controlling.

## Sales Managers Are Administrators—A Distinct Skill

A sales manager is first and foremost a manager—an administrator—and management is a distinct skill. Only during the past few decades has management (or administration, and we use these terms synonymously) been recognized as a separate body of knowledge. One of the ironies of sales force management is that sales managers were usually promoted into the executive ranks because of their talent as salespeople. But from then on their success or failure depended on their administrative skills—skills that may or may not have been developed during their time as sales reps.

### Sales Ability Is Not Enough
Although many people with outstanding technical abilities make good administrators, there is considerable evidence that sales talent alone does not make a good manager. This is the same in many fields. In the sports world, for example, many successful managers and coaches were only av-

erage players. In the sales field, it is widely recognized that the best sales-person may not even be a passable sales manager.[7] The very factors that create an outstanding salesperson often cause failure as an administrator. For example, many successful salespeople have strong, aggressive personalities. This can be a liability when working closely with others in an organization. Also, the detail and paperwork that most sales personalities detest are essential duties of a sales manager. However, we should not jump to the conclusion that top sales producers never make good sales managers. A firm's top salespeople certainly should be considered when a management opportunity develops.

While sales skills alone do not make a good administrator, some proficiency in the field is needed. It is difficult to imagine a successful sales manager who has little or no knowledge of selling. Also, the sales force must be confident that the sales manager can lead the group; successful sales experience can inspire such confidence.

### Management Can Be Learned

One top executive who was a leader in the Young Presidents Organization confessed to a group of business students that she was a terrible manager in her first job. She set out to overcome this deficiency by volunteering for charitable work. In this way, she learned how to organize people and get them to cooperate.

Another young president reported that he learned a great deal about administration by studying executives and how they behaved in managing their enterprises. Observing the tactical behavior of both successful and unsuccessful managers helped him form ideas about managing people. The continuing growth of management development programs indicates that there is a body of management knowledge that can be taught and learned.

## Levels of Sales Management Positions

In the administrative structure of many firms with outside sales forces, several executive levels are involved in sales force management, as shown in Figure 1-6. The title of *sales manager* may be applied to positions on any of these levels. *Field sales manager* is a loosely used term typically applied to any sales executive who manages an outside (in-the-field) sales force or to an executive located in branch offices (in the field) away from company headquarters.

### Lower-Level Sales Executives

The entry-level sales management position, especially in traditional firms with a large sales force, is typically that of a *sales supervisor*. This person provides day-to-day supervision, advice, and training for a small number of salespeople in a limited geographical area—usually part of a sales district. In firms that have adopted a team selling approach, the

■ **FIGURE 1-6**

**The executive ladder in personal selling**

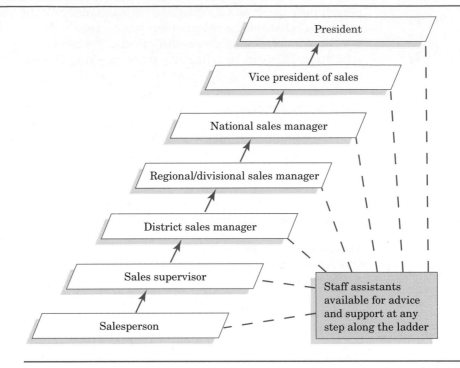

first managerial position is typically a *client team leader,* who coordinates the efforts of a multifunctional team. Usually the customer team leaders are people with client sales or service experience.

The next step up the executive ladder is the position of *district sales manager.* This person manages the activities of sales supervisors or team leaders and also participates in some sales planning and evaluation activities in the district. In firms that do not have sales supervisors, the district sales manager is the entry-level management position. In those firms which are primarily using team selling, the district manager position may be eliminated.

### Middle-Level Sales Executives

These positions usually carry the title of *regional* or *divisional sales manager.* This executive normally is responsible for managing several sales districts. Sometimes this job title is *branch manager,* especially when the branch office carries product inventory and performs physical distribution activities. This position may also be eliminated in a firm which is using team selling.

### Top-Level Sales Executives

The highest executive in sales management is most often called the *vice president of sales.* This executive reports to the vice president of market-

■ **FIGURE 1-7**

**The executive
ladder in team
selling**

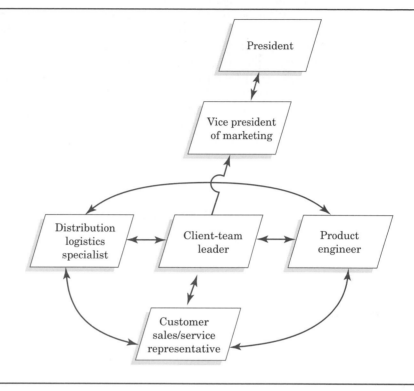

ing or directly to the president. The vice president of sales is responsible
for designing an organization's long-run sales strategies and other companywide strategic sales planning activities. This executive acts as the
sales department's liaison to the top executive in finance, production, and
other major functional areas of the firm.

Just below the vice president of sales may be the *national sales manager*. The national sales manager heads the companywide sales force operations and is the executive to whom the regional sales managers report.
The general sales manager thus acts as liaison between the *strategic* planning of top sales and marketing management and the *tactical* planning involved in operating regional sales forces.

### Flatter Organizations
It is important to note that many organizations are becoming flatter; that
is, they have eliminated some of the levels of management. Typically
these are the organizations using cross-functional teams to serve their
clients. As noted above, team leaders replace lower-level management positions, and often the middle levels are eliminated as well. Thus the team
leader may report directly to the vice president of sales or marketing (see
Figure 1-7).

### Staff Sales Management Positions

In addition to the sales management positions discussed, most medium- and large-sized companies employ staff executives to head activities that provide assistance to the sales executives and the sales force. Sales training, sales planning, and sales and marketing cost analyses are examples of these staff activities. A key point is that these executives have only an advisory relationship with the line sales executive and the sales force. Staff executives do not have line authority in the sales executive hierarchy. However, within a staff activity area—sales training, for example—the staff executives do have line authority over the people in that area.

## Sales Managers' Jobs Differ from Other Management Jobs

Probably the most significant differentiating feature of an outside personal selling job is that the salespeople work away from the company's main facilities. Thus sales managers cannot directly supervise each rep's work in person on a daily basis. The geographical deployment of an outside sales force makes sales managers' jobs different in several respects from other management jobs.

In sales training, for example, a sales manager can provide on-the-job training usually to only one person at a time, so other training tools and methods must be used. Communication with outside salespeople is often more difficult because it is not face-to-face communication. Similarly, motivating a sales force is a problem when a sales manager cannot regularly spend one-on-one time with the salespeople.

Another problem is evaluating a sales rep's performance when the sales manager cannot personally see the rep's work. It is also difficult to monitor the ethical behavior of workers who are geographically separated from the company. Finally, sales managers frequently face morale problems among outside salespeople. Being physically separated from co-workers, the sales reps don't have the same group morale support network as do inside employees.

## ◨ IMPORTANCE OF PERSONAL SELLING AND SALES MANAGEMENT

From any viewpoint in our total economy, in an individual organization, or even to you as a student, personal selling, and consequently its management, are tremendously important. As "Red" Motley, a noted sales trainer and writer, once said, "Nothing happens until somebody sells something."

### In Our Economy

For the past 70 years, except during World War II and the immediate postwar period, a strong *buyers' market* has existed in the United States. That is, the available supply of products and services has far surpassed the demand. There has been relatively little difficulty in producing most goods. The real problem has been in selling them. Particularly during recessions, business people soon realize that it is a slowdown in selling that forces cutbacks in production.

For further evidence of the importance of selling in our economy, take a look at the numbers. About 12 percent of the civilian working-age population is employed in sales occupations. That comes out to more than 26 *million* people. There are about 3 million outside sales jobs. Compare that to total employment in advertising, which is about 500 thousand.

## In an Individual Organization

When a firm stresses marketing management, executive attention is devoted to sales and market planning. Such emphasis may be well placed, but ordinarily the sales force in the field must carry out the sales plan. No plan is of much value unless it is implemented properly. If salespeople cannot sell successfully because they are improperly selected, trained, or compensated, then the efforts devoted to sales planning are of little value. About the only exceptions are firms that do not rely on their own sales force. Instead, they primarily use advertising or agent middlemen, such as brokers or manufacturers' agents, to move the products. Since the sales force is critical to the success of a concern's marketing venture, sound management of these representatives is important.

The cost of managing and operating a sales force is usually the largest single operating expense for most firms. Public attention and criticism often focus on the amounts a firm spends for television or magazine advertising. Yet a firm's total advertising expenditures may be only 3 percent or 4 percent of net sales. The total expenses related to salespeople may be 15 percent or 20 percent of net sales.

## To You, the Student

Okay, so selling and sales management are important in our economy and in an individual organization. But why should you study sales management? What's in it for you?

The primary reason is related to your career aspirations. There are more positions available in sales than in any other professional occupation. As a result, there are also a lot of sales management jobs in today's world. A firm with a medium-sized or large sales force has many sales executive positions (sales supervisors, sales team leaders, district sales managers, regional sales managers) but only a few executives in finance, production, personnel, advertising, or marketing research. And the pay is usually much higher in sales management jobs.

An added career-related reason for studying sales management is that you soon may be involved in these activities. Within two or three years after graduation, you may be serving as a sales supervisor or a district sales manager. Even as a salesperson, you may engage in managerial activities, such as visiting your alma mater to do employee recruiting. You may be asked to do some sales forecasting for your territory or to offer suggestions regarding a proposed compensation or quota plan.

## ◼ SALES FORCE MANAGEMENT IN THE TWENTY-FIRST CENTURY

Earlier in this chapter we noted that personal selling has assumed broader and more professional dimensions. We also observed that the people who manage the personal selling effort have significantly broadened their management activities. Now sales managers are planning for the first decade of the 21st century. To be successful in the competitive environment in the years ahead, sales executives must develop greater expertise in the following areas. Each of these areas is discussed in varying depth later in the book.

- **Sales management skills.** During the 21st century, more companies will respond to the changes in customer buying patterns by utilizing *selling teams*. Coordinating the efforts of these teams and motivating them is a task very different from supervising and motivating the individual sales rep. Collaboration and consensus building will be essential skills for the manager in the next millennium.

  Additionally, many sales managers will be asked to manage increasingly *complex channels of distribution*. They will oversee a hybrid sales force which includes field sales reps, tellsellers, and electronic sellers. Their jobs—organizing and coordinating the efforts of these diverse salespeople—will become more strategic in nature. The successful sales managers of the 21st century will be adaptive and strategic in their thinking.

- **An international perspective when selling at home or abroad.** Today the U.S. market has reached the saturation point for many consumer and industrial products. At the same time, many global markets are emerging and growing rapidly. By the year 2000, the economies of the eastern Asian countries will equal that of the United States. Growth for many companies in the 21st century will come from their development of these international markets. Some companies, such as Coca-Cola, Colgate-Palmolive, and Avon, are already earning the greatest proportion of their revenues outside the United States. Small companies are also selling globally, with more than 20 percent of them reporting international exports.[8] When an American firm goes international in its selling and sales management, it may be playing a whole different ball game. Differences in cultures and ways of doing business in foreign countries pose real challenges for American sales management.

  Additionally, in the United States, American sellers face increasing competition from many foreign firms. This competition is bound to increase (1) as economies expand in Asian and eastern European countries such as Korea, Taiwan, Thailand, China, Hungary, and Poland; (2) as a result of the European Community (Common Market) becoming a unified trading market in 1992; and (3) as a result of the United

States passing NAFTA (North American Free Trade Agreement) in 1993, which eliminated many of the trade barriers between the United States, Canada, and Mexico. Sales executives must manage their sales forces to meet foreign competition in this country and to improve their company's personal selling efforts in other countries.

■ **Management of women and minorities.** More women and minorities are embarking on careers in personal selling and are advancing into sales management positions. In the early 1980s only 10 percent of outside salespeople were women. Now that figure is at 24 percent. However, there is considerable imbalance in the number of saleswomen among the various industries (see Figure 1-8).[9] There have been women in sales management positions for many years, but their number has been relatively small. However, the growing number of female sales reps is beginning to translate into promotions to sales management in many companies and industries. To remain competitive, sales managers need to capitalize on the strengths of women in selling and to be aware of what women want in a sales job. Minority groups present a different set of challenges for sales management because minorities have been more difficult to recruit in large numbers for outside sales jobs.

The bottom line for sales managers of women and minority groups is this: These groups are here to stay in selling, and they must be managed effectively. As a matter of self-interest, sales managers cannot afford to waste the brain power (and selling power) of over half of our population. Moreover, executives simply will not be able to adequately fill the available sales jobs in the foreseeable future unless they recruit qualified women and minorities. In the year 2000 one-third of the American population is expected to be part of a minority group, according to Department of Labor estimates.

■ **Effective use of electronic communication systems and computer-based technology.** In the United States, 2.2 million salespeople use some type of computer technology to enhance their sales performance. This number is expected to grow by 40 percent a year.[10] During the next decade, sales force automation will become commonplace. Innovations—laptop computers, electronic data exchange, and desktop video conferencing—and the Internet are enabling salespeople and sales managers to improve their productivity. To compete effectively in the future, salespeople and managers alike will have to adopt the latest technologies. However, it should be noted that "technology can make some things more efficient, but it can't replace face-to-face contact."[11]

■ **Ethical behavior and social responsibility.** Each person in business operates within a personal moral framework, the business ethical framework of the company and the industry, and a framework imposed by society. Of the five topics covered in this final section of the chapter, the topic of ethics is probably the most necessary, but also the most difficult to

■ **FIGURE 1-8**

| Women in the sales force | Product or Service | Percentage of Sales Reps | Percentage of Sales Managers |
|---|---|---|---|
| | Consumer products | 28.3% | 16.5% |
| | Consumer services | 30.5 | 17.3 |
| | Industrial products | 17.8 | 9.8 |
| | Industrial services | 23.7 | 12.9 |
| | Office products | 27.5 | 17.0 |
| | Office services | 30.5 | 16.1 |
| | **Industry** | | |
| | Hotel and other lodging places | 65.3% | 46.0% |
| | Communications | 41.4 | 25.5 |
| | Health services | 35.5 | 28.6 |
| | Office equipment | 19.6 | 15.1 |
| | Retail | 21.9 | 11.7 |
| | Business services | 27.5 | 15.6 |
| | Insurance | 33.8 | 18.6 |
| | Printing and publishing | 26.3 | 6.1 |
| | Trucking and warehousing | 15.5 | 0.1 |
| | Paper and allied products | 16.4 | 0.0 |
| | Educational services | 30.7 | 8.3 |
| | Electronics | 22.8 | 12.7 |
| | Fabricated metals | 12.4 | 11.4 |
| | Wholesale (consumer) | 12.2 | 7.5 |
| | Wholesale (industrial) | 20.7 | 9.8 |
| | Manufacturing | 17.1 | 7.4 |
| | Chemicals | 13.7 | 4.3 |
| | Instruments | 14.3 | 4.7 |
| | Machinery | 6.1 | 2.8 |
| | **Overall** | **24.1%** | **13.2%** |

manage. Ethics are defined differently by various companies and industries, and also by different societies. Nevertheless, any institution in our socioeconomic system must operate within socially acceptable limits of ethical behavior; society will penalize any unethical institution and the people in it.

For centuries, the institution of business, and especially its personal-selling component, has been accused periodically of unethical behavior. Yet it is commonly accepted that outside selling today is on an ethical plane far above that of a few decades ago and in a different world from a century or two in the past. Today, sales managers have no choice but to strive to maintain their ethical standards in personal selling and sales management, for the alternative can put them out of business or even into prison.

# ■ SUMMARY

This is a book about managing a sales force—that is, managing the personal-selling component of an organization's marketing program. Specifically, this book deals with the management of an outside sales force where the salespeople go to the customer. This contrasts with across-the-counter selling where the customers come to the salespeople. By any measure—people employed, dollars spent, or sales generated—personal selling is by far the most important element in a company's promotional mix.

In the face of intense competition, many companies today practice relationship marketing or relationship selling, which is very different from the traditional transaction-oriented selling which focused on the one-time sale of the product. In contrast, relationship selling focuses on developing trust in a few selected accounts over an extended period of time.

There are a wide variety of sales jobs in which salespeople work for a wide variety of companies, selling many different products, and serving a wide variety of customers. The sales job is also different in a number of ways from other jobs. Further, a new type of sales representative is emerging who acts as a marketing consultant for the customer and for his or her own firm.

The role of the sales manager is also expanding. The primary responsibility of an administrator is to staff the organization with the right people. The manager must also place a priority on the development of people. Today, the most successful sales managers are seen as team leaders rather than bosses.

Sales managers are administrators, and administration (management) is a distinct skill. Sales talent alone does not make a good manager but management can be learned. There are several levels of sales management positions and sales managers' jobs also differ from other management positions.

The importance of personal selling and sales management may be viewed from the perspective of our total economy, individual organizations, or individuals such as yourself. To manage a sales force effectively into the 21st century, sales executives must develop greater expertise in the following areas: (1) sales management skills; (2) international perspectives; (3) management of women and minorities; (4) use of electronic communication systems and computer-based technology; and (5) ethical behavior and social responsibility of salespeople and sales managers.

## Key Terms

| | | |
|---|---|---|
| Communications mix | Outside order-taker | Sales facilitation |
| Consultive salesperson | Outside sales force | Sales maintenance |
| Driver–salesperson | Promotional mix | Sales support |
| Electronic marketing | Relationship marketing | Telemarketing |
| Inside order-taker | Relationship selling | Transaction selling |
| Marketing mix | Sales development | Value-added components |
| Missionary salesperson | Sales engineer | |

# ■ QUESTIONS AND PROBLEMS

1. Explain how changes in purchasing patterns have changed the nature of the selling task.

2. What is an outside sales force? Is this type of sales force used only by producers and wholesalers? Is it used only in business-to-business selling?

3. How does relationship-oriented selling differ from transaction-oriented selling?

4. Based on the seven classifications of sales jobs listed in this chapter, answer these questions:
   a. In which types of jobs is the sales rep most free of close supervision?
   b. Which types of jobs are likely to be the highest paid?
   c. For which groups is a high degree of motivation most necessary?

5. We said that today's professional sales representative is a marketing consultant and a manager of a market—his or her territory. Explain how a sales rep can be a marketing consultant and a manager.

6. What can sales managers do to increase the professionalism of their salespeople?

7. How does a sales job differ from other jobs?

8. Assume that it is the year 2001 and you are a middle-level sales manager. Tell us something about your job.

9. Why do many successful salespeople fail to become successful sales managers?

10. Assume that you are a sales manager. What characteristics would you look for, or what criteria would you use, when promoting a salesperson to the position of district sales manager?

11. It has been said that "nothing happens until somebody sells something." How would you explain this to a student who is majoring in accounting, finance, or engineering?

12. Should a nonmarketing major take a course in personal selling? In sales management?

13. Review your activities of the past week and identify those in which you did some personal selling.

14. How can salespeople and sales managers use computers in their jobs?

# ■ EXPERIENTIAL EXERCISES

A. Interview sales managers from three different companies concerning their responsibilities and what they do. Compare and contrast their positions. Then explain which one you would prefer and why.

B. Interview a salesperson from each of three different companies about the nature of their selling responsibilities and their relationships with their customers. Then describe each of these sales positions and explain whether the selling is more similar to transactional selling or to relationship selling and why.

# ■ REFERENCES

1. John R. Emshwiller, "Suppliers Struggle to Improve Quality as Big Firms Slash Their Vendor Roles," *The Wall Street Journal,* August 16, 1991, p. B1.

2. Benson P. Shapiro, Adrian J. Slywotzky, and Stephan X. Doyle, "Strategic Sales Management: A Boardroom Issue," *Harvard Business School Case Study* (Boston: Harvard Business School, 1994).

3. James Champy, "Heading in New Directions," *Sales & Marketing Management,* January 1997, pp. 32–33.

4. Geoffrey Brewer and Christine Galea, "The Top 25," *Sales & Marketing Management,* November 1996, pp. 38–70.

5. Rolph E. Anderson, "Personal Selling and Sales Management in the New Millennium,"

*Personal Selling & Sales Management,* Fall 1996, pp. 17–32.

6. Ibid.

7. Bill Kelley, "From Sales Person to Manager: Transition and Travail," *Sales & Marketing Management,* February 1992, pp. 32–36.

8. Anderson, "Personal Selling."

9. Christian P. Heide, *Dartnell's 29th Sales Force Compensation Survey 1996–1997* (Chicago: Dartnell Corp., 1996), p. 171.

10. Scott De Garmo, "Becoming a Sales Leader," *Selling Success,* May 1996, p. 4.

11. Jack Flavey, "The Art of Selling," *The Wall Street Journal,* July 15, 1996, p. A12.

---

## Case 1-1

### THOMPSON PLASTICS
### Making the transition from salesperson to sales manager

Thompson Plastics is an eight-million-dollar family-owned corporation which takes pride in its quality products and customer relationships. The company manufactures plastics products, resins and adhesives, and custom moldings. The plastics, which are the largest part of Thompson's business, include polyvinyl chloride (PVC) sheets, acrylic sheets, acetate, polypropylene, and nylon. Thompson also manufactures 15 different resins and adhesives as well as custom-made vacuum molding products for other manufacturers.

Thompson sells its products to various manufacturers and retailers in the Buffalo, New York, metropolitan market. Sales to other manufacturers account for approximately 77 percent of its sales, and sales to retailers account for the remainder. Thompson has several competitors in the Buffalo market but has maintained slow, consistent growth over the past several years. Thompson's strategy is to maintain its market share by concentrating on its existing customers with quality products and personal service.

The company has a simple line-type organization that is relatively small. The president, John Thompson, heads up the organization. Reporting to him are the vice presidents of manufacturing, finance, operations, and marketing. The vice president of marketing is Lorna Kelley. Reporting to her is the sales manager, Ted Cook, who oversees the sales operations and the seven salespeople employed by Thompson.

Ted Cook was recently promoted into the manager's job. Thompson has a policy of promoting from within and Ted was selected from among the salespeople based on the strong recommendation of Lorna Kelley. She felt that even though he was not the top salesperson, he was the best choice to move into management. He clearly had the best administrative skills of the group, he often took a leadership role in helping the younger reps, and he was respected by all the other reps. In her mind, Ted had seemed to be the logical choice; but now she was wondering if she had made a mistake.

The sales manager for Thompson has a large amount of the responsibility for planning the sales effort and total responsibility for organizing and managing the sales force. In the area of planning, he (or she) assists in the preparation of the sales forecast. He compiles territory estimates by customer and by product, based on past history, forecasts of economic conditions, and competitive developments. Based on the final forecasts, he also prepares the expense budgets and the sales quotas for the individual reps. He then breaks these budgets down into monthly and quarterly dollar figures, which he uses in evaluating the reps and determining their incentive pay.

The sales manager has total responsibility for recruiting and selecting new salespeople when there is an open territory. He places the advertisements in the local newspapers, screens the applicants based on their résumés, interviews those who appear to have the qualifications to fill the job, selects the candidate, and makes the job offer. The sales manager then spends two to three weeks training the new salesperson. This involves everything from acquainting the new rep with company objectives, production capabilities, and operating policies to teaching product knowledge and selling skills. During the training period, the new rep accompanies the manager on a number of typical sales calls.

Supervision, motivation, and evaluation are essential components of this position. The manager makes sure that the reps are allocating their time properly and that they are keeping current with regard to their product and industry knowledge. He is responsible for weekly sales meetings and continuing training programs. He must also spend time in the field with each rep in order to evaluate performance. In conjunction with the evaluation, he designs and administers the recognition and compensation programs. Of course, the sales manager also acts as a troubleshooter when any of the reps needs assistance with an account.

In the past, the sales managers at Thompson had always retained some of their keys accounts. However, Lorna felt that because the size of the sales force had doubled in the last few years and because the responsibilities of the sales manager had expanded, it was time that the sales manager devote 100 percent of his time to managing the sales effort. Therefore, when she offered the manager's position to Ted Cook, she asked him to give up all of his selling responsibilities. His compensation package would consist of salary, plus a commission on all the reps' sales, plus a bonus for making the sales and expense targets. This package would more than compensate for the loss of income from his sales commissions.

Ted was really excited about the opportunity to become Thompson's sales manager. But he was somewhat surprised that he had been chosen because he did not have seniority among the reps. However, when Lorna told him about giving up all of his accounts, he countered that he didn't want to do that and that it was not in Thompson's best interests. Lorna recalled his comment: "If customer relationships are as important as we say they are, then I should retain several of my key accounts in which I have developed strong relationships over the past several years. I am certain we would lose our position as a favored supplier if we assigned these accounts to a new rep. It isn't that I'm any better than the next rep; it's just that it takes time to gain their trust and nurture these relationships."

Of course Ted had also wanted to know why there had been this change in policy. When Lorna explain her reasoning, Ted suggested that keeping several of his accounts would actually help him be a better manager because he would be more knowledgeable about what was going on in the marketplace. When Lorna relented, Ted took the job and kept his largest accounts. The smaller customers were split among the territories contiguous to his.

At first this arrangement worked pretty well. However, in the last several months Ted began having problems with both the managing and the selling aspects of his job. His paperwork was way behind, his sales figures had slipped a little, and one of the reps had complained to Lorna about the lack of support from Ted.

Lorna did not have a good solution. If she forced Ted to give up his accounts, she thought there was a good chance he might quit Thompson. If he quit, she really did not have anybody else she felt she could put in his position. She would have both a manager and a rep to replace. If she asked him to give up the manager's job and go back into full-time selling, he might quit in that situation as well.

**Question:**

1. Should Lorna ask Ted to give up his accounts? How do you think Lorna should handle this problem?

---

*Case 1-2*

## THE CORNELL COMPANY

### Selection of a sales manager

Mrs. Paula Ruiz, vice president of marketing for the Cornell Company of Chicago, Illinois, knew she had to make a decision on whom to select to manage the company's 56-person sales force. Seven months previously, the former sales manager resigned to accept the sales managership for Cornell's major competitor. Since that time Mrs. Ruiz had assumed direct control of the sales force, but she clearly saw that in doing so she was not only neglecting her other responsibilities but also doing a poor job of managing the sales force.

Mrs. Ruiz's search for a new sales manager had narrowed down to two people, Gordon Price and Janice Wilson, both of whom seemed eminently qualified for the job.

The Cornell Company was one of the nation's leading manufacturers of special-purpose metal fasteners and metal fastening systems used by metal fabricating manufacturers. The sales reps worked closely with both the engineers and purchasing agents of customers' organizations in developing product designs and specifications for solving their problems. While there was some calling on new accounts, the bulk of the sales rep's time was spent working with longstanding established accounts.

The sales manager was charged with the full responsibility for maintaining an effective field sales force, which included hiring, firing, training, supervising, compensating, controlling, and evaluating the salespeople. The manager was accountable for all the department's paperwork, which included budget preparation, expense account auditing, and sales force planning. At times the manager had to work closely with sales reps in handling special accounts or particularly important or difficult contracts. There were no field supervisors to help the reps; however, close communications were maintained with them by the home office through the extensive use of modern electronic technology.

Each rep had a portable computer, mobile telephone, and fax machine, which allowed immediate contact with the home office and its databases. Technical information was immediately available to all sales reps by accessing the company's mainframe computer, which contained an extensive technical database. Every company employee could be accessed by electronic mail. The sales manager had an assistant in the home office who handled all communications between the reps and the manager. A large portion of the manager's time was spent in meetings with other members of management to coordinate sales force activities with all other functions of the business. The manager had to work particularly closely with Mrs. Ruiz.

Mrs. Ruiz had taken the files on the two prospective managers home for the weekend to contemplate her decision. She had decided to announce her selection Monday morning.

As she reviewed Gordon Price's file, she fully realized that if Gordon were not made sales manager some repercussions might be felt. Gordy was not only the firm's best sales rep but was well regarded throughout the organization. He had sold for the company for 15 years and prior to that had worked in production for 4 years after graduation from high school. Now 37 years old, he had outsold all other reps for the last 10 years and always exceeded quotas by more than 20 percent, even in difficult times. Since the sales force was paid on a commission basis, Gordy had become moderately wealthy. His average earnings over the past decade exceeded $100,000; last year he earned $135,000. Gordon was married to an understanding woman of considerable charm. Their three children were in high school and to Mrs. Ruiz's knowledge were outstanding youngsters. The Prices were extremely adept at entertaining and socializing with people. Hardly a month passed that they did not have some sort of social event at their home.

Although Gordon had not attended college, Mrs. Ruiz knew that he was intelligent and had acquired considerable business know-how. He had accumulated an impressive library of business books and had participated in many meaningful self-improvement programs.

When he learned of the previous sales manager's resignation, Gordon had come directly to Mrs. Ruiz and requested the position. He outlined his achievements for the company and then gave a brief account of the goals that he would work toward as manager. Mrs. Ruiz recalled acknowledging at the time that Gordon was certainly a prime candidate for the job and that he could be assured that he would be given every consideration. However, she told Gordon that the decision was not entirely hers to make. The president had suggested that a thorough search be made in order to ensure that the best person available was placed in the position, since he felt keenly that the company had prospered largely because of its excellent sales force and he wanted to do nothing to jeopardize that success formula.

Privately, Mrs. Ruiz had some reservations about making Gordy sales manager but she was hesitant to bring her thoughts into the open for fear of engendering animosities that would later haunt her. First, she was fearful that if she promoted Gordy she would be losing a good sales rep and getting a poor sales manager. She had seen it happen in other companies, and sales management literature was full of warnings that top salespeople may not make good sales managers. The two jobs required different skills. Second, Mrs. Ruiz was worried that Gordon would be unhappy with the sales manager's salary of $90,000, despite his insistence that he would be happy with it. Third, she was afraid that Gordy's preference for customer contact would result in his not staying in the office enough to do the required paperwork. Finally, she was disturbed by Gordy's relationships with the other reps. He was extremely well liked by the men, who felt that he "would give you the shirt off his back" if you needed it. However, a few of the 14 women on the sales force had communicated to her that they felt that Gordy was a bit too macho for their liking. However, none of the women had indicated that Gordon had been anything but very proper and pleasant in his behavior toward them.

Gordon had forced Mrs. Ruiz to make a selection soon, appearing in her office Friday morning to issue a rather strong ultimatum: He had been offered a sales managership with a significant competitor and had to give an answer in two weeks. He made it clear that he did not want to leave but he would do so to become a sales manager if that opportunity was not to be his with the Cornell Company. Mrs. Ruiz inwardly rebelled at this holdup ploy but realized that it was a fair tactic. The last sales manager had given no warning of his impending departure. She thought that at least it was nice to be forewarned for a change.

Mrs. Ruiz proceeded to review her other leading candidate, Janice Wilson, with whom she had been acquainted for more than four years. They were members of several clubs together and, while not close friends, had known each other from their college days. Janice was the sales manager for an electronic instrumentation company and had developed an enviable reputation in the industry for building an outstanding sales force. She was 32 years old, married, with two young children. While she had a most agreeable disposition, all evidence indicated that she ran a tight ship. She demanded outstanding performance and seemed to get it.

Mrs. Ruiz casually mentioned her job opening to Mrs. Wilson one day at one of their club meetings on the off chance that she might know some outstanding person whom she could recommend for the job. Mrs. Wilson had hesitated for a moment, then replied, "Let's talk."

She then confided that her firm was about to be acquired by a larger firm and she was not at all enthralled about what she knew of its management. "They are not my kind of people," she went on to say. "From what I know of you and your operation, I think I would like very much to be considered for the job."

After two hours spent contemplating the pros and cons of selecting each person, Mrs. Ruiz was still undecided.

**Question:**

**1.** Whom would you make sales manager?

# CHAPTER 2

# Strategic Sales Force Management

*Everything in strategy is very simple, but that does not mean that everything is very easy.*

**Karl von Clausewitz, Prussian strategist**

Too many people think of sales as an activity that is separate from marketing strategy. They don't understand how sales operations fit into the marketing plan and how that fits into the total corporate plan. Even worse, marketing and sales personnel often operate as if they are engaged in some sort of win/lose contest in which neither will cooperate with the other. However, in order to achieve marketing objectives, the sales force must be seen as an integral part of the marketing strategy . . . the part which carries out the strategy. Marketing and sales personnel must understand that they are on the same team.[1]

A chief operating officer (COO) of a biotech enterprise whose 75-person sales force was fueling the company's rapid growth into the Fortune 500 recently noted, "I need many of my present sales people to develop insights into the company's strategic plans so they can be my managers of the future. We're going to need dozens of them."

This executive neatly highlighted the purpose of this chapter—to place sales force management within the context of the total marketing program. To make wise strategic decisions about the sales force, the sales manager must understand how the field-selling effort fits into the total marketing plan and how that plan fits into total corporate strategy.

## ◼ THE MARKETING SYSTEM

A marketing system operates within a framework of forces—its environment. Two sets of these forces are external to the company and another two sets are internal. Their relationship is seen in Figure 2-1.

### External Environment

Six macroenvironmental forces impinge considerably on any company's marketing system, yet they generally are *not* controllable by management. This set of forces includes:

**■ FIGURE 2-1**          **A company's complete marketing system: a framework of internal resources operating within a set of external forces**

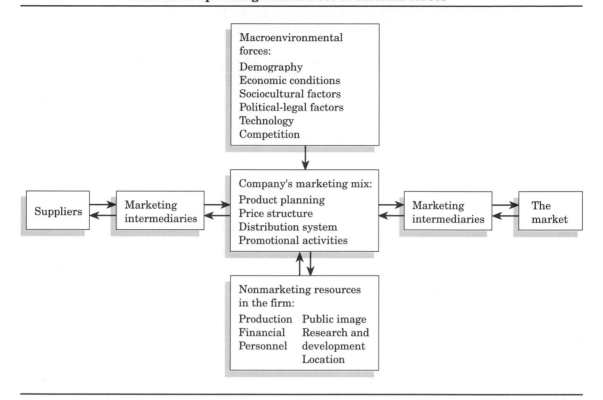

- Demography
- Economic conditions
- Sociocultural factors
- Political–legal factors
- Technology
- Competition

In addition, a company faces a set of three external forces that are a *direct* part of the firm's marketing system. These are the company's market, its suppliers, and marketing intermediaries (primarily middlemen). While generally classed as uncontrollable, these three elements are susceptible to a greater degree of company influence than are the other six. Note the two-way flows between the company and these three external elements in Figure 2-1. The company receives products and promotional messages from its suppliers. In return, the company sends payments and marketing information. The same types of exchanges occur between the company and its market. Any of these exchanges can go through one or more middlemen.

## Internal Variables in Marketing Systems

To reach its marketing goals, management has at its disposal two sets of internal, controllable forces: (1) the company's resources in nonmarketing areas and (2) the components of its **marketing mix**—its product, price structure, distribution system, and promotional activities. Figure 2-1 shows these internal forces in relation to the forces in the external environment. The result is the company's total marketing system set within its environment.

The term *marketing mix* describes the combination of four ingredients that constitute the core of a company's marketing system. When effectively blended, these four—product, price, distribution, and promotion—form a marketing program designed to provide want-satisfying goods and services to the company's market.

Promotional activities form a separate submix that we call the *promotional mix* or the *communications mix* in the company's marketing program. The major elements in the promotional mix are the company's advertising, sales promotion, and personal-selling effort.

## THE MARKETING CONCEPT AND MARKETING MANAGEMENT

As businesspeople have come to recognize marketing's vital importance to a firm's success, a way of business thinking—a philosophy—has evolved. This is called the **marketing concept,** and it is based on three fundamental beliefs, as seen in Figure 2-2:

1. Company planning and operations should be *customer* or *marketing oriented.*
2. Marketing activities in a firm should be *organizationally coordinated.*
3. The goal of the organization should be to generate *profitable sales volume over the long run.*

In its fullest sense, the marketing concept is a business philosophy that makes the customers' want satisfaction the economic and social justification for the firm's existence. Thus company activities should focus on finding out what the customers want, satisfying those wants, and making a profit over the long run.

As we noted in Chapter 1, more firms are *customer oriented* today than in the past. A firm that is customer oriented has adopted the mar-

■ **FIGURE 2-2**

**The marketing concept's three foundation stones**

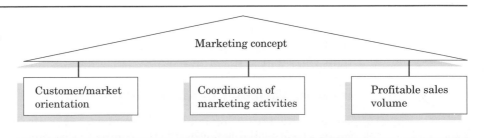

keting concept as its business philosophy. It has used the philosophy to guide both the planning process and the implementation of strategies and tactics necessary for achieving its goals.

## Marketing Management and Its Evolution

For a business enterprise to realize the full benefits of the marketing concept, its marketing activities must be coordinated. The chief marketing executive is responsible for planning, implementing, and coordinating all marketing activities and integrating them into the overall operations of the firm. This process is called **marketing management.**

Since the Industrial Revolution, marketing management in American business has evolved through three stages. A fourth is now emerging. Many companies are still in one of the earlier stages, however. The following diagram shows the four stages in the evolution of marketing management:

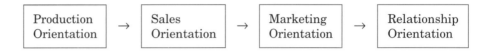

### Production-Oriented Stage
During the first stage, a company is typically production oriented. The executives in production and engineering shape the company's objectives and planning. The function of the sales department is simply to sell the production output at the price set by production and financial executives. During this period manufacturers have sales departments—marketing is not recognized—headed by a sales manager. This organizational pattern was predominant in the United States until about the start of the Great Depression in the 1930s.

### Sales-Orientation Stage
The Depression made it quite clear that the main problem in our economy was no longer the ability to make or grow enough products. Rather, the problem was selling this output. Unfortunately, during this same period selling acquired much of its bad reputation. This was the age of the "hard sell." Even today, many organizations believe they must operate with a hard-sell philosophy. As long as companies operate with a hard-sell philosophy, there will be continued (and justified) criticism of selling and marketing.

### Marketing-Orientation Stage
In the third stage, companies use coordinated marketing management directed toward the twin goals of customer satisfaction and profitable sales volume. Attention focuses on marketing rather than on selling. The top executive is a marketing manager or the vice president of marketing. In this

**Company
organization
chart
embracing the
concept of
marketing
management**

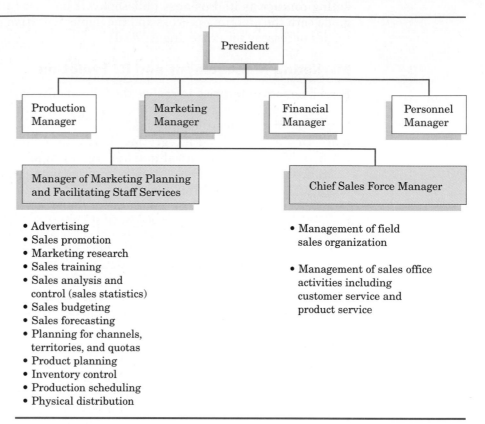

At this point all activities have been integrated under a single marketing manager. Organizationally, the company has adopted the marketing concept.

stage, several activities traditionally the province of other executives become the responsibility of the marketing manager (see Figure 2-3). For instance, inventory control, warehousing, and aspects of product planning are often turned over to the marketing manager.

### Relationship-Orientation Stage

This stage is characterized by relationship building. The buyer and seller make a commitment to each other to do business over a long time period rather than view each sale as a discrete transaction. Salespeople become consultants to their customers. Their goal is to improve the customer's overall profitability rather than just sell products. To build these relationships, salespeople strive to earn the trust of their customers. As noted in Chapter 1, marketing in this orientation is referred to as *relationship marketing*. Companies that are practicing relationship marketing have put the marketing concept into practice.

## Relationship Marketing

To practice relationship marketing, companies must place a priority on four major components of their marketing and sales efforts: understanding customer expectations, building service partnerships, empowering employees, and total quality management.[2] Each of these is discussed below.

- **Understanding customer expectations.** Companies must be able to identify what customers want and market a product to them that exceeds their expectations. To do this, it is necessary for firms to systematically collect precise information about their customers' needs and desires. Salespeople are often responsible for collecting this information.

- **Building service partnerships.** Companies must work closely with their customers to add information and services beyond their traditional products to increase the value of their offerings to customers. This means that salespeople must develop close, collaborative relationships with their buyers in which both parties work toward a common goal. Salespeople must be open and honest with customers. They must be "bias free," making only those recommendations which are in the best interests of both.

- **Empowering employees.** Companies must encourage and reward their salespeople for taking initiative and using creativity in helping solve customer problems. Thus salespeople must have the skills, responsibility, and authority to make decisions which better serve their customers. Further, managers must foster an environment in which salespeople do fear losing their jobs if they make a mistake.

- **Total quality management.** This is the process by which the company strives to improve customer satisfaction through the continuous improvement of all its operations. All decisions are made for the expressed purpose of improving customer satisfaction. These decisions are based on the information that salespeople and selling teams collect from their customers and transmit back to their companies, such as product inquiries, specifications, problems, and changing customer needs. This information is provided by salespeople to various departments in their own organizations, such as product design, production, accounting, and/or shipping. People in these departments who use this information to make improvements are in essence the salesperson's *internal customers*. To compete effectively, salespeople must provide both their external and internal customers relevant, accurate, and timely information.

If a company is successful in implementing a relationship marketing program, it can expect to have higher quality products, higher customer satisfaction, more loyal customers, and greater profitability.[3] As more and

---

### How to Practice Relationship Marketing

1. Salespeople should establish continuous dialogue with their customers to define their current and future needs.

2. Assign permanent contact personnel within your company to each customer; empower them to resolve customers' problems.

3. Use customer standards, such as the number of product returns, the number of complaints, the time to handle complaints, the number of billing errors, and on-time deliveries, to drive plans and customer relationships.

4. Measure customer satisfaction on an ongoing basis.

Source: Adapted from Norton Paley, "Romancing Your Customers," *Sales & Marketing Management,* March 1996, pp. 30–31.

---

more companies focus on customer relations and satisfaction as a measure of the effectiveness of their marketing programs, sales managers and salespeople will be expected to assume greater responsibility for directing and coordinating the marketing efforts of the firm.

### Integrating Marketing and Sales Functions

From a strategic perspective, it is essential that marketing and sales are closely aligned. The sales force is an invaluable source of information which marketing should draw upon in designing product/market strategies. For example, the executive vice president for Service Master Consumer Products, whose divisions include Merry Maids, Terminix, and Trugreen–Chemlawn, credits feedback from the sales force in helping the company design the marketing strategy that led to one-stop shopping for all of their products.[4]

Also, marketing is charged with the responsibility of providing the sales force with the marketing tools they need to sell more effectively, such as advertising, support services, and sales promotions. But if salespeople don't like a particular tool, they probably won't use it—or at least they won't use it as effectively as they could.

Salespeople have the primary responsibility for implementing marketing strategies. They will ultimately determine the success or failure of those strategies. Therefore, it is important that marketing seeks input from the sales force throughout the planning process. The Campbell Soup Company provides an interesting example of a company which took an unusual step in order to make this happen. It regionalized its marketing programs by placing the marketing management staff organization into the regional sales offices.

The marketing concept holds that sales activities are a part of marketing. Consequently, a company should do more than simply coordinate its sales and marketing activities. Management should fully *integrate* these two functions. One key to successfully implementing the market concept is management's ability to effectively integrate selling—the prime revenue-generating activity—with other marketing activities.

## Integrating Production and Sales

Sales plans provide the basis for production forecasts—materials requirements and production schedules are developed based on sales forecasts. Therefore, production and sales must integrate their plans in order to avoid operational problems. Fulfilling customer orders also requires that sales and production coordinate their activities. However, a recent survey of manufacturers reports that 37 percent of companies do not coordinate their planning processes.[5]

In these companies, marketing and production agree on general objectives, such as improving profit margins, but they disagree on specific actions or strategies to meet the goals. Some of this disagreement is caused by the fact that each group has a different orientation. The sales group is "sales" oriented and they want as many different products as possible to satisfy their customers. The production orientation is focused on cost and technology.

To solve these problems, companies must institute procedures that will establish communication and coordination links between the two functions. These links are essential for firms seeking to improve customer satisfaction.

## ■ STRATEGIC PLANNING

When shaping sales force management strategy, sales executives are guided and limited by both the firm's total company planning and its strategic marketing planning. For example, in the early 1990s, IBM made some significant changes in its overall strategic approach to the personal computer market. For several years IBM was interested in selling networks to big businesses and more or less ignored the individual, the educational, and the small-business market segments that Apple Computer solicited. However, Apple's success in its markets forced IBM to reconsider its own company strategies. IBM altered its marketing strategies to reflect the new company strategies, and IBM sales management planning also soon reflected those changes.

Three concepts—objectives, strategies, and tactics—are the heart of planning at any level in the organizational hierarchy. All sales managers should have a thorough understanding of these concepts—what they are and how to use them.

### Objectives

**Objectives** are the goals around which a strategic plan is formulated. A plan needs goals. Without them, it is impossible to create a meaningful plan. Objectives must be more than platitudes. Such cliches as "We should be of service to our customers and treat our employees fairly" are only hazy guideposts for making business decisions. To be useful, objectives must be specific and measurable.

Once the firm's objectives are agreed on, all decisions should align with them. Decisions incompatible with objectives only hinder realization of goals. This alignment seems simple and obvious, but it is not so easy to achieve. For instance, goals of a 15 percent return on investment and a 10 percent annual growth rate can clash. Heublein, Inc., encountered this difficulty when it acquired Hamms beer. One of Heublein's objectives was a 15 percent rate of return on its investment. It also had ambitious growth objectives. Hamms beer's large sales volume fit the company's growth objective. However, profits in the beer business are far less than 15 percent—Hamms realized about a 5 percent return on investment. To satisfy the growth objective, Heublein would have to sacrifice the profit objective. A few years after acquiring it, Heublein sold Hamms at a loss.

## Strategies

The terms *objectives, strategies,* and *tactics* gain more meaning when viewed in relation to each other, as in Figure 2-4. Objectives are set first and then **strategies,** or plans of action, are developed to achieve the objectives. For instance, the sales manager may have the goal of achieving a certain dollar volume of sales in a coming period. She proceeds to formulate strategies to accomplish this goal. This may include entering new markets or covering the existing markets more intensely.

The strategies chosen should be followed with some degree of perseverance. Some strategies require time to be effective. Impatient managers eager for results may not allow certain programs time to bear fruit. These managers often take new products off the market before the products have had a fair chance to develop a following. One sales manager fired a

■ **FIGURE 2-4**

**Relationship of objectives, strategies, and tactics**

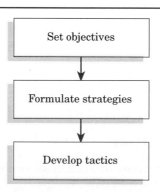

**This sales manager and his rep discuss their sales strategy for the Rome market.**

© Index Stock Photos

rep who had been sent to open up a new territory because dealers were not buying the product as fast as the manager had expected. The fault was not that the sales rep was inefficient, but rather that the manager had unrealistic expectations.

## Tactics

After all the talking is done, the resulting plans (strategies) must be implemented. Some work must be done. **Tactics** are the activities which must be performed by people in order to carry out the strategy.

There are no perfect tactics, and in most situations there is no one best tactic that should be used. Rather, managers must evaluate the situation and choose those tactics which they feel are consistent with the strategy and have the highest probability of success at that point in time.

Generally when a company changes its strategies, it must also change its tactics. However, many administrators use the same tactics repeatedly, regardless of the circumstances, because the tactics worked for them in the past. But success can be lulling. There comes a time when the tactic will not work, and that is usually the most critical time.

The classic example of using an inappropriate sales tactic is a company which has changed its sales strategy from straight product selling to an emphasis on relationship selling and yet does not make any changes in its compensation plan to reflect the changes in selling responsibilities. The following discussion of strategic planning further illustrates the relationship among objectives, strategies, and tactics at different levels within the corporation.

# STRATEGIC PLANNING AT THE COMPANY, MARKETING, AND SALES FORCE LEVELS

Several of the administrative concepts that we just discussed are involved in the strategic planning process for the total company, its marketing program, and its sales force operations. The strategic planning on all levels in a firm should be well integrated and highly coordinated. In any organization, the planning should start at the top and guide the entire organization. Thus decisions at the top shape the strategic management of the marketing program. Marketing planning, in turn, determines the strategic course of sales force management.[6]

## Strategic Planning for the Total Company

Strategic planning for the total company involves determining the organization's mission, the broad objectives (goals) that will enable the company to fulfill its mission, and the strategies and tactics needed to achieve the objectives. Thus strategic planning starts with identifying the organization's broad, fundamental **mission**—management should decide, essentially, "What business are we in?" and "What business should we be in?" The answers to these two questions may or may not be the same. A television manufacturer may say it is in the indoor entertainment business. But after further analysis of its market opportunities, management may say its mission is to be in the entertainment and education business.

Once the company's mission is determined, management can set broad goals consistent with that mission. For example, the company may aim to earn a 20 percent return on investment next year or to increase its market share from the present 8 percent to 20 percent in three years.

The next step is to select the strategy to be used to reach the goal. As examples, consider the following relationships:

| Goals | Possible Strategies |
|---|---|
| 1. Earn 20 percent return on investment next year. | *a.* Reduce production and marketing costs. |
| | *b.* Increase rate of capital turnover |
| 2. Increase market share from present 8 percent to 20 percent in three years. | *a.* Intensify marketing efforts in domestic markets. |
| | *b.* Expand into foreign markets. |
| | *c.* Buy out a competitor. |

The tactics selected to implement the strategy would, of course, depend on the strategy chosen. Thus if the strategy is to reduce marketing costs, management can use such tactics as (1) cutting advertising expenses by 10 percent or (2) closing two branch offices. To implement the strategy of intensifying the domestic marketing effort, management might (1) add 20 more sales reps or (2) change the compensation plan to provide greater motivation for the sales force.

## Strategic Marketing Planning

Once the total company planning process is completed, essentially the same procedure can be repeated for the marketing program. The goals, strategies, and tactics at the marketing level are closely related to those at the corporate level. For example, a corporate strategy often translates into a marketing goal. To illustrate:

| Company Goal | Company Strategy | Marketing Strategy |
|---|---|---|
| 1. Earn 20 percent return on investment. | Cut marketing costs by 15 percent this year. | Reduce direct selling efforts by using wholesalers to reach small accounts. |
| 2. Increase market share from present 8 percent to 20 percent. | Intensify marketing efforts in domestic markets. | Enter new markets. |

## Sales Force Strategy

Once the strategic planning process for the entire marketing program has been completed, the role of the sales force has largely been established. That is, the goals, strategies, and tactics adopted by sales managers generally are limited and guided by the strategic marketing plan. To illustrate:

*Corporate goal:*  Increase market share from 8 percent to 20 percent in two years.

*Corporate strategy (marketing goal):*  Intensify market efforts in domestic markets to increase sales volume by $3 million next year.

*Marketing strategy (sales force goal):*  
a. Enter new geographic markets and sell to new types of customers, or
b. Cover existing geographic markets more aggressively.

Now, whether the company elects to pursue marketing strategy (sales force goal) *a* or *b* will make a big difference in the choice of sales force strategies and tactics. Tactical decisions in the areas of organizational design, selection, training, compensation, supervision, and evaluation must all be aligned with the sales strategy. These principles may be illustrated as follows:

| Marketing Strategy | Sales Force Strategy | Sales Force Tactics |
|---|---|---|
| *a.* Enter new markets. | Build long-term customer relations. | 1. Stress missionary selling in sales training and supervision. 2. Stress salary element in compensation plan. |
| *b.* Sell aggressively in existing markets. | Increase sales force motivation. | 1. Conduct more sales contests. 2. Stress commission feature in pay plan. 3. Increase field supervision. |

In many companies, this strategic sales force planning is continued down the organizational hierarchy. That is, sales force goals and strategies are established for regional sales divisions, and even for individual sales reps and key accounts.

## STRATEGIC TRENDS

Several strategic developments in marketing management that have evolved in the 1990s will have a major impact on sales strategies throughout the next decade. First, many companies are adding new channels of distribution to existing ones in order to expand market coverage and lower costs. Second, many firms are interested in buying whole systems rather than stand alone products as solutions to their problems. Third, a number of companies are using varied relationship strategies with different classes of customers. Fourth, many companies have adopted a team selling approach. All four of these trends impact sales force management, as we discuss next.

### Multiple Sales Channels

To maintain existing customer bases, cut costs, and expand market coverage, many firms are restructuring their sales operations to use multiple sales channels. A company may employ a direct-sales force as well as distributors. The same firm may also use direct mail, telemarketing, and electronic mail. These methods may be used to reach different segments of customers or to perform various selling tasks necessary to efficiently serve one segment.

Originally IBM's selling tasks were handled by their direct sales force only. But as IBM faced increasing competition, it expanded its sales efforts to include independent dealers, catalogs, direct mail, and telemarketing.

Apple Computer, on the other hand, started with a dealer network and later added a direct-sales force. Mary Kay has added telemarketing to its more traditional personal selling methods. Each of these companies created a *hybrid* sales system to reach different segments of buyers.

The objective in designing these systems is to determine what mix of selling methods can best accomplish the selling tasks. Often it is possible to use less expensive selling methods for tasks that do not require face-to-face contact. The trade-off which must be considered is between the need for personalized customer service and the cost of providing that service. Chapter 3 explores these options further.

The addition of new sales channels requires changes in the structure and policies of the sales organization. Often these changes will be accompanied by a certain amount of resistance from the existing salespeople. Sales managers must manage this conflict as well as the coordination within and across channels. Specific guidelines must be established which clearly delineate who is responsible for which customers and/or tasks in the hybrid system. Utilizing multiple channels undoubtedly makes the sales manager's job more complex. But in spite of the potential problems, the use of multiple channels is likely to increase throughout the next decade.

## Multiple Relationship Strategies

Along with using multiple channels of distribution, many companies are segmenting their customers on the basis of the relationship the company has (or wants to develop) with the customer. The relationship can vary from one in which the sale is just an individual transaction to one in which the company develops a close long-term relationship or even a partnership with the customer.

In **transaction selling,** salespeople emphasize the product, its quality, and the price. Generally, this kind of sale involves products which are not very complex, and the dollar amount of each sale is low. In **relationship selling,** salespeople develop in-depth knowledge of their customers' company and business. They help customers identify problems and they work with customers to find mutually beneficial solutions. In a **partnership,** companies form strategic alliances in order to achieve joint goals. In a partnering relationship, the salesperson is responsible for overseeing the coordination and integration of the efforts of the two partners.

These relationships vary in terms of the degree of *commitment to the customer* and the *cost of serving the customer,* as outlined in Figure 2-5. In a transaction sale both the commitment and the selling costs are at a minimum, whereas in a partnership the commitment and costs are very high.[7] Therefore, many companies are using different relationship strategies to serve different customers. DuPont, for example, segments its customers according to the relationship strategy which it has identified as

■ **FIGURE 2-5**

**Multiple
relationship
strategies**

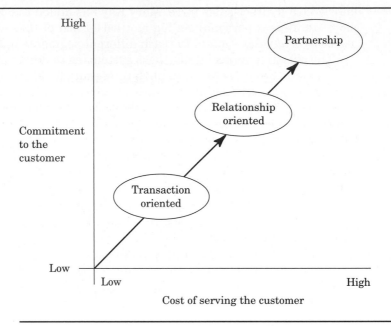

Source: Adapted from presentation by Gerald J. Bauer of E. I. du Pont de Nemours & Company, "Sales Enhancement Process," 1996.

being the most effective for that customer.[8] Motorola has three different sales forces which serve its *business* customers, its *major customers,* and its *partners.*[9]

## Systems Selling

Most customers are facing severe cost pressures as a result of intensified global competition. To reduce costs, companies are adopting new purchasing practices. In today's markets, customers are looking to suppliers for solutions to their problems, not just products.

**Systems selling** is a strategy adopted by firms in response to the customer's desire for solutions. This strategy involves selling a total package of goods and services and the related expertise—a system—to solve a customer's problem. The idea is that the system will satisfy the buyer's needs more effectively than will selling individual products separately. The sellers not only differentiate their offering by providing a high level of value added, but increase the costs of that customer switching to a new supplier.[10]

Xerox, for example, which originally sold individual products, today uses a systems selling approach. After studying the customer's office information and operating problems, Xerox recommends an integrated system of products and services to solve that customer's problems.

## AN INTERNATIONAL PERSPECTIVE

Emerging markets in such places as eastern Europe and China; trade agreements with Canada, Mexico, and much of western Europe; and the increase in foreign competition within the United States are drawing U.S. companies into the global marketplace. As larger companies begin to globalize, their suppliers will be forced to adopt a global strategy as well. Future success for many companies is linked to their ability to compete in international markets.

In these markets, U.S. companies face intensified competition, shorter product life cycles, higher quality standards, and rapid technological changes. The key to success in these markets is building effective relationships with customers. In many global markets, there is a much greater emphasis on developing interpersonal relationships between buyers and sellers than there is in the United States. The more successful international firms place a greater emphasis on customer service, using it as a base upon which they develop strong relationships with their customers.

Unfortunately, many U.S. firms have relied on technological aspects of their products to give them a competitive advantage. Because of this technical orientation, many of these firms have not adequately developed the service component of their marketing mix. To be competitive in the global marketplace, U.S. firms must develop strategies which encompass a strong customer service component.

Sources: Sergey Frank, "Gaining a Global Outlook," *Sales & Marketing Management,* January 1992, pp. 52–57; and A. Coskum Samli, Laurence W. Jacobs, and James Wills, "What Presale and Postsale Services Do You Need to Be Competitive?" *Industrial Marketing Management,* February 1993, pp. 33–41.

In some cases the seller buys components or complementary products from other suppliers and assembles them into a package for the buyer. These sellers are often referred to as **value-added resellers (VAR).**[11] Some corporations do not want to perform any function that is not directly related to making or marketing their own products. They delegate the entire purchasing process for some projects to a **systems integrator.** This person (or firm) is responsible for an entire project, from conception to implementation and follow-up services.[12] General Motors, for example, has teamed up with Fanuc, a supplier of paint spray guns and spray-booth equipment, to provide solutions to their complex painting needs. When Harnischfer Engineers, a supplier of cranes and storage-retrieval machines, determined that even its most sophisticated customers lacked the expertise to design an automated materials handling system, it revised its entire business strategy to become a systems integrator. Instead of selling machines and equipment, Harnischfer now sells plantwide materials handling systems.[13]

Thus many firms who used to sell directly to the end user are now selling to VARs or competing to be one of the suppliers for a systems integrator.

### Team Selling

Because customers are searching for integrated solutions to problems, the purchasing process has become more complex. As a result, the buying decision is no longer being made by an individual. Rather, it is often being made by a group of functional specialists who view the purchase from a strategic perspective. This group of people is sometimes referred to as the **buying center.**

Because these individuals represent numerous technical and managerial functions, it is difficult for one salesperson to satisfy all of the individuals involved.[14] As a result, many sellers are adopting a strategy of **team selling** in order to match the expertise of the buyer team. The seller team is composed of one or more salespeople as well as other functional specialists, such as design engineers, financial experts, customer service representatives, quality control engineers—anyone and everyone who can contribute to finding the best solutions to a particular customer's problems. A team-selling approach is especially appropriate when a company has also adopted a strategy of selling systems. MCI, which sells telecommunications systems, usually uses a team-selling approach. Purabil, a leading maker of temperature and humidity control systems, uses sales teams to sell to systems integrators. The organization of these selling teams will be discussed in greater detail in Chapter 4.[15]

## Marketing Management's Social Responsibility

Social and economic conditions in the 1990s have led to another important development in the evolution of marketing management. Marketing executives must act in a socially responsible manner if they wish to succeed, or even survive, in this era. External pressures—consumer discontent, concern for environmental problems, and political–legal forces—influence marketing programs in countless firms.

Arco developed and markets an unleaded regular gasoline with low emissions in response to great pressure from environmentalists. The auto industry made many technical and design changes in its products in response to governmental and public pressure for safer vehicles. Grocery chains responded quickly to complaints about harmful chemicals sprayed on produce. Ralph's, a California supermarket chain, promotes its produce as being free of such chemicals. This book is printed on partially recycled paper. It would be difficult to find any firm that has not somehow had to alter its marketing behavior in response to external pressures.

Viewed more broadly, there is a growing concern for the management of human resources. We sense a change in emphasis from materialism to humanitarianism in our society. One mark of an affluent society is a shift in consumption from products to services and a shift in cultural emphasis from things to people. As we look forward to the 21st century, marketing management must be concerned with creating and delivering a better quality of *life,* rather than only a better material standard of *living.*

# ■ Summary

Modern sales managers understand that they are but one link in the total marketing strategy for the firm. Moreover, they understand the place of the firm's marketing strategy within the company's total strategic plan.

In addition, both the manager and the reps should understand the external environmental forces that affect their operations. One must be sensitive to the social, economic, technical, and governmental forces that are at work in our society. They must also understand their markets, their suppliers, and the marketing intermediaries (wholesalers and retailers).

Personal selling is part of the promotional mix, which is part of the marketing mix.

With the advent of the marketing concept and its acceptance by most businesses, the job of the sales manager has been changed. Now sales operations are but one portion of the firm's total marketing program. Marketing has evolved through several stages. It is now in the relationship-oriented stage, whereby buyers and sellers make long-term commitments to do business with each other.

Setting specific, clear-cut objectives is an essential step in the management of a company. Once the company's goals are set, management can develop appropriate strategies for achieving those objectives. Tactics are the organizational behavior that executes the strategy.

Strategic planning on all levels in a firm should be coordinated. This planning should start at the top and guide the entire organization. Thus decisions at the top shape strategic planning in the marketing program. Then the marketing planning determines the strategic course of sales force management.

Several strategic trends which have evolved during the 1990s are shaping the strategy of sales organizations. In response to intensified competition and changes in customer purchasing patterns, many firms are now using multiple sales channels to reach a broader customer base and multiple sales strategies to sell to different customers. Also, many companies have adopted systems-selling and team-selling strategies in order to better serve the needs of their customers. Finally, today's managers must act in a socially responsible manner if they wish to succeed.

## Key Terms

| | | |
|---|---|---|
| Buying center | Objectives | Systems selling |
| Marketing concept | Partnerships | Tactics |
| Marketing management | Relationship selling | Team selling |
| Marketing mix | Strategies | Transaction selling |
| Mission | Systems integrator | Value-added resellers (VAR) |

## QUESTIONS AND PROBLEMS

1. How can top management keep the sales manager abreast of changes in the environment that affect the company? How can the sales manager pass such information on to the sales force?

2. We said company planning should be customer oriented. Exactly what does that mean? In what way or by what stretch of the imagination might the planning of the firm's employee benefit package be affected by customer considerations?

3. Why should a company be concerned about the profitability of its customers?

4. What are some ways in which sales managers can empower their salespeople?

5. How do marketing people depend on salespeople? How do salespeople depend on marketing people?

6. Why should a sales manager prepare an annual operating plan?

7. If you, as a sales manager, were required to prepare an annual operating plan, what would you include in the plan?

8. As a sales rep, you are required to develop an annual sales plan for your territory. What would you include in your plan? *Hint:* Think in terms of objectives, strategies, and tactics.

9. What role does the quality of the information you possess have in your tactical behavior?

10. In what way is the existence of a sales force the reflection of a strategy?

11. One management writer observed that it is folly to expect behavior A when rewarding behavior B. How might his insight be applied to the problem of aligning sales force behavior with corporate goals?

12. What are some of the ways sales managers can limit the amount of conflict between various distributors if their company is using a multiple-channel strategy?

13. How should a company decide whether to use transaction selling or relationship selling or develop partnerships with each of its customers?

14. How does a manager reward the team members in a team-selling situation?

15. How can team selling help a firm implement a strategy of systems selling?

 EXPERIENTIAL EXERCISES

A. Interview a marketing or product manager for a firm. Ask him or her to identify the primary sales objective for one of their products. Ask one of their sales managers and one of the sales representatives the same question for the same product. Compare and contrast their viewpoints.

B. Using one company as a source of information, explore how the marketing and sales activities for a new product differ from those of an older product.

## ■ REFERENCES

1. Rolph E. Anderson, "Personal Selling and Sales Management in the New Millennium," *Journal of Personal Selling and Sales Management,* Fall 1996, pp. 17–32.

2. Joel R. Evans and Richard L. Laskins, "The Relationship Marketing Process: A Conceptualization and Application," *Industrial Marketing Management* 23 (1994), pp. 439–52.

3. Ibid.

4. Craig Palubiak, "There's No Hole in This Plan," *Sales and Marketing Management,* November 1996, pp. 28–29.

5. Paul A. Konijnendijk, "Dependence and Conflict between Production and Sales," *Industrial Marketing Management,* August 1993, pp. 161–65.

6. William Strahle, Rosann L. Spiro, and Frank Acito, "Marketing and Sales Strategy: Strategic Alignment and Implementation," *Journal of Personal Selling & Sales Management,* Winter 1996.

7. Gerald J. Bauer, "Sales Enhancement Process," presentation at the New Horizons in Personal Selling and Sales Management Conference, American Marketing Association Selling and Sales Management Strategic Interest Group, Lake Buena Vista, Florida, July 1996.

8. Ibid.

9. Neil Rackham, presentation at Indiana University, November 1996.

10. Stanley J. Paliwoda and Andrea J. Bonaccorsi, "Systems Selling in the Aircraft Industry," *Industrial Marketing Management,* May 1993, pp. 155–60.

11. Marvin Everett, "Systems Integrators: Marketing's New Maestros," *Sales & Marketing Management,* November 1990, pp. 50–60.

12. Ibid.

13. Ibid.

14. S. Joe Puri and Pradeep Korgaonkar, "Couple the Buying and Selling Teams," *Industrial Marketing Management,* November 1991, pp. 311–17.

15. Everett, "Systems Integrators."

---

*Case 2-1*

## MATSUSHITA ELECTRIC CORPORATION OF AMERICA
### Sales force strategy

John Cunningham was the national sales manager of the Lighting Products Department, Special Products Division, of Matsushita Electric Corporation, a huge industrial complex in Japan with total sales worldwide of ¥6,660 billion ($60 billion). He was immediately concerned with the operational sales strategy for a new line of compact, energy-efficient, fluorescent light bulbs (lamps) for both the consumer and industrial markets. The company had many years of experience selling lamps in the Orient, where it was a major factor in the market. For strategic reasons, Matsushita marketed its wide line of consumer and industrial products in the United States under the trade name Panasonic.

John Cunningham, after graduation as a marketing major from the University of South Florida in 1978, began his career selling light bulbs (lamps) for Westinghouse and subsequently North American Phillips when it purchased the lamp division from Westinghouse. His outstanding sales record attracted the attention of Mitsubishi, which was trying to build distribution for a new line of energy-efficient light bulbs it had developed. However, that venture was terminated when the new bulbs were found to infringe on patents held by Phillips. Mitsubishi transferred John to selling its gigantic Diamond Vision television screens now seen in most of the sports stadiums in the country. His outstanding performance attracted the attention of the managers of Matsushita's light bulb operations, who were looking for someone to manage sales and distribution in the United States. After much conversation, several interviews, and a thorough investigation, John was hired. While his previous experience working for a Japanese company, combined with his knowledge of the Japanese business culture, were important factors in his selection, his outstanding sales record and establishment of a distribution network with Mitsubishi's compact fluorescent lamp operation was instrumental in the hiring decision.

Matsushita's basic marketing strategy was to introduce compact, energy-efficient, fluorescent lamps. A 15-watt fluorescent lamp would provide the same lumens (light) as a 75-watt incandescent lamp, thus yielding significant savings in power consumption. Such savings were important in the Far East markets where electricity costs were much higher than in the United States. Further, the life of the lamp was about 10 times that of an incandescent lamp. Research in the United States indicated that most people considered longevity the product's prime benefit. Social, political, and economic forces strongly supported such energy-saving innovations.

Despite John's outstanding performance, Panasonic's share of the U.S. consumer lamp market was small. It was a new player in a very competitive market dominated by such powerful names as General Electric and Phillips. Even such a name as Westinghouse had been driven out of the business. At a meeting at the company's headquarters in Osaka, Japan in late 1996, he was asked a direct question by one of the firm's top executives: "What would it take for us to significantly increase our share of the market for our fluorescent bulbs?"

John knew that he was expected to make the company a major player in the market; Matsushita management did not like being a minor factor in any of its markets. John had studied the situation intensely and was waiting with his answer. "We need to develop an electronic chip to replace the ballast. Present ballasts hum, flicker when started, are bulky, and are not rheostatable. They are either off or on. If a small electronic chip could be designed to replace the traditional ballast, we'd have a technological feature that would significantly increase our market share."

John's superiors took note of his request and within a short time the company R&D people gave him exactly what he had requested—a small electronic chip to replace the ballast in fluorescent bulbs. It could be available for distribution in August 1997. A planning meeting was held in Osaka at which John was asked to provide sales forecasts and budgets for marketing the new line of lamps. John was responsible only for the marketing of lamps under the Panasonic brand name. Matsushita also sold huge quantities of goods directly to other manufacturers and to large distributive organizations that sold them under their own brand names. For example, while Matsushita sold compact disc machines under its brand name Panasonic, it also made essentially the same product, with minor cosmetic alterations, for many other companies to market under their brand names. Matsushita company policy was to encourage OEM sales since it was felt that by so doing the company would be able to sell a much larger portion of the total market.

One basic corporate goal was to keep the factories in Japan busy, at full employment. Matsushita was not caught up with the penchant of many American corporations for controlling significant shares of a market through their own brands. It would sell to any firm that could provide significant volume for the factories.

John was informed at the meeting that the new technology would be offered to all other manufacturers. General Electric would have the same technology to sell as Panasonic. John was somewhat dismayed but knew that he could do nothing about the policy. However, he negotiated two concessions. First, he was able to have his sales quotas reduced in view of the increased competition. Second, he was able to get a one-year lead time over the competition. Panasonic would have the innovation exclusively for one year before Matsushita would sell it to anyone else. John had some sales force planning to do.

The new bulbs would be sold through the channels that traditionally sold light bulbs: hardware stores, discount stores, supermarkets, drugstores, light fixture outlets, electrical wholesalers, industrial distributors, and so on. Many of these retail markets were dominated by such huge and powerful mass merchandising firms as Kmart, Wal-Mart, Home Depot, and the drug and grocery chains. All of these firms were national accounts. The task before John was to get adequate distribution of the new bulb in such distributive systems quickly while Panasonic had exclusive control of the product. It would require building a large sales system quickly.

John was inclined to build the sales system using manufacturers' rep organizations that had existing relationships with the target distributive organizations. Using such rep organizations was within Panasonic policy. Its small-appliance division sold Panasonic's wide line of appliances through independent sales reps who called on essentially the same trades targeted by the lamp division.

However, one of John's peers in the Panasonic organization initiated a casual conversation at a company social event during which he suggested that perhaps now would be a good time for the company to consider hiring its own salespeople to sell directly to the particularly large national accounts such as Wal-Mart, Sears, Kmart, Home Depot, and others of such size. Such a sales force could also sell to the distributors that sold to smaller retail groups and could cover OEM buyers. He argued, "It's time for us to get some experience in managing a sales organization and we could well afford it on the 5 percent of sales we would have to pay the reps. And we'd have more control over them than we would the reps!" John nodded but said nothing.

### Questions:

1. Should Panasonic initiate some efforts to build its own sales force to sell to selected target markets and distributor networks?

2. If not, what course of action would you recommend to John?

*Case 2-2*

## COMPUTER TRAINING INSTITUTES, INC.
### A vendor relationship problem

Larry Rugg, president of Computer Training Institutes, Inc. (CTI), of Atlanta, Georgia, had just finished a telephone conversation with Mark Ruiz, president of PC Publications, Inc., of San Jose, California. Ruiz had asked Rugg for a personal appointment at 9:00 A.M. the following Monday to discuss the relationships between their two companies.

CTI operated 36 trade schools in large metropolitan areas, teaching high school graduates how to use computers. The education was strongly career oriented, leading to entry-level jobs in corporate computer operations. CTI's rapidly growing organization was highly profitable, a reflection of the good placement of its graduates. In addition to teaching students how to use computers, CTI also provided some basic business training in such areas as marketing, accounting, and finance. Rugg had discovered that the firms that hired CTI graduates greatly preferred them because they understood overall business operations better than others seeking the same jobs. They were prepared to accept other responsibilities in the organization.

Books and other educational materials were furnished as part of the tuition. Naturally, CTI bought the books as cheaply as possible. It was usually able to buy them for about 40 percent off list price. Not only were book costs high, but considerable time and effort were required to procure and distribute them. Separate negotiations had to be carried on with more than 15 publishers.

A month earlier, Rugg had hired Karin Bradley to assume total responsibility for managing the book program. He had discovered Bradley while buying some books from PC Publications; she had been PC's general manager for three years. However, Bradley had told Rugg that she and Ruiz were not getting along well at all. Bradley said she was looking for another job and would appreciate it if Rugg would keep his eye open for a position that would be good for her. Rugg agreed to do so. He thought about the situation for two days and then invited Bradley to Atlanta for an interview. She went and was offered a position that was most attractive to her.

When the time came for CTI to renew the PC Publications' contract, Ruiz strongly objected to the price demands made by Bradley: 60 percent off list price. Ruiz hung up the telephone on her, saying, "I'll talk with your boss about this and some other things too." Rugg answered Ruiz's telephone call on Friday afternoon. Ruiz let it be known that he wanted to negotiate with Rugg only. He claimed that Bradley was being deliberately unreasonable in retaliation for some of the conflicts they had while she was working for him. When asked about them, he would not provide any specifics on what those conflicts were. He made it clear that he was not only unhappy that Bradley had hired a PC employee, but that the person was using inside information to PC's disadvantage.

Rugg insisted that Bradley was in total charge of the book-buying operation and that Ruiz would have to deal with her. Finally, Ruiz proclaimed, "I'm flying to Atlanta and will see you at 9 o'clock Monday morning." Rugg agreed to the meeting only to end the conversation. Rugg was well aware of Bradley's demand for a 60 percent discount, and the reason for it. It seemed as if the vendor's gross margins could allow such a discount for the volume of books being sold. Unfortunately, Bradley was in New York buying books from some large New York publishers.

Rugg leaned back in his chair, looking out over the wooded Georgia landscape. He wondered how he should handle the matter.

**Questions:**

1. Evaluate the situation from a tactical viewpoint.

2. Precisely how should Rugg handle this matter?

# CHAPTER 3

# The Personal Selling Process

Losing is simply learning how to win.
**Ted Turner**

It is difficult to manage a sales force intelligently without a good grasp of the selling process. While heated debates over the sales manager's need for significant and successful sales experience have raged off and on in marketing for decades, good judgment favors the manager who is competent and knowledgeable about the field being administered. Thus some exposure to selling seems warranted for students of sales management. Additionally, sales training programs basically teach selling. It would be difficult to plan and conduct a sales training program without knowing how to sell.

In Chapter 1, we noted the wide array of activities which salespeople perform. In this chapter we focus on just those activities which are related to generating sales and satisfying customers. As you can see from Figure 3-1, the average sales professional works about 47 hours per week. During a typical week salespeople spend 56 percent of their time performing selling activities and another 25 percent of their time following up their sales with service calls. If we consider that service is a part

■ **FIGURE 3-1**

**Salesperson's average time allocation**

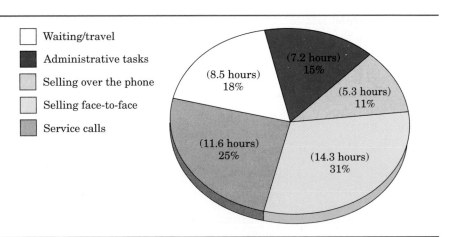

Source: Christem P. Herde, *Dartnell's 29th Sales Force Compensation Survey 1996–1997* (Chicago, IL: Dartnell Press), p. 177.

of the selling process, salespeople spend approximately 31 hours in selling related activities each week versus a little less than 16 hours performing the nonselling aspects of their jobs.

One of the first ideas a sales rep needs to understand is that there are no magic sales techniques. No one method can be used to close every sale. The recommended techniques are simply those that experience has indicated seem to work better than others in certain situations.

The actual selling process can be likened to a chain, each link of which must be closed successfully, or the seller will fail to get the order. However, each step overlaps others, and their sequence may be altered to meet the situation at hand.

The eight steps of the sales process are:

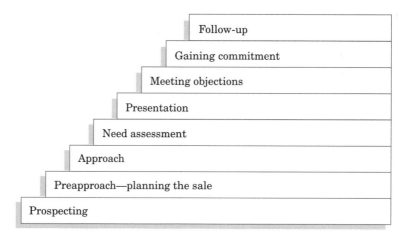

| Follow-up |
| Gaining commitment |
| Meeting objections |
| Presentation |
| Need assessment |
| Approach |
| Preapproach—planning the sale |
| Prospecting |

## PROSPECTING

Succeeding in today's competitive environment means that a company must constantly be finding new customers. A salesperson's basic strategy should be to spend as much time as possible with excellent prospects—people who recognize their need and are ready to buy. As Phil Clark, former IBM regional sales manager in Dallas, succinctly told his sales force, "The idea is that through our advertising and promotional efforts we stand on a ladder shouting loudly all over Dallas, 'Everyone who is ready to buy a computer please raise their hands.' Then we go sell one to each person who responds."

**Prospecting** is the method or system by which salespeople learn the names of people who need the product and can afford it. There are two steps in successful prospecting. The first step is generating leads—identifying potential customers. The second step is qualifying leads according to who is most likely to buy.

## Identifying Leads

Names and addresses of good prospects can be obtained in a number of ways:

- Referrals from customers—salespeople indicate that their number one source of referrals is their existing customers, who provide nearly two-thirds of their leads.[1]
- Referrals from internal company sources such as the sales manager, the marketing department, or the telemarketing department—customer inquiries may be generated from company advertising, direct mail, trade shows, and teleprospecting efforts. Salespeople report that these sources provide approximately 23 percent of their leads.[2]
- Referrals from external referral agencies—some companies turn to outside agencies, such as Contact Software International, for the generation and qualification of leads.
- Published directories—trade associations, the government, local chambers of commerce, the yellow pages all are good sources of prospects. Many of the directories are available on the Internet.
- Networking by the salesperson—salespeople often use their friends and acquaintances to make new contacts. Many salespeople join professional and civic organizations in part to meet new people who may be potential customers or who may be able to provide leads.
- Cold canvassing—salespeople make unannounced calls on businesses which may need the products which the rep sells. The popularity of this approach is declining because it is very time consuming and not very cost effective due to the high rejection rate. This approach does not allow the salesperson to *qualify* the account before calling. However for certain widely used products, such as office supplies, this approach can work well.

## Qualifying Leads

Whatever the source of the lead, it is important that the lead be qualified. Philosophically, professional salespeople do not want to bother people who have no need for their products. Moreover, it is very expensive for salespeople to make calls which have little chance of success because the customer does not need or want or cannot afford the products. In order to qualify a prospect, the salesperson or the person providing the referral should determine whether the prospect is a good one. To determine this, the prospect must satisfy three conditions:

1. The customer has a need for the products which are being sold.
2. The customer can afford to buy the products.
3. The customer is receptive to being called upon by the salesperson.

---

### Marketing Identifies; Sales Closes

Generating inquiries with advertising, direct mail, trade shows, and other media is only half the marketing department's job. It must also determine which leads are bona fide leads, sparing salespeople the drudgery of sifting a glut of time-consuming unqualified leads.

---

Traditionally, sales reps were expected to find their own prospects. That was part of the selling process, part of the job—a most important part of it. Today, however, many companies realize that the marketing department is in the best position to develop effective prospecting systems for the sales force. Recent surveys show that 45 percent of the people who make an inquiry to a company about a product or service buy it from that company or a competitor within 12 months. Another 25 percent are planning on buying it (see Figure 3-2). So in fact these leads are hot prospects. Moreover, the success of company promotional programs in generating good leads (prospects) has centralized the prospecting systems. Today many companies use telemarketing to help salespeople identify and qualify customers.

Sales reps generally appreciate being relieved of the burden of developing a prospecting system, and the company benefits when its reps can spend more time actually making sales presentations to qualified prospects. Yet reports suggest that only 10 percent to 15 percent of all business and industrial leads receive personal follow-ups.[3] To convert a qualified lead to a sale, salespeople must follow up the lead. In general, salespeople get more than 80 percent of the business if they follow up a customer inquiry (see Figure 3-3).

■ **FIGURE 3-2**

---

**Lead conversion ratio: inquiry to decision 12 months after inquiring**

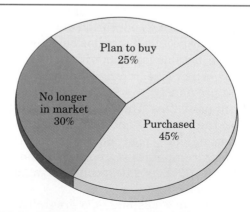

Plan to buy 25%

No longer in market 30%

Purchased 45%

---

Source: Bob Donath, James K. Obermayer, Carolyn K. Dixon, and Richard A. Crocker, "When Your Prospect Calls," *Marketing Management* 3, no. 2 (1994).

■ **FIGURE 3-3**

**The value of inquiry follow-up**

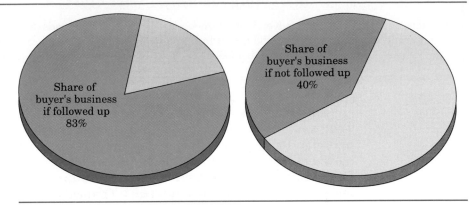

Source: Bob Donath, James K. Obermayer, Carolyn K. Dixon, and Richard A. Crocker, "When Your Prospect Calls," *Marketing Management* 3, no. 2 (1994).

## PREAPPROACH—PLANNING THE SALE

This preapproach step includes all the information-gathering activities which salespeople perform to learn relevant facts about the prospects and their needs and situation. Then, based on this information, salespeople plan their sales presentations, selecting the most appropriate objective for each call.

### Customer Research

The sales rep should learn everything possible about the business of the prospective customer—its size, its present purchasing practices, the location of its plants, the names of its executives, and, most important, the *names of people who make the buying decision as well those who influence the purchase.* It is also helpful to learn something about the buyers' background, such as education and social affiliations, or their personalities. If the prospective buyer has been having problems, the seller should, if possible, become familiar with them.

When researching a current customer or one which has been called on previously by a salesperson from your company, start by reading the company files. They should provide a wealth of background information on the company and possibly on the buyers as well—sales records, correspondence, past sales call reports, and other relevant information. Many companies store information about their customers in a database to which their salespeople have easy access using laptop or notebook computers.

For new customers, a great deal of the information may be obtained easily using the Internet or on-line information services such as LEXIS-NEXIS, DIALOG, and Dow Jones News/Retrieval. Other sources include trade magazines, industrial directories, magazine and newspaper articles, chambers of commerce, and government publications, as well as the annual reports of companies. Sometimes the company's current suppliers, customers, and certain employees can provide information.

The goal of customer research is for salespeople to know as much as they can about the company, the decision makers, and their needs before making that first call. As Kenneth Ranucci, a senior account executive at Contempo Design, says, "In-depth research into prospects makes salespeople stand out."[4]

### Planning the Sales Presentation

The most important part of planning the sales presentation is defining the objective or goal for the particular call. The goal is not necessarily to close or complete the sale on each call. In fact salespeople report that on the average it takes four calls to close a sale.[5] However, on each call, the salesperson does want to obtain from the buyer some *type of commitment for action which moves the sale forward*. That should be the goal. For example, the salesperson may try to obtain a list of the customer's vendor selection criteria or get the buyer to set up a meeting with some of the other people who will be involved in the decision. The objective may be any agreement on an action that moves the sale forward.

Salespeople may also plan how they are going to approach the buyer and what kind of questions they want to ask. It is important that salespeople recognize differences across selling situations and adapt their presentations accordingly. Based on their precall customer research, they will make a tentative judgment as to which of their products best meet their customers' needs and then formulate a tentative plan for presenting the features and benefits of those products. Of course the information gained by salespeople during the actual call may often cause them to alter their initial objectives and/or plans. This is called **adaptive selling.**[6]

## ■ THE APPROACH

Once the sales rep has the name of a prospect and adequate preapproach information, the next step is the actual approach. It is important to make an appointment to see the buyer. This increases the chances that the salesperson will have the buyer's attention during their meeting.

A good approach makes a favorable impression on the buyer and establishes some degree of rapport between the salesperson and the buyer. In order to make a favorable impression with customers in the United States, the salesperson should have a firm handshake, be professionally attired, and make good eye contact. Usually each call starts with an introduction (unless the salesperson has called on this customer before) and a limited amount of small talk. Sometimes salespeople will draw attention

---

### A Typical Day in the Life of a Compaq Salesperson

The sales rep starts her day at home, checking the network for electronic mail and activity affecting her customers. She then gathers the material she needs for the day's meetings, using her notebook computer, which includes appointments, telephone numbers, charts, illustrations, and graphics. With the notebook computer, she can access the company's database on the road.

After about three or four sales calls, she returns home to complete her paper work and update the company database with the latest information about her customers. She also e-mails one of the tech reps to assist one of her customers in solving a technical question that he had.

Source: R. Lee Sullivan, "The Office That Never Closes," *Forbes,* May 23, 1994, p. 212.

---

to their products by handing the buyer a sample or by highlighting some benefit in which the buyer will likely be interested.

The approach usually takes up only the first minute or so of a call, but it can make or break the entire presentation. If the approach fails, the salesperson often does not get a chance to give a presentation. At the end of the approach, the salesperson must gain the buyer's agreement to move into the need assessment stage of the call.

## NEED ASSESSMENT

Companies and consumers purchase products and services to satisfy needs or to solve problems. In a business situation, the company's purchases are always related to the need to improve performance—to become more efficient and effective at fulfilling customer needs. Need assessment is the stage in which the *salesperson must discover, clarify, and understand the buyer's needs*. The best way to uncover and understand needs is by asking questions. In fact, research has determined that the more questions salespeople ask, the more likely it is that they will be successful.[7]

There are several types of questions which salespeople can use to encourage their buyers to reveal and discuss their needs:[8]

- **Situational questions.** These are questions which ask for factual information about the buyer's current situation. Salespeople ask these questions to get ideas about how the customers might be able to use their products. If salespeople do a good job of researching the customer during their precall planning, then they are able to use fewer situational questions. Examples of these are:
  
  *a.* How often do you change the cutting oil in your drill presses?
  
  *b.* Who is involved in the purchase decision for this product?
  
  *c.* How much inventory of this product do you carry?

- **Problem discovery questions.** These are questions used to uncover potential problems, difficulties, or dissatisfaction that the customer is experiencing that the salesperson's products and services can solve. Salespeople use these questions to uncover customer needs around which they can build their presentation. Examples of these are:

*a.* Which part of your production process is the most difficult in terms of controlling quality?

*b.* Have you experienced any delays in getting those materials from your current suppliers?

*c.* Have you experienced any problems in servicing your presses?

- **Problem impact questions.** These are questions about the impact that the buyer's problem will have on various aspects of their operations. Salespeople ask these questions to make the buyer think about the consequences of *not* solving the problem. These questions help the buyer see that the seriousness of the problem justifies the time and money it will take to achieve a solution. Examples of these are:

*a.* What impact do the quality consistency problems have on your production costs?

*b.* What affect do the delays in receiving the materials have on your operations?

*c.* How do these maintenance problems affect your operations?

- **Solution value question.** These questions ask about the value or the importance of a solution to a problem uncovered earlier in the conversation. Salespeople use these to reinforce the importance of the problem and to help the buyer assess the value of a solution. Examples of these are:

*a.* If the rejection rate on your quality inspection was reduced to under 1 percent, how much would that save you?

*b.* How much are your production costs increased by material stockouts?

*c.* How important is reducing downtime to minimizing your production costs?

- **Confirmatory questions.** Finally, these questions ask for confirmation from buyers that they are interested in hearing about how your products will help them. Salespeople may use confirmatory questions to make the transition into their presentation of their products' features and benefits. Examples of these questions are:

*a.* So you would be interested in a maintenance program that would minimize your downtime, is that correct?

*b.* If I can provide evidence to you that our products would significantly lower your rejection rate, would you be interested in that?

Salespeople ask these questions in the logical order just presented. The situational questions should be asked first, followed by the problem discovery questions, the problem impact questions, the solution value

---

### Talk, Talk, Talk, Talk: Try a Little Listening

While many corporate slogans promote the notion of listening to the customer, a recent study of 432 corporate buyers by Communispond, Inc., revealed that salespeople are not good listeners. Nearly half of the buyers said that salespeople are "too talky." The buyers also felt that salespeople do not know how to ask the right questions about their companies' needs.

Only 1 percent of the respondents said that the salespeople they deal with have "excellent" sales skills, while 69 percent rated them poor or merely fair at their jobs. Not too surprisingly, these corporate buyers reported that one of the major reasons they switched vendors was because their sales representative was "out-of-touch."

Buyers are interested in purchasing products to meet the needs of their firms; but if salespeople do not listen to their buyers, they will not be able to target their presentations to the appropriate needs.

Source: *The Wall Street Journal,* March 22, 1990, p. B1.

---

questions, and then the confirmatory questions. Each type naturally leads to the following type and each one helps build the buyer's interest in hearing about the solutions the salesperson has to offer. It should be noted that studies of 35,000 sales calls by Neil Rackham demonstrate that the most successful salespeople are those who use fewer situational questions and more problem discovery, impact, and solution value questions.

## THE PRESENTATION

Once salespeople have assessed the needs and desires of their customers, they move into the main body of the sale, the presentation. The **presentation** is primarily a discussion of those product and/or service features, advantages, and benefits which the customers have indicated are important to them. While most presentations are oral, they often include written proposals and supporting material as well as visual aids. The goal of the presentation is for salespeople to convince their customers that their company's products or service will satisfy their needs better than those of a competitor.

**Features** describe the characteristics of the product or service, **advantages** describe how the feature changes the performance of the product or service, and **benefits** describe how the advantage will help the buyer. For each feature and advantage that a salesperson presents, he should also present one or more benefits of that feature to the buyer. In fact the benefits which are presented by the salesperson should be those that address specific needs mentioned by the customer. Listed below are some examples of products, their features, advantages, and benefits:

**This salesperson is using her laptop to retrieve information for her customer.**

© Jim Pickerell/Westlight

| Product | Feature | Advantage | Benefit |
|---|---|---|---|
| Copy machine | Ten service reps | Fast service | Saves time |
| Shoes | Inventory control system | Reduces need for inventory | Saves money |
| Motor oil | Rust inhibitor | Oil and engine have longer life | Saves money |
| Forklift truck | One-month trial | Ensures product meets needs | Saves money and time |

## Product Demonstrations

A good sales presentation is built around a forceful product demonstration. Reps should demonstrate everything possible during the presentation. Today there are numerous software packages which can be used with notebook or laptop computers to make full-color presentations that include sound effects, personalized graphics, and full-motion video testimonials.

American Airlines recently equipped its 500 sales reps worldwide with high-powered notebook computers and presentation software that incorporates graphics, sound, and video. Where the company used to spend more than $100,000, using an external production firm, to put together an important presentation, reps can now do it themselves for under $5,000. The software enables reps to develop professional-looking, cost-effective, multimedia presentations. The new tools are so easy to use that the most technophobic rep can and will use them.[9] However, there is a danger in forgetting that even the glitziest multimedia presentation cannot take the place of the personal touch and understanding that the rep brings to the presentation.

## Prepared Sales Presentations

The advisability of using a prepared sales presentation, better known as a canned sales talk, is debatable. Without doubt, a prepared presentation done

---

## Turning Software into Stunning Presentations

Just because you have the top-of-the-line software doesn't guarantee that you will have a top-notch presentation. To unlock the potential of the software, you must follow the same basic principles which apply to making all good presentations:

- **Be prepared and organized.** If your thoughts are disorganized, your presentation will be as well. You must organize the templates in a logical manner and you must *plan* what you are going to say around them.
- **Practice.** If you want it to be good, you must practice the presentation. Just running through it once will not result in an

outstanding presentation. The more you practice, the smoother it will be.

- **Repetition, repetition.** It is important to repeat the most important points in your presentation. Develop several main themes in your presentation and come back to them more than once.
- **Avoid information overload.** Remember that not everything in your presentation warrants a template. Just as important, do not overload the template. The slides should be simple. Use bullet points and lay them out in a logical fashion.

Source: Tom Dellecave, Jr., "Now Showing," *Sales & Marketing Management,* February 1996, pp. 68–71.

---

poorly and without feeling is a dismal experience. However, many firms do use them successfully. The prepared presentation has several advantages:

- It gives new salespeople confidence.
- It can utilize tested sales techniques that have proven effective.
- It gives some assurance that the complete story will be told.
- It greatly simplifies sales training.

The use of a prepared presentation does *not* mean that sales reps cannot use their own words. Above all, the salesperson's own feelings and personality should be evident in the presentation.

### Developing Effective Presentations

The task of developing a presentation is not an easy one. Some simple advice may be helpful here.

- **Keep the presentation simple.** The temptation to tell everything is overwhelming. Don't do it. The prospect can absorb only a limited amount of information at any one time. Don't overload his system.
- **Talk the prospect's language.** Don't build the presentation around industry jargon or product model numbers. If customers don't understand what the rep is talking about, they seldom say so. That would be an admission of ignorance. They usually pretend to understand and then say, "I'll have to think it over for a while."
- **Stress the application of the product or service to the prospect's situation.** Tailor the presentation to the application or person at hand. Even within the same firm, different individuals place

different priorities on what is important about the product. You must adapt your presentation to the situation and person.

- **Above all, seek credibility at every turn.** The entire presentation is nothing if it is not believed. Each statement must be credible. Prove points one by one. A critical point is not complete until the prospect believes it. The real key to successful selling lies in this credibility.

# MEETING OBJECTIONS

Objections are encountered in practically every presentation. They should be welcomed because they indicate that the prospect has some interest in the proposition. A prospect who is not interested in buying seldom raises any objections, silently going along with the presentation but saying at the end, "I'm not interested in your deal." There are several important techniques which should be used in responding to a buyer objection:

- *Listen* to the buyer. It is important that you listen actively. Do not assume that you know what the buyer is going to say. Encourage the buyer to talk. This helps to get the objection out in the open.
- *Clarify* the objection. Repeat and clarify the objection by asking for more information, using questions such as "Let me see if I understand you correctly, [repeating the objection as you understand it]. Is that correct?" The buyer may confirm that you are correct in your understanding or provide additional information. Sometimes this step can uncover a misunderstanding that the buyer has about your product and/or service.
- *Respect* the buyer's concern. Acknowledge that you understand and appreciate the concerns. Remember that the buyer is not attacking you personally, so you should not become defensive.
- *Respond* to the objection. It is important that you respond to the buyer's concern. The specific response to the objection depends on the type of objection it is. The most common types of objections and specific strategies for handling them are discussed next.

## Price or Value Objections

Buyers who say "I don't need it" or "it costs too much" are indicating that they don't think the *value* of solving the problem or meeting the need is *worth the cost.* In this case, the salesperson must convince the buyer of the importance of the problem and of the value of the solution. It may be necessary to go back to the need assessment part of the call to ask some additional problem impact and solution value types of questions to increase the buyer's perception of the seriousness of the problem and the importance of a solution. If the buyer acknowledges the importance of the problem but still feels that the company can't afford it or it is not a price-competitive solution, then the salesperson can offer some price value comparisons of alternative solutions.

## Product/Service Objections

Sometimes the buyer acknowledges the importance of a problem but doubts whether the product or service can solve his problem or improve his operations. The buyer may disagree with the salesperson's assessment or, in some cases, even doubt the genuineness of the salesperson. In this case the salesperson needs to convince the buyer that her product will do what she says. She must demonstrate or prove that the product has the capability to fulfill the need. Some of the proof-providing tactics are to offer the buyer

- case histories
- testimonials
- independent tests
- a demonstration
- trial use
- expert opinion

Some objections relate to needs that your product *cannot satisfy*. In this case, it is best to first acknowledge that your product or service cannot meet the particular need. Then try to increase the perceived value of your product by reemphasizing those important needs which your product can meet.

## Procrastinating Objections

Procrastinating objections can be difficult to overcome. Some such objections are:

- Let me think about it a while.
- I have to talk it over with my boss.
- I have to wait until the next budget cycle.
- I have some other reps to talk to before I make a decision.

Procrastinating prospects use such excuses to avoid acting on a proposition immediately or to avoid admitting that they don't have the authority to make the decision.

In door-to-door selling, a sale that cannot be closed on one call usually has little chance of completion. In many business sales, however, the prospect cannot be pushed into a sale without creating considerable ill will. The amount of aggressiveness must be modified to fit the prospect and the situation. In some situations, the sales rep must be patient or lose the sale. Some people will not be pushed or rushed. In these situations, *the best strategy is to ask for a commitment for some future action which will move the sale forward.* For example, the salesperson might ask for a meeting with the buyer and his boss or with whoever else seems to have substantial influence over the decision.

## Hidden Objections

Prospects may state their objections to a proposition openly and give the salesperson a chance to answer them. This is an ideal circumstance, because everything is out in the open and the salesperson does not need to read the prospect's mind. Unfortunately, prospects often hide their real reasons for not buying. Further, stated objections may be phony. A prospect may say she does not like the looks of your product, when she really thinks your price is too high. The rep must determine the real barrier to the sale to be able to overcome it.

Some salespeople have developed special methods for getting the prospect to disclose what is blocking the sale. One saleswoman uses what she calls her "appeal for honesty" tactic. She says to the reluctant prospect, "You expect me to be honest with you, as you should. But haven't I the same right—to expect you to be honest with me? Now honestly, what is bothering you about the proposition?" However, *the best technique for discovering hidden objections is to keep the prospect talking by asking questions.*

As we noted earlier in the planning section, it is often necessary for salespeople to change their original objectives and strategies for the sales call. Salespeople must recognize the need and be willing to adapt their presentations when the buyer's objections signal that they may have initially chosen the wrong strategies. Another important principle to remember in handling most objections is to avoid arguments at any cost. The sales rep should ask questions that help clarify the prospect's thinking. This provides insights into the precise obstacles that are hindering the sale. Even if prospects are dead wrong, sales reps should never offend them. A sales rep can win an argument only to lose the sale.

## GAINING COMMITMENT

At some point after the salesperson has convinced the buyer that his or her products at least warrant further attention, *the salesperson must ask the buyer to commit to some action which moves you further toward the sale.* This is called **gaining commitment.** In a relatively simple sale, which usually requires only one call, it is important for the salesperson to get a commitment from the buyer to purchase the product on the first call or she will have lost the sale. Some of the techniques which are often used to close these transaction sales are highlighted in the nearby box.

However, sales of most business products are more complex and usually require more than one call. In fact, some large, complex sales may take several years to complete. Therefore, in these kinds of calls, a salesperson's final objective should be to get the buyer to agree to some action which moves the buyer closer to the sale. For example, the buyer may agree to see a demonstration or to review the specifications or to try a sample. The key to obtaining commitment is *first to plan realistic objectives for each sales call* and *second to ask for a commitment.* If the salesperson doesn't ask, then he or she won't move the sale forward.

At some point the salesperson can ask for an action that in effect finalizes the sale. For example, the salesperson may simply ask, "Can I

---

### Common Sales Closes

#### The Assumptive Close

Many salespeople rely on the assumptive close—they merely assume prospects are going to buy and begin taking orders by asking such questions as:

Now, what size do you want?

When can we deliver this—today or tomorrow morning?

Will three dozen be enough, or should I send four?

If the prospect answers such questions, the close is under way.

#### Special-Offer Close

Some sales managers give their sales force a special customer offer each time around the territory. The 3M Company's Scotch Tape division has used this closing tactic. If the special deal were a billfold, the sales rep might say, "If you put in this specially priced dealer display today, we will include this billfold."

#### Summary Close

Another frequently used close is to provide a summary of the benefits that the buyer has already acknowledged and then to suggest an action for finalizing the sale. For example, the dialogue could follow this pattern:

**Salesperson:** You have agreed that our products will be easier for the consumer to use and that our advertising support will convince the retailers to stock the product, correct?

**Dealer Prospect:** Then I suggest that you place your first order today so that you have it on the retailer's shelves when our advertising campaign kicks off.

---

place an order for you today?" Sometimes the buyer may volunteer to take an action which moves the sale forward or even finalizes the sale. For example, the buyer may say, "We've decided that we need to make a change and we think your company is in the best position to serve our needs." But often, it does not happen this way and the salesperson must ask for the commitment.

## FOLLOW-UP

Reps must learn that the sale is not over when they get the order. Good sales reps follow up in various ways. They make certain that they have answered all the buyer's questions and that the buyer understands the details of the contract. If the merchandise is delivered at a later date, the reps are present at the time of delivery or call soon afterward to ensure that everything is in order.

Good follow-up is the key to building a loyal clientele, which ultimately results in a handsome income for the salesperson. Satisfied customers voluntarily provide more business. People truly appreciate being served by good salespeople. Once they locate a person who pleases them, they are not likely to forget that individual in the future.

# ◼ SUMMARY

As part of their jobs, salespeople perform a wide variety of activities. Typically salespeople spend 67 percent of their time on selling or service activities and the remainder on the other administrative aspects of their jobs.

The sales process has eight steps. The first of these is prospecting, which involves identifying and qualifying leads. There are a number of possible methods of generating leads. The most frequent source of leads is existing customers. In order to qualify a prospect—to decide if the prospect is a good one—it must be determined whether the prospect has a need for the product, can afford to buy the product, and is receptive to being called upon by the salesperson.

The second step is precall planning. This includes all of the information-gathering activities which salespeople perform to learn about their prospective customers. Then, based on this research, salespeople plan their presentations. As a part of their plan, they must decide what the objective for the call is as well as how they are going to approach the buyer and what kind of questions they will ask.

The third step is the approach, during which the salesperson meets the buyer, introduces himself, engages in momentary small talk, and, most important, gains the buyer's agreement to move forward into the need assessment part of the presentation.

During the fourth step, identified as "need assessment," the salesperson must discover, clarify, and understand the buyer's needs. The salesperson uses a variety of questions to encourage buyers to reveal their needs.

The presentation of the product or service and its features and benefits is the next step. The general goal for salespeople is to convince their customers that their company's products and services will satisfy the customers' needs better than those of a competitor. Today many salespeople use computers to help them make effective presentations.

The sixth step is handling the buyers' objections. Buyers often question the price or value of the product, or they may not believe that the product will improve their operations. The salesperson must be able to overcome these objections as well as others. Sometimes salespersons will find it necessary to adapt their presentations in order to move the presentation forward.

At the seventh step, the salesperson must ask the buyer to commit to some action which will move the buyer closer to the sale. Often it takes multiple calls before the buyer is ready to commit to the sale. Even after getting the order, the salesperson must always follow up, the eighth step, to ensure that the customer is satisfied.

## Key Terms

| | | |
|---|---|---|
| Adaptive selling | Features | Problem impact questions |
| Advantages | Gaining commitment | Prospecting |
| Approach | Identifying leads | Situational questions |
| Benefits | Presentation | Solution value questions |
| Confirmatory questions | Problem discovery questions | Qualifying leads |

## ▣ QUESTIONS AND PROBLEMS

1. What percentage of their time do salespeople spend performing selling activities and servicing their accounts?

2. Should marketing or sales be responsible for generating leads?

3. How does the salesperson determine if the lead is a good prospect?

4. Should the salesperson try to close on every call? Why or why not?

5. Identify what type of question each of the following is:

   a. If your inventory could be reduced by 20 percent, how much would that save you?

   b. Can you tell me how you recruit your new salespeople?

   c. How does the turnover in your sales force affect your operations?

   d. Have you experienced any problems in servicing your office equipment?

6. Identify a feature, an advantage, and a benefit for the following products: a camera, a backpack, fat-free ice cream, and lawn care service.

7. What are the advantages and disadvantages of using prepared, or "canned," sales presentations? Give examples of when using a canned presentation might be better than using a less structured presentation.

8. If the salesperson doesn't believe that the customer is being honest about what she doesn't like about the product, what should he do?

9. If the customer says to the salesperson, "You seem like a nice guy and I would like to buy from you personally, but I don't think your company is worth a nickel!" what should the salesperson say?

10. It has often been said that salespeople are born, not made. Do you agree or disagree? Explain why.

## ▣ EXPERIENTIAL EXERCISES

**A.** Spend a day with a salesperson from two different companies.
   1. Report in itinerary form how you spent each day.
   2. Describe each job, comparing and contrasting both.
   3. Tell which position you would prefer and why.

**B.** Identify prospects for a new brand of special occasion and novelty cards.

**C.** Pick a product which is normally sold by a salesperson. Talk to a customer who has just purchased or has been considering purchasing the product and find out the important characteristics of the salesperson from the customer's point of view.

## ◼ REFERENCES

1. Allen Lucas, "Leading Edge," *Sales & Marketing Management,* June 1995, pp. 13–14.

2. Ibid.

3. Bob Donath, James W. Obermayer, Carolyn K. Dixon, and Richard A. Crocker, "When Your Prospect Calls," *Marketing Management* 3, no. 2 (1994), pp. 27–28.

4. Ginger Trumfio, "Opening Doors," *Sales & Marketing Management,* May 1994, p. 81.

5. Christian P. Heide, *Dartnell's 29th Sales Force Compensation Survey 1996–1997* (Chicago: Dartnell Press, 1997), p. 216.

6. Rosann L. Spiro and Barton A. Weitz, "Adaptive Selling: Conceptualization, Measurement, and Nomological Validity," *Journal of Marketing Research,* February 1990, pp. 61–69.

7. Neil Rackham, *The Spin Selling Fieldbook* (New York: McGraw-Hill, 1996).

8. This discussion is based to a large extent on concepts developed by Neil Rackham which were based on a research study by the Huthwaite Corporation of 35,000 sales calls. These ideas were originally reported in the book *Spin Selling* (ibid.).

9. Tom Dellecave, Jr., "Now Showing," *Sales & Marketing Management,* February 1996, pp. 68–71.

---

*Case 3-1*

## GEM TOOLS, INC.

### Evaluating sales leads

"It's a jungle out there, where only the savviest operators survive," George likes to tell his troops. As division sales vice president of his company, George is proud of his devoted effort and the reputation he has earned as a "real hands-on guy." He enjoys his regular Friday after-lunch ritual, a relaxed time to phone friends to arrange weekend plans as he sifts the pile of sales lead forms that accumulate during the week.

Passing by in the hallway, Janice, the company's new marketing communications director, stops to watch George at work through his open office door. What she sees alarms her.

With a wastebasket positioned strategically alongside his desk, George plucks forms from the stack before him. He squints at each thoughtfully for a few seconds and lays some respectfully on another much smaller pile that he will send to his road warriors in the field. But he flicks most of the forms disdainfully into the trash. George is screening advertising inquiries, raw leads from trade publication reader service cards indiscriminately passed on by marketing communications to the sales department.

"Those leads cost us 28 bucks apiece!" Janice protests, striding into George's office like cavalry to the rescue. She works hard to run an advertising campaign to excite the marketplace and motivate likely buyers to ask for more information. Brochure requests have skyrocketed. Inquiry counts have soared. It's a numbers game to Janice, and she boasts about her marketing communications program's sizzling scoreboard.

---

This case was reprinted with permission from Bob Donath, James W. Obermayer, Carolyn K. Dixon, and Richard A. Crocker, "When Your Prospect Calls," *Marketing Management Magazine,* 1994, pp. 27–28.

But Janice worries that salespeople, and boss George in particular, view the extra volume as an imposition, possibly even a threat. Not that anyone has said anything; it's just that tone of voice she hears from salespeople on those rare occasions when she travels to the field.

"How can you tell so quickly who's a good lead and who's not—who's going to buy and who's not?" Janice demands. She wants to add, but doesn't, that the sales department is breaking the rules. Each inquiry should be followed up with a salesperson's phone call, she believes, maybe even a visit. That's the sales department's job. Summarily trashing leads without checking them out defeats her program at the start, Janice seethes.

She worries because she doesn't really know what happens to all those names and addresses her department shovels to George's office across the hall. Spending so little time making calls on prospects with salespeople, Janice never sees how most of the inquiries she forwards actually frustrate salespeople, waste their time, and justify their muttering that "the leads are no good."

George tries to protect his people with his home-grown lead-qualification system. "It's easy to tell which are which, with my experience," George calmly answers Janice,

a parent educating a child. "Sit here and let me show you how it's done."

George slides a lead from the stack and with a flourish offers it for their mutual inspection. "See, this has no phone number; he's obviously not a serious buyer." George flips the lead card into the wastebasket triumphantly.

"Here's another one 600 miles away from our nearest office—so we can't follow it up right away. We'll call on them when one of our people gets up there next month," George promises without conviction.

"This one's for a $200 meter, and we sell $200,000 complete power systems," George holds the lead with two fingers at arms' length as if it were vilely soiled. "Let this guy call back later if he just wants the meter."

On it goes, George's decision rules enraging Janice.

The marketing communications director frets over the fate of the advertising inquiry database she wants to create, so she can earn recognition upstairs for the inquiry count's rapid growth. Janice also knows she will not win points arguing with the senior sales executive, so she remains silent.

*Questions:*

1. Who is right, Janice or George?
2. What would you recommend to Janice and to George?

---

*Case 3-2*

## FLETCHER ELECTRIC, INC.

Molly Stevens, account manager for Fletcher, was pondering her next move with Tymco, her largest account. Fletcher manu-

From: Barton Weitz, Stephen B. Castleberry, and John F. Tanner, Jr., *Selling,* 3rd ed., Chicago: Richard D. Irwin.

factures a line of pumps, electric motors, and controls that are sold to companies that use Fletcher's parts in manufacturing all kinds of equipment. Tymco, a maker of street sweepers and other specialized industrial products, had purchased Fletcher controls for the last five years, but also purchased controls from several small distributors for specific applications when Fletcher's products could not meet the specifications. Stevens originally sold the controls by proving to the engineering department that Fletcher's quality could meet their specifications and demonstrating the controls' accuracy and long life. Then she convinced the purchasing agent that the pricing would be more stable with one major vendor than with multiple distributors. Since then, Stevens has heard no complaints about Fletcher's products. Tymco even allowed a trade magazine to write an article about Tymco's experience with Fletcher controls.

Early last year, Stevens persuaded the purchasing agent for Tymco to switch to Fletcher electric motors for several applications. Although engineering was not involved in this decision, Stevens had to prove to the purchasing agent that the products were as good as the ones they were currently purchasing. Stevens estimated that Fletcher had about 30 percent of the Tymco motor business, 30 percent went to Visa SA from Mexico, and the remainder of the business belonged to Smart & Company, which actually distributed several lines of electric motors imported from the Pacific Rim.

Last month, Stevens received a call from the director of engineering asking for a meeting to discuss some issues with Fletcher motors. She was delighted, because one of the Fletcher engineers had suggested combining Fletcher motors and controls and shipping the units as one assembly. Stevens believed such a meeting would be a perfect opportunity to present the new idea. She created and presented a proposal to the engineering department that, if accepted, would mean doubling Fletcher's share of the electric motor business. The proposal would require some redesign by Tymco, but the savings over two years would be more than the redesign costs. After that, Tymco could increase profits on those products by about 3 percent. But several engineers pointed out that Fletcher was unwilling to manufacture controls for all of Tymco's needs, and they were reluctant to make such a change with a company that was not willing to work more closely with them. In addition, one engineer seemed very unhappy that the purchasing department had switched to Fletcher motors. She thought the reject rate of 2 percent was too high; all of Tymco's other vendors were achieving fewer than 1 percent rejects. At the conclusion of the meeting, the director of engineering said to Stevens, "Molly, we've enjoyed a long and good relationship with Fletcher. And your idea is a good one. Right now, though, I don't think Fletcher is the company we should do that with. But we'll consider it and let you know."

### Questions

1. In what stage of partnering is the relationship between Fletcher and Tymco?

2. Is there anything Stevens could have done to set the stage for better acceptance of her proposal?

3. What should she do right now? If her visionary objective is to develop a strategic partnership with Tymco, is it still realistic? What should she do to achieve that visionary objective?

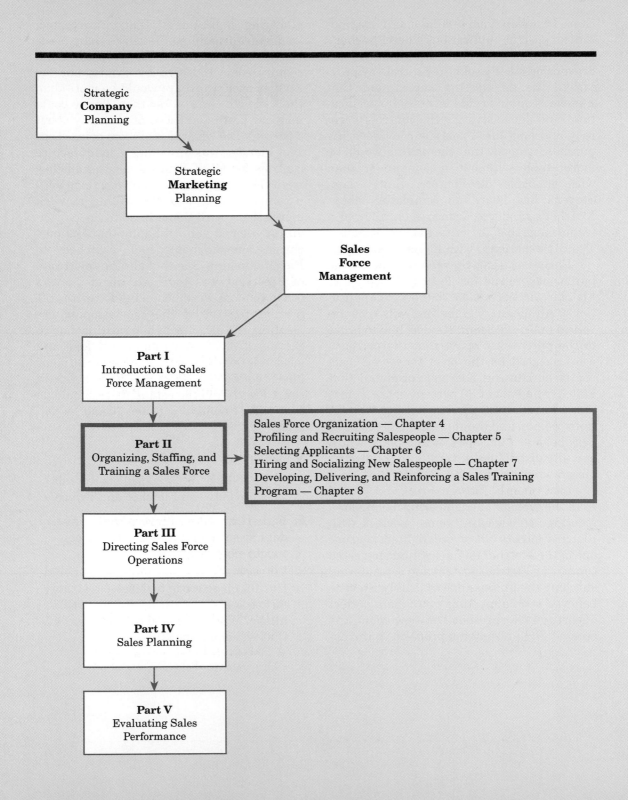

Strategic **Company** Planning

Strategic **Marketing** Planning

**Sales Force Management**

**Part I**
Introduction to Sales Force Management

**Part II**
Organizing, Staffing, and Training a Sales Force

Sales Force Organization — Chapter 4
Profiling and Recruiting Salespeople — Chapter 5
Selecting Applicants — Chapter 6
Hiring and Socializing New Salespeople — Chapter 7
Developing, Delivering, and Reinforcing a Sales Training Program — Chapter 8

**Part III**
Directing Sales Force Operations

**Part IV**
Sales Planning

**Part V**
Evaluating Sales Performance

# PART II

# ORGANIZING, STAFFING, AND TRAINING A SALES FORCE

Most sales executives devote the bulk of their time to organizing, developing, and directing the activities and people involved in *operating* a sales force. This is the stage in the management process in which the sales organization actually *implements* the strategic planning designed to help the company reach its sales goals.

Sales operations—the topic of Parts II and III of this book—include organizing and staffing the sales force and training the salespeople. In addition, sales operations include designing compensation and expense plans for the sales force, motivating the group, leading and supervising their field-selling activities.

Part II consists of five chapters covering the organization, staffing, and training activities of sales force management. Chapter 4 deals with sales force organization—the characteristics of a good organization, the basic types of organization, the organizational specialization within a sales department, and other organizational options such as national account management, selling teams, and independent sales organizations. Organizational options for international sales are also discussed.

Staffing the sales force—selecting the right people—is the most important activity in the entire management process. Selection involves determining the kind of people wanted, recruiting applicants (Chapter 5), and selecting salespeople from the applicants (Chapter 6). Those selected must then be hired and immediately assimilated and socialized into the organization (Chapter 7).

Chapter 8 is devoted to sales training activities. First the need for training assessment is discussed followed by program design, reinforcement, and evaluation.

# CHAPTER 4

# Sales Force Organization

"Love the one you're with. . . ."
**Steven Stills**

In the management process, you must first decide where you want to go and then figure out how to get there. In more formal terms, management should first establish its objectives and then plan the appropriate strategies and tactics to reach those goals. To implement this planning, the activities and people must be properly arranged and effectively coordinated. This is where the concept of organization comes in. The fundamentals of organization are essentially the same whether we are talking about organizing a sales force, a production department, a sorority, or any other group involved in a common effort.

## NATURE OF SALES ORGANIZATIONS

An **organization** is simply an arrangement—a working structure—of activities involving a group of people. The goal is to arrange these activities so that the people involved can act *together* better than they can *individually*.

Organizational changes occur in companies' sales and marketing efforts as firms find that their existing structures are inappropriate to implement the marketing concept. As we noted in Chapter 2, one idea underlying the marketing concept is that all marketing activities should be organizationally integrated and coordinated.

In recent years, many firms have restructured their sales organizations to make them more responsive to the changing needs and, in some cases, demands of their customers. Companies are doing this by organizing around their customers. As noted by the president of U.S. Power Plant, "If you want to be a customer-driven company, you have to design the sales organization from the outside in, around individual buyers rather than around your products."[1]

The trend is toward flatter organizations in which coordination across activities is more important than top-down control. In these organizations, salespeople are often part of customer-focused, cross-functional teams designed to serve specific customers. These changes are occurring because companies are changing the way they do business with their suppliers. These organizational trends are discussed in detail later in the chapter.

**SALES FORCE ORGANIZATION AND STRATEGIC PLANNING**

A close relationship exists between a company's sales force organizational structure and its strategic marketing and sales force planning. The organizational structure has a direct and significant bearing on the implementation of strategic planning. The key here is to design an organizational structure that will help to successfully implement the strategic marketing and sales force planning.

An **organizational structure**—whether it is for a sales force or any other group involved in a joint effort to meet a goal—is a control and coordination mechanism. In addition to its organizational structure, management has several other mechanisms to direct the efforts of its sales force—its compensation plan, training program, and supervisory techniques, among others. But the organizational structure looms large because it typically is set up before these other mechanisms are established. Consequently, any mistakes in organization can result in reduced efficiencies in selection, compensation, training, and other tools of managerial control and guidance.

Therefore, as a control mechanism, the organizational structure guides the company—or in some cases, the sales force—in carrying out the strategic planning to pursue marketing and sales force goals. Often a sales force fails to reach its goals because the organizational structure hinders the effective implementation of the strategic sales force planning.

To illustrate, assume that a company's sales goal is to increase its market share to 20 percent next year. The company's key sales strategy is to increase its sales to large, national accounts by 30 percent over last year. However, the sales force is structured so that each rep's efforts are spread thinly over accounts of all sizes. No key executives are assigned to sell to national accounts. Under these organizational conditions, it is doubtful that this company will successfully implement its plan.

 **CHARACTERISTICS OF A GOOD ORGANIZATION**

Some management generalizations that characterize a good organization are summarized in the box "Principles of Organization Design." These features apply to organizations in any field—not just sales management—and they are useful when designing a new organization or revising an existing one. A company's formal organizational structure may comply with all or most of the desirable characteristics. However, in the real world most firms need an additional element to make the formal structure work well. That key element is an **informal organization.**

### Role of an Informal Organization

A healthy organization is a self-adjusting one. Through its own devices, it finds ways to get a job done with minimum effort. A formal organization's

## Principles of Organization Design

- **Organizational structure should reflect a marketing orientation.** When designing a sales organization, management should focus first on the market and sales force. Executives should consider the selling and marketing tasks necessary to capitalize on the market demand and to serve the firm's customers. From this base, an organizational structure can be built.

- **Organization should be built around activities, not around people.** This goal sometimes is very difficult to achieve because it may be almost impossible to avoid some organizing around people—that is, making "people adaptations" in the structure.

- **Responsibility and authority should be related properly.** When you give someone a job to do, also give the person the tools to do it. Responsibility for each activity should be clearly spelled out and assigned to some individual. Then the necessary authority should be delegated to that person.

- **Span of executive control should be reasonable.** By span of executive control, we mean the number of subordinates who report directly to one executive. What constitutes a "reasonable" span of control depends on the nature of the subordinates' jobs and the abilities of the executives and subordinates. As a guideline, the span should be small—usually not more than six or eight people. However, there are many exceptions, and the recent trend to fewer organizational levels of management has resulted in broader spans of control at each level.

- **Organization should be stable, but flexible.** An organization should be like a tree—firmly rooted, but flexible enough so that a strong wind won't break it. *Stability* in an organization means having trained executive replacements available when needed. *Flexibility* refers more to short-run situations such as seasonal fluctuations in the number of workers needed. An organization might subcontract some work during peak seasons or hire a temporary sales force to deliver samples of new products.

- **Activities should be balanced and coordinated.** Good *balance* does not mean that all organizational units should be equal. Balance means not letting one unit become unduly more important than another. You don't stress the offense to the neglect of the defense, for example. In sales management, effective *coordination* is needed (1) between sales and nonmarketing departments as well as (2) between sales and other marketing units. Some examples:

  Sales ↔ production: Sales furnishes accurate sales forecasts; production provides dependable production schedules.

  Sales ↔ finance and accounting: These units collaborate in controlling selling costs and setting credit policy.

  Sales ↔ advertising: Advertising can generate leads to prospective customers and make them more receptive to sales force calls. Sales reps can tell retailers how the producer's ads will bring people to the store.

well-being is maintained by the system known as the informal organization structure. This structure represents how things really get done in a company, not how they are supposed to be done according to a formal organization chart.

The following example shows how an informal organization actually works. A sales manager's secretary opens a letter from a customer complaining about an overcharge on an order. If the lines of the formal organization chart were followed, the secretary would refer the letter to the sales manager. This manager would relay the message up through executive echelons until it reached the administrator in charge of the chief executives in sales and accounting. This top administrator would forward the complaint down through channels to the appropriate person in the billing division. The answer would follow the reverse path up and down through channels until the sales manager's secretary received it and could notify the customer. Such procedures are rather ridiculous, and most organizations would not follow them. Instead, the informal structure would be used. The sales manager's secretary would simply telephone or walk over to see a clerk in the billing department to find out what happened to the customer's order.

The informal organization also gives richer meaning to some time-honored principles of organization. For example, a person should have only one boss. Fundamentally, this is a sound generalization. Yet the informal structure adds dimensions of practicality and flexibility to this principle. Actually, we all have many bosses, each having authority over different activities.

## ◼ BASIC TYPES OF ORGANIZATIONS

Most sales organizations can be classified mainly into one of four basic categories:

- A **line organization.**
- A **line-and-staff organization.**
- A **functional organization.**
- A **horizontal organization.**

Figure 4-1 describes these categories, explains when each is likely to be used, and states their major advantages and limitations. Figures 4-2 and 4-3 depict line-and-staff and functional sales organizations. Finally, Figure 4-4 shows the horizontal organizational form. The horizontal structure, which has recently been adopted by some of the biggest companies in the United States, such as AT&T, Du Pont, General Electric, and Motorola, is described further in the box on page 90.[2] Kraft Corporation recently restructured into a hybrid organization in

■ **FIGURE 4-1**      **Basic types of organization—their nature, uses, and merits**

| | Organization Type | |
|---|---|---|
| | **Line** | **Line-and-Staff** |
| **Nature** | Simplest form of organization. Authority flows from chief executive to first subordinate, then to second subordinate, and so on down. | Take a line organization and add staff assistants who are specialists in various areas—advertising or marketing research, for example. The staff executive is responsible for all planning connected with the specialized activity, but has only an advisory relationship with sales managers and sales reps. The same staff executive—an advertising manager, for example—has line authority over people in the advertising department, but is in a staff-authority (advisory) relationship with the sales force. |
| **When used** | In very small firms or within a small department in a larger company. | Probably the most widely used basic form of organization in sales departments today. Likely to be used when any of the following conditions exist:<br><br>■ Sales force is large.<br><br>■ Market is regional or national.<br><br>■ Line of products is varied.<br><br>■ Number of customers is large. |
| **Relative merits** | Low-cost operation; quick decision making; highly centralized authority. Lack of managerial specialization and frequently no replacement for top executive, who is the owner of the firm. | Provides benefits of division of labor and executive specialization. Total cost of organization can be high, especially when staff assistants have their own departments. Decision making is slower. A potential problem: strong staff executives may want to assume line authority instead of staying in an advisory role. |

■ **FIGURE 4-1**          **(continued)**

## Organization Type

| Functional | Horizontal |
|---|---|
| A step beyond line-and-staff structure in that each activity specialist—advertising or sales promotion, for example—has line authority over the activity in relations with the sales force. Suppose a credit manager wants the salespeople to make collections on delinquent accounts. A staff executive can only *recommend* to the general manager that the reps do this job. A functional executive has line authority to *order* the assistant sales manager or the salespeople to do the job. | Eliminates both management levels and departmental boundaries. A small group of senior executives at the top overseeing the support functions like human resources, finance, and long-term planning. Everyone else is a member of cross-functional teams which perform core processes such as product development and sales and fulfillment. These teams are self-managed. |
| Large company with varied product lines and/or markets. The key is to limit the number of executives who may use the functional line authority. The more people giving orders to the sales force, for example, the more opportunity there is for trouble. | By large and small companies seeking greater efficiencies and customer responsiveness. Firms which are establishing long-term partnering relationships with their customers are the most likely to adopt a horizontal structure. Various cross-functional teams work with customers' teams to solve problems and create opportunities for greater productivity and growth. |
| Advantages of specialization of labor plus the assurances that functional executives' plans and programs will be carried out because the executives can order that this be done. The major drawback is that line sales executives and the salespeople may get orders from more than one person. | Reduces supervision and eliminates activities that are not necessary for the process. Costs are reduced and customer responsiveness is greatly enhanced. |

■ **FIGURE 4-2**

**Line-and-staff sales organization**

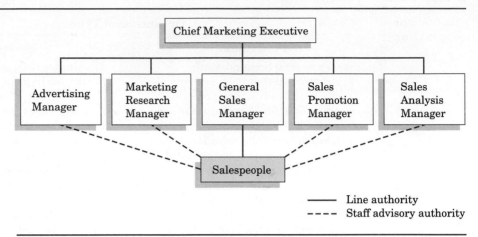

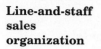

■ **FIGURE 4-3**

**Functional sales organization**

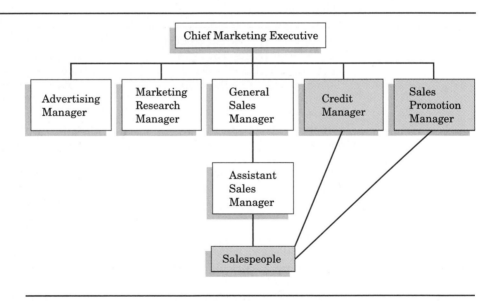

which functional staff personnel provide advice to the horizontal customer teams.[3] Usually most medium- and large-sized firms will expand one of the basic structures in some specialized way so that the sales force can be more effective. We discuss specialization in sales organizations in the next section.

■ **FIGURE 4-4**

**The horizontal corporation**

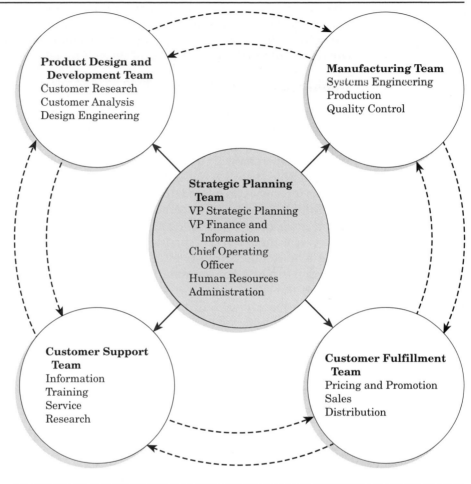

**Product Design and Development Team**
Customer Research
Customer Analysis
Design Engineering

**Manufacturing Team**
Systems Engineering
Production
Quality Control

**Strategic Planning Team**
VP Strategic Planning
VP Finance and Information
Chief Operating Officer
Human Resources
Administration

**Customer Support Team**
Information
Training
Service
Research

**Customer Fulfillment Team**
Pricing and Promotion
Sales
Distribution

## ■ SPECIALIZATION WITHIN A SALES DEPARTMENT

In the organizational examples discussed earlier, the sales force has not been divided on any basis. As a sales force grows, the job of the executive managing the sales force becomes more difficult. The number and complexity of a company's products and/or markets may also call for some organizational division if the sales effort is to be effective.

The most common way to divide sales responsibilities is to split the sales force on some basis of sales specialization. There is a definite trend toward the use of specialized sales forces in the United States. The key strategic question here is what should be the *basis* of the specialization—geography, type of product, market-based divisions, or other criteria. To make this decision, management should carefully analyze many factors, including sales force abilities, market and customer considerations, nature of the product, and demands of the selling job.

## Geographical Specialization

Probably the most widely used system for dividing responsibility and line authority over sales operations is the **geographic organization**—the sales force is grouped on the basis of geographical territories. In this type of structure, each salesperson is assigned a separate geographical area, called a *territory,* in which to sell. A reasonable number of salespeople representing contiguous territories are placed under a territorial executive who reports to the general sales manager. The territorial sales executive is usually called a *regional* or *district sales manager.* Companies with large sales forces often have two or three levels of territorial sales executives, as in Figure 4-5.

A firm can benefit in many ways from territorial specialization in its sales department. For example, this structure usually ensures better coverage of the entire market, as well as better control over the sales force and sales operations. A firm can better meet local competition and adjust to local conditions by having an executive responsible for a limited segment of the market. Local management also can act more rapidly in servicing customers and handling their problems.

■ **FIGURE 4-5**

**Geographical
sales
organization**

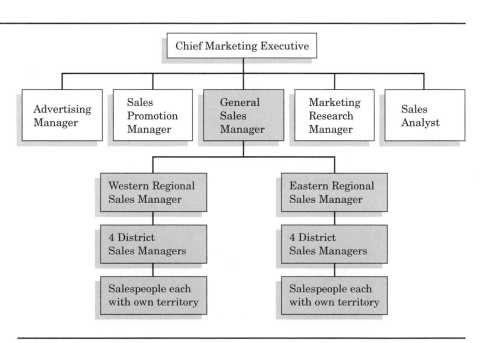

A drawback in a geographical sales organization is that there is usually no specialization of marketing activities. Each district manager, for example, may have to work in advertising, sales promotion, and marketing research, in addition to managing a sales force.

## Product Specialization

The type of product sold is another frequently used basis for dividing the responsibilities and activities within a sales department. The two most widely used structures featuring product specialization are product operating and product staff organizations.

### Product Operating Specialization

In the company represented in Figure 4-6, products have been separated into three groups. Salespeople in one group sell only the products included in group A. All sales reps in group A report directly to the sales manager of product group A, who in turn is responsible to the general sales manager. The three product sales managers are strictly line operating executives; they have no staff assistants. The staff executives in advertising, for example, are located in the home office and are not specialized by product.

This type of organization is likely to be used when a company is selling:

- A variety of complex, technical products, as in the electronics field.
- Many thousands of products—a hardware wholesaler, for example.
- Very dissimilar, unrelated products—a rubber company may use three sales forces to sell (*a*) truck and auto tires, (*b*) rubber footwear, and (*c*) industrial rubber products such as belts, bushings, and insulating materials.

■ **FIGURE 4-6**

**Sales organization with product-specialized sales force**

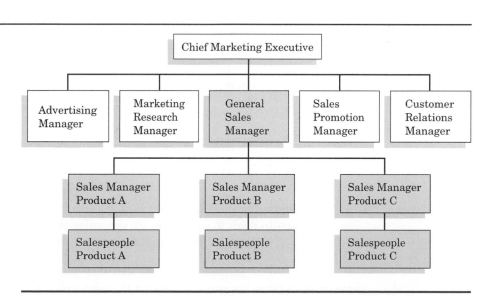

## The Horizontal Corporation

In search of greater productivity, many companies are changing the fundamental way that work gets done in their organizations. Companies such as AT&T, Du Pont, Eastman Chemical, Ryder Systems, and Xerox are moving toward horizontal organizational structures.

General Electric's chairman, John F. Welch, says that their new **"boundaryless"** organization has "reduced costs, shortened (product development) cycle time, and increased company responsiveness to its customers." GE's $3 billion lighting business scrapped a more traditional hierarchical organization in favor of a horizontal one in which a senior team of 9 or 10 people oversee 100 processes or programs worldwide, from new-product design to improving production efficiency. Every team is made up of people who perform different activities, such as selling, pricing, and shipping. The members work together to accomplish the objectives of the process or program, such as sales and fulfillment.

The key elements of this new organizational structure are:

- **Organize around process, not task.** Instead of creating functional departments, organize around the key processes, such as new-product development, sales and fulfillment, and customer support, with specific performance goals.
- **Reduce the number of management levels.** To reduce supervision, combine tasks and eliminate those which do not add value. Use as few teams as possible to perform a process.

- **Use teams to manage everything.** Use teams as the main organizational unit. Make the teams manage themselves and hold them accountable for measurable performance goals.
- **Let customers drive performance.** Make customer satisfaction, not profitability, the measure of performance.
- **Reward team performance.** Change the evaluation and reward systems to reward team results, not just individual performance.
- **Maximize supplier and customer contact.** Make sure that employees have direct, regular contact with suppliers and customers. Include customers and suppliers on internal teams when they can contribute.
- **Inform and train all employees.** Share all information with employees and train them in how to use it in their own process team.

It should be noted that no companies have completely eliminated functions, such as sales, advertising, or research. Rather, most organizations have been reshaped as a cross between the horizontal structure and one of the more traditional structures. But the horizontal corporation is gaining in popularity and is considered by some to be the wave of the future.

Source: This discussion has been based to a large extent on the cover story in *Business Week,* "The Horizontal Corporation," by John A. Byrne, December 20, 1993, pp. 76–81.

The major advantage of this form of organization is the specialized attention given to each product line by the sales force. Also, each line gets more executive attention because one person is responsible for a particular product group.

Probably the biggest drawback is that sometimes more than one salesperson from a company calls on the same customer. Not only is this duplication of coverage expensive, it also can evoke ill will from the customers. This structure also has the same weakness as the geographic type in that the product sales managers have no staff assistants in advertising, sales promotion, or other specialized marketing activities.

### Product Staff Specialization

Figure 4-7 illustrates a line-and-staff organizational structure that is commonly used when management wants to use staff assistants who specialize by products. The company in Figure 4-7 has three staff executives, called **product managers** or **category managers.** Each bears responsibility for planning and developing a marketing program for a separate group of products. These people have no line authority over the sales force or the sales force managers. They can only advise and make recommendations to the line managers. The sales force is not specialized by products. Instead, each salesperson sells the products of all three product managers.

A company can use this structure when it wants some of the advantages of specialization by product line at the planning level, but does not need the specialization at the selling level. Thus in one stroke the product staff organization corrects two of the weaknesses in a product-operating structure: (1) the problems of duplicate calls on a customer and (2) the lack of specialization in planning the functional activities. Of course, a product staff organization loses any advantage of having salespeople specialize in a limited line of products.

## Market Specialization

Many companies divide the line authority in their sales departments on the basis of type of customer, classed either by industry or by channel of distribution. For example, a division of Kimberly-Clark that sells Huggies

■ **FIGURE 4-7**     **Sales organization with product managers as staff specialists**

diapers, Kleenex tissues, and a variety of feminine products uses separate sales forces to reach mass merchandisers, grocery stores, and military post exchanges (PXs). Sonitrol, a security alarm maker, divides its reps into two groups: the account managers who hunt for new business and the client salespeople, who regularly service and survey new accounts.[4]

A sales organization featuring **market specialization** is illustrated in Figure 4-8. The sales manager in charge of each industry group is a line-operating executive with authority over one group of salespeople. These executives have no staff assistants under them. Each sales rep sells the full line of products used by the customer group.

The use of market specialization in sales organizational structures has increased in recent years, while product specialization, at least in some industries, has declined. This trend is expected to continue. Certainly market specialization is consistent with the customer orientation philosophy that underlies the marketing concept. Among the companies that already have made the market-specialization move in their sales organizations are such well-known names as Xerox, IBM, NCR, Hewlett-Packard, General Foods, and General Electric.

Xerox embarked on an ambitious three- to five-year program that eventually had its 4,000 to 5,000 sales reps selling the company's full line of office-automation products. In effect, the company switched from a product-oriented sales organization, consisting of several product sales forces, to a market-oriented structure. The company spent between $10 million and $20 million a year in its training program to implement this organizational change.

■ **FIGURE 4-8**

**Sales organization specialized by type of customer**

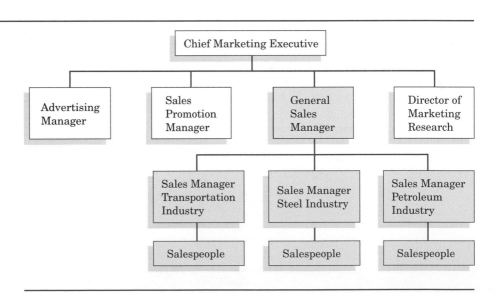

IBM reconfigured its sales force by industry; that is, reps are now assigned by industry, not necessarily by geography. Now its reps are industry experts who sell primarily to customers within specific industries. This focus on customers is widely credited for the company's double-digit sales growth. As one IBM client executive noted, "Customers were demanding that we focus our organization more closely on their industries, so IBM changed its organization to meet their demands. Now we have intimate knowledge of their businesses."[5]

Although it overcomes some of the disadvantages of product specialization and conflict of interest between channels, the customer type of organization does have some limitations. It causes overlap in territorial coverage and therefore is costly. Also, unless separating the sales force by markets results in some product specialization, the customer-based organization may include the disadvantages of full-line selling.

## Combination of Organizational Bases

In the examples of organizational bases given earlier, we assumed that a company divides its sales force on only one basis, such as territory, product, or market. Actually, many firms use some combination drawn from the structures already discussed. For example, a firm may combine geographical specialization with product staff specializations (through the use of product managers). Or a sales force may combine market specialization with geographical specialization.

As we look ahead at sales management in the 2000s, it is evident that the trend toward specialized sales forces will continue. The basis of specialization—geography, product, market, or a combination—may vary from company to company, but some specialization is needed to remain competitive during this decade. In the following section we discuss additional organizational alternatives that can benefit a company's selling effort.

# ADDITIONAL STRATEGIC ORGANIZATIONAL ALTERNATIVES

In our discussion of organizational structures, we looked at an outside sales force that makes calls *in person* on accounts (customers). We implied that the reps are alone when they make these face-to-face sales calls. And we did not consider the impact of the size of the account on these organizational structures.

However, there are additional selling strategies with significant organizational implications that do include such factors as (1) account size, (2) team selling, (3) outside selling without in-person sales calls, and (4) the use of independent agents. (See Figure 4-9.) These organizational alternatives, which have attracted increasing managerial attention in recent years, are likely to gain even greater acceptance as we move through the next decade.

■ **FIGURE 4-9**

**Organizational
options for the
next decade**

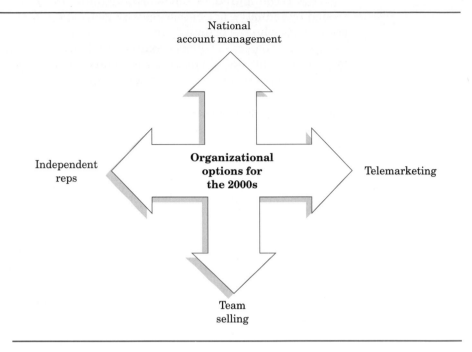

## National Account Management

Many companies have developed separate structures and programs within their organizations for dealing with major accounts—that is, their large-volume customers. Some firms use the term **national account management (NAM)** to describe these large customers; others use the terms *house account, corporate account,* or *major account.* These customers can range from a large firm with only a local or regional market to a company that is multinational. Whatever the title, these customers are extremely important to a seller because they usually account for a disproportionately large share of a seller's sales volume and profit. In addition to their large buying size, major customers are also differentiated by the *complexity* of their buying process.

Several factors contribute to the complexity of the buying–selling process of major accounts. On the buyer's side, people in different geographical locations may be involved in the buying process. Even at one site, several executives, including top management, may influence the buying decision. Price concessions, special services, and custom-made products may be demanded by large buyers. Salespeople in different geographical areas may be calling on the same customer, and many customers do not want the confusion of dealing with a different salesperson and a different contract for each site. Similar conditions on the seller's side add to the complexity and potential confusion. The large dollar volume involved usually attracts executives from other functional areas, and maybe even the president.

Obviously there is a dramatic need for close organizational coordination both within the seller's company and between the buyer and seller. Many sales executives believe that the major accounts are too important to be handled only by the average territorial sales rep. Consequently, many companies are modifying their sales organizations to provide better treatment for these accounts.[6] Three commonly used organizational approaches are:

- **A separate sales force.** In recent years many firms have established separate sales forces to sell to key accounts. A variation is to have the major-account salespeople call on customers' home offices while using the regular sales force to service the customers' branch and field offices. DataCard Corporation, a marketer of hi-tech machines for personalizing credit cards and encoding names on magnetic strips, has an "elite corps" of national account managers who call on "name accounts," such as Citibank and Texaco. Their other sales force consist of 60 territorial reps who call mainly on health care facilities and small retailers.[7]

  Hewlett-Packard splits its sales force into three groups: the red team, the blue team, and the green team. The red team goes after only strategically important accounts in targeted industries, usually market leaders; the green team calls on the wholesalers and distributors who are used to sell to the smaller accounts; and the blue team includes telesales and some other less important accounts which don't fit in the other categories.[8]

  In contrast, Xerox national account managers work hand-in-hand with the local reps to develop strategies for approaching the customer on both the national and local level.[9] Nalco Chemical, a billion-dollar manufacturer of specialty chemicals, has 15 national account managers who are responsible for calling on top corporate executives. However, the district reps, calling on the local plants, usually close the sale.[10]

- **Use of executives.** Some companies use their top sales and marketing executives or their field sales executives for major-account selling. This approach is an alternative for firms that cannot afford a separate sales force. A company that has only a few large customers may also find this approach useful. By sending its top executives to call on key accounts, a company uses a person with the authority to make decisions about prices and allocation of manufacturing facilities. On the other hand, executive time spent on servicing key accounts is time taken away from planning and other management activities.

- **A separate division.** A company may establish a separate division to deal with its key accounts. This option has been used by some apparel manufacturers that produce and sell private-label clothing for the

*Introduction to*

## MAJESTIC PLASTICS COMPANY

### A series of operating problems facing a sales manager

This company formerly was the Majestic Glass Company, a manufacturer of glass bottles, jars, and other containers. Over the years, however, management saw the handwriting on the wall as the market demand for glass containers declined and, concurrently, the demand for plastic packaging increased substantially. Consequently, in 1993 the company's factory in eastern Ohio was completely converted to the production of plastic containers, and the company was appropriately renamed as Majestic Plastics Company. Bottles for cosmetics and toiletries accounted for the bulk of the company's sales volume. However, containers for soft drinks, milk, food products, medicine, and shoe polish also were important in Majestic's product mix.

Clyde D. Brion was the company's general sales manager, and he directed 18 salespeople, each based in a different city. Each sales rep was paid a commission of 10 percent on all sales in his or her territory. The reps received an additional 5 percent on orders from new customers, provided the order was larger than a specified minimum quantity. In addition, the company paid all reasonable travel and entertainment expenses that were incurred by the reps.

Orders from large and regular customers were shipped directly from the Majestic factory to users' plants by rail. For smaller and infrequent buyers, stocks of standard bottles and jars were maintained in warehouses owned by public warehouse companies. At these warehouses, Brion also rented desk space with telephone and basic secretarial services for each sales rep. This arrangement, in effect, provided Majestic Plastics with regional sales branches and product inventory in 18 cities.

Competition was keen in the container industry. Several large firms produced plastic bottles and jars. Competition also came from containers made of glass, metal, or paper. It was especially important that the Majestic sales force be alert to new business possibilities, that they follow up leads and market tips quickly, and that they offer maximum service. It was Majestic's policy to meet competitors' prices, but not to undercut a competitor willfully in order to steal business.

At the time you are studying this case, Brion faced several problems in the operation of his sales force. He was anxious to solve each one promptly and correctly. Brion also wanted to set up safeguards against recurrence of the problem. At the same time, he wanted to establish a policy for dealing with the problem, should it arise again.

Fifteen of these operating problems facing Brion appear at various places in this text. In each instance, the particular problem is located at a relevant place in the chapter. The first in the series is a problem in organization, and it follows right after this introduction.

Note: The concept of Majestic Plastics operating problems is based on earlier writings of Prof. Phillip McVey, then at the University of Nebraska-Lincoln.

large general-merchandise chains such as Sears, Wards, and JC Penney. This organizational structure has the advantage of integrating the manufacturing and marketing (including the sales) activities related to the major accounts. On the other hand, this structure is expensive because it duplicates other units in the selling firm.

*A Day-to-Day Operating Problem*
## MAJESTIC PLASTICS COMPANY (A)
### Location of authority

Clyde Brion, general sales manager of the Majestic Plastics Company, received the following letter from Centra Wineries, Inc., a San Francisco firm which had bought standard-line Majestic bottles for many years:

April 9
Mr. Clyde D. Brion, General Sales Manager
Majestic Plastics Company
Lancaster, Ohio 43130

Dear Mr. Brion:

We have decided reluctantly that we must remove your company from our list of acceptable container vendors unless you can provide sales service more in keeping with our needs.

Please understand that this action in no way implies dissatisfaction with Majestic bottles or with your San Francisco representative, Mr. Harlow Britt.

As you know, the domestic wine industry is a fiercely competitive, fast-moving, low-margin business. We operate on a system of guaranteed resale prices to our distributors and dealers. Consequently, any competitive price-cutting pressures must be met by trimming our costs. Such a small saving as 3 cents per unfilled bottle may on occasion make the difference between profitable and unprofitable business for us.

Similarly, to escape storage costs we never stock more than our immediate requirements of unfilled bottles. We depend upon bottle manufacturers to provide guaranteed deliveries to us on very short notice—never more than 10 days.

While Mr. Britt is very helpful, we find that he lacks authority to adjust your prices to meet our needs, or to guarantee on-time deliveries to us at your risk. He tells us that he must have your written approval on these questions, and the time required to obtain it may be 24 to 72 hours.

We hope you can give Mr. Britt the authority he needs to retain our patronage.

Yours truly,
V. Collasini
Centra Wineries, Inc.

Brion checked his records on this customer and learned that the average elapsed time from order date to delivery date was 19 days. On orders which Britt had marked *"rush"* and Brion had expedited, the average elapsed time had been nine days. No deliveries had been guaranteed.

**Question:** Now what does Clyde Brion do? Answer the letter.

---

National accounts management programs are not always successful. The box titled "Creating a National Accounts Program" provides several key steps toward establishing a successful program.

## Buying Centers and Team Selling

In Chapter 1 we stated that growing expertise among buyers will continue to challenge strategic sales management during the 21st century and beyond. Many business and governmental organizations have already

**This team of sales representatives discusses the call they just made on one of their major accounts.**

developed and implemented the concept of a buying center in their buying process. The **buying center** may be defined as all the individuals involved in the purchasing decision process. Thus a buying center usually includes people who play any of the following roles:

- *Users* of the product.
- *Influencers,* who set the product specifications.
- *Deciders,* who make the actual purchasing decision.
- *Gatekeepers,* who control the flow of purchasing information.
- *Buyers* (purchasing agents), who process the purchase orders.

As noted in Chapter 2, a growing number of firms are using selling teams to call on the various individuals in the buying center. A **selling team** is a group of people representing the sales department and other functional areas in the firm, such as finance, production, and R&D.

### Organizational Options for Team Selling

The organizational arrangements for team selling are quite flexible. Usually the functional specialists and management levels on the selling team match those from the buying center in any given purchase–sale transaction. Therefore, the functional and executive composition of a selling team varies from company to company, and from one selling situation to another within a given firm.

Companies like IBM, DEC, and Tandem, which sell customized combinations of computer hardware and software, use teams of salespeople and technical experts who work closely with the customer's buying team.[11] At IBM, for example, client executives manage teams which in-

---

## Creating a National Accounts Program

1. *Top-management commitment.* It takes time to develop an effective NAM program, so executives must believe in it enough to give it time to flourish.

2. *A culture of customer service.* It is much easier to develop a NAM program if a culture of customer service already exists.

3. *A culture of cooperation.* Satisfying the needs of national accounts requires that all departments work well together.

4. *Involve everybody in the program's development.* When the strategy is being developed, everyone who deals with the customer should be involved in the planning.

5. *Always communicate to the salespeople.* Salespeople need to be continuously updated on everything that concerns the account.

6. *Compensate people properly.* When salespeople assume the role of a national account manager, the compensation plan should be changed to reflect the change in their responsibilities.

7. *The program must have both a structure and a strategy.* The program must be well-defined and it must have goals, which are communicated throughout the organization.

Source: Adapted from Andy Cohen, "Managing," *Sales & Marketing Management,* April 1996, p. 79.

---

clude product reps, systems engineers, and consultants.[12] At 3M Corporation, cross-functional teams have been formulated for each of the company's regions; these teams include people from logistics, management information systems, and sales.[13] Black & Decker has special sale teams, which include a salesperson, a marketer, an information systems expert, a sales forecaster, and a financial analyst, just to serve its Wal-Mart and Home Depot accounts.[14]

In recent years, there has been a trend toward including representatives from the customer's organization on the team. General Electric creates large teams which are both cross-functional and cross-company in order to service its important customers. It formed a 140-person cross-company team to help one customer, Southern California Edison, reduce the downtime on its steam turbine generators, which were purchased from GE. The team consisted of 60 GE people and the remainder were from Southern California Edison. Baxter International has gone even further by jointly setting targets and sharing the savings or the extra costs.[15] In these cases, the two companies have entered into a partnership as described in Chapter 2.

Some companies establish a separate location where sales teams meet with customer buying teams. At these **selling centers,** the selling team presents an integrated program which matches the account's needs. The agenda for the program is usually developed in consultation with the buying team. Xerox believes that the atmosphere at its six centers, called *executive briefing centers,* stimulates openness, which improves communication and thus the relationship with the buying team.[16]

## Keys to Successful Team Selling

- **Begin slowly.** Choose a few large customers with whom you already have a good relationship and involve them in the team creation process.
- **Choose team members who understand and support the concept.** Those people who seek out the ideas and assistance of others and who are willing to help others are good candidates for team members.
- **Demonstrate management support.** The managers in the functional groups from which the members are drawn must support the team. They must encourage full participation and equality in member status.
- **Give the team the skills to enable them to succeed.** To make the transition from individual to cross-functional selling, training should be provided in the areas of teamwork, communication, and consensus building, as well as in major account selling and product or service training if needed.
- **Provide meaningful team incentives.** Being on a team which is responsible for a major account is a big responsibility and the rewards should match the risks. Don't change the basic compensation structure, but provide the team with an additional incentive which everyone shares.

Source: Adapted from Cathy Hyatt Hills, "Making the Team," *Sales & Marketing Management,* February 1992, pp. 56–57.

### Strategic Considerations

A number of factors must be considered if a company chooses to adopt a team-selling approach. The size and the functional diversity of the team must be established. Management must determine how it will reward the individuals on the team as well as the team itself. To a large extent these decisions should be based on the strategic objectives for the team. For example, if one of the primary responsibilities of the team will be to provide a great amount of after-sale support and if that support will be provided by people other than the salesperson, it is often effective to include the support staff as part of a sales team. This enables the support personnel to develop a better understanding of the customer's support needs relatively quickly. Furthermore, with their expertise, support people can help "close" the sale.

However, there are some general guidelines that may affect these decisions. It has been found that individuals tend to exert less effort as team size increases, so there is some rationale for limiting the size of the team. On the other hand, there is evidence that greater skill diversity is related to increased effort and interaction on the part of the team members. Therefore, it is a good idea to form teams with individuals who are from several different functional areas or departments within the firm.

Team selling is not the best alternative in every situation. It is expensive and consequently is used only when there is potential for high sales volume and profit. For example, companies may use teams to call on their major accounts but not on their lower volume accounts. Even then, team selling is likely to be used only in complex situations involving a large capital expenditure, a long-term contract, customized products and services, or a new account. We call these *new-task* situations. *Routine* selling situations—even for large amounts—are likely to be handled by a sales rep and a purchasing agent working together, with no team involved. The in-between situations—*modified rebuys,* we call them—may involve a selling team, but with fewer members than in new-buy situations.

The overriding consideration in the decision to use sales teams should be whether the approach is consistent with the needs of the buyer. If your important customers or potential customers are using buying teams for their complex purchasing decisions, then your firm should consider using multifunctional sales teams to call on these customers.

## Independent Sales Organizations

Most producers use some type of wholesaling or retailing middlemen to get their products to the final customer. According to the Census of Retail Trade, less than 5 percent of the dollar volume of products bought by household consumers are purchased directly from producers. In business goods, the dollar volume of direct sales—producer to business user—is very high. But most business-goods producers also use some type of wholesaling middleman.[17] Most producers, then, rely in part on using someone else's sales force to move the product to market. At the same time, these middlemen must be sold on representing a certain producer and selling the producer's products. In effect, a middleman's organization becomes both a customer and a sales force for this producer.

The two major categories of these independent sales forces are merchant middlemen (wholesalers and retailers) and agents. Additionally, most wholesaling middlemen (merchant wholesalers and agents) have outside sales forces—sales forces that go to the customer. Therefore, the management of these sales forces is within the scope of this book. However, at this point we are interested only in the sales force organizational relationships between a producer and these middleman companies.

### Independent Agents

Many producers, either with or without their own sales forces, rely heavily on the sales forces of independent agents to reach the market. These agents are wholesaling middlemen who do not take ownership title to the products they sell, and they usually do not carry inventory stocks. Agent middlemen are paid a commission on the sales they make. Consequently, the commission is a variable expense to a producer—that is, a producer doesn't pay if no sale is made.

The most widely used type of agent is a **manufacturer's representative,** also called a *manufacturer's agent* or simply a *rep.* A single producer usually uses several manufacturers' agents, each having a specified geographical territory. Each agent has its own sales force and generally represents several manufacturers of related, but not directly competing products. Manufacturers' reps are most often used in the following situations:

**?**   **AN ETHICAL DILEMMA**

A strong regional manufacturer decided several years ago to expand into a new geographic area. Although the company served all of its current customers with its own sales force, it chose to use a manufacturer's rep to expand into the new territory. The company was not certain how long it would take to build up the business in the new area, and using a rep organization would enable the company to limit its expenses during this developmental period.

During the next several years, the rep did an outstanding job of opening up new accounts for the manufacturer. The rep was well liked by her customers, and the company was very satisfied with the amount of effort which had been devoted by the rep to the company's products. In fact, management readily acknowledged that the rep's knowledge of the customers in that market had clearly been the primary factor which enabled the company to penetrate this market with such rapid success.

Sales in this territory were now at a level which was large enough to support the company's own rep and the company was *not* planning on renewing its contractual arrangement with the rep. Rather, it would replace the rep with one of their own salespeople.

Is this company acting ethically if it replaces the independent rep with one of its own salespeople?

- When a manufacturer does not have a sales force; the rep then does all the selling.
- When a producer wants to introduce a new product, but for some reason does not want its existing sales force to handle it.
- When a company wants to enter a new market that is not yet sufficiently developed for the seller to use its own sales force.
- When it is not cost effective for a company to use its own reps to call on certain accounts because the sales potential does not justify the cost.

From a producer's point of view, there are advantages in using the sales forces of manufacturers' agents. These reps know their market and have already established relations with prospective accounts. An individual producer, on the other hand, especially one new in the market, probably will not have the same access to customers. Another benefit of using reps is that it is less expensive in sparsely populated markets or for smaller accounts or where the producer has a limited line of products.

National Semiconductor is a firm which uses independent reps to call on its 75,000 smaller accounts which purchase $20,000 to $200,000 worth of products each year. These reps supplement the 130 company reps who call on the larger accounts.[18]

**Brokers** are another type of independent agent that is used extensively, at least in some industries. The prime responsibility of brokers is to bring sellers and buyers together. Brokers can also furnish considerable market information regarding prices, products, and market conditions. Brokers may represent either the seller (90 percent of the time) or the buyer (10 percent), but not both parties in the same transaction.

Brokers are used in marketing services as well as products. Hotels, airlines, and resorts, for example, make extensive use of travel agents as a sales force. Brokers play a major role in the sale of stocks, bonds, and other financial services.

### Wholesale Distributors

Wholesalers are another type of independent sales organization that producers may use to reach their final customers. Wholesalers—also called *jobbers, distributors,* or *industrial distributors,* depending on the industry—are middlemen who take ownership title to the products they sell. They also carry a physical inventory of these products. Distributors may represent only one producer, but most often they represent many producers of related and competing products. A large percentage of producers, especially producers of business (industrial) products, use distributors.

Distributors can be very useful in selling situations where (1) individual sales are small, (2) the buying process is not highly specialized, or (3) rapid delivery and local service facilities are important.

### The Decision to Use Independent versus Company Reps

This decision depends on the specific market the firm is trying to serve. As a basis for making the decision, a company must establish clear objectives for each of the markets it is targeting. Then it must develop strategies to achieve those objectives. The strategies will dictate whether the company should use direct salespeople, independent reps, or some combination of both.

Often the decision revolves around three considerations:

- Which is most effective in achieving your objectives for that market.
- Which method is the most economical.
- Which gives you the necessary amount of control in order to achieve your objectives.

The answer to which method is most effective in achieving your objectives depends directly on what the objective is. For example, if the primary objective is to quickly achieve wide distribution for a new product, manufacturers' reps may be the best alternative for a company without an established company sales force. If the long-term objective is to develop partnerships with a certain group of customers, then it is probably best to serve them directly even though this may be an expensive alternative.

As illustrated in Figure 4-10, the answer to which is the most economical method is a function of (1) the potential volume in the particular market and (2) the number of company salespeople which would be required to serve that market. It can also be seen that the direct sales force has a variable cost-to-sales ratio, and the independents have a fixed cost-to-sales ratio. When sales are low, the direct cost-to-sales ratio will be high, but it decreases as volume rises, whereas the ratio for the independents stays the same regardless of the volume. Because of this, the use of

■ **FIGURE 4-10**     **Company sales reps versus independent sales reps: a cost analysis**

| Number of Company Salespeople | Territory Volume | | | |
| --- | --- | --- | --- | --- |
| | **$500,000** | **$1M** | **$2M** | **$3M** |
| | Cost of Sales | | | |
| One | $60,000 | $60,000 | $60,000 | $60,000 |
| | 12%* | 6% | 3% | 2% |
| Two | $120,000 | $120,000 | $120,000 | $120,000 |
| | 24% | 12% | 6% | 4% |
| Independent Rep Commission | Territory Volume | | | |
| | **$500,000** | **$1M** | **$2M** | **$3M** |
| | Cost of Sales | | | |
| 5% | $25,000 | $50,000 | $100,000 | $150,000 |
| | 5% | 5% | 5% | 5% |
| 7.5% | $37,500 | $75,000 | $150,000 | $225,000 |
| | 7.5% | 7.5% | 7.5% | 7.5% |

*Cost as a percent of total sales.

Notes: Annual cost figures for direct sales are based on a salary of $45,000 plus $15,000 expenses per salesperson. This does not include the costs of branch office facilities and personnel or fringe benefits normally paid to direct salespeople. The number of independent reps covering the same territory may vary, but the commission percentage as a ratio to sales would remain the same.

Source: *Sales & Marketing Management,* June 1991.

direct salespeople becomes more economical at higher volumes. Generally, the volume in a market must be fairly substantial before a company can cover the costs of serving the customers with direct salespeople.

The question of control should be decided on the basis of how much control is needed to achieve the desired objectives. When a firm uses independent reps, it loses control over the amount of time devoted to its product lines because these reps usually represent more than one company. It also loses control over the approach and attention given to its customers. If the firm's customers each require a specialized approach and a great deal of attention, the use of independent reps may not be the way to achieve its sales objectives. However, control in itself is not an objective; sometimes the objectives may be achieved more efficiently and effectively using independent reps.

*Choosing an Independent Agent*   It is important to pick the very best agent available. In particular, the agent should be one who best matches the market strategy and the culture of the parent organization. The goals of the two organizations should be compatible and the selling philosophies of the two should be the same. However, in a recent survey of 334 manufacturers who use agents, 59 percent of them reported that they were *not* compatible or had marginal compatibility with their sales agents.[19] In order to be compatible, a parent company should devote the same amount of resources (time and money) to the selection of its independent agents as it would to the selection of its own company reps.

*Managing the Independent Sales Force*    It is difficult enough to run your own sales force, but you face further organizational challenges when you use independent sales forces—whether agents or distributors. The biggest and perhaps the most obvious challenge is the one mentioned above—that the producer has very little control over the independent sales force. This factor creates at least two managerial problems. First, a producer must compete with other firms for the selling time of the agent's or distributor's salespeople. This is a particularly tough challenge if the manufacturer and its products are not well known. A second problem is that it is difficult to get manufacturers' reps to service an account and perform non-selling activities because they get no commission for such work.

There is no perfect solution to this problem because the top independent agents will have their choice of companies to represent. They do not need your company to survive and will not put up with attempts to control their actions. Therefore, the best strategy is to provide your reps with the proper amount of support. This may involve training the salespeople of the agent or distributor. The manufacturer can also provide technical product information and can have a missionary sales force that does promotional work supporting the middleman's efforts. Providing the appropriate level of support will alleviate the control problems. Furthermore, it is important to work with the reps as partners, making joint decisions on issues that affect the sales of products in the markets which the reps serve.

## Telemarketing and Electronic Marketing

In Chapter 1 we said that this book deals with the management of a sales force that goes to the customer. But an increasing number of firms—both large and small—have moved some outside selling efforts to within the company. Instead of face-to-face sales calls, salespeople are "going to the customer" by using telephones, fax machines, television, and computers.

Telephone selling is not new. What is new today, however, is the innovative use of communication systems to aid the selling effort and other marketing activities. The terms **telemarketing** and **electronic marketing** are used to describe these communication systems. Generally telemarketing refers to telephone sales where the customer is contacted by a telemarketing person. However, in electronic marketing the contact with the customer is through the Internet, e-mail, or other computerized systems. *Marketing News* reported that in 1995 companies spent approximately $54 billion on telemarketing calls to customers and secured sales from these calls of $386 billion.[20] The use of telemarketing and electronic marketing is likely to increase in the coming years.

Two main reasons for the growing use of telemarketing as a form of sales force specialization are: (1) many buyers prefer it over personal sales calls in certain selling situations and (2) many marketers find that it increases selling efficiency. For a buyer, placing routine reorders or new orders for standardized products by telephone or computer takes less time than in-person sales calls. Sellers face increasingly high costs keeping salespeople on the road. So any selling done by telemarketing reduces that expense. Also, using telemarketing for routine selling allows the field sales force to devote more time to developmental selling, major account selling, and other more profitable selling activities.

In some cases, the telemarketing salespeople are the only salespeople. For example, Dell Computer Co., with over $500 million in personal computer sales, launched its business through telephone sales and still does the majority of its business through this channel.[21] Blue Star Industries, a company which markets specialized oil field and pollution control materials, uses only the telephone to reach its customers.[22]

Some companies, such as Hewlett-Packard and IBM, use telephone reps to handle smaller or lower priority sales so that the direct rep can concentrate on bigger potential accounts.[23] In these selling programs, often referred to as **telesales** or **telephone account management,** the rep is responsible for qualifying customers as to their sales potential, assessing their needs, recommending products and services, taking orders, and providing customer service.

Many companies use telemarketing to assist the sales force. Estimates of the increases in sales in these situations range anywhere from 10 percent to 400 percent. Shachihata, which sells preinked rubber stamps through independent reps, created a consumer development department whose sole function is to take the company's leads and generate appointments for the reps. This led to an increase in appointments of four to five times the number generated the previous year.[24] The Santa Fe Railway Co. is another company that uses a telemarketing group to generate leads and qualify prospective buyers. The field sales force follows up on these leads. Other companies use telemarketing to provide after-sale service to customers. General Electric is famous for its "Answer Center," whose 250 telephone operators answer 3 million inquiries a year concerning GE products which the customers have purchased or are considering purchasing.[25]

The selling activities which can be performed by telemarketing are summarized below:

- Identify prospective customers.
- Screen, qualify, and refer sales leads.
- Solicit sales.
- Order-processing.
- Product service support.
- Account management.
- Customer relations.

In most companies, telemarketing is *not* the exclusive method used to generate and service sales. It has not replaced the direct selling effort, but rather it is used to supplement the direct efforts in some way. As we noted in Chapter 2, many companies are using multiple selling channels to reach customers more efficiently. Telemarketing is often one of the channels.

# ORGANIZING FOR INTERNATIONAL SALES

As we move into the 21st century, increasing numbers of American companies are engaging in international marketing. Since 1986 the level of U.S. exports has risen at a rate four times that of the increase in gross domestic product (GDP), and U.S. company investment in foreign operations has doubled in the same time period to over $500 billion.[26] Additionally, international trade is being encouraged by a number of trade agreements which are lessening the trade barriers around the world. The most important of these is the **General Agreement on Tariffs and Trade (GATT),** which governs trade among 90 countries. For the United States the **North American Free Trade Agreement (NAFTA)** signed in 1993 is also important because it eliminated many of the trade barriers between the United States, Canada, and Mexico. The increasing foreign investment and exports as well as reduction of trade barriers means that more firms are developing global sales operations.

The individual company decides to sell its products overseas for many different reasons. It may be in response to a customer request or because the home market is saturated or simply because of excess capacity. Whatever the reason, it is important that the company's sales efforts are part of a long-term international strategy that has the full support of senior management. The plan must examine whether there is a need or demand for its products and how the company will sell its products abroad. A company has essentially three options with regard to distributing its products internationally: (1) It can turn over the export of its product to home-country middlemen, (2) it can partner with foreign country middlemen, or (3) it can establish its own company sales force in the foreign country.

## Home-Country Middlemen

Depending on the products, there are a number of export middlemen, located in the producing firm's country, who provide international marketing services from a domestic base. Firms such as **export merchants, trading companies, export management companies, agents, brokers,** and **distributors** all offer international sales and distribution services for those companies which do not wish to become immediately involved in the complexities of international sales or which want to sell abroad with a minimum financial and management commitment.

Even in the case of minimum involvement, the company must make a number of critical sales management decisions. The appropriate agent or distributor must be identified and an agreement must be reached with regard

## AN INTERNATIONAL PERSPECTIVE

Even when a company chooses to employ its own sales force, it still must decide whether to hire foreign reps or reps from its own country. Foreign nationals are familiar with the local customs and culture but unfamiliar with the product and the company's marketing practices. The company reps, on the other hand, know the product and the company but are unfamiliar with the local customs and culture.

The answer to this question can be found by examining the needs and desires of the customers. Research on similarity in sales has generally demonstrated that, all other things being equal, the customers would rather be served by someone who is similar to themselves. Therefore it is probably better to hire a national from your target market unless there are some overriding reasons not to. For example, some products are so complex that the salespeople may require extensive training and/or experience before they can sell these products. It may not be economically feasible to provide the amount of in-depth training which would be needed if the company hires inexperienced nationals or it may not be possible to find enough qualified individuals in the target country.

If a company does hire foreign nationals, it should provide adequate product and company training. Likewise, if a company hires reps from its own country, it should provide extensive training in the cultural norms of the foreign market.

to the services to be provided and their compensation. It may also be necessary to train personnel and to establish a system for monitoring sales results.

### Foreign-Country Middlemen

Many small and midsized firms which decide that they want to establish a sales organization in a foreign country cannot afford to employ their own international sales forces. Therefore, many manufacturers set up a network of manufacturers' agents, distributors (wholesalers), and/or dealers (retailers) in foreign markets. In many cases these independent organizations are already selling other products and services in the target country. In addition to personal selling, these middlemen perform many services, including advertising, providing market information, making repairs, collecting invoices, and settling disputes. In return, the American firms usually grant exclusive territorial sales rights and may grant one wholesaler the sole distributorship for an entire country.

In foreign markets without sufficient sales potential to justify establishing a company sales force, such as those in developing countries, distributors are used. Other markets are so large geographically that independent reps may be used to cover the outlying areas of the country and company salespeople are used in the population centers.

Cultural diversity also affects this decision. Some markets which are multilingual and culturally heterogeneous require several different reps to deal with customers from the varying cultural groups. This is often the case in the markets in Southeast Asia.

Foreign middlemen are generally less aggressive and perform fewer marketing activities than their American counterparts. But some of the factors described above often make it difficult for the company to bypass foreign middlemen.

If a company decides to use foreign-company middlemen, it must first identify the prospective candidates. Sources of information for locating foreign middlemen include

- U.S. Department of Commerce
- Foreign consulates
- Foreign chambers of commerce
- Business publications
- Published directories
- Middleman associations

After identifying candidates, the company must select the middleman. In making the selection the firm should consider the nature of the prospective distributor's business. In other words, do the company's products fit with the prospective distributor's current products? The company should also consider the distributor's current volume of sales, its financial strength, and its managerial capability and stability.[27]

## Company Sales Force Located Abroad

In a country where the volume and profit potential warrants it and government regulations allow it, an American firm may establish its own company sales force. Only the largest companies, those with at least $500 million in sales, should consider the possibility of establishing their own sales force in a foreign market.[28] These sales forces may sell directly to the final customers or they may sell through local distributors and dealers. Using its own sales force enables a company to (1) promote products more aggressively and (2) control its sales effort more completely.

For products which are technically or chemically complex, the manufacturer may feel that company-employed salespeople are necessary to ensure that the proper training and assistance are provided to the customer. The company's legal liability with regard to the use of these kinds of products is another factor that may cause the company to use its own salespeople.

# ■ SUMMARY

An organization is an arrangement of activities involving a group of people. The goal is to arrange the activities so that the people who are involved can work *together* better than they can individually. The sales force organizational structure has a significant influence on the implementation of a company's strategic planning.

The general characteristics of a good organization are (1) an organizational structure that reflects a market orientation; (2); an organization that is built around activities and not around the people performing these activities; (3) responsibilities that are clearly spelled out, and sufficient authority granted to meet the responsibility; (4) a reasonable span of executive control; (5) stability combined with flexibility; and (6) balanced and coordinated activities both *within* the sales department and between sales and nonmarketing departments.

Most sales organizations can be classified into one of three basic categories: a line organization, a line-and-staff organization, or a functional organization. A line organization is the simplest form of organization and is often appropriate for small firms. A line-and-staff organization enables a company to use staff assistants who are specialists in various areas of marketing. A functional organization carries specialization a step further by giving more line authority to the executive specialists. There is also a new horizontal structure which is being used by a number of firms. It is a much flatter organization with fewer levels of management.

In most medium- and large-sized companies, the sales forces are divided on some basis of sales specialization. The most frequently used bases are (1) geographical territories, (2) type of product sold, (3) classes of customer, or (4) some combination of these categories.

Giving each sales representative the responsibility for his or her own geographical territory is probably the most widely used form of sales force specialization. Specializing a sales force by type of product sold is often used when a company sells unrelated products, highly technical products, or several thousands of products. Product specialization may also involve the organizational concept of a product manager. Specialization by markets may be done on a channel-of-distribution basis or on an industry basis.

In the organization of an outside sales force, the use of the following four organizational strategies is increasing: national account management, team selling, independent sales forces, and telemarketing. For national account management, firms may use a separate sales force or executives, or they may establish a separate division. Selling teams comprised of people from several departments are being used to match the needs of customer buying centers. Sometimes a firm cannot afford or does not want to have its own sales force. Then it will use some type of independent agent. Telemarketing is sometimes used as the primary selling method, but often it is used to assist the sales force.

Organizing for international sales also presents some difficult challenges for sales management. Companies must decide whether to use independent selling organizations in the home country or in the foreign country or to employ their own salespeople. Even if the company decides to use its own salespeople, it must still determine whether it will hire reps from its own country or foreign nationals.

## Key Terms

| | | |
|---|---|---|
| Broker | Functional organization | Line-and-staff organization |
| Buying center | General Agreement on | Line organization |
| Distributors | Tariffs and Trade (GATT) | Manufacturer's |
| Electronic marketing | Geographic organization | representative |
| Export management | Horizontal organization | Market specialization |
| companies | Independent agent | North American Free Trade |
| Export merchants | Informal organization | Agreement (NAFTA) |

National account
  management (NAM)
Organization
Organizational structure
Product-line specialization
Product or category
  manager

Product operating
  specialization
Product staff specialization
Selling center
Selling team
Telemarketing

Telephone account
  management
Telesales
Trading company
Wholesale distributor

## QUESTIONS AND PROBLEMS

1. Explain how coordination can be effectively secured between the sales department and each of the following departments: production, engineering and design, personnel, finance, export sales.

2. What are the reasons for the lack of coordination that sometimes exists between advertising executives and field sales managers? What are some proposals for developing better coordination between these two groups?

3. The choice of organizational structure is influenced by factors such as:
   a. Size of the company.
   b. Nature of the products.
   c. Nature and density of the market.
   d. Ability of executives.
   e. Financial condition of the company.
   Explain how each of these conditions may affect the choice of structure.

4. In your opinion, what are the best policies or procedures for solving the following problems, which are often found in a line-and-staff organization?
   a. A strong-willed staff executive tries to take on line authority instead of remaining an adviser.
   b. A line executive consistently bypasses or ignores advice from staff departments.

5. What type of organizational specialization within the sales department do you recommend in each of the following companies?
   a. Manufacturer of high-quality women's sportswear with 100 salespeople selling to department stores and specialty stores throughout the nation.
   b. Plumbing wholesaler covering the southeast quarter of the country with 50 salespeople.
   c. Manufacturer of chemicals used in fertilizers with 35 salespeople selling to 500 accounts located throughout the country.
   d. Manufacturer of office machines with 1,000 salespeople.

6. A regional hardware wholesaler in Detroit, Michigan, employed 20 salespeople, each of whom sold the full line of products. It became apparent that the list of products was simply too long for one person to sell effectively. The company felt it had a choice of
   a. reorganizing the sales force by product lines or
   b. adding more representatives, reducing each person's territory, but still having each carry the full line.
   What do you recommend?

7. A manufacturer of small aircraft designed for executive transportation in large companies has decided to implement the concept of a selling center. What people in this company should be on the selling teams? What problems is this firm likely to encounter when it uses team selling?

8. How does the quote at the beginning of the chapter, "Love the one you're with," relate to the concepts discussed in the first four chapters?

9. *a.* What courses of action would you propose for a company that wants to get its manufacturers' reps to devote more time to selling the company's products?

   *b.* A manufacturer of small motors uses industrial distributors to reach its market. What can this producer do to encourage the distributors to spend more time selling the company's products?

10. A manufacturer of playground equipment now uses its own sales force to sell directly to customer groups such as city park departments, school districts, private day nurseries, and companies that maintain day-care centers for employees' children. This producer would like to install a telemarketing system to reduce some of its field-selling costs. What problems is this seller likely to encounter in the telemarketing move? What recommendations do you have for solving these problems?

11. A manufacturer of pharmaceuticals wants to market its products in the EC. Its sales are currently $400,000. How should the company enter this market, with its own sales force or with some type of independent distributor? Support your choice.

12. A U.S. manufacturer of industrial tools wants to market its products overseas. It is considering establishing sales organizations in several different countries. In which of the countries listed below do you think this manufacturer should use an independent selling organization rather than its own sales force?

    *a.* Switzerland.

    *b.* Malaysia.

    *c.* Spain.

    *d.* China.

## ◼ EXPERIENTIAL EXERCISES

**A.** Obtain an organizational chart for a firm which sells consumer products and a firm which sells industrial products. Compare and contrast the sales organization structure in terms of span of control, centralization, specialization, line-and-staff components, and so on.

**B.** Contact an executive from any small organization and ask about the formal organizational relationships. *Without seeing the firm's organizational chart* (if there is one), draw an organizational chart based on the information given to you by the executive. Does this organization violate any of the principles of organizational design? Compare your organizational chart to the firm's official chart.

**C.** Contact a manufacturers rep for any type of product (they are usually listed in the yellow pages of most major cities); find out what criteria reps use to select the manufacturers they are willing to represent. Also determine what types of assistance the various manufacturers they represent provide to the manufacturers' rep.

## REFERENCES

1. Patricia Sellars, "How to Remake Your Sales Force," *Fortune,* May 4, 1992, pp. 98–103.

2. John A. Byrne, "The Horizontal Corporation," *Business Week,* December 20, 1993, pp. 76–81.

3. George S. Day, "Aligning the Organization to the Market," Prakash Nedungadi Memorial Lecture, Indiana University School of Business, January 1997.

4. Geoffrey Brewer, "Love the Ones You're With," *Sales & Marketing Management,* February 1997, pp. 40–41.

5. ____, "Brain Power," *Sales & Marketing Management,* May 1997, pp. 39–41.

6. Andy Cohen, "Managing," *Sales & Marketing Management,* April 1996, pp. 77–79.

7. Martin Everett, "Send in the Specialists," *Sales & Marketing Management,* April 1991, pp. 44–49.

8. Daniel S. Levine, "Justice Served," *Sales & Marketing Management,* May 1995, pp. 53–58.

9. Kerry J. Rottenberger-Murtha, "The Lean and the Green," *Sales & Marketing Management,* February 1993, pp. 68–71.

10. Everett, "Send in the Specialists."

11. Cathy Hyatt Hills, "Making the Team," *Sales & Marketing Management,* February 1992, pp. 54–57.

12. Brewer, "Love the Ones You're With."

13. Rahul Jacob, "Why Some Customers Are More Equal Than Others," *Fortune,* September 19, 1994, pp. 215–20.

14. Sellars, "How to Remake Your Sales Force."

15. Jacob, "Why Some Customers Are More Equal Than Others."

16. Joseph Conlin, "Teaming Up," *Sales & Marketing Management,* October 1993, pp. 98–104.

17. "Sales Manager Survey," *Agency Sales Magazine,* February 1993, pp. 9–13.

18. Melissa Campanelli, "Agents of Change," *Sales & Marketing Management,* February 1995, pp. 71–75.

19. "Sales Manager Survey."

20. Author, "Telemarketing Cited as Chief Form of Direct Marketing," *Marketing News,* January 1, 1996, p. 9.

21. Chad Rubel, "Data-Base Strategies Pay Off in More Sales," *Marketing News,* May 20, 1996, p. 6.

22. Roger Ricklefs, "Working at Home Proves Too Cozy for Entrepreneur," *The Wall Street Journal,* September 12, 1996, p. B2.

23. Tim Clark, "A Sales Force Weaves New Strategies," *Business Marketing,* May 1993, pp. 26, 32.

24. John F. Yarbrough, "Salvaging a Lousy Year," *Sales & Marketing Management,* July 1996, p. 72.

25. Aimee L. Stern, "Telemarketing Polishes Its Image," *Sales & Marketing Management,* June 1991, pp. 107–10.

26. Rob Norton, "Strategies for the Export Boom," *Fortune,* August 22, 1994, pp. 124–31.

27. For suggestions regarding the selection of qualified distributors in foreign markets, see Eugene H. Fram, "We Can Do a Better Job of Selecting International Distributors," *Journal of Business and Industrial Marketing,* Spring 1992, pp. 61–70.

28. Lawrence Richter Quinn, "Global Warning," *Sales & Marketing Management,* April 1997, pp. 54–58.

*Case 4-1*

## TRICON INDUSTRIES*

Organizing the Sales Force

Laura Thompson, the vice president and general manager for the Heavy Duty Products (HDP) Division of Tricon Industries, was shaken. She had been heading up a task force of Tricon's divisional vice presidents. The committee's charge was to make recommendations with regard to possible changes in the organizational structure of Tricon's three divisions.

Jon Belth, the vice president of the Braking Systems Division, had just left Laura's office. He had accused Laura of taking a position on the possible reorganization which was not in the company's best interests, but rather served the purpose of consolidating her power and authority. Laura felt that this was an unfair accusation, but she also felt that she understood why Jon would make such an accusation. Jon felt threatened. If there was some type of consolidation of the marketing and sales efforts of the three divisions, his position might not exist under the new structure. And if the number of managerial positions were reduced overall, he might be out of a job. Laura knew that her position was at risk as well, but that she was less likely to be let go than Jon.

Although Laura recognized that there were a number of problems associated with any reorganization that the committee might recommend, she was committed to move forward with the discussions and subsequent recommendations. If there were disagreements, these would be acknowledged in the report to Peter Gray, the chief executive officer of Tricon, who had created the task force.

Tricon Industries is a diversified company whose products serve the construction and transportation industries as well as numerous other general industrial markets. The Heavy Duty Products Division produces brake linings for on-road trucks, and its primary customers are OEM axle manufacturers such as Spicer and Mercedes and trailer manufacturers such as Fruehauf and Monon. HDP's strategy is to seek approval for its products at the OEM level in order to push them through the channel to the large national trucking fleets such as Consolidated Freightways and Roadway. It also targets the aftermarket sales by convincing the fleets to specify HDP products as replacements when the original brake linings wear out. This division, which has sales of $81.8 million, is the largest and oldest of the three divisions.

In 1994, Tricon purchased the off-highway braking division of an international construction equipment manufacturer and created the Braking Systems Division (BSD). This division designs and manufactures braking system products for construction and mining original equipment manufacturers (OEMs) throughout the world and is a leading supplier of genuine replacement parts to the aftermarket. OEM customers include worldwide companies such as Caterpillar, Komatsu Dresser, and John Deere. BSD is currently establishing a worldwide network of distributors that will provide sales, installation, and service support to the OEM and aftermarket customers. With sales of $50 million, BSD is the most international of the divisions.

Specialty Products Division (SPD), the smallest of Tricon's divisions, has sales of

---

*Adapted from a case prepared by John Hiel and Julie Singh under the direction of Rosann L. Spiro.

$20 million. It was acquired in 1993 because of its high growth potential. In addition to braking products, the division's product lines include driving applications, such as clutches, as well as extruded products. The business segments served by the division include industrial drives and motor brakes, light aircraft, lawn and garden, and recreational vehicles. These applications are primarily low-volume specialty applications.

Each division has its own dedicated sales representatives, who are assigned to geographic territories. In the HDP and BSD divisions, the sales engineers are assigned to either the OEM or the aftermarket customers. (See Exhibit 4-A for Tricon's organizational chart.) In the OEM market, the sales reps sell directly to the manufacturers; in the aftermarket, the reps call on independent distributors. There are currently 23 sales reps serving the three divisions. Each salesperson is responsible for serving his or her existing customers as well as for finding new customers.

Laura realized that the BS and SP divisions had been purchased because their product lines, technologies, and markets were seen as complementary to HDP's existing competencies. However, these acquisitions took place without a formal plan for integration. For the most part, each division continues to operate fairly independently; as a result, Tricon is not taking advantage of the potential synergies which exist between the companies. Laura felt that consolidation of the sales forces offered the greatest opportunity for achieving some of the synergies.

However, the prevailing philosophy has been that there are sufficient differences between the various product lines and customers to justify separate organizations. Jon had argued, "Our current structure allows our sales engineers to provide specialized attention to our customers." Laura acknowledged that Jon was correct, but she argued that the negatives of the current structure outweighed the benefits. As she stated in the recent meeting, "Many of our customers are called on by more than one sales engineer from Tricon. This duplication of effort is not only very expensive, but it may be hindering our customer relationships. Some of our customers are confused about which division to call with questions or problems, and some of them just don't want to deal with more than one rep from the same company."

Laura knew that she must sell the benefits of consolidation over the objections of Jon and possibly others. Although she felt that she could present a convincing case for consolidation, she knew that designing an acceptable structure for the new sales organization would be a challenge. There were clearly a number of options, and she wasn't certain which would best meet the needs of Tricon and its customers.

*Questions:*

1. Should Tricon consolidate its sales forces?

2. If Tricon were to reorganize its sales forces, what are the options and which structure would you recommend?

■ **EXHIBIT 4-A**   Tricon organizational chart

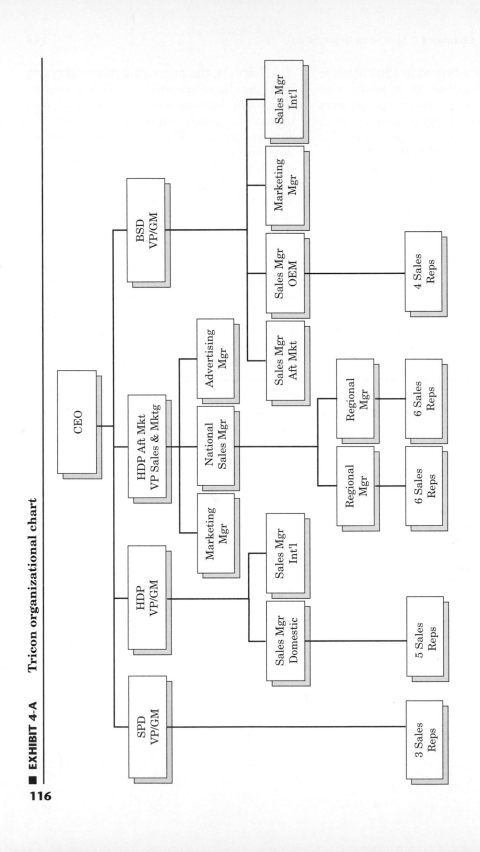

*Case 4-2*

## MICROPLASTICS, INC.
### Need for reorganization

"Perhaps a bit of history regarding our sales organization will help you in your coming weeks as our new sales manager," said Don Lopez, president of Microplastics, Inc., to Katie Curry, the firm's new sales manager. The company had been organized in 1988 to manufacture to specification small plastic parts which were sold directly to other manufacturers, particularly high-technology industries.

Lopez continued, "It seems as if our sales force has been in a constant state of upheaval for the past five years. A year hasn't gone by but what we reorganized it some way or another. But nothing seems to work. Let me go back to 1988 and trace our troubles for you. Our growth had been great in the early days of our industry. We had little direct competition and we were making plenty of money, sold everything we could make. Then competition came into the market and we hit a recession. Sales dropped 40 percent and profits turned to losses. At first we thought that it was happening to everyone, but soon we discovered that our competitors were not being hit as hard as we were. Their salespeople seemed to be able to sell into accounts where our people couldn't.

"We became most unhappy with our sales organization, which at the time consisted of 28 people who reported to one sales manager. We fired the sales manager and brought in a man from one of our most successful competitors. It cost some money to get him, but we were willing to pay it. Well, right off the bat this bozo wants to hire three assistant sales managers to supervise the sales force, a sales training director to train them, a sales analyst for the home office, and a home-office sales engineer to back up the field sales force technically."

"That's a lot of money," Katie Curry commented when Lopez paused. "How did he justify it to you?"

"I remember it well because it scared me to death," Lopez said. "He said that if we wanted to be a big-time company we would have to do things the way the big boys do them. He insisted that the key to success was to back up the field people with tremendous support from the home office and supervise them closely in the field."

"Well, how did it work out?"

"Need you ask? Sales stayed about the same but our costs skyrocketed. We lost our shirts. I never saw such confusion. No one seemed to know what they were supposed to do. So we fired the sales manager and promoted one of the sales reps to the job. He immediately cleaned out all of the staff the other fellow had hired so we were back to square one. But not quite."

"Oh, did the new manager make some changes?" Curry asked.

"He felt that our real problem was that the reps couldn't sell to all types of customers, so he divided them into two groups. The first bunch of 10 reps was to sell to the large manufacturers, where there was a lot of engineering work to be done with the customer's people. The second group was to cover the smaller assemblers where engineering was not so important, where you dealt with the owner directly," Lopez explained.

"What happened?"

"Mass confusion! The reps didn't want to give up their customers, so they held onto them as long as they could. And it didn't seem to help sales. We didn't sell any more large accounts than we were previously selling. The guy got tired of managing and asked to go back into the field where he felt he knew what to do.

"You can bet that the next sales manager was selected with a lot more care," Lopez continued. "We interviewed more than 20 people until we found this fellow who had a terrific record over at National Plastics. We thought we had a barn burner in him. He came in, surveyed the situation, and wrote a report for me on what had to be done."

"You're shaking your head. What went wrong?" Curry inquired.

"He personally spent a day with each sales representative to diagnose what was wrong with the operation," said Lopez. "On the basis of his judgment, 19 of our reps were incompetent, with no hope of ever becoming the type of salesperson he thought was needed to do the job. He planned to fire them immediately. Then he would call in the remaining nine reps for an intensive training program to teach them how to sell the way he wanted them to. I remember vividly how he leaned over my desk with his fists clenched and sternly said, 'My sales force will sell the way I want them to sell or they won't be around.' Well, we had some words over that report," Lopez said. "I just could not let him fire 16 people who had been with us from the beginning and who had helped us build the company. I wanted him to train all of them, but he said it couldn't be done. They just weren't his 'type of people.' That kind of talk really gets my goat. He was putting these people down like they were dirt, and I told him so. Well, one thing led to another, and there went the new sales manager."

"And you had no inkling of this aspect of his personality before hiring him?" Curry asked.

Lopez drew a deep breath and confessed, "I must say that we did. His previous boss described him as one tough, driving guy who was hard to live with but who really got results. I guess all we wanted to hear was that he got results. We didn't stop to think about how he got them."

"And so here we are," Katie summarized. "You want to know what I have discovered and what I intend to do about it."

"That's it!" said Lopez. "Have you anything to report yet?"

"It's a bit premature now to lay out a program for you," she replied, "but the seeds of it are in everything that has happened previously. I'll be ready next Friday for a report on my proposed program."

"Fair enough," said Lopez.

Katie had already made up her mind about what needed to be done, but did not want to reveal it until she had figured out how to go about it. She had quickly related to everything that had been told her. The sales manager who had wanted to reorganize for some staff support was right. The span of control was ridiculous, and the reps were getting little support from the home office. The second manager had been right in seeing that the reps were not equally effective in selling to all types of customers. The third manager was certainly correct in his appraisal of the reps. The sales force had some people with mediocre talents. For the most part, they were a seedy crew that looked good in the early days of the industry before competition became a factor in the market. But she realized that there would be little she could do about this problem immediately. It would have to be worked on over a period of time. For the time being, she had to develop a means for working with these people and that seemed to call for some sort of reorganization.

### Question:

1. What changes should the new sales manager recommend?

*Case 4-3*

## EXCEL TOOLS, INC.
### Sales organization for new products and markets

Excel Tools planned to introduce several new products during the late 1990s, some for the consumer market and others for industrial users. Both the sales volume and the number of sales calls on industrial users had been declining. Consequently, the field sales manager, Roger Cook, was wondering whether the present organizational structure of the sales force was appropriate for meeting the increasingly difficult competition being encountered from both domestic and international competitors and for exploiting the expanded market opportunities provided by the new product lines.

Excel Tools was a large manufacturer of a widely diversified assortment of products, most of which were sold to the industrial market. Except for power tools, the company had little experience with consumer products. Excel had diversified both by acquiring existing companies and by expanding its own product lines. Sales in 1994 were $950 million. In addition to power tools, the company made and marketed such products as meters and valves for the gas, oil, and water industries; taxi meters; parking meters; iron and steel castings; and sewer cleaning equipment. With its home offices in Cincinnati, Ohio, the company operated manufacturing facilities in 11 states and 5 foreign countries. Excel marketed electrical and pneumatic power tools, both portable and stationary models. These products were sold to both consumer and industrial markets. Separate Excel-owned brands were used to differentiate the portable tools from the stationary models. In addition, the firm manufactured power tools under retailers' brands, such as Sears' Craftsman label. Sales in the power tool division totaled $190 million in 1994.

Competitive gaps existed in the product assortment offered each of these markets, but the new product lines were intended to fill these gaps. In the consumer market, a new low-priced line was intended to complement the product group that previously consisted only of upscale, higher priced units. A new line of portable tools was intended to round out the product assortment designed primarily for industrial users. While sales declined in 1992 and 1993, management's long-range planning projected that the sales volume of power tools would double by the year 2000. Major competition was expected to continue from such companies as Black & Decker, Stanley, Rockwell Manufacturing Company, and the producers of Skill power tools.

As vice president of sales for the power tool division, Cook was responsible for achieving the sales goals set for all power tools, including those sold through distributors (wholesalers) in the United States and abroad and those sold directly to private-brand customers and to large chain-store organizations and discount retailers. Reporting to Cook were 10 regional sales managers in the United States, covering approximately 100 territories. International sales, which had been rising, were under the direction of Pierre Dubnow in the Paris office. The domestic salespeople under each regional manager were divided into two groups on the basis of product lines—portable or stationary tools. Both groups of salespeople called on many different types of wholesalers. These included automotive wholesalers, hardware wholesalers, builders' supply houses, machine tool distributors, and any other types of industrial distributors or consumer goods wholesalers whose customers might constitute a reasonably sized market for Excel power tools. Reps in either sales force also might call on retail dealers in a promotional or missionary capacity. The salespeople might perform such assignments as demonstrating the proper tool for a given job, setting up in-store promotions, arranging for the dealers to participate in Excel's cooperative television and newspaper advertising programs, or training dealer salespeople to sell Excel tools more effectively.

Several factors prompted Cook to review the division's organizational structure. With its ambitious new programs to extend its lines, the company was, in effect, expanding both its consumer and industrial markets. The broader product assortment, however, made each of the sales forces less specialized than before.

This was occurring at the same time that Excel's competitors were moving toward more specialized sales organizations. Excel's biggest competitor—the largest company in the industry—had divided its sales force into four specialized groups. Smaller competitors marketed a more limited line of power tools, so their sales force efforts automatically were more specialized than Excel's.

Moreover, the greatly increased importance of large national accounts, such as Wal-Mart, K mart, Sears, and Home Depot, had placed great pressure on the firms selling to them to assign sales reps to service each firm. Excel had not yet altered its structure to accommodate national account selling. Something would have to be done about this organizational need.

The recent decline in sales volume was another factor prompting Cook to review the division's organizational structure, although he recognized that the structure might have had no relation to the decline in sales. Cook also was aware of a common disadvantage to a product-type sales organization—namely, two sales reps, each with a separate product line, may be calling on the same account. In Excel's case there had been instances of conflicts and lack of coordination between the portable tool reps and those who sold the stationary tools in setting up cooperative advertising and other promotional programs.

To get more specialized selling efforts, Cook was considering an organizational structure in which each of the existing sales forces would be divided into two groups, according to class of customer. Thus the company would have four sales forces, the same as its biggest competitor. Existing and potential accounts would be analyzed to determine whether they served industrial or consumer markets. Then they would be divided accordingly and separate sales forces would be assigned to each customer group. Each industrial account, for example, would be called on by an industrial portable tool sales rep and an industrial stationary tool rep. Cook realized that this four-way division of the sales force would mean adding new people. Such a structure might also entail a different supervisory arrangement at the regional-manager level.

The increased specialization of effort would be a definite plus factor. Interviews with some of the salespeople indicated that most of the reps preferred to work in one market or the other. That is, they preferred to do industrial selling or to do the sales and promotional work involved with the distributors and merchants in the consumer market. Rarely was anyone encountered who liked to sell in both markets equally.

An alternative being considered was to keep the double sales force structure but divide the reps on a customer basis rather than by products. For example, one sales group would sell both portable and stationary power tools, but only to industrial accounts. In this arrangement, Excel would hope to develop account specialists and, at the same time, have only one rep call on a given account. Organizing the sales force by customer group meant that each rep would cease to be a product specialist. A rep now selling only portable tools would have to learn about selling stationary tools. However, often specialization by customer resulted in product specialization because the account bought either only portable or only stationary tools. Mr. Cook also was considering other organizational arrangements. One suggestion he was considering was to continue with the existing structure but supplement it with better programs for motivating and supervising the salespeople.

The sales manager in the Chicago regional office, Charles Webster, had a different proposal—that the company abandon its specialized sales forces and, instead, give each rep a smaller geographical territory to sell both portable and stationary tools to all classes of customers in the territory. Webster argued that neither the customer groups nor the product lines were different enough to warrant the costs and problems that resulted from specialization.

Regardless of the organizational structure finally selected—but assuming Excel continued with more than one sales force whether it was specialized by customer, product, or some other basis—there would still be an organizational question involving the regional managers. Cook was wondering whether to continue with one regional manager over all groups of salespeople in a given region or to establish separate managers for each group of reps in a region. If the sales force were further specialized, this would put increased responsibility on the regional managers under the present system. Furthermore, Excel's major competitor was using specialized managers along with its more specialized sales force. The fundamental problem was this: At what level should the organization be divided on whatever basis selected? At the level of the field salespeople only? At the regional manager level? Or conceivably at the field sales manager level, with a separate field sales manager for each major group of sales reps? Cook also was considering the possibility of using product managers or customer-group managers in a staff capacity to plan merchandising and promotional programs, and to otherwise support the field-selling effort.

*Questions:*

1. What type of sales force organization should Excel Tools, Inc., adopt?
2. Based on your decision, what regional manager structure should the company adopt?

# CHAPTER 5

# Profiling and Recruiting Salespeople

Eagles don't flock. You have to find them one at a time.

**Ross Perot**

Billions of dollars have been spent on research to improve the recruiting and selection of salespeople. Though the process has been improved, selecting those who would be successful remains one of the greatest costs and challenges to sales management today. The costs to a company which does a poor job of selecting reps are staggering. They may include the costs of advertising and possibly using an employment agency; the time to screen, interview, and assess candidates; training for the position and paying the salary of those who are hired. These costs are all wasted if that individual doesn't perform or doesn't like the job and leaves the company. [1] Additionally, there are the opportunity costs of lost sales. A poorly motivated, ineffective rep can damage a company's reputation and ruin established relationships with customers. These relationships may take years to reestablish, and the costs in terms of lost revenues may be devastating.

Nevertheless, too many managers make hiring decisions based solely on what "feels right" rather than on objectively determined criteria. Additionally, many managers start recruiting when someone is leaving rather than establishing an ongoing recruiting program. As a result, they often end up settling for someone just to fill the open position.

We believe that staffing—the selection of personnel at any level in an organization—is the most important activity in the management process. Consequently, the most important responsibility of administrators is to staff their organization with the right people. Obviously, recruiting and selecting salespeople is not a sales manager's *only* job, but it is the *most important* one. The hiring process warrants much more thought and preparation than managers usually give it. Ideally, managers should always be recruiting.

## ■ SALES FORCE SELECTION AND STRATEGIC PLANNING

In most organizations, the sales force is the one group that directly generates the revenues for the organization. Thus the sales force is directly involved in carrying out the company's strategic marketing plans. How

## Management Challenges for the Year 2000

According to the Hudson Institute, a research institute which studied corporate reactions to emerging work force issues, the number of entry-level workers will decline and significant changes in the composition of the work force of the future will occur in the next few years. For example, the sales force of the future will be drawn from an older and more culturally diverse group of people. This means that competition for sales people will be tougher, training them will cost more, and motivating and retaining them will be more difficult. Thirty percent of the companies studied reported difficulties in recruiting and expected them to continue throughout the nineties. Companies will be challenged to adapt their recruiting plans, selection procedures, and motivational practices to develop an effective sales force in the year 2000.

Source: Jeffrey D. Smith, "Radical Changes in Store for the Workforce 2000," *Sales & Marketing Management,* November 1990, p. 122.

well these plans are implemented depends to a great extent on the choice of salespeople to do the implementing. Certainly the selection process and the type of salespeople hired should be consistent with the company's strategic marketing planning. In fact, the entire sales force selection process should implement the firm's marketing and sales force planning.

Let's look at some practical applications of the relationship between sales force selection and strategic marketing planning. Assume that a company's goal is to maintain its leading market position and its market share. One major marketing strategy may be to provide considerable service to existing accounts. The sales rep's job consists primarily of existing-account maintenance rather than new-account development. This affects selection because the two tasks—maintenance and development—usually call for different types of salespeople.

As another example, the company may adopt a strategy of promoting from within as part of its strategic planning for the development of future executives. This strategy should influence management when it decides on hiring qualifications and recruiting sources for salespeople. Hiring older, experienced sales reps at high salaries probably would not be a sound way to implement this promoting-from-within strategy.

The selection process should also be strategically integrated with all aspects of sales force management. To illustrate, if a company has no sales training program, it should not recruit inexperienced students just graduating from college. If management prefers to hire people right from college, the firm had better institute a training program.

## IMPORTANCE OF A GOOD SELECTION PROGRAM

Good selection is of vital importance to the firm because it is the sales force that directly generates revenues for the firm. Moreover, selection is the starting point for developing an effective and efficient group of people who will be responsible for generating those revenues. In this section, we further explore the reasons why a good sales selection program is essential.

- **Good selection addresses the problem of getting good people.** For many reasons, there is a scarcity of qualified salespeople. Selling, for example, does not have the high social prestige of some other careers. Indeed, a survey of students in a large introductory marketing class found that most students viewed selling in a negative way, associating it with door-to-door activities or with less than desirable personal traits, such as being pushy or obnoxious.[2] Furthermore, many young people are not aware of the opportunities provided by jobs in outside selling. They often equate selling with clerking in a retail store.

- **Good selection improves sales force performance.** The salesperson-recruiting process has a strong impact on profits. When a firm hires a salesperson whose performance is just acceptable rather than outstanding, it is forgoing additional sales revenues and profits that the outstanding rep would have generated. Also, a good selection program is likely to reduce sales force turnover and thus lead to improved sales performance.

- **Good selection promotes cost savings.** Both direct and indirect cost benefits derive from a good selection program. Substantial *direct* cost savings are often generated when sales force turnover is reduced. A beginning salesperson may cost a company well over $100,000 before reaching productive status. These figures include recruiting and selection costs, the salesperson's salary and travel expenses, and a share of the training and supervision costs. The *indirect* costs of poor selection are insidious because they don't show up in accounting records. Here we are talking about lost sales—sales that would have been made if a rep had been selected more carefully.

- **Good selection eases other managerial tasks.** Proper training, compensation, supervision, and motivation are vital to successful management of a sales force. However, if a company selects the right people for the sales job, training is easier, less supervision is required, and motivation is less difficult.

- **Sales managers are no better than their sales force.** Under comparable product and market conditions, a slightly inferior sales force may outperform a better one because the first one has a much more able manager. An executive with a very poor sales force, however, cannot surpass a competitor who has much better salespeople, no matter how good the first executive may be.

## ◼ THE LAW AND SALES FORCE SELECTION

Increasingly, firms are held responsible for the legality of their recruiting and selection policies. Although certain aspects of the selection process may be performed by the human resources department, the final hiring decisions are most often made by the sales manager. Sales managers must therefore understand the complex laws which govern sales force selection policies. The particular laws and other regulations that are directly related to sales force selection are summarized in Figure 5-1.

These laws and related regulatory guidelines emphasize two concepts in employment: **nondiscrimination** and **affirmative action.** *Nondiscrimination* requires elimination of all existing discriminatory conditions, whether intentional or inadvertent. *Affirmative action* requires the employer to do more than ensure neutrality in regard to race, sex, and national origin. It requires the employer to *make additional efforts* to recruit, employ, and promote qualified members of groups formerly excluded. These efforts must be made even if that exclusion cannot be traced to discriminatory actions of the employer.

The guidelines set by the Equal Employment Opportunity Commission (EEOC) and the Office of Federal Contract Compliance (OFCC) cover the full scope of sales force selection activities—setting hiring specifications and recruiting and processing applicants. They also set prescribed limits regarding the use of various tools in the selection procedure, such as application blanks, interviews, and tests. Either agency may audit a firm to determine whether the firm is complying with the regulations.

---

■ **FIGURE 5-1**

| Key laws and regulations affecting a sales force | **Civil Rights Act of 1964**<br>Prohibits discrimination based on race, color, religion, nationality, or sex.<br>**Federal Contract Compliance, Executive Orders**<br>Ensures that federal contractors and subcontractors with 50 or more employees will comply with federal legislation and submit affirmative action plans.<br>**Age Discrimination in Employment Act (1967)**<br>Prohibits discrimination based on age.<br>**Fair Employment Opportunity Act (1972)**<br>Established the Equal Employment Opportunity Commission (EEOC) to ensure compliance with the Civil Rights Act for firms with 25 workers or more.<br>**Rehabilitation Act of 1973**<br>Requires affirmative action to hire and promote handicapped persons if the firm employs 50 or more workers and is seeking federal contracts in excess of $50,000.<br>**Vietnam Era Veterans Readjustment Act (1974)**<br>Requires affirmative action to hire Vietnam veterans and disabled veterans of any war by firms holding contracts in excess of $10,000.<br>**Uniform Guidelines on Employment Selection Procedures (1978)**<br>The EEOC, the U.S. Civil Service, and the Departments of Justice and Labor jointly issued these guidelines to prevent discriminatory practices in hiring.<br>**Americans with Disabilities Act (1990)**<br>Prohibits discrimination based on handicaps or disabilities (either physical or mental). |
| --- | --- |

---

*A Day-to-Day Operating Problem*

## MAJESTIC PLASTICS COMPANY (A)

### Adding minority reps to the sales force

There were seldom any vacancies on the Majestic Plastics Company sales force, and Clyde Brion, general sales manager, was proud of that fact. He had several applications from available recruits on an informal waiting list, and he tried to keep the facts on these applicants up to date. Occasionally unsolicited applications were received, and some were from unusual types of applicants. For example, Brion had once been urged to hire an ex-convict. Currently Majestic's sales force was composed of 14 men and 4 women, all of whom were white (Caucasian). On more than one occasion, Brion had been asked why the company had no minority sales reps. When such questions were asked by Majestic executives, by customers, or by public officials, Brion believed he could not ignore them.

One afternoon Brion was asked to come to the office of the company president, Boyd Russell. He found himself in a conference with Russell, several other department heads, and two men who were introduced as representatives of the Affirmative Action Program in the Department of Health and Human Services (HHS).

The visitors explained that the Majestic Plastics Company had been loyally served for many years by minority workers in the factory, on the custodial staff, and in a few cases in clerical jobs. However, no minority people held supervisory, sales, or managerial jobs. The HHS representatives directly requested that the company place some minorities in each of these categories or suffer censure through national publicity. When asked if qualified minority reps could be found, the visitors displayed well-prepared dossiers on several people. As nearly as Brion could judge during a quick examination of these files, the people easily met the minimum standards he had maintained in sales force recruiting.

The meeting continued after the visitors left. Brion said that a minority salesperson might find "rough sledding" on the sales force, and some customers might be resentful toward the rep. Brion also pointed out that there were no openings on the sales force now or in the near future. To accommodate a new rep, Brion said he would be forced either to discharge a salesperson now at work or create a new and unnecessary territory.

In closing the meeting, Russell said, "We'll have to look at this thing positively. Life could get mighty unpleasant for us if we don't!"

**Question:** What action should Clyde Brion take in this situation?

Note: See the introduction to this series of problems in Chapter 4 for the necessary background on the company, its market, and its competition.

Probably the greatest problem these agencies pose for sales executives is that the burden of proof to show that a company is complying with the regulations generally rests with the company. That is, the firm must be able to demonstrate (if called on to do so) that its recruiting and selection processes are *not* discriminatory and that all of its selection requirements, sources, and tools are predictive of performance in a given sales job. These issues are discussed in subsequent sections.

■ **FIGURE 5-2**    **Sales force staffing process**

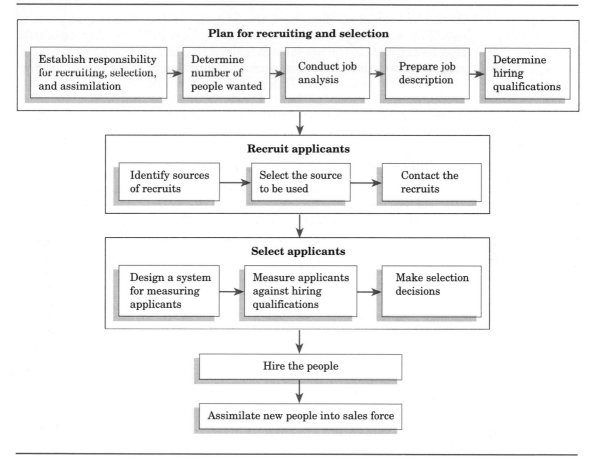

## SCOPE OF SALES FORCE STAFFING PROCESS

There are five major activities involved in staffing a sales force:

1. *Plan* the recruiting and selection process.
2. *Recruit* an adequate number of applicants.
3. *Select* the most qualified applicants.
4. *Hire* those people who have been selected.
5. *Assimilate* the new hires into the company.

The flowchart in Figure 5-2 illustrates these major activities; this chapter and the next two are devoted to this topic. You will notice in Figure 5-2 that planning and selecting are broken down into several related steps described below.

### The Planning Phase of the Process

As can be seen in the flowchart, the first step of the planning phase is to establish responsibility for recruiting and selection. These responsibilities may be assigned to the top sales executive, the field sales manager, the human resources department, or some combination of these positions. Second, the number and type of people needed must be determined. This involves an analysis of the market and the job and the preparation of a written job description. The qualifications necessary to fill the job must also be established.

### The Recruiting Phase of the Process

This step includes identifying sources of recruits which are consistent with the type of person desired, selecting the source to be used, and contacting the recruits. Selection entails an evaluation of the effectiveness of the potential source versus the costs associated with using that source.

### The Selection Phase of the Process

This stage has three steps. First, it is necessary to establish a procedure for measuring the recruits against the standards that were established in the planning phase. Second, the system must be put into effect in order to make the actual selections, which is the third step. Selection is covered in Chapter 6.

### The Hiring and Assimilation Phases of the Process

After you have made an offer to a recruit, the job is not done. Sometimes the recruits have other job offers and you must convince them that your company offers them the best opportunity. The staffing process is complete when the new salespeople are successfully assimilated into your organization. Hiring and assimilation are covered in Chapter 7.

## ESTABLISH RESPONSIBILITY FOR RECRUITING, SELECTION, AND ASSIMILATION

Management must decide who will be responsible for making the recruiting and selection decisions and who will be responsible for assimilating the new hires into the organization. How these decisions are made is often related to the size of the firm and to the nature of the selling task. In a small firm, for example, it is usually the top-level sales executive or even the president who makes these decisions. Since the sales force is small, these decisions do not place too much of a burden on any one executive.

In a large firm, however, the large number of territories and the normal turnover in those territories means that the job of recruiting and selecting new salespeople will be a continuous one. It would be very difficult for any one executive to make all of these decisions; therefore, the decisions are usually shifted to lower-level sales managers. Additionally, in large firms the human resources department usually assists managers with their recruiting and selection responsibilities. The human resources department may do all of the recruiting and initial screening of the recruits. But it is usually the sales manager who makes the final hiring decisions.

## ■ DETERMINE THE NUMBER OF PEOPLE WANTED

A company should try to accurately determine how many sales reps it needs and then hire that number. It should not employ more than are needed with the intent of weeding out some as time goes by. This indicates that the firm has no faith in its selection system and is using performance on the job as an additional selection tool.

Sales personnel needs should be forecast well in advance of the time the people will actually be employed. This policy forces the various sales units to plan systematically. It also allows better programming of recruiting, interviewing, and other steps in the selection procedure.

Additionally, management should first review any changes in the company's strategic marketing plan to determine how the plan will affect the number of salespeople needed. For example, is the company planning to continue with the present channels-of-distribution structure? A firm now using manufacturers' reps in a certain region may be planning to replace these reps with a company sales force. Another strategic issue relates to relevant financial conditions in sales force size. Is the company planning to cut sales force costs by using a telemarketing system and reducing the size of the outside sales force?

For the specific estimates of the number of new salespeople that must be hired, management should consider the following factors, which are depicted in Figure 5-3:

- Reps needed for planned expansions into new territories minus reps withdrawn from territories which are being eliminated or folded into other territories.
- Promotions out of the sales force.
- Expected retirements from the sales force.
- Expected turnover, including terminations and resignations.

The manager adds the total number for each of these categories to estimate the number of new reps which will have to be hired. See the example in Figure 5-3. The question of how many reps are needed to cover a particular area is discussed in Chapter 15 on sales territories.

■ **FIGURE 5-3**      **Determining the number of sales people needed**

| | | | **Strategic Plans** | | | |
|---|---|---|---|---|---|---|
| **New territories** | **– Eliminate/ combine territories** | **+ Promotions** | **+ Retire- ments** | **+ Termination/ resigna- tions** | **= Total new reps needed** |
| Expansion into Texas. Reps needed: | MN and RI territories combined. Reps elimi- nated: | 2 promo- tions ex- pected: | 2 retire- ments ex- pected: | 1 termina- tion ex- pected: | |
| 4 | – 1 | + 2 | + 2 | + 1 | = 8 |

## ◼ DETERMINE THE TYPE OF PEOPLE WANTED

A sales manager needs detailed specifications when selecting salespeople. Otherwise, he or she cannot know what to look for. Certainly, a company should be as careful in buying the services of men and women as it is in buying the products these people use or sell.

There are three tasks associated with determining the type of people wanted:

- **Job analysis**—the actual task of determining what constitutes a given job.
- **Job description**—the document that sets forth the findings of the job analysis.
- **Job qualifications** (sometimes called *hiring specifications*)—the specific, personal qualifications and characteristics applicants should possess to be selected for the given job.

These tasks are detailed next.

### Job Analysis

Before the selection process is developed a thorough job analysis should be conducted. It should clearly identify all of the specific tasks which salespeople will perform. Additionally, it should provide information on which activities are critical for job success.

This analysis may be conducted by any member of the sales organization, by someone from the human resources department, or by an outside specialist. An effective analysis of a sales job usually requires extensive observation and interviewing. The person conducting this analysis should spend time traveling with several salespeople as they make their calls.

The analyst also should interview many of the people who in some way interact with the reps in the sales job. The analyst should start interviewing with the reps themselves and then include sales force managers, customers, and other executives who are directly involved with the personal selling activities of the company. Also, salespeople can complete time and duty sheets on which they record all of their activities and the specific times they performed the activities for a specified time period.

## Job Description

Once the job is analyzed, the resultant description should be put in writing. The job analysis and subsequent written description must be done in great detail. It is not enough to say that the salesperson is supposed to sell the product, call on the customers, or build goodwill toward the company.

### Scope of Job Description

Most well-prepared job descriptions have similar items of information. The following points are usually covered:

- *Title of job.* A complete description so there is no vagueness, especially in a company that has several different types of sales jobs.
- *Organizational relationship.* To whom do the salespeople report?
- *Types of products and services sold.*
- *Types of customers called on.* This includes the type of personnel on whom the rep will call, such as purchasing agents, engineers, and plant managers.
- *Duties and responsibilities related to the job.* Planning activities, actual selling activities, customer servicing tasks, clerical duties, and self-management responsibilities.
- *Job demands.* The mental and physical demands of the job, such as the amount of travel, autonomy, and stress.
- *Hiring specifications.* While job qualifications technically are not part of a job analysis, there is merit in presenting the job duties and the job qualifications in one document.

Exhibits 5-A and 5-B (on pages 150–154) are examples of sales job descriptions for two sales positions. Exhibit 5-A is the job description for a Xerox Corporation marketing representative. Exhibit 5-B is called a "charter of accountability" and the position is a passenger sales representative (for an international airline).

### Uses of Job Description

The job analysis and the resultant written job description thus become the first two steps in the selection process. As such, they provide strategic guidance for the steps that follow. Recruiters cannot talk intelligently to prospective applicants if they do not know in detail what the job involves. A firm cannot develop application forms, psychological tests, and other selection tools if it has not first analyzed the job. If hiring criteria and selection tools are developed through job analysis, misplacement and turnover can be reduced. [3]

However, hiring is only one of the many uses for a job description. *It is probably the most important single tool used in the operation of a sales force.* A job analysis should be the foundation of a sales training program. By studying the description, the executive in charge of sales training knows in detail what the salespeople's duties are and what they must learn. Job descriptions are also used in developing compensation plans. If management does not have a clear idea of what the sales force is supposed to do, it is difficult to design a sound compensation structure. Also, a salesperson's periodic performance ratings will be more meaningful if the company designs an evaluation form that includes many of the detailed aspects of the sales job. Finally, a good job description enables management to determine whether each salesperson has a reasonable work load.

## Qualifications Needed to Fill the Job

### Most Difficult Part of Selection Function

The next step in a selection program—determining the qualifications needed to fill the job—is probably the most difficult part of the entire selection process. This is because there is no generally accepted profile for success across selling positions. A review of more than 400 studies investigating the relationship between performance and personal characteristics concluded the following:

- Demographic characteristics (age, sex) and physical characteristics do little to explain salesperson performance. This suggests that some of the commonly held stereotypes about salespeople are inaccurate.
- Education and experience, commonly used as criteria to select salespeople, also do little to explain salesperson performance.
- Personal history, such as number of brothers and sisters or extracurricular activities, though a better predictor than demographics, explained only 20 percent of the variance in performance.
- Job skills and experience are generally better predictors of success than aptitudes, motivation, or background.
- The strength of the relationship between many of the characteristics and performance varies significantly across types of customers and types of products sold.[4] Another recent study has shown that the skills which distinguish outstanding salespeople in one firm are not the same as those in another firm. [5]

The general conclusion from this research is that the determinants of sales performance are job specific. That means that different sales positions require different qualifications. Therefore, each company should establish its own individualized set of hiring requirements for each class of sales job in that firm. Furthermore, a sales rep who fails in *one* company or territory may not necessarily fail in *all* companies or territories. Many people have become successful with one firm after failing in an earlier environment. Even within a given firm, salespeople sometimes perform poorly in one territory (because of social, religious, or other environmental factors) but are successful after transferring to another region.

### Are There Generally Desirable Characteristics for Salespeople?

Though every selling situation is different, most managers and customers agree that there are some generally desirable characteristics for salespeople.[6] These characteristics are presented in Figure 5-4, "Buyers' Top 10 Salesperson Traits."

It is also generally acknowledged that the salesperson of the future must be much more knowledgeable about electronic communications and technology.[7] Salespeople will have access to electronic data banks with product, customer, and competitive information. They will also have multimedia options for making presentations to their customers. Salespeople will need to be comfortable with the technology in order to utilize the information options in a comprehensive manner.

Experts predict that team selling, which now accounts for 20 percent to 30 percent of all sales, will account for 70 percent to 80 percent of all sales in the future.[8] This shift has had an important impact on the type of salesperson desired. A study of 26 of the leading corporations, including General Electric and AT&T, found that the *"ability to work on a team"* was a job requirement.[9] The nearby box, "Recruiting for the Team," highlights some additional changes.

Even though there are some generally desirable traits, we emphasize again that it is important for each company to develop its own set of criteria for selecting salespeople. The following major categories of traits are those for which specifics should be developed.

- Mental capacities (planning and problem-solving ability)
- Physical characteristics (appearance, neatness)
- Experience (sales and other business experience)
- Education (number of years, degrees, majors)

---

■ **FIGURE 5-4**

---

**Buyers' top 10 salesperson traits**

| | |
|---|---|
| ■ Knowledge | ■ Empathy |
| ■ Organization | ■ Promptness |
| ■ Follow-through | ■ Problem solver |
| ■ Punctuality | ■ Willingness to work hard |
| ■ Energy | ■ Honesty |

---

Source: A survey of members of the National Association of Purchasing Managers, "The Buyers' Top Ten," *Sales Manager's Bulletin,* May 30, 1993, p. 3.

---

### Recruiting for the Team

In this reengineered business environment, many companies are choosing partners, not products. Customers are demanding more value-added services and more follow up after the sale than one person can provide. Teaming is essential!

Character traits long associated with salespeople, such as independence, self-sufficiency, and a need to control, are now considered a handicap in the new selling order. Companies now seek salespeople who are very adaptable, with a willingness to share and put the group's goal above their own . . . selfless behavior. The sales world has changed from an "I" orientation to a "We" orientation.

Source: Adapted from Mary Connors, "From 'I' and 'Me' to 'Us' and 'We' :The Future Belongs to the Team," *Selling*, July/August 1995, pp. 52–53.

---

- Personality traits (persuasiveness, adaptiveness)
- Skills (communication, interpersonal, technological, job-specific)
- Socioenvironmental factors (interests, activities, memberships in organizations)

When dealing with qualifications in any of the preceding categories, management must be careful to comply with laws regarding nondiscrimination in employment. Many qualifications that once were used to screen sales force applicants, such as age, marital status, and ethnic background, can no longer be used. Exceptions exist if the company can show that these requirements are bona fide occupational qualifications (BFOQ). For example, an arrest (or even a conviction) cannot be used to screen out an applicant unless the company can demonstrate the validity of the qualification.

## Methods of Determining Qualifications

There is no satisfactory method for every company to use in determining the qualifications needed in its sales force. Several different procedures are currently being used. Some are adaptable for companies that have large sales forces and have been in business for some time, so that recorded histories of background and performance are available. Other methods may be used by firms that are large or small, old or new. Some of these methods are discussed in this section.

### *Study of Job Description*
Many hiring specifications can be deduced from a carefully prepared job description. Job description statements about the degree of sales supervision, for instance, indicate that the salesperson should have the resourcefulness to work alone. Statements about the nature of the product, viewed in light of the company's training program, indicate something about the desired technical background or experience qualifications.

### Analysis of Personal Histories

A company in business for several years and with a large sales force can determine its job qualifications by analyzing the personal histories of its present and past salespeople. The age and size requirements for the company are necessary to get a sample of histories large enough to make the findings reasonably reliable. The procedure is to analyze various characteristics of good and poor sales reps to determine whether there are certain traits present in the good reps and absent in the poor ones. These traits of the good sales reps are then presumed to be some of those required for success, and they would be used to develop a **job profile** of the kind of person the firm is seeking.[10] Figure 5-5 briefly describes the procedure for making an analysis of personal histories, along with a simple illustration.

In Figure 5-5, two characteristics—age at time of hiring and amount of education—are used to illustrate how personal histories can be studied. Similar analyses may be made for any other trait believed to influence success in selling in a given company. The firm could study environmental and experience factors in much the same manner as age and education. Mental abilities may be quantified by means of intelligence tests. General appearance could be measured by giving a person a rating on neatness and appropriate dress, and test scores can be used to measure personality traits.

This personal-history information can be analyzed using the method demonstrated in Figure 5-5 or by using a more sophisticated statistical technique called discriminant analysis. This type of analysis identifies characteristics which vary significantly between the groups. Once these distinguishing characteristics have been identified for a particular sales force, they can be used to develop a profile of the successful salesperson. The Tennant Company, which sells industrial floor products through a direct sales force of about 100 persons, encourages its sales managers to develop their own individualized profiles using techniques similar to those described above.[11]

Based on an analysis of its current sales consultants, Anderson Consulting totally revised its selection criteria. The company discovered that students with part-time jobs and extracurricular activities were more likely to succeed than those with higher grade-point averages.[12]

## ◼ RECRUITING AND ITS IMPORTANCE

After determining the number and type of salespeople wanted, the next major step in selecting a sales force is to recruit applicants for the position to be filled. **Recruiting** includes all activities involved in securing individuals who will apply for the job. The concept does not include the actual selection of people by means of interviews, tests, or other hiring tools. That step is the topic of Chapter 6. A sound selection program cannot

■ **FIGURE 5-5**      **A personal-history analysis—the process with examples**

**The three-step process:**
1. List all present and past salespeople; include their (a) *selection records* (application blanks and interview results, for example) and (b) *performance records* (sales results, quotas, and job evaluations).
2. Divide all salespeople into two or three groups, depending on management's judgment of their sales ability. In our example, the reps are divided into two categories—good and poor. Possible classification criteria include sales volume, percentage of sales quota attained, gross margin, ratio of expenses to sales, and missionary selling activities.
3. List each trait that influences success in selling. Then decide if there is any significant difference in how much of the trait good salespeople possess in contrast to the poor ones. Differences between good and poor performers in such qualifications as age at time of hiring or previous sales experience are easily determined. However, it is much more difficult to measure differences in personality traits in the two groups. This step is time-consuming and must be done carefully.

**Now for our example:**
1. Two characteristics—age at time of hiring and amount of education—are used to illustrate a personal-history analysis.
2. A sample of 600 past and present salespeople was used, 360 of whom were considered good.
3. Age and education brackets were established; then each of the 600 was placed in the correct bracket for the rep's age at time of hiring and amount of education. The results are shown in the following two tables.

| **A. Age when Hired** | | | | | **B. Previous Education** | | | | |
|---|---|---|---|---|---|---|---|---|---|
| **Number of Reps** | | | | | | **Number of Reps** | | | |
| Good Reps | Poor Reps | Total | Percent of Good Reps | | | Good Reps | Poor Reps | Total | Percent of Good Reps |
| Under 25 | 30 | 70 | 100 | 30 | Some high school | 30 | 70 | 100 | 30 |
| 25–35 | 180 | 20 | 200 | 90 | High school graduate | 250 | 25 | 275 | 91 |
| 36–45 | 100 | 50 | 150 | 66⅔ | Some college | 20 | 80 | 100 | 20 |
| 46–55 | 40 | 60 | 100 | 40 | College graduate | 55 | 45 | 100 | 55 |
| Over 55 | 10 | 40 | 50 | 20 | Postgraduate study | 5 | 20 | 25 | 20 |
| Total | 360 | 240 | 600 | | Total | 360 | 240 | 600 | |

4. From Table A, we find that those sales reps most likely to succeed in this company were between 25 and 35 years of age when hired. Ninety percent of these people were good sales reps. Those reps who were under 25 or over 55 when hired seem to perform the most poorly.
5. In Table B, we find that high school graduates seem to have the right amount of education for future sales success. A person who started high school or college, but did not graduate, seems to be a particularly poor risk.
6. From the findings on the tables, it is probable that some years of business experience are necessary in this company. If 18 is the average age of high school graduates and 25 to 35 is the best hiring-age range, then the years in between have to be accounted for.

exist without a well-planned and well-operated system for recruiting applicants. If recruiting is done haphazardly, a company runs the risk of overlooking good sources of prospective salespeople. Also there is a risk of hiring unsuitable people simply because the firm must select immediately from the available applicants.

The importance of recruiting grows in relation to increases in the costs of selecting salespeople and maintaining them in the field. Certainly, the direct costs of recruiting—costs such as maintaining recruiting teams and placing recruiting advertisements—are increasing. But more important than the *direct* cost of recruiting is the effect that recruiting may have on the *total* costs of selection and training. For example, it may be desirable to *increase* the cost of the recruiting activity if it results in finding better-quality applicants.

The costs of having an open territory are also great. *If a firm must do a significant amount of recruiting, it should be done continuously.* Even when no immediate need for new salespeople exists, the firm should develop a list of potential recruits. Then when an opening does occur, the time and costs of filling that territory will be relatively low. Sales managers should be proactive in their recruiting efforts. They should anticipate openings, look constantly for potential recruits, and keep a file on those who might be able to fill a future need. As J. Doug Clopton, a regional manager for Hershey's Chocolate, stated, "The best time to recruit is *before* you have an opening."[13]

## Need for Many Recruits

A philosophy to follow in recruiting is to get enough qualified applicants to maximize the chances of finding the right person for a job. The shortage of qualified sales representatives makes it imperative for a business to screen several people for each opening. The following is a useful rule of thumb to determine the number of recruits needed to select one salesperson:

- Recruit 20 people who are interested in the job.
- A review of application blanks will eliminate 10. The initial interview will eliminate another 6 or 7. The 3 or 4 finalists are screened further by interviews, tests, and other selection tools.
- One person is finally hired.

## Find and Maintain Good Recruiting Sources

Most firms actively recruit sales reps from many sources. To determine the best sources, a recruiter should first find out where the company's best salespeople came from in the past. This assumes that there has been no substantial change in the job description or job qualifications. The evaluation of current sources will be discussed at the end of this chapter.

If the company is recruiting for the first time or if its current sources are inadequate, then the job description and hiring specifications provide a useful starting point. These documents reveal factors that affect the recruiter's choice of recruiting sources. For example, the educational qualifications for the job may indicate whether colleges are a good source for recruits. If industry knowledge is a requirement, the recruiter may consider employees from other departments within the company.

Once satisfactory sources are located, management should maintain a continuing relationship with them, even during periods when the firm is not hiring. Firms that want college graduates should keep in touch with professors who have furnished assistance in the past. Customers who have supplied leads to good people should be reminded periodically of the company's gratitude and encouraged to suggest more prospects.

## RECRUITING SOURCES OF SALES REPRESENTATIVES

Some frequently used recruiting sources or leads to sources, as shown in Figure 5-6, are:

- Referrals
- Within the company
- Other companies (competitors, customers, noncompetitors)
- Educational institutions
- Advertisements
- Employment agencies
- Computerized databases
- Voluntary applicants
- Part-time workers

### Referrals

A referral is a recommendation by one individual that another be hired for a position. Referrals often come from someone included in one of the other sources just listed, but they may come from other people as well. Because they are the preferred source of sales recruits, we will discuss them separately.

In a recent survey asking managers where they find their best salespeople, 47 percent of the respondents indicated that referrals were their best source.[14] There is a good reason for this. Most referrals come from someone who works for the company. They know the job requirements and the recruit. Chances are pretty good that the recommended candidate will have the necessary skills as well as fit within the company culture. The current salespeople, for example, are an excellent source of leads to new recruits. They clearly know the job and the company, and they often meet reps and employees from other companies.

■ **FIGURE 5-6**

**Sources of sales force recruits**

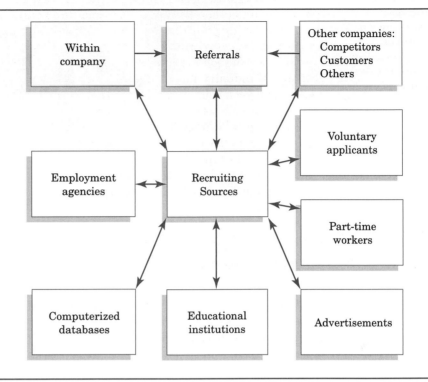

The big disadvantage of using referrals is that you may not get enough of them. Jim Miller, the CEO of BT Miller Business Systems, has found a good way to combat this problem. An employee is rewarded with monetary compensation if a person he or she recommends stays more than 90 days. He believes that using referrals sustains his company's culture.[15] Again, it should be noted that referrals often come from one of the sources discussed below.

## Within the Company

Some companies recruit their sales force from workers in their production plants or offices. Management has been able to observe these people and evaluate their potential as sales reps. These workers are acquainted with the product and also have been indoctrinated in company policies and programs. Their values fit with the company culture. One study, which assessed the value of hiring from various sources, found that salespeople hired from within the company will yield more long-run profits than those from any other source.[16] This is due in part to the fact that they are the least costly to recruit and train. Hiring salespeople from within the company can also be a great morale booster, because most plant and office workers consider transfer to the sales department as a promotion.[17]

This sales manager interviews a potential candidate for an open sales position.

## Other Companies: Competitors, Customers, Noncompetitors

A *competitor's* sales force is a major recruiting source for salespeople. However, there are different views about recruiting competitors' salespeople. On the one hand, they know the product and the market very well. They are also experienced sellers and therefore require little training. On the other hand, it may be harder for these people to unlearn old practices and make the adjustment to a new environment. Also, for some managers, recruiting from a competitor's sales force may present an ethical dilemma as described in the box above.

A firm may seek leads to prospects from its *customers.* Purchasing agents are often good sources of names. They have some knowledge of the abilities of the sales reps who call on them. Customers' employees themselves may be a source of salespeople. Often, retail clerks make good salespeople for wholesalers and manufacturers. These clerks know the product. They also know something of the behavior of the retailers—the market to which the hiring firm sells. Shopsmith, Inc., a $43 million manufacturer of woodworking equipment, uses direct mail campaigns to its 3,000 customers to recruit new salespeople. This costs the firm less than if it advertised the position.[18]

Sales reps working for *noncompeting companies* are another source, particularly if they (1) are selling products related to those sold by the recruiting firm or (2) are selling to the same market. A salesperson working for a supplier of the recruiting firm, for example, is a potential source of recruits. Presumably, recruits from this source have some sales ability and need less training.

Recruiting from other firms raises some questions. Hiring the good employees of a customer obviously has drawbacks. The task must be handled very diplomatically to avoid losing the customer. A firm that hires

**?** **AN ETHICAL DILEMMA**

Qualified salespeople are hard to find, especially experienced salespeople who are familiar with a recruiter's industry. One way to get such people is to aggressively recruit them from a competitor's sales force. Not only do these reps know the business, but they also might bring along some of their customers. Competitors object strongly to this "pirating," as they call it. They have spent much money training these reps, and now they lose the benefit of the reps' sales productivity. The recruiting companies believe that taking salespeople from competitors is no different from taking customers—that's called competition. Is it ethical for a sales manager to directly approach a competitor's sales rep with a job offer?

from the outside should determine (1) why the applicants are interested in changing jobs and (2) why they want to work for the hiring company. Applicants may figure that the quickest way to success is to move from one company to another.

### Educational Institutions

Colleges and universities are frequently used as a source of recruits for sales positions. However, according to a recent survey of students enrolled in personal selling classes at four universities, many students know very little about most of the companies that recruit on campus. This is because the recruiters assume the students are familiar with their companies and do nothing to establish a high profile among the students. Indeed, many students find it ironic that companies looking for sales/marketing candidates don't know how to market themselves.[19]

On the other hand, some companies have developed distinctive identities with college students by speaking to classes and student organizations, participating in job fairs or on advisory boards to marketing departments, and providing scholarships and summer internship opportunities. Some firms such as IBM and Deloitte & Touche provide diskettes as part of their recruiting materials.[20]

The recruiter who interviews the students also plays a critical role in attracting them to sales jobs. Yet too often the recruiter emphasizes aspects of the job which are not the most important to the students. Students say that these recruiters violate a basic principle of selling: Know your customer.[21] Recruiters must be flexible and emphasize those job attributes which are important to the students, as summarized in Figure 5-7.

### Advertisements

Newspapers and trade journals are the most widely used media in which ads for selling jobs are placed. Some companies use advertisements to recruit high-caliber salespeople for particularly challenging jobs. However,

■ **FIGURE 5-7**

| Differences in student and recruiter perceptions of important attributes for selecting a sales position | Importance Rank | Attributes as Selected by the: | |
| --- | --- | --- | --- |
| | | Student | Recruiter |
| | 1 | Job satisfaction | Training program |
| | 2 | Fit with goals | Advancement opportunity |
| | 3 | Recruiter morale | Recruiter morale |
| | 4 | Company financial stability | Company reputation |
| | 5 | Company reputation | Fit with goals |
| | 6 | Employees voice own views | Job satisfaction |
| | 7 | Job security | Defined career path |
| | 8 | Cost-of-living increases | Recruiter friendly |
| | 9 | Defined hiring process | Company financially friendly |
| | 10 | Recruiter shows interest | Salary |
| | 11 | Recruiter friendly | Defined hiring process |
| | 12 | Advancement opportunity | Recruiter shows interest |
| | 13 | Employee creativity | Student activities |
| | 14 | Salary | Job security |
| | 15 | Training program | Recruiter personality |

Source: Dan C. Weilbaker and Nancy J. Merritt, "Attracting Graduates to Sales Positions: The Role of Recruiter Knowledge," *Journal of Personal Selling & Sales Management,* Fall 1992, pp. 49–58.

most firms that use advertising—particularly in newspapers—are trying to fill the less attractive type of sales job, such as in-home selling or clerking in a retail store.

Advertisements ordinarily produce many applicants, but the average quality of the applicants is questionable. The cost of reaching these recruits is low. However, additional screening may be needed to weed out those who are clearly unqualified.

The quality of prospects recruited by advertisements may be raised by careful selection of media and by proper information placed in the copy. For example, by buying space in a trade journal rather than in a daily newspaper, a firm is automatically more selective in its search. The more information given in the notice, the more it serves as a screening device.

To be effective, a recruiting ad must *attract attention and have credibility.* An advertisement that does not get read, or one that is read but is not considered believable and sincere, is wasted effort.

Now, what information should be included in a recruiting advertisement? Here are some points to consider.

■ **Company name.** The answer is, it all depends. By placing their names in their ads, well-known firms may attract applicants who otherwise would not answer a blind ad. But companies with a poor public image (such as some in-home sellers) often must hide their identities in an ad to attract prospects.

- **Product.** Usually yes, unless it is a product (gravestones and cemetery lots, perhaps) that is likely to turn away prospects who otherwise might be interested once they learned more about the company and the job opportunities.
- **Territory.** Yes, especially if it is not in the area where the ad is run.
- **Hiring qualifications.** Include enough of them so the ad serves as a useful screening device. But keep in mind the legal guidelines when stating any hiring requirements. As a general rule, all ads should carry the "Equal Opportunity Employer M/F" line.
- **Compensation plan, expense plan, and fringe benefits.** Include some information in these areas, especially if it is a strong point. A company paying straight salary is more likely to mention this point than is one that pays straight commission.
- **How to contact the employer.** The ad must have a phone number or a mailing address.

Five recruiting ads are shown in Exhibit 5-C at the end of this chapter. Take a look at them and decide which ones are good, which are poor, and why.

## Employment Agencies

Agencies that place salespeople are a frequently used source of recruits. If the agency is carefully selected and good relations are established with it, the dividends can be satisfying. The agency can do some of the initial screening, because presumably it will abide by the job specifications given. Fees usually range from 10 percent to 40 percent of the new employee's first year's compensation and increase as the compensation goes up. Agencies where the fee is paid by the employer probably attract a better quality of sales recruit. The employer's cost for the agency's fee may be offset by the savings in the advertising and initial screening activities done by the agency.

## Computerized Databases

*Résumé search services* use the computer to sort through thousands of current résumés, looking for specific characteristics. Then they pass on the selected résumés to the recruiting company. These firms charge far less than agencies do, and they guarantee qualified candidates. If there is no match, the company using the service doesn't have to pay anything. [22]

Many companies are using the *Internet* to recruit for sales positions. The largest Internet recruiting site is the Online Career Center (OCC), a nonprofit recruitment and human resources database that posts job listings from companies such as Sprint, Compaq, and R. R. Donnelly & Sons, to name a few. More than 1,600 postings are for sales or marketing positions. It also contains up to 24,000 résumés at any given time. The Job Web is another recruiting site, sponsored by the National Association of Colleges, which is targeted at college students. Most of the recruiting sites offer key word searches by state, locality, industry, company, or title. [23]

## Voluntary Applicants

Some organizations do no recruiting advertising. Instead they answer situation-wanted advertisements placed by people who are looking for sales jobs, or they hire people who walk in and say, "I want to sell for your company." These firms are interested in people who show enough initiative to seek out a job rather than waiting for one to come to them. Voluntary applicants are an excellent source of sales recruits. In addition to their initiative, they usually possess a high degree of self-confidence and self-reliance.

## Part-Time Workers

The use of part-time salespeople in outside selling jobs is increasing. They are easy to contact, readily available, and usually can work flexible hours. For example, in-home selling firms such as Mary Kay and Amway frequently use students or homemakers as salespeople.

# ■ DIVERSITY

For outside selling jobs, firms can recruit minorities or women by using any of the sources that we discussed in the preceding section. In this section, however, we call special attention to minorities and women as recruiting sources for two reasons. First, these groups are underemployed in outside sales jobs. That is, the percentage of minorities and women in outside sales jobs is far below their percentage in the total population. Second, the changing economic, demographic, and legal conditions in this country are bringing major changes to the sales field. As reported earlier in the box titled "Management Challenges for the Year 2000," the Hudson Institute predicts that the composition of the work force will change to include a more culturally diverse group of people. The sales force of the future will be drawn from this culturally diverse group of workers, including women, American-born minorities, and immigrants.

## Minority Groups

Many executives report only limited success in attracting minority groups to outside sales jobs. In fact, the outside sales force typically has the lowest percentage of minority employees of any department in a company. For example, a recent survey of 200 companies found that 62 percent of the firms had less than 5 percent African Americans employed as salespeople. Many companies cite two reasons for this low percentage: (1) not many African Americans apply and (2) they don't have adequate recruiting sources. But Lawrence Graham, a professor of African-American studies, says, "The truth is, they're just not tapping into the right sources." Groups such as the Urban League and the National Black MBA Association, as well as most business schools, have resource centers with hundreds of résumés on file. [24]

As noted earlier, there are legal reasons to practice diversity. The Equal Employment Opportunity Commission, which strives to ensure that minorities have the same opportunities as whites, investigates as many as 30,000 cases of racial discrimination each year. In many cases companies are forced to pay stiff fines and implement diversity programs. But practicing diversity is also good business. As minorities make up more of the labor force, so too will they be a greater percentage of the purchasing population. For some companies, such as AT&T and Levi Strauss, diversity is seen not only as the right thing to do, but also as a key to success. [25]

## Women

Reports on the perceptions and experiences of sales executives concerning the problems and performance of women in outside selling jobs are interesting and enlightening. Overall, these experiences and perceptions have been quite favorable. Furthermore, this favorable reaction is not limited to consumer products companies or service industries. Women also are performing well as sales recruits in industrial sales jobs. Many companies that may have originally recruited women as the "politically correct" thing to do have found that women are a vast untapped resource with a significant positive effect on the bottom line.[26]

Yet women are still grossly underrepresented in most outside sales forces. Women account for about 50 percent of the total labor force, yet in few companies do they account for more than 25 percent of the outside sales force. Looking at sales management ranks, the picture is even worse—on the average only 13 percent are women.[27] There still are personal and professional factors that inhibit the movement of women into outside sales forces.

Nevertheless, the influx of women into outside sales forces will continue to increase during the next decade. To counter the expected shortage of qualified salespeople, management must strongly recruit from the population segment that will comprise over 50 percent of the labor force in the year 2000.

## LEGAL CONSIDERATIONS

The federal legislation summarized in Figure 5-1 prohibits discrimination based on age, race, religion, sex, or national origin and requires affirmative action toward minorities, veterans, and handicapped persons. These groups are considered to be "protected classes" of people. If an applicant from one of these groups is rejected for a particular job, he or she may file a discrimination suit against the employer. If the company has a proportionately low number of people from this group as employees, that may be enough to establish discrimination. However, it would not be discriminatory if the position has been widely advertised and few people from this group applied.

Discrimination charges can also be based primarily on the sources which are used to recruit salespeople. If a firm uses sources that have few people from the protected classes, this in itself may be a basis for a discrimination charge. For example, if a firm hires salespeople only from within the firm and the firm employs predominantly white males, then this recruiting practice may be discriminatory even if there wasn't any intent to discriminate.

The easiest way the firm can protect itself from the discrimination charges described above is to recruit from multiple sources, some of which are intended to reach the protected classes. Similarly, the firm must be very careful not to use any language in advertising the position which could be construed as discriminatory.

## ■ RECRUITING EVALUATION

To better direct its focus in the management of its recruiting sources, a company should continually evaluate the effectiveness of its recruiting program. To conduct this evaluation, management might use some form of matrix approach such as the one in Figure 5-8. This information should

■ **FIGURE 5-8**      **Recruiting evaluation matrix**

| Recruiting Sources | Evaluation Criteria | | | | | | |
|---|---|---|---|---|---|---|---|
| | Consistent with Strategic Planning? | Number Recruits | Number Hired | Percent Retained after 3 Years | Cost | Frequency of Use | Rep's Performance after 2 Years |
| Referrals | | | | | | | |
| Within company | | | | | | | |
| Other companies Competitors Customers Noncompetitors | | | | | | | |
| Educational institutions | | | | | | | |
| Advertisements | | | | | | | |
| Employment agencies | | | | | | | |
| Voluntary applicants | | | | | | | |
| Computerized databases | | | | | | | |

enable management to determine which sources produced the best recruits. This approach lends itself to computer technology, which can aid in the evaluation process. A spin-off benefit of recruiting evaluation is that it can be used in the performance ratings of sales executives who are involved in recruiting. That is, some companies use "recruiting effectiveness" as one factor in evaluating a sales manager's judgment and promotability.

## ■ SUMMARY

In the Preface and again in Chapter 1, we stated one of our basic philosophies—selecting the right people (staffing the organization) is the most important step in the management process. Sales force selection should be coordinated with an organization's strategic marketing and sales force planning because the sales force often plays a major role in implementing the plans. Sales executives must understand the various civil rights laws and other government regulations that have a substantial impact on all phases of sales force selection.

The sales selection task is a five-step process. First, management determines how many and what kind of people are wanted. The second step is to recruit a number of applicants. The third step involves processing these applicants and selecting the most qualified. Then those selected must be hired and assimilated into the organization.

Management can determine the *number* of salespeople to be hired by conducting an analysis based on the company's past experiences and future expectations. To determine the *type* of person wanted, management should first conduct a job analysis and then write a job description for each position to be filled.

Determining the qualifications needed to fill the job is the most difficult part of the sales selection process. As yet, we simply have not been able to isolate the traits that make for success in selling. However, we do know that it is important to develop *individualized* hiring specifications for a given job in a given firm. As a starting point, management should study the job descriptions. They should also analyze the personal histories of their present and past salespeople to identify those characteristics which distinguish the successful reps from the less successful ones.

After determining the number and kind of salespeople wanted, the next major step in sales force selection is to recruit several applicants for the job. A well-planned, well-operated recruiting system is essential for a successful selection program. A company must identify the sources that are likely to produce good recruits and maintain a continuing relationship with these sources, even during periods when the firm is not hiring.

Many managers feel that referrals are the best source of sales recruits. These referrals may come from many places including within the company doing the recruiting. Often the present sales force is an excellent source of leads to new recruits. Also, some companies recruit new salespeople from employees in their offices or factories.

Another major source of recruits is other companies—competitors, customers, or noncompetitors. A company may try to hire a competitors' salespeople. Or a firm's customers may supply recruiting leads. Some companies will hire customers' employees, although this must be done very carefully. Another source is salespeople working for noncompeting firms.

Many companies recruit salespeople from educational institutions—universities, community colleges, high schools, or vocational–technical schools. Some firms rely on advertisements to reach prospective applicants. For some types of sales jobs, employment agencies can provide good prospects.

Increasingly, firms are using computer-aided searches to identify candidates. Résumé search services will perform the search for a fee, or managers can access several job banks on the Internet.

Voluntary (walk-in) applicants can be an excellent source, but usually there are not enough of these people. Part-time workers, such as students or homemakers, are excellent candidates for certain selling jobs.

Increasingly, companies are looking to women and minority groups as sources of applicants for sales jobs. This trend is expected to continue and to intensify. A company should periodically evaluate the effectiveness of its recruiting program to ensure that it is using the best sources available.

## Key Terms

| | | |
|---|---|---|
| Affirmative action | Job profile | Recruiting evaluation |
| Diversity | Job qualifications | Recruiting sources |
| Job analysis | Nondiscrimination | Selection |
| Job description | Recruiting | |

 ## QUESTIONS AND PROBLEMS

1. "Salespeople are born, not made." Do you agree? If so, why does a firm need a training program or sales supervisors? If you do not agree, why is so much stress placed on the importance of good selection? Perhaps a firm should spend far less time and money on selection and instead place the effort in a training program.

2. With the advent of "team" selling, what personal attributes might play a greater role in the salesperson's success?

3. Assume that you have just opened a dental supply house which manufactures dentures and other dental correction devices. What criteria would be important in selecting salespeople to sell for your company?

4. If a person wants to be a top-notch professional career sales rep and has no interest in being a manager, is a college education necessary? Discuss. If your answer is no, why do so many firms recruit salespeople from colleges, and why is a college education so often listed as a qualification for a sales job?

5. Assume that a company wants to hire a sales engineer—that is, fill a position where the major emphasis is on technical product knowledge. Should this firm recruit engineers and train them to sell, or recruit sales reps and teach

them the necessary technical information and abilities?

6. Prepare a list of the qualifications you feel are necessary to fill the sales job described in Exhibit 5-B.

7. Is it ethical for a sales manager to directly approach a competitor's salesperson with an outright offer of a better job?

8. How would the sources and methods of recruiting salespeople *differ* among the following firms?

   a. A company selling precision instruments to the petroleum industry.

   b. A coffee roaster and canner in Denver selling to wholesalers and retailers in the Southwest and the Rocky Mountain regions.

   c. A national firm selling kitchenware by the party-plan method.

   d. A luggage manufacturer selling a high-grade product nationally through selected retail outlets.

9. One manufacturer of dictating machines recruits only experienced people and does no recruiting among graduating college students. A competitor recruits extensively among colleges in its search for salespeople. How do you account for the difference in sources used by firms selling essentially the same products?

10. The following companies are looking for product salespeople and decide to use advertising to recruit applicants. For each firm, you are asked to select the specific advertising media and to write a recruiting advertisement for one of those media. You may supply whatever additional facts you need.

    a. Manufacturers' agent handling lighting fixtures for both the industrial and consumer markets.

    b. Manufacturer of outboard motors.

    c. Wholesaler of lumber and building materials.

11. What sources should be used to recruit sales reps to fill the jobs described in Exhibits 5-A and 5-B?

12. Evaluate the five recruiting advertisements for salespeople shown in Exhibit 5-C.

## EXPERIENTIAL EXERCISES

A. After interviewing some of the sales force and/or the appropriate executives, prepare a detailed job description on one of the following jobs.

   a. Automobile dealer salesperson.

   b. Driver–salesperson for local soft drink bottler.

   c. Missionary salesperson for manufacturer.

   d. Salesperson for some type of wholesaler.

B. Prepare a list of qualifications needed to fill each job you analyzed and described in the preceding exercise.

■ **EXHIBIT 5-A**     **Job description—marketing representative for Xerox Corp.**

## JOB DESCRIPTION

*Primary Function:* To achieve assigned sales operating plan objectives in Group III establishments by: prospecting new accounts, developing and maintaining customer rapport, identifying customer requirements for office equipment, matching customer requirements to existing Xerox equipment via written proposals, demonstrating Xerox equipment, signing orders for equipment, resolving customer problems, ensuring proper installation of equipment, training customers on the proper use of equipment, and performing customer care calls to ensure customer satisfaction.

*Source of Supervision:* Marketing/Sales Manager

## JOB DUTIES AND RESPONSIBILITIES

### Conducts Customer Prospecting Calls

■ Plans, organizes, and prioritizes the following activities on a regular basis: customer prospecting calls, customer appointments, customer care visits, customer follow-up calls, customer training, demonstrations, and internal meetings.
■ Performs 15–30 customer prospecting calls (cold calls) per day to identify potential new business or develop customer rapport with previous contacts.
■ Asks office personnel questions to identify key decision maker(s) (e.g., office manager).
■ Asks probing questions and listens to customers' responses to identify potential office equipment requirements.
■ Documents customer information (e.g., customer's name and location, type of existing office equipment, customer requirements for new office equipment) on an account profile form to create a record of all customer prospects.
■ Distributes business cards, sales brochures, and promotional information to customer locations to establish contact with potential customers.

### Conducts Customer Appointments

■ Schedules appointments with customers to further identify customer requirements for office equipment.
■ Gathers information to identify customers' requirements for office equipment by asking probing questions (e.g., current copying and/or FAX equipment used, satisfaction with current equipment, lease agreement on current equipment, number of copies per month, type of copying done, the amount of work that is sent out for outside copying, future needs for copying and/or FAX equipment).
■ Answers customers' questions about Xerox equipment and service.
■ Verbally presents information to customers using brochures and other written materials (e.g., price lists) to inform customers about Xerox equipment and service.
■ Documents results of customer calls and necessary actions needed to advance the call through the sales cycle.

### Conducts Customer Call Follow-Up

■ Seeks information to answer customers' questions from various resources (e.g., written documentation, field support personnel, sales managers, and other sales representatives).
■ Returns customer telephone calls to answer questions and provide information.
■ Writes follow-up thank you letters to customers summarizing the key points of customer calls.
■ Mails information (e.g., flyers, brochures) to customers regarding new office equipment and sales promotions.

### Develops Written Sales Proposals

- Discusses customer requirements with sales managers and other sales representatives to obtain information and develop a strategy for meeting customer requirements.
- Inputs information into sale range pricing database to obtain information regarding the cost and financing of office equipment.
- Calculates finance factors using basic mathematics $(+, -, \times, \div)$ and finance principles to obtain cost of ownership information.
- Writes sales proposals that recommend office equipment and provide product, service, and financial information to meet customers' requirements.
- Types sales proposals using a 6085 computer terminal (if necessary).

### Performs Product Demonstrations

- Schedules appointments with customers to demonstrate equipment.
- Cleans and checks equipment to ensure equipment performance quality (e.g., copy quality, free from jamming).
- Tailors demonstration to meet identified customer requirements.
- Obtains information about competitors' equipment and integrates this information into demonstration.
- Practices demonstration to ensure that equipment is working properly.
- Performs demonstration for customer by presenting product information, running customer applications on the equipment, answering customer questions, and probing the customer for additional requirements.

### Negotiates Close of Sale

- Discusses terms of lease or sale of equipment with customer to clarify all costs of ownership.
- Obtains written commitment from customer to lease or purchase equipment by asking questions to obtain customer information (e.g., desire to purchase equipment, customer location, contact person, billing specifications) needed to complete order form.
- Reviews information on equipment order form with customer to clearly specify the terms of the agreement and ensure information accuracy.
- Answers all customer questions regarding the terms of the lease or sale of the equipment.

### Completes Paperwork to Place Customer Orders for Equipment

- Communicates order information to customer administration representatives, billing representatives, and credit representatives to ensure timely processing of customer order for equipment.
- Obtains additional information from customers to clarify any problems with equipment orders.
- Discusses possible dates for equipment installation with scheduler and confirms installation date with customers.
- Initiates follow-up communications with all order-to-install personnel to ensure the accurate and timely processing of customer orders and equipment installation.

### Assists in the Installation of Equipment (if necessary)

- Measures space requirements to ensure sufficient space is available for equipment installation.
- Assists Customer Service Engineers (CSEs) with the installation of equipment.

■ **EXHIBIT 5-A**     *(concluded)*

## Trains Key Operators and Other Equipment Users

- Presents an overview of equipment features and capabilities to customers.
- Demonstrates proper use of the equipment by running specific customer applications.
- Answers customer questions regarding the operation of equipment, servicing of equipment, ordering of supplies, and trouble-shooting equipment problems.

## Maintains Rapport with Customers

- Conducts periodic post-sale customer care visits to answer customer questions, solve customer problems, maintain rapport with customers, and identify any additional office equipment needs.
- Obtains information and contacts the appropriate personnel to resolve customer problems and ensure customer satisfaction.

## Participates in Quality Improvement Activities

- Attends planning and review meetings and territory reviews to help forecast sales and develop strategies for closing sales cycles.
- Attends team meetings and participates in developing creative solutions to existing problems.
- Writes and delivers presentations in order to share information with other sales representatives and managers.
- Uses the tools of Leadership Through Quality to improve work processes and solve problems.

## JOB PREREQUISITES

Must possess a Bachelors degree or have 2–3 years of relevant sales experience. Must pass all parts of the qualifying test battery for the Marketing Representative position regarding written and verbal communication skills, planning and organization skills, presentation skills, listening ability, problem-solving ability, mathematics/finance skills, and customer relations skills.

The above statements reflect primary activities that are necessary for success in Marketing Representative positions, and shall not be considered a detailed description of all job requirements. The purpose of this job description is to serve only as a basis for developing a new selection process for Marketing Representatives and to provide job applicants with a detailed description of the work requirements.

Source: Used with permission of Xerox Corporation.

■ **EXHIBIT 5-B**      **Job description—sales representative for an international airline**

## CHARTER OF ACCOUNTABILITY

*Position:* Passenger Sales Representative
*Reports to:* Regional Passenger Sales Manager

### 1. Mission
The mission of the Passenger Sales Representative is to generate sales of passenger services and products while optimizing yield and traffic mix levels and achieving the targeted cost/revenue ratio; and to provide professional, prompt, and reliable service to the existing and potential customer base.

### 2. Policy Guidelines
The activities of the Passenger Sales Representative are governed by the policies, procedures, and guidelines established by the Regional and District management and Headquarters; the corporate Personnel Manual and all other related company manuals; and with DOT, FAA, IATAN, ARC, and all other applicable governmental and industry rules and regulations.

### 3. Authority
The Passenger Sales Representative is authorized to sell passenger products and services; to identify and develop new sources of traffic; to represent the company in all first level sales contract negotiations; and to perform the activities listed in Section 5.

### 4. Accountability
The Passenger Sales Representative is accountable for:

- Evaluation of the assigned territory's market potential and competitive influences.
- Preparation of a realistic sales budget.
- Identification and development of new sources of traffic.
- Planning and execution of an effective time and territory management system.
- Achievement of the passenger sales volume/yield targets.
- Negotiation of cost-effective contracts with select agents and corporate/leisure accounts.
- Participation at industry trade shows scheduled within the assigned territory.
- Production of group travel bookings with a high percentage of passenger materialization.
- Accurate and timely presentation of required reports.
- Comprehensive knowledge of all company products and services.
- Quality and professionalism of customer service activities and effectiveness of sales techniques.

### 5. Responsibilities
The Passenger Sales Representative is responsible to:

- Evaluate the market potential of the assigned territory and prepare an attainable sales budget complete with its applicable cost budget.
- Identify potential opportunities for new sources of traffic through market research data and sales leads; develop and implement appropriate strategies.
- Achieve agreed-upon passenger revenue targets through a planned and systematic sales campaign—targeting high-potential accounts, evaluating actual versus expected production for each account, and taking corrective action when required.
- Negotiate advantageous commission contracts with select agents and corporate/leisure accounts.
- Develop call plans based upon production levels and geographic location of accounts; set account goals and strategies; prepare seasonal analysis of time usage and adjust to optimize available time.

■ **EXHIBIT 5-B**     *(concluded)*

- Prepare call strategies and make presentations to corporate, leisure, and agency sales sources and develop group packages and programs to meet their special needs.
- Attend and participate in industry trade shows scheduled within the assigned territory; set up and man the booth; pack material for next location; and submit report on results for future consideration.
- Generate group travel business; negotiate commission and number of blocked seats; complete precall forms; monitor space confirmation; reduce/adjust block space to ensure high passenger materialization.
- Track and report on the competitive influences and market conditions in the territory and recommend actions to counteract competitive activities.
- Project a positive and professional image when representing the company at appropriate industry functions and associations; establish and maintain cooperative working relationships with industry counterparts.
- Coordinate with other district and regional personnel for the planning and implementation of media projects, agent reward systems, and other marketing activities.
- Maintain all pertinent records and prepare ad hoc and periodic reports for management review and decision-making purposes.

6. **Position Scope**

| No. of staff | Cost Budget | Sales Budget |
|---|---|---|
| 0 | $100,000 | $4,000,000 |

## ■ REFERENCES

1. E. James Randall and Cindy H. Randall, "Review of Salesperson Selection Techniques and Criteria: A Managerial Approach," *International Journal of Research in Marketing* 7 (1990), pp. 81–95.

2. Charles Butler, "Why the Bad Rap?" *Sales & Marketing Management,* June 1996, p. 30.

3. Randall and Randall, "Review of Salesperson Selection Techniques and Criteria."

4. Neil M. Ford, Orville Walker, Jr., Gilbert A. Churchill Jr., and Steve W. Hartley, "Selecting Successful Salespeople: A Meta-Analysis of Biographical and Psychological Criteria," *Review of Marketing,* ed. Michael Houston (Chicago: American Marketing Association, 1988), pp. 90–133.

5. Thomas Rollins, "How to Tell Competent Salespeople from the Other Kind," *Sales & Marketing Management,* September 1990, pp. 116–18.

6. "The Buyers' Top Ten," *Sales Manager's Bulletin,* May 30, 1993, p. 33.

7. "Technology Raises Bar for Sales Jobs; Know Your Dress Code," *The Wall Street Journal,* January 21, 1997, p. B1.

8. Mary Connors, "From 'I' and 'Me' to 'Us' and 'We': The Future Belongs to the Team," *Selling,* July/August 1995, pp. 52–53.

9. Geoffrey Brewer, "Brain Power," *Sales & Marketing Management,* May 1997, pp. 39–48.

10. Randall and Randall, "Review of Salesperson Selection Techniques and Criteria."

11. Timothy Trow, "The Secret to a Good Hire: Profiling," *Sales & Marketing Management,* May 1990, pp. 44–46.

12. Nina Munk and Suzanne Oliver, "Think Fast," *Forbes,* March 24, 1997, pp. 146–51.

13. J. Doug Clopton, "Becoming Proactive about Recruiting," *Sales & Marketing Management,* September 1992, pp. 93–97.

■ **EXHIBIT 5-C** **Advertisements for sales positions**

14. Julia Lawlor, "Highly Classified," *Sales & Marketing Management,* March 1995, p. 84.

15. Barry J. Farber, "On the Lookout," *Sales & Marketing Management,* October 1995, pp. 34–35.

16. René Y. Darmon, "Where Do the Best Sales Force Profit Producers Come From?" *Journal of Personal Selling & Sales Management,* Summer 1993, pp. 17–30.

17. Shankar Ganesan, Barton A. Weitz, and George John, "Hiring and Promotion Policies in Sales Force Management: Some Antecedents and Consequences," *Journal of Personal Selling & Sales Management,* Spring 1993, pp. 15–26.

18. "Need Help? Try Asking Your Customers," *Sales & Marketing Management,* April 1991, p. 25.

19. Danielle Service, "Poor Marks for Recruiters," *Sales & Marketing Management,* June 1995, p. 77.

20. Ginger Trumifio, "Recruiting Goes High Tech," *Sales & Marketing Management,* April 1995.

21. Service, "Poor Marks for Recruiters."

22. Phaedra Hise, "Hiring Through Résumé Databases," *Inc.,* May 1993, p. 30.

23. Ginger Trumifio, "Should Your Company Hire Online?" *Sales & Marketing Management,* May 1994.

24. Allison Lucas and William Duke, "Race Matters," *Sales & Marketing Management,* September 1996, pp. 51–62.

25. Ibid.

26. Christian P. Heide, *Dartnell's 29th Sales Force Compensation Survey* (Chicago: Dartnell Corporation, 1997), pp. 168–71.

27. Bill Kelley, "Selling in a Man's World," *Sales & Marketing Management,* January 1991, pp. 28–35.

---

*Case 5-1*

## COMPUTER SERVICES CORPORATION
### Improving the recruiting process

Paul Robbins, national sales manager for Computer Services Corporation, commonly known as CSC, was very frustrated. The company's recruiting efforts this past spring had not yielded the number of recruits the company needed to fill its open territories. This was not a new problem; it was a repeat of similar problems the company faced the previous year, but this year the need for recruits was even greater and the results had been worse. While some districts did better than others, the recruiting efforts across sales districts had not been as effective as they needed to be. Out of every four offers CSC had made, three had been turned down.

Located in Dallas, Texas, CSC manufactures and markets a full line of business forms, computer hardware and software, machine ribbons, computer accessories, and a host of other office products and services. The entire line—well over 6,000 products—is sold to a broad base of customers. For example, 50 percent of the country's phone bills are printed by CSC; UPS shipping forms are another CSC product. This diverse product line has contributed to the tremendous success of the company. CSC has been in business for 30 years, and management is extremely proud of their 15 consecutive years of earnings and sales growth.

CSC considers itself a customer-oriented company. The sales organization is responsible for implementing CSC's strategy of being a full-service, high-quality supplier. Because reorders provide the majority of sales for their primary products, it is imperative that the sales representatives maintain regular and close contact with their customers. To facilitate this close contact, CSC has 105 sales offices throughout the United States. Each office has a district sales manager who reports to one of eight regional managers. The regional managers report to the national sales manager. Most of the sales managers have six or seven salespeople reporting to them.

The salespeople are authorized to sell the entire CSC product line. Each rep is responsible for a specific geographic area. The reps must learn their customers' business and identify ways to help their customers improve their operations and profits. Then they design the forms and sell the products that will improve the customer's operations.

The salespeople are usually compensated on a base salary plus commission. It usually takes about two years to reach the point where the commissions become significant. At that point, the reps can elect to shift their income to a higher proportion of commission. Most of the senior salespeople are on straight commission, and many earn more than $100,000 per year. There is no limit on how much a rep can earn.

Turnover at CSC is much lower than the industry average. The reps are well trained and well paid. The low turnover rates suggest that they are relatively satisfied with the supportive environment of CSC. As Paul had noted to one of his sales managers, "CSC does not have any problem in retaining its reps. The problem is just getting recruits to commit to CSC in the first place."

CSC recruits exclusively from business majors at one or two of the universities which are located in each of the regional areas. For example, in the Houston District Sales Office, the sales managers recruit at the University of Texas and at the University of Houston. The sales managers who have or are anticipating open territories in-

terview 10 to 15 candidates each at one or two campuses. There is no generally agreed-upon set of qualifications or format for conducting the interviews. Each manager is free to conduct the interviews in the way that best suits him or her. After the first round of campus interviews, the manager will invite two to four recruits to the district office for a second round of interviews.

During the district office interviews, the recruits meet with several district staff personnel and spend time with one of the sales representatives. If a regional manager is available, the recruits will interview with one of them as well. Then, based on the outcome of the second round of interviews, the sales manager will usually make two to three offers. Currently the average offer is for $22,000, which applies to the salesperson's first six months. At that time, the salary drops to $20,000 and the potential to earn commission becomes available to the rep. Typically, the average first-year rep will make about $24,000 with salary and commission combined.

However, a lot of quality people are not accepting CSC's offers. Rather they are accepting offers for similar positions with some of the marketing giants like P&G and Johnson & Johnson. The higher starting salaries and company cars these companies offer are attracting recruits. Typically these offers are $5,000 to $6,000 more per year then CSC.

Paul knows that one logical solution to their recruiting problems is to offer starting salaries which are comparable to the other companies. However, his boss, Joe Cannon, is not going to support this idea for several reasons. First of all, the budget for the year has already been set, and raising starting salaries would mean a substantial increase in marketing costs. But even more important is CSC's hiring philosophy of "bringing them in hungry." CSC has always tried to hire people who are "money-motivated," who are excited by the unlimited earning potential at CSC. In fact, management has intentionally kept starting salaries below market so that it is the long-term potential and not the starting salary which attracts recruits to CSC.

Paul had to admit that CSC's hiring philosophy seemed to work well. The low turnover and large commissions earned by

the salespeople attest to its success. Yet he was also certain that unless he did something, the company would continue to spend an excessive amount of time and money on recruiting with dismal results.

**Question:**

Should Paul be concerned about the recruiting results? If so, what changes should Paul make or recommend to improve the results.

---

*Case 5-2*

### EVERGREEN LIFE INSURANCE COMPANY*
Pressure to add a male to an all-female sales force

Louise Marshall was the manager of a highly successful regional sales office of the Evergreen Life Insurance Company. In fact, her region was doing so well that she decided to add another person to the sales force. Her request for an additional rep was approved by the home office. In authorizing the hiring of a new rep, however, the home office strongly recommended—in fact, virtually required—that the new salesperson be a man. There were eight people in the regional office managed by Marshall: four sales reps and four staff assistants, all women. Marshall intended to promote one of the staff assistants when an opening developed in the sales force. The home-office hiring edict thus posed a problem for her.

The Evergreen Life Insurance Company was founded in San Francisco in 1950. During its first 20 years, the company concentrated its marketing efforts in a five-state area—California, Arizona, Nevada, Oregon, and Washington. During the next 20 years, Evergreen expanded into other regions. One

of the newer markets was the region managed by Louise Marshall—a five-state area in the Rocky Mountains with offices in Denver, Colorado.

Evergreen sold a full line of life insurance, including term insurance and a variety of whole-life policies. In recent years, sales had been especially brisk in single-premium policies and various annuity policies. This was partly because of certain income tax advantages provided by these policies. Evergreen wrote both individual-life and group-life policies.

Two channels of distribution are widely used in marketing life insurance. Some companies use their own sales force to sell directly to prospective policyholders. Other firms reach customers through independent insurance brokers. Evergreen relied on an extensive network of brokers to reach its market. These organizations ranged from small, one-office firms to large chain brokers with offices in many locations. These independent brokers were critically important to Evergreen's success. Life insurance customers who bought from a broker usually did business with only one or two brokers.

---
*Adapted from a case prepared by Lewis Fowler under the direction of Professor William J. Stanton.

These customers often relied heavily on the brokers for advice, recommendations, and other insurance services. Each broker typically represented several different insurance companies, all of which competed for the broker's selling time. Furthermore, the insurance companies that Evergreen competed against generally offered about the same product in terms of benefits and premium costs. Often the only important differentiating feature was the service provided by the insurance company to its brokers and its policyholders. Evergreen used its own sales force to deal directly with the network of insurance brokers. In fact, part of an Evergreen rep's job was to contact and sign up new brokers to sell and service Evergreen's insurance policies. To motivate these brokers to devote time to selling Evergreen policies and to service these policyholders well, Evergreen realized that it must give the brokers all possible assistance. Evergreen prided itself on the high quality of service provided by its sales reps to the brokers.

Louise Marshall was only the second manager in the seven-year history of Evergreen's Rocky Mountain regional office. She had been hired four years previously to replace the original manager, whose market development had not met Evergreen's expectations. Marshall had three years of previous experience in the industry as an agent (salesperson) in the Denver, Colorado, office of a large national insurance firm. When Marshall first joined Evergreen, she thought that her job title as a manager was a bit of an exaggeration. "In addition to being the manager of one office assistant, I also was Evergreen's entire sales force in this vast region. As a sales rep, my job was to contact independent insurance brokers and persuade them to offer Evergreen's policies to their customers," she commented. But during her four years with Evergreen, Louise Marshall proved to be a top per-

former. She transformed a region with a dismal record into one that consistently exceeded goals. Her boss in San Francisco viewed Marshall as a strong-willed, intelligent, hard-working overachiever. She devoted her spare time to expanding her knowledge of the life insurance industry, its products, and its markets. She wrote articles for industry journals and conducted classes for persons studying to get their state licenses or professional certificates. By so doing, Marshall had become recognized as an "expert in insurance" by many in the industry. This favorable recognition also brought calls from competitors who wanted to hire her. Currently she was earning $100,000 a year—half in salary and half in commissions.

As a reflection of Marshall's successful market development, her work force had expanded considerably. The primary task of the outside reps continued to be to service the independent brokers and to recruit additional ones. The inside sales staff processed all newly written policies and provided information and other services to support the brokers and the salespeople. To minimize travel time in their huge region, all of Marshall's people used telephones and computers extensively to provide service for brokers and to establish new accounts. Louise believed that her people were highly motivated and worked hard. Two sales reps said that the group's high motivation was a result of Marshall's management style. Her aggressive, yet polite style seemed to appeal to her staff. They looked up to her as a successful professional person and someone to emulate because of her prestige and earning power.

Marshall's management style was geared to the development of the people under her. She assigned a project to a staff member and expected that person to complete the job on her own. These workers learned how to provide the services needed by the brokers. Marshall trained her staff in the management of information needed in their work—how to find, organize, analyze, and disseminate this information. In effect, Marshall was preparing her people to assume a job like hers in the future. The sales reps and staff assistants all knew this, and consequently they liked and respected Louise Marshall and enjoyed their work environment.

The four salespeople earned $40,000 to $60,000 yearly in salary and commissions. The four staff assistants were paid an hourly wage, which averaged $26,000 a year.

All of Marshall's staff were between 26 and 38 years of age. The workers often socialized together after work because they had similar social interests, were close in age, and had similar career aspirations. Marshall encouraged their social activities, believing they helped to develop a tightly knit group with high morale.

Evergreen's sales forecast for 1995 in the Rocky Mountain region projected a significant increase over 1994. To meet this forecast, Marshall requested an additional salesperson who was to be paid a salary of $25,000 plus a commission for the first year.

The home office approved Marshall's request, but stipulated that the new salesperson must be a man. Evergreen's general sales manager, Philip Norden, believed it was time to introduce a male into Marshall's group. The Rocky Mountain regional market was expected to grow considerably over the next 5 to 10 years. Consequently, Evergreen would continue to add sales reps in that region. Norden believed that as Marshall continued to add women, it would be increasingly difficult to assimilate a male into the Denver regional sales office. Norden also wanted to get some men into that region because he believed that many of the

brokers still preferred to deal with a man. Norden's male-only stipulation infuriated Louise Marshall. She said she had a hard-working, effectively motivated staff that was giving an above-average performance for the company.

"What more do those home-office jokers want?" she said. "My people are motivated because they see insurance sales as a career that can earn them good money. None of them has a college education, and they all have worked since high school. I have especially motivated my four inside people by holding out the possibility that in time they can move into field selling. In fact, right now Holly Allis is fully qualified to move into the new sales position, and she knows she is ready for the job. What happens to her morale if we pass her by? In fact, what happens to the morale of all of my people if I bring in an outsider to do a job that any member of my inside staff would take in a second? How will my tight-knit work family react if that outsider is a man?"

Nevertheless, Louise Marshall proceeded to interview several people—all males—for the new sales position. She decided that, if she had to hire a man, Glenn Lufkin was the best prospect. However, she still wondered if she should try to convince the home office to promote Holly Allis into the job. Marshall was about to enter the peak season for insurance selling so she realized a decision had to be made quickly. Before discussing the situation further with the home office, Marshall summarized the qualifications of Lufkin and Allis as follows: Glenn Lufkin was 28 years old and had five years' experience in the insurance industry. He had a dual undergraduate degree in marketing/finance from the University of Colorado and was presently working at the Denver branch office of a large Chicago insurance brokerage firm. Three of Lufkin's five years with the firm had been spent with the technical support staff in Chicago. This gave him a thorough knowledge of life insurance policies and the insurance industry. For the last two years, Lufkin had worked as a sales representative at the Denver branch office and sold primarily to large groups. He was successful as a sales representative but felt he could make more money in Evergreen's type of operation.

Glenn was single and enjoyed the single lifestyle. He liked to ski in Colorado and enjoyed the activities the western area offered. He had no immediate plans for marriage and dated several women. Glenn currently earned $30,000 a year.

Holly Allis was the oldest (31) and most experienced staff assistant. She had thorough technical knowledge of Evergreen's policies and had received her insurance agent's license. She had been with Evergreen for two years before Louise Marshall was hired. It was through Marshall's management practices that Allis had learned so much about the insurance industry. Allis wanted a position such as Marshall's soon, even if it was for another company. Louise knew this and had increased Allis's responsibilities with the brokers to develop her sales skills.

Holly's husband supported her ambitions. They had always planned to be a dual-career family. He felt that with their child in a good day-care facility and by sharing home responsibilities, Holly could pursue her career ambitions. Holly had lived in the Denver area for 20 years, and considered it her home. Holly currently earned $28,000 annually.

**Questions:**

1. Should Louise Marshall hire Glenn Lufkin or should she try to convince management to approve the promotion of Holly Allis?

2. If Glenn Lufkin is hired, what recommendations do you have for assimilating him into Louise Marshall's work group?

---

*Case 5-3*

## PEERLESS GENERATORS, INC.
### Developing a recruiting program

Jim Shaw, sales manager for Peerless Generators, recognized that he was fortunate to still have his job. Most of the company's top management had been replaced with people from the Multitech Company when the two firms merged operations in March 1990. Roger Konstant, the new president of Peerless Generators, had told Jim that the only thing that saved him was that Jim's performance in operating an industrial sales force was far superior to that of anyone in the Multitech sales management organization. Now Jim was approaching Konstant's office for a meeting that was suddenly called on a Monday morning in early May 1994. "Good morning, Jim! Hope you were able to enjoy the weekend," Roger Konstant greeted him warmly. "Yeah, wasn't the weather great? Got in a couple of rounds of golf," Jim replied with a smile.

"Great! Never can tell what the weather is going to be like this time of year here in Cleveland," Konstant observed. He continued, "Jim, I've got to catch a plane to the coast so I'll have to be quick about this."

Jim's stomach tightened. He thought, don't tell me . . . not now.

Konstant said quickly, "Seems you've impressed the Multitech people more than we knew. I've been on the phone for two hours with Jane Conover, who heads their marketing organization. It seems that she has been dissatisfied with their field sales operations for some time but has not been able to get their sales force turned around to her liking. She has had a marketing consulting firm, Marketing Associates, study the problems, and they have submitted their report. They believe that Multitech's sales force has not lived up to expectations because the firm has not been hiring the right people. They claim that this poor selection record is the result of a poor recruiting program. The consultants recommend that the firm's recruiting program be overhauled."

He continued, "Now, as for you! The consultants recommended that an outside party be brought in to develop the new recruiting program. I'm sure they had themselves in mind for the job, but Conover recalled the terrific recruiting program you installed here at Peerless and wants you to come in to do it. You're due in New York tomorrow morning. You have a 10 o'clock meeting with Jane Conover. A copy of the consultants' report will be waiting for you at the Plaza. All reservations have been made for you. Pick up your tickets downstairs; you're out of here at 6, so go home for the rest of the day. You'll need the rest. Got to run now."

And Roger Konstant was gone. Jim wondered if this was how the new management always operated as he returned to his office to give his people instructions for his unexpected absence.

Jim Shaw did not know Jane Conover, nor did he really know much about Multitech sales operations. He wasn't really sure what all the company sold or to whom they sold it. He would soon find out. Jim arrived at the Plaza in New York and was getting settled in his room when the telephone rang. Conover had sent her assistant to the hotel to brief Shaw about company operations.

The assistant, Stu Jackson, was in the lobby now, loaded down with materials for Shaw's information. Jim listened carefully for the next two hours while Jackson briefed him on Multitech sales operations and plans.

It developed that the firm's problems with its sales operations were far more extensive than Jim had been led to believe. "Top management is not happy with sales operations in any of its 12 companies. Studies have continually shown that the firm's sales performance in each of its markets is below average for that industry. Evidently, we're just not very good at selling our goods," stated Stu Jackson.

He continued, "We hire more than 600 sales reps in total for the whole system, but the turnover is killing us. We lose 25 percent a year. Right now we just hire on a catch-as-catch-can basis. The field sales managers hire reps to replace those we lose as best they can. We can discern no pattern, except that they do tend to hire reps from other technically oriented firms and from competitors." Jim nodded as Stu continued, "On top of all that mess, top management has launched a strategic expansion program that schedules us to hire a total of 100 new sales reps each year for the whole system."

"Why do you keep speaking of the company as a whole and not of the individual firms? Doesn't each firm have its own distinctive needs?" Jim asked.

"Not really. They all sell highly technical equipment to the electronics industry. Each company was a successful high-tech start-up that we purchased when the entrepreneur or the investors were ready to cash out. We considered combining all the sales forces, but it proved to be not the thing to do. Each has its own niche in the market and deals with separate technology. And company policy is to allow the firms that we take over to keep their own identity."

When Stu had completed his briefing, Jim asked, "Do you know exactly what Conover wants me to do?"

"I think she wants you to tell her what to do. She just wants the problems solved," Stu replied.

Jim nodded and thanked Stu for working so late to help him out. Jim knew that sleep might be elusive that night—he had much to mull over. He knew he would stall for time by asking Jane Conover to tell him as much as possible about the situation so he could discern her thoughts on the matter.

The next morning Conover quickly took over the meeting once the usual formalities had been observed. "I need a plan. Tell me how to solve this problem, but do it quickly. I'm being pressed hard from the top about our field sales operations and I am afraid that field sales are not my cup of tea. I came up through marketing and product management at General Electric. You're free to write your own ticket in the deal. Pick your role. Use my budget. Stu is yours if you want him. He'll handle your budget and arrangements. Can I have your report next week?"

Jim was silent for a moment, trying to process all this information while looking reasonably intelligent. He finally replied, "I'll do better than that. I'll tell you tomorrow what I propose to do." Jim did not want to stick around New York for a week. He had already made up his mind that he did not want to work separately with each subsidiary; it would involve too much traveling and too much time. He contemplated developing a model recruiting program for each of the firm's sales managers to follow. It would tell each sales manager how to develop a recruiting program for his or her operation. Jane Conover smiled and said, "See you tomorrow at 9."

*Questions:*

1. Outline what a model recruiting program should cover.
2. What career opportunities does this event provide Jim Shaw?

# CHAPTER 6

# Selecting Applicants

The worst mistake a manager can make is to make a bad hire.

**Anonymous**

In our **selection** process, we have determined the number and type of salespeople needed, and applicants have been recruited. Now management is ready for the third and final stage in the sales selection function. This step involves (1) the development of a system for matching the applicants with the predetermined requirements and (2) the actual use of this system to select the salespeople. The major selection tools are:

- Application blanks
- Personal interviews
- Psychological tests
- References and credit reports
- Assessment centers

## ◼ SELECTING APPLICANTS AND STRATEGIC PLANNING

Selecting applicants is an integral part of implementing the strategic sales force planning. If the selection stage is handled effectively, it can help ensure successful sales performance. On the other hand, a poor job in processing applicants can hinder implementation, even though determining qualifications and recruiting were done well. Matching company needs and applicants' potential is very important to the strategic and tactical aspects of sales force management.

The key here and the central theme of this chapter is for management (1) to select the best processing tools and then (2) to use them effectively to match the applicant with the hiring specifications.

The sequence in which selection tools are used varies among companies. Initial screening (beyond that done in recruiting) may start with an application blank, an interview, or some form of test. The purpose of the initial screen is to eliminate undesirable recruits quickly and inexpensively. Therefore, no matter which technique is used first, it is usually brief—a short application blank, a brief interview, or a simple test that can be administered and interpreted quickly. This procedure follows the general idea that the *least costly selection tools should be used first.*

Since no single selection tool is adequate by itself, a series should be used to carefully determine an applicant's qualifications. In many cases, one tool can be used to complement or to verify information derived from another. Some pertinent data ordinarily come only through an interview, while other traits are discerned only by testing.

The tools a company uses to process its sales recruits should fit the particular needs of the firm. Standardized forms (application blanks, interview forms, and so on) prepared for general use are usually less effective than those a company develops itself.

These tools and procedures are only *aids* to sound executive judgment and not *substitutes* for it. They can eliminate obviously unqualified candidates and generally spot extremely capable individuals. However, for the mass of recruits between these extremes, the tools currently used can only predict those who should be successful in the job. As a result, executive judgment still plays a critical role in selecting sales representatives from among those who have the potential to be successful.

## ■ LEGAL CONSIDERATIONS

The legislation summarized in Chapter 5 protects certain classes of people against discrimination. As a result of these laws and their enforcement by the EEOC and the OFCC, there is certain information which should *not* be requested during the selection process. These inquiries are outlined in Figure 6-1. Additionally, preemployment medical screening should not be conducted until after the offer has been extended. The job offer should be made contingent on the physical, if and only if the medical requirements are related to job performance.

Hiring decisions may no longer be made on "gut feeling." Title VII of the Civil Rights Act of 1964 provides that the selection of employees must be based on objective criteria. These criteria must be (1) independently measurable, (2) job related, and (3) predictive of performance.[1]

Companies subject to affirmative action guidelines must keep an "applicant flowchart," which lists the processed applicants by sex and ethnic group. If there is a disproportionately high rate of rejection of women or minority applicants, each step in the hiring process may be reviewed to determine which tool is producing this result. Once identified, the particular tool must undergo a validation procedure if management wants to continue using it.

**Validation** is the statistical process of measuring the extent to which a given selection tool or hiring qualification is a predictor of, or is related to, job performance. To reduce selection mistakes and possible legal hassles later, we recommend that companies validate their selection tools *before* using them. This increases management's chances of using the best available selection criteria. Moreover, if a company is later charged with discrimination, validation is the best defense possible.

Many questions formerly asked on application blanks and during interviews either are no longer permitted or must be handled very carefully. Sometimes questions in sensitive areas are asked after the person is

■ **FIGURE 6-1**

| What to ask and what not to ask | Do not ask: | Lawful inquiries: |
| --- | --- | --- |
| | ■ The applicant's age. | ■ How many years of experience do you have? |
| | ■ If the applicant has children or the ages of the children. | ■ Why do you want the job? |
| | ■ Who will care for the children if the applicant is hired? | ■ Can you do extensive traveling? |
| | ■ The applicant's race or a question directly or indirectly indicating race. | ■ What languages do you speak? |
| | ■ The applicant's height or weight. | |
| | ■ An applicant's citizenship. | ■ Whether the applicant is a citizen or resident alien of the United States. |
| | ■ Whether the applicant was ever arrested. | ■ Questions about convictions if they relate to the fitness of the applicant to do the job. |
| | ■ Whether the applicant is married, single, divorced, widowed. | ■ Whether the applicant should be addressed as Mr., Mrs., Ms., or Miss. |
| | ■ The applicant's religious affiliation. | ■ Questions about the applicant's goals. |
| | ■ What the applicant's spouse does. | ■ Questions regarding specific skills. |
| | ■ The applicant's maiden name or her father's surname. | ■ What the applicant didn't like about a job and why the applicant left a job. |
| | ■ The names and/or addresses of any relative of an adult applicant. | |
| | ■ If the applicant belongs to a specific organization, if that would indicate race, religion, or ancestry. | ■ Questions regarding education and schools attended. |
| | ■ If the applicant owns or rents. | |
| | ■ With whom the applicant lives. | |
| | ■ Whether a woman would be comfortable supervising a man. | ■ If the applicant would be comfortable supervising others. |

Source: *Approaches to Affirmative Action,* Bureau of National Affairs, Inc.

hired, as in the case of age and marital status for insurance purposes. Questions in sensitive areas may be asked *during* these interviews, however, if they relate to **bona fide occupational qualifications** (BFOQs). Age and sex may be BFOQs, for example, if the sales job calls for a salesman to model the line of menswear he is selling. If a certain ethnic background and ability to speak a certain foreign language are BFOQs, then obviously questions pertaining to these factors are perfectly appropriate. To summarize, any question asked or hiring qualification required must be "job relevant"—that is, it must be important to the job.

*A Day-to-Day Operating Problem*

## MAJESTIC PLASTICS COMPANY (C)

### Request to rehire a former sales rep, now in penitentiary

Clyde Brion, general sales manager for Majestic Plastics Company, was visited in his office by Mrs. Edgar Jenner. She was accompanied by a man who identified himself as a parole officer of the Ohio State Department of Correction. As Brion knew, Mrs. Jenner was the wife of a former Majestic salesman based in Detroit. At this time Jenner was in the Ohio Penitentiary serving the third year of a seven-year sentence for manslaughter committed while driving a car under the influence of liquor. The case had attracted much newspaper attention because the victim was a pretty teenage daughter of a U.S. senator. She was struck down crossing a quiet street on her way to church where she was to have been a bridesmaid at the wedding of another senator's daughter.

Except for an attempt to escape custody during his trial, Jenner had been a docile prisoner. The parole officer described him as remorseful, morose, and worried about his wife as well as about his own future. A doctor at the penitentiary had found him free of any addiction to alcohol. The doctor had recommended that Jenner be freed, if he could return to his regular work in familiar surroundings. Mrs. Jenner asked Brion to rehire her husband.

Until his conviction, Jenner had been a satisfactory sales rep for Majestic. In sales volume, his territory had never ranked higher than ninth among the 18 territories, despite his six years on the sales force. The Detroit area was believed to have considerably more potential than he was able to tap. Jenner had used his drawing account regularly, saying that he needed extra money to pay medical bills on his wife's long illness.

The Detroit territory had not been permanently filled since Jenner had left it. Because it was relatively close to the Majestic home offices, Brion had preferred to use it as a training territory for new salespeople, supervised by himself.

**Question:** Should Clyde Brion rehire Edgar Jenner?

Note: See the introduction to this series of problems in Chapter 4 for the necessary background on the company, its market, and its competition.

## APPLICATION BLANKS

### Reasons for Using Application Blanks

The **application blank,** or personal-history record, as it is sometimes called, is one of the two most widely used selection tools. (The other is the interview.) Sometimes a firm uses two blanks, a short one and a longer, more detailed one. The short form ordinarily is used only as an initial screening device.

A longer blank may be used as an initial screen or for other purposes. The facts stated on the form can be the basis for probing in an interview. For instance, the interviewer can ask several questions about job experience stated on the blank. Later the data on the blank can be used to reevaluate the characteristics needed for the job. One national pharmaceutical firm uses data on the application blank to screen for high performers who will stay with the firm. Based on an analysis of the application information for their current and past salespeople, they weight certain characteristics more heavily than others.[2]

## Information Asked for on Application Blanks

A company ordinarily should ask only for information it intends to use now or later. Unless a question relates to some standard or job qualification, its presence on a blank is debatable. However, sometimes a question may be needed to complete personal records. A seven-part classification of sales job qualifications—mental, physical, experience, education, personality, skills, and environmental—was proposed in Chapter 5. An application blank is an excellent tool for getting significant information in three of those categories—physical, experience, and environmental.

When a certain *physical condition* is a bona fide occupational qualification, a company might ask questions about it. For example:

- The job requires frequent lifting of 60-pound objects. Can you safely perform such a task?
- The job requires much driving of a car and physical activity when calling on customers. Do you have any physical problem that would interfere with the performance of such activities?

On an application blank, **experience requirements** are usually divided into two groups, educational background and work experience. Companies ask questions about educational background because they believe that applicants' performance in school tells something about their mental abilities and personality traits. Anyone who has graduated from high school or college (depending on the firm's requirements) is presumed to have the necessary basic intelligence. A course of study indicates much about a person's interests. Working one's way, at least partially, through school may indicate self-reliance and industry.

Most application blanks ask for information about the candidate's employment history, including periods of unemployment. If a company has certain experience qualifications, the application blank is a good tool for determining whether a candidate meets these requirements. Companies also usually like to know the reasons why a person left each previous job. If possible, a prospective employer should check on this point with someone other than the applicant.

Companies ordinarily are interested in the **environmental qualifications** of prospective employees. Questions may be asked on topics such as the following:

- Membership in social, service, and business organizations.
- Offices held in organizations.
- Outside interests, hobbies, athletic endeavors, and others.

(Once again, remember that questions about age, marital status, religion, or any of the points discussed above must comply with federal laws and regulations.)

Information on the prospect's environment can be extremely helpful because it reveals something about the person's interests, capabilities, and personality. Active participation in organizations may indicate ability to meet and mix with people. Holding office may imply leadership traits and administrative abilities.

## ◼ PERSONAL INTERVIEWS

### Nature and Purpose

Virtually no salesperson is ever hired without a personal interview, and there are no satisfactory substitutes for this procedure. Much has been written about the use of weighted application blanks, various kinds of tests, and other aids in hiring. But none of these tools completely takes the place of getting to know applicants personally by talking to them.

A personal interview is used basically to determine a person's fitness for a job. Moreover, personal interviews disclose characteristics that are not always observable by other means. An interview is probably the best way to find out about the recruit's conversational ability, speaking voice, and social intelligence. By seeing the applicant in person, an executive can appraise physical characteristics such as general appearance and care given to clothes. Certain personality traits may also be observed. The applicant's poise under the strain of an interview may be noted, along with any tendency to dominate or lead a conversation.

Another purpose in interviewing is to interpret and get further information about facts stated on the application blank. For example, the applicant may have stated that he was a district manager in a previous job. The prospective employer may ask what his responsibilities were and how many employees he supervised.

Fundamentally, all the questions asked during an interview are aimed at learning four points about the applicant:

- Is this person capable of excelling at this job?
- How badly does this applicant want the job?
- Will the job help this person to realize his or her goals?
- Will this applicant work to his or her fullest ability?

In general, the inquiries are intended to examine the applicant's past behavior, experiences, environment, and motivation. Another set of questions typically deals with an applicant's goals, strategies, and tactics for the future. Within these broad categories, each firm must select those inquiries which are pertinent for its sales positions.

Finally, the interview is not only a means by which a company determines an applicant's fitness for a job; the interview also offers an employer the opportunity to "sell" the position and the company to the recruit. The interviewer can help applicants learn about the nature of the job, the compensation, the type of training and supervision provided, and the opportunities for the future so that they will be interested in the job.

## Reliability of Personal Interviews as Predictors of Success

Interviews are the most widely used selection tool. Although for many occupations interviews are not good predictors of an applicant's subsequent job performance, studies have found that they can be good predictors of success in the sales job.[3] This is in part due to the fact that the sales job requires skills similar to those which are on display in the interview. Also, it has been discovered that behavioral/performance-based interviews are better predictors of success in the sales job than other types of interviews.[4] (This type of interview is discussed in a subsequent section.)

Too often, however, interviews are not as effective as they could be. The inherent weakness in the interviewing process is that it is heavily dependent on the behavior of the interviewer. Unfortunately, many people do not know how to interview an applicant effectively, nor do they know how to interpret an applicant's responses. An interviewer's reactions, for example, can greatly affect an applicant's responses. It is so important, and yet so difficult, for an interviewer to remain completely neutral and consistent through a series of interviews with several applicants. Another problem is that an interviewer's impression of an applicant may be based on "gut" reaction instead of on an objective evaluation of the candidate's qualifications. This reaction is highly subjective and therefore may not be consistent with the impression that other interviewers have. Still another behavioral consideration is that most interviewers talk too much, listen too little, and ask the wrong questions. These factors tend to lower the value of the interviewing process as a selection tool. Consequently, most interviewers do not accomplish their intended goal of matching applicants with hiring specifications, and thus predicting job performance. Yet a well-planned, properly conducted interview is a valid predictor of performance and should always be used in the selection process.

## Improving the Validity of Interviews

There are ways to offset these weaknesses and improve the validity of interviews as predictors of job performance. It is important to thoroughly review the applicant's resume or application before proceeding further in the selection process. Sometimes companies use a telephone interview or a brief interview (such as a campus interview or a job fair interview) as part of the initial screening process. The screening step can weed out obviously unqualified or uninterested candidates. It may also highlight certain aspects of the candidate's background which are in need of further investigation.

It is also important to have more than one interview with each candidate. In general, a company should not depend on a single interview, a single interviewer, or a single place for the interviewing. This idea is based on the assumption that the more time spent with prospective recruits and the more people who talk with them, the greater the opportunity to get to know them well. Additionally, interviewers should use standardized rating forms that they fill out after each interview with an applicant. Later, the information on these forms can be reviewed, evaluated, and used for making comparisons among the applicants.

Another step is to train interviewers on how to conduct interviews and how to use rating forms. Practice interviews with a follow-up group discussion in training sessions can increase the consistency of applicant ratings by the interviewers. Additional suggestions for improving the interviewing process are discussed below.

## Interview Structure

Selection interviews can differ, depending on the extent to which the questions are detailed in advance and the conversation is guided by the interviewer. At one end of the scale is the totally structured or guided interview and at the other end is the informal, nondirected type.

### Guided Interviews

The procedure in a guided interview is highly standardized. All interviewers for a firm use the same guide sheet containing a series of questions. The interviewer asks these questions and makes notations concerning the candidate's responses. The guided interview seeks to overcome problems encountered in using personal interviews as a selection technique. Many sales executives engaged in selection activities do not know what questions to ask. They may know the qualifications for the job but they do not know what questions will tell them whether the applicant possesses these characteristics.

Also, because all of the applicants are asked the same questions and their responses are recorded, the interviewer can readily compare and rate the candidates. Furthermore, several interviewers, interviewing the same set or a different set of candidates, have a good basis for comparing their evaluations. Some people criticize the guided interview as being inflexible. But this is not necessarily the case. Trained interviewers can use their judgment and make slight modifications without detracting from the full value of the guided form.

### Nondirected Interviews

At the other end of the structured interview scale is the informal, nondirected one. Ordinarily, the interviewer asks a few questions to get the applicant talking on certain subjects, such as his or her business experiences, home life, or school activities. The interviewer does very little talking—just enough to keep the conversation rolling. The theory is that significant characteristics come to light if the applicant is encouraged to speak freely.

The major problem with the nondirected interview is that much time may be wasted unearthing little information. Some of what an applicant says may be irrelevant or impossible to evaluate. This type of interview requires far more interpretive skill on the part of the interviewer than the structured form. There is no written record to be passed on to someone else for appraisal. Also, the values of standardization are lost in the nondirected interview.

Most firms today use an interview format somewhere between the guided and the nondirected interview such as those described in the next section.

## Interview Focus

Over the past several years, new types of interviews have emerged which focus on the applicant's behavior. One type poses questions concerning the candidates' past or intended behaviors which relate to their sales aptitude. Another focuses on the candidates' performance of selling related exercises.

### Behaviorally Based Interviews

Questions which focus on *past behaviors* are based on the premise that what a person has done in the past is indicative of what he or she will do in the future. Applicants who have performed successfully in the past are expected to be successful in the new job. Companies such as Polaroid and TRW are using this type of behavioral interviewing.[5] Examples of traditional and behaviorally based questions are:

| Traditional | Behaviorally Based |
|---|---|
| ■ Do you get along with people? | ■ Tell me about any incident in your last job that caused conflict with a customer; what did you do to work things out? |
| ■ What qualities do you think are important for success in this job? | ■ Give me a specific example of a job situation in which you had to use your problem-solving abilities. |
| ■ What is your biggest weakness? | ■ Tell me about your greatest failure. |

---

## Hiring for Team Synergy

A candidate for a team selling position should possess a different set of characteristics than a sales rep who works individually. One critical dimension is how well the person works with others. Another is how well a person will fit into the existing culture of the team. The best way to answer these kind of questions is to ask the people who know the team members best. **Ask the team!** Involve the team members in determining qualifications, conducting interviews, and providing selection recommendations. Some experts are convinced that it is the best way to ensure that the synergy of an excellent team can continue when team members leave and other people are hired.

Source: Adapted from Paul Ludwick, "Teams by Design: Hiring for Synergy," *Public Management,* September 1995, pp. 9–14.

---

Focusing on past behaviors is valid if the new job is similar to the old one. However, if the applicants have not had experiences similar to those in the new job, then exploring past behavior becomes less useful. In this case it may be better to ask about *intended behaviors—how applicants think they would behave in job-related situations. This type of question is based on the premise that people's behavioral intentions are related to their subsequent behavior.*

### Performance-Based Interviews

Some companies ask candidates to perform *exercises simulating selling situations.* For example, at Copyrite, Inc., candidates first review the annual report and videotapes on the company. Then they are asked to "sell the interviewer on the company from what they have learned." The Office Place, an office supply and equipment dealer, gives candidates a product ID number and asks them to be prepared to make a presentation on that product during their interviews.[6] These exercises are valuable in showing how much time, effort, skill, and creativity the candidates bring to these presentations.

### Stress Interviews

The stress interview is one in which the interviewer intentionally places the applicant under stress. For example, the applicant may be handed an object such as a pen or a notebook and asked to "sell" it to the interviewer. In recent years, a number of companies have been asking interviewees to solve brainteasers and riddles in order to gauge their ability to think quickly and creatively. The answer isn't as important as how one gets there.[7] (Test yourself on the examples in the box titled "Brainteasers.") In some cases, the interviewer may be intentionally rude, silent, or overly aggressive in questioning just to see how the candidate will react. The ultimate performance-based, stressful exercise is one in which the candidate rides with a rep to observe several cold calls and then is asked to make a cold call on his or her own.

---

### Brainteasers

- You have 12 balls, and one has a different weight than the others. Using a two-plate scale only three times, how would you figure out which ball was different and whether it was lighter or heavier? (McKinsey & Co.)
- How many barbers are there in Chicago? (McKinsey & Co.)

- Why are manhole covers round? (Microsoft)
- You are in a room with three light switches. Each one controls one light in the next room. You must figure out which switch controls which bulb. You may flick only two switches, and you may enter the room only once. (Boston Consulting Group)

---

These techniques give the interviewer some idea of how the candidate will behave under the stress encountered in the sales job. However, these methods can also aggravate applicants and lessen their interest in the job.

### Timing of the Interview

#### During Initial Screening

Companies often use an interview as the initial screening device. For example, when recruiting teams visit college campuses, one or more team members may briefly interview a prospect to determine whether that person should be considered further. Initial screening interviews should last only 15 or 20 minutes. Figure 6-2 is a copy of the form that the Xerox Corporation uses to evaluate a campus interview.

Because interviewing takes executives' valuable time, the interviewer should quickly find out if the recruit is uninterested or unqualified. This information may be determined, first, by giving a brief job description and, second, by asking a few questions to see if the recruit meets the minimum requirements. Figure 6-3 is the patterned interview form used by Xerox when a telephone interview is the initial screening device.

#### At Later Stages

Firms that do a thorough selection job ordinarily interview applicants several times before they are hired. After applicants pass through the initial screen, but before a final decision can be reached, much remains to be learned about them. In turn, they must be told many things about the job. The more time spent with prospective recruits and the more people who talk with them, the greater the opportunity to get to know them well.

## PSYCHOLOGICAL TESTING

Psychological testing is another major tool often used in the sales selection process. Typically a company uses a battery of these tests rather than a single test. Over the years, psychological testing has undoubtedly been

■ **FIGURE 6-2** **Campus interview—evaluation report**

## XEROX   **Campus Interview — Evaluation Report**

| C | Social Security Number | Applicant's First Name | MI | Last Name | Major | Interview Date Mo. Day Yr |
|---|---|---|---|---|---|---|
| 1 | 10 | 11 20 | 21 22 | 38 | 39 41 | 42 47 |

| 1 | | | | | | |

| EEO Code | Sex | Degree | Position Interest | College Code | Graduate Date Mo. Day Yr |
|---|---|---|---|---|---|
| 48 | 49 | 50 | 51 69 | 70 73 | 74 79 |

| Interviewer Name (Print) | Employee No. | Org.(ISG, XBS, RTG, etc.) | School |
|---|---|---|---|

**Interviewer's Recommendation (Circle One)**

80
[1] Invite     Days Avail _____

80                      80
[2] Write-Off      [3] Refer _____

80
[4] Employment Department Use Only

To Whom/For What

1.

2.

3.

### Evaluation Criteria

**Evaluation (Circle Level)**

| Evaluation Criteria | (Does Not Meet Xerox Standards) | | (Meets Xerox Standards) | | (Exceeds Xerox Standards) |
|---|---|---|---|---|---|
| **Aggressiveness and Enthusiasm** | 1 | 2 | 3 | 4 | 5 |
| **Communication Skills** | 1 | 2 | 3 | 4 | 5 |
| **Record of Success** | 1 | 2 | 3 | 4 | 5 |
| **Rational Thought Process** | 1 | 2 | 3 | 4 | 5 |
| **Maturity** | 1 | 2 | 3 | 4 | 5 |
| **Overall Evaluation** | 1 | 2 | 3 | 4 | 5 |

### Summary of Applicant's Qualifications

Apparent Strengths:

Apparent Weaknesses:

Areas Requiring Clarification:

**Major Codes: Col. 39-41**

| | |
|---|---|
| 305 Finance Gen. | 720 Metallurgy |
| 410 Engr Chem. | 803 Economics Gen. |
| 422 Engr Electro | 815 Political Sc. |
| 428 Engr Industr. | 899 Social Sci. |
| 434 Engr Mchncl. | 309 Economic Bus. |
| 312 Marketing | 420 Engr Electri. |
| 844 Humanities | 704 Chemistry |
| 331 Mgt. General | 729 Physics |
| 399 Business Gen. | |

See College Major Code Table for additional codes.

**EEO Codes: Col. 48**

1 - Black
2 - Asian or Pacific Islanders
3 - American Indian or Alaskan Native
4 - Hispanic
5 - White

**Degrees: Col. 48**

1 - Associate
2 - Bachelor
3 - Master
4 - Doctorate

**Sex: Col 49**

M - Male
F - Female

**College Codes: Col. 70-73**

See College Code Table for Alphabetical List of codes.

■ **FIGURE 6-3**     **Telephone screen evaluation**

---

## XEROX       **Telephone screen evaluation**

| Applicant | Interviewer | Date |
|---|---|---|
|  |  |  |

1. Would you tell me about your current job?  (Determine whether the applicant has related experience, training, interest, etc.)

2. Why are you looking for a job at this time?  (Determine whether reasons are acceptable.)

3. Why are you looking for this particular job at Xerox?  (Determine whether the applicant's perceptions of the job are sufficiently accurate.)

4. What background, qualifications, and abilities do you feel you have which would enable you to be successful on this job?  (Determine whether the applicant can sell him/herself and whether these qualifications are beneficial.)

5. What are your salary expectations?  (Determine whether the applicant is realistic.)

6. Where do you expect to be five years from now?  (Determine whether the applicant has sufficient ambition.)

7. When would you be able to start with Xerox?  (Determine whether this fits into manpower needs.)

Summary of Applicant's Qualifications

Apparent Strengths:

Apparent Weaknesses:

Interviewer's Recommendations

A. Recommended for testing:       ☐ Yes    ☐ No

B. Areas requiring clarification in additional interviews:

---

the most controversial of all the selection tools. Today the added burden of complying with legal guidelines has increased the complexity and controversy surrounding the use of testing in sales force selection.

Despite the complexity and controversy, the use of tests as a selection tool is becoming increasingly popular. A *Sales & Marketing Management* survey reported that 50 percent of the companies responding are using some type of testing for selecting salespeople.[8] The increased use of tests has occurred for several reasons. First, employers have become more knowledgeable about the legal requirements surrounding the use of tests. Second, some studies have shown that testing is a better predictor of job performance than any other selection tool.[9] Finally, as the cost of making a poor selection decision continues to rise, employers are turning to testing as an additional means of improving their selection decisions.

## Legal Aspects of Testing

Although federal legislation put restraints on the use of testing in the selection process, *testing is legal.* In fact, a testing and selection order issued by the OFCC (Office of Federal Contract Compliance) says that "properly validated and standardized employee selection procedures can significantly contribute to the implementation of nondiscriminatory personnel policies" and that "professionally developed tests . . . may significantly aid in the development and maintenance of an efficient work force." The key phrases in this quotation are *properly validated* and *professionally developed.* These requirements are discussed below.

## A Framework for Testing

Ideally, tests should be used to provide objective information about a candidate's skills and abilities. This information can and should be used to support what is discovered in the interview process or to uncover areas to explore during the interview. It is important to remember that no test can predict with 100 percent accuracy. Therefore, the results should *not* be used as the sole acceptance or knockout factor. Accordingly, the test results should not include a hiring recommendation. Rather, it is the responsibility of the hiring manager to decide if the psychological profile is correct for the job in question.[10]

### Selecting and Developing Tests

In building a good testing program, a company should use tests which measure the criteria developed during the planning phase of the hiring process. The firm can develop its own in-house tests with the aid of company or outside psychologists. Alternatively, it can use tests professionally developed by outside consulting firms such as the Klein Behavioral Science Consultants or the ATI company. Typically, tests developed outside have a broad usage base, which makes validation less complicated and less costly.

## Main Types of Tests Used in Sales Force Selection

- **Mental intelligence tests.** Intended to measure a person's native intelligence (IQ—intelligence quotient) and general ability to learn. Some examples of these tests are (1) the Otis Self-Administering Test of Mental Ability and (2) the Wonderlic Personnel Test.
- **Aptitude tests.** Designed to measure a person's aptitude for selling. This category also includes tests that measure social aptitude (social intelligence). Some examples are (1) the Sales Aptitude Checklist, (2) the General Sales Aptitude Test, and (3) the Diplomacy Test of Empathy.
- **Interest tests.** Designed to measure or compare a person's interests with the interests of successful people in specific occupations. Some examples are (1) the Strong-Campbell Interest Inventory and (2) the Kuder Occupational Interest Survey.
- **Personality tests.** Intended to measure various personality traits. These tests are the most risky and difficult to validate because of our inability to identify the traits needed for a particular sales job. Some examples of these tests are (1) the Bernreuter Personality Inventory, (2) the Edwards Personal Preference Schedule, (3) the Multiple Personal Inventory, and (4) the Gordon Personal Profile.

However, many testing specialists and managers agree that the variable requirements of different sales jobs call for customized tests. For example, Infonet Services, a data communications services provider, has found that its marketing reps who bring in new business have different personalities and aptitudes than its account development reps who work with current customers. Therefore, the company tests for different characteristics for each position.[11]

Each test which is used as part of the selection process should be validated. As discussed in Chapter 5, this means that the company should be able to demonstrate a relationship between test results and the performance of its salespeople. If the company is using standard tests supplied by an outside consulting firm, the supplier should provide proof of the tests' validity. If the company has developed customized tests, it must validate them.

### Problems in Testing[12]

Most testing procedures generate the concept of an average or normal type of employee. The implication is that this person is the best to hire for a given job. The danger is that a potentially successful sales representative may be screened out simply because he or she does not fit the stereotype. Testing may eliminate the truly creative person, who may not fall in the average or normal range in testing. At the same time, creativity may be the very trait that would make that person an outstanding sales representative.

---

### Conditions When Testing Is Most Effective

A program for testing in sales selection is most likely to be effective when any of the following conditions exist:

- The firm hires a relatively large number of salespeople and management wants to improve its success ratio.
- The company is hiring young, inexperienced people about whom little is known. (If experienced reps are being selected, their performance records rather than test results should be the criterion.)
- The executives who interview recruits are not adept at discovering personality traits and selling aptitudes. Normally, executives with a great deal of experience in hiring do

a much better job of interviewing than an administrator who is new at the job.

- In companies where the cost of failure is high, the expense of testing may be considered a small investment to ensure that no one slips through the selection screen. If the testing procedure catches just one failure a year who would otherwise have been hired, the costs of the testing may be justified.
- The executives can competently interpret the psychologist's recommendations and feel free to act on their own judgment regardless of the tests.

---

Another problem with testing is that tests are sometimes used as the sole deciding knockout factor. An applicant may look good based on interviews, the application blanks, and reference checks. But if the test scores are especially low, management may be reluctant to hire that person.

Tests are sometimes misused because executives fail to apply the concept of a *range* of scores. For many kinds of tests, psychologists agree that a range of scores is acceptable. All who fall within that range should be judged as *equally qualified for the job*. Unfortunately, most people tend to feel that a person scoring near the high end of the acceptable range is a better prospect than one scoring in the lower part of that range.

Another factor to watch for in testing is that applicants can fake the answers on some tests, especially on some personality or interest tests. Reasonably intelligent applicants for a sales job know they should indicate a preference for mixing with people, in contrast to staying home and reading a good book. Cultural bias is another situation that can creep into tests. A person may score poorly, not because of a lack of interest, aptitude, or native intelligence, but only because the test included questions that assumed a certain cultural background.

## REFERENCES AND OTHER OUTSIDE SOURCES

When processing applicants for sales jobs, an administrator can get help from two general sources of information outside the company. In the first, the applicant furnishes the leads; this is called a **reference.** In the other, the company solicits information on its own initiative; this source includes credit and insurance reports, school records, and motor vehicle histories.

Reference checks may be made by letter, telephone, or personal visit, and each method has some limitations. A personal visit may take too much time, and it is not practical unless the reference is located near the prospective employer. Using a personal visit or the telephone is advantageous because nothing is in writing. However, some companies will not supply information to a stranger over the telephone. A letter is probably used more frequently than the two other methods, but often it is of very little value. Firms hesitate to put anything derogatory in writing. This leads us to the big problem today with any kind of a reference check. Companies are extremely leery about giving out meaningful information regarding former employees. In fact, many companies now have strict reference policies which, in effect, put a tight rein on the employee information that they release. This situation has developed because of fear of being sued by the employee for defamation of character. Despite the obstacles, management should not bypass this tool. If only one significant fact is uncovered, it makes the effort worthwhile.

When talking with an applicant's former employer, a key question to ask is: Would you rehire this person? Additional questions which may provide some insights are: In which areas does the applicant need improvement? Why did the applicant leave? Did performance in the applicant's territory go up or down after he or she left? Generally employers give very positive references only to those people who deserve them and say little except to verify information about those whose performance was inadequate.

Most people list as references only those people who they are confident will give them a positive reference. In order to get a more balanced picture of the candidate, you can ask the reference for the names of several other people who would be familiar with the applicant's work. Also, if you are hiring salespeople with experience, the best reference source is the candidate's previous customers. They are best able to provide an accurate picture of what kind of salesperson the candidate is. Questions which should be asked are: How would you rank this person compared to other salespeople who currently call on you? Was this person genuinely interested in serving your needs? Was the candidate efficient and dependable?

A special source of outside information is the **credit report,** or a report from some other investigating agency. These agencies specialize in preemployment investigative interviews with former employers, co-workers, neighbors, and creditors. Reports from local credit bureaus, through their affiliation with their national association, can provide a wealth of information on a prospective salesperson. Often, former employers and other references give information to a credit bureau that they would not divulge to a prospective employer. Several companies—Equifax, Fidelifacts, Metropolitan New York, for example—specialize in providing preemployment data to employers. Using information from several different databases, they provide summaries of the applicant's financial condition, criminal and driving records, and employment history.[13]

---

## Drug Testing and Drug Use

One controversial issue related to the sales selection process today is whether an applicant should be tested for drug use before a hiring decision is made. If the answer is yes, then the next question is: If the applicant tests positive, is this an automatic knockout factor in the selection process? Or, if the applicant is otherwise highly qualified, will the person be hired with the understanding that he or she will undergo counseling or other drug treatment? Whatever the answers to these questions, this point seems clear: A company should have a clearly stated policy about drug testing and drug use for its sales force and also its sales managers. Despite their controversial nature, these are issues that sales managers will very likely have to face in the 1990s.*

*For a report on the extent and costs of the drug abuse problem in the nation's sales force, see W. E. Patton III, "Drug Abuse in the Sales Force," *Journal of Personal Selling & Sales Management,* August 1988, pp. 21–33.

---

Today, reference checks and other forms of background investigation are critical because, sad to say, too many job applicants lie about their backgrounds. Some applicants lie about their educational record, their past salaries, and/or their past job responsibilities. Career fraud—that's the fancy name for it—often goes undetected, simply because many companies don't take the time and effort needed to do a thorough background check.

### Legal Considerations

Essentially any inquiry which is illegal to ask a candidate directly is also illegal to ask a reference. All of the inquiries should be job related. One step which can be taken to lessen the legal liability which occurs in checking references is to ask the candidate to sign a release form which gives you permission to contact previous employers, educational institutions, and any others you may wish to contact. Employers may run credit checks on applicants without informing them. But if candidates are rejected on the basis of a credit check, they must be informed of this.

## ASSESSMENT CENTERS

The assessment-center technique is another hiring tool that a company can use as part of its sales force selection process. The main factor limiting the use of this technique is probably its high cost. The **assessment-center** technique is a centralized, comprehensive evaluation procedure involving tests, interviews, and simulation exercises such as business games, discussion groups, role playing, and individual presentations. This technique is conducted by trained executive observers and usually takes from one to three days. These observers then take another one to three days to evaluate the applicant–participants and their performance. Assessment centers have been used primarily to evaluate people for promotion within a firm, to aid in an individual's professional development, and

## AN INTERNATIONAL PERSPECTIVE

In the United States, most corporations are able to find qualified personnel for sales positions. However, when American companies go overseas it is often very difficult to find qualified salespeople. There are significant differences between the U.S. and foreign cultures that make selecting salespeople for international territories a complex problem. For example, in many foreign countries the amount of education that most people have is much more varied than in the United States, where 45 percent of the 18- to 21-year-olds have some form of college education. In developing countries in particular, there is a lack of college-educated personnel and technically trained personnel. Also ethnic background, religion, and social class all exert much more influence on business practices in foreign countries than in the United States. Thus matching the salesperson with the customer in terms of their socioeconomic backgrounds becomes more important. Below are a few examples of how the culture of the country makes the task of selecting salespeople more complicated:

- **Mexico, Peru, El Salvador.** These countries are characterized by ethnic diversity.

Skin color is often used to ascribe status (lighter-skinned people of European ancestry are preferred over the indigenous darker-skinned Indian people) and more respect is given to those of higher social status. Therefore, for salespeople to be effective, they must be selected to "match" their customers in terms of social status.

- **Belgium.** This country is comprised of people of either Flemish or French culture. In selecting salespeople it is important to choose those who speak both languages.
- **Malaysia.** Recruiters should be aware that there are social tensions between the Malays, who comprise 55 percent of the population, and the Chinese, who represent only 33 percent of the population but dominate business and commerce.
- **India.** A strong social caste system and a multitude of languages tend to fragment the market and make it difficult for reps to sell outside their own social and language groups.

Source: This discussion is based to a large extent on an article by John S. Hill and Meg Birdseye, "Salesperson Selection in Multinational Corporations: An Empirical Study," *Journal of Personal Selling & Sales Management*, Summer 1989, pp. 39–47.

to evaluate training programs. However, this technique also has been used in selecting new salespeople. For example, one company, using an assessment center, was able to accurately predict the performance of 79 percent of its newly hired salespeople.[14]

## REACHING A DECISION ABOUT AN APPLICANT

When all the steps in the selection process have been completed, one thing remains to be done. A company must decide whether to make a job offer. This decision involves a review of everything known about each applicant. What detailed impressions have they made? What are their qualifications, and what is their potential? What do they want, and what can the firm offer them? This last point is far broader than just the monetary aspects of the job. It involves all the hopes and ambitions of each applicant

**Recruiting reps for foreign assignments, whether they are nationals or internationals, is difficult.**

as matched against the opportunities and rewards offered by the job and the company.

At this stage, it is important that the company not leave any applicant dangling. If the firm clearly has decided *not* to hire a certain applicant, an executive should gently, but clearly, tell the person. To those applicants who are still in contention for the job, an executive might say something like this at the close of an interview: "As you know, we have several people applying for this position. My hope is that we will move along in the process and be able to notify you one way or another in two weeks."

If the decision is to hire a certain person, the next step is to make a formal offer and persuade the person to accept it. The actual hiring process, after an applicant has been selected, is covered in the following chapter along with assimilating the new rep into the company.

## SUMMARY

The last step in the sales force selection process involves (1) developing a system of tools and procedures to measure the applicants against the predetermined hiring specifications and then (2) actually putting this system into operation to select the salespeople. Processing applicants is a key activity in implementing a company's strategic planning. When using any selec-

tion tool, management must make certain that it is complying with all pertinent laws and regulatory guidelines.

The application blank and the personal interview are the two most widely used selection tools. A short application blank may be used as an initial screening device. A longer application blank is a primary source of personal history information that can be used in hiring and in other phases of sales operations. An application blank is an excellent tool for getting information in three major categories of job qualifications, namely, the applicant's physical condition, experience background, and environmental information.

The personal interview, which is the most widely used of all selection tools, is designed to answer four questions regarding an applicant: (1) Is the person capable of excelling at this job? (2) How badly does the person want the job? (3) Will the job help the person realize his or her goals? (4) Will the person work to his or her fullest ability?

Often interviews are not an accurate predictor of job performance because most people don't know how to interview. The predictive validity can be improved by using more than one interviewer, more than one interview, in more than one place. Training the interviewers, providing a reasonable amount of structure to the interview, and using behaviorally based interviews can also improve the process.

Interviews may vary according to (1) the degree to which the interviews are structured; (2) the degree to which the interviews are behaviorally based; (3) at what stages in the selection process the interviews are made.

Psychological testing is another major selection tool, and researchers consider it the best tool for predicting job performance. The most commonly used tests cover four areas—mental intelligence, aptitudes, interests, and personality. There are some problems in using tests as part of the hiring process. Also, testing is more likely to be successful when certain conditions exist.

Reference checks are widely used in the sales selection process. A personal visit or a phone call to a reference usually is a better method than letter writing. A key question to ask is whether the reference person would hire the applicant. Assessment centers were the final hiring tool discussed briefly in this chapter.

## Key Terms

Application blanks

Assessment centers

Bona fide occupational
 qualification (BFOQ)

Credit report

Environmental
 qualifications

Experience requirements

Personal interviews

Psychological tests

References

Selection

Validation

## ■ QUESTIONS AND PROBLEMS

1. "Careful selection is important but not essential in building an effective sales force. Improper selection of salespeople can be overcome by a good training program, sound supervision, or an excellent compensation program." Do you agree? Discuss.

2. One sales executive claims he "knows a good rep when he sees one," and therefore he does not like to be bothered by

so-called scientific selection processes. What can you offer to refute this claim? Would your answer be any different if you knew that this sales manager had a low rate of turnover in his sales force and was running a highly profitable operation?

3. " In the "Application for Sales Position" form that an aptitude testing firm has prepared, the following questions are

asked. In each case, what do you think is the purpose of the question?

*a.* What is the most monotonous task you ever did?

*b.* In people you like, what do you like about them?

*c.* What has been the outstanding disappointment in your life?

*d.* What is your best friend's strongest criticism of you?

4. How may the limitations of the interview be eliminated, reduced, or counterbalanced?

5. When interviewing an applicant for a sales job, management ordinarily should be vitally interested in complete answers to the following three points:

*a.* How badly does the applicant want or need the job?

*b.* Can the job furnish him with the success he wants or offer him the opportunity to realize his goals in life?

*c.* Will he strive to achieve the level of work his capacity will allow?

Prepare a series of questions an interviewer might ask with respect to each of these points.

6. What are the potential drawbacks in soliciting references from a candidate's former customers?

7. Can you eliminate the personal biases and prejudices of interviewers so they will conduct an interview impartially?

8. Suppose that halfway through your interview for a job in which you are very interested, the interviewer says "I don't think you are right for this job." How would you respond?

9. What is the point of asking a recruit during an interview, "How many golf balls would it take to fill the swimming pool used at the Atlanta Olympics?"

10. The following traits are generally considered undesirable in a salesperson. What tools can management use to determine whether an applicant possesses any of these characteristics? If you feel that an interview or application blank can be used in this case, what questions should be asked?

*a.* Failed in a business.

*b.* Has a history of not staying in one job very long.

*c.* Was not able to pass an insurance physical examination.

*d.* Has financial problems.

*e.* Does not get along well with other people; is the lone-wolf type.

11. Under what conditions would you recommend that a company use a battery of tests as part of its procedures for selecting salespeople?

12. What are some of the problems or dangers in using tests as part of the sales force selection process?

13. Many sales managers claim that the real factor that determines whether people will be successful in selling is their motivation for hard work. Where is this motivational factor measured in psychological testing? How should sales managers determine a person's motivation to do a good job?

14. Some managers believe that the reference is not very helpful as a selection tool. Do you agree with this appraisal? If so, why do you think it continues to be used by virtually every firm that is hiring salespeople or other employees?

15. How could a candidate's ethical standards be evaluated in the interview process?

## ■ EXPERIENTIAL EXERCISES

**A.** Interview three recruiters from three different companies. (These should be companies with whom *you will not have interviews.*) Ask them to describe the qualities they are looking for in the candidates they interview. Ask them what questions, exercises, and/or other strategies they use to get at this information.

**B.** Soon many of you will be interviewed by companies that recruit graduating students. The interviewer might ask the following questions. What is each question trying to determine, and how would you answer it?

*a.* Why do you want to work for this company?

*b.* Why should we hire you?

*c.* How much do you hope to be earning in three years?

*d.* If you come to work for us, what kind of a job do you expect to have with us in three years?

## ■ REFERENCES

1. C. David Shepard and James C. Heartfield, "Discrimination Issues in the Selection of Salespeople: A Review and Managerial Suggestions," *Journal of Personal Selling & Sales Management* (Fall 1991), pp. 67–75.

2. Myron Gable, Charles Hollon, and Frank Dangello, "Increasing the Utility of the Application Blank: Relationship between Job Application and Turnover of Salespeople," *Journal of Personal Selling & Sales Management* (Summer 1992), pp. 39–55.

3. E. James Randall and Cindy H. Randall, "Review of Salesperson Selection Techniques and Criteria: A Managerial Approach," *International Journal of Research in Marketing* 7 (1990), pp. 81–95.

4. Julia Lawlor, "Highly Classified," *Sales & Marketing Management,* March 1995, pp. 75–85; and Jeff A. Weekly and Joseph A. Gier, "Reliability and Validity of the Situational Interview for a Sales Position," *Journal of Applied Psychology* 72 (1987), pp. 484–87.

5. "All the Right Moves for Interviewers," *Business Week,* September 17, 1990, p. 156; and

James M. Jenks and Brian L. P. Zevnik, "ABCs of Job Interviewing," *Harvard Business Review,* July-August 1989, pp. 38–42.

6. William Keenan Jr., "Who Has the Right Stuff?" *Sales & Marketing Management,* August 1993, pp. 28–29.

7. Nina Munk and Suzanne Oliver, "Think Fast," *Forbes,* March 24, 1997, pp. 146–51.

8. William Keenan Jr., "Time is Everything," *Sales & Marketing Management,* August 1993, pp. 60–63.

9. Richard Nelson, "Maybe It's Time to Take Another Look at Tests as a Selection Tool?" *Journal of Personal Selling & Sales Management,* August 1987, pp. 33–38.

10. Geoffrey Brewer, "Professionally Speaking," *Sales & Marketing Management,* February 1996, p. 27.

11. Kate Betrand, "Hiring Tests: Sales Manager's Dream or Nightmare?" *Business Marketing,* July 1990, pp. 36–42.

12. For additional information on evaluating and using tests, see "Standards for Educational and Psychological Testing," from the American

Psychological Association, Washington, DC; and "Principles for Validation and Use of Personal Selection Procedures," from the Society for Industrial and Organizational Psychology Association Inc., an American Psychological Association division in Arlington Heights, IL.

13. Jeffery Rothfeder, "Looking for a Job? You May Be Out Before You Go In," *Business Week,* September 24, 1990, pp. 128, 130.

14. E. James Randall and Cindy H. Randall, "Review of Salesperson Selection Techniques and Criteria: A Managerial Approach," *International Journal of Research in Marketing* 7 (1990), pp. 81–95.

---

*Case 6-1*

## THE SWEET HOME WOOD PRODUCTS COMPANY

### Selecting a sales representative

"You're putting me on, now aren't you? These aren't really the three choices you've come down to, are they? You're either testing me or teasing me. Which is it?" Earl Goddard, president of The Sweet Home Wood Products Company of Sweet Home, Oregon, was quizzing his operations manager, Wes Wilson, about the three individuals whose names had been submitted for Goddard's consideration to hire as the firm's sales rep in Southern California.

The company had been formed in 1950. Among its first products were cedar shingles, which found widespread acceptance in the huge and rapidly growing Southern California real estate market of the 1950s. However, during the 1970s and 1980s wood shingles came under attack from many sources. Fire departments strongly recommended that they be banned since they had proven to be great fire hazards during the annual fire season suffered each summer and fall by the residents of the area. Insurance companies, consumer advocates, and various legislators strongly opposed their use in both the new construction and replacement markets. Many people who owned homes with wood shingles sought to replace them with fireproof shingles.

Many firms rushed into the market with some form of concrete shingles. However, there were some problems. The concrete shingles were heavier, often much heavier, than wood shingles, thus preventing their use on most houses. The structures had not been engineered to support such weight loads. Moreover, the early concrete shingles were brittle and thus would break when walked upon by the various repair people who had to go on the roofs. Moreover, since they had no nail-holding power, holes had to be drilled through the concrete so they could be attached to the roof nailing strips.

Earl had studied the problem for several years and had continually experimented with new forms of shingles that would answer all of these problems. In the late 1980s he had perfected a process to produce shingles made by bonding wood fibers with cement, such as is used to make concrete. The resulting product was fireproof, long lasting, resilient, held nails, and was light in weight. While the new shingle was slightly heavier than dry wood shakes, it was much lighter than wet wood shakes. Wood shakes gain much water weight during rains and damp weather, whereas the new shingle did not absorb any water. Thus the new shingle could be used to replace wood shakes without structural strengthening. Earl called the new shingle Cemwood. Several product line extensions using the new technology formed the bulk of the company's sales in the early 1990s. It was this product line that the new sales rep would be selling in Southern California.

All sales were made through reputable roofing contractors. The job entailed working closely with the roofing contractors in selling the product to large customers. A rep had to train the roofer's employees in proper installation techniques and troubleshooting tasks; respond to customers' warranty claims; and educate the fire and building authorities, the zoning commissions, and the politicians about the virtues of Cemwood. For example, during the past month the San Diego sales rep had helped Mike Petronelli, owner of Petronelli Roofing Company, make a sale of Cemwood shingles for reroofing 500 homes in a gated planned community. The total volume was 12,500 squares of shingles (a square is 100 square feet) for a shingle sales value of about $4 million over the next four years. At the same time, a previous customer had complained that the Cemwood shingles that had just been installed were discoloring, turning white. The sales rep inspected the job and discovered that the white coloring was the result of the alkali leaching out as a result of the cement curing. The shingles had been rushed to the job without sufficient time to cure properly. The discoloration would disappear—wash out—with the rains. On another job the sales rep had to solve a problem caused by improper installation; he spent half a day training the roofers to handle such problems.

The job paid a salary of $50,000 a year, plus a bonus based on company profitability. All expenses were paid. The previous sales rep had resigned to form his own roofing company in Ventura, California.

Earl continued, "How in the world is it possible for you to come up with three such different people for me to pick from? It seems to me that the job forces us to hire people just like the ones we now have—ones that have been so successful. We have the pattern, let's just use it."

Wes waited to make sure that Earl was through talking before trying to answer any of the questions posed him. "No, I'm not pulling your leg. No, I am not teasing you or testing you. It's no joke. This is serious stuff. Take a good look at these three people. Each has a good case."

"I have! One's an old man, one's a pushy female, and one's a college dude who wants my job. Come on, they can't all be equal candidates for the job. What gives?" Earl asked.

"Each has a story. Depends on what we want to buy!" Wes explained.

"Why don't you save me some time and tell me the case for each of them. What about the old man? We can't have a 60-year-old guy climbing around on roofs. It's too dangerous. And how many years is he going to work for us?" Earl began.

"You're referring to Boris, of course, and you ought to look at him. They aren't making 60-year-olds like they used to. He's in great physical shape. Stronger than either of us. I know that isn't saying much, but this guy is a physical specimen. Pumps iron, takes pills, runs forever, looks like he's 40! But that's not his story. The fact is that this guy has been in roofing all his life and he really knows it inside out. All his former employers say nothing but good about him. His sales record has been outstanding. He tried retiring but couldn't stand it. Says he's going to work till he drops. The guy can do a great job for us."

"So hire him! Why look at the next two?" Earl asked.

"Good question. Perhaps I can answer it. Let's consider Eric first. He's got it all. He's smart, ambitious, personable, has good work habits and values, everything you want your kid to be. I think he is management material and you know how thin we are in the ranks of management. We need more managers to support our growth. Look at the quality control problems we've been having in trying to expand production. That happened because we had some management decisions being made by the warehouse workers. Eric can be with us here in Sweet Home after two or three years in sales. Maybe sooner!"

"Then, why not hire him as a management trainee and forget him as a sales trainee?" Earl inquired.

Wes replied, "You know the budget won't allow it right now. Maybe we can slot a trainee in for next year but by then Eric will be working elsewhere. This is what we have for him right now and it has the compensation he needs. He won't come for a trainee's pay."

"OK! Now let's talk about Beth," Earl urged.

Wes responded, "Beth is a hard-working, down-to-earth person who needs to work for a living to support her family. She's tough physically; she has worked in construction and on roofs for some time. All her previous employers speak highly of her and I have talked with them personally. She is currently selling tile for VIP Tile company and is their top producer, but she isn't satisfied with her pay. We can pay her substantially more. She lives right in the middle of the territory so she won't have to move. Her kids are grown, but her husband is an invalid, and they need income. She is a very determined lady. Everyone who interviewed her came away with the feeling that she would and could do the job. So there we are. Three great prospective hires and enough money to hire only one of them. What do you want to do, boss?"

**Question:**

Which person would you first try to hire?

---

*Case 6-2*

### DELTA PRODUCTS COMPANY
#### Selection of sales representation

"We were formerly employed at TRW—Jim was in microelectronics marketing as a salesperson, and I worked inside to provide technical assistance and service to Jim's accounts. We were a team. Our division was directly hit with the defense and aerospace reductions in 1993. We were terminated. They call us displaced workers." Christina Alvarez, with her partner Jim Reynolds, were explaining their sales proposition to Tom Shilling, marketing manager for the Delta Products Company.

She continued, "But we have had enough of working for other companies. We decided to form our own marketing company, Pacific Technical Sales. We will do for other companies exactly what we did for TRW. That is, we will sell microelectronic devices, except we will do it for a commission instead of a salary and all the benefits. And we'll do it for several noncompeting companies. You will not sell anything for another company that you are prepared to make. No conflicts of interest!"

Jim Reynolds came in on cue. "We propose to represent your firm in California, Arizona, and Nevada for a commission base of 5 percent. That rate will be renegotiated for significant contracts in which highly competitive bidding is encountered."

Tom Shilling asked, "And what about business that walks through our door in which you played no role?"

Christina replied, "Each week we would furnish you a list of the firms that we have contacted and we would be protected on those accounts for six months. Everything is spelled out in this portfolio that explains who we are, what we have done, and what we can do for you."

"I know you need time to consider our proposal for it is a departure from your previous policy of having your own salesperson in the field. However, since your local sales rep no longer is with you and market conditions have changed considerably, we think you should consider retaining our firm instead of hiring another salesperson," Jim declared. He continued, "Is it convenient for you to see us next Monday morning at 11 for your answer?"

Tom studied his bulging day book and replied, "Monday is really bad for me. I'm all jammed up. Besides, I need more time to consult with the boss about it. This would be a pretty big change for us to make. I can hire salespeople without talking it over with anyone, but you are another matter. No, I'll have to do a lot of talking with some people before I can give you an answer. Let's make it next Thursday morning at 11."

Alvarez and Reynolds departed as Shilling rose and cordially walked them to the front door. He said, "I'll take your portfolio home tonight and give it a close look and tomorrow I'll get with Mr. Gross, our president, about it."

Shilling intended to encourage the two people because he faced a serious problem

trying to maintain field sales representation in the highly competitive, declining markets being faced.

Delta Products Company designed and manufactured small electronic devices for other manufacturers that incorporated them into whatever products they made. It did business all over the world; international sales accounted for 35 percent of its business. Sales in California, Arizona, and Nevada had accounted for about 10 percent of its sales during the 1980s but had dropped to only 4 percent by 1993 because of the firm's historical dependence on sales to firms in the defense and aerospace industries. Tom had already started strong sales programs to solicit business from new accounts outside the defense/aerospace industry.

However, the cost of the field sales force had become a burden. Shilling had terminated the firm's salesperson, Herb Hawkins, for the California/Arizona/Nevada region. Herb's selling costs had soared way out of line because of a significant drop in sales in the region. His total selling costs for 1992 had been $192,466, of which $85,000 had been his salary. No bonuses had been paid since his performance had been below expectations. The bulk of his expenses had been for automotive and entertainment costs. Herb had been with Delta since its inception in 1972. He was its leading producer for years when his territory was the focus of much defense and aerospace activity.

In a rather disturbing meeting with Herb, Jim had reviewed the situation with him and declared that the company could no longer afford $192,000 to cover his territory. He then told Herb that the firm could afford to pay only 5 percent of sales for field-selling costs. Based on Herb's 1992 sales volume, this meant a total cost of $116,000. Consequently, he had told Herb that his 1994 salary would be $50,000 plus some bonuses for meeting quotas, with an expense allowance not to exceed $60,000. No more lavish entertaining and no more paying more than $30,000 for a car! Herb had a strong preference for driving an expensive car, a vehicle costing well in excess of what could be deducted for income tax purposes.

Herb had rejected the offer. Since he was 63 years old, he had decided to take early retirement. The combination of his company pension plan, his savings, and Social Security exceeded what was being offered him, so he retired.

Shilling did not immediately begin a search for Herb's replacement. He felt that he could use the savings from not having a salesperson in the area to help meet his budget deficits for the year. He was in no hurry to replace Herb since he felt he and the staff could serve the existing accounts from the home office in Redondo Beach, California. However, while attending a trade show Shilling had occasion to renew acquaintance with Brian Snowcroft, with whom he had worked closely when they both were at Hughes Aircraft in the early 1970s. He thought highly of Brian's talents and knowledge of the industry. He recalled Brian's background: He had graduated from Arizona State with a degree in electrical engineering. After starting to work for Hughes in Tucson, Arizona, on a classified technical project, he had been thrust into contract relationships because of his excellent customer skills. He enjoyed great success with Hughes but was about to be put adrift due to the cutbacks Hughes was making. He was looking for work. He had only three more months before he was going to be on the street looking for work.

Shilling told Brian of his situation with Herb and asked him if he would be interested in it. Brian did not say no, and he was not indignant when told of the reduced compensation package. He was told he would not have to move to Redondo Beach but could cover the territory from his home in Tucson. It was left that, if Brian was interested in the job and wanted to talk about it some more, he would call Shilling.

Sunday night Tom Shilling settled down in his lounge chair to study the Alvarez–Reynolds proposal. He was impressed with it. Friday afternoon he had called a friend of his at TRW to ask her to investigate the records of both Alverez and Reynolds at TRW. She had reported back within the hour that their records were spotless. They were both well thought of and highly recommended. They had been terminated only because of the cutback of all employees.

As he was thinking about the matter the telephone rang. It was Brian Snowcroft. He had been laid off that afternoon, much sooner than he had anticipated. He was now interested in the job. However, he said that he would have to have a minimum salary of $65,000 to be able to survive financially. He said that he had been making in excess of $85,000 a year for the past five years. With his high fixed costs plus having two kids in college, he needed more than $65,000 a year to stay financially above water.

The two men talked for more than 30 minutes about the job and the situation. Shilling let Brian know that he was also under great financial pressure and was being forced to make some cutbacks that he was reluctant to make, but such were the times. Shilling signed off by saying that he would get back to Brian the following week.

In a way Shilling was grateful that Brian had called for it helped him focus his thinking on the problem at hand. The thought crossed his mind that perhaps he should abandon efforts to fill the position with an experienced salesperson and hire a beginner right out of an engineering college, someone he could pay a beginning salary of perhaps $25,000 a year. However, he wondered if the additional delay of having to start a search for a college graduate might upset his boss, who had indicated some apprehension over the firm's lack of a sales rep in the area. Tom did not want to look indecisive.

He rose from his chair to go to the window to gaze at the blue Pacific below him as he pondered the problem.

*Questions:*

What course of action should Tom Shilling follow regarding the vacant position?

---

*Case 6-3*

### BAY AUTOMOTIVE PARTS CENTER
#### Selection of inside salesperson

"The job calls for someone with a great telephone voice and an easy way of talking with people. I want someone our customers will really want to talk with," Bill Monk, owner of Bay Automotive Parts Center, declared to Linda, his partner and spouse.

Linda was in charge of office operations, which included handling all incoming sales orders. Bill handled the outside sales operations while their three children, Ken, Kay, and Kate, ages 25, 27, and 29, respectively, ran the distribution center. Kate was in charge of purchasing and inventory management. Kay managed warehouse operations and order picking. Ken managed the receiving and shipping department. Much to their parents' dismay, none of their offspring had much interest in the sales end of the business.

Each time an opening on the three-person inside sales force came up, Linda had pressured her children to get some experience in sales. She thought that their taking turns on the inside sales desk would be good training. They resisted her overtures. They maintained that it was too important a job for their inexperienced efforts. Moreover, none of the children was blessed with a good speaking voice. Consequently, Bay Automotive was looking for an inside salesperson to

fill the vacancy that developed when Sal Nunzio retired.

Bay Automotive Parts Center of Baltimore, Maryland, was a large independent distributor of automotive parts in the Chesapeake Bay area, with sales in excess of $25 million a year. It had an outside sales force of five reps who called on local area garages and parts dealers. Bill handled the significant accounts himself. However, on a day-to-day basis the bulk of the orders came in by telephone to people who took the orders. Normally, the three inside salespeople could handle the incoming orders, but usually there were times during the day when Linda and/or Bill would have to handle some overload calls.

Linda, resigned to selecting a new inside salesperson, had considered 11 people for the job, two people from within the firm and nine recruited from other sources. From those people, Linda had narrowed her choices to three people, each of whom represented different prototypes for the job.

First, there was Larry, an older man with considerable experience in the automotive business, both in repair and in parts sales. For the previous two years he had worked the inside desk for a parts distributor in Detroit. He quit that job to move to

Baltimore to be closer to his children and grandchildren. He knew the auto parts business and was considered by his previous employers to be a reliable employee. He could go to work immediately with little training. The firm's compensation package, which was slightly below the market for such jobs, was satisfactory to him. He was ready to go to work.

The second person under consideration was Dorothy, who was working in a telemarketing "boiler room" selling health insurance. She was good at it but disliked what she was selling. She voiced serious concerns about the scripts she had to read to the prospects. She had said in her interview, "I want to sell legitimate products to people who really need them."

Dorothy was a local person who had graduated in 1990 from the University of Maryland, majoring in the dramatic arts. Her speaking voice and stage presence were superb. She was quick-witted and able to handle herself quite well with all sorts of people. While she had shown a slight surprise at the firm's compensation package, she seemed to accept it. Linda wondered how long Dorothy would stay interested in the job. But she thought that whatever that time would be, it would be well worth it for what she and the other people would learn from her about telemarketing. Linda secretly hoped some of Dorothy's polish would rub off on Kay and Kate.

The third person being considered was Bill Cassidy, who had worked for Bay Automotive for more than 10 years in various capacities. He was currently filling orders and reported to Kay Monk. When he learned of the vacancy, Bill came to Linda and said he wanted the job. He was sure he could do it, he wanted the higher earnings, and he wanted to get into sales and develop his skills. He had been a loyal worker with good work habits. The Monks held him in high regard and really wanted to help him but were not certain that this was the best way to do it—for either him or the firm. While Bill had helped out on incoming sales calls when things got too busy for the regular crew to handle, he was not famous for having a melodious voice.

Linda assembled what she had developed on each of the candidates for the job and laid the information before the family after an evening meal. An extensive discussion followed. Each candidate had his or her supporters. Ken really liked Dorothy but for the wrong reasons. Finally Bill said, "As I see it, it comes down to a question of (1) do we hire an old parts pro who knows what to do and can do it now, (2) do we go for the modern telemarketing professional who might be able to teach us a thing or two, or (3) do we reward our loyal employee and friend who wants to improve himself. Is that it?"

They all nodded in agreement and then tried to avoid making a decision.

*Question:*

Who should be selected for the job?

# CHAPTER 7

# Hiring and Socializing New Salespeople

You can't build a business if you have a revolving door.
**Harvey McKay**

The costly recruiting and selection process can be completely nullified if the person or people selected do not accept the firm's offer of a sales job. If they do come to work for the company, all efforts can be undone if the recruits are not properly integrated into the organization. This chapter covers the hiring and introduction of the new person into the work group. People are often more motivated by social than economic forces. We will show how this affects their reactions to their initial relationships with superiors and co-workers.

## ◼ HIRING[1]

Selection and **hiring** are not synonymous. Often the firm's job offer is rejected. Naturally, the rejection rate varies tremendously among firms, depending upon the attractiveness of the job offered. For firms offering relatively low-paid, routine selling jobs with little potential, the acceptance rate may be less than 10 percent. This places great pressure on the sales manager to generate a large number of acceptable recruits. At the other end of the scale, some sales jobs are so attractive that rejections are rare. The rejection rate is also partially a result of how well the hiring process is executed.

The time involved in the hiring process directly affects its efficiency. If you are slow in making offers, some recruits will accept other offers because they cannot afford to gamble on getting yours.

A well-designed hiring process properly implemented tells the recruit that the firm is well managed and that it really wants the recruit as an employee. Sometimes firms inadvertently send a message of indifference to the recruit: "It's no big deal one way or the other to us if you take the job." Remember that everyone likes to feel important. As a result, people seek work environments in which they are made to feel that they somehow make a difference; that they are important to the company.

## Preoffer Planning

Some thought should be given to the offer process before actual recruit contacts begin. First, the acceptable recruits should be ranked. Next, some thought should be given to how the offer(s) will be extended. Finally, contingency plans should be developed.

### Ranking the Recruits

Two lists should be developed: the first is a list of the recruits in the order of the firm's preference for them; the second is a list of the recruits in the order of their preference for the firm. The second list can be developed by the firm's interviewers, based on how interested the recruits seemed in joining the firm during the interviews.

A dilemma arises when the person the firm wants most is not interested in the job. Does the firm waste time making offers to recruits who are unlikely to accept them? This takes time that might be spent in making offers to candidates who are more likely to accept them. Such judgments must be made by the sales manager on the basis of the situation. The decision depends on the depth of the list, the decrease in quality as people of lesser rank are considered, how much money is involved, the time factors faced by the recruits and the sales managers, and competing offers from other firms. A sales manager often finds the labor market highly competitive. Recruits may have other attractive offers to which they must respond promptly. As a result, the manager is under pressure to make offers to people who are likely to accept them. The time pressures under which the manager operates frequently dictate what offers are made, often to the detriment of the hiring process.

### What Will Be Included in the Offer?

Of course the most important part of the offer is the compensation which the salesperson will be paid. The type and amount of compensation is covered in detail in Chapter 10. The offer should also include the other benefits which will be part of the employment package. These might include any or all of the following: insurance, retirement contributions, vacation pay, educational benefits, profit sharing, a company car.

In many cases, to alleviate some of the inconveniences of moving, the new employee's moving and relocation expenses are also paid. Most large companies usually pay for the following moving expenses when they transfer employees:

- Packing and moving all household furnishings and equipment, with insurance to cover any damage.
- Meals, lodgings, and first-class transportation by land or air for the entire family and for family pets.
- Brokers' commissions and legal fees for buying or selling homes.

- Entire expense of housing the employee and family in a hotel for several weeks after arrival. Thereafter the company pays the difference between charges for hotel rooms and normal rental costs if other living space has not been found.

- Installation of appliances in the new home and allowances toward refitting draperies, carpeting, and blinds.

- A reasonable number of personal trips between the new and old location when the employee is separated from the family for a long time.

- A trip for the spouse to visit the new location to look for a new house and expenses while house hunting.

Moving people into certain high-cost urban areas such as southern California, Washington, DC, New York City, and the San Francisco area poses a serious economic problem to both the firm and the employee. Often the economics of the situation make it difficult for new employees to move into such areas and maintain their previous standard of living. Moreover, firms may find it quite expensive to move their people into such areas because they must offer cost-of-living allowances, mortgage interest differential payments, and tax bonuses in order to induce employees to accept assignments in these high-cost areas. To avoid these problems, many firms today meet their personnel needs in high-cost areas by hiring people already living in the area. This avoids the economic aspects of relocation as well as the social ones.

A number of firms are also offering to help the potential employee's spouse or significant other find a job. While this may not necessarily need to be a part of the formal offer, it may be a very important consideration in the candidate's decision. As more families have two people who are pursuing careers, it is important that both people are able to find good employment opportunities in the same location. If an employer is willing to help the other person identify job opportunities, this will certainly create a very positive impression on the candidate. Moreover, if the spouse or significant other is able to find employment, it may be the factor which causes the recruit to accept one firm's offer over another attractive offer.[2]

### How Will the Offer Be Extended?

Who will make the offer? How will it be made? Will a contract be offered? Some firms want the sales manager for whom the recruit will be working to make the offer. Other firms leave such matters to professionals in the human resources department. Sometimes higher-level executives, even the company president, may make the offer in the hope of impressing the recruit with the importance of the job offer.

Most job offers are initially made over the telephone. Before making that call, it is important for the sales manager to make two decisions: How much time will be allowed for acceptance and what concessions will be made if the recruit wants to negotiate some of the terms of the deal. Once

---

## AN INTERNATIONAL PERSPECTIVE

A new job not only affects the person accepting the job; it may affect two, three, or four other people as well. Certainly the person with the new position welcomes the opportunity. However, the spouse may face leaving a good job for a lesser position or, even worse, no job. Their children too are affected by the need to leave their schools and friends. When the new position is a foreign one, these problems are compounded by the challenge of facing an unfamiliar culture. If candidates feel that their families will be unhappy, they may not accept the offer. The National Foreign Trade Council reports that 81 percent of relocation candidates turn down the opportunity because of family-related problems.

To attract salespeople to foreign assignments, the company must provide support for the entire family. In some cases, financial support may not be as important as helping the spouse find a job or helping the family find schools for the children. It is also important that the company provide the family with predeparture cultural training so that their expectations will be realistic.

Source: Michele Marchetti, "Enticing Families to Move Overseas," *Sales & Marketing Management,* September 1996, pp. 44–45.

---

on the telephone, the manager will have to make some quick decisions about these matters. Prior consideration greatly facilitates a smooth telephone offer. A formal letter follows only if the telephone offer is accepted. This letter is very important and requires careful wording since it becomes a contract.

Aggressive managers often prefer to make job offers in person. This puts more pressure on the recruit to respond favorably and quickly. It is quite easy for the recruit to avoid giving direct answers over the telephone. Moreover, the telephone does not allow the manager to "read" the recruit's body language to make additional judgments about the negotiations.

### Extending the Offer

Many small, but important, details must be anticipated in making the offer. Experience dictates a process that a manager should follow to seem professional in the eyes of the recruit (see Figure 7-1).

First, *review the job*. Go over the job opportunity with the recruit. Details are easily forgotten. Recruits can be overloaded with so much information from several companies that they forget the specifics of your job opening. Be careful not to oversell the job at this point, and do not make promises you can't keep. Always be able to deliver more than you promise.

Then, *ask for questions*. Now let the recruit talk. This is the time to clear away any misunderstandings about the job. Possible objections may be detected at this point from the questions being asked. Answer the questions as if the recruit had the job: "Yes, your expense account would be unlimited."

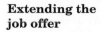

**Extending the
job offer**

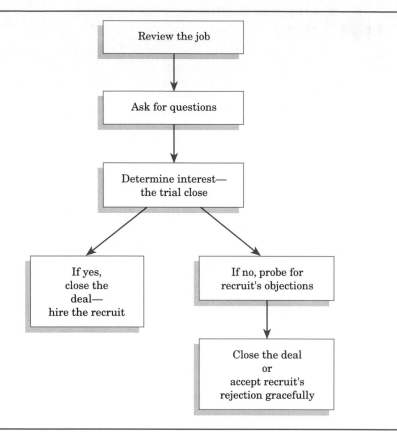

Next, try to *determine interest*. In selling, it is called a *trial close*. "Are you interested in working for us? Do you want the job?" Such questions should bring out whatever objections are lurking in the recruit's mind.[3]

If the recruit seems to have a positive interest in the job, then a question such as, "If we made you an offer, would you accept it?" is appropriate. If a yes answer is given, the deal can be closed. If the answer is no, the manager may want to *probe for objections*. What is blocking the deal? Sometimes little problems that can be easily answered stand in the way of final acceptance.

Many times the recruit will stall. Perhaps some other offers are pending. The person will accept your job offer if another offer is not received. Such situations don't do much for the manager's ego, but they exist and must be tolerated. After all, if no else wanted to hire the person you selected, you might have reason to question your choice. Few things make the manager's competitive juices run as much as seeking a sales rep that other companies also want. Questions such as, "Can you give me an answer by Friday?" may help pin down the recruit to your schedule.

*A Day-to-Day Operating Problem*

**MAJESTIC PLASTICS COMPANY (D)**

### Extending a job offer

"I need some time to think about your offer, Mr. Brion. I feel that changing jobs is a serious matter and don't want to act precipitously. It does appeal to me and definitely would be a step up for me. Can I give you an answer March 1st?" asked Sharon Axe in her reply to Clyde Brion's job offer over the telephone on a dreary day in early February 1990.

Brion had been under considerable pressure from his boss to hire a woman sales rep for the sales territory that had been vacated when one of the firm's older reps had retired. He had recruited and interviewed four experienced saleswomen, all of whom were qualified for the job. However, Axe stood out as the most promising person for the job.

After consultation with his boss, Brion had called Sharon to make her the firm's standard job offer. He was somewhat surprised with her

request for time to think about it; he thought that she wanted the job and was eager to get going.

He also was eager to get the position filled because many of the accounts in the territory had voiced some concern about the company's inattention to their needs during the past few weeks. Brion had been trying to cover the territory as best he could, but the time he could spend doing it was limited.

Brion stalled for a few moments, making some pleasant remarks about how happy he was that she liked Majestic Plastics, but he had to give her a reply *now*.

**Question:** Exactly what should Clyde Brion say to Sharon Axe?

Note: See the introduction to this series of problems in Chapter 4 for the necessary background on the company, its market, and its competition.

---

If the recruit rejects the offer, the manager should *accept the decision with grace.* Don't make the person feel guilty with some comment such as, "If you won't accept our offer, why did you apply with us?"

 ## SOCIALIZATION

**Socialization** is the process through which the new recruits take on the values and attitudes of the people who are already working for the firm. This process begins before recruits go to work for the company and continues until they are fully assimilated into the company's culture. Successful socialization of recruits and new salespeople helps them adjust to their new jobs. More important, it also leads to salespeople being more involved and satisfied with their jobs in the long run.

### Preemployment Socialization

Before accepting the offer and during the preemployment period, the recruits will start thinking about the experiences they are about to encounter, and they will begin to prepare themselves mentally. It is critical that the candidates be provided with realistic **job previews** which allow them to make informed employment decisions. Providing the recruit accurate information about the job and the company helps him or her to have realistic expectations about the challenges to be faced and the level of effort and the kinds of skills required to meet these challenges (see Figure 7-2). If the recruit accepts the offer, this realism at the preemployment stage will lead to greater satisfaction with the job and commitment to the company.[4]

Most firms start indoctrinating the recruit the minute initial contact is made. Booklets describe the operations of the company and its distinctive qualities. These publications are part of the recruiting process described in Chapter 5. Further introductory work is done in the selection interviews, as shown in Chapter 6. The sales executive describes many aspects of the company's operations and answers the recruit's questions. If these activities are thorough, trainees will know something about the organization before starting work.

Many firms go a step further in presenting a realistic picture by asking the recruit to view a videotape of the salesperson on the job. Northwestern Mutual Life, IBM, and Deloitte and Touche are among the firms providing the recruits with interactive diskettes which are filled with information on the job and the company. Deloitte and Touche information categories include information on the company's mission and shared values statement, an overview of the firm, details on training, employee benefits, and professional development opportunities.[5] Some firms ask recruits to spend a day making calls with a salesperson so that they will have a more realistic perspective of what the job entails.

Procter & Gamble, Ford Motor Co., American Express, Dow Brands, Northern Telecom, and many other companies that hire college graduates for sales positions offer summer internships for students. These internships allow the student to learn about the company before they must make a long-term commitment. Likewise, many of these companies are relying

■ **FIGURE 7-2**     **Details of the Job**

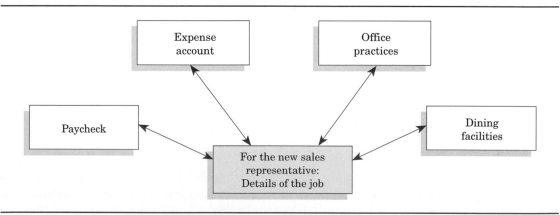

more on internships to help them assess whether the potential employees can do the job and whether they fit into the culture of the company.[6]

The more recruits understand about the company and its culture before making a decision, the more effective their self-selection will be. That is, those people who fit in the company's culture are more likely to accept the offer than those who don't. Also, the more information recruits get at this stage, the smoother their assimilation into the organization will be.

## Assimilation

The second stage in the socialization process begins when the recruits accept the position. Now they must be **assimilated** into the organization. They must learn how to perform the tasks associated with their jobs and they must become familiar with the people in various work groups with whom they must interact in order to do their jobs effectively. In many companies a great deal of this information will be covered in an initial training program. However, the socialization that should take place at this stage cannot be accomplished exclusively through training. There must be a conscious effort made to provide recruits with information, experience, and the personal attention which will enable them to understand the informal as well as the formal norms and values of the corporate culture. Various orientation programs and policies which help the firm do this are described below.

## ORIENTATION INFORMATION

Some firms prepare detailed booklets about the company's history, the executives, the product line, and the various financial, health, and recreational programs available. If such a publication is given to the recruit when he or she is hired, the recruit can read and absorb its contents before coming to work. This information will help the newcomer begin to feel like a member of the organization. Immediately on reporting for work, there are several issues which should be covered as part of the employee's orientation.

### The Paycheck

The pocketbook is a quick way to a good attitude. Misunderstandings concerning the paycheck can make anyone suspicious. It is discouraging for a sales trainee, who knows his or her earnings are $1,800 a month, to receive a check for $1,370. The rep realizes that some income tax and social security tax must come out of the $1,800 but feels that "There must be some error; taxes wouldn't be that much." A trainee should be told when and how payment will be made. All deductions should be itemized so that the rep knows exactly what to expect.

**This new rep gets a warm welcome.**

Firms that pay their salespeople on a straight commission often provide reps, particularly new ones, with a *drawing account,* which should be explained in detail. Such accounts allow the person to draw money from the company in anticipation of future commissions. Some of the pertinent problems are:

- What happens if the rep gets too far in debt?
- What happens if the rep leaves the company while still owing money on the drawing account?
- Just how are future commissions used to offset the money advanced?

## The Expense Account

Serious misunderstandings can arise over expense accounts. The new rep must be told precisely what can and cannot be put on the expense sheet and in what manner the money will be paid. Can it be drawn prior to incurring the expenses or will it be paid after filing the report?

If certain tacit limitations are placed on various items, these should be made clear. The manager also might tell new employees how to recover money spent on selling expenses that do not clearly fall in allowable categories but nevertheless were incurred working for the firm.

## Office Practices

Office facilities and supplies should be checked to see that the new rep has everything needed and knows how to replenish supplies. Some office practices and policies do not have official sanction but nevertheless have considerable force. Most groups have informal policies on gift funds, betting, parties, and other activities incidental to the job. The new employee should be briefed on these by a co-worker. If the manager did so, it might seem to give them official sanction. When the boss explains the TGIF (Thank God It's Friday) get-togethers, for example, the employee may feel that he or she must participate.

## Dining Facilities

If the company maintains dining facilities, their use should be explained. New sales reps need to know if they can use the executive dining room to entertain customers. Some firms make arrangements with restaurants to accommodate the sales force and their customers, with the bill forwarded directly to the firm. These arrangements also need to be explained.

## What Is Going to Happen Next?

Trainees are eager to know as much as possible about what the company plans to do with them. They greatly appreciate a schedule of their training. Imagine the impact made by the manager who briefly discusses a vague or generalized training program, in contrast to that of the manager who tells the trainee precisely what will happen during the next few weeks.

The new person's status in the firm must be made clear to everyone. To accomplish this, many firms distribute an information sheet on each new employee that tells what he or she will be doing for the company.

A new rep needs to know from whom to take orders. The entire organizational plan should be explained so the rep knows his or her relationship to others, who else reports to the rep's immediate boss, and who the boss reports to in the department and the company. The support staff must be informed of their relationship to the new person. Those who report to the same boss must become acquainted with their new workmate, and other employees should also be informed about the position the new rep occupies.

Introductions are a two-way street—a new salesperson is eager to meet other employees, and they want to meet him or her. The introductions should be so arranged that those involved have enough time to do more than just say hello. A short chat with each person is helpful. It allows people to get more than a quick impression of each other, and it helps them to remember names. Present employees should be given background information on the new salesperson so that they can converse on some common ground. The new rep should be briefed on the people to be met—who they are, what they do, and what their interests are.

The administrator must keep in mind that if a sales manager does not show the new person respect and consideration, the other employees probably will not do so either. In a sense, the manager's attitude establishes the new rep's informal status in the group.

Consider the case of a new sales recruit who is young, just out of school, and who requires considerable training and experience. The sales manager's idle remark, such as, "Oh, he will be okay in time, but right now he is just a green kid," can set the key for the rep's treatment by other employees. The new rep is pegged as incompetent and from then on may have a difficult time with the group. For some, this rep will never live down the initial unflattering stereotype.

Conversely, if the manager should mention that a new sales rep is a top-notch prospect with a great potential, the newcomer will be regarded in a different light. Such compliments must be handled judiciously, of course, so that other employees do not become jealous or feel threatened by the new rep.

## ORIENTATION EXPERIENCE

It is especially difficult to assimilate new sales reps when they are thrust into a sales territory with no home-office training. The new person has little opportunity to become integrated with the work group. In such situations, so-called lone wolves are born. While many sales managers complain that their salespeople are not team players, little has been done to make them part of a team. For this reason, it is usually advisable to keep new salespeople around the home office long enough to get to know the employees in supporting departments very well.

After an initial descriptive introduction to the business, the home-office trainee usually begins a program of familiarization with the firm's operations. This is the initial stage of training, which is discussed in Chapter 8. This phase of the socialization program is often so comprehensive that the trainee spends significant time in each of the firm's functional units. Not only does the person get to know the people in the firm, but he or she also learns how the company operates. For example, new sales hires for Global Mail Ltd., a deliverer of international mail, spend one to three days each with the customer-service, accounting, operations, and telesales staffs. These new reps work on the loading dock, process bills, answer customer inquiries . . . they learn all of the steps involved in satisfying the customer.[7]

### Need for Effective Communication

For some years now, the importance of effective communication has been stressed in management theory. It is especially relevant when new reps join a sales force.

#### *Vertical Channels of Communication*
The first weeks on the job are difficult for all. The new recruit has questions, uncertainties, and insecurities. The manager must do extra work to get the recruit started. Co-workers may have to make allowances for the new employee's lack of experience.

The first few days are particularly trying, since the new person has not had time to develop communications with the other members of the organization and must look to the manager for answers. The manager should give as much time as possible to starting the trainee in the right direction. A good technique is to confer with the new employee at the beginning of each day, for a time, to answer questions and present new material. The trainee should be encouraged to ask questions about the job and the company.

New sales reps appreciate this attention. It makes them feel wanted and valued by the company—something most individuals earnestly seek. One of the quickest ways to affect people's attitudes adversely is to ignore them. New reps may interpret this lack of attention to mean that the sales manager does not care about them. The truth probably is that the executive is just preoccupied with operational problems. It comes as quite a blow to new workers to encounter such apparent lack of interest, since they were given so much attention while they were being interviewed. Suddenly the honeymoon is over. Now they think it was just sales talk, and they should have known better than to be taken in by it. The wise sales manager will try to prolong the honeymoon for a while until the new people can take their places in the organization. The nearby box presents a case history which demonstrates the importance of these points.

The actual case history is indicative of what happens when a sales manager is not aware of the needs of a new representative. If new sales reps are not closely supervised and trained during the first few weeks on the job, they may become discouraged and quit. Although it might seem that new employees would enjoy "working" without supervision, this is not the case. They are eager to learn the profession and get into the field so they can find a place in the organization.

### Horizontal Channels of Communication

Sales managers should not force trainees to rely on the grapevine to find out what is going on in the organization and what is expected of them. However, the trainees have no alternative if they are not given proper communication channels. Instead of having access to vertical communication channels, they are forced to use horizontal ones. That is, they seek information from other people on their own level. In the example of the college graduate who went to work for the manufacturer, there was a lack of contact between subordinates and superiors. It had gone so far that the boss was surrounded with barriers to keep subordinates away.

When new people are forced to go to unofficial sources for instruction, the executive runs the risk that they will pick up wrong or undesirable information. Moreover, their allegiances become divided. The informant in effect assumes some managerial functions, and the recruit comes to rely

## The First Few Days on the Job: A College Graduate Who Went to Work for a Large Manufacturer of Industrial Products

On my first day at work I knew nobody except my boss and his assistant. I was given a little glass-enclosed office along the same line as some other such offices. People were working all over the place, but I didn't know who they were or what they were doing. I had been introduced to my boss's secretary and was told she would take care of me. I wasn't quite sure what he meant by that, and I discovered that she wasn't either, for she was no help. I could not get a letter typed by her. Later I made friends with another secretary who was new on the job and in the same position as I was. She typed all my stuff and really looked after me. She would come in and dust off my desk and generally be my secretary. I am certain that she was supposed to be doing something else, but no one seemed to know what was going on, and I had no objection to having a secretary, so that was that. I guess we had been shoved together because of everyone's complete indifference to our plight.

I tried to look busy and kept reading all sorts of reports that were stacked around, but I had been given little direction. When I reported for work, the boss said, "Here is a marketing consultant's report on a new product we are thinking of making. Read it and give me your impressions." That was the last I saw of him for three weeks, since he had to go out of town. I completed the report in two days. I really went over it and did some outside investigation on my own. But there was a limit to what I could do with it, so I quickly ran out of work to do.

Then I hit upon doing library research on the subject and started going down to the city library. It was a good place to loaf, and I enjoyed getting into a lot of books I had never realized existed. It was quite an education, but it came to an end in time, and still I had no work to do or anyone to tell me to do something.

I started to go to the movies in the afternoon, getting back just in time to punch out on the clock. Can you imagine that: all of us had to punch in and out on a time clock. It was

ridiculous, since it accomplished nothing. I felt rather guilty about going to the movies in the afternoons, but it was better than sitting around the office with everyone looking at you and wondering what you were supposed to be doing.

The secretary of my boss's boss thought she ran the place. She really gave me a bad time when she saw me goofing off. Boy, those icy stares of hers were enough to freeze the devil himself. I tried to get to see the top boss about my plight, but she would not let me near him. He was always "in a conference" or "out of town" or something like that. I knew that they were lies because I had seen him cutting it up a bit on several occasions in there, but what could I do? The secretary controlled the door to his office, and we didn't meet anywhere. I had to eat in the cafeteria while he was in the big shot's dining room. We couldn't even use the same rest rooms. Boy, was he ever guarded!

Well, to make a long story short, it did not take me long to decide that I would quit at the end of summer and go back to graduate school. I made up my mind in late June and told them the first of August that I thought I needed more schooling. They gave me an exit interview, and personnel asked me how I liked the company and all that stuff. I kept my tongue and said it was fine and that I had learned a lot but I felt incompetent and wanted to know more about marketing since I had majored in another subject in school. He said he was sorry to see me go and that he thought I had a good future with the firm and all that bunk. Even my boss never tumbled to the real reason why I quit. It never dawned on him that he had not said over 100 words to me during the whole three months I worked for him. To top it off, I had not moved to town yet but was commuting 100 miles a day to work, and they did not even know it. The boss was surprised when I told him the commuting problem was getting me down. Well, there were a lot more little things, but that is the basic story of what actually happened to me.

on this source for information. For instance, in the earlier example, the new secretary came to the new sales rep for work instructions; in fact, he became her manager. Her allegiance was transferred in part to her source of guidance.

The problem is further complicated because those employees who actively solicit listeners frequently may not be the ones with whom the recruit should be associated. Often, it is the malcontents, the office politicians, and the downright incompetents who are excessively interested in that type of activity. Instructional and policy information should come from management; moreover, it should be prompt and accurate.

## ■ MEETING SOCIAL AND PSYCHOLOGICAL NEEDS

An individual's assimilation into the organization involves considerably more than just getting started on the job. He or she should be socially integrated into the new environment. A manager who forgets that people are essentially social animals is destined for disappointing results. For many people, their social and psychological needs overrule their economic requirements. Ester Perry, an IBM Global Accounts Manager, says that her number one priority is retaining her sales personnel.[8] They often leave for reasons which aren't economic. Sometimes they leave because they perceive that their positions within the company are not secure. Sometimes they don't understand or agree with the company strategy. To some extent, these kinds of problems can be alleviated with proper communication and integration of sales personnel into the organization. Such efforts must begin when the salesperson is hired.

Newly hired salespeople may be under a lot of stress the first few months. Frequently they are thrust into a strange city, their children are upset, their new home is not as comfortable as the old one—conditions that hardly foster efficiency at work. For this reason, many managers hire only local people for a territory. They do not want to force employees to move from their environment, feeling that people are far more effective if left among their friends and in their areas of acquaintance. This policy is sometimes difficult to maintain, however. In many instances a firm can't find a qualified person in the local market and is thus forced to move someone.

The sales manager is in a position to cushion the shock of social uprooting by providing some social activities and contacts. The manager should take positive steps to see that recruits and their families get into activities in which they are interested. The golfer should be worked into a foursome and the bridge player invited to join some group.

The job itself also plays an important social role. Co-workers are an obvious reference group because employees often spend more time with their co-workers than their families. People often derive a great deal of satisfaction from the personal relationships they develop on the job. The sales manager can help new employees initiate these relationships by bringing them together with their co-workers in social situations. The story below illustrates the importance of personal relationships on the job. A vice president of marketing for a sizable consumer goods concern was elated when he persuaded a nationally prominent market research expert to join the company. Two years later the boss was hurt and bewildered when the woman resigned to go with a competitor. "They bought her from us," was the rationalization; but in reality the researcher never felt she was part of the team. Her version, however, was as follows:

> He was the weirdest boss I've ever had. When he hired me, you'd have thought we were really going to do some great things together. Then every time I tried to get approval for some project, he'd throw cold water on it. I had no social and precious little professional contact with the man during my two years with him. We had him and his wife over twice for some parties, but you know, I don't even know where he lives or what his home phone number is. I can't work for a guy like that. I need good, close relationships with my boss to do my job as I want to do it.

One entrepreneur built a business around IBM's penchant for moving its employees frequently. In Boulder, Colorado, the home of a large IBM installation, Marisa Everakes started New Places/New Faces of Boulder, which charges $600 per person to help the families of IBM employees transferred to Boulder integrate into the community. Even though IBM maintains that it has an excellent assimilation program of its own, Everakes says such programs don't even begin to address what's at the root of the problem: loneliness.

## Socialization and Cultural Diversity

Early in the equal opportunity–affirmative action movement, managers worried about how well women and minority trainees would integrate into the sales force. Those fears have subsided for the most part. For example, one study of industrial saleswomen indicated that, contrary to original worries, women encountered little difficulty with their peers or customers who, by and large, were supportive.[9] However, as sales recruits become more culturally diverse in the remainder of this decade, managers will need to pay more attention to their assimilation and socialization within the organization.

The initial introduction of the new minority rep to the work group is particularly critical. The reception, status, and initial relationships of these new hires will depend to a large extent on how management regards them and on the work group's perception of management's attitude. If these new reps have been hired in token observance of equal rights or affirmative action laws, that attitude will be communicated to the work group. This is a poor basis for good working relationships.

Companies should develop programs to facilitate the smooth entry and socialization of these individuals into the work group. Below, three programs are described which have been used by a number of companies to achieve these objectives.

## Mentoring New Employees

A **mentor** is someone with knowledge, experience, position, or power who provides personal counseling and career guidance for younger employees. Many of the nation's major companies, such as Xerox, General Electric, and Pacific Bell, have formal mentoring programs. The goal of these programs is to make the employees feel comfortable in their new jobs, to teach them the corporate culture, to give them someone to whom they can turn when they need support or advice, and in some cases to push them up the corporate ladder.

There are three types of mentoring programs. The first is one in which a senior manager is assigned to each of the new sales reps for a period of a year or sometimes a little longer. This manager advises, teaches, and helps the rep learn the corporate culture. Because this person is supposed to be a friend as well as an adviser, the mentor is never the employee's direct boss. Rather, a mentor is chosen who does not have the authority to fire or promote the employee.

Another form of mentoring involves co-workers who are chosen to be the new reps' advisers/trainers. Senior salespeople are assigned to the new sales reps and are expected to "teach them the ropes." In some cases, especially small companies, the mentor is also the primary trainer, teaching product knowledge and basic selling skills. Again because of the importance of the personal relationship between the mentor and the employee, care is taken to assign a mentor who does not or will not have any direct authority over the new rep.

The third type of mentoring is an informal process in which a senior executive selects a younger salesperson or manager and helps him or her climb the corporate ladder. A well-placed mentor inside the company can protect the reps' interests in the company's political arena as well as help them advance if their talents warrant it. The mentor knows the cast of characters and can provide valuable advice.

It is comforting to know that some firms recognize the difficulties encountered by the newly hired employee in being integrated into both the company and the community and are *doing* something about it.

# ◼ SUMMARY

If management is sincere in its statements about the importance of people to its success, it seems only logical that it would be sensitive to new employees' needs during the first few months on the job. This sensitivity begins with the hiring process. Once acceptable recruits have been identified, the hiring process begins. Much can go wrong in hiring people, particularly highly desirable people. If the hiring process is not well thought out and executed, all the good work done in recruiting and selecting may be nullified.

During preoffer planning, the acceptable recruits should be ranked. Then what will be included in the offer and how it will be extended must be decided. In extending the offer, the recruiter should (1) review the job, (2) ask for questions, (3) try to determine interest, (4) if the candidate seems positive, make the offer, and (5) if necessary, probe for objections.

Much of the sales recruit's long-run success with a company depends on how well he or she is socialized and assimilated into the work group during the first few months on the job. There is much to learn about the

company, its people, and how things are done in the organization. The initial socialization begins during the preemployment period as the reps hear and read about the jobs they will soon begin. The second stage is the actual assimilation into the firm. During this period, salespeople should be given information concerning their paychecks, expense accounts, office practices, dining facilities, and their schedule of activities for the upcoming weeks. Then the reps should become familiar with the firm's operation and employees. Both vertical and horizontal communication are important during this period.

In order to retain salespeople, they must be socially integrated into the firm. The desire for social acceptance in the work group is so strong that the recruit who fails to gain it will probably quit. The sales manager can help employees initiate relationships by bringing the new employees together with their co-workers in social situations. Sales managers can also use various mentoring programs to help with the socialization and assimilation of new reps.

## Key Terms

Assimilation

Hiring

Horizontal channels of
communication

Job previews

Mentor

Socialization

Vertical channels of
communication

# ◼ QUESTIONS AND PROBLEMS

1. One recruit you want to hire stands out above all the others you interviewed. You make her an offer that is standard throughout your medium-sized company, which has a commis-

sioned sales force of 33 reps. The recruit wants a higher initial salary for the first year before going onto a commission. Normally, all trainees are paid $2,500 a month plus expenses for the first year. The recruit demands $3,000. The average commissioned sales rep makes $84,000 a year after four years in the field. What would you do?

2. A prized recruit to whom you have made an attractive offer stalls about giving an answer. You request that the recruit answer within a week. The recruit demurs and asserts, "I'll need three weeks." What do you say or do? Explain your attitudes in this matter.

3. A manager may find it advisable to supervise distribution of status symbols. What are some of these status symbols and why should the manager be concerned with them?

4. One sales manager commented that the man in the story related by a college graduate about his first few days at work was just a spoiled brat who simply was not capable of doing an honest day's work, and that the firm was fortunate in getting rid of him. He said that it was not the sales manager's job to wet-nurse each employee. A person must be able to take a job and work without all the coddling sometimes recommended. Does this chapter distort the actual need for introductory activities out of proportion to the real problem in industry? Why not adopt a sink-or-swim philosophy on the mat-

ter? If a person is really good, why is all of this attention needed?

5. What are some of the actions a sales manager can take to provide new employees with social contacts and activities?

6. A sales manager made the following statement: "I don't lose any sleep over it when one of my reps leaves for another position. Generally, it's those people who don't quite fit in who leave." Evaluate this manager's statement.

7. Should the sales manager warn the trainee about listening to or being influenced by other people in the organization for whom the manager has particularly low regard?

8. With the introduction of more women to sales positions, what special problems might arise in assimilating them into an all-male sales force?

9. To what extent can members of the peer group facilitate a trainee's assimilation into the work group? How could management encourage such efforts?

10. One manager maintained, "You can always spot the malcontents in our organization—just watch to see who runs to befriend the new person." Evaluate that statement. If it is true, of what significance is it to the new person?

## ◼ EXPERIENTIAL EXERCISES

A. **Step 1:** Interview 10 of your peers to ask them what are or will be the most important considerations in their job search decisions.

   **Step 2:** Develop a brief questionnaire which asks respondents to rank the factors uncovered in Step 1.

   **Step 3:** Administer the questionnaire to 20 of your peers. Summarize the results in a report.

B. **Step 1:** Change the wording on the questionnaire developed above from "Rank the criteria below according to their importance to you in accepting a job" to "Rank the criteria below according to the importance that you feel that students will place on them in their job searches."

**Step 2:** Administer the questionnaire to 20 recruiters who visit your campus.

**Step 3:** Summarize the results in a brief report. Also in your report, compare the responses of the recruiters to the responses of your peers.

## ■ REFERENCES

1. Much of this section is based on the excellent work of Robert D. Goddard, Jeremy Fox, and W. E. Patton, "The Job-Hire Sale," *Personnel Administrator,* June 1989, pp. 120–24.

2. "As More Men Become 'Trailing Spouses,' " *The Wall Street Journal,* April 13, 1993, p. A1.

3. This presentation assumes that the sales manager must "sell" recruits on working for the firm. In many instances, sales jobs are so attractive that the roles are reversed. The applicant must try to "sell" the manager on hiring him or her.

4. William Kennan Jr., "Time Is Everything," *Sales & Marketing Management,* August 1993, pp. 60–61.

5. Ginger Trumfio, "Recruiting Goes High Tech," *Sales & Marketing Management,* April 1995, pp. 42–44.

6. As reported by the Indiana University School of Business Placement Office, 1997.

7. "A 'Finishing School' for Sales Reps," *Inc.,* October 1992, p. 30.

8. Ester Perry, New Horizons in Personal Selling and Sales Management Conference, American Marketing Association, 1996.

9. Bill Kelley, "Selling in a Man's World," *Sales & Marketing Management,* January 1991, pp. 28–35.

---

*Case 7-1*

### UNIVERSAL COMPUTERS

### Evaluation of hiring procedures

Fran Long, branch sales manager, walked into her office at Universal Computer's southeastern regional headquarters in Atlanta, Georgia. She had spent the previous week in the field working with some of her sales reps who were having trouble with some key accounts. While she had kept in close contact by telephone with her office staff during the week, her paperwork had stacked up. The in-basket was overflowing. She groaned as she surveyed the work ahead of her that morning, but got to it immediately. She turned the basket upside down and began processing the paper—first in, first dealt with.

After reading and processing several intercompany memos, suddenly a letter from Sharon Altman caught her attention. Sharon, a marketing major, had graduated from one of the state's universities with an outstanding record while working full time in the school's computer department. After on-campus interviews with her, she was invited for a series of personal interviews at the company's Atlanta offices. She made an excellent impression on everyone in the company who had interviewed her, and everything on her résumé checked out satisfactorily. Consequently, she was offered a job as a sales trainee at the market rate for such people. She was given two weeks to accept the offer which had been made in a letter sent to her three days after her interview. She had been informed verbally that she would be receiving the offer. She requested two weeks to answer, which was granted.

After working through all the nice commentary about how great Universal was and how much she was impressed with Fran and all the people she had met, Sharon got to the bottom line—she had accepted a sales job with another firm.

Fran was displeased. She had made a great effort to recruit Sharon and thought that she had been successful. Sharon had given no indication that she was considering another job. Fran considered calling her immediately to find out what happened, but looked at the stack of papers to be processed and decided to postpone taking any action that day. She wanted to think about it for a while.

Fifteen documents later she was looking at another letter rejecting a job offer she had made to a young man from North Carolina. Again, the story was about the same. An outstanding prospective sales rep was made an offer when he indicated that he wanted one. Fran was puzzled by this rejection because the young man fit the stereotypical person the company was famous for hiring. He was a Universal man from his haircut down to his shoes. What's going on here, Fran wondered.

By noon Fran had finished with the in-basket and wished she had stayed home. Three more people to whom job offers had been made unexpectedly rejected them to accept other opportunities. Fran knew she had a problem on her hands because hiring good people was the lifeblood of the business. The firm had been built on its ability to attract, train, and keep a highly effective sales force.

Universal Computers was one of the world's largest computer companies, with offices in every major city in the world. Its growth and profitability had been the envy of the international business world. Unfortunately, during the previous two years it had encountered financial difficulties as its revenues suffered from competitive intrusions into its markets, as well as from a sluggish economy. Massive cutbacks in budgets and personnel were made by management. Changes in top management rocked the business world. The price of its stock dropped by more than 50 percent.

Its sales management program had been copied extensively by its competitors. Universal was a household word. Fran thought, "You just don't reject an offer from us, particularly in these tough times. And above all you don't play games with us." She recognized that these recruits had used the Universal offers for bargaining with other firms. She had used the same tactic in reverse when she came to work for Universal 10 years previously.

With five sales trainee positions to fill, Fran had interviewed 22 people for the openings. There were eight other recruits who were considered acceptable to hire, but they were not considered nearly as promising as the recruits who had received the offers. She arranged for a meeting that afternoon with everyone involved in the selection process.

After explaining what had happened to the offers that they had made, Fran said, "I want to discuss three things right now. What went wrong? What should we do right now? And how do we keep this same thing from happening in the future?"

The discussion was spirited as each person had some opinions. The group thought that there was nothing wrong with its selection process. The procedures that had worked so well for years were followed. Those recruits were given the royal treatment. No insincerity from the recruits in wanting to work for Universal was detected: All of them seemed to be bona fide recruits.

The group wondered if they made a mistake by not putting more pressure on the recruits. Perhaps they should not give them so much time to consider the offer, and maybe they should get a verbal acceptance before making a written offer.

"Good deeds never go unpunished!" observed Fran's operations manager. He continued, "We were nice guys. Maybe we should quit being so nice. Competition is getting rough as we well know and that holds true for people as well as markets."

Fran's assistant demurred. "Do we really want to hire anyone who really doesn't want to work for us? I think not. I just can't see pressuring anyone to come to work for us. It hasn't come to that, has it?"

Fran nodded and asked, "To what extent have our current competitive and financial problems played a role in this matter? Let's face it, we avoided all discussion of it with these people. We pretend it doesn't exist. But it does. Should we get it out on the table and talk about it with these people or would that be washing our dirty linen in public?" She did not wait for an answer, but hurried on to the immediate problem: "How do we go about making the next offers? Should we bring them in to Atlanta again and get their acceptance on the spot? If we don't fill these five slots will we look bad in New York when this year's sales training program begins?" She said the words, but she really wondered if they should be hiring available bodies to fill slots instead of waiting until the right people could be hired. After all, the world wouldn't end if they weren't able to fill their sales trainee positions with college graduates. She knew that there were a lot of good people on the streets looking for jobs.

*Questions:*

1. Why did the applicants reject Universal's job offer?

2. If Fran wants to hire five trainees from those who have already been interviewed, how should it be done?

3. If you were in Fran's position, exactly what actions would you take?

---

*Case 7-2*

## PACIFIC PAPER PRODUCTS

### Indoctrination of new salespeople

"I'm getting too old for this job. Everything seems to have changed. I don't seem to be able to manage things the same way I used to," Mo Martin complained to his long-time friend, Bernie, who was a bit weary of Mo's never-ending complaints about the ways of the modern world.

Mo Martin, vice president of sales for Pacific Paper Products, had started his career in sales with the paper division of Weyerhaeuser, the huge wood products company, when he graduated from college in 1961. After completing the company training program, he was assigned to the firm's Southern California regional office where he enjoyed a stellar sales career through a combination of hard work and a large, fast-growing territory. Weyerhaeuser was known as an excellent company to work for and Mo was enjoying much success in his sales career. However, he became progressively dissatisfied with his status at Weyerhaeuser as his peers in his training program were being promoted into various management positions while he was still selling. He kept asking his boss about it, and he was continually told that the company felt that his superior selling skills would best benefit the company if he remained in selling. He was given several large key accounts for which he was solely responsible. One of those accounts was Pacific Paper, a paper wholesaler. Mo eventually became close friends with its owner, who persuaded Mo to work for him as vice president of sales. Starting in 1973, Mo Martin established himself as an excellent sales manager by most indexes one might want to use: sales increases, profit margins, selling costs, turnover, and modernization of the sales system.

Mo's traditional management style was to develop close personal relationships with his people. There was much socializing among the sales force that was located in the Southern California region. Sales meetings were often held in Palm Springs or San Diego, at which golf tournaments were usually featured. The company sponsored several charity celebrity golf tournaments at which the salespeople played significant roles by inviting various key customers to play.

Mo spent much time in the field working closely with the sales reps. He tried to spend at least one day every three months with each of the firm's 33 sales reps. Every birthday, anniversary, wedding, graduation, or other memorable event in a rep's family was recognized with appropriate gifts or cards.

The sales group was diverse, with 10 reps from minority groups and four women. The first woman was hired in 1991. Mo was aware that the women had not assimilated into the sales force at all well even though their sales performances were good. As he had said when asked why he had hired them, "They were the best of the applicants."

He normally went out of his way to help new sales reps become part of the work group. He kept close daily contact with new reps, helping them with whatever personal problems they were encountering in changing their jobs. He had made personal loans to some new reps who were having financial troubles. Mo said, "They can't sell effectively if they're worried about their family or finances. Anything I can do to help them become effective salespeople and happily accepted in our work group will eventually pay us big dividends."

However, Mo had quickly detected that his management style was not well accepted among the women he had hired. While they had not come to him as a group, individually they had let him know that they did not play golf and did not like to go to a bar with him to talk over the day's sales calls. Moreover, they were not really interested in socializing that much with the other sales reps, or even having much ado made over their birthdays. Mo had held a surprise birthday party for Ruth Spencer on her fortieth birthday. She was not amused, as they say, and she let him know about it.

Bernie was well aware of Mo's problems as they exchanged confidences almost daily—they were neighbors and socialized extensively. Bernie kept observing that times had changed and Mo had to change with them. "What worked for you before may not work for you now. Maybe some people only want to work for you; they don't want to be your buddies. They only wanted a job, not a social life," Bernie told him.

"Yeah, I know you're right, but how about me and what I want. I enjoy my job so much because it's so much fun working and playing with my people. If I can't have fun and do it my way, why do it? Maybe I should take early retirement and say to heck with it."

"Hold the phone, Mo. Don't go off the deep end just yet. I know someone who might be able to help you with your problem. I met this woman management consul-

tant who specializes in advising managers on these matters. Talk to her. And talk to some other people, too. I think there are some things you can do to get some perspective on your situation."

*Question:*

**1.** What advice would you give Mo Martin?

# CHAPTER 8

# Developing, Delivering, and Reinforcing a Sales Training Program

Those who seek mentoring will rule the great expanse under heaven.
**Shu Ching, Chinese Book of History**

The training program is a vital link in the process of converting the recruit into a productive sales rep. The money which is spent on recruiting and selecting salespeople may be wasted if their selection is not followed up with the proper training programs. Additionally, experienced reps may not improve or even maintain their productivity if they are not provided with an adequate amount of continual training.

In this chapter we discuss developing and conducting a sales training program. Chapter 3 provides additional details about the personal selling process. Successful sales training programs consist of four phases: **training assessment, program design, reinforcement,** and **evaluation.** In each phase sales executives must make a number of decisions, as seen in Figure 8-1.

The four basic types of training programs are (1) initial or indoctrination training, (2) refresher courses, (3) continuous training programs, and (4) executive development programs. The decisions which the executive makes with regard to training vary with the type of program being considered.

## THE VALUE OF SALES TRAINING

In a recent survey, sales executives ranked proper training as the second most important factor ensuring a salesperson's success.[1] They rated a good/positive attitude as the most important factor. But salespeople's attitudes toward their jobs are affected by the amount and quality of training they have received. Several others of the "success" factors, such as knowledge and identifying customer needs, are also directly related to the amount of

The authors wish to acknowledge the contributions of Dick Canada, Chairperson of Dartmouth Group Ltd., to this chapter. A former National Sales Training Manager for Xerox, Dick offered ideas, as well as reviewing and improving those of the authors.

■ **FIGURE 8-1**

**Phases of developing and conducting sales force training**

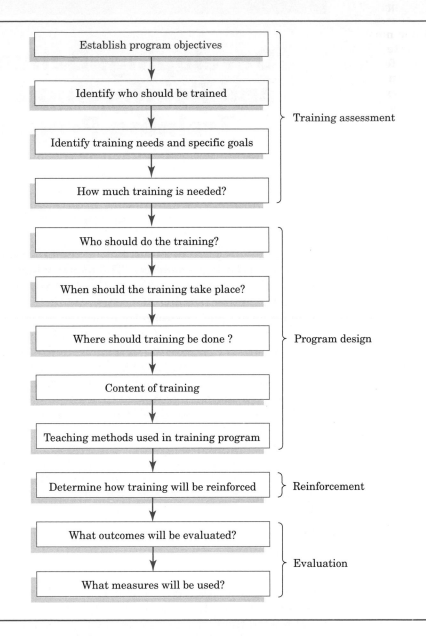

Training assessment
- Establish program objectives
- Identify who should be trained
- Identify training needs and specific goals
- How much training is needed?

Program design
- Who should do the training?
- When should the training take place?
- Where should training be done?
- Content of training
- Teaching methods used in training program

Reinforcement
- Determine how training will be reinforced

Evaluation
- What outcomes will be evaluated?
- What measures will be used?

training a salesperson has received. (See Figure 8-2.) Therefore, the impact of training on success is even greater than the number two ranking suggests.

In the same survey, executives also rated the most significant factors contributing to the failure of salespeople. With the exception of sufficient effort, each of the other top reasons for failure is directly related to defi-

■ **FIGURE 8-2**

| Single most important factor for ensuring a salesperson's success | Factor | Percent Mentioning |
|---|---|---|
| | 1. Good/positive attitude | 13 |
| | 2. Proper training | 10 |
| | 3. Good work habits/hard work | 8 |
| | 4. Motivation/self-motivation | 7 |
| | 5. Knowledge (customer, market, competition, product) | 5 |
| | 6. Dedication/desire to succeed | 5 |
| | 7. Identifying customer needs | 5 |
| | 8. Customer-oriented sales approach | 5 |

Source: Thomas N. Ingram, Charles H. Schwepker Jr., and Don Hutson, "Why Salespeople Fail," *Industrial Marketing Management,* August 1992, pp. 225–30.

ciencies which can be corrected through training. Training may even lead to greater effort. As salespeople develop greater self-confidence through training, they may be encouraged to put forth more effort.

Salespeople themselves agree that training is important. In a survey conducted by *Marketing News,* new salespeople reported that a lack of training was the major cause of dissatisfaction. The survey found that turnover was very high among new and younger salespeople. Even more important, the survey also found that customers rated 70 percent of sales personnel as only moderately effective to ineffective.[2] Despite the reported relationship between sales training and sales productivity, studies report that over one-third of business firms do no sales training, and many other firms provide only on-the-job-training.[3]

Yet many other companies are investing heavily in sales training programs. In fact the number of hours spent by U.S. corporations on sales training now exceeds the amount spent on executive, senior, and middle-management–level training.[4] The average annual investment in training ranges from $1,600 to $23,300 per salesperson.[5] Yet, given the number of customers who say that the salespeople who serve them are not very effective, it is apparent that many sales training programs are not imparting the skills necessary to achieve success in sales.

There are three main reasons why this is happening. First, many companies design training programs without a thorough assessment of training needs. Second, the buyer's preferences for and evaluations of salespeople are typically ignored in the design of most sales programs.[6] Third, managers and trainers do not continually reinforce the behaviors which have been covered in the training programs. This lack of skill reinforcement leads to minimal behavioral change by the salesperson.[7] Xerox Corporation has for years been recognized as possessing one of the finest sales training programs in the world, yet Xerox found an 87 percent loss of skills 30 days after the initial instruction.[8] In other words, some companies may be spending a lot of money on training, but they are not spending those dollars carefully enough to be effective.

It should also be noted that frequently companies use training as the solution to problems that cannot be "cured" through training.[9] For example, if the reps are performing poorly, it may be because the company is selecting the wrong type of person for the job. If sales are low, it may be due to a poor marketing strategy. Training is not a panacea, but it can lead to significant improvements in performance if it is properly designed, implemented, and reinforced. In the remainder of this chapter we discuss how to design, deliver, and reinforce an effective sales training program.

## ▉ SALES TRAINING AND STRATEGIC PLANNING

Many aspects of sales training are affected by the company's strategic marketing plan. The sales training program—when properly coordinated with the firm's marketing objectives and strategies—can aid in implementing the company's strategic marketing plan.

In today's competitive marketplace, customers are demanding more from their suppliers in terms of quality and service. In response to these pressures, firms are placing greater strategic emphasis on developing long-term partnerships with their customers. Rather than just selling products and/or services, salespeople are expected to build relationships and provide solutions to their customers' problems. As a result, the selling process is much more interactive and more situation specific. Salespeople have to know more about the product and more about the customer. Many firms have adopted team-selling strategies in order to respond to customers' ever-increasing expectations. In team-selling approaches, the salesperson works much more closely with people from other areas in the firm, such as manufacturing, engineering, and/or research.

As a result of these new strategies, sales training has become much broader in scope, covering topics such as quality management, teamwork, and other interpersonal skills necessary for building relationships.

The firm's marketing strategies and objectives provide the basis for establishing sales training objectives. The sales training objectives must be consistent with the firm's marketing objectives. For example, a marketing objective of increasing market share by 20 percent calls for a different training program than the objective of maintaining market share by providing better service to existing customers.

If a company makes a major change in its sales organizational structure, an intensive training program for experienced sales reps may be needed. This sort of situation occurred when Xerox embarked on a three- to five-year program to train all 4,000 of its reps to sell the full product line rather than a selected part of the line as they had been doing in the past.

# ■ TRAINING ASSESSMENT

In the **training assessment** phase, sales executives must determine:

- What are the training program objectives?
- Who should be trained?
- What are the training needs of the individual rep?
- How much training is needed?

## Training Program Objectives

Most companies expect to influence the productivity of their field sales organizations through the design and delivery of their training programs. But training programs may have other objectives as well. They include a lower turnover rate, better morale, more effective communication, improved customer relations, and better self-management. These objectives are shown graphically in Figure 8-3 and described below.

- **Increased sales productivity.** Companies try to improve their return on sales investment by improving the productivity of their sales-

---

**■ FIGURE 8-3**

**Objectives of sales training programs**

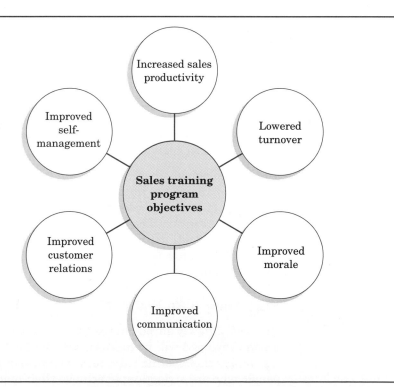

people. This can be done by increasing sales per salesperson or by lowering costs. Training is frequently used to accomplish greater sales per salesperson and sometimes used to lower costs.

- **Lower turnover.** Good training programs lower job turnover because well-trained people are less likely to fail. A well-thought-out training program prepares trainees for the realities of a life in sales—including the fact that discouragement and disappointment are to be expected early in a sales career. The trainee who can handle the early problems is less likely to become discouraged and quit.

- **Better morale.** Closely tied to turnover is the matter of morale. People who are thrust into the business world without proper training or preparation are likely to suffer from poor morale. Lack of purpose is another reason for poor morale. Hence a major objective of a sales training program should be to give trainees some idea about their purpose in the company and in society.

- **Improved communication.** Training is used to ensure that salespeople understand the importance of the information they provide to the company concerning their customers and the marketplace. They need to know how the information will be used and how it affects the performance of the firm.

- **Improved customer relations.** A good training program helps trainees become aware of the importance of establishing and maintaining good customer relations. They should learn how to avoid overselling, how to determine which products are needed, and how to adjust complaints.

- **Improved self-management.** Management has become increasingly interested in how employees use their time. The goal is to learn how to produce more output from the relatively few hours available for working. Salespeople must be organized and allocate their time effectively in order to be successful.

Technological advances in recent years have provided sales reps with great opportunities to improve their productivity. Computers, particularly laptop computers, will play an increasingly important role in selling during the 21st century. They allow the rep to access the company's databases and communicate with the operating sales system. Properly used, they can be of immense benefit. However, the reps must learn how to use the new technology.

## Who Should Be Trained?

Obviously, newly hired company sales reps require some training. How much they need will be discussed in the next section. The need for training among the existing sales force is not so obvious. But usually there are people who are struggling to achieve their objectives. They need help, and the company can profit by giving it to them.

Of course, things continually change. New products are introduced, markets shift, and buyers change. These and other changes require re-training the sales force to handle the new developments. But even without such changes, every salesperson can benefit from appropriate sales training. Even the most experienced or skilled salesperson can benefit from refresher courses. Sales training is most effective with those reps who have a strong desire and commitment to learn coupled with a specific lack of skills or knowledge.

Generally speaking a company will achieve its best investment return when it gives priority to training the middle 60 percent of its sales force (see Figure 8-4). People who are in the top 20 percent of a field sales force usually are not going to increase their performance substantially above the level they are currently achieving. By the same logic, sales reps who are consistently in the lowest 20 percent of the organization may be in the wrong job, a problem which cannot be helped through training.[10]

At times it is also important to train people who are not the company's employees: independent manufacturers' representatives, distributors, dealers, and users. For example, manufacturers' representatives promote

■ **FIGURE 8-4**

**Best return on investment in the training of salespeople**

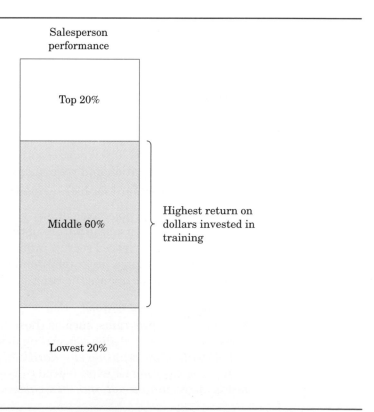

Salesperson performance

Top 20%

Middle 60%

Highest return on dollars invested in training

Lowest 20%

those products that are easiest to sell or that have the highest commissions. Experience shows that the products that are easiest to sell are those with which the rep is most familiar. Usually the rep is most familiar with the products which are best supported by their manufacturers. These agents and distributors want and expect support from the companies they represent. Firms that give it to them send several valuable messages: We want you to make money with our line; we will support you in the best way we can; and we want you to be part of our organization.

One medical equipment and supply company will not allow any physician to buy or use its products until the physician has gone through the company's training program. This policy is part of the firm's program to lessen medical product liability litigation. It has worked; the company has had no suits to date.

## Identifying Training Needs and Setting Specific Goals

To say that the purpose of a training program is to increase sales productivity is so general that it serves only as a hazy guidepost for making decisions. The manager must break down the broad objectives into *specific goals,* such as improving product knowledge, prospecting methods, probing, or relationship building. Meeting these separate goals should result in achieving the broad objectives.

The assessment of training needs is the most important step in designing a sales training program. The identification of training needs provides the starting point for setting training goals and designing the program. The analysis is used to identify weaknesses in selling skills and then programs are designed to eliminate these weaknesses.

Setting these specific objectives serves several other important purposes:

- Helps the trainer and trainee focus on the purpose of the training.
- Guides prioritization and sequencing of training.
- Provides a standard for measuring training effectiveness.[11]

Naturally, the objectives of any segment of a sales training program will vary depending on the nature of the trainee. The program designed to convert an inexperienced recruit into a professional sales rep will be more comprehensive than a program intended to refresh the selling skills of an experienced rep or update the existing sales force on new products.

### Standardization and Customization

Some training programs, such as those for inexperienced reps or those for disseminating knowledge concerning new products or policies, can be provided to *all of the reps in a standardized form.* However, a significant portion of the training for experienced reps should be based on *identifying the needs of the individual and then customizing a curriculum to meet those individual needs.* G. D. Searle, a medical supply company, has improved the effectiveness of its training through customization. Each of its 1,100 salespeople, in consultation with their sales managers, may select from a variety of courses according to their needs.[12]

### Sources of Information

Many sources can and should be used to gather the information concerning training needs. The most frequently used source is management judgment. While these assessments may be accurate, it is important for a firm to systematically collect information from a number of other sources as well. Performance measures, such as sales volume, number of calls, selling expenses, and customer complaints, can help managers assess training needs.

Interviews with or surveys of salespeople and customers can also provide valuable insights. For example, several divisions of the 3M Company use customer questionnaires as the basis for identifying individual training needs. Each salesperson delivers the questionnaires to a selected group of about six customers, who are asked to assess the importance of a variety of skills to the selling relationship and to rate the salesperson's application of these skills. Questionnaires on which the customers rate a particular skill as important but report the salesperson's application as low suggest areas in which the salesperson can use additional training.[13]

Another method of assessing training needs is to conduct a **difficulty analysis** of the sales job. In this analysis the sales manager attempts to discover what difficulties are encountered in the field. Then, proper training can be devised to help overcome those problems. The difficulty analysis is conducted by going into the field and interviewing sales reps about their problems. Frequently, the investigator reviews a series of calls in which the reps failed to get orders. In each instance, an attempt is made to discover just what caused the failure. If the analysis discloses that the rep is picking poor prospects, for example, additional training on prospecting would be required.

## How Much Training Is Needed?

The amount of training needed depends on the training objectives. A half-day program might suffice to introduce the reps to a new promotional program, whereas two or three days might be needed to teach the features and benefits of a new product or service. A program with the objective of improving the sales reps' customer orientation may require three or four days, but a program designed to teach basic selling skills to inexperienced recruits may take as long as six months.

Generally, inexperienced recruits not only need to learn about their companies and the products they are selling, but they also need to learn basic selling techniques. Some recruits who have had sales experience may require less training. However, sometimes these recruits may have inadequate knowledge of specific selling techniques that are most appropriate for their current selling assignment. This situation would call for considerably more training.

Most training programs for new hires are from three to six months, with the average cost ranging from a low of $1,600 to a high of $23,400 per rep; $23,400 is the amount which, on the average, it costs to train a pharmaceutical sales rep. As you might expect, the more technical the products are, the longer the training for new recruits.[14]

In the case of continual training, there is a trade-off which must be considered between the gains that should result from training and the lost sales which may result from the rep's absence from the field. Of course, the long-term perspective suggests that the benefits from training will, in the long run, outweigh any short-term losses. But there is a limit to how long and how often you can pull a rep out of the field and not affect the level of customer service. Surveys show that the amount of continual training varies from providing a low of 12 hours per year to providing 100 hours per year for an experienced rep.[15]

# PROGRAM DESIGN

In the program design phase, the following questions must be answered:

- Who should do the training?
- When should the training take place?
- Where should it be done?
- What should the content of the training be?
- What teaching methods should be used?

## Who Should Do the Training?

Three basic sources of trainers are regular line executives, staff personnel, and outside specialists. Any one or a combination of them can be used successfully. It is not uncommon for a firm to use all three, each for different purposes. It is very important to remember in choosing trainers that the quality of the teaching itself will have a greater impact on what is learned than the content of the training.

### Line Personnel
Training by line personnel consists of instruction by such executives as senior sales representatives, field supervisors, territorial managers, or sales managers who are in direct command of the sales force.

Some firms have made effective use of peer training. They set up situations in which inexperienced people are partially trained by their peers on the sales force. It works well if the sales force is skilled and has a vested interest in developing the new person's selling ability.

*A Day-to-Day Operating Problem*

## MAJESTIC PLASTICS COMPANY (E)

### Training for an experienced sales rep

Clyde Brion, general sales manager for the Majestic Plastics Company, had a problem. One of the company's veteran sales reps, Bobby Day, had announced his refusal to attend any sales training courses. Majestic had seen sales and customer satisfaction slip in some of its key territories over the last two years. This had prompted Clyde Brion to hire an outside training specialist to conduct a five-day sales seminar for the company's 18 sales reps. Clyde hoped that through the use of case studies, videotape, and role playing, his reps would improve on their interpersonal and overall "selling skills."

Bobby Day, however, didn't like the idea. He told Clyde Brion, "I've been one of this company's top salespeople for 23 years. The last thing I need is to leave my territory for a week just to get some silly training. Leave the training to the new kids. I lose commissions when I'm not out there selling. Five days out of the territory is money out of my pocket."

In reviewing Bobby Day's performance over the last several years, Clyde had to admit that Day was one of Majestic's better reps. After graduating from a midwestern community college, Day started his sales career in the life insurance industry. In his third year on the job, he sold one of Majestic's executives a term-life policy. The executive was so impressed with Day that he offered him a position in Majestic's growing sales force. Day accepted and began his career in the Washington, D.C., area before being reassigned to the bustling New Jersey territory. He has been there ever since, winning five "Salesperson of the Year" awards. Although many people within Majestic feel Day is not much of a "team player," Majestic's CEO boastfully refers to Day as his "Lone Wolf Superstar."

**Question:** What should Clyde Brion say to Bobby Day?

Source: This case was prepared by Steven Reed under the direction of Professor R. Spiro.

*Advantages.*   Line sales executives' words carry much more authority than those of staff people or outside specialists, since the trainees know that these people have had successful sales experience. When the boss does the training, a certain unity of action is achieved because there can be no mistaking what the supervisor expects. Furthermore, recruits can be trained to sell the way the manager wants them to sell. Line executives who train their own salespeople can evaluate each person's ability better than administrators who do not participate in the training program. Also, better rapport can be established between the executive and the sales force, since training affords a wonderful opportunity to become acquainted.

*Disadvantages.*   The disadvantages of using line personnel are lack of time and lack of teaching ability. The pressures of other activities force the manager to give, at best, only partial attention to the training program. This can be harmful to trainee morale. If a line executive is to do the training, adequate time must be available to do it properly.

A line executive may know a great deal about selling but be unable to teach others about it. Neither of these disadvantages is serious, however, since both can be remedied by proper managerial action. Line administrators can be given the necessary time for training. And teachers are not necessarily born; they also can be trained.

### Staff Trainers

Staff trainers can be hired specifically to conduct training programs, or staff people who hold other jobs in personnel, production, or office management can take this on. We will focus on the specially hired sales trainer, since use of other staff personnel ordinarily is not recommended. Members of the personnel department are seldom qualified to conduct a sales training program. They may be involved in certain phases of the instruction, such as furnishing company information or handling the physical arrangements of the program. However, entrusting them with the technical details of the training program is generally unwise.

*Advantages.*    A trainer specifically hired to handle the training program can attend to the details, prepare the necessary materials, and give the trainee the attention required. Frequently, it is less expensive to hire a specialized staff training officer than it is to add the additional line executives needed to allow them more time for training activities.

*Disadvantages.*    In theory, the staff trainer lacks control over the trainees and does not speak with the authority of a line executive. However, in practice, this is an academic point, since the trainees know that the trainer has the backing of the boss.

Companies incur additional cost in maintaining a separate training department. The median salary of the trainer alone will be about $60,000 per year, depending on his or her qualifications. This limits the number of firms that can afford to hire a sales trainer; smaller companies cannot afford the cost.

### Outside Training Specialists

Practically every large city has firms that specialize in sales training. Their scope varies widely. Some will establish and administer an entire training program, while others specialize in teaching sales techniques. Sometimes these training firms specialize in a very narrow field. For example, some organizations do nothing but train real estate brokers or insurance agents or retail sales clerks.

Small and medium-sized firms often turn the entire training of their sales reps in selling techniques over to outside firms. Xerox Learning Systems was a major supplier of such services. A glance at the Yellow Pages for any large metropolitan area will disclose a number of such sales training organizations.

The key to successfully using an outside specialist is to select the one which is right for your firm. The following steps can help ensure that you do so:[16]

- Preview or audit the program.
- Get references.
- Select only those programs which allow you to customize.
- Set specific objectives.
- Ask for specifics in terms of what results the company can expect.

Self-development programs are also important in training a sales force. Many firms pay part or all of the cost of approved educational programs or seminars. Sometimes they furnish subscriptions to educational services and newsletters. The basic idea is that the company benefits from better-educated employees.

## When Training Should Take Place

There are two basic attitudes toward the timing of training. Some executives believe that no one should be placed in the field who is not fully trained, not only in product and company knowledge but also in selling techniques. Training programs for new salespeople may last from a few weeks to as much as a year or more before the salespeople are sent into the field. Sales managers may have trainees work for a while in either production or service to acquire product knowledge.

Other managers want the recruit to exhibit a desire to sell before investing in training that person. Some insurance companies require a new agent to sell a certain amount of life insurance before going to a sales school. The first training program is only a basic course. After that, the agent must again go into the field and sell successfully before attending more advanced schools for underwriters.

This philosophy has considerable educational and managerial merit. From the educational point of view, it is much easier to train people who have had some field experience than those who have none. People who have experience in facing problems are eager to get answers to them. If many prospects have told them that the price is too high, for example, they will be eager to find out how to cope with that objection.

From a managerial point of view, weak prospective salespeople are usually eliminated if they must sell before being trained. By putting new employees in the field first, the manager also has the opportunity to determine how much and what type of training they really need. The only trouble is that many people who might have been successful had they been given proper instruction may be eliminated by this push-them-off-the-dock method.

About the only time that delayed training should be used is in situations where product knowledge is easily acquired and the prospect does not require a polished selling approach. Delayed training is usually practiced by firms whose customers are sold only once, with each sale being of little importance to total volume. If a sales rep botches a particular sale, the company is not seriously injured.

The need for training does not end with completion of the initial program. Most sales authorities see training as a continual function. It never ceases; it only changes form. Salespeople continually need refresher courses. Often some of the continual training is used to reinforce the initial training. The need for reinforcement of training is discussed in a later section.

## Where Training Should Take Place

The basic problem in deciding on the training program's location is determining the extent to which it should be centralized. Unless there is some reason for centralizing training in one location, it should be decentralized. Centralized training is usually more expensive and requires more organizational effort than training in the field.

### Decentralized Training

Decentralized training can take several forms: (1) field sales office instruction, (2) use of senior salespeople, (3) on-the-job training, (4) sales seminars or clinics, or (5) self-guided assignments.

*Advantages.*    The advantages of decentralized sales training are many. First and foremost, it is usually less expensive than centralized training. The trainee remains in the field to work while learning, and the company avoids the substantial expense of supporting both the trainee and a central school staff.

Second, there is definite educational merit to decentralized training. Education requires time. Studies prove that cram courses are inefficient since the students quickly forget much of what they learn. A decentralized program can match instruction to the speed at which the trainee can learn the material. The limit on how much effective training can be accomplished in the shorter time frame of a centralized program has caused companies like Xerox, Motorola, ARCO, and many others to decentralize training efforts as much as possible.

Third, decentralized training has considerable managerial benefits because the branch manager or an assistant is usually directly responsible. If the branch managers do a good job, trainees gain confidence in their leadership. At the same time, the managers have a good opportunity to evaluate each of the trainees.

Many companies are turning to self-guided instruction. These programs are not only cost effective and self-paced; they can also be customized to address the training needs of the individual rep. This is particularly useful for continual training.

*Disadvantages.*    First, the major weakness of decentralized training, and it is a big one, is that the branch or field manager may not be able to perform the training role properly. Time demands, combined with lack of training skills or the desire to train, may make the field manager an inept trainer.

Second, if complex or expensive equipment is needed in the training program, it may not be available in the field. For example, one interocular lens company had to set up an operating room to train its reps about eye surgery.

### Centralized Training

Centralized sales training may be presented in organized schools or in periodic sales meetings at a central location, often the home office. Some large companies that hire many sales reps each year maintain permanent centralized sales schools. NCR's training camp, called Sugar Camp, is an example of such an installation. Xerox's International Training Center in Leesburg, Virginia, is another. Smaller concerns typically conduct one or two sales schools a year in the home office, each lasting three or four weeks.

*Advantages.*    In centralized training, highly skilled personnel are usually available to teach. Also, proximity to the plant or the home office allows the trainees to become acquainted with home-office personnel and manufacturing facilities. It is important for them to meet the top executives. Centralized training certainly saves executive time because there isn't any travel time for them. Also, a centralized school normally has more formal facilities for training than are available in the field. The needed equipment and materials are handy for the instructor's use. Another significant advantage is that the trainees can get to know one another. An esprit de corps can develop among the members of the class, and this is conducive to good morale.

From an educational standpoint, removing trainees from the home setting, so they are not subject to the distractions of home life, has some merit. They can focus attention on learning how to be better salespeople.

*Disadvantages.*    Centralized training has two main weaknesses. First, as was noted, it is expensive to take people out of the field and support them while training. Second, the amount of time a person can be kept at a central training location is limited. Moreover, trainees eventually become bored. When boredom sets in, education stops. Also, some people do not want to be away from their families for extended periods.

## Content of Training

The primary purposes of most sales training programs are to teach people to sell or to improve their current selling skills. Therefore, a significant

---

### The Best of Both . . . A Staggered Approach to Training

Some companies overcome the disadvantages of using either centralized or decentralized training by designing a program which incorporates both. Johnson Controls Inc. (JCI), headquartered in Milwaukee, is one of these companies. It has recruits start out with one month in Milwaukee for orientation, then three weeks in the regional offices learning about equipment and engineering, three more weeks in Milwaukee learning installation and estimating skills, seven weeks in the branch office (three with an engineer in the field and four making calls with the rep's direct manager), another three in Milwaukee honing presentation and relationship-building skills, four more weeks of making sales calls with a mentor, and finally a two-week simulation in Milwaukee where trainees get graded on their sales competencies.

Source: Andy Cohen, "Talent Scout," *Sales & Marketing Management,* December 1996, pp. 54–57.

---

amount of the content of most training programs is devoted to product knowledge and persuasive communication skills. However, several factors other than the mastery of the persuasion process affect success or failure in selling. These are the trainee's attitude toward the selling job and the training, knowledge of the company, knowledge of customers, knowledge of competitive products, business knowledge, relationship-building skills, team-selling skills, computer assisted–selling skills, time-management skills, and knowledge of the legal constraints on selling. They should also be covered in sales training programs. Not every training program should necessarily cover all of them at one time. Rather, the specific content of the training will vary depending on the objectives of that particular training session. Each of the factors just mentioned is discussed below.

#### Attitudes toward Training

For training to have its greatest impact, it is important to first instill in the trainees a thorough understanding of the nature and importance of the selling job and of their role in achieving the company's overall objectives. Some trainees may hold certain beliefs about selling and about training which are not accurate, and these beliefs will hinder their learning. For example, some people believe that salespeople are born with sales ability and that sales training for anyone else is largely a waste of time. This is simply not true. Other commonly held myths about selling are shown in Figure 8-5. Salespeople must also understand the importance of their role in the company. They are the primary communication link between the company and its customers. Often they are the only people in the firm directly responsible for generating revenue. Without communication between the firm and its customers and without the revenues generated by the sales reps, the firm would not exist.

■ **FIGURE 8-5**

| | |
|---|---|
| **Prevalent myths about the selling process** | **Myth No. 1.**   **Salespeople are born—not made.** This simply is not true. Such great sales forces as IBM, Xerox, and Procter & Gamble are based on excellent sales training programs. These firms hire young people who are largely without sales experience or skills and teach them how to sell. |

**Myth No. 1.**   **Salespeople are born—not made.**
This simply is not true. Such great sales forces as IBM, Xerox, and Procter & Gamble are based on excellent sales training programs. These firms hire young people who are largely without sales experience or skills and teach them how to sell.

**Myth No. 2.**   **Salespeople must be good talkers.**
On the contrary: Good salespeople are good listeners. The prospect has the information the sales rep needs; all the rep has to do is learn to ask the right questions, then listen to what the prospect says. (See the box labeled "Talk, Talk, Talk" in Chapter 3.)

**Myth No. 3.**   **Selling is a matter of knowing the right techniques or tricks.**
Unfortunately, there are no "magic" selling techniques, and methods that work for some reps do not work for others. Success in selling is more than mastering techniques; it is a result of several potent factors such as work habits, attitudes, products sold, and markets covered.

**Myth No. 4.**   **A good salesperson can sell anything.**
Not so! A successful sales career results when the individual sells the "right" product made by the "right" company to the "right" people. Any salesperson can prosper in a substantial number of jobs, and it pays handsomely when reps match their talents to prospective jobs.

**Myth No. 5.**   **A good salesperson can sell ice to an Eskimo.**
Selling is not a sport in which a sales rep tries to unload unwanted goods on an unwilling buyer who cannot pay for them. Good selling starts by finding someone who needs the product and can afford it. In other words, good salespeople call on good prospects.

**Myth No. 6.**   **People don't want to buy.**
Not so! People want new cars, nice houses, new clothing, sports equipment—all sorts of things. Industrial buyers *must* buy all the things their companies need for operations. People wait for the salesperson to show them how his or her proposition will benefit them.

*Knowledge about the Company*

All trainees need a certain amount of information about the company's history, its goals, and its organization, policies, and procedures. It is important for the trainee to understand the history and the current mission of the firm. This background information helps the reps develop a sense of pride about their companies. It also helps them to understand and adopt the values of top management as their own.

Trainees need to be shown how to work within the corporate system— who to contact to get things done and how the system operates. They need to be taught the company policies and procedures—and the reasons for them. When sales reps understand the reasons behind the procedures, they are more likely to adhere to them, and they can do a better job of explaining them to the customers.

### Product Knowledge and Application

A large part of training is usually devoted to providing knowledge about the products and services to be sold and their applications. Ordinarily, the amount of this training varies according to the products' technical complexity.

The trainees must know about the products they sell and understand the varied applications of those products. It is one thing to be familiar with the features of the product and quite another to be able to apply this information in the field to solve customer problems.

Today, much product information is put into a computer database which can be accessed directly by the sales rep. Many reps now carry portable laptop or notebook computers with them on sales calls. This makes it possible for them to call up whatever product information they need right in the customer's office.

### Knowledge of Competitive Products

Salespeople should know their competitive products as well as their own because they must sell against them. Detailed knowledge of competing products allows sales reps to design presentations to stress the advantages of their products over the competitors.

### Knowledge of Customers

In today's competitive environment, salespeople must be *customer oriented* in order to be successful. Therefore, the trainees must understand their customers' businesses. Each customer has a different set of priorities and problems, and the salesperson must be able to recognize and respond to all of them. Also, within each account there are usually several different people with whom the salesperson must work. The rep must be knowledgeable of the priorities and preferences of all those people who may have some influence on the decision. Furthermore, reps must have a thorough knowledge of the people and businesses to whom their customers are selling.

### Knowledge of Business Principles

Many salespeople are held accountable for the profitability of their territories. Also, as has been noted in many of the earlier chapters, salespeople often serve as consultants to their customers. Therefore, it is important that they understand basic business practices which underlie the operations of their own companies as well as their customers' companies. Baxter Healthcare, a leading supplier of products for the health care industry, includes business knowledge in its sales training for both salespeople and account managers. The sessions cover such topics as distribution fundamentals, pricing fundamentals, and finance for profit.[17]

### Relationship-Building Skills

Many companies are focusing on developing long-term relationships with selected accounts. The salesperson must be trained to help identify these accounts and to nurture the relationships with these customers. Managing each account for long-term profitability rather than for the short-term sale requires salespeople to prioritize their activities differently. They must work with customers to anticipate and identify problems and find mutually beneficial solutions. This requires a great degree of mutual openness, trust, and commitment, which is not usually found in transaction selling.

### Team-Selling Skills

Many salespeople work as part of a team. The skills which are critical to the successful performance of a team are not the same set as those which are critical for reps selling on their own. For example, being sensitive to the needs of others, accepting the shortcomings of others, cooperation, keeping others informed, being receptive to the ideas of others, and placing team success above individual success are a few of the elements on which training must focus. Many companies incorporate sessions which build sensitivity and trust among fellow teammates.

### Time-Management Skills

Most salespeople are given a great amount of autonomy to manage their territories. Not only must they allocate their time among their customers, they must also allocate their time among the various aspects of their jobs—specifically selling, service, and administrative responsibilities. The primary training objective is to convince the salespeople that ineffective use of their time can significantly reduce their productivity.

### Computer-Assisted Selling

Many companies are training salespeople to use computer programs to help them allocate their time between accounts, to develop their call

**This group of employees is participating in team-selling boot camp exercises to teach them the skills and attitudes necessary for effective team selling.**

## AN INTERNATIONAL PERSPECTIVE

How are multinational corporations training Americans to work overseas? Essentially most American companies are not training the people who are placed in international assignments. A recent survey of practices shows that 70 percent of U.S. managers and 90 percent of their families are sent overseas without any cross-cultural training at all. The study also found that between 16 and 40 percent of these managers return home before they are supposed to due to poor performance or inability to adjust.

In the same study, the researchers reviewed a variety of cross-cultural programs. They concluded overwhelmingly that such programs do increase cross-cultural skill development, ad-

justment, and job performance. The authors further recommend the following:

1. These programs should be considered a necessity. The costs are small compared to the potential loss for an earlier-than-planned return or the lost business due to cross-cultural incompetency.
2. Cross-cultural training should be provided to the whole family to alleviate family adjustment problems.
3. The programs should be experiential, participative, and behavioral using simulations, role playing, and field trips.

Source: Mary Munter, "Cross-Cultural Communication for Managers," *Business Horizons,* May-June 1993, pp. 69–78.

schedules, and to handle many of the administrative details of their jobs, such as placing orders, submitting call itineraries and reports, and developing specifications and quotations. Laptops are also being used by many salespeople as an integral part of their presentations. As the performance of sales activities becomes more dependent upon the use of computers, companies are providing training classes which build computer literacy.

### Legal Constraints on Selling

Properly trained, salespeople can reduce their companies' exposure to product liability and false promotion litigation and increase the chances of a successful defense if a suit occurs. They can also lessen the chance that charges of price discrimination or unfair competition will be brought against the company.

Claims in the area of product liability have been increasing rapidly and the costs of settling these claims is rising. Many are over $1 million. Salespeople should be instructed to adopt the following practices to protect against product liability claims and false promotional charges:

- Always make accurate, understandable statements regarding product warnings, characteristics, and use.
- Avoid making exaggerated claims.
- Review sales literature, warnings, and labels to be sure they are accurate and complete.

With regard to price discrimination, the Robinson–Patman Act of 1936 makes it illegal to offer different prices for the same product or service to different customers unless those differences are cost justified or the price is offered to meet a competitive price. It is important that salespeople are taught the circumstances under which they may offer reduced prices to customers and the documentation that they must have to substantiate the reason for doing so. In fact, salespeople must be careful to offer the same programs of technical, managerial, and/or promotional assistance to all customers (unless the volume of their business cost justifies treating them differently); otherwise they open up themselves and their companies to charges of unfair competition.

### Selling Skills

Finally, of course, the trainees must develop the selling skills and techniques that enable them to effectively communicate with and persuade their customers. These skills were discussed in detail in Chapter 3.

## Training Techniques

Several different teaching methods may be used to present material in a sales training program (see Figure 8-5). Keep in mind that all methods of presentation are not equally effective for all parts of the training.

### Lectures

The lecture method can present more information in a shorter time to a larger number of students than any of the other techniques. A *limited* amount of lecturing has a place in most sales training programs. Although company information and some product knowledge can be presented in

■ **FIGURE 8-6**

**Presentation techniques in sales training programs**

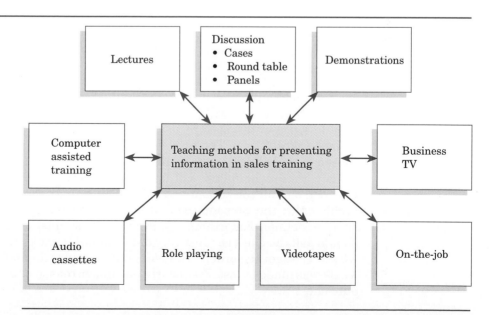

published material, some lecturing is usually necessary. Also, a lecture is frequently the best way to present a basic outline of a subject.

Although selling techniques are best taught by participation methods, short lectures introducing students to the underlying problems and principles can be extremely helpful.

### Discussion

Discussion should play a large role in any sales training program, since it gives the students an opportunity to discuss their own problems. It is the best method for making the experiences of competent salespeople available to trainees. It is also the best method for letting experienced sales reps exchange thoughts and know-how.

Discussions can take several forms. Many are simply open talks on various topics between the teacher and the students, with the teacher controlling the discussion and stimulating it. However, cases, roundtables, and panels can also be used to stimulate and facilitate discussions.

### Demonstrations

Demonstrations can be used to great advantage in teaching both product knowledge and selling techniques. What better way to teach how a product operates than to actually demonstrate its use? Instead of just telling about the different types of questions that can be used to probe for information, for example, they can be demonstrated before the class. Trainees can be shown how to handle innumerable selling situations that are difficult to describe.

### Role Playing

In role playing, the trainee attempts to sell a product to a hypothetical prospect. This type of learning-by-doing education can be highly effective in teaching selling techniques, particularly in initial training programs.

In handling the role-playing sessions, the trainer must explain the importance of taking criticism the right way. Students must be convinced that the critiques will help them become more effective. They must realize that many problems have no cut-and-dried answers and that the suggestions they receive will give them other options to handle problems. The first few presentations are usually poor, but they get better as each trainee takes a turn. The teacher must inform the class that the person chosen to lead off will make more mistakes than will those who follow. Obviously, those who follow will learn from observing the mistakes of the first person and the second and so on. The trainer should focus on major problems in the presentation rather than spending too much time on smaller details. For example, one of the first questions the instructor should ask the class is: "Just why did Joan fail to make the sale?" or "Just why did Joe get the order?" Students must acquire an ability to see where a sale was made or lost. Frequently, one major reason or event decided the outcome.

A few companies, such as the Du Pont High Performance Films, use role playing on a continual basis to *practice* critical, issue-oriented sales calls just prior to making these calls.[18]

### Audio Cassettes

Most sales representatives do lots of driving between accounts and many companies feel that this driving time can be used for professional development through the use of audio cassettes. Companies such as 3M and G. D. Searle provide their sales forces with audio cassettes which cover a wide range of topics.[19] Selling techniques, time management, and motivational speeches are a few of the topics which are typically covered. Many companies purchase their tapes from outside suppliers, but some companies choose to produce their own.

### Video-Enhanced Training

Video-enhanced training programs use videotapes and complementary written materials to train and test salespeople. The major advantages of using this method are the cost and time savings. The use of this technology has increased dramatically over the last few years. Uniroyal, Xerox, and Travelers Insurance are among the firms using this technology for sales training. Motorola uses videos to train salespeople on four different topics: product information, company information, market information, and sales techniques. Tapes on these topics are mailed to as many as 1,000 salespeople, who conduct a self-study of the videos and complementary text. Then, when they feel they have mastered the material, they take an open-book exam which is included with the materials. They transmit their multiple-choice answers to Motorola via a toll-free number. Representatives who successfully complete the test are given special acknowledgment in an annual recognition program. Their results are also considered as part of their formal performance and merit reviews.[20]

### Computer-Assisted Training

Some companies use interactive video technology for training. This technology combines computer, laser disk, and video technology. The videos present sales situations to the trainee in which an actor playing the role of the buyer makes a comment or poses a question. The trainee is asked to respond by selecting an option from a possible set of responses which are presented on the screen. Based upon the option chosen, another scene appears (for another choice) or a review of the lesson material is presented. The entire scenario, including the trainee's responses, is recorded on video for review by the trainee or an instructor.

A number of firms are investing in interactive videos. Motorola uses an interactive system to teach major account selling, while Massachusetts Mutual Life Insurance Company uses the technology to train the large number of new salespeople they hire each year. BellSouth is using interactive videos to teach the steps of the sales process.

There are significant cost savings in using interactive systems for training. These savings stem from the fact that using the videos reportedly lessens the time it takes to learn a given skill by as much as 50 percent. However, the costs to develop these programs are high.[21]

### Business TV

This form of training, in which training programs are broadcast live via satellite, is becoming popular with companies that operate their own television networks. Using television and telephone technology, salespeople across the country (or countries) can tune in and ask questions or exchange ideas with the on-camera presenters. Eastman Kodak, Texas Instruments, IBM, Aetna, AT&T, and Federal Express all rely on business TV for sales communications and training.[22]

### On-the-Job Training

On-the-job sales training is the most popular form of sales training. Eighty-two percent of the companies surveyed by Dartnell use on-the-job training.[23] Generally, the procedure is for the trainee to observe a senior rep or sales supervisor making several sales calls. Then the sales trainee makes several calls and the senior rep or supervisor observes and coaches the rep. Then they discuss what took place during that call and what the trainee could have done more effectively. This method places the student in a more realistic situation than the other techniques discussed. Usually this method is used as the final stage of the trainee's sales education.

## REINFORCEMENT

Most salespeople won't change their behaviors as a result of training unless there is some ongoing coaching and reinforcement. In fact, as noted earlier in the chapter, Xerox found that most of their salespeople retain only 13 percent of the information learned in training after 30 days unless it was reinforced. Yet in many companies this reinforcement doesn't occur as frequently as it should, largely because managers don't place a priority on this activity. They don't have time, they are uncomfortable, or they don't know how to provide constructive feedback, and rarely are they recognized or rewarded for their efforts in the skill development area.[24]

There are many ways to reinforce training, including all of the methods which have been discussed. The most frequently used method is for the sales manager to serve as a coach, reinforcing training efforts during actual calls. Some companies use senior salespeople to coach new reps. If a manager for Ciba-Geigy Pharmaceuticals observes that a rep needs additional training, the rep will be paired with a Certified Field Skills Coach, who is a salesperson, to work on developing skills.[25]

Some companies follow up the training session with refresher classes designed to reinforce the original program. Other companies use video-enhanced methods and computer-assisted methods to reinforce formal training sessions. These methods lower the costs of reinforcing training. Whatever method is used, it is important to build some type of reinforcement into the overall training program.

# TRAINING EVALUATION

Finally, during the evaluation phase, sales executives must assess the effectiveness of their training programs. In doing so, they must decide:

- What outcomes will be evaluated?
- How will these outcomes be measured?

## Outcomes and Measures

It is important to evaluate the effectiveness of training in terms of the objectives for which it was designed. This evaluation is necessary in terms of assessing the value of the training and in terms of improving the design of future programs. A variety of outcomes can be measured to evaluate training programs. They generally fall into one of the four following categories:[26]

- **Reactions.** These outcomes indicate, in a subjective manner, whether those who participated in the training thought it achieved the stated objectives and generally whether it was worthwhile. These reactions may be measured via verbal comments or questionnaires from the trainees, their supervisors, or the training staff.
- **Learning.** This outcome equates to how much information was learned and usually involves the trainee taking some type of test. There may be a "before" and "after" the training test or just one test taken after the training is completed.
- **Behavior.** These outcomes provide an assessment of whether the trainee's behavior has changed in substantial ways. This appraisal is usually conducted by a supervisor who can observe the behavior of the rep. It may also include a self-assessment or input from customers.
- **Results.** These are indicators of whether the training is transferring to improved performance results. This is the ultimate test of whether the benefits of training outweigh the costs. Such measures as increased sales and profitability, better customer retention and penetration, and numbers of new accounts can be used to assess bottom-line results.

A recent survey of evaluation methods reported that many firms are overdependent on testing knowledge learned to evaluate their training programs.[27] While it is important to measure this as part of a systematic evaluation program, it is as important to use the other types of measures as well. Otherwise, the sales manager will not be able to relate training outcomes to performance in the field.

#  Summary

A successful training program consists of three phases: training assessment, program design, reinforcement and evaluation. Training is an important factor contributing to the success of salespeople. A good program begins by establishing program objectives and then determining who should be trained. Once it is determined who will be trained, an assessment must be made of the individuals' training needs. This is the key to how much training will be needed.

During the program design phase, the company must decide who will do the training, where and when it will be conducted, what topics will be covered and what methods will be used. While line personnel have distinctive advantages as sales trainers, they often lack the teaching skills essential to a training program. Thus training is often the responsibility of staff sales trainers.

Although initial training is often conducted centrally, most sales training is provided on the job. New reps need enough initial training to do a respectable job. However, there are advantages to delaying training until the new person has some experience that can be carried into the classroom.

Training programs cover a wide range of topics, such as selling skills and knowledge of the product, company, customer, competitors, business principles, relationship-building skills, team selling, time management, computer-assisted selling, and legal constraints.

Among the many different methods used to train salespeople are lectures, discussions, demonstrations, role playing, audio cassettes, video-enhanced training, computer-assisted training, business TV, and on-the-job training.

It is very important that companies provide a method for systematically reinforcing their training programs. Otherwise salespeople are unlikely to change their behavior.

Increasingly, top management is demanding that training programs prove their worth. Training evaluation may take place on four levels: the reactions of the salespeople, their learning, their behavioral change, and improved performance results.

## Key Terms

| | | |
|---|---|---|
| Centralized training | Evaluation | Reinforcement |
| Decentralized training | On-the-job training | Training assessment |
| Difficulty analysis | Program design | Training content |

# Questions and Problems

1. "I don't have any training program. I just hire salespeople who have already proven successful for other companies and turn them loose. I let the big corporations do all my training for me and then just hire away their best people." This was the attitude expressed by the sales manager of one relatively small office machines agency. Is this a sound policy? What are some of the strengths and weaknesses of this position?

2. "Salespeople are born, not made. It's futile to try to train a person to be a salesperson, so I don't." How would you answer a sales manager who said this to you if you were trying to get him to hire you as a sales trainer?

3. "The school of hard knocks is the best training school for salespeople. I just shove them off the dock. Those that have it in them will learn selling on their own, and those who don't have it in them, well, we don't want them around the company anyway." How would you answer a manager who said this?

4. How can the sales manager keep top-notch sales reps interested in continual training programs?

5. You have been made sales trainer for a firm with 125 salespeople. How would you determine their specific training needs?

6. How can the sales manager determine the excellence of the various instructors in the firm's training program?

7. You read an article about interactive video sales training and liked its message. You feel that it may be beneficial to you in your job as sales trainer to Large, Inc. Unfortunately, you know only what you read about it. You want to know much more. Exactly what would you have to learn about applying interactive video technology to your sales training programs?

8. How would you motivate a manager to spend more time with new reps reinforcing the skills practiced in the formal training program?

9. How should the sales trainer go about establishing the agenda or curriculum for a refresher course?

10. How would you go about proving the cost-effectiveness of your sales training program?

## EXPERIENTIAL EXERCISES

**A.** Identify a business and a position within that business which deals with the public. For example, it could be a bank and a loan officer or a bank teller; or it could be a grocery store and a grocery bagger, or a meat cutter, or a checkout clerk; or a sales clerk at a Gap store; or a sales rep for the local beer distributor. Volunteer to prepare a written assessment of the typical training needs of a new person for that position. Don't forget to talk to people within and outside the company who deal with the person in that position, and don't forget to talk to some of the people who currently hold that position.

**B.** Describe the training for a field sales position, focusing on the following elements: who and how many participate, what content is covered, who conducts the training, what techniques are used, how long it lasts, where it is conducted, the costs associated with the training, whether there is any reinforcement after the training, and how the training is evaluated.

## ◼ REFERENCES

1. Thomas N. Ingram, Charles H. Schwepker Jr., and Don Hutson, "Why Salespeople Fail," *Industrial Marketing Management,* August 1992, pp. 225–30.

2. Marlene L. Rossman, "Marketers Must Realize That Selling Is a Real Job," *Marketing News,* March 5, 1990, p. 26.

3. S. Joe Puri, "Where Industrial Sales Training Is Weak," *Industrial Marketing Management,* May 1993, pp. 101–8; Rossman, "Selling Is a Real Job."

4. Puri, "Where Industrial Sales Training Is Weak."

5. *Dartnell's 27th Sales Force Compensation Survey* (Chicago: Dartnell Corporation, 1997), p. 143.

6. Puri, "Where Industrial Sales Training Is Weak."

7. Mike Zaruba, "Why Most Sales Training Doesn't Work," *Sales & Marketing Executive Report,* April 16, 1997, p. 6; Iris Randall, "How to Build a Premier Sales Staff," *Black Enterprise,* February 1993, pp. 154–55.

8. Neil Rackham and Richard Ruff, *Managing Major Sales* (New York: Harper Business, 1991), p. 130.

9. Robert E. Ayrer, "Why Sales Training Doesn't Work!" *American Salesman,* December 1995, pp. 9–12.

10. Conversations with Dick Canada, Chairperson, Dartmouth Group, Ltd., Indianapolis, Indiana, 1997.

11. Earl D. Honeycutt Jr., Vince Howe, and Thomas N. Ingram, "Shortcomings of Sales Training Programs," *Industrial Marketing Management,* May 1993, pp. 117–23.

12. Andy Cohen, "Ending School Daze," *Sales & Marketing Management,* November 1996, p. 32.

13. William Keenan Jr., "Getting Customers into the A.C.T.," *Sales & Marketing Management,* February 1995, pp. 58–63.

14. Christen P. Heide, *Dartnell's 29th Sales Force Compensation Survey* (Chicago: Dartnell Corporation, 1997), p. 143.

15. Ibid., p. 145.

16. Adapted from Bill Kelley, "Trained to Sell," *Human Resource Executive,* July 1992, p. 5.

17. Mark Vuturo, "Teams: It's Process Alignment, Not Functional Alignment," Presentation at the New Horizons in Personal Selling and Sales Management Conference, American Marketing Association Selling and Sales Management Strategic Interest Group, Lake Buena Vista, Florida, July 1996.

18. Jay Kennedy, "Practicing Sales Excellence," *Sales & Marketing Management Executive Report,* March 5, 1997, p. 6.

19. Cohen, "Ending School Daze"; Keenan, "Getting Customers into the A.C.T."

20. Earl D. Honeycutt Jr., Tom McCarty, and Vince Howe, "Sales Technology Applications: Self-Paced Video Enhanced Training: A Case Study," *Journal of Personal Selling & Sales Management,* Winter 1993, pp. 73–77.

21. Warren S. Martin and Ben Collins, "Sales Technology Applications: Interactive Video Technology in Sales Training: A Case Study," *Journal of Personal Selling & Sales Management,* Summer 1991, pp. 61–66.

22. Kerry J. Rotterback, "Sales Training Enters the Space Age," *Sales & Marketing Management,* October 1990, pp. 46–50.

23. *Dartnell's 27th Survey,* p. 141.

24. Rackham and Ruff, *Managing Major Sales.*

25. Earl D. Honeycutt Jr., John B. Ford, and John F. Tanner Jr., "Who Trains Salespeople?" *Industrial Marketing Management,* February 1994, pp. 65–70.

26. Donald Kirkpatrick, *Evaluating Training Programs: The Four Levels* (New York: Berrett-Koehler Publishers, 1992).

27. Honeycutt, Ford, and Tanner, "Who Trains Salespeople?"

*Case 8-1*

## CENTAURI PLANETARY SYSTEMS, LTD.*
### Cross-cultural sales training

Centauri Planetary Systems, Ltd., is headquartered in Sussex, Massachusetts, which is one of several communities located along the northwestern section of the beltway circling Boston. Centauri was founded with a capital investment of $500,000 during the early 1980s and was an alternative manufacturer of both DOS and Mac operating systems. Almost from the start, Centauri's profits were attractive. Most financial analysts attributed its initial growth to the founder's foresight in not standardizing on one operating system.

Today, Centauri still designs and sells software operating systems as well as other software products that enable users to connect to the World Wide Web. It has 30 offices throughout the United States and six sales offices located in Europe. For its first 12 years it was a privately held corporation. A few years ago, Centauri went public to further fund the research of interactive and multifunctional devices with an initial offering of $12.50 on the NASDAQ.

Recently, Centauri's success has been linked to strongly differentiated product features. Its salespeople have been fortunate in having differentiated products that generate such strong interest on the part of more than 150 manufacturers and nearly 2.5 million users. Senior management recognizes that this revenue stream cannot continue in the hypercompetitive business environment that exists today. During the last three years, four competitors have appeared. Two have incorporated in the New England area—one only four blocks from

Centauri's offices. The other two companies are located in Palo Alto, California, and Dallas, Texas.

Sales revenue last year was $2.4 billion with a net profit of $7 million. Revenue was down 12 percent while net profit plummeted 26 percent. Centauri senior management attributed this downturn not only to the price sensitivity in the computer marketplace but also to the emergence of four competitors that were quickly making inroads into at least half of Centauri's major accounts. A total of 112 clients were identified as major accounts—that is, organizations that purchased at least $500,000 in software packages from Centauri in the last year.

Almost a decade ago, Jill St. Claire received her B.S. degree from Boston College with a major in mathematics and a minor in computer science. She then joined Centauri as an account representative specializing in developing international markets. One of Centauri's best-performing salespeople, Jill achieved the company's highest level of sales performance four out of her first five years. Five years ago she was promoted to first-line sales manager in Centauri's Washington, D.C., office. A year ago Jill was promoted to regional vice president for the Northeast Region.

During a recent meeting, Nick Romanato, the senior vice president of marketing, recommended that Jill, with her experience in the overseas marketplace, would be a good choice to head up international operations. The European market, which comprises nearly 24 percent of Centauri revenues, had been struggling to stay in the black. Part of this downturn has been at-

---

*This case was prepared by Dick Canada, Chairperson of the Dartmouth Group, Ltd., Indianapolis, Indiana.

tributed to the entrance into the European market of two of the four new competitors. Poor decisions to invest in the emerging markets within eastern Europe also contributed to profitability problems.

Other problems resulted from placing a new manager in the position two years ago. The old saying that a good sales representative does not always make a good manager held true in this case. As a result, Centauri was considering withdrawing from the European market or, at the very least, reducing its sales force by 50 percent. Let's get rid of the "dead weight" on the international side continues to be Romanato's mantra. But Nick Romanato has indicated the company's support, as well as his own, in placing Ms. St. Claire at the helm of European operations.

The European reps have an average tenure of just over two years in their current positions. However, the teams' average length of time in sales is closer to seven. Jill St. Claire feels she has a relatively experienced team that should not be having the performance problems that exist.

Upon assuming control of her position, Jill initiated a new management process by which she carefully tracks account activity. Twice a month she either meets or speaks with each rep to assess the current status of accounts and determine any strategic action steps necessary to develop those accounts. This process served Jill well as manager in the D.C. office.

In addition, Jill redesigned the reps' compensation plan to be more in line with the direction of the company and the changing market in Europe. Each of these steps increased the performance of the team slightly. However, Jill was still looking to improve the bottom line of the European market. She felt a key item that was hampering performance was the reps' lack of sales skill and knowledge.

Her periodic account reviews suggested to Jill that the reps were deficient in their selling skills, but she wasn't able to pinpoint the problem. To do so, Jill decided to thoroughly assess the skill level and ability of her salespeople. During the next couple of months, she traveled with each of the 12 salespeople at least twice and observed them making new business sales calls. Jill also conducted interviews with some of Centauri's larger clients and prospects to complete the picture of how her salespeople were behaving in the field.

As a result of her field observations and interviews, Jill identified two problems:

- Reps are unable to effectively uncover and develop the customer's needs. Sometimes customers tell the rep what they need, but if the rep is trying to develop new business, his or her lack of questioning skills becomes a severe roadblock.

- Reps give too much information too soon in their calls. Before the rep knows what the customer needs or is interested in, he or she jumps in with product solutions and starts telling the prospect how wonderful Centauri's product and service support are.

### Question:

Jill wants to conduct a training seminar to address these particular issues, but she doesn't have sufficient funding in her budget. She needs to submit a proposal to Nick Romanato to secure the necessary working capital. Prepare a proposal to Nick from Jill to persuade him to free up funding for the training.

*Case 8-2*

## IMAGINATIVE STAFFING, INC. (A)

### Training program for a selling team

"I'm not sure what's going on around me right now, but it seems as if somebody is trying to tell me something." Angie Roberts, CEO of Imaginative Staffing, Inc., of New York City, expressed her thoughts to her assistant, Nicole Gamin. She didn't wait for an answer but continued, "I met some marketing professor at a party the other night and he seemed to think he was holding class about what's new in selling. He kept babbling something about team selling. I wasn't sure what he was talking about at first. Maybe he had some professional ball team he wanted to sell to someone with more dollars than sense. But then I caught the drift that he was talking about a way to make sales presentations.

"Then last night I read an article in one of the trade journals about team selling. To top it off, my daughter informed me that she was forming a team with some of her Girl Scout friends to sell their cookies this year. Is there some kind of message for us in all this?" she asked Nicole.

Nicole smiled and answered innocuously, "Maybe so!" She had a long list of daily agenda items to go over with her boss and really didn't want to get involved with a discussion about the merits of team selling. "Now let's go over what must be done today."

"You're putting me off because you don't like me to mess up your plans for the day. Well, it won't work. I want to know more about team selling so put it on the agenda somewhere for today," Roberts insisted.

"All right, you're having lunch with your executive committee. Let's put it on the agenda for that meeting." Nicole evidently had said the right thing because her boss immediately got down to the business at hand,

planning the day. Mondays were always busy. Not only did all departments start each week with a short meeting to plan the week, but the head of each department met with the CEO for lunch during which company-wide matters were discussed. Roberts felt strongly that these Monday lunches were important. They allowed her to learn what was going on in the company as well as to foster communications between her and the other managers in the organization.

Imaginative Staffing, Inc., was a temporary-services firm in New York City. Formed in 1990, it had grown to $17 million in revenues. Besides herself and her assistant, Nicole, the company had a chief financial officer, a sales director, four sales reps, an operations manager, 10 account managers, five administrative assistants, and a receptionist.

One reason Roberts had perceived the team-selling messages was that for some time she had been frustrated by the length of time it took to close a sale with a good prospect. On the average, it took about six months of hard work to make a sale to a major customer. One of the sales reps would make the contact and do all of the selling, sometimes with the help of the sales director if the situation seemed to warrant it.

Large and small corporations made extensive use of temporary help for one or more of several reasons: (1) to fill in for workers who, for some reason, were unable to work, (2) to handle overload conditions, or (3) to take care of seasonal peak workloads. In the current legal environment, many organizations were reluctant to hire permanent employees until there was a clear-cut, long-run need for them. Such factors as benefit packages, insurance, unemployment claims, and termination difficulties made management think seriously about hiring people as employees.

The lunch meeting proceeded smoothly as the group ate and disposed of the agenda items in order. When the last item, team selling, came up, members of the group looked at each other with puzzlement. What was it about? Only Susan Borland, the sales director, knew what team selling was. She was not eager to take the lead in the discussion, preferring instead to sit back to find out what was on Roberts's mind. She did not have long to wait.

The CEO began, "You may wonder why I have put this item on the agenda, so I'll not keep you wondering. For some time I have not been satisfied with our selling effort. It seems to take too much time to gain the confidence of prospective accounts to the extent that they feel comfortable with us. We are relatively new in this market. They don't know us. I've heard and read about team selling as a system that might be of use to us. I want to know exactly what it is and if it is something we should be using."

"It's interesting that you bring this up today because I just had a breakfast meeting with a sales team for Colony Cablevision," Susan Borland said. She continued, "As you know, I'm on the board of directors of my homeowners' association. We have over 1,000 homes in our planned development, most of whom individually subscribe to a cable television system at an average cost of about $45 a month. Now we have been approached by Colony to enter into a bulk billing deal in which all the homeowners will be billed by the association at an attractive price, less than $20 a month for the package. Well, they flew in one of the top managers from their home office to join with the local manager, the local technical engineer, the local marketing manager, and the

person who would be our account manager. Each of them made a presentation, and I must say it was effective. I think the board bought it. Anyway, at the time I wondered if this was something we should be doing."

The meeting was interrupted by the receptionist informing several of the managers that their 1:30 appointments were waiting. As they stood up to leave, Roberts asked Borland to prepare a plan for developing and training a sales team for the group to consider at some meeting in the near future.

Susan Borland had been with the company from its beginning. In the early days she did whatever needed to be done, but as the firm grew and was able to hire people to do specific jobs, she devoted more and more of her time to sales. At first she was the firm's only salesperson, but as the company grew she was able to hire more sales reps and she spent increasingly more time in the office, yet still helped the sales reps whenever they needed it. She was interested in her assignment and intended to get on it that afternoon with the help of her assistant, Judy Morgan.

After briefing Judy about the team-selling assignment, she told her to go to the library and research the subject. "Find out everything you can about it and who is using it."

That evening, Susan was talking about the day with a friend and the conversation drifted into team selling. The friend, a sales rep for a leading software company, was familiar with the concept since his firm used it to sell to important accounts. He advised, "Don't put too many people on the team or things can get confusing to the prospect. On one of our first team sales calls, we had seven people in there pitching. It was a disaster. The prospect was overwhelmed with information, much of which was useless. Our people weren't trained. We had some of the programming people in there and you can imagine their selling skills. They just wouldn't talk about what the prospect wanted to hear, they just talked in their lingo."

Susan listened. She had already decided who should be on the sales team, but now she realized that some of these people would require training.

*Questions:*

1. Should Imaginative Staffing, Inc., adopt a team-selling system for selling to important accounts?

2. If so, who should be on the team?

3. What training would be needed by the team? To what extent should the team's presentation be planned?

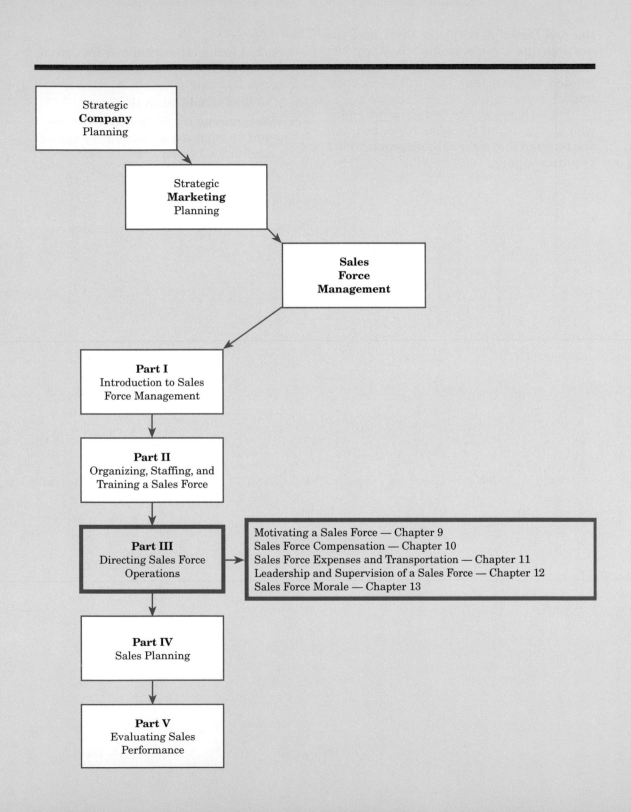

Strategic **Company** Planning

Strategic **Marketing** Planning

**Sales Force Management**

**Part I**
Introduction to Sales Force Management

**Part II**
Organizing, Staffing, and Training a Sales Force

**Part III**
Directing Sales Force Operations

Motivating a Sales Force — Chapter 9
Sales Force Compensation — Chapter 10
Sales Force Expenses and Transportation — Chapter 11
Leadership and Supervision of a Sales Force — Chapter 12
Sales Force Morale — Chapter 13

**Part IV**
Sales Planning

**Part V**
Evaluating Sales Performance

# DIRECTING SALES FORCE OPERATIONS

In Part II we dealt with organizing, staffing, and training a sales force as the first group of activities involved in *operating* a sales force. Part III continues with operational activities that are part of *implementing* a company's strategic sales force planning. Part III consists of five chapters involving *directing* sales force operations.

Chapter 9 deals with sales force motivation—behavioral concepts in motivation and motivational tools, including sales meetings and contests. In Chapter 10 we present the topic of sales force compensation—the objectives and requirements of a compensation plan, the steps in designing a plan, the question of compensation *level,* and the *methods* of compensating a sales force. The problem of sales reps' expense plans and transportation are covered in Chapter 11. Chapter 12 is devoted to the leadership and supervision of a sales force—leadership characteristics and styles and supervisory tools and techniques. The final chapter in Part III covers various aspects of sales force morale.

# CHAPTER 9

# Motivating a Sales Force

I believe I can fly, I believe I can touch the sky!
**R. Kelly, Space Jam**

All motivation is self-motivation. Salespeople cannot be motivated unless they want to be. The challenge for management is to identify, understand, and channel the motivation which their salespeople possess. A sales manager acts as a catalyst, providing both the stimulation for salespeople to feel motivated and the proper rewards so that they continue to feel motivated.

## ■ MOTIVATION—WHAT IS IT?

To better understand the behavioral concept of motivation, let's first ask, Why do people act as they do? Or, Why does a person act at all? The answer: He or she is seeking, consciously or unconsciously, to fulfill some physiological or psychological need. All behavior starts with an aroused (or stimulated) need. Hunger, security, or a desire for prestige are examples of needs.

These needs may originate within the person or they may be stimulated by an external force. For example, you may simply become hungry or you may see an ad for food that makes you hungry. In either case, once the need is aroused you will be motivated—you will want to take some action. *The desire to expend effort to fulfill a need* is what we call **motivation.** In terms of the sales job, motivation is the effort salespeople want to make toward various aspects of their jobs.

### Dimensions of Sales Motivation

Motivational effort is generally thought to include three dimensions: intensity, persistence, and choice.[1] *Intensity* refers to the amount of effort the salesperson expends on a given task; *persistence* refers to how long the salesperson will continue to put forth effort; and *choice* refers to the salesperson's choice of specific actions to accomplish job-related tasks. For example, a salesperson may decide to focus on a particular customer (choice). She may increase the number of calls she makes on this customer (intensity) until she gets the first order (persistence). As noted in Figure 9-1, the choice of a specific action may affect the intensity and persistence. Likewise, intensity and persistence may affect the choice of specific actions.

**Motivational effort**

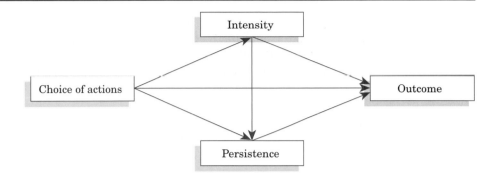

The sales job consists of a large variety of complex and diverse tasks. Because of this, it is important that the sales rep's efforts be channeled in a direction consistent with the company's strategic plan. Therefore, the *direction* of the salesperson's effort is as important as the intensity and persistence of that effort.

### Motivation and Strategic Planning

A sales manager concerned with motivating salespeople finds that the most complex task is getting them to expend effort on activities consistent with the strategic planning of the firm. Many salespeople don't need external stimulation to work hard and long; their internal needs motivate them to do so. However, every sales rep must be externally motivated to perform actions that support the strategic objectives of the firm. For example, if a company's strategic plan calls for changing its customer mix, a sales staff must be motivated to change its allocation of calls in a way that is consistent with the strategic change.

## ■ IMPORTANCE OF MOTIVATION

The nature of the sales job, the individuality of salespeople, the diversity of company goals, and the continuing changes in the marketplace make motivating sales reps a particularly difficult and important task.

### Unique Nature of the Sales Job

Salespeople experience a wonderful sense of exhilaration when they make a sale. But they must also frequently deal with the frustration and rejection of not making the sale. Even very good reps don't make every sale. Also, while many customers are gracious, courteous, and thoughtful in their dealings with salespeople, some are rude, demanding, and even threatening.

Salespeople spend a large amount of time by themselves calling on customers and traveling between accounts. This means that most of the time they are away from any kind of support from their peers or leaders, and they often feel isolated and detached from their companies. Consequently, they usually require more motivation than is needed for other jobs to reach the performance level management desires.

### Individuality of Salespeople

Sales reps have their own personal goals, problems, strengths, and weaknesses. Each rep may respond differently to a given motivating force. Ideally, the company should develop a separate motivational package for each sales rep; but a totally tailor-made approach poses major practical problems. In reality, management must develop a motivational mix that appeals to a whole group but also has the flexibility to appeal to the varying individual needs.

A related point is that the sales reps themselves may not know why they react as they do to a given motivator, or they may be unwilling to admit what these reasons are. For example, a salesperson may engage in a certain selling task because it satisfies her ego. Rather than admit this, however, she will say that she is motivated by a desire to serve her customers.

### Diversity in Company Goals

A company usually has many diverse sales goals, and these goals may even conflict with each other. One goal may be to correct an imbalanced inventory and another may be to have the sales force do missionary selling to strengthen long-term customer relations. These two goals conflict somewhat and require different motivating forces. With diverse goals such as these, developing an effective combination of motivators is difficult.

### Changes in Market Environment

Changes in the market environment can make it difficult for management to develop the right mix of sales force motivational methods. What motivates reps today may not work next month because of changes in market conditions. Conversely, sales executives can face motivational problems when market conditions remain stable for an extended period of time. In this situation, the same motivators may lose their effectiveness.

## BEHAVIORAL CONCEPTS IN MOTIVATION

Finding an effective combination of motivators may be easier if a sales executive understands some of the behavioral factors that affect sales force motivation.

The motivational process begins with an aroused need, but, as depicted in Figure 9-2, three conditions must exist before an unfulfilled need

■ **FIGURE 9-2**

**Motivational conditions**

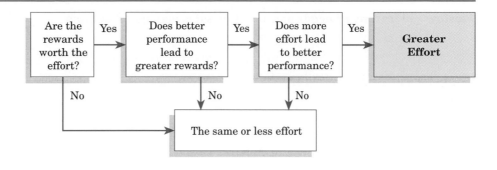

leads to enhanced sales performance.[2] First, salespeople must feel the rewards are desirable—that is, they will satisfy some need. Second, they must believe that gaining these rewards is based on their performance, and they must understand exactly what performance is required to get the rewards. Finally, sales reps must believe that the performance goals upon which the rewards are based are attainable. In other words, the reps must feel that if they try (expend effort), they can achieve the goals that have been set for them.

The behavioral factors that relate to the individual's needs and to the conditional links between performance and rewards and between effort and performance are discussed below.

### Understanding Individual Needs

Managers must know what salespeople's needs are before determining how to motivate them to satisfy those needs. Motivational programs often fail because they appeal to the wrong needs. Two motivational theories offer classification systems that can help managers recognize and understand different kinds of needs.

### Hierarchy of Needs Theory

In his hierarchy of needs theory, A. H. Maslow proposed five levels of needs that every individual seeks to satisfy.[3] These basic needs, presented in Figure 9-3, can be satisfied with extrinsic and intrinsic rewards.

**Extrinsic rewards** (such as pay and recognition) are provided by others. **Intrinsic rewards** come from performing the sales task itself. For example, when a salesperson has feelings of accomplishment because he landed a big account, that is an intrinsic reward. The bonus he receives for landing that account is an extrinsic reward. Potential sales management actions or rewards that can help satisfy the needs described by Maslow are also presented in Figure 9-3. Some of these needs are considered more basic than others. For example, physiological and safety needs are the

■ **FIGURE 9-3**

Maslow's hierarchy of needs and possible sales managers' actions

**Fulfilled through:** Self development, challenge.
**Managerial actions:** Provide/offer advanced training, assignments to special projects, more responsibility and authority.

Self-actualization needs

**Fulfilled through:** Status, recognition.
**Managerial actions:** Recognize sales rep achievements personally and publicly through title changes, commendation letters, promotions.

Esteem needs

**Fulfilled through:** Affiliation, friendship, acceptance.
**Managerial actions:** Use team selling, hold social functions, distribute employee newsletters, hold sales meetings, mentoring.

Social needs

**Fulfilled through:** Job security, safety, income security.
**Managerial actions:** Provide safe work environment, set mutually agreed-upon performance standards, communicate job performance expectations and consequences of failure to perform.

Safety needs

**Fulfilled through:** Food, shelter, clothing, health care.
**Managerial actions:** Provide/offer adequate income and good benefits package.

Physiological needs

most basic needs; social needs are more basic than esteem and self-actualization needs. Thus the needs form a hierarchy, as shown in Figure 9-3. Until the more basic needs of safety and security are fairly well satisfied, the higher-order needs will not be aroused.

### Dual-Factor Theory

Another theory of motivation, developed by Frederick Hertzberg, is also based on the idea that people have needs that they will seek to satisfy through their behavior.[4] However, Hertzberg's dual-factor theory groups sources of satisfaction and dissatisfaction into only two groups, **hygiene factors** and **motivation factors.** Examples of **hygiene factors** (which correspond to Maslow's lower-order needs) are company policies, supervision, and working conditions. They are called hygiene factors because they deal with the condition of the work environment rather than the work it-self. Examples of **motivation factors** (which correspond to Maslow's higher-order needs) are recognition, responsibility, challenge, and opportunities for growth. These factors are part of the job itself and are called motivation factors because they must be present for the salesperson to feel motivated.

Pay can be both a hygiene and a motivation factor. Adequate and competitive salary levels overall are considered a hygiene factor, whereas commissions or raises directly related to performance are viewed as a form of recognition—part of motivation.

Inadequate levels of hygiene factors will cause a sales force to be dissatisfied. And, while adequate levels of these factors will lead to the absence of (or less) dissatisfaction, they will not serve to motivate the reps. Only the higher-order factors lead to motivation.

## Reward Evaluation

Understanding how to appeal to a salesperson's needs is a very complex task. Each rep is unique and has a different combination of needs. Therefore, company rewards and incentives valued by one rep may not be valued by another. As shown in Figure 9-4, often sales managers do not know the relative value placed on various incentives by their salespeople. Several factors detailed below help illustrate how sales reps evaluate rewards.

### Are the Rewards Worth the Effort?

For company rewards and incentives to have an impact on motivation, salespeople must *value* these rewards. In other words, they must feel that the rewards are worth the effort.

■ **FIGURE 9-4**

| What motivates your employees | Ranked by Employees | Ranked by Manager |
|---|---|---|
| | 1. Interesting work | 1. Compensation |
| | 2. Appreciation of work done | 2. Job security |
| | 3. Being well-informed | 3. Growth and promotion opportunities |
| | 4. Job security | 4. Good working conditions |
| | 5. Compensation | 5. Interesting work |
| | 6. Growth and promotion opportunities | 6. Personal loyalty to employees |
| | 7. Good working conditions | 7. Tactful discipline |
| | 8. Personal loyalty to employees | 8. Appreciation of work done |
| | 9. Tactful discipline | 9. Help with personal problems |
| | 10. Help with personal problems | 10. Being well-informed |

Source: Kenneth A. Kovack, "Employee Motivation, Addressing a Crucial Factor in Your Organization's Performance," working paper, George Mason University, Fairfax, Virginia, 1997. This study involved 1,000 employees and their managers.

Assume that a given sales rep, working under a straight salary compensation plan, reached her sales goal. Suppose the reward is a congratulatory pat on the back from management and a formal recognition award for the best sales performance of the period. This rep may say to herself, "This honor award would be fine if I were bucking for a promotion or if I wanted to boost my status with management or my co-workers; but what I really want is more money—a nice bonus or a salary increase for my outstanding performance." At the end of this thought process, the rep decides that the reward for reaching her goal is not worth the effort. Management thus should establish a reward structure that is likely to be attractive to their sales force.

It is also important for the manager to realize that different people value different rewards. The more closely the manager can match the assignment and the rewards with what the individual rep values, the more motivated the rep will be.

### Are the Rewards Equitable?

A significant factor in salespeople's evaluation of rewards is whether or not they feel the rewards are equitable. Reps compare their performance and rewards with those of their fellow salespeople and ask themselves whether they are being treated fairly. Equity theory suggests that if a salesperson feels that reps whose efforts and performance are not as good as his are receiving greater rewards, he may decrease his efforts. Rewards perceived to be inequitable are unlikely to be a motivating force. And there is a strong possibility that where significant inequities are perceived to exist, salespeople will leave rather than continue to be treated unfairly.

## Performance/Reward: A Conditional Link

Not only must sales reps value rewards; they must feel that attaining them is conditional upon performance. If the rewards are pretty much the same regardless of how good or bad that performance is, then these rewards will not be effective motivators.

Salespeople must also understand exactly what they must do to get a particular reward. This is often difficult because much of their job activity involves dealing with people outside the company (namely, customers) and because they usually work with little or no direct supervision. As a result, there can be considerable *ambiguity* and *conflict* in the salesperson's role.

### Role Ambiguity

Often sales reps are not sure what is expected of them. For example, reps may be uncertain of their authority to meet price competition or to grant credit. They may be unclear about their organizational relationship with staff executives. A marketing research manager may ask the reps to perform some duties in the field; the reps may not know how much time and energy should be devoted to such requests.

### Role Conflict

Role conflict stems from two sources. One source is that a sales rep is trying to serve two masters—the company and the customer. Because these two often have different and conflicting interests, a rep can get caught in the middle. For example, a customer wants lenient credit terms, but the credit manager wants to deal in short-term credit with stringent terms. Or a customer expects gifts and lavish entertainment, but the rep's management, fearful of bribery accusations, wants to cut back on these items.

Another potential source of conflict lies in the varying demands placed on the sales reps by different groups within their own companies. For example, the marketing department may push the reps to follow up on the leads generated by the return of the trade publication reader interest cards, but the sales department wants the reps to concentrate on existing customers.

Sales managers must make sure that each salesperson understands what is expected. Writing clear and detailed job descriptions and letting the sales force participate in setting their own goals are ways of decreasing role ambiguity and conflict.

**Management by objectives (MBO)** is a supervisory technique used by many companies to increase the sales staff's understanding and acceptance of the criteria by which they will be evaluated. In MBO, the manager and salesperson set mutually agreed-upon performance goals. Sales reps who participate in an MBO program are more likely to know what is expected of them and to feel that their goals are attainable and equitable than those who do not take part in such a program.

The importance of having the sales force know what is expected of them and how to handle various situations goes beyond improved performance. Research has demonstrated that when salespeople have a clear understanding of their roles, not only is their performance higher; their job satisfaction is higher and their propensity to leave is lower.[5]

### Performance Evaluation

Sales managers must first design a reward structure in which greater rewards are tied to better performance. The evaluation process should be linked to the reward system, and sales managers should make every effort to keep the process as objective as possible. The goals should be clear, concise, and measurable. Every sales rep should be made aware of the criteria and the process that will be used to evaluate them. Finally, sales managers must work with each rep on an individual basis to make sure that she or he has accurate understanding about what is expected and what the rewards are. To be motivated, salespeople must believe that improved performance will lead to greater rewards.

## Effort/Performance: A Conditional Link

Salespeople must also believe that if they expend greater effort, it will lead to improved performance. If they believe this, they will be motivated to put forth greater effort. Otherwise, reps will not expend that effort regardless of the potential for reward. In other words, if salespeople don't believe their additional efforts will make a difference, they won't try. The accuracy of the sales staff's perceptions concerning effort and performance determines whether motivation can lead to improved performance.

Suppose, for example, a salesperson believes that making a greater number of calls will lead to improved performance, when in fact what the rep really needs to do is to improve the quality of the calls or to call on a different mix of customers. The salesperson may be motivated to make the additional calls, but this will not lead to significantly improved performance. Salespeople must have accurate perceptions of which activities will lead to improved performance. Similarly, they must correctly understand the reasons for their successes and failures. Otherwise, it is likely that they will also have inaccurate perceptions of the effort/performance link.

### Perceived Reasons for Success and Failure

Salespeople usually attribute their successes and failures to one or more of the following reasons: ability, effort, strategy (or tactics), luck, or the difficulty of the task.[6] Sales reps will be motivated to do different things, depending upon the **attributions** for success or failure they have made. For example, if a salesperson feels that he did not reach his goals because he did not put forth enough effort, he will be motivated to work harder—to work more hours and/or to call on more accounts. However, if he feels that he lost sales because of the particular presentation he was using, he will change his strategy by adapting his presentation. Changing strategies is sometimes called "working smarter."

If sales reps feel their failures are due to lack of ability, they should be motivated to seek advice or help. But they may instead just become frustrated and make even less effort or none at all. If they feel that the difficulty of the task contributed to their failure, they may be motivated to work harder or to work smarter. However, if they feel that the task is impossible, or that the goal is unreasonable, they will be frustrated and less motivated. Figure 9-5 summarizes these attributes and their impact on selling behavior.

Sales managers can help their people recognize which activities lead to improved performance and help them make correct attributions for success and failure through training, counseling, and day-to-day coaching. It is also important that attainable goals are set. More important, sales managers themselves must understand that encouraging their salespeople to work harder is not the only or necessarily the best path to success. Motivating sales reps to understand customer differences, think about alternative sales strategies, and be adaptive when the situation calls for it may lead to better results.[7]

## Salesperson Characteristics

Salespeople's needs, their evaluation of rewards, and their perceptions of the conditional links described above are influenced by the personal characteristics described below.

■ **FIGURE 9-5**

**Salespeople's perceived reasons for failure and their motivational impact**

| | Motivational Impact | |
|---|---|---|
| **Perceived Reasons** | **Positive** | **Negative** |
| Ability | Seek help; get additional training; ask for supervisor's assistance | Become frustrated and discouraged; give up |
| Effort | Work harder; make more calls; work longer hours | No change in behavior |
| Strategy | Change selling strategy; adapt the presentation | No change in behavior |
| Task difficulty | Work harder; change strategies; or seek help | Become frustrated and discouraged; give up |
| Luck | None | None |

### Demographics

Age, family size, income, and education affect the value that salespeople place on various rewards. For example, sales reps relatively satisfied with their current income level may be more interested in such things as status, freedom, and self-development than in pay and benefits. Others, less satisfied, may be very concerned about their income levels. Salespeople with greater education may place a higher value on opportunities for training and advancement than others.

### Psychological Traits

Some psychological traits relate to how the sales rep evaluates rewards. For example, a rep with a high need for achievement will be motivated by greater responsibility and challenge. Other traits impact the person's perceptions of the effort-performance link. Salespeople with high levels of self-esteem, for example, will feel confident about their efforts to improve performance.

### Experience

Another factor that impacts the salespeople's perceptions is experience. The more experience they have in sales, the more understanding reps will have about what kind of effort leads to improved performance and about what performance levels are necessary to attain the rewards they desire.

### Career Stages

Studies have shown that salespeople's needs change as they progress through their careers.[8] The career stages are related to demographic changes. In the early **exploration stage** of their careers, sales reps are very achievement oriented and are particularly interested in advancement and growth opportunities. During the **establishment stage** of the career

## Team Selling

The success or lack of success of team selling can often be explained by the willingness of the individuals on the team to cooperate with the team efforts. What motivates an individual to cooperate in team-selling efforts?

**Belief in the goal.** The individual must think that the goals of the team are worthwhile. A person who does not believe in the goal probably won't work very hard to achieve it.

**Belief that cooperation will lead to the goal.** The person must feel that the group has the ability to carry out the goal and that cooperation is necessary in order to be successful. If the salesperson feels that the team has been given an impossible task or unrealistic goals, motivation will be low.

**Belief that the benefits to the individual of cooperating will outweigh the costs.** The individual must feel the rewards, both extrinsic and intrinsic, outweigh the personal costs of participating. If the salesperson feels that she is not being compensated fairly, then her commitment to the team will be low. The salesperson may attempt to "free-ride" by letting others do her share of the work. The individual must also feel that he or she will have an influence on the team's actions and that his or her participation will make a difference to the team's success.

Source: Adapted from Thomas W. Porter, "Marketing Teams," working paper, Kelley School of Business, Indiana University, 1998.

---

cycle, sales reps usually become committed to their occupations, striving to succeed, to get ahead. Typically this is also the time when family responsibilities become greater. Money and fringe benefits become much more important during this stage, but status, recognition, and intrinsic job satisfaction are important as well.

In the **maintenance stage,** sales reps are very valuable to the company because they generally account for a large volume of their company's sales. Yet they are at a stage where their performance may begin to level off, and motivating them becomes particularly important. Salespeople in the maintenance stage are often motivated by job security, job enrichment, and status enhancement.

In the **disengagement stage,** salespeople are mentally preparing for retirement. While these reps have adequate knowledge to perform their jobs, they may have lost the desire to sell. Psychologically they are withdrawing. This attitude may overwhelm their ability to sell. That is, as they lose interest in their jobs, their performance will slip. It is very difficult to motivate reps who have reached the disengagement stage. The best thing the manager can do is to give them some reason for staying involved and committed. Assignment to special projects and/or problems is one way to recognize and use their skills and knowledge.

Thus it is very difficult to predict how any given salesperson will respond to a motivational package. But sales managers should begin by getting to know each rep as an individual in order to understand his or her specific needs. Only then will the sales manager design an effective motivational program. Some companies feel that personal goals are such an important motivator that they tie the achievement of bonuses to both sales goals and personal goals.[9] *Every motivational program should have some elements within it that can be tailored to the individual's needs.*

## ◼ SELECTING EFFECTIVE COMBINATIONS OF MOTIVATIONAL TOOLS

As we noted earlier, for any motivational program to be successful, the sales reps must understand all aspects of their jobs. The reps should have a detailed job description and a careful explanation of what is expected of them. They also need to understand how their accomplishments will be evaluated. The key is to establish specific performance objectives which have been agreed upon and can be measured by both the manager and the rep.

Given a set of performance objectives, management must determine the most effective combination of methods to motivate their salespeople to achieve their objectives. Motivational tools may be divided into two categories: **financially based rewards** and **nonfinancial rewards.** Each type is outlined in Figure 9-6. Note that many of these are found in the ba-

◼ **FIGURE 9-6**

| | |
|---|---|
| **Specific elements in motivation mix** | **Financially based rewards**<br>◼ Basic compensation plan<br>    Salary<br>    Commissions<br>    Bonus payments<br>    Fringe benefits<br>◼ Sales contests<br><br>**Nonfinancial rewards**<br>◼ Recognition awards, such as pins, trophies, certificates<br>◼ Praise and encouragement from management<br>◼ Job enrichment<br>◼ Opportunity for promotion (this may also be a financial reward)<br><br>**Other elements**<br>◼ Sales meetings and conventions<br>◼ Leadership and supervision<br>◼ Sales training programs—induction and continuation<br>◼ Sales mentoring<br>◼ Sales planning elements<br>    Forecasts<br>    Budgets<br>    Quotas<br>    Territories<br>◼ Evaluation of salesperson's performance<br>◼ General management elements<br>    Organizational structure<br>    Management's leadership style<br>    Channels of communication |

sic sales management tasks of planning, training, compensating, and evaluating. Because each of these is discussed in separate chapters, we will devote greater attention to the others in the discussion that follows.

# FINANCIALLY BASED REWARDS

## Compensation

Money is a powerful motivator. Surveys show that salespeople prefer pay raises and cash incentives over any other type of motivational program.[10] These types of rewards are the easiest to administer as well. As a result, many companies—IBM, AT&T, and Procter & Gamble, for example—use lump-sum cash awards for their salespeople.[11] The design of sales force compensation plans is discussed in the next chapter.

## Sales Contests

Sales force contests are short-term incentive programs that use prizes and awards to motivate sales reps to achieve goals specified by management. Contests are a popular motivational device.

A contest should have a clear-cut, definite purpose, such as something management wants the sales force to do that it isn't doing. Contests are best used to achieve such specific goals as getting new accounts, selling specific products, or relieving certain overstocked inventory positions.

In planning and conducting a successful contest, managers must design the contest, select the prizes, and promote the contest.

### Contest Design

The contest should be designed so that each person has an equal opportunity to win. If the average or poor reps learn that the top producers win all the prizes, they will silently withdraw from the competition. Opportunity to win may be equalized through the use of quotas or by allowing for differences in territories and selling abilities. The rep who makes the greatest improvement relative to others is the winner. In this way, even the poorest salesperson has a chance to win.

A variation of the design, described above, is an **open-ended contest** in which there is no limit to the number of people who can win by meeting their preset goals. In this way, people are competing only with themselves. This is in contrast to a **closed-ended contest** in which there are a limited number of winners. Northern Telecom has successfully used an open program, whereas IBM recently used a closed program, which is described in the nearby "International Perspective" box.[12]

Another method of broadening the opportunity to win is to use a **tiered contest.** In this type of program, two or more levels of prizes are awarded. If salespeople perform at or above a certain level, they get a certain prize—say, a trip to Europe. If they achieve at a lower level, they get a different

## AN INTERNATIONAL PERSPECTIVE

IBM recently conducted a global sales contest called "You Sell, You Sail." The contestants were 2,000 IBM reps and 5,000 independent distributors, who sell IBM's midsized computers used by small and medium-sized businesses. These reps and distributors were from 140 countries. The prize . . . a Caribbean cruise!

The overall goal of the contest was year-to-year revenue growth and the winning slots were allocated to IBM's global regions based on their contribution to total sales. But because each of the geographic territories have different ways of doing business, the specific criteria for winning were set by the regions themselves and thus varied somewhat across region. As a result, 200 IBM salespeople (and their guests) from the regions of Europe, Canada, Africa, Asia-Pacific, and the United States set sail together from Miami on a Caribbean cruise.

Source: Melanie Berger, "IBM's Global Sails Program," *Sales & Marketing Management,* February 1997, p. 34.

prize—maybe a trip to the Bahamas. This can be used in conjunction with an open-ended contest in which everyone can win. Tissues Technology, a company that sells and leases surgical lasers, has an incentive program in which there are eight levels of prizes with choices at each level.[13]

### Prizes

Contest success depends to a great extent on the attractiveness of the prizes. Cash prizes, merchandise, and travel are frequently used as incentives. Cash prizes have the advantage of giving the rep the greatest choice in how to use the prize. On the other hand, travel and merchandise are more visible and interesting to promote and publicize. Also, some studies have found these noncash prizes to be more effective for motivating sales reps.[14] In the Tissue Technology contest described above, one of the top prizes is a two-week African safari. One way to increase the choice associated with merchandise is to use a point system where the winners earn points toward merchandise they may select from a catalog.

### Promotion

The sales contest and the prizes which will be given should be widely and continually publicized throughout the duration of the contest. At least 10 percent to 15 percent of the budget for the contest should be spent on promotion. The goal is to keep everyone excited.

### Objections to Contests

While contests can increase sales and boost morale, they may also have some unintended effects. Frequently, sales contests lead to undesirable selling methods, such as overstocking, overselling, and various pressure tactics. In the short run, such tactics may enable a sales rep to win the contest, but in the long run they can cause trouble. Many executives object to contests on the grounds that they create morale problems. To some extent, the open-ended and tiered programs can alleviate the possible morale problems.

*A Day-to-Day Operating Problem*

## MAJESTIC PLASTICS COMPANY (F)

### The sales contest

Bud Cowan, the Majestic sales rep in Dallas, was angry. He wanted to know what Clyde Brion planned to do about the sales contest. Although the $15,000 award had already been delivered to another Majestic rep one month ago, Cowan felt the prize was actually his.

It had been only a year ago that Clyde Brion had dreamed up the idea of a $15,000 contest for the Majestic sales force. Having just introduced the new ROYAL line of plastic containers, the company was interested in seeing sales for the new product get off to a quick start. Clyde had suggested a sales contest, the company's first, whereby the rep selling the most from the ROYAL line would receive a check for $15,000 hand-delivered by the Majestic president.

Having developed the guidelines, Clyde then informed the sales force of the contest, which would last for nine months. The reaction from the reps was quite enthusiastic and in the first month alone, ROYAL line sales exceeded company projections.

With one month to go in the contest, Bud Cowan appeared to be well on his way to winning the prize. He had worked extremely hard introducing the ROYAL line to all his customers in the Dallas area, even going as far as holding ROYAL line seminars on weekends. His efforts appeared to be paying off when out of the blue Wally Thomas, Majestic's rep in Milwaukee, delivered a huge order to his largest account, Badger Foods.

With that order, Wally was able to secure the contest and one month ago had received a $15,000 check presented in a ceremony at company headquarters. This week, however, came a startling development. It seemed that Badger Foods had decided to cancel plans for a new product line and no longer needed the shipment of ROYAL line plastic containers. Having neither opened nor used any of the shipment, Badger was expecting a full refund on the returned goods. This practice was in line with Majestic customer policy and, although disappointed, Majestic did not want to get into any kind of legal battle with one of its best customers.

When asked by Clyde Brion about the lost sale, Wally Thomas expressed shock and disappointment but still felt the $15,000 prize belonged to him. "I sold that order within the contest time frame, fair and square! It's not my problem if a customer changes their mind after I've delivered the product. The boys in headquarters should deal with that! I worked hard and won that contest," Thomas said.

Bud Cowan, however, disagreed. "Thomas played this contest like a fiddle! I'll bet he set that bogus order up with Badger Foods on the first day of the contest. Heck, he's been buddies with those guys for over 20 years. I want that $15,000 and a handshake from the president," demanded Cowan.

**Question:** What should Clyde Brion do to resolve this dilemma?

Note: This case was prepared by Steven Reed, under the direction of R. Spiro.

One of the biggest objections to sales contests is that, almost inevitably, a decline in sales occurs afterward. The sales force cannot keep up the high level of activity indefinitely. Also, some crafty sales reps "stockpile" orders by getting customers to delay orders in the period just before the contest begins. Many questions have been raised about the long-run benefits of a contest. If a contest has achieved wider distribution and new dealerships, a long-run benefit should occur. But if the contest has focused mainly on sales volume, its long-range value is questionable. Lack of permanent accomplishment is not necessarily bad, however. For instance, many contests are designed for short-run purposes such as selling out on overstocked inventory.

In summary, then, contests can be effective motivators, but they must be carefully and thoroughly designed to encourage participation by the greatest number of people.

## NONFINANCIAL REWARDS

Managers often assume that financial incentives are the best motivators and that developing a good compensation package is the only thing they must do to motivate their sales force. However, evidence suggests that sales reps are motivated by both financial and nonfinancial incentives. In fact, there is evidence that money is not always the best motivator.[15] A variety of factors, including job enrichment, recognition, promotion, encouragement, and praise, motivate performance. These factors are discussed below.

### Job Enrichment

Salespeople thrive on challenge. One way managers can challenge reps is by giving them greater responsibility, authority, and control over their jobs. Also, most people like to have variety in their job-related tasks. Doing the same things over and over again quickly becomes boring to someone who is seeking challenge. If managers vary some aspects of the sales job, this can provide a stimulus for increased levels of motivation. Finally, like everyone else, salespeople want to feel that they are performing a meaningful task that will make a significant contribution to their companies and/or to those around them. Managers must make sure that each salesperson understands the importance of his or her contribution to the company's performance.

### Recognition and Honor Awards

A fundamental principle of good human relations is to give full recognition to individuals who deserve commendation. Most salespeople enjoy public recognition of their accomplishments. Plaques, pins, or certificates can be used to recognize accomplishment levels. It is really difficult to give too much recognition to anyone. This is exemplified by the following quote from Joe Rice, a Belden-Stark Brick Corporation sales manager:

> The last trip I qualified for was a trip to Istanbul to meet the president of our parent company. I can afford a trip to Istanbul on my own, but a chance to be recognized as one of the top American salespeople is something you can't put a price on.[16]

**Public recognition of a job well done is a good motivational tool.**

These incentive programs are most effective when they recognize approximately half of the salespeople. If too many people receive the awards, they lose their value; if too few receive them, they may be viewed as too hard to achieve. The awards should be publicized and presented in a public ceremony or banquet. Involvement by top management is also important as this adds significance and prestige to the award.

Often clubs are developed for outstanding producers or those who meet certain goals. Membership in such clubs usually bestows on high achievers the right to various recreational diversions in addition to the ego-gratifying recognition connected with just being in the select group. The life insurance industry has long had its Million Dollar Round Table to recognize agents who sell that amount of life insurance each year. Strohs has a Top Performers Club into which 4 out of the top 88 performers are inducted each year. ADP and Xerox have similar President's Clubs.[17] Membership in these clubs is valued highly by most reps, who consider it a major career accomplishment.

## Promotions

Title changes can be another source of motivation. Changing a rep's title from sales representative to senior sales representative, for example, can be used to recognize different levels of accomplishment. Dow Chemical Company recognizes eight levels of achievement for career salespeople from sales representative to corporate account executive. Each level entails a major increase in responsibility.[18] Of course the possibility of being promoted into management is a motivating factor for many salespeople.

## Encouragement and Praise

The easiest and least expensive form of motivation is personal encouragement and praise from the manager. Small things such as a word of encouragement, a personal note, a pat on the back, or a thank-you for a job well done goes a long way. Most reps like to feel that someone knows and cares about how much extra effort went into heading off the competitive threat to their largest account or how hard they tried, even though they didn't get that new account.

# ◼ SALES MEETINGS

Sales meetings are one of the most commonly used methods of motivating salespeople. Most companies have one or more sales meetings a year and some have them as frequently as once a week. The most important aspect of the sales meeting is communication. It gives sales reps the opportunity to interact with management and with fellow reps and makes them feel part of a team.

## Purposes of Sales Meetings

Management can use sales meetings to communicate the company's long-term goals and strategic objectives and to explain how important the salesperson's role is in achieving these goals. This instills in the sales rep a sense of self-esteem and pride in and identification with the company. This kind of communication is particularly important for salespeople, who are so often physically isolated from their companies. Also, many of them rarely see each other except at sales meetings. Thus the meetings enable them to develop friendships and build team spirit and solidarity.

Sales meetings are also used to inform reps about product changes and new products, to explain new advertising and marketing programs, to provide training, and to inspire the sales staff to work harder and smarter. Meetings such as these can help the sales staff understand what is expected, improve their knowledge and skills, and build confidence in their efforts to succeed.

## Planning for Sales Meetings

Planning is the key to success. A poorly planned sales meeting is probably worse than no meeting at all. A boring, tedious meeting in which salespeople have no opportunity to interact and participate can be demoralizing. This problem can be avoided by careful planning, by using speakers who are effective communicators, and by using a variety of communication formats. Videotapes, small-group discussions, role playing, demonstrations, and question-and-answer sessions can all be effective communication methods. Soliciting input from the reps about what they think should be covered in the meeting can help as well.

# ◼ CHALLENGES AND CHANGES IN SALES FORCE MOTIVATION

One of the most pervasive motivational challenges facing sales force managers is the plateaued salesperson. Another motivational issue, somewhat related to the first, is whether or not to segment the sales force for the purposes of motivation, communication, and administration.

## Plateaued Salespeople

A plateaued salesperson is one who has stopped improving and developing. Often these people (usually but not always in the 40 to 50 age bracket) have performed well in the past, but they reach a point where they seem to lose the drive or even the interest in striving for new goals. This is a significant problem for most sales managers. A survey of sales managers reported that 18 percent of their salespeople are plateaued.[19]

These plateaued people are not performing up to expectations, and it is very difficult to get them to do so. Yet managers are hesitant to terminate them. They often have developed very strong relationships with a few important customers, and they may still generate a large number of sales with these customers without trying very hard. Causes of plateauing, symptoms, and possible solutions are presented below.

### Causes of Plateauing

The lack of upward mobility is the number one cause of plateauing. Salespeople faced with limited opportunities for promotion see their careers coming to a standstill. Other reasons are boredom, perceptions of unfair treatment, burnout, and satisfaction with income levels.

### Symptoms of Plateauing

There are early signs of plateauing. The sales reps may not prospect hard enough or they may not follow through. They seem to be sick or absent more and working fewer hours. They seem to lack energy, time, enthusiasm, creativity, and a sense of humor. Their paperwork may become sloppy, and the sales manager may get more complaints from their customers. Usually these reps are not keeping abreast of new products and technologies. They relish the past and resist changes.

*Possible Solutions for Plateauing*

The first step for a good solution is to recognize the symptoms early. Then it is important for the sales manager to discuss the situation with the rep. The manager must identify the problem and set clear performance expectations. If the rep does not improve his performance, then more creative solutions may be necessary. One solution is to give the salesperson a new assignment, such as coaching new salespeople, gathering competitive intelligence, surveying customers for new product ideas, or developing a new territory. The new responsibilities may relieve the boredom and/or provide a challenge which would excite and motivate the rep. Another alternative is to shift accounts, which forces the sales rep out of a comfortable territory that requires little to maintain into one where he or she must start over. It is the manager's responsibility to take action to get these people out of their ruts. Their experience and skills are too great to waste.

## Sales Force Segmentation

Throughout the chapter, we have stressed the importance of recognizing individual differences. Yet it is impractical to design totally different motivational programs for each salesperson. On the other hand, using one program to motivate every rep may not be very effective. Sales force segmentation offers a balance between the extreme of individual motivation and blanket motivational approaches.[20]

In this approach, the sales force is first segmented or divided into several groups. For example, sales reps can be grouped according to their career stages or their sales expertise. Then an appropriate motivational mix can be designed for each. Compensation, communication, supervision, and recognition incentive programs can all be tailored to the specific needs of the group.

Another approach is for the company to offer several alternative compensation and benefit packages and let each rep choose which program he or she wants. The company can even offer a menu of incentives and benefits, letting reps choose from the list and in effect design their own programs. Segmentation is a means through which managers can provide rewards that appeal to all of the salespeople rather than just some of them.

## MOTIVATION AND PERFORMANCE

It is important to remember that motivation—the desire to expend effort—is not the only requirement for successful sales performance. Salespeople must have the *ability* to perform as well as the motivation to do so.

The ability to perform sales tasks can be acquired or learned through training and experience. Some companies hire only experienced, proven salespeople who already have the necessary skills. But when companies hire inexperienced people, management must provide the training for them to gain the necessary skills. It is not enough for the reps to be motivated; they must also know how to do what is expected of them.

Recruiting and selection procedures are also important. If companies hire inexperienced people, they must be careful to select those with an aptitude for learning sales skills. On the other hand, when companies hire experienced people, they must be certain that those selected have the desired set of skills. It is also important in both cases to select people whose needs are consistent with the demands or rewards of the particular sales job.

The motivational program must be integrated with the entire sales management program. A good motivational program will not compensate for poor recruiting, selection, and training. Motivational policies must be a part of a well-planned and executed sales management program.

## ◾ SUMMARY

All human behavior starts with motivation. That is, the reason people act as they do is because they are motivated. Motivation is the desire to expend effort to fulfill an aroused need. Sales managers are interested in the effort salespeople desire to expend on various activities or tasks associated with the sales job.

Sales executives generally agree that effective motivation of a sales force is essential to the success of any sales organization. The problem lies in finding the right combination of motivators for any given group of salespeople. Sales force motivation is difficult because of the unique nature of the sales job. Also, each rep is an individual who responds differently to a given motivator. Another motivational difficulty occurs when there is a conflict in management's sales goals. Finally, changes in the market or selling environment pose motivational problems.

To motivate salespeople, managers must first understand their needs. Both Maslow's hierarchy of needs theory and Hertzberg's dual-factor theory help managers understand the kinds of needs salespeople have. Managers must also understand how their sales reps evaluate rewards. Salespeople will ask themselves: Are the rewards worth the effort? Are they equitable?

Salespeople must also believe that rewards are based on performance. The role ambiguity and conflict often experienced by salespeople sometimes make it difficult for the reps to understand management's priorities for sales performance. Managers must make sure that salespeople know what is expected and understand what kinds of activities will lead to better performance.

Management's task is to select the right combination of motivators—the right motivational mix for a given sales force. Motivational tools fall into two categories: financially based rewards, such as compensation and sales contests, and nonfinancial rewards. Nonfinancial rewards include job enrichment, recognition and honors, promotions, and encouragement, and praise. Sales meetings are another method commonly used to motivate salespeople.

In the future, the problem of plateaued salespeople will continue to challenge managers. It is important that managers recognize the symptoms of plateauing and work with their plateaued reps to overcome these problems. Sales force segmentation, where people are grouped according to their motivational needs and different rewards are offered to each group, provides an innovative approach to the challenge of motivating salespeople.

It is important to remember that motivation is only one component of successful sales performance. Motivational policies must be incorporated into a well-planned and executed sales management program.

## Key Terms

Attributions
Closed-ended contest
Disengagement stage
Establishment stage
Exploration stage
Extrinsic rewards
Financially based rewards
Hygiene factors

Intrinsic rewards
Job enrichment
Maintenance stage
Management by objectives
   (MBO)
Motivation
Motivation factors
Nonfinancial rewards

Open-ended contest
Plateaued salespeople
Role ambiguity
Role conflict
Sales force segmentation
Sales meetings
Tiered contest

 ## QUESTIONS AND PROBLEMS

1. Define motivation and explain why it is particularly important for salespeople.

2. *a.* List several roles that a sales rep is likely to play.

   *b.* List several different role partners with whom sales reps are typically involved.

3. What types of role conflicts are sales reps likely to experience?

4. What can management do to reduce a salesperson's

   *a.* Role ambiguity?

   *b.* Role conflicts?

5. Explain why persistence is an important dimension of motivation for the sales position.

6. As a sales manager, you perceive that your salespeople have a strong need for security and protection. How is this factor likely to influence your planning regarding the following topics:

   *a.* Type of compensation plan.

   *b.* Personal supervision of salespeople.

   *c.* Continuation of sales training program.

   *d.* Length of quota periods.

   *e.* Evaluation of a salesperson's performance.

7. Explain what kind of behavioral changes can be expected if a salesper-

son attributes failures to luck, effort, strategy, ability, or task difficulty.

8. Explain how the sales manager should handle a rep who is one of the best performers, but is constantly driving all of the other reps crazy with her combative, haughty attitude.

9. "If you pay a salesperson enough, you will have a well-motivated salesperson." Do you agree? Explain.

10. Explain how motivation is related to each of the following aspects of managing a sales force:

    *a.* Supervising the sales force.

    *b.* Setting sales quotas.

    *c.* Recruiting and selecting salespeople.

    *d.* Designing the expense-payment plan.

11. If you were a district sales manager, how would you motivate the following sales reps?

    *a.* An older salesman who is satisfied with his present earnings level. He plans to remain as a career sales rep and retire in six years.

    *b.* An excellent sales rep whose morale is shot because he did not receive an expected promotion. He has been with the company five years.

12. A sales manager once said, "Motivating salespeople is the same as babying them. I am careful to hire only motivated people. This way I don't have to worry about motivating them. Good sales reps don't need any motivation from me—they motivate themselves." What do you think about this philosophy?

## EXPERIENTIAL EXERCISES

**A.** Interview a sales manager, asking what he or she thinks motivates three or four individual reps. Then interview these same reps (one at a time) and ask them what motivates them. Compare their responses with those of their sales manager.

**B.** Design a sales contest for the salespeople who sell advertising for your local school paper, for a local copying service, for a local beverage supplier, for a telemarketing firm, for your school's telemarketing fundraising group, or for a school organization.

## REFERENCES

1. Ruth Kanfer, "Motivation Theory and Industrial Organizational Psychology," in *Handbook of Industrial and Organizational Psychology,* ed. M. D. Dunnette and Leaetta M. Hough (Palo Alto, CA: Consulting Psychologists Press, 1990) pp. 75–170.

2. These conditions are based on expectancy theory concepts developed by Victor H. Vroom, *Work and Motivation* (New York: John Wiley & Sons, 1964), and others; Edward C. Tolman, *Purposive Behavior in Animals and Men* (New York: Appleton-Century-Crofts, 1932); and Kurt Lewin, *The Conceptual Representation and the Measurement of Psychological Forces* (Durham, NC: Duke University Press, 1938). Expectancy theory as a framework for explaining salesperson motivation was popularized by Orville C. Walker, Gilbert A. Churchill Jr., and Neil M. Ford, "Motivation and Performance in Industrial Selling: Present Knowledge and Needed Research," *Journal of Marketing Research,* May 1977, pp. 156–68.

3. A. H. Maslow, *Motivation and Personality,* 2nd ed. (New York: Harper & Row, 1970), Chapters 3–7.

4. Frederick Hertzberg, Bernard Mausner, and Barbara B. Snyderman, *Motivation to Work,* 2nd ed. (New York: John Wiley & Sons, 1959).

5. Jagdip Singh, "Influence of Role Stressors and Job Characteristics on Job Outcomes of Salespeople: A Test of Some Unconventional Hypotheses," *Journal of Marketing,* 1998, in press.

6. Andrea Dixon, Rosann Spiro, and Maqbul Jamil, "When the Customer Says 'No,'" working paper, Kelley School of Business, Bloomington, Indiana, 1998.

7. Jaap Vink and Willem Verbeke, "Adaptive Selling and Organizational Characteristics: Suggestions for Future Research," *Journal of Personal Selling & Sales Management,* Winter 1993, pp. 15–23.

8. William L. Cron, Alan Dubinsky, and Ronald Michaels, "The Influence of Career Stages on Components of Salesperson Motivation," *Journal of Marketing,* January 1988, pp. 78–92.

9. Melanie Berger, "Setting Personal Goals for Employees," *Sales & Marketing Management,* February 1997, pp. 35–36.

10. Sandra Pessman, "Motivation Takes Myriad Forms," *Business Marketing,* November 1993, pp. 47–48.

11. Ibid.

12. Melanie Berger, "When Their Ship Comes In," *Sales & Marketing Management,* April 1997, pp. 61–65.

13. Jeff Baectold and Andrew Osman, "Tissue Technologies," working paper, Kelley School of Business, Bloomington, Indiana, 1997.

14. Vince Alonzo, "Cash Isn't King," *Sales & Marketing Management,* July 1997.

15. Ibid.

16. Vincent Alonzo, "Recognition? Who Needs It?" *Sales & Marketing Management,* February 1997, pp. 26–27.

17. Ibid.; and Edmund O. Lawler, "Xerox Gets Big Splash from Travel," *Business Marketing,* November 1993, pp. 50–52.

18. "Up the Ladder," *Sales Manager's Bulletin,* January 1993, pp. 1–2.

19. Robin T. Peterson, "Beyond the Plateau," *Sales & Marketing Management,* July 1993, pp. 78–82.

20. Thomas N. Ingram and Danny N. Bellenger, "Motivational Segments in the Sales Force," *California Management Review* 24 (Spring 1982), pp. 81–88.

---

*Case 9-1*

## BIOLAB PHARMACEUTICAL COMPANY

### A quest for motivational skills

"How did your interview go today? Are you going to get that promotion you want?" Hobie Dobbs asked his spouse, Kathryn. Although they had been married less than a year, Hobie had been paying close attention and had learned when silence was a definitive answer to one of his questions. This was clearly one of those times. Nothing was said but nothing had to be said, for anger and frustration were etched in her face. She dropped her briefcase on the floor rather loudly as she headed for the refrigerator in search of some moral support. Hobie followed and ventured a suggestion, "The Ben and Jerry's ice cream is at the bottom of the freezer."

It worked! After the second spoonful, she said, "I couldn't believe it. There he sat telling me that I'm not properly motivating my reps. That I cannot be promoted until I learn how to motivate people better. Me, Katie O'Brien."

"It's Dobbs, dear, D O B B S. Let me show you the license."

Kathryn was not amused. "Quit trying to be cute. This is serious. My career is being threatened by a bozo who tells me I can't motivate people well enough to suit him."

Kathryn Dobbs née O'Brien, a senior sales rep for Biolab Pharmaceutical Company, supervised five junior sales reps in her St. Louis, Missouri, territory. She had worked for the company for three years and had an excellent record. Each year she was one of the company's top producers. She was well liked by her peers and subordinates. It seemed to everyone that Kathryn was well on her way to a great management career with Biolab.

Biolab Pharmaceutical Company was a huge, international manufacturer of ethical drugs most noted for its biological and blood-related products. Kathryn reported to Mr. Simpson, district manager, who also worked out of the St. Louis office. Thus Mr. Simpson had more opportunity to observe Kathryn at work than was the case in the relationships between most district managers and their senior salespeople.

Hobie also worked for the company in customer service; he was a pharmacist who could be called on an inbound 800 number by any physician, druggist, or sales rep for product and application information. He and Kathryn became good telephone buddies in her early days with the firm because she relied on him for information.

"Gee, that's kind of general, isn't it? Exactly what does he mean when he says you can't motivate people? You sure don't have any trouble motivating me." Hobie continued, "Did you try to pin him down? Ask him what he was talking about? Get some specifics?"

"Yeah, it was like pulling teeth. He squirmed and had trouble looking me in the eye. He really didn't want to get into it with me, but I wouldn't leave until I understood what he was talking about." Kathryn went on, "He kept saying that my five sales reps were not performing well enough to suit him. He thought they should be producing more results and that the reason they weren't was that I was not motivating them to work harder. He said that they just were not making the calls and making the efforts that they should be."

"And that is your fault, is that it?" Hobie continued, "Who hired them, who trained them, who sets all the compensation policies? But since they made you the senior rep over them, everything is your fault, I suppose. Can you get rid of reps who aren't performing up to expectations?"

Kathryn responded, "No, I can only write them up, give them a bad evaluation."

"Have you done that?" Hobie asked.

Kathryn explained, "No, and I won't. It's true they aren't setting the world on fire, but they're doing all right, about average for trainees. They are busy learning the business right now at their stage of development and I don't see why I should put more pressure on them than they have right now. First, learn the business, then when they know what they are doing they can start working harder."

"Seems reasonable to me. Did you tell Simpson that?"

"Are you kidding? I was so mad I couldn't think, let alone speak. Besides I don't agree with his ideas of motivation. He keeps giving us those Bubba stories about how his old football coach used to motivate him and those other players to go out and die for dear old Mizzou. Then he starts talking about his Marine Corps days and how they motivate people—pride, don't let your buddy down, and all that. He's from another world. Well, we sell drugs to physicians for about 40 hours a week. We're not fighting for our lives and we sure aren't trying to beat the brains out of the competition."

"You seem to know how not to motivate your reps. Now what do you think will motivate them?" Hobie asked.

"I don't want to talk about it any more tonight. I want to think about it. I'll tell you tomorrow morning what I am going to do," and with that Kathryn declared the meeting over.

The next day began much earlier than usual because Kathryn was eager to get her conflict with Mr. Simpson behind her. Confrontation was to be the order of the day. She had decided to attack Simpson's evaluation of her motivational skills directly with him instead of appealing it to his superior as she had a right to do under company policy. She was not interested in getting embroiled in the company's cumbersome bureaucratic processes. She would attack this threat right at its source and if her effort failed, she would resign. She had good reason to believe that she could get a similar job with a competitor so she was not worried about getting another job.

She laid out her plans to Hobie, who listened carefully, saying nothing until she was through talking. Then he asked, "And what are you going to tell Simpson about your motivational philosophies and skills that will change his evaluation of you? What makes you think he is really interested in what you think about how to motivate your people? He seemed to be focused on your reps' input efforts. Hard facts! From what you tell me about him, what reason do you have for thinking that he can change his mind about anything? And by the way, what are you going to say about your motivational philosophies?"

Kathryn responded, "First, I am going to insist that the sales reps' basic motivational structure is pretty well set when we hire them. If they're lazy, we're not going to be able to change it. Furthermore, all sales management literature indicates that a firm's basic compensation plan provides the bulk of its motivational thrust. Add the training program to the mix, and I maintain that as a senior salesperson, sort of a bargain basement supervisor, I have little power to really motivate the reps. Consequently, he is evaluating me on something over which I have little control.

"Next, I know how the game is played. I may win something on appeal, but that will be the real end of my future with the firm. I would have dirtied the nest, made waves, or whatever you men call it. I would be tagged a militant and that would be that. So if my career is not to be with Biolab, so be it. The quicker I get out the better. It would be foolish to stay around and let this guy do a job on me. I don't need it and I don't have to take it. So that's the way it's going to be."

Hobie smiled. He knew it was going to be an interesting day.

**Questions:**

1. Do you concur with Kathryn's plan of action? If not, what changes would you suggest she consider making?
2. Do you agree with her philosophies of motivation? If not, what are your philosophies of motivation?

---

*Case 9-2*

### INTERNATIONAL CHEMICAL INDUSTRIES
#### Use of motivational funds

The following memo from George McCall, vice president of sales operations, was distributed to all regional and district managers.

Each manager should be prepared to give a short presentation to the group during our national sales meeting next week about how the motivational fund for his or her area was spent in 1994. Being new to the organization, I want to familiarize myself with what we are doing in this important area. Moreover, it seems to me that many of you may be doing some things that would be of interest to the other managers.

George's hidden agenda underlying the memo was that he was suspicious that much of the firm's motivational fund was being squandered on ineffectual motivational tactics. He wanted to open up the subject not only to discover what was going on, but also perhaps to develop some uniformity to what everyone was doing.

International Chemical Industries produced and distributed basic chemicals, such as nitrates, sulfur, and potassium, throughout the world. It was one of the world's largest chemical concerns. Its U.S. operations were directed from offices in Houston, Texas. The U.S. sales operations were divided into five regions, each of which contained five districts. Thus there were to be five regional managers and 25 district managers at the meeting the following week.

Historically, management budgeted 3 percent of its sales volume of $722 million for the costs of managing sales operations. Of that amount, 83.3 percent was allotted to field-selling costs, which included the salaries and expenses of both the field sales reps and their field managers. The costs of the regional and district sales offices were covered by the remainder of the sales budget. From that amount, area managers were allotted a small fund of approximately 0.02 percent of sales that could be used for motivational purposes in any manner they desired. For example, the district manager for Chicago spent $70,000 in 1994 on a special motivational program for the area's five reps. (Chicago accounted for 5 percent of the company's U.S. sales volume, or about $36 million.) Each rep who achieved quota for the year received a free trip for two people, all expenses paid, to St. Thomas in the Virgin Islands. All reps won and went together with their spouses for a most successful holiday. The manager planned to institute another such program for 1995. The response to McCall's memo was good. The managers seemed to take delight in relating how they spent their motivational fund. It seemed to McCall that they were in competition with each other to see who could come up with the most innovative plan. McCall was pleased to learn that they had been putting their motivational funds to good use. He was also pleased with the attitudes of the managers. Morale seemed to be high. The managers seemed to relate to each other exceptionally well, except for two isolated cases about which McCall had been made aware by his predecessor and about which he was taking steps to remedy.

In summarizing what he learned from the managers' presentations, he categorized the managers' programs into three groups. Twelve of the district managers had developed some sort of program to reward the sales reps' total effort for the year much along the lines of the Chicago district's program. Seven of the managers used the money for shorter special-purpose programs such as contests to encourage certain desired behavior such as pushing certain products or getting new accounts.

One such program stood out in McCall's mind since it particularly impressed him at the time. The manager of the New York office had become concerned with the tendency of the reps to concentrate on the firm's established accounts. He wanted them to make more calls on potentially new accounts. To that end, he designed a contest to reward those reps who not only called on prospective accounts but who managed to make them new customers. Since it usually took many calls on a prospective account before a sale was made, the contest had been conducted over a two-year period.

Six of the managers used the money for doing several smaller, short-run, action-oriented, one-shot deals. For example, the manager of the Charlotte, North Carolina, district walked into the office one midsummer day waving two season tickets for the city's professional basketball team. She announced, "These go to the person who brings in the first new account this month." That resulted in a flurry of new account activity and a dispute between two reps over who brought in the first new account. The manager settled the argument by giving both of them two season tickets. She made two reps happy. McCall was impressed with her savvy in handling what could have been a sticky situation. On another occasion, she walked in and announced that if the district met its quotas for the quarter, everyone and their families would be treated to a long weekend outing on a chartered boat out of Wilmington. The district sales volume had not been up to plan, but that quickly changed as everyone started working hard for their boat rides.

McCall was not sure which of these models was best for the company, in either the short or long run. He had heard some of the managers talking about how much they liked learning about what the other managers were doing with their motivational money. He wondered if such information should be included in the company's monthly newsletter. How would such information be used? Would a rep in Chicago pressure the manager for a contest that provided season tickets to the Bulls or Bears games after learning of the Charlotte program?

After due consideration, McCall felt that the money was being well spent and wondered if it should be increased. He had such questions as: What returns were being realized from those expenditures? How could he build a case to his superiors for increasing the motivational funds budget? Should he do it across the board or test it by giving an increased budget to a district manager representative of each of the three types of programs that were evidenced?

*Questions:*

1. What would you recommend McCall do about the firm's motivational fund?
2. What policies should McCall establish regarding the motivational fund?

# CHAPTER 10

# Sales Force Compensation

How little you know about the age you live in if you fancy that honey is sweeter than cash in hand.

**Ovid**

As we indicated in the preceding chapter, compensation is the most widely used method of motivating a sales force. Furthermore, research studies clearly show that the sales reps themselves much prefer pay raises to other performance rewards such as promotion opportunities, fringe benefits, or recognition awards.[1] Yet over the years a stream of research studies, interviews with executives, and other reports have consistently stated that many companies are dissatisfied with their sales force compensation plan. Consequently, in this chapter we study sales force compensation, suggesting ways that sales executives can reduce their frustrations in administering this very important element in a sales force management program.

The structure for sales force compensation looks something like this:

- Financial compensation.
    - *Direct* payment of money.
    - *Indirect* payment—paid vacations or company-financed insurance programs, for example.
- Nonfinancial compensation.
    - *Opportunity* to advance in the job.
    - *Recognition* inside and outside the firm.
    - *Enjoyment* of the job.

Most of our discussion in this chapter will deal with *direct* payments of *financial* compensation.

The compensation problem is twofold. A company must determine both the *level* of earnings and the *method* of paying its sales force. By **level of earnings** we mean the total dollar income paid to each sales representative for a given period of time. The **method of compensation** is the plan by which the workers earn or reach the intended level. One company may use a straight salary method of payment, for instance, while another may choose to pay a salary plus a commission.

# SALES FORCE COMPENSATION AND STRATEGIC PLANNING

A close relationship exists between a company's strategic marketing planning and its sales force compensation plan. The compensation plan has a direct bearing on the successful *implementation* of the marketing plan. As an example of this relationship, assume that a manufacturer of industrial machinery is planning to enter a new market to increase the firm's market share. A straight salary compensation plan probably would help to implement this strategy. On the other hand, a stronger incentive—perhaps a large commission—might be necessary when the strategy calls for aggressive selling to liquidate excess inventories.

To get its salespeople to aid in successfully implementing its strategic marketing plan, management needs to coordinate its sales compensation plans with the company's goals. But it is surprising how often a firm has a sales compensation system that is at odds with management's stated goals. Many firms, for example, typically say that they want a sales compensation plan that "emphasizes profitability." Yet these plans often have a commission component based on sales volume, rather than on gross margin or some other measure of profit. Other sales execs say that they want their salespeople to meet customer needs, but compensate them only on meeting sales quotas.[2]

To implement its strategic marketing plans, management also should recognize that companies and their market positions change over time. Consequently, a sales compensation plan also should change to reflect the company's evolution in its business environment. One type of pay plan is needed when a firm is just getting started and it wants to reach and maintain a certain level of sales revenue. Another type of plan will be required later when this company is realigning territories, introducing new products, and adding new channels of distribution or new types of middlemen.[3]

As we noted in Chapter 2, companies are changing the way they do business. Successful companies in the 21st century will focus on developing long-term relationships with their customers. Sales efforts must shift to reflect these changes; and because sales efforts must change, compensation plans must be revised as well. Instead of being rewarded for selling as much as possible and winning market share, salespeople will be rewarded for building penetration of each customer, keeping customers longer, and increasing the value of each customer.[4]

# OBJECTIVES OF A COMPENSATION PLAN

The objectives of a good compensation plan, as seen in Figure 10-1, may be viewed from the perspective of the company as well as from the perspective of the individual salesperson. These objectives are not mutually

■ **FIGURE 10-1**     **What a good sales compensation plan should do**

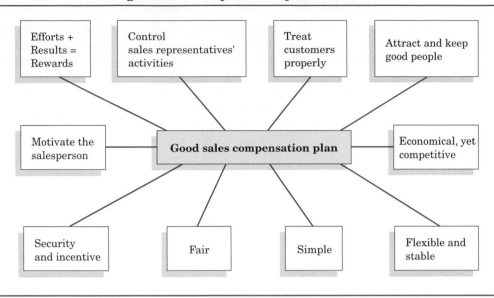

exclusive. In some situations, one goal may conflict with another. All, however, are valuable guidelines for a sales executive to recognize and follow.

## The Company's Perspective

We begin by considering objectives from the company perspective.

### To Motivate Salespeople

Companies want to encourage salespeople to reach and exceed their goals. Thus compensation plans are designed to motivate salespeople to perform. According to a recent survey, most companies do a relatively good job of using the sales compensation plan to motivate their salespeople. Seventy percent of those surveyed reported that their plans were effective or very effective. However, the remaining 30 percent reported that the plans which they use are not effective or at best only somewhat effective.[5] Clearly, designing a plan that motivates salespeople to meet or exceed their goals is not an easy task.

### To Correlate Efforts and Results with Rewards

This is an ideal that most companies constantly seek, yet seldom achieve. In the United States, in practically any situation—whether it be in business, politics, athletics, or social life—we usually pay off on *results* and not on *efforts*. It is nice, of course, if the results are commensurate with the efforts. But the key to rewards in most cases is results—also called performance or productivity.

This situation can be very problematic. A person can work very hard (expending much effort) but get little reward because the results of that effort are minimal. It could be that the results are minimal due to factors beyond the control of the salesperson. In reverse, we all know of situations where seemingly little effort has brought big results and consequently big rewards.

The problem in sales management is that it is frequently hard to equate efforts with results. Sometimes it is difficult even to measure results. For example, a given amount of effort on the part of salesperson Bill Garner may result in $50,000 of sales. The same amount and quality of work put forth by Sue Anderson may not result in any sales. Instead, Sue is building the foundation for profitable future business with a customer. However, this relationship may not be reflected in sales until some months or even years later.

### To Control Salespeople's Activities

A good pay plan should act as an unseen supervisor of a sales force by enabling management to control and direct the sales reps' activities. Today, this usually means motivating the reps to ensure a fully balanced selling effort. As a business becomes more customer focused, its salespeople tend to become territorial marketing managers. This, in turn, means that they must be motivated to do a *total* selling job. That is, the compensation plan must offer incentives flexible enough to cover such varied tasks as full-time selling, missionary work, or controlling selling expenses.

### To Ensure Proper Treatment of Customers

In the next decade, companies will be increasingly competing on the basis of customer service. A seller's ability to maintain strong, long-term relationships with customers depends largely upon providing customer service that results in a high level of customer satisfaction. A good compensation plan is one that motivates salespeople to treat customers properly, thus providing customer satisfaction. Improper treatment of customers is a sure way to lose them to competitors.

### To Attract and Keep Competent Salespeople

A good pay plan helps build the quality of a sales force that the company wants. A good compensation plan should assist in *attracting* the caliber of reps wanted by the company. A sound plan should also help to keep desirable people.

### To Be Economical Yet Competitive

From management's standpoint, a compensation plan should be economical to administer. Furthermore, a firm wants to keep its sales force expenses in line with those of competitors. Otherwise, the firm will have to increase the price of its product or suffer decreased profit margins.

### To Be Flexible and Stable

A compensation plan should be sufficiently flexible to meet the needs of individual territories, products, and salespeople. Not all territories present the same opportunity. A representative in a territory where the company is the leader should ordinarily not be compensated by the same method as a rep in a newly entered district. Flexibility also is needed to adjust for differences in products. Some products are staples and can be sold by taking orders for frequent repeat sales. Others are sold one to a customer and much creative selling is needed.

At the same time, the basic plan should possess stability. The basic pay plan should contain features that enable a company to meet changing conditions without having to change the basic plan. For example, the basic plan may include three categories of commission rates—high, medium, and low percentages—to reflect differences in profitability among products. However, a product category may be changed from time to time as competition and other external factors affect its profitability. These category reassignments can be made without changing the basic pay plan at all.

## The Salesperson's Perspective

The salesperson's perspective may differ from the company's perspective.

### A Secure Income and an Incentive Income

Every plan should provide a regular income, at least at a minimum level. The principle behind this point is that sales reps should not have to worry about how to meet living expenses. If they have a bad month, if they are in seasonal doldrums, or if they are sick and cannot work for a period, they should have some income. However, this steady income should not be so high that it lessens the desire for incentive pay.

In addition to a regular income, a good pay plan should furnish an incentive to elicit above-minimum performance. Most people do better when offered a reward for some specific action than when no incentive is involved. It should be noted that it is not possible to design a workable system that offers the greatest degree of both security and incentive. The concepts are mutually incompatible. In practice, the company must develop a compromise structure.

### Simplicity

Simplicity is a hallmark of a good compensation plan. However, sometimes simplicity and flexibility are conflicting goals. That is, a plan that is simple may not be sufficiently flexible, and a plan with adequate flexibility may achieve that goal at the expense of simplicity. A plan should be simple enough for salespeople to understand readily; they should be able to figure out what their incomes will be. In general, there should be *no more than three measures* combined to calculate the reps' compensation.[6]

### Fairness

A good compensation plan must treat the salespeople in an equitable manner. Nothing will destroy salespeople's morale faster than feeling that their pay is inequitable. One way to ensure fairness in a plan is to strive to base it as much as possible on measurable factors that are controllable by the sales force. The next section covers this point further.

# DESIGNING A SALES COMPENSATION PLAN

The steps in designing a pay plan for a sales force are shown in Figure 10-2. However, before designing a new pay plan or revising an existing one, a sales executive should review a few fundamental points. These are presented below, followed by a discussion of the first three steps of designing the plan—reviewing the job description, identifying the plan's specific objectives, and determining the job elements that are controllable by the reps and objectively measurable.

## Some Useful Generalizations

- **There are inherent conflicts in the objectives of most compensation plans.** Sales executives want a plan that maximizes the sales reps' income and at the same time minimizes the company's outlay. Or they want one plan to give the sales force security and stability of income as well as incentive. In each situation, the desires are diametrically opposite. About all a manager can do is adjust the pay plan until a reasonably satisfactory compromise is reached.

- **No single plan fits all situations.** Consequently, a firm should have a plan tailor-made for its own specific objectives. There may be considerable similarity in the general features of plans used by several firms, but the details should reflect the individual objectives of each company.

■ **FIGURE 10-2**     **Steps in designing a sales compensation plan**

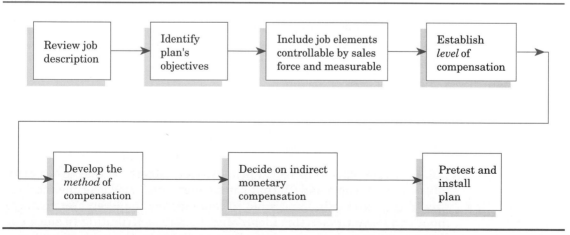

Many companies also need more than one compensation plan because of differences in types of sales jobs, territories, or products.

- **It is very important to achieve external parity in salespeople's earnings.** Management should pay its sales force at a level competitive with salespeople in other firms. An excellent source of information on this point is the Dartnell Corporation's annual *Survey of Sales Force Compensation*. This survey reports average annual pay levels (1) by industry and by company sales size, (2) for several levels of salespeople.

- **Management should solicit suggestions from the sales force regarding the compensation plan.** Salespeople are more likely to accept a plan if they were consulted about it during its design and development.

### Review Job Description

The first step in the design of a new compensation plan, or the revision of an established one, is to carefully review the detailed job description. This should disclose the exact nature, scope, and probable difficulty of the job. A separate description should be included for each selling position, such as sales engineer, missionary salesperson, or sales trainee. The job descriptions indicate what services and abilities the business is paying for.

### Identify Specific Objectives of Plan

Part of the job of designing a compensation plan is deciding *specifically* what it is intended to accomplish. It is not enough to say that the goal is to get an honest day's work for a day's pay or to attract good people. These are examples of the broad, general type of objective referred to earlier—objectives *every* plan should attempt to accomplish. Following are examples of specific objectives.

- Increase volume by 10 percent.
- Increase sales volume of a certain class of products by 10 percent.
- Obtain 10 new accounts.
- Stimulate missionary work.
- Develop a new territory.

### Include Job Elements Controllable by Sales Force and Objectively Measurable

Compensation should be based primarily on factors (1) that are controllable by salespeople and (2) that can be measured. However meritorious, this ideal is virtually impossible to implement completely. Yet management can move toward this ideal. Most factors contributing to sales success are only partially or not at all controllable by the sales force. Salespeople have some control over their sales volume, for instance, but this control is limited by product attributes and company pricing policies. The point is that a firm should try to base most of each salesperson's compensation on factors over which the rep has a maximum of control.

The next step is to give as much consideration as possible to the elements that can be measured objectively. For example, sales, selling expense, calls made, new accounts brought in, displays set up, or gross margin contributed are all quantitatively measurable. In contrast, such activities as building goodwill or training dealer salespeople are not easily evaluated, even though they are largely controllable by the sales representatives. This is not to say that these factors should be ignored in compensation matters.

## ESTABLISHING THE LEVEL OF COMPENSATION

One of the two key tasks in designing a pay plan is to determine the *level* of compensation (the other is to develop the *method*). The level of pay means the average earnings of the salespeople over a given period. In many respects, the level is more important than the method. People usually are more interested in *how much* they've earned, rather than *how* they earned it. To the company, the level of income is the direct sales cost. Management is interested in the compensation level because that is what attracts most salespeople. If reps believe that they will not be able to earn enough, they probably won't be attracted to the job regardless of the method used. On the other hand, they may take a job that pays well, even though the firm does not offer the combination of salary and commission they prefer.

### Factors Influencing Level of Compensation

There is no clearly prevailing pay rate for a sales job, as there is for certain office or factory jobs. However, compensation levels for salespeople do vary considerably among different *industries.* Figure 10-3 shows some examples of this spread. In the insurance industry, the median earnings of senior sales reps (five or more years of experience) were $86,900 in 1996. At the lower end of the scale, median earnings were $50,800 in banking and $59,100 in the wholesaling of consumer goods. None of these figures include benefits (insurance and pension, for example), which averaged $7,548 per sales rep across all industries.

The *method* of compensation has a bearing on the *level* of compensation. Salespeople who work under a straight salary plan typically earn less than reps who are paid a straight commission or some form of combination plan.

The level of sales compensation is also closely related to the *experience* of the salesperson. This is understandable because the more experienced representatives have usually developed more skills. As a result, their productivity should be higher.

■ **FIGURE 10-3**    **Median compensation levels for senior salespeople, selected industries, 1996**

| Industry | Median Compensation* | Industry | Median Compensation* |
|---|---|---|---|
| Insurance | $86,900 | Chemicals | $72,400 |
| Communications | 82,300 | Real estate | 69,600 |
| Electronics | 81,200 | Machinery | 65,700 |
| Paper and allied products | 81,400 | Wholesaling (industrial goods) | 63,700 |
| Health services | 77,600 | Wholesaling (consumer goods) | 59,100 |
| Investments | 76,400 | Retail | 54,500 |
| Rubber/plastics | 74,800 | Banking | 50,800 |
| Printing and publishing | 73,100 | | |

*Does not include average benefits of $7,548 in 1996.

Source: *Dartnell's 29th Sales Force Compensation Survey* (Chicago: Dartnell Corporation, 1997), p. 49.

## DEVELOPING THE METHOD OF COMPENSATION

The other key task in designing a sales compensation plan (besides setting the pay *level*) is to develop the *method* by which the reps will be paid. The building blocks available to management when constructing a sales compensation plan include the following elements:

- Salaries
- Commissions
- Drawing accounts
- Bonuses
- Profit sharing
- Indirect monetary benefits (e.g., vacation and insurance)
- Expenses

Some of these components are incentives for the sales force; others offer stability and security in earnings; still others may help the firm control sales costs. The more elements used in building a plan, the more complex it is, as seen in Figure 10-4. *Although there is a box for expenses in the figure, ordinarily reimbursement for travel and other business expenses incurred by salespeople should be kept separate from their compensation.* The two elements usually cause enough problems on their own without combining them. Sales force expenses are covered in the next chapter.

### Basic Types of Compensation Plans

Fundamentally, there are only three widely used methods of compensating a sales force.

■ **FIGURE 10-4**

**Building blocks
for a sales
compensation
plan**

| | | Others | |
| | | Company car | |
| | Profit sharing | Pension | |
| | Bonus | Moving expenses | |
| | Drawing account | Insurance | Other business expenses |
| Salary | Commission | Paid vacation | Travel |
| **Security** | **Incentives** | **Benefits** | **Expenses** |

1. *A straight **salary**—*a fixed element related to a unit of time during which the salesperson is working.

2. *A straight **commission**—*a variable element related to the performance of a specific unit of work.

3. *Some combination of compensation elements.*

Over the past 40 years, there has been significant growth in plans that combine salary with an incentive feature. This trend has been primarily at the expense of straight salary and straight commission plans. Today about 75 percent of all companies use some form of combination plan to pay their sales forces.

These generalized statements do not reveal the wide variations among different industries. Primary metals firms, for example, tend to prefer straight salary plans. At the other extreme, companies marketing financial services, especially securities brokers, are heavy users of straight commission plans. Surveys of salespeople indicate that the reps themselves strongly endorse some form of combination plan.

***Emphasis Shifting from Volume to Profits and Customer Satisfaction***
Traditionally, sales compensation plans have been geared to generate sales volume. Today, however, there has been a shift away from sales volume *alone* toward *profitable* sales volume. Over 50 percent of the firms provide an incentive to their salespeople that specifically rewards profitable sales.[7] The rise of profit consciousness probably coincides with the profit squeeze faced by many firms. Executives have seen that an *increase* in sales is sometimes accompanied by a *decrease* in company profits. Consequently, they realize that sales volume alone is a poor indicator of a salesperson's value to the firm.

When designing incentive plans that stress profits, many firms adopt the gross-margin approach. That is, the commission or other incentive is based on the gross margin (net sales less cost of goods sold) resulting from a sales rep's total sales. Many other firms still base their commission payments on sales volume. However, these commission plans are often structured to stress the sales of profitable products.

Customer satisfaction is an important objective for sales organizations. IBM, Xerox, and Saturn are among the firms that now include in their compensation plans a component which measures *customer satisfaction*.[8] The firms which use this measure of performance must be sure that salespeople, rather than the products, distribution, or other dimensions, are the primary factor influencing customer satisfaction ratings.

## Straight Salary Plans

A salary is a direct monetary reward paid for performing certain duties over a *period of time*. The amount of payment is related to a unit of time rather than to the work accomplished. A salary is a fixed element in a pay plan. That is, in each pay period, the same amount of money is paid to a sales rep, regardless of that person's sales, missionary efforts, or other measures of productivity.

### Strengths of Straight Salary Plans

Assured regularity of income gives the salesperson a considerable degree of security. A salary plan also provides stability of earnings, without the wide fluctuations often found in commission plans.

The assurance of a regular, stable income can do much to develop loyal, well-satisfied salespeople. Sales forces on straight salary usually have lower turnover rates than those on commission. Also, management can direct the sales force into various activities more easily under a salary plan than under any other method of compensation.

Because people on salary are less likely to be concerned with immediate sales volume, they can give proper consideration to the customers' interests. Also, customers often react more favorably to a salesperson if they know he or she is on straight salary.

### Limitations and Administrative Problems in the Plans

Often the limitations of a straight salary plan are really not *inherent* weaknesses but only a reflection of poor administration. One good example is the frequent objection that a salary plan provides no direct incentive to the sales force. True, a salary plan does not offer the strong, direct incentive that a commission or bonus does. However, part of the failure to furnish incentive usually can be traced to the *frequency* and *bases* of salary adjustment, which are administrative matters. Theoretically, salaries could be revised daily or weekly in relation to the salesperson's performance, but this is not practical. The problem is that companies sometimes go to the other extreme and do not make adjustments often enough.

Many salary plans fail to provide adequate incentive because the *bases* of adjustment are not sound. Often there is no clear-cut understanding of what constitutes satisfactory performance. Another disadvantage of a straight salary is that it is a fixed cost. There is no direct relationship between salary expense and sales volume. When sales are down, the fixed cost of compensation can be a burden on the firm.

### When a Straight Salary Plan Is Best

Generally speaking, a salary plan is best used when management (1) wants a well-balanced sales job and (2) can supervise and motivate the reps properly. Some of the specific situations for which a straight salary is better suited include:

- Sales recruits are in training or are still so new on the job that they cannot sell enough under a commission to earn a decent income.
- The company wants to enter a new geographical territory or sell a new line of products.
- Several reps must work together for long periods to sell one account.
- The job entails only missionary sales activities.

## Straight Commission Plans

The straight commission plan involves a regular payment for the performance of a *unit of work*. A commission is related to a unit of accomplishment, in contrast to the salary method, which is a fixed payment for a unit of time. A commission is usually based on factors that are largely controllable by the salespeople and consists of three items:

1. A *base* on which performance is measured and payment is made—for example, sales in dollars or units of the product.
2. A *rate,* which is the amount paid for each unit of accomplishment—for example, if a firm pays a nickel in commission for each dollar of sales, the rate is 5 percent.
3. A *starting point* for the commission payments.

The straight commission method may or may not include a provision for advances against future earnings (a drawing account). Essentially, straight commission plans and straight salary plans are diametrical opposites. That is, the strong points of one generally are the weak points of the other.

### Advantages of Straight Commission Plans

Probably the major advantage of the straight commission method of sales compensation is the terrific incentive it gives to the sales force. Many firms have no ceiling on sales reps' commission earnings, so their income opportunities are unlimited. Commission payments also are a strong motivating factor to get the reps to work hard. Typically, a salesperson on commission works more hours each week than one on salary.

A commission plan probably is the best type of pay plan for weeding out ineffective sales reps. Another big advantage to the company is that a commission is a direct response. That is, an expense is incurred only when a sale is made or some other activity is performed.

### Disadvantages of the Plans

The limitations of the commission method of sales compensation mentioned most often can be summed up under one point. It is difficult to supervise and direct the activities of salespeople because they tend to think they are in business for themselves.

Often, under the usual commission structure, the salespeople's only concern is to sell more merchandise, without regard for the interests of the company or the customer. The reps may concentrate on easy-to-sell items and frequently ignore those that are slow moving. Customers may be overstocked or sold more expensive items than necessary. Sales reps often disregard any thought of a fully balanced sales job, and management cannot expect them to do missionary work.

Management is not totally helpless to combat some of these problems. In fact, it can exercise considerable control by judiciously modifying commission rates and bases. For example, to deter the sale of easy-to-sell, low-margin items, it can pay a commission on gross profit. A lower commission rate on easy-to-sell products also reduces the attention they receive.

### When a Straight Commission Plan Is Best

Conditions under which the straight commission method is the best choice can be summarized as follows:

- A company is in a weak financial position and therefore selling costs must be related directly to sales.
- Great incentive is needed to get adequate sales.
- Very little nonselling, missionary work is needed.
- Developing long-term relationships with customers is not required.
- A firm uses part-time salespeople or independent contractors such as manufacturers' agents.

### Aspects of the Commission Method that Require Decisions

Several administrative decisions must be made when a firm uses the commission method, whether it is the only element in a pay plan or part of a combination plan. Below we discuss each of these common decisions—commission bases, commission rates, split commissions, and drawing accounts.

*Commission Bases*   Management must determine what **base** to use for paying commissions. Most bases are related to sales volume, gross margin, or, in some cases, nonselling activities. A commission may be paid on sales as measured in dollars or in units of the product.

A company can focus its reps' attention on *profitable* sales volume by basing the commissions on gross margin. In some firms the commission is based on sales volume. However, by establishing different rates for different product lines, the company, in effect, is stressing the profit feature. That is, higher commission rates are paid on the high-margin products to encourage their sales. Conversely, low rates are paid on sales of low-margin products.

*Rates of Commission*   Management also must determine the **commission rate**—that is, the amount paid for each unit of accomplishment. Rates vary among companies. Even within a given firm, there may be rate differentials among the products or territories. The choice of rates is affected by factors such as (1) the level of income desired for the sales force, (2) the profitability of given products, (3) difficulty in selling a product, or (4) classes of customers.

Rates may be *constant* throughout all stages of sales volume. Or they may be on a sliding scale, going up or down as sales volume increases. A *progressive* rate increases as the volume increases. To illustrate, a business may pay 5 percent on sales up to $20,000 a quarter (three-month period), 7 percent on the next $80,000 (sales from $20,000 to $100,000), and 10 percent on everything over $100,000. A salesperson who had sales of $130,000 for the quarter would receive a commission of $9,600, computed as follows:

| | |
|---|---|
| 5% on first $20,000 | $1,000 |
| 7% on next $80,000 ($20,000 to $100,000) | $5,600 |
| 10% on $30,000 (amount over $100,000) | $3,000 |
| | $9,600 |

■ **FIGURE 10-5**

**Example of progressive and regressive commission rates**

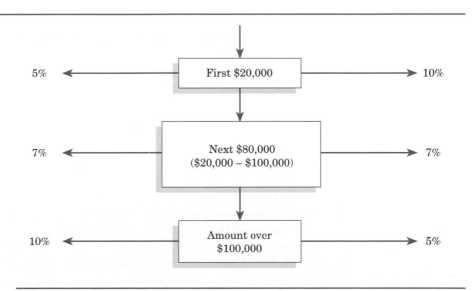

A progressive rate is intended to offer reps a great incentive in that the more they sell, the more they make on each sale. The company usually can afford to step up the rate because only the variable costs increase with each dollar of sales. The larger the sales, the less the overhead charged to each unit of volume. A progressive rate requires careful administration to prevent reps from taking advantage of the system. Reps may postdate or predate orders so all fall in one period. Thus they artfully boost their volume during a given period and consequently qualify for a higher rate on the last orders turned in.

A *regressive* rate works in reverse. The concern may pay 7 percent on the first $20,000 of sales in a given period, 5 percent on the next $20,000, and 3 percent on all sales over $40,000. A regressive rate has some merit if it is hard to get the first order but reorders come frequently and automatically. A regressive rate also may be used to even out the earnings of all salespeople or to reduce the effect of windfall sales. A regressive rate requires careful administration to discourage a salesperson from (1) withholding orders at the end of a commission period when they would command a lower rate and then (2) turning them in at the start of the next period. (See Figure 10-5.)

*Split Commissions*    When two or more salespeople work together on a sale, provision must be made to split any commission or other credit given. Various situations may call for a decision on the issue. It may take a team of three people to complete a sale of some large, technical product. One may be the territorial sales rep, the second a sales engineer or service rep from the home office, and the third the district manager. If a commission or bonus is part of the compensation plan for each of these people, distribution of the credit is a problem. (See the box labeled "Compensating Cross-Functional Selling Teams" for a discussion of other compensation considerations surrounding team selling.)

Geographical location can also complicate the commission division. For example, a salesperson in the Birmingham, Alabama, district may make a sale, but the order is placed through the buyer's home office in Atlanta. To further complicate matters, delivery may be made to plants in Nashville and New Orleans as well as to Birmingham. If each of the four cities is covered by separate sales reps, the sales manager has a real problem in splitting any commission involved. The Birmingham salesperson may want to claim full credit, pointing out that the order basically originated in his territory and through his efforts. At the same time, the Atlanta rep may have been calling on the buyer's home office for some time. The problem of split commissions can be particularly sensitive when central buying offices are concerned. Often, the salespeople in the outlying territories feel that their efforts avail them little.

No simple or generally accepted method exists for handling split credits. Instead, each firm must feel its own way, using executive judgment to arrive at a policy.

---

### Compensating Cross-Functional Selling Teams

Team selling is gaining in prevalence and importance. It requires the joint selling effort of several people, often from different functional areas within the firm. For example, Hallmark's selling teams include members from marketing, sales, finance, logistics, operations, information systems, and customer service. As a result, designing a compensation plan for a selling team can be a truly challenging assignment.

Several principles should be followed in designing a team-based compensation system:

■ **Shared reward.** Some form of shared reward is always necessary. That is, some significant portion of the team members' pay should be variable, based on the team's operating success. But there should be a balance between individually based and team-based compensation.

■ **Role–reward congruence.** Each team member contributes in a different way to the team. Therefore, not all of the team members must be measured and paid in the same manner. The specific performance measures used and the percentage which is team based should be chosen in accordance with the tasks performed by the individuals on the team.

■ **Team-member input.** For teams to succeed, all of the team members must be committed to the team goals and satisfied with the compensation structure. Therefore, it is important to gather input early on from those who will be affected by the pay program.

■ **Peer evaluations.** Part of the evaluation of performance should be based on team members' evaluations of each other's contributions to the overall performance of the team. This helps recognize individual performance and pinpoints freeloaders.

---

*Drawing Accounts*   A **drawing account** is a cash advance made available to a salesperson. The advance may be paid at regular intervals such as weekly or monthly. Or it may be set up as an amount for a rep to draw against as needed during a period. The amount drawn is paid back to the company out of the person's commission earnings during the same period.

A drawing account may or may not be guaranteed. Under a **nonguaranteed** plan, the advance is strictly a loan. Assume that a salesperson does not earn enough in commissions to pay back the advanced funds in one period. Then the balance of the debt is carried over to the next period.

A **guaranteed** drawing account operates in much the same way, with one big exception. At the end of a stated period, if a sales rep's commissions total less than the draw, the loan debt is canceled. It is not carried forward, and the rep starts with a clean slate. Thus a guaranteed draw is much like a salary. A nonguaranteed draw is more widely used than the guaranteed type, because the former is less of a financial burden on a company.

Drawing accounts are used to offset some of the drawbacks of the straight commission plan, because they add a semblance of security and regularity of income. In businesses where sales fluctuate seasonally, an advance can help carry a sales rep financially through a period of low income resulting from low sales.

### Placing Limits on Earnings

Should management place a ceiling, or limit, on the earnings of its sales-people? This question will most likely arise when part or all of the compensation plan is based on commission. Actually, earnings limits for salespeople are quite common among American businesses.

The executives that favor caps on salespeople's earnings put forth some compelling arguments. For example, no sales reps—even star salespersons—should earn more than their bosses. Otherwise, there would be adverse effects on executive morale and questions about the boss's managerial fitness. Furthermore, if they are paid too much, top-performing sales reps may turn down a promotion into management, if this means a cut in pay. Another argument is that reps should not benefit from windfall sales—a particularly large single order in his or her territory—especially when the rep made no significant contributions, put forth no special effort, or had no influence or control over the sale.

The reasons for having no ceilings or limitations on sales earnings seem to outweigh the arguments favoring them. The more a salesperson earns, the more the company makes, particularly if the earnings are in the form of a bonus or commission. The idea of a ceiling seems totally alien to the philosophy of selling. A firm ordinarily does not limit sales of its products to $x$ dollars a year. Yet, placing limits on sales reps' incomes has the same effect.

If management does decide to curb the earnings of its salespeople, several methods besides establishing a ceiling on earnings are available. One approach is to reduce commissions or bonus payments on all sales. Or the firm may establish a system of regressive commission rates, whereby successively lower commission rates are paid as sales volume increases beyond a given level. Windfall accounts may be classified as house accounts. These accounts are turned over to the territorial sales manager, and the salesperson receives no earnings credit for sales to them. Management may even change its basic compensation plan to place less emphasis on the incentive features and more on the fixed element of salary.

## Combination Plans

Today, some form of combination pay plan is used to compensate about 75 percent of all sales forces. Broadly speaking, the purpose of any combination plan is to overcome the weaknesses of a single method, while at the same time keeping its strong points. Most of the combined plans fall within the following categories:

- Salary plus commission and/or bonus.
- Commission with guaranteed drawing account.
- Commission and bonus.

*A Day-to-Day Operating Problem*

## MAJESTIC PLASTICS COMPANY (G)

### Reps selling too many low-profit products

Over the past several days the top executives in the Majestic Plastics Company had been conducting their annual performance review of the company's operations. The company president, Boyd Russell, sat in on most of these sessions and periodically became quite involved in some of the departmental reviews. The sales department was the one currently under discussion, and Clyde Brion, the general sales manager, was the focus of attention. Overall, the sales and profit results were satisfactory, but the executives noted what they thought was a problem in two sales territories. One was centered in Boston, where Louise Shannon was the rep, and the other was in Chicago, which was Henry Sadowski's territory.

In each of these territories, the sales reps' total sales volume was satisfactory. The problem was that the bulk of their sales volume was in low-profit products—that is, products whose gross margin was well below the company's desired average. Then the chief financial officer, Oliver Twombly, recalled that this same situation had been brought up at last year's performance review. Clyde Brion realized he was on the spot with his fellow executives, including the president.

Top management really did not want to change the basic compensation plan (straight commission on sales volume) because, over the

company as a whole, it apparently had been working okay. And Brion concurred in this decision. He pointed out that Shannon and Sadowski consistently met their total sales quotas, and each had won a sales contest designed to stimulate total sales. But their performance was not balanced. They went way over quota on low-margin products and generally failed to meet quota on high-margin goods. They were not selling a desirable mix of products, nor were they generating their share of new accounts. Basically they were getting large, repeat orders from a few established accounts. And Shannon and Sadowski generally were neglecting the newer products that were the foundation of the company's future growth.

Brion had been aware of this situation for some time. But he never gave the problem the attention it deserved, partly because the two reps' total sales volume was satisfactory and partly because he had other brushfires to put out. Now he was convinced that he had better do something and do it quickly.

**Question:** What should Clyde Brion do to remedy the imbalanced sales performance of Louise Shannon and Henry Sadowski?

Note: See the introduction to this series of problems in Chapter 4 for background information on the company, its market, and its competition.

In a combination pay plan, what portion should be incentive and what portion salary? The answer depends on the nature of the selling tasks and the company's marketing goals. The incentive portion should be larger when a company is trying to increase its sales or gross margin, especially in the short run. The salary element is larger when management emphasizes customer servicing, a fully balanced selling effort, or team selling. The incentive portion in combination plans is most often in the 30 percent to 40 percent range. It has been increasing over the past two decades and will probably continue to increase slightly in the next decade.[9]

**This sales manager congratulates his sales person on his first bonus.**

Combination plans introduce a component that we have not yet discussed—namely, a bonus. The word *bonus* is probably the most loosely used word in the compensation vocabulary. As a result, it is sometimes difficult to accurately assess the extent to which it is used in pay plans. A **bonus** is a lump-sum payment for an above-normal performance. Because of its nature, a bonus cannot be used alone, but instead, must always be combined with another element such as a salary or commission. Strictly speaking, management need not announce in advance either the amount of the bonus or the basis for distributing it.

However, most sales bonuses are intended to stimulate the sales force to perform certain tasks by offering an incentive. Unless the plan is explained fully in advance, management will gain nothing by giving a bonus. The most commonly used basis for paying a bonus is the measure of a salesperson's performance against a quota—typically, a sales volume quota or an expense quota. A sales rep may get a cash bonus of $x$ dollars for going 10 percent over quota. More than 47 percent of the firms participating in Dartnell's annual compensation survey use some type of bonus in their compensation.[10]

### Salary Plus Commission

This plan is probably used more than any other type of compensation method. However, no generally agreed-on percentage division prevails between the fixed and the variable elements. The salary–commission plan provides the advantages of a salary plus the incentive and flexibility features of a commission. But this plan is more complex and costly to operate because of the increased number of elements involved. Also, the addition of incentive features at the expense of the salary can reduce managerial control over the sales force. In the final analysis, the success of this plan—or of any combination plan, for that matter—depends largely on the balance achieved among the elements.

### Salary Plus Bonus

For the company that wants to control its sales force at all times and still offer some incentive, a salary-plus-bonus plan may be the answer. Usually, the salary element constitutes the major part of the total earnings—much more so than in a salary–commission plan. The salary-plus-bonus arrangement is excellent for the firm that wants to encourage some activity for a short time. For example, a company may want to generate new accounts or push missionary selling work for one product line. Many companies are using bonuses to reward team performance. If the team achieves its goals, then all of the team members receive a bonus. Also, some companies use bonuses to help the sales force focus on long-term corporate objectives such as improving customer satisfaction.[11] A few companies even tie bonuses to the accomplishment of personal goals such as losing weight or learning a foreign language.[12]

### Salary Plus Commission and Bonus

A number of companies use all three components in their compensation plans. This allows them to have a certain degree of control and provide an incentive as well as offer a bonus for the accomplishment of a specific goal.

### Commission with Guaranteed Drawing Account

As explained earlier, a guaranteed drawing account is an advance against commissions. It must be paid back if commissions are large enough in a given period. However, any indebtedness at the end of the period is canceled. In this combination plan, the guaranteed draw is much like a salary, at least from a computational standpoint. A commission with a guaranteed draw is similar to a salary plus a commission on sales that exceed a quota. Assume that a rep was paid a guaranteed draw of $1,000 a month plus a commission of 5 percent on net sales. The rep would start receiving a commission when his sales reached $20,000 a month (which is the amount of sales needed to cover the guaranteed $1,000 at a 5 percent commission rate).

While this plan may be similar to salary plus commission from a computational viewpoint, it has significant psychological differences. First, management probably can adjust the level of the drawing account more easily than the level of salary. Second, the plan has the fixed-cost weakness of a salary without the control advantages, because most salespeople probably link the plan to straight commission.

## Linking the Method to the Objective

As we noted earlier in the chapter, it is very important that the compensation plan be linked to achievement of specific objectives. The choice of which methods to use depends on the specific objectives that have been chosen. To provide examples, we list the objectives that were presented earlier and suggest the best methods to achieve them:

- *Increase volume.* Some form of incentive is usually necessary, such as a commission or a bonus.
- *Increase sales volume of a certain class of products.* A higher rate of commission may be paid on sales of the high-margin items, or whichever line of goods the company is pushing.
- *Obtain new accounts.* A bonus may be paid for every new account brought in, or this activity may be reflected in a higher salary.
- *Stimulate missionary work.* This includes such activities as training dealer salespeople, making demonstrations, or building displays. Some of these efforts can be individually measured, and a commission or bonus can be given for their accomplishment. Efforts that cannot be measured easily may be rewarded by having salary form the bulk of the total compensation.
- *Minimize expenses.* A bonus may be based on how much a sales rep's expenses run below an expense quota or how much they decrease from one period to another.
- *Develop a new territory.* Probably all income should be in the form of salary, at least in the earliest stages of territorial development.

## INDIRECT MONETARY COMPENSATION

Today, most salespeople enjoy the same employee benefits as production and office workers in a company. Young people going into selling today are more security conscious than they were years ago, and management is more sensitive to its social responsibility. Sales executives are realizing that rewards are due in two other general areas. One is **nonfinancial compensation** in the form of honors, recognition, and opportunities for promotion. These features help salespeople develop a sense of self-worth and of belonging to a group.

The other type of reward is an **indirect monetary benefit:** items that have the same effect as money, though payment is less direct than a salary or commission. These items, which are also referred to as *fringe benefits,* include such things as retirement plans, vacation, and insurance. Indeed, what are referred to as "fringe" benefits today are better considered to be a part of the compensation package. These benefits averaged $7,548 per salesperson in 1996, according to *Dartnell's Sales Force Compensation Survey.* This figure is in addition to the average earnings of $65,700 for senior salespeople and $47,400 for intermediate reps.[13] Figure 10-6 shows the most widely used sales force benefits that are paid in part or in total by the company.

Firms also give their salespeople paid holidays and provide paid vacations of varying lengths, depending on the employees' length of service. Paid vacations present a managerial problem in connection with sales-

■ **FIGURE 10-6**      **Company-paid fringe benefits for salespeople**

| Benefit | Percentage of Companies |
|---|---|

Medical insurance — 96%

Group life insurance — 79%

Dental insurance — 69%

Long-term disability — 62%

Pension plan — 57%

Short-term disability — 51%

Profit sharing — 45%

Thrift savings plan — 24%

Employee stock purchase plan — 24%

Source: *Dartnell's 29th Sales Force Compensation Survey* (Chicago: Dartnell Corporation, 1997), p. 137.

people who work partly or entirely on commission. These reps usually do not receive vacation pay that equals their commissions. Firms often give these reps their regular drawing account, which must be repaid from post-vacation earnings. Also, most companies pay a commission to the reps on any sales that come in from their territories while they are on vacation.

Indirect monetary benefits are important in attracting desirable sales applicants. These benefits probably give salespeople a greater degree of security and make them more loyal and more cooperative. Such characteristics undoubtedly have some bearing on a reduction in the turnover rate.

# ■ FINAL STEPS IN DEVELOPMENT OF THE PLAN

## Pretest the Plan

Once management has tentatively selected the method of compensation, the next step is to pretest the entire compensation plan. This involves determining how the proposed plan would have operated if it had been in effect during the previous few years. Management can estimate what the company's cost would have been and what income would have been earned by the salespeople. Pretesting a compensation plan is a simulation exercise that can easily be done on a computer. No amount of pretesting will answer all questions. If the new plan had been in effect, sales might have been quite different.

The commission features of a plan are easier to pretest than the salary elements. If the base salary is increased 20 percent, it is hard to say how much more effective the missionary work will be or how much harder the sales force will work. However, several calculations can be made regarding the commission elements. By assuming various levels of sales for each line of products, management can compute what the compensation cost will be.

### Introduce Plan to Sales Force

Changing a compensation plan—especially if the change is a major one—can be a real culture shock for the sales force. Often, salespeople believe that management is simply trying to reduce selling costs. Thus they look on any changes in the pay plan as a way to lower the sales reps' earnings.

Consequently, management should develop and introduce the new plan the same way porcupines kiss each other—very carefully. If the plan has been carefully developed, then the salespeople already have been asked for suggestions and criticisms. The reasons for changing the previous plan have been thoroughly and candidly discussed.

### Install Plan and Evaluate It Periodically

A compensation plan may be installed throughout the entire sales force, or it may be tested in only one or two territories. If a company cannot conduct a realistic pretest, then it may field test the plan in a few districts under actual selling conditions. Sometimes a company will phase in a new plan over a period of time—three or six months or even a year. This phasing-in period gives the salespeople a chance to adjust to the new plan—to "buy into" the new system.

The final step is to make certain the entire plan will be evaluated frequently to prevent it from becoming outmoded. A common mistake is to spend much time and money developing a good compensation system (or selection or training program) and then allowing the system to become outdated. A person's job often changes over time. Market and product conditions also change. It is only sound management to keep a compensation plan in tune with the times.

## ▪ SUMMARY

Compensation is the most widely used method for motivating a sales force. Most of our discussion involved direct payments of financial compensation. When building a compensation plan, management must determine both the level of earnings and the method of paying the sales force. The sales force pay plan has a significant influence on the implementation of a company's strategic marketing plan.

From the company's perspective, the seven general goals of a good compensation plan are (1) to motivate salespeople, (2) to correlate a person's efforts and results with rewards, (3) to control the salespeople's activities, (4) to ensure proper treatment of customers, (5) to attract and keep competent salespeople, (6) to be economical and competitive, and (7) to be flexible and stable. From the salesperson's perspective, the objectives are (1) to provide both a steady income and an incentive income, (2) to be easy for the sales rep to understand and for the company to administer, and (3) to be fair to the sales rep.

When designing a pay plan, a company first should review its job description to see what the reps are being paid to do. Then management should set specific goals for the pay plan. Compensation ideally should be based on items (1) that are controllable by the sales force and (2) that can be measured objectively.

A major step in building a compensation plan is to establish the *level* of pay for the salespeople. Another major step in designing a compensation plan is to determine the *method* of compensation. Fundamentally, there are only three methods for compensating a sales force: (1) a straight salary, (2) a straight commission, and (3) some combination of compensation elements (salary, commission, bonus, drawing account, expenses, and fringe benefits). Some form of a combination plan is used in about 75 percent of all sales forces.

A straight salary plan ensures a regular, stable income for the sales force. It enables management to direct the sales force into a variety of activities. The main drawback to a straight salary plan is that it does not provide any direct incentive to the sales force. It is also a fixed cost to the company. Generally speaking, a straight salary plan is best used (1) when management wants a fully balanced sales job and (2) when management can supervise the salespeople so that they are properly motivated.

The main advantage of a straight commission plan is the tremendous incentive it gives the sales force *to do what the commission is based on.* To management, a straight commission plan is a variable expense. Under a straight commission plan, it may be difficult to direct the activities of the salespeople. There are several situations where a straight commission plan is best used. With a straight commission pay plan, management must decide on the base and rates for paying the commission. Also, policies are needed regarding split commissions and drawing accounts. Management must also decide whether it will limit its sales reps' earnings.

Combination pay plans typically are a compromise designed to retain as much as possible the strong points and to overcome the weaknesses of straight salary or straight commission. Often combination plans include some type of bonus paid for above normal performance. Most sales compensation plans also include fringe benefits—*indirect financial* rewards such as paid vacations and company insurance plans. The final steps in designing a pay plan involve pretesting the plan, introducing it to the sales force, and actually installing the plan.

## Key Terms

| | | |
|---|---|---|
| Bonus | Guaranteed drawing | Nonfinancial compensation |
| Commission |   account | Nonguaranteed drawing |
| Commission base | Indirect monetary benefit |   account |
| Commission rate | Level of earnings | Salary |
| Drawing account | Method of compensation | |

# ■ QUESTIONS AND PROBLEMS

1. As stated in this chapter, two broad goals of a sound compensation plan are (a) to control and direct sales force activities and (b) to ensure proper treatment of customers. Can these goals be reached by use of any managerial tool or activity other than a good pay plan?

2. Rank the following types of sales jobs by total earnings, showing which type you feel should have the highest level of compensation, which is second, and so on. Justify your rankings.

   a. Missionary sales for a large soap company.

   b. Sales for a steel manufacturer.

   c. Door-to-door cosmetics sales.

   d. Sales by appliance wholesalers to retail stores.

   e. Life insurance sales.

   f. Sales for a manufacturer of office machines.

   g. Sales for a manufacturer of children's clothes, calling on retail department stores and other clothing stores.

   h. Sales for a firm selling conveyor systems.

3. Should the level of sales compensation in a firm with a national market be affected by regional variations in the general wage scale and the cost of living? Will your decision be influenced by the firm's policy regarding geographical differentials for its plant and office employees?

4. In 1994, a firm hired several college graduates for sales jobs at a yearly salary of $32,000 plus travel expenses. By 1998, most of these people were making a salary of $36,500 to $37,000

a year, plus travel expenses. In 1998, the same company hired more graduates and paid them $35,500 a year, plus travel expenses. This was the salary being offered to qualified college grads for entry-level sales jobs in this company's industry in 1998. Thus the people with no experience received almost the same pay as those with four years' experience. Discuss the problems involved in this situation and suggest remedies.

5. Assume that salespeople's earnings in a certain firm have no limit, and a good sales rep can earn more than some of the company's sales managers. What incentive do these salespeople have to move into management? Especially consider those for whom a promotion means a decrease in income.

6. Give some specific examples of how each of the following factors can influence a company's choice of a sales force compensation plan.

   a. Caliber of the salespeople.

   b. Nature of the job.

   c. Financial condition of the company.

7. Following are three problems often faced by sales managers:

   a. Salespeople tend to overemphasize the easy-to-sell parts of multiple product lines in an effort to build sales volume; other, more profitable lines are forced into the background.

   b. Salespeople need to spend more time developing new accounts.

   c. To improve a company's long-term position, salespeople should be doing more missionary work and developing long-term customers to meet expected competition.

Suggest a specific type of compensation plan that may be used to solve each of these problems.

8. What is the economic justification underlying the progressive commission rate? Is there any economic justification for a regressive rate? Which of the two rates is better for stimulating a sales force?

9. What plan would you recommend for each of the following companies in handling split commissions?

 a. Manufacturer of sheets, pillowcases, towels, and related items sells to a department store chain. The order is placed through the chain's buying offices in New York. Delivery is made to stores throughout the country on an order from the department manager in each store. The manufacturer's salespeople call on the units of the chain located in their territories.

 b. Manufacturer of oil well drilling equipment sells to main offices and drilling locations. Salespeople in the area where the product is delivered must service the item.

10. What do you think would be some potential problems in having team members rate each other as part of their performance evaluation?

11. All of a company's employees—sales and otherwise—received paid vacations, except the salespeople on straight commission. Should management establish a policy whereby these reps are given the same benefits? If so, how should management determine the amount to pay the commissioned reps during their vacations?

12. In what respects would a compensation plan differ among salespeople for the following firms?

 a. Manufacturer of small airplanes used by executives.

 b. Wholesaler of office equipment and supplies.

 c. Automobile dealer.

## EXPERIENTIAL EXERCISES

**A.** Call 10 different firms and ask them to identify the methods used to compensate their salespeople.

**B.** Ask 20 of your friends what portion of their compensation they would like to be salary (a fixed component) and what portion they would like to be some type of incentive (commission or bonus) assuming that they were in a sales position. Try to determine why different people have different preferences in this regard.

## REFERENCES

1. For example, see Lawrence B. Chonko, John F. Tanner Jr., and William A. Weeks, "Selling and Sales Management in Action: Reward Preferences of Salespeople," *Journal of Personal Selling & Sales Management,* Summer 1992, pp. 67–75.

2. Roberta Maynard, "What the Numbers May Not Tell You," *Nation's Business,* January 1996, p. 21.

3. Thomas R. Mott, "A Formula for the Future," *Sales & Marketing Management,* June 1993, p. 42.

4. Don Peppers and Martha Rogers, "The Money Trap," *Sales & Marketing Management,* May 1997, pp. 58–60.

5. "Does Your Sales Compensation Plan Motivate Your Salespeople?" *Sales & Marketing Executive Report,* March 5, 1997, p. 1.

6. Michele Marchetti, "Can Reps Win with Your Comp Plan?" *Sales & Marketing Management,* December 1996, p. 29.

7. Christian P. Heide, ed., *Dartnell's 29th Sales Force Compensation Survey* (Chicago: Dartnell Corporation, 1997), pp. 154–55.

8. Arun Sharma, "Customer Satisfaction–Based Incentive Systems: Some Managerial and Salesperson Considerations," *Journal of Personal Selling & Sales Management,* Spring 1997, pp. 61–70.

9. Heide, *Dartnell's 29th Survey,* pp. 40–41.

10. Ibid., p. 43.

11. Michele Marchetti, "Are Reps Motivated by Bonuses?" *Sales & Marketing Management,* February 1997, p. 33.

12. Melanie Berger, "Setting Personal Goals for Employees," *Sales & Marketing Management,* February 1997, pp. 35–36.

13. Heide, *Dartnell's 29th Survey,* pp. 118–19, 49–50.

---

*Case 10-1*

## ID SYSTEMS, INC.

### Directing salespeople's efforts through a compensation system

"Today, world crime escalates daily, with terrorism and hijackings almost commonplace. Bombing, kidnaping, and electronic fraud dominate both national and international news. Add to that the less dramatic, but damaging, cost of white-collar crime, and the conclusion is clear: Never before has absolute identification been so important."

That is the theme of ID Systems, Inc., manufacturer of personal identification systems. The three main product areas are cardkey systems, proximity reader systems, and retina-scanning devices.

The cardkey security systems control who is permitted to enter a defined area and during what time of day they may enter. Each card is coded by means of a microchip within the card. The cards cannot be duplicated, as some with magnetic strips can. The proximity reader systems are based on a concept similar to the cardkey systems. However, instead of carrying a card that must be inserted into a system, the user simply carries a plastic plate, about one inch by two inches, that activates the lock at a certain distance from the door. The retina-scanning device is based on the fact that every pair of eyes has a unique pattern of blood vessels. The identification system compares the retinal scan with a template of characteristics stored in a memory bank. When the template is matched with an acceptable degree of accuracy, access is granted.

The average cardkey or proximity system sells for about $3,000 per door, and the retina scan is around $25,000. The average sale for the company is $60,000 to $75,000. In 1996, ID Systems, with sales of $72 million, controlled 30 percent of the U.S. security market. Its two closest competitors are Schlage with 20 percent of the market and Boye with 15 percent. Seventy-five additional companies each have 3 percent to 4 percent; and another 200 companies, which are not UL (Underwriter's Laboratory) approved, have approximately 5 percent of the market. The demand for security identification systems is exploding, and the market is expected to have sales of $4.4 billion by the year 2000. ID Systems, whose products are becoming more high tech with each new design or improvement, is in an excellent position to compete in the changing marketplace. Its product line is the trend of the future and its potential for sales is enormous.

ID Systems' sales force consists of 24 sales representatives divided into six districts across the United States. Each district has a sales manager, an electrical engineer, and a sales support engineer. There is also an international sales zone. International sales, all through an independent distributor network, comprise 73 percent of ID's sales.

Each sales rep is expected to make 16 calls and to quote four jobs in a week. The sales rep makes the initial call and determines what the customer needs and what will satisfy those needs. Then the sales engineer does a "walk-through" with the rep to make sure the design is technically feasible.

The territories are designed to equalize potential, and each rep has a quota of $1,500,000 per year. The compensation is a base salary of $34,000 plus a graduated commission based on gross sales. For sales of $800,000 and under, the reps receive a 5 percent commission; for sales above $800,000 to $1,200,000, they receive 6 percent; for sales above $1,200,000 to $1,500,000, they receive 8 percent; and for everything over $1,500,000, they get 10 percent.

Cheryl Sites is the vice president of sales for ID Systems. She began her career with the company as a sales rep, progress-

ing through the positions of district manager and regional manager. She has been the VP for several years and is well respected for her market knowledge and sense of fairness in dealing with employees.

Recently, Cheryl has been struggling with a serious problem of how to implement a new marketing and sales strategy. ID Systems had been growing at a healthy rate for the past 10 years. This growth has come primarily from skimming the more profitable and larger accounts on the market. Management realized that there is a tremendous amount of untapped business, and that much of it is located in areas of relatively low population which the sales force does not heavily penetrate. Realistically, it would be difficult for the existing salespeople to cover the more densely populated parts of their territories as well as the outlying areas. On the other hand, these areas by themselves do not have enough volume to support a full-time rep. Therefore, the company had decided to establish a distributor network to supplement the direct sales by the reps.

The salespeople have been given the task of identifying and supporting the distributors for their own territories. The reps are each supposed to have sales of $300,000 each year through their distributor networks. They must locate the distributors, get them set up, support them with their service, and maintain a working relationship with them. They are also expected to help train the distributors' employees.

Cheryl agreed with the new strategy. She felt that it made sense from an overall strategic perspective. She also felt that, in the long run, ID's salespeople would benefit from the opportunity to develop a greater sales base through the distributor network. However, her salespeople seem to view the new strategy from a short-term commission perspective. While the sales reps received the same commissions from sales through their distributors, the prices to the distributors are generally discounted by 40 percent off the normal selling prices. As the reps see it, they are getting significantly less for selling the same amount of product. Furthermore, they know that it takes a lot of additional effort initially to get the distributor set up and that the ongoing support requirements are going to be greater. They do not want to spend time with distributors when they feel they can continue to do well without them.

The reps also do not want the distributors stealing sales from them. Even though the distributors would be selling in areas that the ID reps have not had time to cover, the reps would technically be giving up some of the potential in their territories. If these concerns were not enough, one of the reps said to Cheryl yesterday, "Why should I help find my own replacement?" Apparently, many of the reps are threatened by the establishment of a dealer network. They envision ID eventually selling exclusively through distributors, and having reps who merely service these distributors. Cheryl is also concerned that if she pushes the reps

into setting up some distributors, they may set them up, but they won't support them very well. This could give ID a bad name, making it difficult to establish additional distributors.

Cheryl is considering her options. Her preference is to find some way of motivating the current reps to support the establishment of the distributor network. One way is to change their compensation to provide some short-term incentive to establish and support the distributors. She was not certain what that incentive should be and she was not certain, given the reps' attitude, whether it would work. Another alternative is to hire several new reps whose only responsibility would be to set up and sell through the distributors. Of course, the current reps wouldn't like this idea either. Finally, she could recommend to management that ID change its strategy of establishing a distributor network at this time.

*Question:*

Should Cheryl recommend a change in strategy? If not, what steps should Cheryl take to implement the new strategy?

---

*Case 10-2*

## IMAGINATIVE STAFFING, INC. (B)
### Compensating a sales team

Susan Borland, sales director, and her assistant, Judy Morgan, had been assigned the task of developing a program for team selling the company's services to prospective accounts. As they dug into their task, they encountered particular difficulty with the matter of how to pay the team.

Imaginative Staffing, Inc., was a temporary-services firm in New York City that supplied temporary workers to firms located in the five boroughs. Formed in 1990, it had

grown to $17 million in revenues in 1994. Besides herself and her assistant, Nicole, the company had a chief financial officer, a sales director, four sales reps, an operations manager, ten account managers, five administrative assistants, and a receptionist.

One reason Mrs. Roberts, Imaginative Staffing's president, had become aware of the team-selling concept was that for some time she had been frustrated by the length of time it took to close a sale with a good prospect. On the average, it took about six months of hard work to make a sale to a major customer. One of the sales reps would make the contact and do all of the selling, sometimes with the help of the sales director if the situation seemed to warrant it.

Large and small corporations made extensive use of temporary help for one or more of several reasons: (1) to fill in for workers who, for some reason, were unable to work, (2) to handle overload conditions, or (3) to take care of seasonal peak workloads. In the current legal environment, many organizations were reluctant to hire permanent employees until there was a clear-cut, long-run need for them. Such factors as benefit packages, insurance, unemployment claims, and termination difficulties made management think seriously about hiring people as permanent employees.

Susan and Judy had decided that a selling team should usually consist of at least three people: a sales rep, the person who would be the account's manager, and one person from top management. There was considerable debate on two issues. Should someone from the sales director's office be on the team (Susan or Judy) and who in top management should be involved? In particular, much consideration was given to Angie Roberts's role. Should the president be part of a sales team on an important sale or would that undermine the development of the company's salespeople?

In any event, the matter of paying the people became an issue. Susan thought that there should be no special compensation plan for the selling team. "After all, they are paid a salary for their work and they all get substantial bonuses at the end of the year depending upon how much profit we have made. If they sell more, they'll get paid in their year-end bonus."

Judy demurred, "Two problems here: Delayed payment provides little immediate incentive and the impact upon a person's bonus by any one sale would be slight. I think we need to build some push into this team-selling concept by giving the victors some of the spoils."

Under the existing system, the sales rep who brought in a new account was paid a commission of 10 percent of that account's billings for the first year. The commission was paid at the end of the month in which the money was received from the account. Thereafter, the sales rep received 1 percent of the account's billings. The account manager who took over the managing of the new account was paid a salary plus 1 percent of her account's billings. The company would not accept any account with billings less than $10,000 a year. It had slightly more than 500 active accounts, of which about 100 had billings totaling approximately $11,000,000. The typical new account started out with billings of about $12,000 for the first year, and it grew as it gained experience with the company. It was part of the account manager's job to develop each account's use of the firm's services. This usually involved getting to know the account's special needs and problems and then developing programs for using temporary employees to solve them. It often involved recruiting people with special skills who could work as needed for the accounts that periodically needed those skills. For example, one client required people with the ability to read music. Another required people fluent in Russian.

The reps and the account managers had been receiving earnings based on customer billings. Consequently, both Susan and Judy anticipated problems with them if those earnings were threatened by the team-selling concept. Why would they want to adopt a new selling system that would threaten their earnings? Clearly, they would have to see the system as a way to increase their earnings.

Another problem automatically arose. If the reps and the account managers received incentive compensation based on account billings, how would that affect the attitudes of the other team members? Wouldn't they also want some pay based on the productivity of their work? If that was to be, then how much?

**Questions:**

1. Should the president be part of the selling team when appropriate?

2. Should the team receive compensation for their productivity or should the teamwork be considered part of the job?

3. If you feel that a productivity compensation plan for the sales team is called for, design one.

---

*Case 10-3*

### XEROX CORPORATION

### Limits on sales reps' earnings

When she graduated from the University of Southern California's Entrepreneur Program, Leana Grandy accepted a job as sales trainee with the Xerox Corporation. After completing the training program, in which she received high marks, Grandy was given her choice of several sales assignments. She decided to accept a position selling Xerox copiers to the Los Angeles school system. It was called the K–12 market.

Having just one customer, a very big customer, appealed to Leana. It seemed to simplify the selling job for her, since she had only one system to learn. Moreover, she could focus more intently on the applications of greatest interest to that customer.

Grandy's sales performance was outstanding. At the end of her second year on the job, she led all Xerox sales representatives in sales—she was a star salesperson. Her compensation was commensurately generous. She made in excess of $200,000 during her second year on the job.

Xerox's compensation program provided strong incentives. All reps were assigned sales quotas. If they met their quotas, they were well compensated. However, the real money was to be made by exceeding quotas,

and Grandy exceeded her quotas by a large margin. Those quotas had been set up on the basis of previous sales to the Los Angeles school system. It had been assumed that Leana should sell about the same amount as her predecessor, who had been promoted into management because of her excellent performance.

Grandy was rapidly becoming an independently wealthy woman. Although she had harbored thoughts of breaking away from the corporate world in a few years to establish her own business, she had put such thoughts aside. "I am having too much fun and making too much money to leave this job," she told an undergraduate class of entrepreneur majors she was addressing at the end of her second year on the job.

The class loved her story and learned much from it. When asked to what she attributed her success, Leana replied, "I simply treated my territory as I would if it were my own business. I pretended that I was going into the business of selling copiers to the Los Angeles school system. Then I wrote a business plan for that venture, just like you are writing now for your businesses. Then, I just took the plan and worked it, made it happen. Hey, it works!"

She continued, "I have been asked the same question several times by my managers and I tell them the same story. They are so impressed with it that they now want me to teach it to the trainees. They want me to go into sales training. But that's not where the money is to be found, so I have been fighting it."

The following year Grandy returned to talk with the next class. Conditions on the job had changed a bit. She told the class what she had told the previous year's class, then added, "But a lot happened this past year." She then related that her high earnings were bothering her managers. They had increased her quotas an "unreasonable" amount, which had resulted in a substantial reduction in her total compensation.

"I have come to the conclusion that there is in fact a real ceiling on how much you can earn as a sales rep. Once you reach it, they start cutting you down. I've heard some of the managers talk. It bothers them when you make more money than they do. My manager explained to me that if they let reps make too much money it just ruins them. They think that rich reps will either quit working very hard or will leave the company."

Grandy was asked if she was going to quit over the matter. "It's often tempting when I start thinking about it, but let's face it. I am still making a lot of money, more than I can make by going somewhere else. But I am salting it away fast! I am getting more and more independent. One of these days . . . who knows!"

The students pushed Leana hard about how she really felt about the earnings-ceiling issue. "Down deep I know that if I were in their shoes I would feel the same way about it. And face it, it's true. Once you have a lot of money, it does affect how hard you work. I am not knocking myself out now like I did at first. I've learned that it wouldn't pay off. If I sold more, they would just raise my sales quotas. So I've learned to balance out my efforts. Everybody is happy if you exceed your quotas by 20 percent or so. It's when you are producing 200 percent that management gets all upset."

*Questions:*

1. Should Xerox change its compensation policies? If so, in what way?
2. Why does management become upset when the reps exceed their quotas by large margins?

---

*Case 10-4*

## WALTON ENTERPRISES, INC.
### Revising a sales force compensation plan

Over the past few months, Theodore Doane, vice president of sales and marketing at Walton Enterprises, Inc., and Henry Richman, the sales manager reporting to Doane, had periodically discussed the compensation plan currently used for the company's sales force. They agreed they had talked long enough. It was time for action.

Walton Enterprises was a Midwestern firm that manufactured and marketed two lines of carpet cleaners for industrial uses. One line consisted of six different models of a steam carpet cleaner, known in the industry as an "extractor." The other product line was a series of vacuum cleaners, some of which Walton manufactured and some that were imported from Germany. Walton's sales last year were $6.4 million.

The vacuum that Walton manufactured had to be used with one of the extractors, since the extractor contained the bucket that held the debris. The vacuum did not have a bag of its own like most vacuum cleaners. This tended to make vacuuming a slow process. However, it was extremely efficient because of the tremendous suction from the extractors. The vacuum that Walton imported from Germany was the usual type of vacuum cleaner with a bag. However, it had advanced features—two motors instead of one and a protected belt that prevented it from breaking if the brushes got stuck on a button or a hairpin. This allowed the machine to run longer without repairs than conventional models. Walton sold these vacuum cleaners for about $600. The selling price of Walton's extractors ranged from $1,500 to $11,000. Walton's channel of distribution was from Walton to industrial distributors (usually janitorial supply houses) to industrial users. The distributors took an average markup of 15 percent on their costs (Walton's selling price). Most of the industrial users were janitorial maintenance firms that cleaned carpets in office buildings, schools, hospitals, and hotels/motels. The distributors also sold to building contractors and to companies (other than supermarkets) that rented carpet-cleaning equipment.

The Walton sales force consisted of 10 people who worked out of the home office and reported to the sales manager, Henry Richman. These salespeople paid their own expenses, except for intercity transportation, which was paid by the Walton company. Richman said that the company used this compensation and expense plan because Walton was a small firm and was trying to keep its operating costs as low as possible. By paying a straight commission, the company made its sales compensation ex-

pense a variable cost. Also, Richman believed that people paid on a straight commission basis tended to work harder. They had no salary to rely on.

A Walton sales rep's job had two sets of activities. The first involved finding distributors (janitorial supply houses) and selling them Walton products. These were the wholesalers that sold to the janitorial maintenance firms that cleaned offices and other buildings. The second set of job duties involved activities to make the distributor's selling effort more effective.

To get a distributor to carry the Walton line, a sales rep would first go to a janitorial service that cleaned several office buildings. The rep would give a sales presentation that included a demonstration of the product and then secure an order. The rep took this order to the distributor. With orders from the final user already secured, it would be easier to get the distributor to carry the Walton line.

Once the distributor agreed to handle Walton's products, it was the sales rep's job to keep that distributor actively and effectively selling those products. Because most of these distributors also carried other brands of carpet cleaners along with the Walton products, the reps were constantly trying to persuade the distributors to promote the Walton line over competing brands. This meant that the Walton reps had to make frequent calls on their distributors.

To effectively sell the carpet soil extractors, the reps usually had to conduct sales demonstrations at night. Carpet cleaning was a wet process and therefore took time to dry. If the demonstration was done in the evening, the carpet could dry overnight and not interfere with the business working day. Also, janitorial cleaning crews did most of their work at night. Since they were the final buyers of the Walton extractors, demonstrations had to be directed toward them. Most of the time, the distributors were not willing to put in this extra effort. As a result, the Walton salespeople had to convince the distributors of the need for these night demonstrations in order to maintain sales of Walton products.

Three factors had triggered Doane and Richman's discussions of the sales compensation plan. First, Richman noticed that some of the sales reps were showing signs of dissatisfaction with their jobs. He was concerned because he knew that any decline in the sales reps' morale would adversely affect their working relationships with their distributors.

Second, the company had just begun to import the vacuum cleaners from Germany. Top management was thinking of selling this new product to the consumer market as well as to the industrial market. These executives had not yet decided which channel to use to reach consumers. But Doane and Richman both agreed that a sales rep's duties certainly would be affected by the addition of this new line of German cleaners.

The third factor leading to the compensation discussions was Richman's growing concern that the existing plan failed to motivate the salespeople to do a complete sales job. The straight commission on net sales, he believed, did little to get the sales reps to make night demonstrations or to spend time with the industrial users—the janitorial maintenance firms. Richman said that the plan did not stimulate long-range planning by the reps or their building lasting relationships with the distributors.

Doane felt that the current plan was generally working well. He believed that morale problems should be approached through changes in the sales training program. Doane talked to James Gaston, the manager of sales training, about the morale problem. Jim had done some research in attitude measurement and change. He conducted sales training seminars for Walton's distributors as well as for the sales force. Richman felt that these seminars were beneficial. He said, however, that they were not enough to handle the problems related to the three factors just noted—declining morale, new job duties, and the lack of a complete selling job.

Jim believed that any problem in this situation was not the fault of the compensation plan. He noted that the 10 percent straight commission plan was standard in the industry and that the Walton reps were making good money. Doane, in looking for a compromise, suggested increasing the commission rate another 2 or 3 percent—to a total of 12 or 13 percent. He believed that this added incentive might offset the three growing problems.

Richman felt uneasy with both Gaston's and Doane's proposals. He wondered about introducing a salary element into the plan, along with reducing the commission rate. He also brought up the idea of a quota–bonus plan. Under this proposal, each rep would be assigned a sales volume quota. The rep would receive a 10 percent commission on all sales up to the quota, and a bonus of maybe 3 percent on all volume exceeding the quota. The quota would be set on a quarterly basis. Thus the reps would start fresh every three months in their quest for a bonus.

Doane preferred not to bring quota-setting problems into the compensation plan. But he was also getting anxious to settle the compensation question. He felt that Walton had a good sales force. Many of the reps had been with the company for several years and Doane did not want to lose them now. Consequently, he asked Henry Richman to come up with a solid proposal regarding the sales force compensation plan.

### Question:

What plan should Walton Enterprises use to compensate its sales force?

# CHAPTER 11

# Sales Force Expenses and Transportation

Our men give their talent to the company and their genius to their expense accounts.

**LIFE magazine**

One sales manager observed that, even when properly managed, sales force expense accounts are a nuisance and, improperly managed, they can amount to grand larceny. This may be an unusually sour view of the situation. However, it points up the problem of establishing and administering a plan for controlling travel and other business expenses incurred by the sales force.

Sales reps are among the few company employees who are allowed to spend the company's money. Furthermore, sales force travel and other business expenses can be quite substantial. In 1998 the cost per sales rep for *meals and lodging alone* averaged about $44,000 in a typical metropolitan area in the United States. This average covered a 5-day, 50-week working period. The cost ranges from about $85,500 in New York City down to around $31,000 to $33,500 in smaller urban centers—places such as Burlington, Vermont or Corpus Christi, Texas.[1]

Remember, too, these figures do *not* include transportation or entertainment. Management often spends another 5 percent to 6 percent of sales on travel and entertainment to bring in an account. For many companies, when we talk about sales force travel and entertainment expenses, we are talking about big money!

## ■ SALES FORCE EXPENSES AND STRATEGIC PLANNING

Expense account policy is one element in a firm's strategic marketing plan. New enterprises are often financially unable to bear the fixed costs of a rep's selling expenses. The entrepreneur wants all costs to be as variable as possible—that is, related to sales volume. Thus, as a matter of strategy, the first reps will likely be offered a deal in which they pay all their own selling costs in exchange for a higher rate of commission. Higher commissions promise the hopeful reps that they will make more money than if the company paid selling expenses. One fact is certain: If the reps pay their own expenses, there will be little waste.

On the other hand, some firms hope to woo customers by treating them lavishly. Through the adroit use of entertainment, the customer is lured into the company's fold and kept there. Other firms want to develop an image of prosperity. They require their reps to go "first class" in their travel and relationships with accounts.

Often firms use expense account policy as a strategic tool for recruiting salespeople. A generous expense account and a company car will attract many financially strapped college graduates. One of the most recent strategic trends is the willingness of companies to pay for items which can lead to increases in salesperson productivity. You can see from Figure 11-1 that a lot more firms are willing to pay for 100 percent of the expense for such things as laptops, car phones, home fax machines, and home photocopiers than they were in the past. These numbers show a sharp increase from those of just two years ago. Clearly this trend will continue as more and more firms utilize sales automation.

## INTERNAL REVENUE SERVICE REGULATIONS

Income tax laws significantly affect the travel, entertainment, and gift expenses of salespeople. Congress and the IRS have progressively tightened the regulations on the deductibility of such expenses for income tax purposes. For many years the government has taken a strong stand on the deductibility of business entertainment expenses. Since 1994, only 50 percent of legitimate business entertainment expenses and only 50 percent of business meals expenses can be deducted when computing a firm's income tax. Furthermore, the tax deductibility of business gifts is limited to $25 per year for each recipient.

Moreover, tax auditors often scrutinize T&E expenses closely because experience has shown that there is a high probability of error in

■ FIGURE 11-1

| **Percentage of companies paying 100 percent of selected selling expenses** | Item | 1994 | 1996 |
|---|---|---|---|
| | Auto co-owned | 16% | 31% |
| | Auto leased | 20 | 40 |
| | Mileage | 37 | 57 |
| | Lodging | 80 | 87 |
| | Entertainment | 81 | 86 |
| | Home photocopier | 16 | 41 |
| | Home fax machine | 25 | 56 |
| | Car phone | 38 | 53 |
| | Laptop | 28 | 66 |

Source: Christian P. Heide, ed., *Dartnell's 29th Sales Force Compensation Survey* (Chicago: Dartnell Corporation, 1997), p. 121.

T&E expenses. Thus taxpayers should keep careful records of all such expenses to support the deductions on their tax returns.

## ■ LEGITIMATE TRAVEL AND BUSINESS EXPENSES

Management should specify in writing the expenses for which the company will pay—not only the broad expense categories, such as transportation or lodging, but also the details within each category. For example, in the case of air travel, management may reimburse only for coach fare. Specific guidelines should let sales reps know whether they must lease the cheapest rental car available. *All* items relating to travel should be clarified beforehand.

When determining allowable items, a good general policy is that the salesperson should be reimbursed (1) for business expenses incurred in connection with work and (2) for personal expenditures that would not have been necessary otherwise. The first part of the policy statement provides for expenditures for entertainment, faxing, office supplies, and transportation. Many of these expenses may be incurred either on the road or while selling in the home-office city. Personal expenditures include such items as overnight lodging, meals, and possibly laundry or valet service away from home. Rather than trying to determine the difference between the cost of meals at home and on the road, most firms pay all meal expenses while the salesperson is traveling.

There is no unanimous agreement on what constitutes a legitimate expense for reimbursement, but we can generalize about major categories of expenses. Usually, companies cover all *transportation* costs incurred on the job and all *lodging* costs incurred while the rep is away from home overnight on business. Companies usually cover the cost of *meals* while traveling out of town, but they frequently limit the amount.

Telephone, faxing, and other *communication* costs are considered legitimate business expenses, as are *office supplies* and *stenographic service.*

Undoubtedly, the most controversial of all expense categories is *entertainment* and *gifts.* The prevailing practice seems to be to allow all necessary and reasonable entertainment expenses. There may be limits in the form of per-person maximums on allowable items, such as meals and theater tickets. Or the entertainment may be restricted to lunches or dinners.

The advent of the 50 percent IRS limit on the deductibility of entertainment expenses has dampened management's enthusiasm for entertaining. Additionally, the soaring costs of entertainment have made management reappraise its entertainment policies. Giving business gifts is a longstanding practice. Surveys show opinions divided on gift giving. Some firms do it because they like to. Other organizations would like to end the practice but feel they would suffer competitively. Limiting the tax deductibility of business gifts has altered the gift-giving practices of many companies. Now many firms limit their gifts to the Christmas season. Also, some organizations do not allow their buyers to accept any gifts—even small ones.

# ■ CHARACTERISTICS OF A SOUND EXPENSE PLAN

A well-conceived and well-executed expense plan has certain general characteristics. Naturally, no perfect plan exists. Every plan has inherent limitations.

## No Net Gain or Loss for the Reps

The expense plan should be designed so that employees neither profit nor lose. A sales rep should net the same income working on the road as at home, an ideal difficult to achieve in practice.

While expense allowances should not be used in lieu of compensation, some firms intentionally follow this practice, with the approval of the sales force. The employee often prefers an increase in a nontaxable expense account to a raise in taxable salary or commissions.

The practice of compensating people by way of the expense account is unwise for at least two reasons. First, it is poor management; it tends to nullify the control feature of a good compensation plan. Second, the practice encourages people to violate tax laws. An expense account is nontaxable only to the extent that it reimburses the employee for legitimate business expenses. If the total allowance exceeds total costs, the excess money is taxable.

## Equitable Treatment of the Reps

Sales reps should be able to maintain approximately the same standard of living on the road as at home. They should not have to sacrifice comfort to stay within expense limits. Sales managers should recognize differences in travel expenses among the different territories. Costs are higher in an Atlantic Seaboard territory than in the Great Plains, for example.

## No Curtailment of Beneficial Activities

A good expense plan should not hamper the performance of selling duties, nor should it curtail activities beneficial to the company. A plan that attempts to set selling expenses as a percentage of sales may discourage a rep from developing a new territory. If expenses are limited to 1 percent of sales, for instance, no one would be eager to go into a new territory where expenses often are abnormally high in relation to early volume.

## Simple and Economical to Administer

A sound expense control plan should be simple and economical to administer. Clerical and administrative expenses should be minimized. Often expense reports require too much unnecessary detail, or they duplicate information requested elsewhere.

### Avoids Disputes

A good expense plan should prevent misunderstandings between management and the sales force. One way to reach this goal is to consult the sales force when establishing or revising an expense-control plan. The plan should be fully explained to the sales force in detail and in writing before it is put into effect. The company should pay promptly or, better yet, make an advance payment available to those who need it.

### Company Control of Expenses and Elimination of Padding

A good plan controls expenses and curtails padding. However, control is not synonymous with stinginess. A sales executive should be able to get all the benefits of control without damaging sales force morale by adopting a Scrooge-like approach.

Expense account padding is a problem most sales managers face at one time or another. Actually, it is more apt to be a *symptom* of a problem in another area. Often, good judgment in other areas will prevent sales reps from abusing their expense accounts. Recognition of achievement, a good training program, and an adequate compensation plan are practices that help eliminate expense account padding.

## ■ METHODS OF CONTROLLING EXPENSES

First, management must decide whether the company will pay for the sales rep's field-selling costs or have the reps pay their own expenses out of their earnings. Most firms pay for travel and business expenses. This practice is almost universally followed if salary is an element in the compensation plan. If the sales reps pay all their own expenses, the chances are that they are compensated by the straight commission method.

### Salespeople Pay Own Expenses

Salespeople paid by a straight commission usually pay their own expenses for two reasons. First, management is willing to pay a certain percentage of sales for the field sales function. It offers the total amount to the sales rep and says, in effect, "What's left over after you pay your costs is yours." Second, some people paid a straight commission are tempted to cheat on an expense account during periods of lean sales.

There are several reasons for letting the sales reps pay their own expenses. They often prefer this plan because it gives them more freedom of operation. They don't have to explain their expenses to management. Many reps believe that there are income tax advantages when paying their own expenses. They can deduct more expenses than if their earnings and expenses are separated by the company. Also, from management's standpoint, the plan is simple and costs nothing to operate.

**AN ETHICAL DILEMMA**

Many companies control their sales reps' travel and other business expenses by using some form of limited-payment plan. That is, management will set a maximum amount that the company will reimburse for specific items such as lodging, meals, entertainment, and laundry. Typically, the reps do not have to furnish receipts that are under the maximum limit. Also, frequently an item—local transportation, for example—may not require a receipt for reimbursement.

Under these limited-payment expense control plans, sometimes the salespeople's expense accounts do not record what *really* happened. A rep may overspend the dinner limit by $10 and then make it up by adding to an underspent breakfast or lunch. One rep padded his taxi expenses (where no receipts were required) to make up what he overspent on food. He claimed that there was no way he could eat properly in that city on the limited amount set by the company. In other cases, reps may underspend the limit on meals or entertainment, but their expense accounts state that they spent the maximum allowed. The reps claim that they should be allowed to economize in order to earn extra money, so long as their job performances and customer services do not suffer.

As a means of getting around the controls built into limited-payment expense plans, are any or all of the above-described practices ethical?

When salespeople pay their own expenses, however, the results may not be what management wants. A company loses considerable control over its reps' activities. For example, the reps are not likely to travel long distances to call on and entertain prospective new accounts who do not offer immediate sales potential.

## Unlimited-Payment Plans

The most widely used method of expense control is to reimburse sales representatives for all legitimate business and travel costs incurred while on company business. There is no limit on total expenses or individual items, but reps are required to submit itemized accounts of their expenditures.

The main advantage of the unlimited method of expense control is its flexibility. Cost differentials between territories, jobs, or products present fewer problems under this plan. Flexibility also makes the plan fair for both salespeople and management, assuming reps report their expenditures honestly and accurately. Furthermore, this plan gives management considerable control over the sales reps' activities. If sales executives want a new territory developed or new accounts called on in out-of-the-way places, the expense plan is no deterrent.

On the other hand, the unlimited method of controlling expenses may not allow management to accurately forecast its direct selling costs. The unlimited feature is an open invitation for some people to be extravagant or pad their expense accounts with unjustifiable items. The plan offers no incentive for a salesperson to economize.

It is questionable whether the unlimited-expense plan leads to more or fewer disputes between management and the sales force than other expense-control systems. The unlimited feature should reduce the number of disagreements, but friction may arise if management questions items on the expense reports. Probably the major need in an unlimited-payment plan is to establish a successful method of controlling the expenses. Certainly a sales manager should analyze the reps' expense reports to determine what is reasonable and practicable.

## Limited-Payment Plans

Two widely used expense-control plans each limit the payments to the sales reps. One such plan places a limit on the amount to be reimbursed *for each expense item.* For example, a company may pay a maximum of $140 a day for lodging, $7 for breakfast, $12 for lunch, and $25 for dinner (or $44 each day for food). The other limited-payment plan provides a *flat sum for a period of time,* such as a day or week. One company may allow $180 a day; another firm may set its flat sum at $900 a week. Management may set the same limits in all its territories, or it may establish different limits to account for territorial cost differentials.

Setting limitations on expense payments has some advantages. These plans especially are suitable when sales reps' activities are routine and travel routes are repetitive. Then the expenses can be more accurately forecasted. These forecasted expense maximums then aid in budget planning. Also, knowing in advance what the limits are should reduce expense-account disputes between management and the sales reps, particularly if the limits are perceived to be fair.

Probably the major problem involved in administering a limited-payment plan is to establish the limits for each item or time period. Management may study past reports to determine the mileage typically covered each day. It may examine hotel and motel directories to establish limits on lodging. A separate study should be conducted for each territory to ensure that the plan reflects regional cost differentials. Also, management should monitor the program to ensure that the limits reflect a territory's current structure. Sales reps should be included in these various deliberations, because limited-pay plans are good only if the sales force believes the limits are equitable.

Other problems typically are encountered in limited-payment plans. High-caliber salespeople may object to such a plan, because they feel that the company does not trust them. Also, the system can be inflexible. A sales rep may have some unusual expense, such as an entertainment item he or she could not escape without losing the account. If entertainment is not an allowable expense, the rep may not be reimbursed. Some companies avoid such inflexibility by allowing these unusual expenses if they are reported separately with an explanatory note.

When management sets limits for each item, the plan may be hard to control. Reps may switch expenditures among expense items. They may attempt to recoup the money spent in excess of the limit for one item by padding the claim for some other item. Also, the plan cannot prevent a cheater from economizing on some expenses and then padding the account up to the allowable limits.

## Combination Plans

The advantages of both the limited and unlimited plans can sometimes be realized by developing a control method that combines the two. Management may set limits on items such as food and lodging, for example, but place no ceiling on transportation. Another combination method is an expense-quota plan. Under this system, management sets a limit on the total allowable expense, but the ceiling is related to some other item on the operating statement, such as net sales. For example, a quota of $2,000 may be set for a month because monthly sales are expected to be $40,000. Expenses can be tied to sales even more directly by allowing sales representatives a monthly expense account not to exceed 5 percent of their net sales. The compensation plan can play some part in this expense-control system by paying a bonus if the rep keeps expenses at an amount under quota.

Expense-quota plans do have the advantage of enabling management to relate sales force expenses to net sales. In this method, management has some control over this direct selling cost. Furthermore, the reps have some operating flexibility within the total expense budget. Reps who have been made expense conscious are not likely to be wasteful.

## CONTROL OF SALES FORCE TRANSPORTATION

One significant expense with little room for discretion is the cost of transportation. Transportation expense decisions are usually clear-cut, based on the costs and the nature of the selling environment. The rep who covers Manhattan must use taxis, buses, and the subway; a car would be next to useless. Without a car in Los Angeles, however, the rep goes nowhere. The situation largely dictates the transportation required. Some aspects are open to managerial control, however.

### Ownership of Automobiles

Since most sales travel is done by automobile, a car has become almost standard equipment. Management may provide company-owned cars, the vehicle may be leased, or salespeople may use their own cars. No one policy for car ownership is best under all conditions. The final decision rests on a consideration of the following factors.

- **Size of sales force.** With a small sales force, simplicity and economy are achieved either by having salespeople use their own cars or by

*A Day-to-Day Operating Problem*

## MAJESTIC PLASTICS COMPANY (H)

### Reduction in travel expenses

Clyde Brion had just finished reading a memo from the president's office, instructing all department managers to reduce their travel expenses. No specific percentage reductions were stated, nor were the managers given any details as to how the reduction was to be achieved. Brion realized that his sales force accounted for a substantial share of the company's total travel expenses, so he recognized the major responsibility being placed on his shoulders. His problem was how to achieve a significant cost reduction without unduly hurting sales force morale.

Brion knew that many other companies were struggling with this same cost-reduction problem. For example, several firms that formerly provided first-class air transportation now required their personnel, including the executives, to fly economy class (coach fare). For his own sales force, Brion wondered if he could use some of the ideas he had picked up in an article in the international edition of *USA Today* (9/22/93).

One substantial cut in air travel costs could be made if the sales reps were to stay over Saturday night on their out-of-town sales calls. On some routes a rep may pay two or three times higher fares by coming home on Friday instead of staying over Saturday night. Some companies now *require* their reps to stay over Saturday night; other firms put this on a *voluntary* basis. Either way poses morale problems. Even on a voluntary basis, a volunteer may incur the ill will of those who think they look bad because they do not volunteer to stay over.

On some airlines the fares are half price if you leave very early in the morning or very late at night. For transportation in town or to the airport, some companies are shifting from taxis to buses. Hotel bills are reduced by having sales people stay at Holiday Inns, rather than the Marriott or Hyatt Hotels. On food, one company saved 19 percent by requiring receipts for expenses as low as $15 instead of $25, because employees had been padding their food expense accounts.

Brion was seriously considering these various alternatives for cost cutting, especially the Saturday-night stayover. He also was wondering what other options he should explore.

**Question:** What specific steps should Clyde Brion take to reduce his sales force travel expenses?

Note: See the introduction to this series of problems in Chapter 4 for the necessary background on the company, its market, and its competition.

leasing cars for them. Only when its sales force is large does a company generally find it advantageous to own the cars.

- **Availability of centralized maintenance and storage facilities.** If a company maintains centralized vehicle storage and repair facilities, it is in a good position to furnish the sales force with cars.

- **Unusual design required.** Some companies require that the cars used by their salespeople be a special color, have a specially constructed body, or carry some form of company advertising. Sometimes the vehicle must double as a sales car and a delivery truck. In these situations, the company should furnish the cars.

- **Control of car's operating condition.** If the company furnishes the car, management is in a better position to demand that it be kept presentable. The company probably provides later-model cars than the average salesperson's own car. However, sales reps may take better care of their own cars than company-owned or leased vehicles.

- **Personal preferences.** Some people are financially able and willing to furnish their own cars for work. When sales reps *must* provide the cars, however, management runs the risk of losing good applicants. Some reps may not want to drive their own cars for company business, or they may not have suitable cars.

- **Annual mileage.** A rep's average annual mileage influences ownership of the automobile. The more miles driven, the more advantageous it becomes for the company to own the cars. The point of indifference varies depending on the cars used and the company's auto-expense allowances. Suppose the company pays a flat 30 cents per mile auto allowance. Management has calculated the cost of owning the preferred model to be $4,000 a year, plus 10 cents a mile. Under these circumstances, the point of indifference would be 20,000 miles. If the salespeople covered less than this mileage, management would probably encourage them to own the cars.

- **Operating cost.** It is hard to generalize on which of the three alternatives—employee-owned, company-owned, or leased—offers the lowest operating cost. It depends to a great extent on rental costs, number of miles driven, and method of reimbursing the sales force. It also is difficult to measure some indirect costs of company ownership, such as the administrative expense of operating the system.

- **Investments.** If the company is not in a strong financial position or does not want to make the investment, it can lease cars or have the salespeople provide their own.

- **Administrative problems.** One major administrative question that comes up when the company furnishes cars is whether they should be available for the reps' personal use and, if so, to what extent. Most companies allow reps to use company cars for personal transportation. Management may or may not suggest some limits. If a company adopts a no-limit policy, reps may not buy their own cars, or they may use the company car as a second family car.

  Use of a company car for private purposes is another indirect monetary payment, the same as group insurance or a paid vacation. Some businesses ask the rep to pay for the gas when driving the car for personal use. Others pay all expenses for both business and private use. Some ask that operating expenses be paid only on long personal trips such as vacations.

Leasing is the easiest way to put the sales force on wheels. The sales executive does not have to be a transportation expert, and the firm avoids the problems of buying the car, maintaining it, and later reselling it.

The IRS's policy greatly encourages leasing automobiles, particularly the more expensive models. Lease payments are deductible, almost without question, while the IRS often contests (in audit) depreciation deductions for expensive company-owned cars. The record-keeping chores are also minimized if the cars are leased.

## Reimbursement Plans for Employee-Owned Cars

Salespeople who use their own cars on company business are often reimbursed for the cost. Three separate types of expenditures are involved in owning and operating a car. One type is *variable costs,* which are generally related directly to the number of miles driven. Examples of these items are gasoline, oil, lubrication, tires, and normal service maintenance. A second class of expenditures is *fixed costs,* which tend to be related to time rather than miles driven. These costs include depreciation, license fees, and insurance. A third group of *miscellaneous expenses* is difficult to standardize. Typical items are tolls, parking, and major repairs. Usually the third type of costs is not incorporated into one of the ordinary automobile expense-control plans. These items are listed separately on the expense account.

Salespeople may be reimbursed for using their cars on company business by some kind of a fixed-allowance plan or by a flexible-payment method.

### Fixed-Allowance Plans

One general type of fixed-allowance plan is based on *mileage* and another on a period of *time.* Under the first, the employee is paid the same amount for each mile driven on company business. The flat rate per mile is used by more companies than any other major plan, although there is a trend toward more flexible methods. Under the other type of fixed-allowance system, a flat sum is paid for each period of time, such as a week or a month, regardless of the number of miles driven. The reimbursements cover both fixed and variable automobile costs.

The fixed-allowance plans have several advantages. They are generally simple and economical to administer. Salespeople know in advance what they will be paid. Also, if payment is based on a flat allowance for a given period of time, the company can budget this expense in advance. People who drive few miles (5,000–10,000) prefer it because they can generally make money under such a plan.

The criticisms of fixed-allowance plans are so severe, however, that we wonder why they remain so popular. Generally speaking, the plans are inflexible and may be unfair to some salespeople. Some may benefit while others lose. The fixed sum for a given time period can be reasonably good only if everyone travels in a routine fashion and costs are the same in each territory. Similarly, the flat-mileage allowance is equitable only if all reps travel about the same number of miles in the same type of cars under the same operating conditions. These conditions are highly unlikely and unrealistic.

Consider the inequities introduced, for example, by variations in the number of miles driven. In the operation of a car, some costs are fixed regardless of the number of miles driven. Therefore, the greater amount of driving, the more miles over which to amortize the fixed costs. So the fixed costs per mile decrease as the total mileage increases. Under a fixed allowance per mile, every additional mile works to the financial benefit of the sales reps. An example is outlined in Figure 11-2. Assuming annual fixed costs of $3,000, variable costs of 12 cents per mile, and a mileage allowance of 25 cents, the results are shown for various annual mileages. If a sales representative drives 5,000 miles per year, he receives $1,250, when the real costs are $3,600. Thus earnings are reduced by $2,350. At the other extreme, a representative who drives 40,000 miles gets $10,000, which is a gain of $2,200 over actual costs. If the representative were paid a fixed sum per month, similar inequities would result but in reverse. That is, a payment of $400 a month would benefit the low-mileage traveler at the expense of the person who drove many miles in a year.

### Flexible-Allowance Plans

To avoid the inherent weaknesses in a fixed-allowance system, companies have developed several flexible plans.

A *graduated-mileage* rate plan pays a different allowance per mile depending on the total miles driven in a time period. For example, one firm pays 30 cents a mile for the first 15,000 miles driven in a year and 20 cents a mile for those over 15,000. Mileage allowances are graduated downward to reflect the fact that total costs per mile decrease as mileage goes up. While a graduated plan corrects some of the faults of a flat-rate method, it usually does not consider differences in territorial costs and types of cars.

Under a plan that *combines an allowance per time period with a mileage rate,* management figures automobile allowances in two parts. Thus the differences between fixed and variable costs of owning and operating a car are reflected in the payment. To cover fixed costs, a flat payment

■ **FIGURE 11-2** **Example of results of flat rate per mile plan under varying annual mileages**

| Annual Mileage | Fixed Cost | Variable Costs at 12 Cents per Mile | Total Costs | Per-Mile Costs | Payment to Representatives at 25 Cents per Mile | Gain or Loss to Representatives |
|---|---|---|---|---|---|---|
| 5,000 | $3,000 | $ 600 | $3,600 | $.72 | $ 1,250 | −$2,350 |
| 10,000 | 3,000 | 1,200 | 4,200 | .42 | 2,500 | −1,700 |
| 20,000 | 3,000 | 2,400 | 5,400 | .27 | 5,000 | − 400 |
| 30,000 | 3,000 | 3,600 | 6,600 | .22 | 7,500 | +900 |
| 40,000 | 3,000 | 4,800 | 7,800 | .195 | 10,000 | +2,200 |

## AN INTERNATIONAL PERSPECTIVE

As they say south of the border and also in Madrid, las diferencias culturas (the cultural differences) face American companies that are managing a sales force in foreign countries. And these differences are not limited to areas of selecting, training, and motivating salespeople. Other areas—renting cars in Europe for sales force transportation, for example—also can be a whole different ballgame.

Unless they are forewarned, sales managers may be surprised by the high costs in Europe—especially the steep prices for fuel and sales taxes. Gasoline runs $4 to $5 for a U.S. gallon. (The last time one of your authors rented a car in Italy, unleaded gas—not super premium—came to $5.35 a gallon, after converting lire to dollars and liters to U.S. gallons.) On auto rentals, the value-added tax—a form of sales tax—in various European countries is as follows:

| | | | |
|---|---|---|---|
| Great Britain | - 17.5 % | Norway | - 22% |
| France | - 18.6% | Sweden | - 25% |
| Holland | - 17.5% | Denmark | - 25% |
| Germany | - 15% | Spain | - 15% |
| Austria | - 21.2% | Italy | - 19% |

Most of the cars of the size that sales reps are likely to rent have stick-shift (not automatic) transmissions and no air conditioning, even in Italy, Spain, or Portugal.

Besides the costs and car equipment, sales reps should be alert for other potential surprises. In Italy, for example, retail stores including nonairport rental agencies typically close for three hours at lunch time. Obviously, this cultural feature must influence a rep's planning for an auto pickup or dropoff. Sometimes the rental location is difficult to find. One major company's location in Rome was tucked away in an underground garage.

The question of additional insurance to cover collision and other damage can be a bone of contention for renters. Some rental agencies require this added insurance, even though the driver is covered by his or her U.S. insurance policy or credit card company.

There also is a question regarding the level of customer service overseas as compared to service in the United States. Car rental executives say that the level of their customer service in Europe is uniformly high. But impartial industry observers do not agree. An American Express Company executive, whose department has to reconcile billing disputes between drivers and rental companies, says that the level of customer service in Europe is below what it should be. As one executive who has lived abroad said regarding the familiar-looking locations, "It's an illusion. You walk in and see the same uniforms and smiling people, and you think you are dealing with home boys, but you're not."

Source: James S. Hirsh, "Renting Cars Abroad Can Drive You Nuts," *The Wall Street Journal*, December 10, 1993, p. B1.

is made for each given time period, such as a week or a month. In addition, variable costs are reimbursed by mileage allowances, which usually are flat rates although they could be graduated. For example, one company pays $300 a month plus 12 cents a mile; another pays $350 a month plus 20 cents a mile over 750 miles a month.

A widely recognized and respected plan was developed more than 50 years ago by the founder of Runzheimer International, a management consulting firm for travel and living costs, headquartered in Rochester, Wisconsin. This company typically divides the United States into several geographic regions and then computes the total annual costs, which in-

■ **FIGURE 11-3**

**Runzheimer annual vehicle costs for a midsized four-door car in selected locations**

| Location | Total Annual Costs |
|---|---|
| Los Angeles, CA | $8,952 |
| Philadelphia, PA | 8,163 |
| Boston, MA | 7,682 |
| Phoenix, AZ | 7,367 |
| Denver, CO | 6,957 |
| Kansas City, KS | 6,782 |
| Minneapolis, MN | 6,668 |
| Atlanta, GA | 6,609 |
| Cleveland, OH | 6,440 |
| Portland, OR | 6,195 |
| Nashville, TN | 6,065 |
| Sioux Falls, SD | 5,813 |

Costs are based on a 1998 Ford Taurus 3.0 L, six-cylinder, four-door sedan equipped with automatic transmission with overdrive, power steering, power disc brakes, tinted glass, AM–FM stereo, cruise control, and air conditioning. Costs include operating costs: fuel, oil, tires, and maintenance; and fixed costs: insurance, depreciation, and license and registration fees. Factors are based on a 4-year, 60,000-mile trade-in cycle.

Source: Runzheimer International, Rochester, Wisconsin.

clude ownership and operating expenses for cars in each of these regions. As an example, Figure 11-3 shows the 1998 cost allowances for a midsized car in 12 selected locations.

In some respects, the Runzheimer plan gives the same results as the graduated mileage system in that the more miles driven, the smaller per-mile allowance. However, the Runzheimer plan is much more accurate because payments reflect variations in types of cars, miles driven, and territorial operating costs. For a midsized car in 1998, for instance, the annual fixed costs varied from $8,952 in Los Angeles down to $5,813 in Sioux Falls, South Dakota. In summary, a **Runzheimer plan** seems to be the most equitable and accurate method for paying salespeople for the use of their cars.

## ■ OTHER METHODS OF EXPENSE CONTROL

Selling costs loom large in the expenses of most firms. While top executives may not be too happy about the cost of sales force compensation, they are even more concerned about their reps' field-selling expenses. At this point we shall note briefly a few additional methods of controlling field-selling expenses (besides the expense account and automobile-allowance plans already discussed in this chapter).

### Training and Enforcement

Right from the start, management should teach the sales reps how the company expects them to spend its money. Any violators of company expense policy should be subject to immediate reprimand or something stronger. Otherwise, the reps will assume that expense account abuse will be overlooked by management.

Some firms make it quite clear from the beginning that expense account fraud will be a basis for dismissal. Moreover, these firms include a section in their job performance evaluations appraising how wisely a rep spends company money. A rep who wants a position in management should develop the image of an honest person who is careful with company money. Management may tolerate some character flaws in its people, but dishonesty is not one of them.

## Credit Cards

Many firms use credit cards to control various expense items. By accepting credit card charges only from a designated list of hotels and restaurants, for example, a company can control the places where its reps sleep and eat. Also, using credit cards means that the reps need to carry less money, thus reducing the risks of loss or theft.

## The Expense Bank Account

In some instances an undue burden is placed on representatives who have to pay their expenses and then wait for reimbursement. They may have to finance three or four weeks' expenses—$2,000 to $4,000. To avoid this, some firms place a certain sum, say $2,000, in a checking account for each representative. The rep pays expenses by drawing on that account. When the account needs replenishment, or at regular intervals, the rep files an expense report. Upon approval of the report, the amount accounted for is deposited in the checking account to bring it back up to the initial sum.

## Change in Nature of Entertainment

The costs of entertaining customers have skyrocketed to ridiculous levels in many areas. It is easy to spend $1,000 entertaining a client for one evening in New York City or Los Angeles.

Consequently, home entertainment, quiet dinners, or small parties offer attractive alternatives to the manager or rep seeking lower entertainment costs. The out-of-pocket costs directly associated with the party are included in the normal expense account. Some firms have simply stopped entertaining clients at Broadway shows or with an expensive night on the town.

## Telemarketing

High field-selling costs are one reason for the rapid expansion of telephone selling tactics—telemarketing. A firm can afford a lot of long-distance telephone calls if it can substantially reduce its field-selling expenses.

In many situations, the sales rep automatically determines whether a telephone call can substitute for a personal visit. Both buyer and seller

## Controlling Expenses: A Five-Step Process

One of the authors was visiting the sales manager of a major publisher while the manager was reviewing some sales rep expense reports. The manager moaned, "OK, you're supposed to be the expert on selling expenses. Here's one for you: How can I devise an expense account that will keep this guy from spending $20 parking in a Wabash Street garage when he could park much cheaper in Grant Park? How do you get reps to treat the company's money as they would their own?"

The author replied, "You don't have an expense account problem in your hand. You have a training and supervision problem. Teach your salespeople how you want the company's money spent and then see that they do it."

The author continued, "Controlling selling expenses can be seen as a five-step process. First, make up your mind that you really want to control the expenses. Some managers like to gripe about how much their sales reps spend, but really don't want to do anything about the system for fear it might affect their own expense account behavior.

"Second, establish selling expense budgets. Some hard facts about field-selling costs must be developed. Often management is simply unaware of how much it costs to operate in the field these days. It's too easy to unfairly judge some sales rep who is honestly trying to operate in the field when one does not know the facts about the matter.

"Third, communicate management's expense standards and practices to the sales force in writing. Leave no room for doubt about what is expected, but allow room for unexpected costs and unusual situations.

"Fourth, set up a routine, automatic auditing system for the expense reports. Most sales managers prefer to control this function rather than have the accounting department do the job.

"Finally, departures from company policy must be recognized and dealt with. In cases where the rep is abusing the expense account or is openly defrauding the company, dismissal is appropriate. Remember that filing false expense reports is fraud. Sometimes a few reps lose sight of this fact."

can benefit because many buyers would much rather deal with the rep in a short time over the telephone than spend an hour listening to the rep's sales pitch. Both parties seek transactional efficiency.

## Careful Travel Planning

Many large companies have established the position of travel manager whose job it is to minimize travel expenses by careful advanced planning. Sales reps or managers sometimes go on sales trips in various directions with little advance notice and no preplanning. Instead, with the help of a travel manager, plus careful routing and planning in advance, much business can be accomplished on each trip along with reduced travel costs.

Some firms whose people must travel extensively by air have developed in-house travel agencies to help lower travel costs. These firms also carefully study the costs of flying from different airports under different conditions. Prices vary greatly almost on a daily basis, depending upon when one travels, how much in advance reservations are made, how long the traveler stays, the airline and the route selected, and the competitive situation at the time.

## ◼ SUMMARY

The handling and control of expense accounts is one of the most sensitive areas in sales management. Expense accounts are strictly regulated by the Internal Revenue Service, which stipulates in some detail what is and is not deductible. Management should identify in writing, and in detail, the expenses it will cover. Normally, sales reps are reimbursed for their business expenses plus some personal costs that would not have been necessary if the reps were at home. A sound expense plan should be simple to administer, neither enrich nor impoverish the reps, and control the level of selling expenses.

Management must decide if the company will pay for the sales force's field-selling costs or if the reps should pay their own expenses. Salespeople working on a straight commission usually pay their own expenses. Under any other compensation plan, however, the company should pay the rep's expenses as an item separate from the compensation plan.

In the most widely used expense-control plan, reps are reimbursed for all legitimate expenses, but they must itemize expenses and document certain large expenditures. Under the other major plan, management either sets limits for certain items (such as food, lodging, and entertainment) or else provides a fixed total allowance for some time period.

A company should develop a plan for controlling the sales force's transportation costs. When the reps travel by car, management must decide whether to own or lease the cars or have the reps use their own cars. If the reps use their own vehicles, the company should formulate a program to reimburse them. Often some form of fixed allowance per mile or per time period is used. However, the preferred method is to develop some system of flexible allowances that considers the variation in the miles each rep drives and the costs of driving in the rep's area.

The greatly increased costs of travel and entertainment have encouraged most companies to attack such expenses aggressively by several means. In many cases, entertainment has been curtailed. Telemarketing has entered the picture as the telephone has become a less expensive means of contacting the market than a field sales call. Travel plans are now more carefully monitored to limit costs than was previously the case.

**Key Terms**

Fixed-allowance plans
Flexible-allowance plans

Limited-payment plan
Runzheimer plan

Unlimited-payment plan

##  QUESTIONS AND PROBLEMS

1. "The expense-control plan should enable our representatives to maintain (at no extra cost to them) the same standard of living while on the road that they enjoy at home," said the sales manager of a metal products manufacturer. Discuss the implications in this statement.

2. When recruiting salespeople, some firms offer the opportunity for additional net income through the expense plan. Evaluate this policy on economic, human relations, and ethical bases.

3. What factors should management consider when deciding what method to

use for controlling and reimbursing sales reps' expenses? Give some examples of how each factor might influence the decision.

4. "I don't make any money when my reps are home. I want them on the road all the time. I want them to live in luxury. Our present gross margin allows us to spend a lot of money so we can make even more money. I don't care what the reps spend just so they are happy and keep selling. All I care about is how much they sell." Comment on this entrepreneur's statement.

5. A company was in dire need of a replacement part that had shut down its production line. A sales rep in the supplier's office was told to deliver it as quickly as possible. She did so in record time. She also received a ticket for speeding (85 miles per hour). On her expense account, she applied for reimbursement of the $150 fine. As sales manager with responsibility for the rep, what would you do?

6. A petroleum firm with a sales force of 300 people planned to sell its fleet of company-owned automobiles and have the salespeople furnish their own cars. What problems are involved in this change?

7. The oil company noted in Question 6 was trying to decide which method should be used to reimburse the sales force for the use of their cars on business. Each rep traveled about 15,000 miles a year. The company was computing the costs on the assumption that they drove midsized cars. The following payment methods were under

consideration. What would be the total annual cost to the firm under each of the three proposals?

   a. A straight 40 cents a mile.

   b. $300 a month plus 18 cents a mile.

   c. The Runzheimer plan. Use Figure 11-3 and assume that the 300-rep sales force was equally divided among territories based around Los Angeles and Philadelphia.

8. In lieu of a salary increase last year, a television manufacturer granted its sales force the privilege of using company cars for any personal purposes, and the company paid all expenses. Previously, the firm had strictly prohibited any personal use of these cars. Discuss all aspects of this policy decision.

9. One publisher was considering leasing small Chevrolet or Dodge cars instead of paying its present 30 cents per mile to sales reps for using their personal cars. Several of the reps were driving economy cars and were willing to take less than 30 cents per mile in order to keep from changing cars. What should the firm do?

10. The major U.S. airlines have frequent-flyer plans which offer awards (free flights or upgraded seats) after a person has accumulated a certain number of miles flying on a given airline. In the case of sales reps who accumulated miles on business travel, who should get these awards—the reps who did the traveling or their companies who paid for the trips? If you give the awards to the reps, should the awards be considered taxable income to the salespeople?

# ◧ EXPERIENTIAL EXERCISES

**A.** Contact a local car dealer to compare the costs of leasing or buying a fleet of 10 cars. Assume that the cars will be midsize American cars and that the salespeople will average 30,000 miles per year.

**B.** Contact sales managers from five different companies. Ask them to explain the expense reimbursement plan for their salespeople.

# ◧ REFERENCES

1. Data in this paragraph are provided by Runzheimer International, a Rochester, Wisconsin–based management consulting firm which specializes in providing information on travel and living costs for all metropolitan areas in the United States.

---

*Case 11-1*

## PAN PACIFIC TRADING COMPANY
### Expense account auditing policy

Kate Cook, sales manager for Pan Pacific Trading Company, wondered what was bothering Larry Cheng, the company's controller. He had asked for a meeting with her concerning sales department expense accounts.

The Pan Pacific Trading Company of San Francisco imported a wide range of consumer products, gift items, wearing apparel, and jewelry from the Pacific Rim nations. Its customers were department stores, gift shops, chain specialty stores, and any other merchant who found the goods attractive. The company's product policies had been most aggressive. It would import anything that management felt would make a good profit. Some of the items defied classification. One profitable item for the Christmas season of 1994 was a novelty from Taiwan—a plastic flower that danced to music.

Since the markets for the firm's imports were so diverse, the company had to encourage buyers for smaller operations to come to Pan Pacific's sales offices. Consequently, the company maintained sales offices at the home office in San Francisco and at the major marts in such cities as New York, Chicago, Dallas, Los Angeles, and Atlanta. Each office was under the direction of a regional sales manager who had the major responsibility of developing that region's markets. The regional managers were paid a modest salary supplemented with a strong incentive system of bonuses that resulted in average earnings in excess of $150,000 a year. Each sales office also had an in-house salesperson who kept the office open each day. There were usually two or three other sales reps who worked large accounts in addition to the regional manager. Everyone was in the office on "Market Days." While the apparel trades held a few market weeks during the year, usually six, the gift trades were different. For example, in Dallas every Friday was market day for gift buyers. In addition, several well-attended gift market weeks were held each year.

Moreover, the daily traffic that stopped by the sales offices was surprisingly large.

Many different merchants who sold the kinds of things imported by the company visited the sales offices.

Larry had requested a two o'clock meeting, and Kate noted that he was prompt as usual. He marched into her office with his large brown attaché case firmly in hand. After the perfunctory greetings, he asked, "Can I spread my papers on your table?" Cook nodded while wondering what this was all about. She resented his failure to tell her the subject of the meeting. Cook was about to say so when he made the appointment, but she decided she would be better off not knowing what was to be discussed. That way, she could always stall and divert him by saying, "Hey, you just sprung this on me. I'll need some time to study it." Kate took pride in her tactical skills, which had served her well as she rose in the company.

Cheng began, "I don't know where to start. Your sales department expense accounts are not only way out of line, but they're illegal. If the IRS audits us, they'll disallow a lot of your expenses. And I mean yours and your department's."

Kate interrupted, "Does Mr. Tsai know of this meeting and your concern with our expense accounts?" Tsai was the founder and president of the company. Cook wanted to discover Cheng's power base and find out how much clout he was carrying in his crusade for lower and cleaner expense accounts. This was not a new issue with him. Cook and Cheng had this same conversation each year about tax time.

Larry answered, "No, this is my area of responsibility. I don't run to the boss every time there's a problem. You know he doesn't want to hear about our problems. He only wants to hear about our solutions to them."

Kate knew that Tsai was not too sympathetic to Cheng's close adherence to the Internal Revenue Code. When Cook had brought the expense account issues to Tsai

before he had told her, "In some ways, it is an advantage to have Cheng the way he is; it keeps us on our toes. He will make certain we know what we are doing. On the other hand, he may be of less use than he could be because he does not believe in our cause. We'll wait and see if he becomes a problem." Cook then understood that Tsai would not appreciate any expense account problems being dumped into his lap. Thereafter, she handled issues as they arose.

"Come on, Larry, you're talking generalities. Get down to specifics. I can't make decisions on such generalities."

"There are so many of them."

"I don't care how many there are, if you want me to do something about each one of them, you'll have to list them. Get me a document that itemizes each of your concerns so I can start to deal with them." Cook smiled to herself. She bought some time to think about the problems that would be on that list. She knew exactly the things that were bothering Larry. She knew the law and IRS policy. She had even gone out of her way to take a seminar on handling expense account deductions for income tax purposes. She knew it was an important part of her job and she was not about to let any accountant push her anywhere she did not absolutely have to go.

Cook also understood the company's tax compliance philosophies. While Tsai insisted on absolute compliance with all laws of the lands in which the company did business, he also recognized that there were many gray areas in which the laws were subject to great differences of interpretation and administration. He saw no reason to penalize his company by attempting to interpret any law in favor of whatever government was involved. He pushed the law to the limit when necessary and then backed off or compromised if the government forced him to do so. Neither he nor Pan Pacific

Trading had ever been charged with any misdeeds. He had told Cook, "Tax audits are inevitable. Count on them! Play the game as tough as you can, but keep good documentation. If a dispute arises, our professional people will settle it as best as they can depending upon the documentation we provide them."

Larry persisted, "Fine, you'll have your itemized list tomorrow. But now I want to tell you the areas that are going to cause us some real problems down the line. First, there's the matter of the cars that everyone drives and deducts. It is quite clear in the law that the government does not want to subsidize the driving of luxury cars. They don't feel you need to be driving a Cadillac to do business. Now, you and all of the regional managers and sales reps are driving luxury cars and the end result is that the company is paying for them. Get our automotive expense account policy within the law!"

Cook did not like Cheng's tone or attitude. She coolly replied, "What we do is not illegal. As I recall, when we began our present policy, no one questioned its legality." She wondered what was bothering Cheng so much about the cars they were driving. She really liked her BMW. Then she recalled that Larry drove a Ford. She also realized that perhaps the biggest danger to the company in the matter was Larry's attitude toward the company's policy. Just after Congress altered the tax code to limit the deductions for the depreciation of automobiles, the company changed its method for handling auto expenses. It started giving each sales manager and rep a flat expense allowance per year that was sufficiently generous so they could afford to drive luxury cars. She knew that several reps rented their cars. She did not know how they handled their tax treatment since such matters were the private, personal concern of each person. The allowance varied depending upon the person and the territory. The New York rep's allowance was much lower than the Los Angeles rep's because she did not even own a car. She either used public transportation or rented a car when she needed one. Cook was given a $15,000 a year allowance. It was treated as income and reported to the IRS on her W-2 form. She then had to take the deductions for its business use. She preferred this system as did all the other managers and reps. Some members of top management had similar car allowances. Larry did not!

Larry continued, "And then there is the matter of your entertainment costs. They are excessive. Any auditor will scream at some of your claims. Sally's (the New York rep) last expense account claimed that she spent $950 entertaining one customer one evening in New York. That's nonsense! And, Kate, I didn't intend to say anything, but those expense reports of yours on that trip you and Mr. Tsai took to Japan . . . well."

Kate knew he was referring to that $4,500 meal they reported when they entertained several of their Japanese suppliers one evening at a fancy Tokyo restaurant on the Ginza. She said nothing about it because she knew she could beat him on that one if he even so much as mentioned it in the itemized list of grievances. Then Cheng launched into the subject of the limitations that had been placed on entertainment expenses by the 1993 tax legislation.

"We need to reexamine our attitudes toward entertainment now that we can only deduct 50 percent of their costs. We are now having to absorb half of our already outrageous entertainment expenses as nondeductible expenses."

Cook dismissed Larry by saying, "I've got to run to a meeting now. I'm eager to see your list."

*Questions:*

1. How should Kate Cook handle this problem with Larry Cheng?

2. Is the company's auto expense policy in violation of the IRS code?

3. Evaluate Larry Cheng's concern with the seemingly high costs for entertainment. What would you do to avoid such high entertainment costs?

---

*Case 11-2*

## LUTZ INTERNATIONAL

### Tactical problems in managing expense accounts

Jim Gomez picked up the large stack of mail and memos that had accumulated over the last 10 days while he had been out of town. He quickly glanced through it to see if there was anything urgent or negotiable. A memo from his boss, Mr. Bannon, grabbed his attention. Almost without thinking, he knew it would be his next assignment. The memo asked Jim to see Bannon as soon as he returned from High Point, North Carolina.

Jim Gomez was a senior consultant for Bannon & Associates, which had offices in New York, Chicago, and Los Angeles. The firm was a partnership of marketing consultants whose reputation over the past two decades had attracted many large firms as steady clients. Gomez worked out of the Chicago office.

Jim Gomez, age 35, started his career as a sales rep for Xerox after graduating from business school. Within five years, he was a regional sales manager. A company program had allowed him to study for his MBA while working. One of his classmates was doing some work for Bannon and needed help; he talked Gomez into moonlighting for Bannon. The firm was impressed with his work and soon made him an offer of a senior consultant position. Gomez liked the variety of tasks encountered in consulting, so he accepted the offer.

As it worked out, he developed a reputation in the field of sales compensation and expenses. His work had been well regarded; he was on the verge of becoming one of the associates, a partner. As he walked down the hall to find out when Bannon would be free to talk, Bannon, who preferred direct action, pulled him into Ann Woodward's office. "Jim, Ann has some expense account problems with the Lutz people. She is bogged down making a marketing audit for their board and can't really take the time to handle it. She uncovered some real bombs ready to explode while doing her audit. They won't wait until the audit is finished. Will you talk with Ann now? She will fill you in on the mess. I have to run for O'Hare. See you next week at the partners' party."

Gomez smiled at that last thought as he made the appropriate noises bidding the boss a safe trip. Jim knew that the Lutz account was important to the firm. Lutz had been a good client for 10 years. The firm paid its bills on time and did not challenge the time charges at every turn. He said to Woodward, "And how can I help keep the Lutz people happy with us?"

"By heading off a real revolt in their sales department over the rep's expense accounts," Ann replied. "Let me fill you in on the gory details."

Jim made himself comfortable on the office sofa as Ann began. "For years, the Lutz sales force has significantly enriched itself with tax-free money by generously padding their expense accounts with the tacit approval of the sales managers, who were doing the same thing. The whole sales department has played fast and loose with their expense accounts."

"So what's new?" Gomez snickered.

"The company controller is what's new. She is as straight as they come. Right by the book, no nonsense. She took one look at the expense sheets, and how they were signed by all the sales managers, and she wants their hides on her barn door. Fired, I think that was one of the words she used. I think I also heard such words as jail, tax fraud, and the IRS. Oh, yes, did I forget to tell you that she is an ex-IRS special agent?"

"Whee! Ain't consulting a barrel of fun!" Jim laughed. "Why in blue blazes did the old man hire her? He knew the company's dirty."

Gomez also knew several other facts from previous experience with the Lutz organization. First, it was a highly profitable organization that made and distributed worldwide a line of electro-optical devices that were well regarded in the industry.

Its success was a dual function of its technology and aggressive selling by 47 sales engineers. Gomez had often wondered about the firm's compensation policies because the reps were not really being paid that well. The plan was largely salary combined with performance bonuses at the end of each year. The bonuses were more related to how much profit the firm made that year than to the performance of the rep. Gomez knew that the reps' expense accounts were huge because they traveled extensively and did much entertaining. Moreover, certain liberties with the law were known to occur in some foreign lands when the situation required that money be given to influential people if business was to be done. Thus management, over the years, had not wanted to look into the reps' expense accounts too closely. No sales rep had ever been questioned about an expense account.

Gomez said, "She can wreck that sales organization if we're not careful. Those reps are highly marketable. All sorts of firms would love to have them, particularly the offshore operators. They know where the business is and how to get it. Ann, why did old man Lutz hire this woman? He had to know. He isn't senile."

Woodward answered, "I asked him just that question. He's scared to death of jail. All that publicity on the Helmsley tax evasion case, with her getting nailed and jailed, has him petrified. He wants to clean up his act before he gets into trouble. And he has a new tax accountant who has been scaring him to boot."

"OK! I guess we'll have to bail him out again. That's what they pay us all that money to do," Gomez responded. "Call your person at Lutz and find out who I should contact first. In the meantime, I'll figure out how I am going to approach this mess. Got to be real careful here. Some real damage could be done if we don't get all the parties satisfied. How much time have I got before the lady blows the whistle?"

"Not much! I'll call her and tell her that you are on the problem with the sales department and that it would be most helpful to the company if she could give us some time to get matters resolved without losing some valuable people," Woodward promised.

Gomez finished his coffee and returned to his office to do some thinking. This was not going to be easy. He wondered how he should approach the problem. Should he try to develop some legal way that the sales force could continue with their expense account practices or should he develop a program for making the company squeaky clean?

*Questions:*

1. What approach should Jim Gomez take in this matter? What should his attitude be?

2. Develop a step-by-step plan for Jim Gomez to propose to the Lutz sales manager and sales force.

3. How should Jim Gomez handle the new controller?

# CHAPTER 12

# Leadership and Supervision of a Sales Force

*I can inspire people to do things I believe in . . . especially when I see someone with ability who isn't trying his hardest!*

**Michael Jordan**

One hallmark of excellent leaders is their ability to motivate people to give their best efforts each day. It's not an easy task. Work can be boring and distractions abound. But an organization bereft of leadership will accomplish little.

## LEADERSHIP—WHAT IS IT?

*Leadership is a process in which one person influences other people's behavior toward the accomplishment of specific goals.* Strong leaders can motivate people to achieve more than they would on their own.

Is leadership essential for a sales manager to be effective? We think so! Someone must be in charge of each organizational unit and provide the leadership necessary for accomplishing the organization's goals. Leadership is the managerial ingredient that makes organizations more effective.

## LEADERSHIP CHARACTERISTICS AND SKILLS

Identifying potential leaders is not easy. An individual's leadership qualities can't always be judged by the performance of the person's administrative unit. As depicted in Figure 12-1, leadership effectiveness is based on a combination of personal characteristics, managerial skills and behaviors, and the situation. Personal characteristics and skills that affect leadership potential are discussed below.

### Personal Characteristics

#### Self-Confidence

Leaders must believe in themselves. To inspire confidence in others, they must set an example. They must have confidence in their abilities and beliefs in order to face the challenges and problems inherent in the sales manager's position.

■ **FIGURE 12-1**

**Leadership effectiveness**

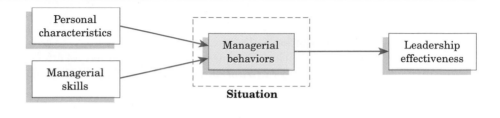

**Situation**

### Initiative
Leaders are independent self-starters who take initiative. They take charge. Leaders welcome change and create change. They are willing and eager to take the risks associated with change.

### Energy
Leaders usually have high energy levels. They are industrious, stepping forward when something needs to be done. Leaders must manage a wide variety of activities and relationships among people. This takes a lot of energy. Also, a very energetic person is perceived by others as highly motivated and enthusiastic. This behavior is contagious and spreads to those surrounding the leader.

### Creativity
Leaders need creativity and imagination. The organization looks to its leaders for solutions to problems—a challenge that often entails creativity and new approaches.

### Maturity
Effective leaders must be more interested in the well-being of their organization and the development of their people than in their own self-importance or domination of others.

## Managerial Skills and Behaviors

### Problem-Solving Skills
Most managers spend a significant amount of time resolving problems. Effective leaders identify specific problems and their causes; they formulate and implement solutions. Such leaders must anticipate, analyze, and make decisions.

### Interpersonal Skills
Interpersonal skills bear heavily on leadership capabilities. Leaders must discover what best motivates each salesperson. To do this, leaders establish good working relationships with their people. They know and treat each salesperson as an individual. This does not mean that leaders

necessarily become good friends with every sales rep. Often they cannot and should not. Instead, leaders develop good business relationships. Leaders must also establish good working relationships with superiors.

### Communication Skills

Communication skills are a critical component of effective leadership. Setting goals, organizing, forecasting, staffing, training, motivating, supervising, evaluating, and controlling the sales force all involve communication. The sales manager continuously transmits information from upper management to the sales force and from the sales force to upper management. This information must be accurate, clear, concise, and timely. An effective leader must have good oral and written communication skills.

### Persuasive Skills

Good leaders rely more on persuasion than on power. They persuade people to do what they want instead of threatening or coercing them. Their ability to persuade is based on the fact that their subordinates admire and respect them.

### Managerial Behaviors

Having certain characteristics and possessing certain skills gives the manager the potential to be an effective leader, but that doesn't necessarily mean that he or she will be one. The measure of good leadership is how the manager behaves. In other words, what the leader does is more important than who she or he is. Good leaders use a wide variety of managerial behaviors. They are listed in Figure 12-2.

■ **FIGURE 12-2**

**Leadership behaviors and styles**

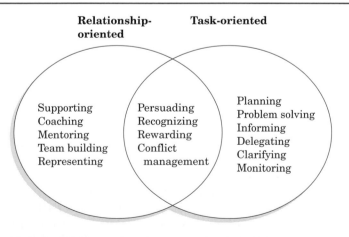

# ■ LEADERSHIP STYLE

The combination of behaviors that a manager typically uses is known as that manager's **leadership style.** Many of these behaviors can be classified into two categories: task-oriented behaviors and relationship-oriented behaviors.[1] As can be seen from Figure 12-2, some behaviors do not fall neatly into one category or the other, but rather reflect both a relationship and a task orientation. We discuss these behaviors next.

## Task-Oriented Style

For the task-oriented leader, the first and most important concern is getting the job done. To achieve this goal, managers use one-way communication to tell their subordinates how, when, where, and what to do. Some of the behaviors in Figure 12-2 are distinctly task-oriented behaviors. For example, planning, clarifying, monitoring, informing, and delegating are all behaviors related to getting the task completed.

Sales managers who have a task-oriented style tend to rely on the authority of their positions and on their ability to reward and punish subordinates to motivate sales reps. Their ability to influence others is primarily based on positional power. Sometimes, this type of leader is referred to as an *autocratic leader*.

## Relationship-Oriented Style

Relationship-oriented leaders are primarily concerned about the welfare of their people. These leaders use two-way communication. They seek input from their subordinates, provide feedback, and allow them to participate in decision making. Relationship-oriented behaviors, shown in Figure 12-2, include supporting, coaching, mentoring, team building, and representing. Sales managers who have relationship-oriented styles rely on their own expertise and personal relationships with their salespeople to persuade them to perform at high levels. Their ability to influence others is based on personal power. These managers are warm, friendly, and approachable; they provide their salespeople with emotional support, psychological stroking, and personal assistance to get things done. Sometimes these managers are called *participative* or *democratic leaders*.

## Situational Leadership

Excellent sales managers use a variety of behaviors to motivate their salespeople. No single leadership style is best in all situations. Rather, they tailor their behaviors to the needs of the individual and the situation.[2] Figure 12-3 is a situational leadership matrix which has been used by several Fortune 500 companies, such as Caterpillar, Shell Oil, and IBM, to train managers.

■ **FIGURE 12-3**

**Basic
leadership
styles**

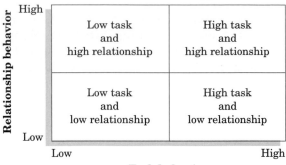

In this model, high and low levels of task and relationship behavior are combined, resulting in four basic leadership styles. Each of these is more appropriate in certain situations than others. The situations are defined, to some extent, by the reps' motivation and ability to do the tasks at hand. An example for each quadrant is given below.

■ **High task and low relationship.** This style is most appropriate for newly hired, inexperienced salespeople. These new reps probably have lots of motivation, but little ability. The sales manager informs the new rep on how to develop a sales presentation.

■ **High task and high relationship.** When salespeople face a new and/or difficult task, they may lack the necessary skills or the desire to take it on. Therefore, it is appropriate for the managers to use both task and relationship behaviors to guide and motivate them.

■ **Low task and high relationship.** This style is most effective when the manager wants to motivate salespeople to perform at higher levels or to do certain aspects of their jobs better. The manager may mentor, coach, or provide other support.

■ **Low task and low relationship.** For high-performing salespeople who prize their autonomy and freedom, the sales manager should just let them do their job, providing little or no direction.

Effective leaders have high concern both for the task and for people. But the key to successful leadership is in knowing when to use task and relationship behaviors. When situational leadership is applied correctly, it enhances leadership effectiveness.

## Charismatic Leadership

Some leaders have a remarkable ability to get others to believe in their vision for the future. Their words and actions transform the basic values, be-

---

### Leading the Team

The selling team is often led by a salesperson or sales manager. However, for this leader, the most important role is *not* influencing the customer's buying decision. Rather it is guiding a loose group of people from the whole company who work together to meet the customer's needs. Because of the complexity of the team-selling effort, team leaders must know some-thing about all facets of their company's business and be able to interact with a large variety of people from many areas within the company. Along with technical skills in selling, these leaders must also have experience, continuity, and commitment.

Source: Henry Canaday, "Rules of Success," *Selling Power,* June 1996, pp. 77–83.

---

liefs, and attitudes of their employees in such a way that they are willing to perform beyond the standard levels expected by the organization. These leaders are usually referred to as **charismatic**.[3] Their behaviors, described below, are called **transformational leader behaviors**.[4]

- **Articulate a vision.** Charismatic leaders create a common, compelling vision for guiding the future of their companies. They communicate to subordinates their exciting, challenging future and the company's organizational goal. They get people to work toward a common end, even sometimes at the expense of their personal goals.

- **Challenge the status quo.** These leaders encourage people to think in new directions, to be creative. They set very high—seemingly impossible—goals and express strong confidence in their employees' abilities to achieve those goals.

- **Provide a role model.** Charismatic leaders work as hard or harder than anyone else. They also demonstrate the highest level of integrity. They set an example that is consistent with the values they espouse and with the goals of the organization.

## ■ SUPERVISION—WHAT IS IT?

While leadership refers to the manager's overall approach to motivation, **supervision** is day-to-day operation and control of the sales force. More strictly, it refers only to *direct* working relationships between salespeople and superiors. The sales manager who checks with the salespeople each morning to see what their plans are for the day is *directly* supervising their activities. Many other managerial actions constitute indirect supervision, such as auditing expense accounts or appraising sales performance.

Many large companies employing hundreds, if not thousands, of sales reps often hire field supervisors whose sole assignment is to supervise the reps' field-selling activities. More often, however, this supervisory function is performed by district or regional sales managers as one of their many responsibilities.

# SUPERVISION AND STRATEGIC PLANNING

The amount and nature of the supervision given the sales force is part of the company's strategic marketing plan. Many firms, particularly smaller ones, decide to hire experienced proven performers and then turn them loose with little supervision. Other firms hire inexperienced reps and then supervise them closely.

An important factor in this strategic decision is the importance of any one sale to the firm's welfare. If each sale is vitally important to the firm (as it is for Boeing Aircraft), each rep will be closely supervised. If a sale or even a territory is not that important to total corporate well-being, then management is not likely to spend much money supervising. The supervision decision is a portion of the overall strategic decision as to how important the sales force is in accomplishing the firm's goals.

# REASONS FOR SUPERVISION

## Training and Assistance

The supervisor must make sure that the reps (1) understand what they are expected to do, (2) know how to do it, and (3) have the competence to do it. In many ways, the field supervisor is an on-the-job sales training executive. The most effective sales training takes place over a period of time and is best done in the field while sales reps are actually facing day-to-day problems. Good supervision can do much to develop an inexperienced recruit into a productive sales rep. Additionally, sales reps may need technical help or assistance in certain selling situations.

## Enforcement

Supervision is often used as an enforcement tool to ensure that company policies are being followed. In this role, the supervisor works in much the same capacity as a foreman in the plant—he or she makes sure that reps are doing their jobs properly. Jobs that call for little selling ability and consist mainly of repetitive nonselling duties require close supervision to ensure that the tasks are actually carried out.

## Better Performance and Improved Morale

Some sales managers believe that direct supervision stimulates salespeople to do better work. However, there is a limit to how much an employee can be prodded without becoming resentful. Just knowing that management is aware of one's efforts can be beneficial. Conversely, performance seems to suffer when sales reps know that management has no means of knowing what they are really doing.

**This sales manager is assisting his new representative with an important client.**

It is important to most sales reps to know that someone in the organization cares about and recognizes the work they do. If the supervisor is adept, just the fact that he or she is in personal contact should have a good effect on morale.

## AMOUNT OF SUPERVISION NEEDED

There are dangers in either over- or undersupervising the sales force. Supervision costs are significant, and management does not want to spend more than necessary. Oversupervising hampers the performance of sales representatives. While some supervision can improve morale, too much has the opposite effect. Able, independent sales reps resent managers who hold them on too tight a rein. Many people go into selling to escape such direct control.

The dangers of undersupervision are much the same as those of oversupervision. Morale can suffer, and costs can rise. A sales rep who is not getting the attention or supervision needed to do the job properly is likely to develop a poor attitude. More important, performance is related to supervisory behavior; and without proper supervision to improve performance, such a rep may eventually be fired or quit.

## Factors Determining How Much Supervision Is Needed

The foremost factor in determining how much supervision is required in a given situation is the quality of the sales force. If a firm hires only top-notch recruits or salespeople with proven talents, little supervision may be needed. On the other end of the scale are the newly hired individuals with below-average ability and no selling experience. It would be difficult to give such reps too much supervision. They need the sales training and assistance that a supervisor can provide.

Between these two extremes of sales force quality is an almost unlimited number of variations. In determining the proper amount of supervision to provide, the sales manager must consider several factors, including the importance of one sale in achieving the organization's overall objectives, the geographical distribution of the sales force, the size of the sales force, the compensation plan, and other control mechanisms.

If the importance of any one rep's performance is vital to the firm's overall sales picture, management should make certain that this rep does the job well. For example, one highly technical concern sold large projects to a few big companies through five sales engineers. A sales manager closely supervised their activities daily by e-mail and worked closely with each rep on every project. Each sale was too important to do otherwise.

The geographical distribution of the sales force should be considered in determining the degree of supervision. If the reps are widely dispersed across the country, it may necessitate having a greater number of supervisors than if the reps are concentrated in a metropolitan area.

The size of the sales force also affects the amount and type of supervision management provides. If the sales force is relatively small, many sales managers find that they can handle the job themselves, without supervisors. The larger the sales force, the more necessary it becomes to hire personnel who do nothing but direct salespeople through formal supervisory activities. It should be noted that as more companies are using computerized information networks to communicate with their salespeople, fewer supervisors are needed to direct the activities of the sales force.

The compensation plan and other control mechanisms used can affect the amount of personal supervision needed. In general, management usually finds close supervision more necessary when the reps are being paid largely by salary. A strong, properly designed incentive system can provide many of the benefits of supervision, as can a detailed method for evaluating sales performance.

# ■ TOOLS AND TECHNIQUES OF SUPERVISION

The topic of supervision usually conveys the idea of a field supervisor who is in personal contact with the reps. While this is an important method of supervision, it is only one of several that are used. The tools and techniques used in supervising the sales force include personal contact, sales reports, telecommunications, sales meetings, printed aids, and indirect supervisory aids provided by sales management practices.

## Personal Contact

Typically, the supervisor visits sales reps on the job and tries to help them with whatever problems are evident. The supervisor's objectives and activities when traveling with a rep vary. They include assisting in selling difficult customers or settling grievances, training, and evaluating. It is important to remember that when the sales manager or supervisor accompanies the sales rep on a sales call, the sales rep should still take the lead in directing the conversation and in moving from one agenda item to another.

When supervisors ride with their reps in order to train and evaluate them, there are a variety of things they can and should observe. Supervisors should keep the following questions in mind:

- Is the salesperson prepared for the call?
- Does the salesperson understand the customer's business and specific needs?
- Does the salesperson treat customers respectfully and honestly?
- Does the salesperson know the competition?
- Is the salesperson skillful at gaining commitment?

The supervisors should make notes on their observations of the reps, indicating their strengths and weaknesses. These should be discussed with the rep as soon as possible after the call.[5]

## Sales Reports

Sales reports provide records for monitoring and evaluating sales reps' activity. These reports usually include the number of calls made, number of orders taken, miles traveled, days worked, new prospects called on, and new accounts sold. As a supervisory tool, the sales report is a silent enforcer of company policy. Reps who know they must account for all their activities will feel more secure and comfortable if they stay within company policy.

Frequently reps are required to submit a **call plan,** which reports their itinerary for the upcoming period. This forces reps to organize their

## ? AN ETHICAL DILEMMA

Karee McBride is a sales manager for Precision Tools Inc. in the northeast district. She has been with the company for seven years and has been progressing rapidly up the sales ladder. Originally her sales territories and her first supervisory assignments were in the east district and the north midwest district, respectively. Six months ago, she was promoted to the northeast district as a sales manager. She replaced a manager who had been there for 10 years. The district's performance in the last three of those 10 years had been steadily declining, so the decision was made to replace the district manager.

Shortly after her promotion, Karee spent a great deal of time analyzing the sales results for the district and realized that there were some performance problems which would have to be resolved if the district's overall performance was to improve. One of these problems involved Bob Chay, who had been with the company for 24 years. Although Bob's sales were down slightly this year from the previous year, his sales for the past four years had been flat. At one time Bob had been one of the top producers, gaining new customers each year and cultivating more business at his existing accounts. Now, however, it appeared that Bob was riding on his relationships with his oldest and best accounts. But even the sales to those accounts seemed to be slipping. Karee guessed that these customers would continue to give Bob some of their business out of a sense of obligation based on their long friendship with him. But some of the new business at these accounts was obviously going to other vendors.

Karee had discussed the lack of sales growth with Bob, but he just said that he was not a hot-shot kid anymore and that he was pretty content with his compensation and didn't see the need to work that hard anymore. He also pointed out that his sales were not the lowest in the district. Karee was convinced that there was not a whole lot she was going to be able to do to motivate Bob to do more than he was doing now. She also felt strongly that a new rep could get a lot more growth out of that territory than Bob would or even could.

Bob was eligible for early retirement, but Karee knew that he was not interested in retiring at this time. He was 58. Karee knew that her decision with regard to Bob was complicated by the fact that he was an old friend of her family's. In fact he was the one who had first given her name to the national sales manager and recommended her for the sales job.

What would you do if you were in Karee's situation?

---

activities. These reports show, for example, whether the reps are routing themselves properly, calling on the various classes of customers in the right ratio, and/or developing appropriate objectives for their calls.

These reports are not only used as a supervisory tool, but they are also used to provide much of the data for the marketing information system. As a result, these reports also contain in-depth information on customer problems and needs as well as on competitive activity. Sales managers must ensure that salespeople place a priority on this activity—that they provide timely and accurate information. This reporting activity should be evaluated and rewarded as one of the salesperson's primary responsibilities.

## Telecommunications

Most sales executives supplement their personal contact with sales reps with telecommunications—the telephone, fax messages, voice mail, electronic mail, and computer-based support systems. Many companies use computerized support systems to assist the sales force in performing its many responsibilities. These companies, such as IBM, Hewlett-Packard, and Procter & Gamble, give each of their salespeople a portable, laptop computer which is used to assist the rep in the following areas:

- **Better customer and industry information.** Salespeople and their managers have immediate access to complete customer histories and industry information.
- **Selling assistance.** The systems provide electronic libraries of product information and enhanced capabilities for analyzing customer problems. Price quotes, bids, proposals for service, and installation agreements can be generated automatically.
- **Sales support.** Orders can be entered and tracked very accurately by the salesperson. Correspondence with customers can also be handled more efficiently by the reps using their portable computers.
- **Reporting responsibilities.** Salespeople can submit their call plans and reports, expense reports, and other market intelligence using their laptops.
- **Communication.** The electronic mail capability of these systems enables companies to be in constant communication with their reps regardless of where they are.

At Hewlett-Packard, for example, each of the 900 sales reps has a laptop computer.[6] These computers are programmed to quote prices, write contracts, track orders, and provide product and marketing information.

These systems provide a way to minimize the time spent on report writing. Yet at the same time, they improve the accuracy of the marketing information which is collected. Companies that have computerized support systems report significant improvements in sales force productivity and management effectiveness. IBM reports that its revenue per rep has increased by 30 percent since its sales force began relying on computerized support systems.

## Printed Aids

Sales manuals, bulletins, or company house organs help in supervising the sales force. A good sales manual tells sales reps what to do in various circumstances. Some questions can be answered just as effectively in a publication as they can by personal contact.

## The Virtual Office

In many companies, the only offices salespeople have are their **virtual offices.** In virtual office mode, the sales reps carry their "offices" in their portable computers. All of the information they need to do their jobs is in or can be accessed through their computers. At some companies, such as Intel Corp., the reps are responsible for keeping their account goals and progress toward those goals updated in their computers. At any time, the sales supervisor can call up each rep's records to check that

rep's progress. By utilizing a virtual office, sales reps spend nearly all their time in the field; their visits to a branch or regional office are rare.

As a result, managers and supervisors are also more mobile. In order to train and motivate their salespeople, sales managers spend a lot less time in the office and more time with their reps doing in-the-field coaching.

Source: Thayer C. Taylor, "Going Mobile," *Sales & Marketing Management,* May 1994, pp. 94–101.

## Meetings

Sales meetings, which were discussed in Chapter 9, are another means used to provide supervision. During sales meetings, new procedures, policies, and programs are often explained to the sales reps.

## Indirect Supervisory Aids

Several other managerial tools can be called **indirect supervisory techniques.** They have inherent supervisory powers and work automatically toward company goals—and they can be exceptionally effective. Unlike the field supervisor or other supervisory methods, these indirect techniques travel with the reps everywhere, every minute of the day, and on every call they make. They include:

- **Compensation plans.** By far the most important automatic supervisory tool, the compensation plan encourages reps to do those things that will maximize their earnings.
- **Territories.** Establishment of specific sales territories tells reps what areas they are responsible for.
- **Quotas.** By setting quotas for various product lines or for certain classes of customers, the sales manager can guide sales force activities into desired channels.
- **Expense accounts.** Policies on expenses automatically guide sales force behavior by limiting the amount spent on certain activities.
- **Sales analysis procedures.** Using sales analysis procedures (discussed in Part IV), management can evaluate the performance of each salesperson and then guide or assist the reps who need help on certain points.

# ■ PROBLEMS ENCOUNTERED IN LEADERSHIP AND SUPERVISION

Certain leadership and supervisory problems are commonly encountered. They include poor performance, substance abuse, expense account abuse, other unethical behavior, and sexual harassment.

## Poor Performance

When salespeople are not performing up to standards, the challenge is not to fire them, but rather to help them become productive employees. Often these reps have received extensive training and correcting the problem is less expensive than replacing them. Because of possible discrimination suits, it is also prudent for managers to make sure that they have done everything within reason to help failing employees before firing them.

Although many managers find it difficult to criticize their subordinates, it is often possible to correct a problem just by giving immediate feedback about the problem behavior. This constructive feedback should take place as soon as the manager notices the performance problem. Managers should be very specific about what the problem is. The following steps should be followed in providing effective feedback:[7]

1. State the problem.
2. Get the salesperson's agreement on the problem.
3. Listen to the salesperson's assessment of the problem.
4. Consider extenuating circumstances.
5. Design an action plan for improvement.
6. Get the salesperson's agreement on the action plan.

If the rep's performance does not improve as a result of immediate feedback, the problem should be reviewed in a formal performance appraisal and a plan for improvement should be agreed upon by the manager and the rep. The manager must make it very clear that poor performance is not acceptable. Each step should be documented with written memos detailing what took place. If the problem continues, a counseling session is recommended to review all the previous attempts to encourage improvement. The rep should be given a specified time period to show improvement. Then, if necessary, and with all of the appropriate documentation, the manager must terminate or demote the salesperson.

## Substance Abuse

One of the most difficult personal problems sales managers encounter is the salesperson with an alcohol or drug problem. Unfortunately, some sales jobs lead to excessive drinking because they constantly put the reps

*A Day-to-Day Operating Problem*

## MAJESTIC PLASTICS COMPANY (I)

### A sales rep objects to harassment

Lisa Brannigan, Majestic's sales rep for the Kansas City area, had called her boss, Clyde Brion, requesting an urgent meeting. Lisa was having problems at American Pharmaceuticals (AP), one of Majestic's largest customers. Although she had been named Majestic's top salesperson last year, Lisa's current troubles did not come as a total surprise to Clyde. As he prepared for the meeting, Clyde reviewed the account history at AP.

As a longtime producer of generic drugs, AP represented the type of customer Majestic craved. It was only four years ago, however, that Majestic sales rep Nancy Sloan had been able to convince Charles "Chuck" Spencer, AP's president, of the value of doing business with Majestic. Within one month of replacing Earl Warner as sales rep on the account, Nancy delivered the largest order in Majestic's history. For the next year and a half, Majestic's business with AP grew tremendously.

After breaking all company sales records, however, Nancy Sloan abruptly resigned from Majestic. Citing "personal and family matters," she left to take a job in banking. Although Clyde Brion sensed something more was involved, he quickly replaced Nancy with one of Majestic's brightest stars, Matt Carson.

Matt had graduated with honors from the University of Missouri before joining a national paper supply company. Bright, articulate, and personable, he quickly became his firm's leading sales rep. Deciding to switch industries, he had joined Majestic with flawless credentials. He seemed the ideal choice to replace Nancy Sloan.

Six months later, however, Matt Carson felt something was terribly wrong at the AP account. Although he had increased sales throughout the territory, AP had stopped placing any significant orders with Majestic. Chuck Spencer seemed apathetic toward the new rep and Majestic. For the next three months, Carson solicited the advice of Clyde Brion on how to deal with Spencer and the erosion of one of Majestic's biggest accounts. When all attempts failed, Carson finally approached an AP purchasing manager who told him, "Chuck likes lady reps. I guess he feels more comfortable buying from a woman."

It was then that Brion, under pressure from top management to save the AP account, decided to have Lisa Brannigan switch territories with Matt Carson. Matt adapted well to his new territory in St. Louis while Lisa began to make significant progress in Kansas City, particularly at AP, where she brought in five large orders within three months. But that was over a year ago and now Clyde Brion had to deal with a troubled Lisa Brannigan.

"Spencer keeps making passes at me and yesterday asked me to join him for the weekend at his lake house. He's a 48-year-old rich and powerful bachelor who expects all the women he meets to fall madly in love with him. I've been totally professional with him since the day I joined the account, but I can't take any more of his antics. Either tell him to cool it with the harassment or I'm not calling on AP," Lisa said.

Question: Given that Chuck Spencer has no superior at AP and makes all the large buying decisions, what should Clyde Brion do in response to Lisa's request?

Note: This case was prepared by Steven Reed under the direction of Rosann Spiro.

in social situations where drinking is expected. Such jobs are terrible risks for people who cannot handle alcohol or the temptations of illegal drugs.

Surveys indicate that the problems of drug and alcohol abuse are pervasive and costly. It is estimated that approximately 7 percent of the nation's work force suffers from some form of addiction. Among salespeople, we expect this number to be even higher because salespeople usually work unsupervised in the field. The performance of sales representatives who are alcoholics or drug abusers always suffers. Their work habits are poor and the quality of their work is often unacceptable.

### Detection

The signs of alcohol abuse (the odor, for example) are more obvious than drug abuse, but both may be difficult to detect. Often sales supervisors do not have day-to-day contact with their salespeople, and the problem may go undetected for some time. There are warning signs. Many abusers have alcohol on their breath, slurred speech, they miss appointments, they frequently miss work, and their performance declines. Their behavior at company functions and conventions may also show signs of excessive use of alcohol or drugs.[8]

Some firms (Intel and Exxon, for example) make job offers to applicants contingent on their passing a drug test. Regardless of whether or not a firm uses substance abuse testing, sales supervisors should become familiar with the signs and symptoms of abuse so that they can detect the problems as early as possible.[9]

### Dealing with Abuse

The use of illegal drugs on the job is, of course, never allowed; the consumption of alcohol, which is a legal substance, may be allowed in certain situations, such as entertaining customers. However, the abusive use of either alcohol or drugs invariably leads to performance deficiencies. It is the performance deficiency, not the abuse itself, that the supervisor should address first.

The sales rep should be told that he or she must rectify the performance deficiency or be subject to termination. Then the supervisors can explore the reasons for the deficiency with the rep. When it is possible to get an admission of an abuse problem, the sales manager can recommend that the salesperson seek assistance from a professional substance abuse program. Sales managers should not attempt to provide counseling—they are not trained to deal with these problems. If salespeople refuse treatment or do not make satisfactory progress in the treatment and if their performance does not improve, termination may be appropriate.

Some companies have formal policies for dealing with alcohol and drug abuse, but many do not. If there is no company policy, sales managers should develop their own formal, written policies. These policies should be clearly communicated to the sales force.

## Expense Accounts

Expense accounts can lead to costly problems for management. The folk-lore of selling is full of tales of sales expense accounts and their fictional contents. Expense account policies should be clearly set forth when sales-people are hired. Companies that expect the sales force to be honest make it clear that cheating on an expense account is grounds for dismissal. Then they consistently back up that policy with action.

When the sales manager discovers discrepancies in a rep's expense ac-counts, the manager should review the situation with the rep to be certain it is not simply an error or a misunderstanding of allowable expenses. Some managers simply disallow expenses they feel are not in order. Oth-ers go over the expense report with the rep, putting the rep on notice that the expense reports are being watched. But such matters are sensitive, and the sales manager must deal with each case as the situation warrants.

## Unethical Behavior

Padding expense accounts is one type of unethical behavior. But there are others—for example, recommending unnecessarily high product quality levels or inventory levels, selling out-of-production items without inform-ing the customer, or providing misleading information on competitors. Sales managers who overlook such unethical practices are asking for trou-ble. While the immediate consequences of allowing such behavior may not seem too great, this practice will likely result in more serious long-term consequences such as lawsuits and negative publicity.

Managers must take immediate action to put an end to unethical be-havior. The same steps suggested earlier for problematic performance should be followed in correcting unethical behavior.

## Sexual Harassment[10]

In 1980, the Equal Employment Opportunities Commission (EEOC) is-sued guidelines which interpret sexual harassment as a form of discrimi-nation. Since that time, the number of sexual harassment cases filed has been steadily increasing. Sexual harassment cases ranked fourth among the unlawful employment practices filed with the EEOC. Further, the an-nual cost of the problem to the average Fortune 500 company is estimated at $6.7 million due to turnover, absenteeism, and reduced productivity (le-gal expenses are not included in this number).

It is important that sales managers take proactive steps to prevent sexual harassment, recognize it when it does take place, and put a stop to the harassment when it occurs.

The EEOC defines sexual harassment as follows:

> Unwelcome sexual advances, requests for sexual favors, and other verbal or physical conduct of a sexual nature constitute sex-ual harassment when any of the following criteria are met:

1. submission to such conduct is made either explicitly or implicitly a term or condition of an individual's employment;

2. submission to or rejection of such conduct by an individual is used as a basis for employment decisions affecting that individual;

3. such conduct has the purpose or effect of unreasonably interfering with an individual's work performance or creating an intimidating, hostile, or offensive working environment.

Companies are not only responsible for creating an environment which does not condone sexual harassment by its employees; they are also responsible for *third-party harassment,* that is, harassment by clients and customers. If managers or supervisors are aware of the harassment by customers or even if they should have been aware of it, they have a responsibility to take actions to protect the employee from further harassment. These actions may include reassigning employees, requesting that customers stop the inappropriate behaviors, and/or advising them that the company can no longer serve them without a commitment to refrain from such behaviors.

In order to create an environment which discourages sexual harassment, companies should develop comprehensive policies against sexual harassment. These policies should include statements about the behaviors which are prohibited; the penalties for misconduct; the procedures for making, investigating, and resolving complaints; and procedures for education and training. Sales managers should be knowledgeable of these policies and ensure that they are followed.

## ■ SUMMARY

Leadership—a process in which one person influences other people's behavior toward the accomplishment of specific goals—is essential for a sales manager to be effective. Leadership is based upon personal characteristics, managerial skills and behaviors, and the situation. The personal characteristics include high levels of self-confidence, initiative, energy, creativity, and maturity. Appropriate problem-solving, social, communication, and persuasive skills are also necessary for an effective leader.

Managerial behavior can be divided into two categories: task-oriented behavior and relationship-oriented behavior. The situation will determine the appropriate levels of each managerial behavior. Charismatic leaders are able to get others to perform beyond the standard levels expected by the organization. They use transformational behaviors such as articulating a vision, challenging the status quo, and acting as a role model. In team selling, the role of the team leader is to direct a loose group of people from the whole company who work together to serve the customer.

Supervision entails a multitude of activities that the sales manager undertakes daily to ensure that the sales force operates effectively. While the ultimate goal of supervision is to increase sales while reducing costs, several secondary purposes are served in reaching that ultimate goal. Much supervision revolves around training and developing the individual's potential. The other side of supervision entails enforcing company policies and monitoring sales force activities to make certain they comply with management's wishes.

Most sales management operations rely heavily on indirect supervisory techniques such as the compensation plan, sales territories, quotas, expense account policies, and the reporting systems established by the company.

The amount of personal supervision imposed on a sales force is largely a function of the caliber of the sales reps. Typically, highly talented salespeople require very little supervision, whereas people in low-level sales jobs require far more.

Some frequent problems encountered by leaders include poor performance, substance abuse, expense misappropriation, other unethical behavior, and sexual harassment. Each problem needs to be dealt with when detected to avoid potentially serious consequences.

## Key Terms

Call plan
Charismatic leader
Indirect supervisory
   techniques
Leadership

Leadership style
Relationship-oriented style
Sexual harassment
Situational leadership
Substance abuse

Supervision
Task-oriented style
Transformational leader
   behavior
Virtual office

 ## QUESTIONS AND PROBLEMS

1. What are the personal characteristics necessary for an effective leader? Will possessing these characteristics alone ensure success as a manager? If not, what other elements need to be considered?

2. What type of leadership style would you use in the following situations? Why?

   *a.* Terry is one of your best sales representatives. She has eight years of experience and has proven her abilities many times.

   *b.* Diane graduated with a marketing degree within the past year, but she has limited sales experience.

   *c.* John is a veteran employee. In recent months, however, you notice his performance stagnating.

3. How could a field supervisor determine why a certain rep was performing unsatisfactorily?

4. Bill Jolton, a salesman for a large national soap company, informs his immediate supervisor that he is quitting at the end of the month. The supervisor is surprised to learn this, since she thought that Jolton was doing a good job and was happy with his work. The supervisor would like to keep Jolton with the firm, for she thinks Jolton shows exceptional promise. How should the supervisor handle the situation?

5. As sales management moves into the telecommunications age, you, a recently hired marketing department trainee, have been assigned the task of preparing a report on how management can use the existing state-of-the-

art communications equipment to improve supervision of the sales force. What suggestions would you make?

6. A sales manager of a large metropolitan automobile dealership required his sales force of eight people to meet each morning at 9:00 A.M. for about 30 minutes to plan their activities for the day. During this meeting, he asked each rep to tell what he or she intended to accomplish that day. Were these meetings sound? What was the manager's goal in setting up such meetings?

7. What is the difference between a situational leader and a charismatic leader?

8. Should sales team leaders always have sales experience or can they come

from other functional areas of the firm?

9. You notice that Mike, one of your sales representatives, has been consistently unproductive for the past two months. You have heard rumors indicating that Mike may be abusing alcohol or drugs; however, no proof is available. What actions should you take? Why?

10. One of your sales reps, Nancy, claims that one of your other reps, Bill, has been sexually harassing her and she has asked you to do something about it. You have talked to Bill and he denies it. What should you do now?

## ◼ EXPERIENTIAL EXERCISES

**A.** Pick a classmate and describe what personal characteristics, skills and/or behaviors this person exhibits that would make him or her an effective leader. Also describe any characteristics and/or behaviors that would make this classmate less effective.

**B.** Interview two business managers who you know to determine whether they are more of a task- or a relationship-oriented leader. (Hint: It might be useful to ask them how frequently they use certain behaviors to direct the efforts of their salespeople.) Describe the differences between the two managers.

## ◼ REFERENCES

1. Paul Hersey and Kenneth R. Blanchard, *Management of Organizational Behavior: Utilizing Human Resources,* 5th ed. (Englewood Cliffs, NJ: Prentice Hall, 1988).

2. "Put Your Skills to the Test," *Sales & Marketing Management,* September 1994, pp. 132–33.

3. Patricia Sellers, "What Exactly Is Charisma?" *Fortune,* January 15, 1996, pp. 68–77.

4. "It should be noted that transformational behaviors are in contrast to task and relationship oriented behaviors both of which are categorized as transactional behaviors. Transactional behaviors are those by which the leader provides rewards in exchange for the subordinate's effort." Scott MacKenzie, Greg Rich, and Philip Podsakoff, "Transformational and Transactional Leadership and Sales Performance," working paper, Kelley School of Business, Indiana University, Bloomington, Indiana, 1998.

5. Rex C. Houze, "Effective Sales Management," *American Salesman,* May 1995, pp. 3–5.

6. Edmund O. Lawler, "Sales Force Rearms with Portables," *Business Marketing,* July 1993, p. 46.

7. Tom Quick, *Making Your Sales Team No. 1* (New York: AMACOM, 1992).

8. Wayne Friedman, "That Demon Alcohol," *Sales & Marketing Management,* December 1996, pp. 42–47.

9. The National Clearinghouse for Drug Abuse Information (NCDAI) provides written materials on issues surrounding substance abuse problems. They may be obtained at no cost by writing to: NCDAI, P.O. Box 416, Kensington, MD 20795.

10. This discussion is based to a large extent on an article by Cathy Owens Swift and Russell L. Kent, "Sexual Harassment: Ramifications for Sales Managers," *Journal of Personal Selling & Sales Management,* Winter 1994, pp. 77–88.

---

*Case 12-1*

## JUPITER SPECIALTIES

Developing a sales information system

Mike Bachman, the vice president of sales for Jupiter Specialties, recalled his earlier conversation with Pete Poorman, the CEO of Jupiter Specialties. Mike had told his boss that the sales information system was a mess and that he felt it would be best if they designed a new system from scratch. Mr. Poorman reminded him that the company has spent a lot of money designing this system just a few years ago; he went on to inform Mike that it was providing all the information he thought they could possibly use, and it was doing so in a timely manner. "We know everything about how our products are performing and we have a great deal of specific information about each customer."

He ended with, "What more could you possibly want?" "That is just the problem," Mike had told his boss. "We have an overload of information, and because of that the reps either aren't using it at all or they are spending too much time trying to use it." His boss again told him that he was not in favor of scrapping the present system, but he asked Mike to prepare a report detailing the problems and said he would consider it.

Jupiter Specialties is a national distributor of gifts and novelties. Jupiter's customer base is composed of 30,000 retail stores, primarily in the gift and bookstore trades, located throughout the United States. The company is a primary vendor for department stores including Neiman Marcus, Saks Fifth Avenue, Dayton-Hudson, Marshall Fields, and Lord & Taylor. Jupiter, whose sales growth has been averaging 8 percent to 10 percent a year, currently has sales of $30 million and is expecting its growth to continue over the next decade.

Pete Poorman, one of the company's founders, is the chairperson and CEO. Reporting to him are the vice presidents for sales, administration, accounting, manufacturing, and marketing. These managers are responsible for understanding specific corporate strategies, raising questions concerning potential problems, and helping to establish schedules for projects. They are also accountable for planning the implementation of decisions involving the employees under their direction and maintaining communication between departments. Mike Bachman is the newest of the vice presidents, having been with the company nine months.

Reporting to the VP of sales are four regional managers who oversee the district managers and key account activity in four U.S. sales regions: East, Midwest, South, and West. There are 15 district managers who are responsible for training new sales representatives and maintaining ongoing support of the field sales personnel. The district managers, who are responsible for maintaining the quota requirements of the field staff, report to the regional managers, but Mike Bachman frequently communicates directly with the DMs.

Jupiter currently has 75 field sales representatives, called sales consultants. The consultants are responsible for selling Jupiter's product line to various independent and chain retailers. They are paid on a salary plus commission plus group bonus basis. On the average, the individual consultant is responsible for a territory quota of $400,000.

---

■ **EXHIBIT 12-1**    **Sales information system: monthly reports**

**Sales by Territory**

Sales Summary—monthly sales by the rep
YTD Sales Summary—YTD sales vs. previous year by the rep
Sales by Product Category—monthly sales by product category by the rep
Sales by Region—monthly sales by region
Quota Summary—percentage of quota achieved by the rep
Quota by County—percentage quota achieved by county by the rep
YTD Rep Ranking—sales rank based on YTD sales for all reps
Rep Commission Statement—monthly commissions earned
Regional Bonus Statement—group bonus earned by region
Incentive Summary—summary of incentive monies earned by the rep
Gross Sales Comparison—gross sales by reps
Net Territory Comparison—net sales by reps

**Individual Accounts**

Merchant Inventory Plans—plans for periodic changeover of customer's inventory
Qualified/Nonqualified Quarterly Report—information regarding timing for inventory changeovers at qualified and nonqualified accounts
Retail Product Analysis—account performance information which details product contribution to customer gross profit
Product Category Summary—performance information on specific product categories by account
Account Action Report—suggested merchandising actions based on inventory turnover data by account
Account Activity Report—monthly sales activity by account
Region Account Ranking—account ranking by sales for the region
Region Account Ranking by Rep—account ranking by rep for the region

**Credit Status**

Accounts to Collection—accounts which have been turned over to collection for late payment
Accounts in Previous Collection—accounts previously turned over to collection
Cost of Sales

Administrative personnel at corporate headquarters in Asheville, North Carolina, are responsible for field sales force support. The staff collects information from its operations in the field and uses it to generate a series of reports which track the performance of individual sales representatives, customer accounts, and products. These reports have been designed to be used directly by the sales force to improve their ability to service customers and organize their selling effort.

The reports can be classified into three distinct categories. (See Exhibit 12-1 for a listing of the reports.) The first category contains information related to the sales in each territory. The reps can use this information to track sales quotas by county on a monthly, year-to-date, and product basis. They can also compare this year's performance with the previous year. The reps also receive quarterly reports on their sales ranking compared to other reps and on their region's ranking compared to other regions as well as reports on their commissions and regional bonuses to date.

The second category of information tracks the performance of individual accounts. These reports are intended to help the salespeople improve the service rendered to specific accounts and to pinpoint where selling effort is needed or might be most productive. For example, one report contains overall sales, turnover, and margin information for a specific account; another report provides the same information by product and product categories; and others detail specific suggestions for periodic changeover of the customer's inventory.

The third category of reports contains information on the credit status of individual accounts. These reports are used for determining how reliable customers have been in their dealings with Jupiter and whether the customer qualifies for larger inventories of product.

Mike recognized that some of the reports were in fact useful to the reps. The "Retail Product Analysis" report enabled the rep to show the customer precisely how much Jupiter's products contribute to their gross profit, and the "Sales by Category" report can help the rep develop effective selling strategies. However, many of the salespeople complained that there were too many reports and that there was too much information in most of them. One rep stated that she received much more data than she was capable of absorbing and analyzing. Another described stacks of old reports which he would not examine in a timely manner, if at all.

*Question:*

1. What should Mike Bachman recommend to his boss Pete Poorman concerning the sales information system?

---

*Case 12-2*

## KAPFER EQUIPMENT COMPANY

Declining performance of good sales rep

"Johnny's been one of our outstanding reps for the past 10 years. I can't believe what I've just learned," Tom Grant, sales manager, said to Jackie Kapfer, partner and co-manager of the Kapfer Equipment Company of Lincoln, Nebraska.

"And what is that?" she asked.

"He's been moonlighting on us for the past six months. He's a partner in an apartment construction project over in Sioux City with an old buddy of his. That's why his sales have been so bad these past few months. He's not working full time for us anymore."

Kapfer Equipment distributed a wide line of heavy-duty equipment, machines, and tools to the construction trades, governments, mining companies, and the oil industry in a five-state area around Nebraska. Its customers were anyone who had a large-scale construction project to build. The company had a long and good relationship with the 15 manufacturers it represented. Its lines included such items as crawler tractors, excavator–shovels, motor graders, cranes, backhoes, off-highway trucks, loaders, rollers, compactors, conveyors, pavers, and asphalt equipment.

The company had been founded by Otto Kapfer in 1920 and passed to his son, Max, in 1945. Max's two children, Dirk and Jacklyn, had taken over the enterprise in 1985 upon Max's retirement. Dirk worked with the suppliers and the service side of the business while Jacklyn, who was called Jackie by everyone but her mother, ran daily operations.

The 22-person sales force sold the entire line of products and services to every type of customer in the rep's assigned territory. It was a difficult job because it included many different types of products and customers.

John Knight had joined the company in 1984 after five years as a salesperson for Caterpillar. Prior to that he had worked as an engineer in heavy construction, mostly building the interstate highway system. He had graduated from Iowa State University in 1970 with a degree in civil engineering.

Since John had developed many valuable contacts in the Omaha area from his work for one of the area's largest construction companies, he was assigned that territory. He met his quotas the first year and exceeded them by 23 percent the second. He became the company's second most productive sales rep, consistently exceeding his sales quotas. Tom Grant had considered him

managerial timber. It was thought that he might become sales manager if Grant ever left the company or was promoted to a higher position in the company.

Jacklyn asked, "How did you find out about John's apartment project?"

"Well, six months ago his sales fell 30 percent below quota. He blamed the economy but said that things would pick up soon, for me not to worry. Well, when somebody tells me not to worry, that's when I really start worrying. I pulled out his activity reports. He wasn't making the calls like he used to make. Something was wrong. And you know we require a report on every situation where we don't get the order but some other company does. I knew of some business that John Deere had sold that we bid on so I looked for the report on it. No reports! So I go see him."

Jacklyn asked, "Why didn't you call him in? Why waste your time going over to Omaha?"

"Because all the evidence would be in Omaha. It's easy for a guy to lie to you in the office. In the field where the bodies are buried it's easier to get to the truth. I went to his house unannounced. No one was there, but a neighbor told me that John was probably at his apartment project. She gave me the address. I went over and caught him red-handed working on the roof with his partner. Did he ever look sheepish!"

Grant paused for effect and then continued, "He came down and we had a long, very frank talk. I was so mad I wanted to fire him on the spot. If he wasn't so big, I might have decked him. I kept my cool but he knew I was mad.

"His story was that he got caught in the apartment project by the real estate recession. Initially he was only an investor in the deal his friend had put together, but they ran into trouble. Their permanent financing collapsed when the bank got into some trouble with the Feds. Also the insurance company that was furnishing the construction money was about to pull the plug on them, so they had to get the project finished fast for what little money they had. So John and his partner had been working themselves to complete the project to save themselves. He insisted that it would be done in a month and that he would then be back at work at full speed. He pleaded for his job. He said he really liked to work for us. He also said he would continue to do an outstanding job for us if we would just give him a little room right now to get out of the mess he was in."

"What did you say to that?" Jacklyn asked.

"I told him how I felt about how he had treated us and that I thought he had used very bad judgment in how he handled his problem. However, I said that I would think about it and let him know my decision tonight."

"And what have you decided?"

"I decided to talk it over with you and Dirk first. After all, he has been one of the company's valuable earning assets. You wouldn't like it if I sold the warehouse out from under you without you knowing it, would you?"

Jacklyn replied, "Look, I know you have made up your mind what you want to do. So tell me and I'll put in my two cent's worth if I feel like it."

*Questions:*

1. Should John Knight be fired?
2. If not, what should Grant do about the situation?

# CHAPTER 13

# Sales Force Morale

If people feel they are treated fairly and with respect because you've created a positive atmosphere, that goes so far toward keeping people happy.

**Karen Hitchcock, Sales Manager**

Leaders in all sorts of enterprises—business, sports, and the military—have long extolled the importance of morale in building effective organizations. Groups with only mediocre talent have achieved great results because their people had excellent morale. Conversely, talented people with poor morale seldom achieve much. Morale should be of great concern to every manager. But what is this intangible force we call morale?

## THE NATURE AND IMPORTANCE OF MORALE

The word **morale** is commonly used to designate an individual's mental and emotional attitudes toward his or her environment. Major elements of this environment include the family, business associates, the employer, neighbors, and the community. When attitudes are positive, morale is said to be good, or high; when they are negative, morale is considered to be poor, or low.

High morale is associated with attitudes of satisfaction, desire to attain, and willingness to strive for the goals of a particular group or organization. Conversely, the attitudes associated with low morale are dissatisfaction, desire to leave, and a lack of concern for or interest in the goals of the organization.[1]

**Group morale** involves a sense of common purpose, while individual morale concerns one person's state of psychological well-being. High group morale reflects the belief of individuals in the group that group goals can be attained and are compatible with individual goals. This is sometimes called **esprit de corps.**[2]

The sales manager must be alert to both. Group morale may be healthy, but individuals in the group can harbor poor attitudes for a number of reasons. Everyone does not prosper even in the best of situations, and everyone is not unhappy in the worst of them.

One factor that limits the manager's ability to work with the sales force as a whole is that, in many instances, salespeople may be geographically distributed. If they are, they may have little face-to-face contact with one another, and also limited contact with the manager. Therefore, the sales executive often deals with salespeople's attitudes on an individual basis. However, group morale should also be a primary concern.

**Foundations of high sales force morale**

| Common goals | Attainable goals |
|---|---|
| Compatible with personal goals | |

Group attitudes toward work are important for both economic and social reasons. From the economic standpoint, productivity is likely to be higher in groups whose members have relatively good morale. It does not always follow that high morale results in high productivity, however. A group may have a good attitude but poor results. Nevertheless, productivity is usually higher for employees who have good mental attitudes toward their jobs.

From a social point of view, people who develop negative attitudes toward work can make life miserable not only for themselves, but also for those around them. Life is too short to be spent working in an unpleasant environment. The proposition that good morale should be promoted in the work environment for its sake alone certainly has merit.

## ■ MORALE AND STRATEGIC PLANNING

The strategic role morale plays in an organization reflects top management's values—part of what modern management theorists call **corporate culture.** Managers in some firms are not concerned with morale. Their corporate culture is most concerned with group and individual output. Some managers think morale is unimportant. Others feel that there is little they can do to improve morale so they do not include building good organizational morale in their marketing strategy. One owner of 16 units of a large fast-food franchise stated that his labor turnover was 500 percent a year. "We can only pay them minimum wage and they have to work fast and hard, so you can guess what our morale is. What can I do about it?"

On the other hand, some firms make high morale a keystone in their marketing strategy. These companies practice **internal marketing,** which is *attracting, developing, motivating, and retaining qualified employees through jobs which satisfy their needs.* They treat their employees as internal customers and their strategy is to shape jobs to fit human needs. By adhering to this strategy, companies are able to build fiercely loyal, highly effective sales forces.[3]

Honeywell Corporation uses a variety of programs to build company morale. Workers can nominate each other for the "Chairman's Achievement Award," which is a monetary prize of $100 given out by the CEO several times a year. They also give out annual awards to "great" people managers ($3,000), top salespeople (a trip to a resort), excellent service technicians ($1,000), and employees who have done extensive community service ($500 to a nonprofit organization of the employee's choice).[4]

# ◼ FACTORS SHAPING SALES FORCE MORALE

Sales force morale is determined primarily by four components. The first is the corporate culture. The second is the rep's perceptions and beliefs about the work environment. This is often called the **organizational climate,** or work climate. The third is the sales rep's **job satisfaction.** The fourth component—perhaps the most important for group morale—is the **social interaction** among the reps.[5]

Many aspects of these factors were discussed in the chapters on motivation and leadership. However, to better understand the causes and effects of sales force morale, the specific relationship of these four factors to sales force morale is discussed below and depicted in Figure 13–1.

## Corporate Culture

The corporate culture describes managerial norms of behavior. In turn these norms guide salespeople's attitudes and behavior. Salespeople learn these norms by observing their managers and co-workers. For example, if the sales manager doesn't work very hard, then the salespeople probably

◼ **FIGURE 13-1**    **Factors shaping sales force morale**

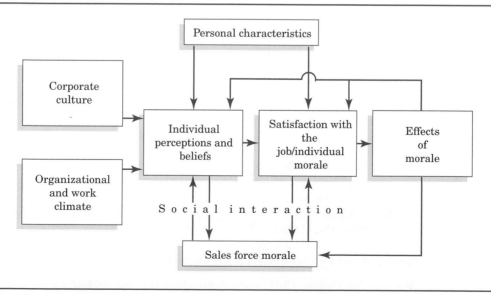

won't work very hard either. When the corporate culture contributes positively to company performance, then the effect on morale will be high, and vice versa.

## Organizational/Work Climate

Climate is a set of characteristics that describes the way a particular organization or work group deals with its members and its environment. The work climate of a particular group such as the sales force may or may not be consistent with the organizational climate. Although both are important to morale, the work group climate of the sales force is probably most important for sales force morale. Climate characteristics may be grouped into the following four categories: individual responsibility and authority; structure; reward orientation; and consideration, warmth, and support.

*Individual responsibility and authority* refers to the responsibility given to individuals within the group or organization and the opportunities for exercising individual initiative. As we noted in Chapter 9, salespeople thrive on challenge, and one good way to challenge them is to give them greater responsibility, authority, and control in their jobs. Hewlett-Packard practices **empowerment** because its management believes that employees feel best about a company that gives them a sense of control.[6]

Sales positions may have more or less **job structure,** depending on organizational policies that guide and/or restrict the salesperson's actions. To some extent, the structure provided through procedural rules helps salespeople have a clearer understanding of their jobs and therefore reduces conflict and ambiguity. On the other hand, too many restrictions and too much supervision will stifle personal growth and creativity and may hamper the sales rep's performance. Recent research has shown that strict regulations have a negative impact on esprit de corps.[7]

**Reward orientation** describes the company's policies on pay and promotions. Are salaries, raises, bonuses, and promotions competitive and equitable? It is difficult to instill a good attitude among the members of the sales force when their pay is not commensurate with their activities. The compensation plan must be fair, offer some security and incentive, and otherwise meet the requirements of a sound compensation plan discussed earlier.

*Consideration, warmth, and support* refers to a style of leadership in a work climate where managers support and nurture their subordinates. In this situation, salespeople feel that their managers are sincerely concerned with the welfare of their people. Some companies provide career counseling and mentoring programs which build employee loyalty to each other and to the company.[8]

## Individual Perceptions and Beliefs

As seen in Figure 13–1, each individual has his or her own perceptions and beliefs about the work climate, and these beliefs influence the individual's morale. For example, two salespeople working for the same manager may feel differently about the manager's leadership style. One rep may feel that the amount and style of supervision is just right, while another may find it stifling. Taken together, however, those beliefs shared or accepted by most of the sales force will reflect and affect their group morale.

## Satisfaction with the Job

The individual's satisfaction with various aspects of his or her job is the second component affecting sales force morale. Whereas climate is a description of work characteristics, *satisfaction* is the individual's *emotional* and *evaluative* feelings toward various dimensions of the job.

The work climate obviously influences the potential for more or less job satisfaction. But people can have similar beliefs about their work environment and yet have very different levels of satisfaction with their jobs. This is because the work climate is only one of the influences on job satisfaction. Individual differences in age, education, health, career stage, tenure, financial status, family life, personality, and values have a great impact on whether individuals find their jobs more or less satisfying. As explained in earlier chapters, this is why motivational programs must to some extent be tailored to the individual.

Most of the dimensions of satisfaction reflect various aspects of the work climate, while a few of them concern other aspects of the job. The specific job dimensions that contribute to the salesperson's overall level of job satisfaction are shown in Figure 13–2 and described below.

### Nature of the Job

In sales work, the job and the individual must be matched. Employees who feel unproductive will be dissatisfied. The job should provide variety, challenge, an opportunity to learn, and a certain amount of autonomy and control. Additionally, some people will be dissatisfied because they are not able to deal with the pressures and frustrations of a sales job.

### Pay

Both the level and method of compensation can cause satisfaction or dissatisfaction. Salespeople are in continual contact with reps who work for other firms, and they are in a good position to know what other firms are paying. If the comparison is continually unfavorable, the reps will realize that they are working for a low-paying concern and could do better elsewhere.

Compensation methods, as discussed in Chapter 10, will also cause dissatisfaction if they are not based on equitable measures of performance. *Quotas,* for example, which often have a direct bearing on the rep's compensation, can be a major source of dissatisfaction. Reps must believe quotas are fair and based on a logical analysis of their territories.

■ **FIGURE 13-2**

**Dimensions of job satisfaction**

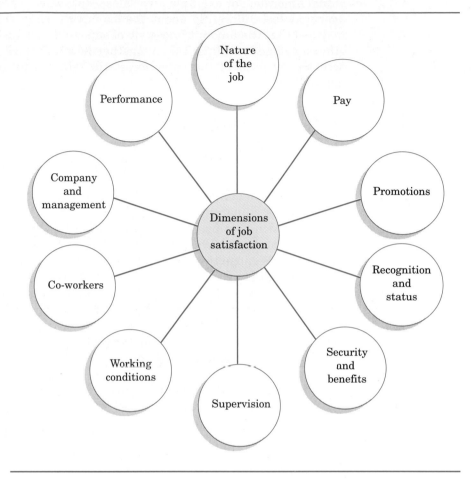

### Promotions

Both the lack of opportunity for promotions and the basis for promotions can cause dissatisfaction. As in the case of pay, promotions should be based on equitable evaluations of performance and managerial potential. Perceptions of *unfairness* are an important cause of dissatisfaction.

### Recognition and Status

Insufficient recognition for performance can create dissatisfaction. People like to be recognized for a job well done. This provides tangible evidence that management appreciates an individual's efforts. Also, most people like to feel that they are an important part of the organization and that they are making a worthwhile contribution. No one enjoys feeling inconsequential. Sales managers who seek the opinions and advice of their salespeople make them feel that they are an important part of the organization.

### Security and Benefits

An individual who is afraid of losing his or her job cannot operate at any-where near a normal level of productivity. Anyone who has ever been in this situation can appreciate the fears and emotional stress that go with such a feeling. The manager who can alleviate these fears does a lot to raise job satisfaction.

### Supervision

As noted earlier, overly restrictive supervisory policies lead to frustration and dissatisfaction. On the other hand, too little supervision can also cause problems. Supervisors themselves, because of their administrative skill and leadership style, can have a tremendous positive or negative im-pact on salespeople's overall job satisfaction. Sales reps who do not respect and/or dislike their immediate supervisor will harbor a lot of dissatisfac-tion even if they like the job itself. In contrast, those who respect and like their supervisors will often be fairly satisfied even in the face of other job frustrations.

### Working Conditions

Many reps work primarily outside the home office. Consequently, their working conditions consist largely of the car they use for travel and the style of living the company's expense account allows them to maintain. Firms should allow their salespeople to drive good cars and provide them with satisfactory expense accounts.

### Co-Workers

While many salespeople often work alone, they still need the support of those around them. Such support helps to ease the pressures and frustra-tions that sales reps often face. Team selling is an organizational option which promotes interdependence and cooperation among employees.

### Company and Management

Most salespeople realize that their productivity and welfare depend to some degree on the competence of the company's managers and on the sta-bility and growth of the company. If they lose confidence in management, reps cannot avoid developing a poor attitude toward the company and the job. Additionally, salespeople need to understand and believe in the goals to which they contribute. Therefore, management should be open and hon-est about the company's operations and should provide salespeople with a clear vision of company goals.

### Performance

Good performance itself can also lead to satisfaction. If salespeople are successful, they will undoubtedly be more satisfied with their jobs than if they are not successful. Additionally, some companies set high expecta-tions because they believe that highly motivated people love to overcome challenges.[9]

*A Day-to-Day Operating Problem*

## MAJESTIC PLASTICS COMPANY (J)

### Team morale

As the general sales manager of Majestic Plastics, Clyde Brion was overseeing the sales team which was working with one of Majestic Plastics' largest accounts to develop several new containers for them. The new container designs were one of the many cost-saving initiatives that Majestic had been working on with this customer. Clyde asked Rob Singer, who had been calling on this customer's largest facility in St. Louis, to serve on the team along with several other people.

Rob had an outstanding record as a salesperson. His relationships with the personnel at the customer's St. Louis facility were excellent. He seemed to be a perfect choice for this special assignment. However, in the team's first two meetings Rob had not contributed to the smooth functioning of the team. In fact he had been a source of irritation. His ideas were pretty good, but he was unwilling to listen to anybody else's ideas. He is opinionated and argumentative. He either ignores suggestions from others or scoffs at them. He had even done this to Clyde. He acted as if he was the only person in the world whose opinion counts for anything.

Rob's behavior is detrimental to the team effort, yet his ideas are good and his experience with and knowledge of this customer could be a very valuable resource for the team.

**Question:** What action do you think Clyde should take to remedy this situation?

## Social Interaction

As noted above and as seen in Figure 13–1, overall job satisfaction stems from an individual's feelings toward various aspects of the work climate and job described above and from individual differences in personal characteristics. These feelings of satisfaction, which could be labeled individual morale, directly influence sales force morale. If most of the salespeople are, in general, satisfied with their jobs, sales force morale will be high.

But morale of the sales force as a group is *not* necessarily the same as the average of the individuals' levels of satisfaction. Group morale is a shared attitude among salespeople about their company and its goals. This shared attitude results to a large extent from the **social interaction** among members of the sales force. The expression "one rotten apple can spoil the barrel" illustrates how one person can have undue influence on the rest of the group. One person, through his or her energy and/or enthusiasm, can also exert a strong positive influence on a group. The attitudes of new salespeople will be greatly influenced by the prevalent attitudes of the current salespeople. While individual satisfaction or morale is important, it is the social interaction among people that transforms individual beliefs and feelings into group morale.

---

### Team Selling Promotes Positive Morale

Salespeople who work on teams develop a strong sense of interdependence among the team members. People become loyal to one another and to the company. At Hershey Chocolate all of the sales incentives are based on team efforts. These group efforts lead to greater feelings of organizational identification, pride, and commitment.

As Jeffrey McIlnes, the CEO of Einson Freeman, Inc., states, "The way I see it, if they

are loyal to the team, they'll be loyal to the company." Such loyalty goes hand in hand with high morale.

Source: Bill Kelley, "Putting Incentives in Their Place," *Sales & Marketing Management,* September 1992, pp. 98–104; and Geoffrey Brewer, "Seven Secrets to Building Employee Loyalty," *Performance,* December 1995, p. 23.

---

## EFFECTS OF SALES FORCE MORALE

Sales force morale exerts a strong influence on individual morale. Good group morale can improve the attitude of a sales rep whose morale is sagging. In the same way, an individual with a positive outlook can affect the morale of the group. As depicted in Figure 13–1, the relationship between individual attitudes and group morale is a *reciprocal* one. This is why the manager must be concerned with both individual and group morale.

**The interdependence of this sales team helps meet the customer's needs and leads to high group morale.**

## Low Morale

A sales representative with a poor attitude toward the job and the company develops an antimanagerial orientation. For real or imagined reasons, such people regard the company as an adversary and attempt to retaliate against management suggestions. They may even deliberately attempt to influence other reps' attitudes. And when sales force morale is low, a company can suffer in many areas.

### Excessive Turnover

One of the most widely recognized indexes for measuring morale in a firm is employee turnover. The theory is that most people with poor attitudes toward their jobs become so dissatisfied that they seek employment elsewhere. Observation indicates that there is little turnover among salespeople with high morale. A few salespeople may leave just because they have a better offer, but the number of people quitting is still a good measure of the state of morale in an organization.

### Increased Expenses

Salespeople who do not have a good attitude toward their employers seldom control their expenses. Such reps may openly state that they intend to get everything they can from the company. When poor morale not only lowers sales volume but also increases expenses, it puts dual pressure on profits.

### Complaint Behavior

Salespeople who have poor morale are apt to magnify minor complaints. Things that normally would go unnoticed in an organization with good morale can become points of contention in other groups. Salespeople who fail to perceive the real cause of their morale problems may complain about whatever is at hand.

### Development of Outside Interests

Unfortunately many individuals with poor morale do not quit. For various economic and social reasons, they continue working for years at a job they detest. Some of them cannot find as good a job elsewhere. Others do not want to leave the location. Usually in such situations, dissatisfied employees develop outside interests—they look elsewhere for their satisfaction in life. They spend as little time as possible on the job and do a minimum amount of work.

### Unsatisfactory Sales Performance

Probably no job in an entire company is so directly dependent on good morale as sales. No one with a poor attitude toward the job can sell effectively. Experienced sales managers know that when a sales rep's volume declines in relation to the rest of the sales force, the first place to look for trouble is in the individual. A rep's mental attitude is reflected throughout the sales presentation. A poor attitude can destroy the effectiveness of a sales presentation and result in lost sales.

**?**  **AN ETHICAL DILEMMA**

Dick Walters, who was the district sales manager for a medium-sized distributor of home building products, was facing a tough decision. One of his reps, Lauren Schultz, had started with the company as a sales rep and in a relatively short time had become one of the top reps in terms of sales results. After five years in sales, she was promoted to the position of staff sales trainer. After two years as a staff trainer, she returned to a field sales position as a senior sales representative, handling several major accounts. Although her performance as a trainer had been satisfactory, she made it clear that she was not interested in any other staff assignments. She had been back in field sales for a year and recently told Dick that her goal was to become a district manager.

Lauren was still one of the top reps in terms of sales. But Dick was convinced, based on her performance as a trainer and in her territory, that she did not have the necessary administrative and people skills to be a good manager. In her formal reviews, she had always been rated low on the administrative aspects of her job. Dick also felt that she was a "loner" who preferred to work on her own. He did not feel that he could recommend her for a promotion. On the other hand, she felt she deserved to be promoted.

Dick did not want to lose Lauren. Yet he knew that if he told her that he would not recommend her for a management position, she would probably leave. Currently, there were not any positions open and there wouldn't be any for some time. Dick was considering whether or not to tell Lauren that he would not recommend her for the next opening.

What, if anything, should Dick tell Lauren?

## High Morale

One effect of high sales force morale is, of course, eliminating the negative consequences associated with poor morale. However, high morale can lead to additional positive outcomes for the company.

### Organizational Commitment

When morale and the accompanying satisfaction are high, salespeople are more committed to the organization. They are more involved in their jobs and have a stronger sense of identification with the company. These salespeople believe in the values and goals of the organization and are willing to exert extra effort on behalf of the organization.[10]

### Citizenship Behaviors

When morale is good, salespeople are more likely to engage in citizenship behaviors of a discretionary nature that are not part of the salesperson's formal job requirements. For example, sales reps will be more willing to help others with their tasks or problems and will try to avoid interpersonal conflicts by being courteous and respectful of the rights of others. They may also be more conscientious, work longer hours, do more than is expected, and be more willing to tolerate problems without complaining. Citizenship behaviors have been shown to be related to overall sales force productivity.[11]

*Performance*

High sales force morale can provide a catalyst for performance above the norm through individual satisfaction or through a commitment to the group. Sometimes individuals will strive for the sake of the group as much as for themselves.

# ■ SPECIAL PROBLEMS IN MORALE

From time to time, virtually every sales manager faces special morale problems that are difficult to handle, including employee dissatisfaction with promotions, severance, the aging employee, and job titles.

## Dissatisfaction with Promotions

Administrators often face the dilemma of choosing from among several equally qualified individuals for only one opening in the executive hierarchy. Such situations often generate poor attitudes among previously good employees. This problem also exists when the opening is filled by someone from outside the organization. Individuals who are doing a good job are disappointed if they don't receive a promotion they feel they should have.

This problem has no easy solution. Often it has no solution. Some of these good people quit when a promotion is not forthcoming. If there are equally deserving reps, managers should explain to those who didn't get promoted why the other rep did and reassure these reps that they are in line for a promotion in the future.

The situation is even worse when the sales force generally believes the company has promoted the wrong candidate. Promotion of an individual who others consider undeserving can undermine morale. The promotion of an undeserving person also creates problems when he or she attempts to exercise managerial authority over former peers. Promotional decisions should be as objective as possible.

## Severance

Many administrators cannot face the task of firing an employee. The sales manager who does not approach this problem correctly can ruin the morale of the entire organization. Others will easily identify with the discharged individual and regard the situation as unfair, whether or not ample cause exists for such feelings.

Firing is a sensitive issue. When employees are fired they may legally challenge their release as a wrongful termination. In some companies, sales reps are seldom fired but instead encouraged to resign. In either case, it is important that managers document the unsatisfactory performance of the reps. In general, the appropriate policy is to first give the rep a warning and a chance to improve performance before he or she is terminated. The steps which were discussed in the previous chapter for handling poorly

## AN INTERNATIONAL PERSPECTIVE

### Culture Shock

An overseas assignment can have an enormous impact on a sales manager's or salesperson's morale. During the first few months of the assignment abroad, most expatriates experience culture shock. Although culture shock is a normal process, it can have some negative consequences for the employee. Culture shock usually evolves through four distinct stages:

- **Initial euphoria.** During this period, which lasts from a week or two to a month, everything is new and exciting. The recent arrivee is impressed by the numerous similarities between his or her home culture and the new one.
- **Irritation and hostility.** During this period, expatriates' focus turns from similarities to differences, which become very troubling. This can cause them to withdraw and build barriers between themselves and the local population.
- **Gradual adjustment.** The expatriate becomes comfortable with those behaviors and norms that once seemed threatening. Sometimes individuals develop negative attitudes toward certain aspects of their own home culture.
- **Adaptation and biculturalism.** The expatriate learns to appreciate the foreign culture as well as his or her own.

The negative impact of culture shock on the employee can be lessened by predeparture cross-cultural training for expatriates and their families, by language training, and by providing a support network to ease the adjustment to the foreign location.

Source: Adapted from Jack Cough and Maureen Rabbit, "Culture Shock," Global Connection, Summer 1997, with permission from the Global Information Network, Kelley School of Business, Indiana University.

performing salespeople should be followed. It is critical from the perspective of building morale that all of the reps know what is expected of them, and that managers apply the same standards to all of the reps.

### Handling Older Salespeople

The ethical and sensitive yet businesslike handling of older salespeople has plagued many managers and has a direct bearing on the morale of all sales representatives in the firm. There is considerable evidence to support maintaining the older sales rep's place in most sales organizations. While they may not be able to cover the territory they once did, often their selling efficiency and profitability can match those of any other person in the organization. Most of these reps do not expect to make the earnings they once did, and frequently they accept a reduction of territory or workload in exchange for the assurance that they will not be forced into retirement. Chapter 9 suggested some ideas for motivating the older rep.

### Titles

What should management call the person who sells the firm's product? Many executives consider this question today because of the changing realities of selling and its impact on morale. As management has become more sensitive to the psychological side of business operations, it has become aware that many potential salespeople resent being called salesmen or saleswomen. They want other titles, more indicative of their actual work. So organizations now try to ensure that titles accurately depict the work done and at the same time bestow status.

Some popular alternative titles for salespeople are:

- Sales engineer
- Sales consultant
- Technical representative
- Factory sales representative
- District or territory manager
- Account representative
- Management representative
- Sales coordinator
- Marketing representative
- Sales associate
- Area sales manager
- Market specialist

The new titles provide more status with the customer and improve the person's self-image. And the new titles are more descriptive of the selling job.

## DETERMINING THE CAUSE OF POOR MORALE

The sales manager may know that morale is poor but not know the reasons for it. Four actions can shed light on some possible causes.

### Provide an Outlet for Complaints

First, the sales manager must offer salespeople an outlet for their complaints, either formally or informally. Some common grievance may be discovered from these complaints. Sometimes it is advisable to question reps informally at a company social event. Often a sales rep will not complain while working but will open up about what is bothering him or her at a cocktail party or a ball game.

### Take Complaints Seriously

Whatever a rep tells the manager should never be belittled or dismissed as trivial. Although the complaint may be silly to the manager, it is probably serious to the employee. If the sales manager does not listen understandingly and then do something about valid complaints, the reps will soon learn that talking gains them nothing.

### Conduct Opinion and Attitude Surveys

Firms often conduct opinion and attitude surveys among employees to determine morale. Company managers or independent consulting agencies may administer these studies. Such surveys do have validity if they are done properly. However, employees are often reluctant to reveal their real attitudes, even to a supposedly independent interviewer.

### Use Exit Interviews

Proponents of exit interviews maintain that the departing employee will open up and tell the employer the reasons for leaving and his or her true attitudes toward the company. Others feel that these interviews do not uncover the true reasons salespeople quit. Most employees know that they need a recommendation from past employers to get future jobs. Because of this, they may be unwilling to openly discuss their dissatisfaction.

This does not mean that exit interviews should be discontinued, for if they are properly handled, they can provide some insight about morale. If the interviewer does not accept the surface reason the employee gives for leaving, the real reasons may be discovered by probing. It depends on (1) the rapport the interviewer can establish with the departing employee and (2) how much confidence the worker has that any revelations made will not adversely affect future recommendations. One firm conducts exit interviews several months after the employee leaves. The theory is that this gives the employees time to evaluate what went wrong in the firm and also time to get whatever recommendations they need from the firm.

## THE MORALE-BUILDING PROCESS

This chapter has discussed the effects of morale and the factors that cause it. Little has been said of how the sales manager can constructively affect the morale of the sales force. It can be done by avoiding the negative situations discussed earlier. However, there are several other ways to help build a good attitude among salespeople, including integrating interests, having a good communication system, and developing a strong corporate culture and a supportive organizational climate.

### Integrating Interests

Building morale in the work environment depends on showing people that they can achieve their personal objectives in life by working for the organization. This is known as the process of **integrating interests** and begins at the time of hiring. It is folly to hire anyone for whom the company cannot provide a work experience that the person will consider a *success*. The sales manager must make a frank analysis of exactly what the firm can furnish its people and then provide a realistic picture of the sales job when recruiting potential employees.

It is almost impossible for a manager to alter an individual's personal interests to conform with what the company has to offer. This can be done only by the individual. Thus, about the only control the administrator has over this aspect of morale is to hire individuals whose needs conform with what the company has to offer. Hewlett-Packard spends tremendous resources on the recruiting and selection process to ensure that there is a fit between the company and the recruit.[12]

## Communication

Good communication is crucial to many aspects of sales management. When channels of communication are absent or faulty, neither management nor the sales force knows what the other thinks.

Managerial policies should ensure that there is ample opportunity for both downward and upward communication within the formal structure of the organization. Informal communication can also play an important role in promoting high morale. Sales managers must be accessible and open to ideas from their salespeople. This not only strengthens morale, but, as noted earlier, provides a means of monitoring morale.

## Developing a Strong Corporate Culture and Positive Organizational Climate

Sales managers can promote a strong, positive culture. Sales managers should let the staff know that they are committed to the organization and its goals through their words and actions. They should display a sense of pride in the company, its products, and its people. If managers demonstrate and verbalize their vision, commitment, and pride, salespeople will likely develop similar values.

Managers can also promote a sense of esprit de corps through team projects or group competitions (say, district against district), sales meetings and conventions, newsletters, honor banquets, or involvement in community projects. These group activities lead to a greater feeling of organizational identification, pride, and commitment.

Finally, the best way for the individual manager to enhance the organizational climate is to be supportive. When managers are supportive, salespeople feel their leaders are sincerely interested in their well-being and development.

## ■ SUMMARY

Morale refers to the mental and emotional attitudes of an individual toward his or her environment. Maintaining high individual and group morale is a key area of concern in managing a sales force. Group morale is sometimes called esprit de corps. High sales force morale results from establishing common goals that are attainable and compatible with personal goals.

Attitudes toward work are important for both economic and social reasons. High morale plays an important role in the success of the sales force. Four components determine sales force morale: the corporate culture, the organization or work climate, the individual's satisfaction, and social interaction.

The corporate culture describes the managerial norms of behavior. Organization or work climate refers to a description of work characteristics consisting of individual autonomy and control; structure; reward orientation; and consideration, warmth, and support. The individual's satisfaction with his or her job reflects emotional or evaluative feelings toward the nature of the job, pay, promotions, recognition and status, security and benefits, supervision, working conditions, co-workers, company and management, and performance. Finally, social interaction refers to the interaction between members of the sales force.

The levels of sales force morale range from low to high. Typical results of low morale include excessive turnover, increased expenses, complaint behavior, development of outside interests, and unsatisfactory sales performance. High morale, on the other hand, increases organizational commitment, citizenship behavior, and performance.

Some special morale issues sales managers must consider include employee dissatisfaction with promotions, severance, handling of older salespeople, and titles. Techniques that help identify morale problems involve providing an outlet for complaints, conducting opinion and attitude surveys, and administering exit interviews. Sales force morale should be nurtured through integrating interests, communication, and developing a strong corporate culture and positive organizational climate.

## Key Terms

Citizenship behaviors
Corporate culture
Empowerment
Esprit de corps
Group morale

Internal marketing
Integrating interests
Job satisfaction
Job structure
Morale

Organizational commitment
Organizational climate
Reward orientation
Social interaction

## ■ QUESTIONS AND PROBLEMS

1. A branch manager of a large, nationally known appliance manufacturer said: "There's no problem in getting sales reps. Sales reps are things. You buy them like you buy merchandise. You put them on straight commission, and they either cut the mustard or get out. After you've been through a few hundred of them, you will have your good sales force." Comment on this philosophy, bearing in mind that this manager's branch has been over quota each year he has managed it, whereas before it was a sick operation.

2. Explain the differences between organizational work climate and individual satisfaction.

3. How does the corporate culture affect sales force morale?

4. How can the sales manager encourage a salesperson to resign?

5. How can the sales manager integrate the interests of the individual and the organization?

6. Why would a sales rep be disloyal to the firm?

7. Managers are continually told to listen to their people and to be sensitive to the signals they send. But managers can listen without hearing a thing. What does it mean to listen?

8. Classify the following as examples of either organizational work climate or individual satisfaction, and indicate the appropriate dimension.

   a. Corporation XYZ provides its employees with a great deal of responsibility.

   b. Mitchell was pleased that he had received a congratulatory memo and an award for superior performance.

    *c.* Alpha Beta's compensation for its employees is below the industry average.

    *d.* Mary feels that the company-owned 1984 Pinto she drives for her sales calls does not make a very good impression on her customers.

**9.** How can the manager give the sales force more status within the organization?

## ■ EXPERIENTIAL EXERCISES

**A.** Develop a questionnaire to measure the extent to which salespeople are satisfied with various aspects of their jobs. Administer this questionnaire to the salespeople from one company. Analyze and report the results. Also make suggestions regarding what the company could do to improve satisfaction.

**B.** Develop a questionnaire to measure the morale of any group to which you belong. Report the results, suggesting ways to improve morale.

## ■ REFERENCES

**1.** Edwin A. Locke, "The Nature and Causes of Job Satisfaction," in *Handbook of Industrial and Organizational Psychology,* ed. M. D. Dinette (New York: John Wiley & Sons, 1983), pp. 1297–1349.

**2.** Thomas E. Boy, Robert F. Lunch, and Due K. Schuller, "Fostering Esprit de Corps in Marketing," *Marketing Management,* Spring 1997, pp. 21–27.

**3.** Leonard L. Berry and A. Parasuraman, "Services Marketing Starts from Within," *Marketing Management,* Winter 1992, pp. 25–34.

**4.** Geoffrey Brewer, "Seven Secrets to Building Employee Loyalty," *Performance,* December 1995, pp. 20–27.

**5.** Rosann L. Spiro, "Sales Force Morale: A Reconceptualization and Model," working paper, Kelley School of Business, Indiana University Bloomington, IN, 1997.

**6.** Brewer, "Seven Secrets."

**7.** Boy, Lunch, and Schuller, "Fostering Esprit de Corps."

**8.** Brewer, "Seven Secrets." and M.M, "Buddy System," *Sales & Marketing Management,* January 1997, p. 37.

**9.** Brewer, "Seven Secrets," pp. 21–22.

**10.** Larry J. Williams and Stella E. Anderson, "Job Satisfaction and Organizational Commitment as Predictors of Organizational Citizenship and In-Role Behavior," *Journal of Management,* September 1991, pp. 601–17.

**11.** Phillip M. Podsakoff and Scott B. MacKenzie, "Organizational Citizenship Behaviors and Sales Unit Effectiveness," *Journal of Marketing Research,* August 1994, pp. 351–63.

**12.** Donald W. Jackson Jr. and Stephen S. Tax, "Managing the Industrial Sales Force Culture," *Journal of Business & Industrial Marketing* 10 (1995), pp. 34–47.

*Case 13-1*

## PRUDENTIAL SECURITIES
### Impact of unfavorable publicity on sales force morale

"I'm sorry but I can't take any more of this situation. I feel betrayed by top management. They lied to us about those limited partnerships and so in turn I lied to my customers, many of them longtime, close friends. Some of them have lost a lot of money because of what I told them. Now some of them are screaming at me. I've lost several accounts and I think that it is only beginning. Today it's the energy partnerships. Tomorrow, what? The real estate and the aircraft leasing partnerships? Are we going to go through the same thing? I've got to leave. I can't work under these conditions. I've enjoyed working for you personally and I know you've done your best. I hope you understand." Ted Knoll was handing his letter of resignation to Cynthia Carlist, his boss and the manager of one of the Prudential's branch brokerages in southern California.

"I'm sorry that things haven't worked out the way you wanted them, but under the circumstances and considering how you feel, I understand. Good luck!" With that Ted left the office as Cynthia Carlist leaned back in her chair and looked once again at the latest article in *Business Week*. This article dealt with the company's difficulties with the Securities and Exchange Commission (SEC) over a series of oil and gas limited partnerships the company had developed and marketed in the early 1980s. As she reread some of the key passages in the article she wondered if Ted's resignation was just the beginning of many more separations.

She had been thankful that so far there was little visible impact on the account executives. In fact, the company's turnover, which historically was 20 percent a year (in-

dustry average was 14 percent), was down to about 15 percent. She attributed this drop in employee turnover to the highly fortunate economic conditions being enjoyed by the industry in this summer of 1993. The Dow Jones average hit an all-time high. Brokers were doing a record business. Much money was being made so the account executives weren't eager to cut down their money tree.

Nonetheless, she thought she should talk with some of her key people about the situation. She strolled into Roland Paffco's office late that afternoon after the market closed. He was an executive vice president and one of the branch's leading producers. She opened the conversation by telling him of Ted's resignation.

"Yeah, I knew he was going to do it. He had spent a lot of time talking to me about it. He was really upset by all of this mess. No need to tell you what he said, but that speech in Santa Monica last week didn't help a bit," Roland remarked.

He was referring to a speech given by the company's CEO at a meeting of 150 of the firm's leading producers in southern California. The subject of the meeting was supposedly mutual funds, but the CEO gave a significant speech about the firm's problems with the limited partnerships in which he insisted that the company had done nothing wrong. He expected that the problems would soon be behind them with a settlement the company was negotiating with the SEC.

Roland said, "Ted didn't believe him. In fact, he reacted adversely. He told me that he felt he was just being lied to again and that these troubles were not going to go away as easily as top management thinks."

Cynthia asked, "How are your clients reacting?"

Roland replied, "I've had a few of them tell me rather sternly what they thought and I've lost some business. It's tough to sit there under that judicial gag order that was placed on us and not give any advice to our customers when we made that first buyout offer. One of my best customers really lit into me when he said that he kept his account with us for the service we are supposed to give yet when he really needed it, we were under a gag rule not to give it. And I could say nothing. He told me of his decision not to accept the buyout. I smiled and said that I had always been impressed with his intelligence. That seemed to give him some satisfaction. At least he still has two accounts with us, but he has switched about half of his account to Schwab." (Schwab is a large discount securities dealer.)

"What do you think we ought to do about it?" Cynthia asked. "Is there anything I can do to help us through this problem? Anything I should be telling my bosses about what we need to be doing?"

Cynthia's questions prompted Roland to say, "Let me give this some thought and get back to you with some ideas first thing tomorrow morning."

**Questions:**

1. What actions could branch managers take in situations such as those being faced by the Prudential Securities account executives?

2. What would you recommend Cynthia Carlist do in handling the situation?

3. What organizational problems might Roland Paffco encounter if he becomes too involved in this matter?

---

*Case 13-2*

### TAYLOR ELECTRONICS COMPANY*
### Sales rep resists a change in job status

In the face of intensified competition, the Taylor Electronics Company's sales revenues and market share, and consequently its net profit, were declining. To meet this situation, Taylor's top management decided to cut costs and reduce the firm's market coverage in various ways. As a part of these moves, Lloyd Williams, a divisional sales manager, was given the unenviable task of downsizing the sales force. Rose Blanchard, one of the salespeople affected by this staff

reduction, refused to go along with it. She rejected the alternatives offered by the company and threatened to sue Taylor on the grounds of sex and age discrimination. At that point, Lloyd Williams wondered what course of action should be taken.

The Taylor Electronics Company was a large manufacturer of highly technical telecommunications equipment. The company was also extensively involved in servicing the equipment it produced and sold. The Taylor product line included computers, telephones, fax machines, and other communications equipment. Taylor's products

---

*Adapted from a case prepared by Bryce Lloyd under the direction of Prof. William J. Stanton.

were designed to be integrated as a complete office information and communication system. They were designed for use by large businesses, small firms, and individual consumers.

The target market for the sales division headed by Lloyd Williams consisted primarily of household consumers and, to some extent, small businesses. Taylor used two competing channels of distribution to reach this market. One involved selling through a series of Taylor-owned retail outlets. The other involved selling through independent retail outlets such as electronics stores, department stores, and hardware stores. Williams's divisional sales force sold to both types of outlets—the company-owned stores and the independent stores—as well as selling directly to small firms. The salespeople were responsible for developing new accounts and maintaining established accounts. Thus the reps had to sell, install, operate, and service the equipment.

Historically, Taylor, along with a few giant firms such as American Telephone and Telegraph Company (AT&T) and International Telephone and Telegraph Company (ITT), accounted for virtually all of the sales of telecommunications equipment. However, technological innovations (satellites, lasers, and fiber optics, for example) and political-legal forces (the breakup of AT&T, for example) had significantly altered the telecommunications industry. Taylor's reputation for quality products and service remained as high as ever, but the company faced numerous effective competitors in the market, in contrast to the less competitive environment of the past.

The net effect of these environmental forces and industry changes was to reduce Taylor's market share and, consequently, to increase the pressure on Lloyd Williams's division. Sales in Williams's division were projected to remain level or to decline as the new competitors continued to nibble at Taylor's market share. At the same time, operating expenses were increasing as Taylor sought to meet these new competitive challenges. Also, older manufacturing facilities caused some production costs to remain high.

Taylor's top management adopted three courses of action to stem the decline in profits. First, some manufacturing operations were moved to lower-cost foreign locations. Second, the company closed the Taylor-owned retailing outlets that were operating at a loss. And third, the company stopped selling to independent retailers where the sales results did not meet Taylor's profit goals. The net effect of the second and third moves was that Taylor did not need as large a sales force as previously. Consequently, some salespeople would have to be moved to other positions or locations or simply be let go.

As a divisional sales manager, Lloyd Williams was given the responsibility and authority to determine which sales positions were no longer necessary. The difficulty of this task was compounded by the fact that Taylor had a long history of excellent employee-management relationships. Employees generally felt a great deal of loyalty to the company and had been treated fairly throughout the years.

The broad guidelines for downsizing the sales force, as set by top management and endorsed by Williams, were based on job function and location. Williams was not allowed to consider such factors as seniority or past job performance. By consistently administering its guidelines and thoroughly communicating with the employees, management hoped to minimize the disruption, minimize the negative impact on employee morale, and still preserve the employee skills needed for the future.

Employees whose jobs were eliminated were offered three options. The first option allowed the employee to take an early retirement with benefits, including a lump sum settlement. Under the second option the employee would accept a lateral move to another division or location, if possible. The third alternative was to accept a demotion within the division or a demotion and a move to another division. People would not lose their jobs just to find room for another employee.

Under the company's guidelines, Williams determined that four sales positions had to be eliminated. Two of these reps took the third option, accepting a demotion in the same geographical division. One rep, an older man, selected the alternative of early retirement.

The fourth rep, Rose Blanchard, did not wish to go quietly. Blanchard had worked as a Taylor sales rep for 12 years, and she had previously worked in sales for another firm in the industry. Blanchard was 59 years old, married, and had no children. She was the principal breadwinner of her family, as her husband had suffered a debilitating injury some 20 years ago. She was a successful sales rep who consistently produced good results. Williams hated to eliminate her position, but her territory no longer called for a rep to handle it exclusively. Williams tried very hard to find her a new position.

The problem was that Blanchard could not afford to retire, nor did she want to. She refused to move, as she and her husband owned quite a bit of land in the area. Blanchard also would not stand for a demotion back to a "lousy office job," as she put it. Williams had found several positions for her in other divisions, but Blanchard refused to relocate geographically.

Williams knew that he could face legal problems if Blanchard were let go. Not only was she a female, but she was also an older employee. "Great," Williams thought, "an age and sex discrimination lawsuit!" Williams knew that his guidelines for eliminating Blanchard's job were fair—but would a jury agree?

Blanchard proposed that she be given Tom Rafferty's territory because she had been with the company longer and had done a better job. Rafferty had been with Taylor for four years, since his graduation from college. Although he was not at all well liked by his peers, his performance results were considered satisfactory.

However, Lloyd Williams felt that he could not release Rafferty just because Blanchard wanted his job. In this downsizing process, company policy stated that no employee was to be bumped from his or her position to accommodate someone else.

As Williams left the office, one further demoralizing thought came to mind. "The only rep who was let go from my division and from the company was Sam Anderson, who accepted the early retirement option. But Anderson may have felt that he was pushed into that choice. So chalk up one more for Blanchard's potential sex and age discrimination suit!"

*Question:*

How should Lloyd Williams handle the Rose Blanchard situation?

*Case 13-3*

## THE CLUB AT MORNINGSIDE
### Impact of difficult economic times

"I don't know how I can keep our salespeople working for us under the circumstances. We haven't sold a single home in over a year. They've made no money, yet we have to keep the sales office open every day." Kyle Coltman was talking about the plight of Morningside's three-person sales force to Pat Smith, an associate in another real estate venture that had been completed some 10 years previously.

Morningside was a planned, gated community of 357 homes built around a Jack Nicklaus Signature golf course located in Rancho Mirage, California. The first homes built in 1989 were priced between $500,000 and $800,000 and they sold in an orderly manner. By 1993, the homes being built were priced from $1,000,000 to $1,800,000. Morningside was created by a partnership of Trojan Ventures and Equitable Life Insurance Company. Trojan Ventures was a partnership headed by Ed Johnson and Kyle Coltman. Mr. Johnson had retired. Equitable bought out Trojan's interests in 1992 but retained Kyle Coltman to wind up the Morningside venture. There were 27 homes yet to sell, priced between $1,500,000 and $1,800,000. The lower-priced homes had been sold.

Equitable was following the same procedures that had been used in developing The Springs, its highly successful, planned, gated community across the street on Morningside Drive. In each case, Trojan Ventures retained the rights to operate a resale office as well as a model home and sales complex on the premises.

The sales complex at Morningside had to be staffed seven days a week from 8 A.M. to dusk. It required at least three people in order to have at least one person there at all times. Usually, a receptionist was also needed. The resale office located at The Springs had only two people staffing it. However, it was no longer concerned with operating a model home complex, but only with resales.

In the summer of 1998 Morningside had 84 homes out of 815 units in the development that were for sale in the $350,000 to $500,000 price bracket. It sold 33 units in 1997 for an average price of $420,000. The real estate agent would receive half of whatever the brokerage received and that depended upon what broker listed the property. Commissions were split 50–50 between the listing broker and the selling broker. Then each broker would split with the agents who listed and sold the property. An agent who listed and sold a property would receive about 3 percent of the sale price, or $12,000 on a $400,000 home. List and sell a million-dollar home and the agent could pocket $30,000. Much money could be made in good years.

Unfortunately, 1997 was not a good year. Nothing was selling in Morningside. The California real estate depression had hit the development particularly hard. Few people were buying million-dollar homes.

Pat Smith could not refrain from observing, "Kyle, you are priced way over market. You're living in the past. I know that a lot of your profits are sitting there in those houses, but the market doesn't care about that."

"I know that! We need to drop the prices $300,000 or so, but unfortunately now that Equitable is calling all the shots and my boss lives in Atlanta and not here, I'm not free to cut the prices. But I am working on it right now," Kyle admitted. He continued, "I know it's really tough on the agents showing up for work every day when there is no one coming through the models. No action, no sales. What do they do? I can't put them to work on other things, because we don't pay them anything except when they sell a house. We've lost most of our people and I'm afraid that I'll lose the three agents who have stayed loyal if I don't do something. They are hanging around for the money to be made when things pick up again, and we move the remaining 27 houses."

Pat nodded but thought that Kyle was unrealistic. The prices of the remaining homes would have to be lowered much more than Kyle was contemplating. Pat said, "What do the agents say to you about the situation?"

"Every day all I hear is 'lower the prices, lower the prices.' They want to be free to sell them for whatever they can. They'd give them away if I let them," Kyle replied. He asked, "You're supposed to be an expert in managing sales operations. What can I do?"

**Question:**

What advice would you give Mr. Coltman?

---

*Case 13-4*

## OLD DAN RICKER

### Problems with a mature sales rep

"It's time to talk about old Dan. He's not cutting it, not getting the job done these days. You've been protecting him, but I had accounting send up his numbers. He hasn't met a quota for two years. He serves some of our most important accounts. Why haven't you done something about it before this?" Kurt Diamond, CEO of Diamond Housewares, demanded of Dave Mitchell, the company's sales manager.

Diamond Housewares had been formed in 1950 by Mr. Diamond's father to sell a line of imported products, all designed to be used in operating a home. As the years passed, the company began to develop its own products and have them manufactured by subcontractors. As plastic and rubberized goods increasingly displaced metal products in the housewares industry, the company purchased a financially distressed, local plastic injection molding company in Chicago, Illinois. It began making some of its own products. Kurt Diamond spent most of his time in production creating and making new products. Sales were left in the hands of Mr. Mitchell.

The company was financially sound and highly profitable due to the steady introduction of new products that found ready market acceptance. The company did little advertising, preferring instead to spend its promotional money at the houseware industry's trade shows. It maintained sales offices and showrooms in the major trade marts. Dan Ricker was the sales rep working from the Dallas Trade Mart, an important market for the company. One of his key accounts was the J.C. Penney Company, headquartered in Dallas.

Dan Ricker had been hired in 1956 when he graduated from the University of Oklahoma as a marketing major. Dan's father and Kurt's father had been close friends, so Dan and Kurt had known each other most of their lives, but they were not considered close since they had contrasting personalities. Kurt was an introvert and socialized little, while Dan had an outgoing personality and many friends. Dan developed a highly profitable business for the company in the southwestern territory by working long and hard developing the department stores and the emerging mass distributing firms as accounts.

Dave Mitchell was more than a little surprised at Mr. Diamond's sudden interest in Dan Ricker. It was the first time he had taken any interest in the sales force for a long time. Usually he had something to say only when sales were down, which fortunately they seldom were, or when one of Mr. Diamond's new products flopped. Of course, any product failure was the fault of the sales force and had nothing to do with the product. Dave understood how that game was played, which was one reason he had kept his job for so long. He had joined the company in 1959 and was promoted to sales manager in the Chicago home office in 1980 after spending 20 years working out of Pittsburgh, Pennsylvania. He later learned that Mr. Diamond had offered the sales managership to Dan but Dan had turned it down for two reasons: He didn't want to take the pay cut and he didn't want to move to Chicago. Being paid on a straight commission, Dan's earnings had been substantially higher than the sales manager's salary. However, that had changed. His earnings had declined with his sales volume.

Dave paused after Kurt stopped talking and then said, "Do you want an answer or was that just some therapy we went through?" He didn't wait for a verbal answer. One was written on Kurt's face. "OK, no need to give you the Dan Ricker history. We both know how much he has done for us. He's been a top producer for years. And he has been loyal to us. Time and again, some competitor has tried to lure him away from us but he's been one of us all the way. So don't you think we should cut him a little slack, give him time to work out his problems?"

Kurt replied, "I recall a punch line that went 'What have you done for me lately?' And what do you mean problems?" Kurt asked. "What's going on?"

"Evidently more things than Dan can handle all at once. First, you remember his daughter Kay and that guy she married. Well, he lost his job at IBM and hasn't been able to find another one. He's been out of work for a year. They had to sell their home and have moved in with Dan, two kids and all. So now Dan is out about $40,000 a year trying to keep Kay's family intact. If that wasn't enough, his son Matt has gotten into some serious legal trouble with substance abuse and that's also costing Dan a lot of money and worry. To top that off, I'm not so sure about his health. He won't say anything, but he's dragging a bit, doesn't look too good to me."

Dave shook his head as he continued, "I've talked with him about his problems but what can I say. I haven't got any solutions for them except to let him work them out. It'll take some time, but these things will work themselves out. Dan's no fool and he's working on them. Then he'll be back with us full time."

Kurt responded, "Come on. Give me a break. Dan is over the hill. He's a tired old man. Tired of working. Tired of hustling and for what? For a few more bucks for us? Get real!" He continued, "If you don't do something we'll be losing some key accounts. Lose the Penney account and ... well, never mind."

The discussion was suddenly interrupted by a telephone call for Dave. It was from the buyer at J.C. Penney.

### Questions:

1. What should Dave Mitchell do about Dan Ricker?

2. Pretend you're Dan Ricker. What would you do in response to what was recommended in the first question?

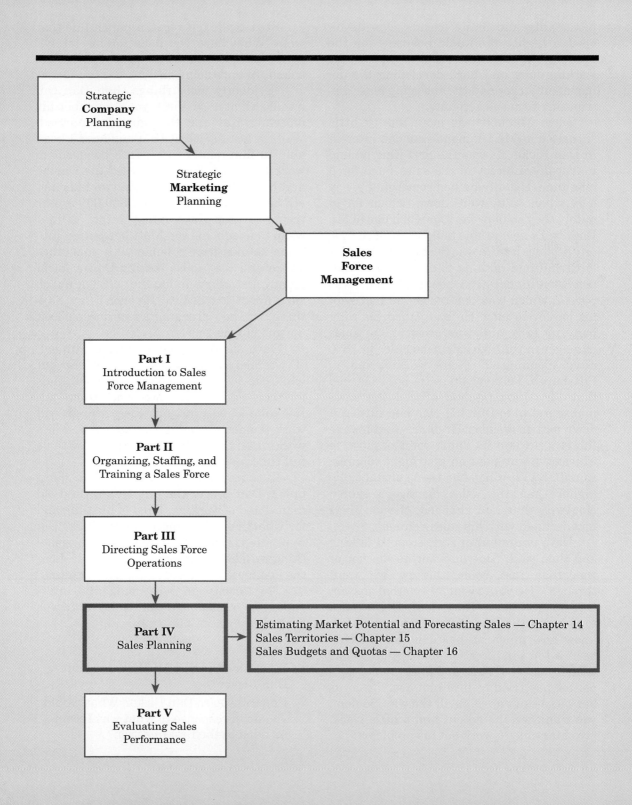

Strategic **Company** Planning

Strategic **Marketing** Planning

**Sales Force Management**

**Part I**
Introduction to Sales Force Management

**Part II**
Organizing, Staffing, and Training a Sales Force

**Part III**
Directing Sales Force Operations

**Part IV**
Sales Planning

Estimating Market Potential and Forecasting Sales — Chapter 14
Sales Territories — Chapter 15
Sales Budgets and Quotas — Chapter 16

**Part V**
Evaluating Sales Performance

# SALES PLANNING

The first stage in the sales management process is planning. This is followed by implementing the plans through sales operations. The process ends with an evaluation of the sales performance. Sales planning involves establishing sales goals and then deciding which strategies and tactics to use to reach them.

However, a company manages its sales force within the context of its total marketing program. Therefore, the path taken in *sales force* planning depends on the company's strategic *marketing* planning. The strategic marketing planning, in turn, depends on the *overall company* planning. Thus, sales executives take their sales planning cues from the firm's strategic marketing planning and corporate planning.

Our coverage of sales planning starts with determining market potentials and sales forecasting in Chapter 14. In Chapter 15, we deal with designing sales territories, assigning sales reps to these territories, and routing the salespeople. Sales budgets and quotas are the topics covered in Chapter 16.

# CHAPTER 14

# Estimating Market Potential and Forecasting Sales

The past is not dead, it isn't even past.
**William Faulkner**

The foundation of the planning efforts of most companies is a sales forecast. The importance of sales forecasting is clearly shown at Otis Elevator Company, a world leader in the development and marketing of elevators and moving stairway systems. According to Heinz Dickens, Sales Manager of International Operations at Otis, sales forecasting at the International Division of Otis begins with estimates of sales for the coming year. These are provided by salespeople and sales managers in the company's territories. Many of the sales territories include whole foreign countries.

Otis, like many large companies, uses its sales forecasts to allocate resources across different functional areas. Production uses sales forecasts to develop production schedules and quantity requirements and to regulate inventories. Finance uses the forecasts to set operating budgets and to project cash flows. Sales forecasts are used by human resources to establish hiring levels and by marketing to allocate resources across different marketing activities.

Sales forecasting at Otis is not an exact science, says Dickens. Adjustments to the forecast for elevators and moving stairways in the International Division are often made as unforeseen events surface, such as wars and changes in governments. These events can dampen or stimulate sales of the company's products. Otis tries to improve forecasting accuracy by including many different types of information in the sales forecasts. For example, monthly reports are compiled on the progress of negotiations between the company and its potential customers in an effort to improve the accuracy of sales forecasts. "Though we may be off-target sometimes," says Dickens, "our manufacturing operation would come to a standstill if we did not produce a reasonably good sales forecast."

The problem confronting Otis Elevator year after year is to develop an accurate sales forecast that helps managers make sound business decisions. In this chapter, we will help you understand the importance of forecasting to the firm, illustrate types of forecasting methods used by firms, and discuss several guidelines on the selection of a sales forecasting method.

# ◼ SALES FORECASTING AND STRATEGIC AND OPERATIONAL PLANNING

The marketing goals and strategies—the core of a marketing plan—must be established before a sales forecast is made. The sales forecasts will differ, depending on whether the marketing goal is to liquidate inventory or to expand the firm's market share by aggressive advertising or some other goal.

Once the sales forecast is prepared, it becomes the key factor in all *operational* planning throughout the company. Forecasting is the basis of sound budgeting. Financial planning for working capital requirements, plant utilization, and other needs is based on anticipated sales. The scheduling of all production resources and facilities, such as setting labor needs and purchasing raw materials, depends on the sales forecast.

# ◼ EXPLANATION OF BASIC TERMS

Before we discuss the methods used in forecasting, we need to define and explain some of the basic terminology used in forecasting sales. Because the terms are closely related and used loosely in business, they frequently cause misunderstandings among managers.

## Market Potential and Sales Potential

What do we mean when we speak of a "potential" market for a product? **Market potential** is the total expected sales of a given product or service for the *entire industry* in a specific market over a stated period of time. To be complete and meaningful, the definition of market potential (and sales potential and the sales forecast, which we will discuss soon) must include four elements:

1. The item being marketed (the product, service, idea, person, or location).
2. Sales for the entire industry in dollars or product units.
3. A specific time period.
4. A specific market delineated either geographically or by type of customer or both.

For example, the market potential for beer in the United States in the year 1999 is expected to be 194 million barrels. Note that the statement about the market potential of beer includes information on each of the four points discussed above. Market potential for beer also could be stated for blue-collar men, white-collar women, or men and women ages 21 to 25 years in the state of Indiana.

**Sales potential** refers to the maximum share (or percentage) of market potential that an *individual firm* can reasonably expect to achieve. For example, Budweiser beer accounted for 40 percent of the approximately

180 million barrels of beer consumed in the United States in 1998. It is reasonable to argue that Budweiser beer's sales potential is close to 40 percent of the market in the coming years. When we speak of a company's sales potential, we must again specify the product, market, and time period.

Market potential is a total-industry concept, while sales potential refers to an individual firm. Thus we may speak of the "market potential" for beer, and the "sales potential" (or market share) for Budweiser beer. Market potential and sales potential are equal in the case of a monopoly. In most industries, however, market potential and sales potential are different since there are many firms competing in the market. As discussed in the next chapter, it is sales potential which provides the basis for designing sales territories.

## Sales Forecast

A **sales forecast** is an estimate of sales (in dollars or units) that an individual firm expects to achieve during a specified forthcoming time period, in a stated market, and under a proposed marketing plan. A forecast may be made for an entire product line or for individual items within the line. Sales may be forecast for a company's total market or for individual market segments.

At first glance, the company's sales potential and sales forecast may appear to be the same. But usually that is not the case. The sales potential is what would be achieved under ideal conditions. The sales forecast typically is less than the sales potential for many different reasons. The company's production facilities may be too limited to allow the firm to reach its full sales potential. Also, the firm's financial resources may be inadequate to realize the full sales potential in the current period.

## Estimating Potentials and Forecasting Sales

For certain strategic decisions, the estimation of the market and sales potential is more relevant than the sales forecast. For example, if a firm wants to decide whether or not to market a particular innovation, it will first estimate the total market potential for that innovation. (Note that in this situation, market potential equals sales potential because there isn't any competition.) If the market potential is large enough, the firm will plan to introduce the innovation. Then, because there isn't any sales history, the firm will forecast sales based on its experience with past product introductions, test market information, and marketing plans for the new product. Decisions about which geographic markets to enter will also be based on estimations of market potentials.

However, once a firm has achieved a certain level of sales in a particular market, the firm usually takes the previously determined potential as a given. It then focuses on developing the most accurate sales forecast possible.

## AN INTERNATIONAL PERSPECTIVE

The western European countries joined together in a common market in 1993. As a result, many of the trade barriers which existed between countries were eliminated and this made it easier for U.S. companies to enter the European market. Potential for U.S. products in these markets is very large. However, viewing this European market as a single entity is shortsighted.

The demand for products across the European community will continue to vary significantly due to differences in preferences, habits, culture, climate, and incomes. Understanding these differences is critical to estimating the potential for U.S. products in Europe. Researchers Ryans and Rau have developed a taxonomy of Euro-consumer clusters that are emerging in Europe. The descriptions of these clusters provides a basis for understanding differences in European buying preferences and patterns.

**Euro-Consumer Clusters**

*Cluster 1:* United Kingdom and Ireland

- Northeastern Europe
- Average income
- Age profile—average of EC
- Common language—English

*Cluster 2:* Central and northern France, southern Belgium, central Germany, and Luxembourg

- North Central Europe—average income
- Low proportion of middle—aged people and high proportion of older people
- French and German languages

*Cluster 3:* Spain and Portugal

- Southwestern Europe
- Young population
- Lower than average income
- Spanish and Portuguese languages

*Cluster 5:* Greece and Southern Italy

- Southeastern Europe
- Lower than average income
- Young population
- Greek and Italian languages

*Cluster 4:* Southern Germany, Northern Italy, Southeastern France

- South Central Europe
- High proportion of middle-aged people
- Higher than average income
- German, French, Italian languages

*Cluster 6:* Denmark, Northern Germany, The Netherlands, and Northern Belgium

- Northern Europe and Switzerland
- Very high income
- High proportion of middle-aged people
- Multilingual—Scandinavian, French, Italian, and German languages

John K. Ryans and Pradeep A. Rau, *Marketing Strategies for the New Europe: A North American Perspective in 1992* (Chicago: American Marketing Association, 1990).

Also it should be noted that the *determination of the sales forecasts and sales budgets* (discussed in Chapter 16) *should be an iterative process.* As mentioned at the beginning of the chapter, the sales forecast provides the basis for preparing detailed sales budgets. However, the amount that the company plans to spend on marketing has a significant impact on the amount of sales the company will be able to achieve. Therefore, changes in marketing expenditures must be incorporated into the preparation of the sales forecasts. In the remainder of this chapter we discuss the procedures for estimating potential and forecasting sales.

# ESTIMATING MARKET AND SALES POTENTIALS

Under conditions of great uncertainty, such as those which exist when a firm is trying to market an innovation, it is very difficult to develop accurate forecasts. Often these estimates are inaccurate. If the innovation hits a market favorably, all projections were probably too low; if it misses the market, no sales projection was sufficiently conservative.

The three fundamental techniques for estimating market and sales potentials for a product are market-factor derivation, surveys of buyer intentions, and test markets. Each of these methods is based on an analysis of the customer. Therefore, the customer analysis is described first, followed by a discussion of each method.

## Customer Analysis

The starting point in any customer analysis is to determine who will use the product and to identify all possible characteristics of the users. A distinction must be made between the person who actually *buys* the product and the individual who *uses* it. The market potential is based on the individual or firm the product is intended for. Although many women buy shirts for men, the market potential for men's shirts is determined by the number of men users, not by the number of women buyers.

Are the users household consumers, industrial users, or both? If they are household consumers, the seller may want to classify them further by demographics such as age, sex, marital status, area of residence, income, occupation, religion, and education. Life-style information may also be used, such as the types of exercise and recreation in which the user is interested. In the case of businesses selling to businesses, information on the types and quantities of products manufactured and sold by the businesses to their end users must be collected. The names and positions of the persons influencing the purchase decision and information about the company's competitors must be gathered. Most companies have compiled such information through periodic contact with their customers or through the use of marketing research.

Performing a customer analysis also requires a determination of why customers are buying the product and their buying habits. Most products are purchased to fulfill some need. Understanding these needs can improve the accuracy of market potential estimates and sales forecasts. For example, consumer sensitivity to the prices of grocery products has resulted in greater sales of private-label products. In response to consumers' concerns about price, consumer product giants, such as Phillip Morris and

Procter & Gamble, chopped prices of their products to stay competitive. In this case, understanding that price is playing an increasingly important role in consumer purchase decisions will help companies make more accurate forecasts.[1] In addition, the frequency of purchase and quantity of units purchased should be determined. Many products are purchased once or twice a week, like milk and bread, while other products are purchased every 8 to 10 years, like air conditioners and water heaters.

## Market-Factor Derivation

The market-factor derivation method for determining the size of a potential market begins with a market factor. A **market factor** is an item or element in a market that (1) causes the demand for a product or service or (2) is related to the demand for it. To illustrate, the number of births is a market factor underlying the demand for playpens. That is, this element is related to the number of playpens that can be sold. Using births as a market factor, a manufacturer of playpens would estimate the sales potential for playpens as follows:

| | |
|---|---|
| Estimated number of births, 2000: | 4,000,000 |
| Times: Percent who buy playpens | $\times$   0.33 |
| Market potential | 1,320,000 |
| Times: Potential market share | $\times$   0.30 |
| Sales potential | 396,000 |

An independent supermarket operator in Nashville, Tennessee, computed the store's sales potential by using *Sales & Marketing Management*'s estimate of food sales in that metropolitan area as the market factor.[2] The store did not sell to the entire area but appealed only to a region in which about 15 percent of the population resided. So the operator estimated the market potential to be about $220 million. Since three other large supermarkets plus some smaller stores competed in that same area, the operator set 20 percent as the store's probable share of the market. Therefore, the sales potential was $44.1 million for the year.

| | |
|---|---|
| Nashville food sales | $1,469,407,000 |
| Times: Percent of market covered | $\times$       0.15 |
| Market potential | $   220,414,800 |
| Times: Potential market share | $\times$       0.20 |
| Sales potential | $     44,082,960 |

This market-factor derivation technique for determining market and sales potentials has several advantages. First, the validity of the method is high. The method is usually founded on some valid statistics that have relatively little error. This is in direct contrast to two methods described later—the survey of buyer intentions and the test-market methods—in which the basic foundations of the process can be criticized. Another favorable aspect of this technique is that it is fairly simple, requires little statistical analysis, and is relatively inexpensive to use.

It should be noted that the market-factor method, like the other methods of estimating potentials, can be used as the basis of the sales forecast. In order to forecast sales, the company must estimate what portion of its sales potential it can reasonably expect to achieve in a given time period.

## Surveys of Buyer Intentions

The survey of buyer intentions technique for determining potentials consists of contacting potential customers and questioning them about whether or not they would purchase the product or service at the price asked.

One manufacturer contemplating the production of an aluminum playpen for babies used this technique. The playpen was to be made exactly like the ordinary wooden playpens on the market, except that aluminum tubing would be used instead of the wooden bars. Since the cost of the unit would be higher than that of the wooden units, the manufacturer wanted to know two things. First, how many people would buy such a product if it were placed on the market at the retail price of $59.95? Second, what did customers think the price of such a product should be?

A survey was conducted through personal interviews with 240 parents of infants. The results showed that 170 of the 240 (approximately 71 percent) were interested in such a product. However, they indicated that the price would have to be $39.95 to capture that size of market. The average (mean) price quoted was $45. However, this price would eliminate half of the respondents who showed interest in the product. At the retail price of $59.95, only 10 people said they would be interested in purchasing the product. Even if all 10 did buy at $59.95, that still represents only 4 percent of the market.

The survey indicated that only about one-third of all childbearing families purchase playpens. This indicates that the total market potential for aluminum playpens would not be more than approximately 52,800 units at best. This figure was derived by multiplying the total number of births per year, 4 million, by 0.33 and taking 4 percent of the result. This simple calculation showed the manufacturer that market interest in the playpen was sufficient to warrant further investigation. The manufacturer had established previously that the firm would be satisfied if it sold only 5,000 units per year. This seemed possible on the basis of the survey.

The primary advantage of this method is that it is based on information obtained directly from the people who will ultimately purchase or not purchase the product or service. Major disadvantages of this method are its cost and time-consuming execution. For the sales manager who needs a quick idea of the market potential of a product, the survey method is not suitable. For the manufacturer who intends to distribute nationally, consumer surveys can easily run into thousands of dollars and take three to six months to complete. Furthermore, surveys of buying intentions are hazardous undertakings. It is easy for the respondents to say that they would buy a certain product. But the acid test is whether or not they are willing to spend money to back up those intentions.

## Test Markets

Test marketing involves introducing and marketing a new product in a market that is similar to the company's other markets. For example, Indianapolis, Indiana, and Columbus, Ohio, are often used as test markets by companies because their socioeconomic and demographic profiles are similar to the profiles of many other cities in the United States. The demand for the product in the test market then will be used to forecast sales of the product in other markets.

Although test markets take considerable time and money, they are probably the most accurate method of estimating the sales potential for certain products. The reason is that a test market actually requires the buyers to spend their money, and this is the acid test of most marketing situations. The other methods discussed require an estimate of what share of the market the product will achieve. Frequently, these estimates are merely guesses. The test market eliminates this guessing.

In the world of new ventures, venture capitalists view the first stage of development in which the product or service is initially offered for sale as a test market. Jerry Zimmer started ZDC, a computerized system for managing and measuring the energy used in master-metered apartment houses, in Boulder, Colorado, with a $60,000 initial investment. He sold about $1 million worth of his systems in the Denver market area during the first year of operation. On the basis of that test, the company was able to raise an additional $500,000 to expand market coverage. The first several years of the life of many new products is essentially a test market that proves that people will buy the product and that it is profitable.

The one obvious advantage of the test-market technique is that it results directly in a sales potential for products under consideration. However, a test market requires a considerable amount of effort and time before results are known. Many products that require extensive investment in fixed assets before they are introduced to the market cannot be evaluated by this method. Similarly, test markets provide poor evaluations of products that require time to gain acceptance or have a low rate of consumption. The test market is used mainly when a relatively small number of units can be produced at a minimum cost.

## ▣ TERRITORY POTENTIALS

Once the total sales potential has been determined, the sales manager usually wants to divide it among the various territorial divisions. This allows the manager to allocate selling efforts properly and to evaluate the relative performance of each district. The usual method for this is to use some pertinent market factor or index broken down by small areas.

A **market index** is a market factor, expressed as a percentage, or in some other quantitative form, relative to some base figure. A market index may be based on two or more market factors. For example, the "buy-

■ **FIGURE 14-1**    *Sales & Marketing Management's* data service information

## Just a sample of all the Data Service gives you.

### POPULATION, EFFECTIVE BUYING INCOME, RETAIL SALES, AND BUYING POWER INDEX [BPI]

| S&MM ESTIMATES METRO AREA County | 12/31/88 Population (Thousands) | % Of US | % Change 1980-88 | Pop Per Sq Mi (Density) | % White | 12/31/88 Households (Thousands) | % Of US | 1988 EBI ($000) | % Of US | 1988 Retail Sales ($000) | % Of US | Buying Power Index (BPI) | EPP (Economy Priced Products) | MPP (Moderate Priced Products) | PPP (Premium Priced Products) |
|---|---|---|---|---|---|---|---|---|---|---|---|---|---|---|---|
| **ALABAMA** | | | | | | | | | | | | | | | |
| ANNISTON | 125.3 | .0505 | 4.6 | 205 | 80.2 | 45.2 | .0489 | 1,109,557 | .0362 | 512,442 | 0313 | .0376 | .0543 | .0488 | .0347 |
| Calhoun | 125.3 | 0505 | 4.6 | 205 | 80.2 | 45.2 | 0489 | 1,109,557 | 0362 | 512,442 | 0313 | 0376 | 0543 | 0488 | 0347 |
| BIRMINGHAM | 934.9 | .3771 | 5.8 | 233 | 70.8 | 357.2 | .3870 | 9,653,194 | .3150 | 5,266,623 | 3216 | .3295 | .4222 | .3737 | .3350 |
| Blount | 42.1 | 0170 | 15.5 | 65 | 97.9 | 15.6 | 0169 | 300,507 | 0098 | 99,422 | 0061 | 0101 | 0204 | 0158 | 0081 |

### TELEVISION MARKETS [ADIs]: TOTALS AND 1993 PROJECTIONS

| S&MM ESTIMATES S&MM ARBITRON TV MARKET (ADI) | 12/31/88 Population (Thous) | % Of US | Projected 12/31/93 Population (Thous) | % Change 1988-1993 | 12/31/88 Households (Thous) | Projected 12/31/93 Households (Thous) | 1988 EBI ($000) | % Of US | Projected 1993 EBI ($000) | 1988 Retail Sales ($000) | Projected 1993 Retail Sales ($000) | Buying Power Index 1988 | 1993 |
|---|---|---|---|---|---|---|---|---|---|---|---|---|---|---|
| **MICHIGAN** | | | | | | | | | | | | | | |
| ALPENA | 42.1 | .0170 | 41.8 | -.7 | 15.9 | 16.4 | 410,460 | .0134 | 605,723 | 201,832 | 282,020 | .0138 | .0132 |
| DETROIT | 4,670.2 | 1.8838 | 4,663.1 | -.2 | 1,727.0 | 1,768.7 | 60,322,475 | 1.9687 | 88,866,408 | 32,818,541 | 48,636,450 | 1.9622 | 1.9094 |
| FLINT - SAGINAW - BAY CITY | 1,266.2 | .5107 | 1,252.2 | -1.1 | 455.8 | 463.0 | 13,238,393 | .4321 | 19,270,380 | 8,035,682 | 11,672,748 | .4652 | .4462 |

ing power index" developed by *Sales & Marketing Management* is based on three factors—population, effective buying income, and retail sales (see Figure 14-1). This index, like many published indexes, provides information broken down in many ways: regions of the country, states, cities, counties, and metropolitan areas. This index is primarily designed to aid the executive in allocating activities among areas.

Figure 14-2 provides an example of how the buying power index is used to allocate total sales potential among territories. A manufacturer of men's suits determined that national sales potential for its suits was $25 million for the next year. The management then determined the percentage of national retail sales that occur in each of its nine sales territories and multiplied the percent by $25 million to yield sales potential on a territory-by-territory basis.

In forecasting sales for industrial products or business-to-business goods or services, the Standard Industrial Classification (SIC) is often used. Anyone doing research in industrial marketing should become familiar with SIC data.

The federal government has classified businesses into a numerical ordering system. Under this system, each firm is assigned a four-digit number on the basis of its main line of business. Then data collected by most government agencies are classified and published by those numbers. For example, as shown in Figure 14-3, SIC 28 contains all chemicals and allied products. The drug segment of that industry carries the three-digit number 283. The pharmaceutical preparations companies are numbered 2834. By referring to 2834 in the SIC, companies selling products to firms in the SIC 2834 can discover how many firms (potential customers) are in-

---

■ **FIGURE 14-2**

**Division of sales potential among territories using retail sales as a market index**

| Territory | Percentage of Total Retail Sales* | Territorial Sales Potential $25M × Col 1 ÷ 100 |
|---|---|---|
| New England | 5.3 | $ 1,325,000 |
| Middle Atlantic | 13.4 | 3,350,000 |
| East North Central | 16.9 | 4,225,000 |
| West North Central | 7.3 | 1,825,000 |
| South Atlantic | 19.2 | 4,800,000 |
| East South Central | 5.7 | 1,425,000 |
| West South Central | 10.5 | 2,675,000 |
| Mountain | 6.4 | 1,600,000 |
| Pacific | 15.3 | 3,825,000 |
| | 100.0 | $25,000,000 |

*From "Survey of Buying Power," *Sales & Marketing Management,* August 1997, p. 54.

■ FIGURE 14-3     **The SIC system**

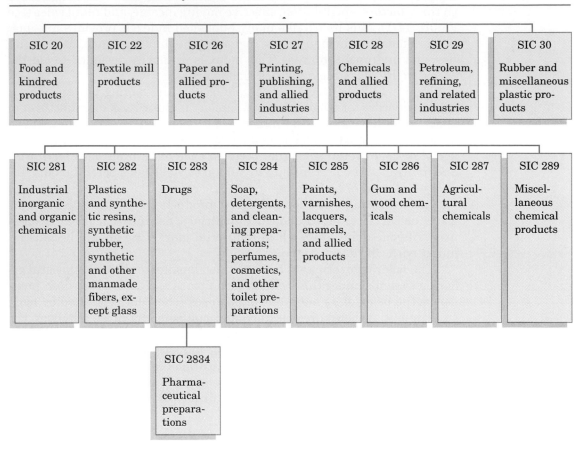

cluded in that category, where they are located, sales volume, the number of employees, and much more. Much of the information can be used to help estimate potentials.

Firms also can use experts to meet their data needs. A large number of commercial data supply and marketing research companies supply information to businesses that can help them with their forecasting needs.

## SALES FORECASTING

After the market or sales potential for a product or service is determined, management can make a sales forecast. This is an essential step in sales planning.

## Importance of Sales Forecasting

As illustrated by the discussion of sales forecasting at Otis Elevator, production, personnel, finance, and all other departments plan their work and determine their requirements for the coming period based on the sales forecast. The sales forecast also plays a critical role in sales force planning. The sales forecast helps sales executives determine the budget for the department, and it also influences sales quotas and compensation of salespeople.

If the forecast is in error, the plans based on it will be too. For example, if it is overly optimistic, the organization can suffer great losses because of overexpenditure of funds in anticipation of revenues that are not forthcoming. If the sales forecast is too low, the firm may not be prepared to provide what the market demands. This means that the company will be forgoing profits and giving its competitors a bigger market share. Clearly, valid sales forecasts can play a major role in the success of the company.

## Difficulty of Sales Forecasting

The difficulty of developing an accurate sales forecast varies from situation to situation. When sales of a product are very stable from one period to the next, a sales forecast for an upcoming period is not difficult to perform. When sales of a product fluctuate dramatically from period to period, accurate sales forecasts are difficult to develop. Accurate sales forecasts are also difficult to attain for new products since a historical sales record is lacking. Developing a sales forecast for an existing product is less difficult since the company has some historical data to guide them in forecasting its sales.

## Sales Forecasting Periods

Sales forecasts are commonly made for periods of three months (quarterly), six months, or one year. Usually the sales forecasting period coincides with the firm's fiscal year since it is used as a basis for planning expenditures. However, some firms find that their operations cycle is considerably shorter than a year and prefer to forecast for that cycle. For example, four cycles or seasons are present in the apparel trades. The firms produce goods for one season and then completely sell out those goods before starting the next season's work. Apparel firms are concerned only with the coming season's activity since they are buying goods and labor for that period only.

Firms usually undertake long-run sales estimates to plan capital expenditures. Top management often seeks knowledge about the long-term sales outlook before undertaking any plant expansion. When the forecasting horizon is short, one year or less, forecasting accuracy is likely to be greater than when the forecasting period is long.

## Factors Influencing the Sales Forecast

The sales forecast must take into consideration changes that have occurred or are anticipated that may affect sales. These changes can be placed in four general categories:

- Marketing plans.
- Conditions within the industry.
- Conditions within the market.
- General business conditions.

### Marketing Plans

Any changes in the price structure, channels of distribution, promotional plans, products, or other internal marketing policies may influence future sales. The forecaster must estimate the quantitative extent of these influences. It may be known, for example, that the firm will soon have to raise prices. Although this action will reduce unit volume, total dollar volume might go up or down, depending on the product's price elasticity. Therefore, formulating a realistic sales forecast is impossible without taking price changes into consideration. If the firm planned to alter its channels of distribution or its advertising expenditures, these actions would influence future sales.

### Conditions within the Industry

A firm obtains its sales volume from total industry sales. Therefore, any change within the industry has an impact on the firm. New producers in an industry may mean that whatever volume they gain must come from existing companies. Thus the sales forecast may have to be revised downward. If a competitor is planning to redesign its line of products, the firm must consider the possibility that the competitor may obtain a larger share of the market during the coming period.

### Market Conditions

If basic demand factors are in a slump, the future sales of the firm will be affected. The firm's manager must be aware of any basic changes in the primary demand for the industry's output. An analysis of future market conditions is particularly important if the concern sells to relatively few industries.

Mor Flo, a manufacturer of solar water heaters, saw its sales potential suddenly multiply several times when the nation suffered shortages of natural gas. And, as the price of gasoline soared, the sales potentials for the makers of compact cars expanded significantly. As gasoline prices dropped in 1986, sales of large cars increased.

*General Business Conditions*

A major influencing factor in future sales development is the general state of the economy. Basically, many of the methods of sales forecasting are simply reflections of overall opinion of what the general economy will be like during the coming period.

# SALES FORECASTING METHODS

The following methods may be used to forecast the sales of a product or service. The methods can be placed in three general categories. Survey methods rely on the opinions of experts, such as sales reps, sales executives, and the customers who will be making purchase decisions. Mathematical methods apply mathematical and statistical techniques to historical data to forecast sales. Operational methods take information about the company's capacity and financial requirements to derive a sales forecast.

- Survey methods:
  - Executive opinion.
  - Sales force composite.
  - Buyers' intentions.
- Mathematical methods:
  - Moving average models.
  - Exponential smoothing models.
  - Regression models.
- Operational methods:
  - Test markets.
  - "Must-do" calculations.
  - Capacity-based calculations.

Figure 14-4 shows the sources of the data for the various methods. Surveys of buyers' intentions and test markets were discussed earlier in the chapter as they are methods which are used both for estimating potentials and for forecasting sales. They will not be discussed again, but each of the other methods is explained below.

## Executive Opinion

The **executive opinion** method of forecasting is the oldest and simplest technique known. It consists of obtaining the views of top executives regarding future sales—views that may or may not be supported by facts. Some administrators may have used forecasting methods, such as those we will discuss soon, to arrive at their opinions. Others may have formed their estimates largely by observation, experience, and intuition.

■ **FIGURE 14-4**

**Sales forecasting methods**

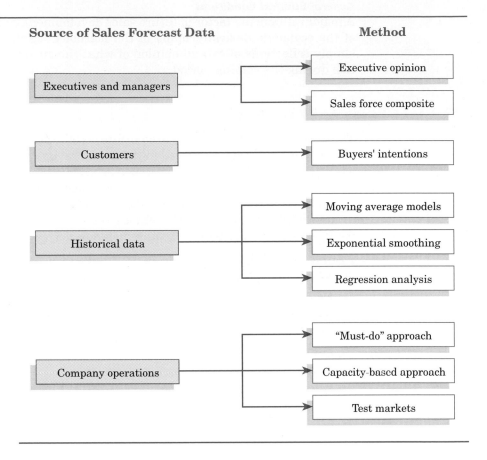

Source of Sales Forecast Data | Method

Executives and managers → Executive opinion / Sales force composite

Customers → Buyers' intentions

Historical data → Moving average models / Exponential smoothing / Regression analysis

Company operations → "Must-do" approach / Capacity-based approach / Test markets

The forecasts made by the executives are averaged to yield one forecast for all executives or the differences are reconciled through discussions among executives. For example, midlevel managers and executives at Blue Cross of California develop sales forecasts every year, beginning in June and ending in October. Any variations in estimating the demand for Blue Cross's products are resolved in a meeting of the managers. The final forecast is then used to develop a financial plan for the coming year.[3]

The major advantage cited for this technique is that it is quick and easy to do. A survey of 150 firms found that 86 percent of the firms surveyed in the study used the executive opinion approach to forecast sales.[4] Perhaps because it is easy to use, the executive opinion method is especially popular among small- and medium-sized companies.

Despite its popularity, the executive opinion approach has several disadvantages. Many managers consider this method to be highly unscientific, little more than educated guesses. Many managers also argue that the executive opinion method requires too much management time since differing forecasts must be reconciled before a final forecast is made. Finally, the opinions of highly placed executives and executives with strong feelings may influence the final forecast more than executives who are more knowledgeable about the company's products.

### The Delphi Technique

A highly publicized technique developed by the Rand Corporation for predicting the future and for forecasting sales is the **Delphi technique.** In administering a Delphi forecast, a panel of "experts"—who are typically managers—is selected. Each expert is asked to make a prediction on some matter. The resulting set of forecasts is fed back to the experts. Then they are asked to make another prediction on the same matter, with the knowledge of the forecasts of the other experts. This process is repeated until the experts arrive at some consensus.[5]

## Sales Force Composite

This method is based on collecting an estimate from each salesperson of the products and/or services they expect to sell in the forecast period. The estimate may be made in consultation with sales executives and customers and/or based on the salesperson's intuition and experience. The individual forecasts of each salesperson are then aggregated to yield an overall forecast for the firm.

The **sales force composite method** places the responsibility for making the forecast in the hands of those who have to make it happen and who are closest to the market. Sales quotas and compensation which are based on these forecasts are likely to be regarded as fair by the reps. However, salespeople are often poor forecasters. They tend to be either overly optimistic or pessimistic. Unfortunately, the sales reps may not only be motivated to understate the forecast if their goals are based on it, but also they are often unaware of broader economic and company forces at work. Finally, the process takes much time from both management and the reps.

## Moving Average Technique

The simplest way to forecast sales is to forecast sales in the coming period to be equal to sales in the last period. Such a forecast assumes that the conditions in the last period will be the same as the conditions in the coming period. It is likely, however, that the factors affecting sales change from period to period. Hence it makes sense to take an average of sales from several periods to construct the sales forecast for the coming period. This approach is called the **moving average technique.** The moving average technique takes the form of the following:

$$\text{Sales}_{t+1} = 1/n(\text{sales}_t + \text{sales}_{t-1} + \ldots + \text{sales}_{t-n})$$

**Sales
managers
often work
with their
salespeople
to develop
accurate
forecasts.**

where sales$_{t+1}$ is forecasted sales, sales$_t$ is sales in the present period, sales$_{t-1}$ is sales in the period immediately past, and so on. The sales of the designated periods are summed and then divided by the number of periods to yield the average. When a forecast is developed for the next period, sales in the oldest period is dropped from the average and is replaced by actual sales in the newest period, hence the name *moving average*. The forecaster determines how many periods will be included in the average.

An example of the moving average technique is shown in Figure 14–5 for a toy manufacturer. Deseasonalized data from the past nine periods were employed. Most companies have historical data to which a moving average model can be applied. A two-period moving average was determined by averaging sales in the present period and the previous period. The first period for which a forecast can be developed was the third period and forecasted sales were $52,000. Sales in period 4 were forecasted to be $63,000. A three-period moving average model is also shown. Note the slight difference in forecasted sales between the two averages, which is to be expected given that an additional period was used to calculate the three-period model.

The most significant advantage of the moving average approach is that it is easy to compute. Moving average models provide accurate forecasts for products with stable sales histories, but are less accurate for products that experience dramatic changes in sales, since the sales forecast is based on an average of sales from several different periods. Moving average models are also unable to reflect the impact of factors that arise

## Seasonality in Sales

To improve the accuracy of sales forecasts, the influence of seasonality on sales must be eliminated. Seasonality refers to changes in sales that occur repeatedly in identifiable periods, such as changes that occur in specific months or quarters of the year. For example, sales of pumpkins, turkeys, and stuffing rise every October and November in anticipation of Thanksgiving, while sales of sunscreens and charcoal increase every spring and summer.

Seasonal influences can obscure the impact (or lack of impact) of company actions and can lead to less accurate sales forecasts. For example, a toy company runs a promotion in the third and fourth quarters of each year. Toy sales always increase in the fourth quarter of every year in response to the holidays. As a result, the company cannot determine whether the increase in sales in the fourth quarter is the result of the promotion or the natural increase in sales due to the holidays,

or both. By correcting for seasonality, the true effect of the company's actions on sales can be ascertained, which can lead to a more accurate sales forecast.

To correct for seasonality, seasonal indexes based on historical data are developed. The charts below provide an example of how an index is developed and applied to data for a small toy manufacturer. In chart A, the average sales of each quarter—$125,000 for the fourth quarter 1998, for example—was found and then divided by the average sales for all quarters—$61,000—to produce a seasonal index for each quarter—2.05 for the fourth quarter, for example. The index is then used to seasonally adjust the actual sales figures, as shown in chart B. Note the differences in sales after the deseasonalization has occurred. For example, sales in the first quarter of the first year are now $48,000 compared to $26,000 if no seasonal adjustment had been made.

### A. Determining seasonality of toy sales*

| | | | Year | | | Quarterly Average | Seasonal Index |
|---|---|---|---|---|---|---|---|
| Qtr | 1994 | 1995 | 1996 | 1997 | 1998 | | |
| 1 | 26 | 30 | 23 | 40 | 45 | 33 | 0.54† |
| 2 | 40 | 31 | 42 | 36 | 50 | 40 | 0.66 |
| 3 | 38 | 50 | 40 | 49 | 60 | 47 | 0.77 |
| 4 | 110 | 124 | 106 | 135 | 150 | 125 | 2.05 |

Overall quarterly average = 61

*In thousands of dollars.
†Quarterly average/overall average = 33/61 = 0.54, 40/61 = 0.66, etc.

### B. Deseasonalized toy sales

| | | | Year | | |
|---|---|---|---|---|---|
| Qtr | 1994 | 1995 | 1996 | 1997 | 1998 |
| 1 | 48* | 56 | 43 | 74 | 83 |
| 2 | 61 | 47 | 64 | 55 | 76 |
| 3 | 49 | 65 | 52 | 64 | 78 |
| 4 | 54 | 60 | 52 | 66 | 73 |

*Actual quarterly sales/seasonal index = 26/0.54 = 48, etc.

■ **FIGURE 14-5**       **Forecasting toy sales using the moving average method**

| Quarter/Year | 3/96 | 4/96 | 1/97 | 2/97 | 3/97 | 4/97 | 1/98 | 2/98 | 3/98 | 4/98 |
|---|---|---|---|---|---|---|---|---|---|---|
| Actual $ sales in thousands (deseasonalized) | 52 | 52 | 74 | 55 | 64 | 66 | 83 | 76 | 78 | |
| Two-period moving average | | | 52* | 63 | 65 | 60 | 65 | 75 | 80 | 77 |
| Three-period moving average | | | | 59† | 60 | 64 | 62 | 71 | 75 | 79 |

*$\frac{52 + 52}{2} = 52$

†$\frac{52 + 52 + 74}{3} = 59.3$

in the forecasted period that were not present in previous periods. For example, the moving average model could not predict a significant decrease in sales for the toy manufacturer due to the unexpected entry of a strong competitor into the market.

### Exponential Smoothing Models

The **exponential smoothing approach** to sales forecasting is closely related to the moving average approach. In moving average models, sales in each of the past periods has the same impact on the sales forecast. In exponential smoothing models, the forecaster can allow sales in certain periods to influence the forecast more than sales in other periods.

The general form of the exponential smoothing model is

$$\text{Sales}_{t+1} = (L) \text{ actual sales}_t + (1 - L)\text{forecasted sales}_t$$

The exponential smoothing model argues that forecasted sales is equal to actual sales in the present period times a smoothing constant $(L)$ plus $(1 - L)$ times forecasted sales in the present period. The key difference between smoothing models and moving average models lies in the application of the smoothing constant $(L)$. A smoothing constant with a high value (0.8) allows more recent periods (represented by actual sales in the present period) to influence the sales forecast more than sales in earlier periods (represented by forecasted sales in the present period), while a constant with a low value (0.2) allows earlier periods to influence forecasted sales more than sales in later periods. The forecaster determines the value of the constant based on a review of the data and the forecaster's intuition and knowledge about the similarity between conditions in the forecasted period and conditions in previous periods.

■ **FIGURE 14-6**    **Forecasting with an exponential smoothing model**

| | 3/96 | 4/96 | 1/97 | 2/97 | 3/97 | 4/97 | 1/98 | 2/98 | 3/98 | 4/98 |
|---|---|---|---|---|---|---|---|---|---|---|
| | | | | | **Quarter/Year** | | | | | |
| Actual sales | 52 | 52 | 74 | 55 | 64 | 66 | 83 | 76 | 78 | |
| Forecasted sales (L = 0.3) | | 52 | 52 | 59 | 58 | 60 | 62 | 68 | 70 | 72* |
| Actual sales | 52 | 52 | 74 | 55 | 64 | 66 | 83 | 76 | 78 | |
| Forecasted sales (L = 0.7) | | 52 | 52 | 67† | 59 | 63 | 65 | 78 | 76 | 77 |

*0.3(78) + 0.7(70) = 72.4
†0.7(74) + 0.3(52) = 67

Returning to the toy manufacturer, the forecaster decides that more weight should be placed on sales from earlier periods so a smoothing constant of 0.3 was selected (see Figure 14-6). Forecasted sales in 4/96 were made equal to actual sales in 3/96 to help start the forecasting process. To calculate forecasted sales in 4/98, 0.3 is multiplied by 78 (actual sales in the present period) and added to 0.7 times 70 (forecasted sales in the present period) to yield 72. If the forecaster had decided that more weight should be placed on sales from later periods, a smoothing constant of 0.7, for example, could have been used. Note the differences in forecasted sales in Figure 14-6 when a smoothing constant of 0.7 is used.

One significant advantage associated with exponential smoothing models over moving average models is that the forecaster can determine the degree to which a particular period can affect forecasted sales. A significant disadvantage associated with exponential smoothing models is that the selection of the smoothing constant is somewhat arbitrary. Despite this limitation, exponential smoothing models are used by a large number of companies to forecast sales.

### Regression Analysis

The final mathematical technique that will be discussed is called **regression analysis.** Often regression is used to project sales trends into the future. In this case, past sales are plotted for each past time period. For example, in Figure 14-7 sales for 1996 and 1997 (on the $x$ axis) are plotted at $7.2 and $9.6 million respectively (on the $y$ axis). Then a straight trend line can be fitted between the points, which minimizes the distances of all the points from the line. This straight trend line can then be extended to project sales in future periods (see Figure 14-7). One way

■ **FIGURE 14-7**

**Projection of sales trend by least squares method**

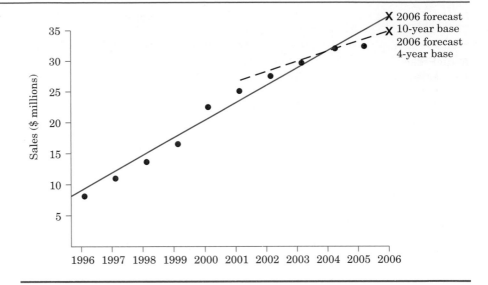

to estimate this line is to draw it freehand on the plot of points. A more accurate method of estimating this line is to use a mathematical **least squares procedure,** which minimizes the errors between actual and predicted sales.

In simple linear regression, the relationship between sales $(Y)$, the dependent variable, and time $(X)$, the independent variable, is represented by a straight line. The equation for this line is $Y = a + bX$, where $a$ represents the intercept of the line on the $y$ axis and $b$ equals the rate at which $Y$ changes for every unit change in $X$. In Figure 14-8, the least squares formulas for estimating $a$ and $b$ from past sales are given. In this example, $a$ equals 4.48 and $b$ equals 3.13. So the projection for 2006, which is the 11th time period $(x = 11)$, is estimated by the formula $Y = 4.48 + 3.13(11)$, which equals \$38.9 million.

The example discussed above uses time as the independent variable, which is common in sales forecasting. But other variables, such as advertising expenditures or numbers of births, could be used if they are related to the sales of the product. When several different variables seem to be important for projecting sales, they can be used simultaneously to project sales. This procedure is called **multiple regression analysis.**

The mathematical complexity of these techniques limits their application in many companies. Yet many firms employ highly trained personnel to use regression models to forecast sales. Also, the availability of software programs designed for nontechnical users has enhanced usage of the technique in many companies.

■ **FIGURE 14-8**

**Sales forecasting: trend projections using least squares method**

| Year | Time Period ($x$) | Sales ($ millions) ($y$) |
|---|---|---|
| 1996 | 1 | 7.2 |
| 1997 | 2 | 9.6 |
| 1998 | 3 | 12.8 |
| 1999 | 4 | 16.3 |
| 2000 | 5 | 21.9 |
| 2001 | 6 | 26.0 |
| 2002 | 7 | 27.9 |
| 2003 | 8 | 30.0 |
| 2004 | 9 | 32.1 |
| 2005 | 10 | 33.3 |

$N = 10$

$$\Sigma x = 55 \qquad \Sigma y = 217.1$$
$$\bar{x} = 5.5 \qquad \bar{y} = 21.7$$
$$(\Sigma x)^2 = 3025 \qquad \Sigma xy = 1452.7$$
$$\Sigma x^2 = 385$$

$$b = \frac{N\Sigma xy - \Sigma x\Sigma y}{N(\Sigma x^2) - (\Sigma x)^2} = \frac{10(1452.7) - (55)(217.1)}{10(385) - 3025} = 3.13$$

$$a = \bar{y} - b\bar{x} \qquad = 21.7 - 3.13(5.5) \qquad = 4.48$$

$$y = a + bx \qquad = 4.48 + 3.13(x) \qquad = \text{Forecasted sales}$$

Forecast for 2006 (10-year base) would be
  $4.48 + 3.13(11) = \$38.9$ million

Forecast for 2006 (4-year base) would be
  $35.4$ million (calculation not shown)

## "Must-Do" Forecasts

Often management forecasts the sales volume it needs to accomplish certain goals. For example, sales forecasts for new products are difficult to develop because historical data on the product's sales do not exist. Hence firms often decide that a reasonable forecast is the sales that must be achieved for the firm to reach its break-even point. In other words, the forecast is based on the sales volume needed to generate sufficient cash to cover fixed and variable costs. At other times management may forecast a level of sales volume that will allow it to achieve some profit goal.

For example, one new service enterprise budgeted its total overhead costs at $165,000 for the first year. The entrepreneur desired a profit of $60,000, which would represent her salary. Thus she projected sales at $225,000 for the year and proceeded to plan on that basis.

## Capacity-Based Forecasts

Sometimes a firm's market is such that it can sell everything it can make or buy. Thus its capacity becomes its sales forecast. For example, the owner of a highly acclaimed restaurant developed a forecast of sales based on the restaurant's seating capacity. The café had seats for 120 people at 30 tables. It was a dinner-only format in which only two seatings per evening were planned. Thus a total of 240 people could be served in each of the 300 nights a year the restaurant was open. There was a waiting list to eat at the restaurant during each night, so empty seats would not be encountered. The average ticket with drinks was forecast at $30. Hence sales for the year were projected at $2,160,000 ($30 times 240 people times 300 nights).

## ■ SOME GUIDING PRINCIPLES FOR FORECASTING

Sales forecasting is a very difficult task. There are some guidelines available to managers that can enhance the accuracy of the sales forecast. They are summarized in Figure 14-9.

### Fit the Method to the Product/Market

Some forecasting techniques work better than others for some products and in some markets. To develop accurate forecasts, it is important to use

■ **FIGURE 14-9**

**Guiding principles for forecasting**

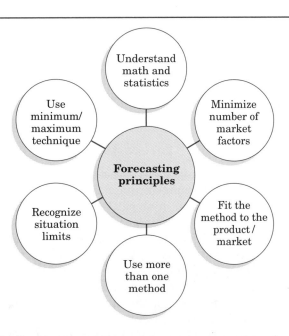

the most appropriate method. Pfizer Animal Health provides a good example of this. The company serves a variety of markets and uses different forecasting methods for different markets. For example, in the poultry market, which is dominated by a few large competitors like Tyson and Perdue, Pfizer's salespeople are very involved in forecasting sales of the product because they are very knowledgeable about any changes taking place in the customer accounts. On the other hand, the cattle market is so fragmented that it is impossible for the salesperson to have intimate knowledge of all of the customers. In this case, the company relies primarily on modeling and trend analysis for its forecasts, where the salespeople provide and confirm some of the information inputted into the analysis.[6] It is important when choosing a forecasting method that sound logic be the basis of the decision.

## Use More than One Method

One way to improve the accuracy of a sales forecast is to use multiple forecasting techniques. For example, United Parcel Service (UPS) uses two approaches. The marketing group develops one forecast based on economic indicators and historical sales data. The salespeople put together an account-by-account sales projection. Then the vice president of sales works with both groups until the differences are reconciled.[7] Similarly, two mathematical methods, such as the moving average method and the exponential smoothing method, could be used to develop a forecast.

## Minimize the Number of Market Factors

In market analysis, simplicity has great virtue. The more factors on which an analysis is based, the more difficult it is to determine exactly what affects the demand for a product. Often the inclusion of many factors in a market index results only in the duplication of a few basic forces. One drug manufacturer computed a market index from the following factors: (1) number of drug stores, (2) population, (3) number of physicians, (4) income, (5) number of hospital beds, and (6) number of people older than 65. Actually, this market index essentially was based on two elements—population and income. Several of the supposed market factors were merely surface indicators of these two basic forces. The number of physicians in an area is a reflection of the population and income of that area. Similarly, the number of drug stores and the number of hospital beds usually depend on population.

Additionally, a large regression model presents the forecaster with many statistical problems and actually can inhibit understanding of the factors that build sales of the product because of its size. A good approach is for the forecaster to discuss the factors that affect sales of the company's products with sales reps, executives, and customers and develop a model consisting of a relatively small set of factors believed to affect sales.

*A Day-to-Day Operating Problem*

## MAJESTIC PLASTICS COMPANY (K)

### Sales reps underestimate sales forecasts

On November 15 each year Clyde Brion was required to submit to top management a forecast of sales for the coming year. To that end, on September 30 each sales rep received a kit containing forms to be used in compiling a forecast of sales for the coming year in the rep's territory along with detailed instructions for their use. The company's sales forecast was then a composite of the sales reps' forecasts. Since the company sold to relatively large industrial concerns and the reps were generally well aware of the conditions in each customer's markets, Brion thought the system had worked rather well. Actual sales each year were within plus or minus 10 percent of the sales forecast.

All company planning, including setting sales quotas, was then based on those sales forecasts. These sales quotas became important because sales force bonuses were based on how well the reps performed in relationship to their quotas. Thus each sales rep's forecast was carefully appraised by management. If it appeared to be off base Brion would go over it with the rep and the two would come to some agreement about what the sales from the rep's territory would be.

As the two top sales reps stepped up to receive their awards at the company Christmas party where year-end bonuses were distributed, some unidentified rep from the back of the room who no doubt had overly partaken of the liquid refreshments yelled, "Sandbaggers!" There was some laughter and some embarrassment.

Clyde Brion said nothing at the time. Later he inquired of a rep with whom he had close rapport, "What was that sandbagging business all about?"

"Come on, Clyde," the rep replied. "Don't play innocent with me. Everyone knows the game and how to play it. Those two guys are just better than others at selling you their forecasts." Brion let the matter drop without comment. But he was deeply bothered by the implication that he was being conned by these two sales reps.

**Question:** What should Clyde Brion do about this matter?

Note: See the introduction to this series of problems in Chapter 4 for the necessary background on the company, its market, and its competition.

## Recognize the Limitations of Forecasting

Managers must be comfortable with the limitations of forecasting. As noted earlier, good sales forecasts are possible for some products more than for others, and in some situations more than in others. For example, good forecasts are very different when the product is innovative and few similar products exist in the market or when the demand for the product is highly variable from period to period. Furthermore, a company can develop a good forecast for the period but fall short of forecasted sales because the company did not implement the marketing plan very well.

### Use the Minimum–Maximum Technique

Sound research strategy dictates the use of both minimum and maximum estimates in all computations in order to obtain a range of variations. Analysts should work up one set of estimates that assumes the worst possible developments in each of the calculations. In doing this, they compute the lowest probable potential market for the product. At the same time, they should estimate what the market potential would be should all things be favorable. They also may prepare other estimates, each based on varying assumptions between the two extremes.

### Understand Mathematics and Statistics

The development of a sales forecast typically involves the use of statistics and mathematics. A sales manager should be sufficiently acquainted with statistical techniques to recognize any serious errors in the material presented.

## ■ REVIEW THE FORECASTING PROCESS

The forecasting process in the company should be reviewed periodically. The first step in the review is to determine the accuracy of past forecasts to learn if changes are needed in the way forecasts are made. If sales forecasts are found to be significantly different from actual sales in the period, a review of the sales forecasting process should be undertaken before more forecasts are made.

The evaluation process then should review the data used in sales forecasting. Poor data collection methods can decrease the quality of the data used for forecasting, or the data may be inappropriate for forecasting sales of the product. For example, a large farm implements company used data provided by sales executives to forecast sales and found the forecasts to be very inaccurate over the years. After a review of the situation, the company decided to collect data from their customers and found that the accuracy of their sales forecasts improved significantly.

## ■ SUMMARY

The sales forecast is the basis of most corporate planning. From the forecast, activities are planned and production levels are determined. Should the forecast be in error, serious consequences may face management.

The company sales forecast is closely related to the market potential of the products or services it sells. Thus the forecasting process begins with understanding the firm's market and sales potentials. The basic techniques for determining market potentials are market-factor estimations, surveys of buyers' intentions, and test markets. Territory potentials are determined by using a market index to approximate the total sales potential among the territories.

Good forecasting rests on a careful analysis of the factors that affect sales of the product. A perceptive analysis of the consumer or user of the product and his or her reasons for purchase should play a significant role in the sales forecasting process. The impact of changes in the firm's marketing plans must also be incorporated into the forecast.

Many different sales forecasting methods are available to managers and a number

of the most widely used methods were discussed in the chapter. One group relies on surveys of executives, customers, and the sales force to derive the forecast. A second group applies mathematical methods to company records or historical data to yield a sales forecast. A third group employs methods linked to the operation of the company to forecast sales. Each of the forecasting methods possesses several advantages and disadvantages, which should be clearly understood by the forecaster and the firm before the forecasting process begins.

## Key Terms

Buyer intentions survey
Capacity-based forecast
Executive opinion forecast
Exponential smoothing
    model
Delphi technique
Least squares procedure

Market factors
Market-factor derivation
Market index
Market potential
Moving average technique
Must-do forecast
Multiple regression analysis

Regression model
Sales force composite
    forecast
Sales forecast
Sales potential

## ◼ QUESTIONS AND PROBLEMS

1. Indicate what market factor or factors you would use to estimate the market potentials for each of the following products: Tiger Shark golf clubs, Scott's fertilizer, Chrysler automatic swimming pool cleaner, Mohawk carpeting, Smith's ski goggles, and a McGraw-Hill economics text.

2. After one year of market testing, the manufacturer of a new food product had sold 4,800 packages in the test city of Louisville, Kentucky. Assuming that the test market is representative of the whole nation, determine national sales of the product.

3. In general, how do sales forecasts based on surveys differ from forecasts based on mathematical methods?

4. Use exponential smoothing with a smoothing constant of 0.8 to predict sales based on the data below. Then forecast sales with a smoothing constant of 0.2.

| Period | | | | | |
|---|---|---|---|---|---|
| 1 | 2 | 3 | 4 | 5 | 6 |
| 24 | 32 | 44 | 24 | 30 | 42 |

5. When should the smoothing constant be large? When should it be small?

6. What are some of the pitfalls in conducting test markets?

7. The following regression model was developed by a professor to help the owner of a restaurant predict sales:

$$Sales = 70.0 + 46.5X_1 + 208.5X_2$$

where sales = $ sales per month

$X_1$ = advertising expenditure per month

$X_2$ = $ value of coupon

Forecast sales if the owner decides to spend $500 on advertising and offers a coupon for $5 off one meal for parties of two or more in a month. Forecast sales if the owner decides to spend $400 on ad-vertising and offers a coupon for $10 off one meal for parties of two or more in a month.

8. A university professor developed a model for predicting the sales of windmills to supply power for businesses and homes. Describe at least five factors that could be in the model.

9. A company's best-selling product line possesses a highly variable sales pattern according to company records. Which sales forecasting technique should be used to provide an accurate sales forecast for the product in the coming period?

10. Should sales reps be paid a substantial bonus for correctly forecasting their sales volumes for a coming period?

## EXPERIENTIAL EXERCISES

**A.** Develop an estimate of the market potential for a business in your community using one of the methods described in the chapter.

**B.** Develop an idea for a new consumer product. Develop an estimate of the market potential for this using census data.

## REFERENCES

1. "Sales of Private Label Goods Keep Rising," *The Wall Street Journal,* October 5, 1993, p. B8.

2. "1997 Survey of Buying Power," *Sales & Marketing Management,* August 1997, p. 143.

3. Deborah Lachman, Kathryn Williams, and Paul Foote, "Forecasting at Blue Cross of California: A Corporate Turnaround," *Journal of Business Forecasting,* Winter 1992–93, pp. 7–9.

4. Paul Herbig, John Milewichz, and Jim Golden, "Forecasting: Who, What, When, Where, and How," *Journal of Business Forecasting,* Summer 1993, pp. 16–21.

5. Bryan Atkin, "Reliable Forecasting in Rapidly Changing Markets," *Navigator* 7 (1996).

6. William Keenan Jr., "Keeping Sales in the Loop," *Sales & Marketing Management,* June 1995, pp. 34–35.

7. William Keenan Jr., "Numbers Racket," *Sales & Marketing Management,* May 1995, p. 70.

*Case 14-1*

## ANDROS INTERCOM
### Revising a sales forecasting approach

"I am very concerned about the accuracy of our sales forecasts in recent years. Last year, for example, we underestimated sales by 16 percent. Based on the faulty sales forecast, we ordered less materials from our suppliers and scheduled less production early in the year, causing us to miss many sales opportunities. I wouldn't be so concerned, but the year before we underestimated sales by 21 percent! I realize sales forecasting is a complex exercise and events can pop up that can dramatically affect a company's sales during the year, but we should be doing a better job in this area. Fay, I want to see some improvement in the coming year." Dinos Andros, founder and president of Andros Intercom, was speaking to Fay Philmus, vice president of sales for Andros. Fay had been in her position only three months, but Dinos was the second person in Andros Intercom to complain to her about the poor forecasts. The first person, John Richman, vice president of finance, was equally blunt in his desire to see the company's sales forecasts improve. He said, "A new salesperson, a new forecaster: good."

Dinos followed John's comment by stating, "Let's meet in two weeks, say on Tuesday the 25th, at 10, to discuss how you plan to forecast sales for the coming year. I'll have John Richman and Ray Forge from production attend as well, to hear what you have to say," he concluded.

Andros Intercom has been in existence for 20 years, manufacturing and marketing internal wall-based communications systems for new homes throughout the states of Maine and New Hampshire. The communications systems are designed so that people in one room can easily talk to people in other rooms or talk to people outside of the home. Andros offers its customers a variety of systems, depending on the type of home and the needs of the home owner. The company, headquartered in Bangor, Maine, prides itself on making the highest quality internal communication systems while offering customers a competitive price. Through clever marketing of its top-quality, but affordable systems, Andros has become the market leader in the Northeast and has enjoyed record profits in each of the last three years.

In response to the president's request, Fay spent a good part of the next week working with her assistant, David Moss, on examining the old forecasting techniques used by the company to forecast company sales over the past 14 years or so. The two managers then worked on developing a new forecasting system for Andros in the week before the meeting. To make a convincing argument on how Andros should forecast in the future, Fay and David prepared a PowerPoint presentation for the meeting.

The 25th finally arrived. Fay and David walked into a crowded conference room for the 10 AM presentation. "Good morning, Fay," Dinos said. A few other people in the room mumbled their hellos.

"Good morning. I brought my assistant David Moss with me for today's meeting. David helped develop forecasts for Spancom and AT&T before joining us about six months ago, and he has helped develop today's presentation." After several people greeted David, Fay started the presentation.

"I would like to begin by reviewing how we have performed our sales forecasts in the past few years. Three methods were employed to develop the final forecast. One involved obtaining information from top executives in the company, based on their intuition, experience, and observations of the business environment. I believe this method was a favorite of my predecessor who sought to have top management partially responsible for the sales forecast." Several people in the crowd snorted with amusement. "Another method involved obtaining information from each of the company's sales representatives. The sales reps' forecasts were then aggregated to yield an overall forecast for the company. Finally, we had our sales reps survey our customers to determine their purchase intentions for the coming year. The three independent forecasts were combined to yield an overall sales forecast for the year," Fay stated.

"In light of our poor forecasting performance in recent years, we would like to propose another approach, which is called regression analysis, that may help improve sales forecasting at Andros. Regression analysis is a mathematical technique where sales, the variable we are trying to forecast, is related to one or more causes of sales, say, price and advertising. Applying regression analysis to a data base will produce a regression line, captured by an equation, which represents all of the data points. The equation is as follows:

$$y = a + b_1 x_1 + b_2 x_2 + b_3 x_3$$

where $y$ is the effect, the number of systems sold, for example: $x_1$, $x_2$, and $x_3$ are actual values or the causes of sales, say prices of our systems and our dollar expenditure on advertising; $a$ is the $y$-intercept or where the regression line passes through the $y$-axis; and $b_1$, $b_2$, and $b_3$ are called coefficients which measure the change in $y$ or sales associated with a unit change in $x_1$ or $x_2$ or $x_3$ assuming that all of the other causes remain constant. To forecast, you just plug in the values for $x_1$, $x_2$, and $x_3$ and multiply

them by their respective coefficients, sum them and add (or subtract) the $y$-intercept to generate a sales forecast. For example, forecasting with a regression model that looks like $y = 10 + 20x_1 + 30x_2$ requires the forecaster to plug in values for $x_1 + x_2$, say 40 and 50, to yield a forecast of 240. We will then combine the results of our regression model and the survey of our customers by our sales reps to develop a final forecast," Fay exclaimed.

Fay continued, "Please note that this approach recommends dropping sales forecasts developed by the individual sales rep and company executives and eliminating purchase intention data from our customers in the forecasting process. After speaking with a variety of people on this issue, it seems the sales reps were being less than candid about their sales forecasts and those of their customers by underestimating demand for our products to help them meet their quotas."

"Wait! You are recommending that we move away from using the input of our customers and our sales force who know the business very well, and our executives, people who also know the business from top to bottom, and move toward a more mathematical approach that is untested and hard for most of us to understand?" cried one manager.

Another manager said, "I understand it. By using regression analysis, you're just saying that the future is going to be like the past. But I question that! My salespeople may be overly pessimistic about sales prospects sometimes, but they do provide us with some valuable information on future sales."

Fay replied patiently, "We are not recommending this approach. We are offering it as an alternative to existing sales forecasting approaches. We feel using regression analysis is a much simpler sales forecasting approach and one that will produce an accurate forecast. Hear me out on this for a minute. The regression model we developed using data from company records and the U.S. government argues that sales is affected by the dollar amount spent on advertising by Andros, the average price for our products after discounts have been taken by our customers, and the number of housing starts in Maine and New Hampshire. Advertising and price are variables that we manipulate to build sales, while housing starts is a good variable to use because our systems are placed almost exclusively in new homes. To develop a forecast, we ran the regression model using a program called Excel that is contained in Windows 95."

"This approach can forecast better than we have been forecasting in the past?" asked one manager.

"If the regression analysis is well conceived, we believe error can be cut significantly," Fay stated. "Here is the database we are using to develop the regression model."

"After entering the data in the format shown above, the model produced a sales forecast that is very close to the actual sales levels obtained by Andros in 1995 and 1996," Fay stated.

Fay stopped a minute to let the audience absorb her presentation. "So there it is. My team and I have given you one approach for forecasting sales. Please let us know which approach you think Andros should take. We can try the old approach again this year or go with something different, like the approach we have presented to you today. We will support your decision either way," Fay concluded.

"Wait a second," John Richman exclaimed. "You and your team are supposed to be the experts, yet you are telling us, the nonforecasting crowd, that we are the decision makers? I think you should make the forecasting decision and we'll live with it, at least until we can determine the accuracy of the forecast."

| Year | Unit Sales | Advertising ($ millions) | Price | New Hampshire & Maine Housing Starts (thousands) |
|------|------------|--------------------------|-------|--------------------------------------------------|
|      | $y$ | $x_1$ | $x_2$ | $x_3$ |
| 1983 | 559 | .2 | 3,005 | 11.0 |
| 1984 | 648 | .3 | 2,985 | 11.0 |
| 1985 | 661 | .32 | 2,878 | 11.1 |
| 1986 | 682 | .33 | 3,013 | 12.5 |
| 1987 | 870 | .4 | 2,799 | 13.0 |
| 1988 | 885 | .41 | 3,100 | 13.0 |
| 1989 | 849 | .51 | 2,913 | 14.2 |
| 1990 | 1,045 | .5 | 2,888 | 16.4 |
| 1991 | 1,115 | .51 | 2,999 | 19.5 |
| 1992 | 1,251 | .57 | 2,794 | 20.7 |
| 1993 | 1,302 | .59 | 2,819 | 22.2 |
| 1994 | 1,444 | .60 | 2,883 | 22.1 |
| 1995 | 1,542 | .60 | 2,851 | 23.0 |
| 1996 | 1,443 | .59 | 3,082 | 32.4 |
| 1997 | 1,990 | .80 | 3,003 | 32.3 |

N=15

$\Sigma Y = 16286$    $\Sigma x_1 = 7.23$    $\Sigma x_2 = 44012$    $\Sigma x_3 = 274.40$

"I agree," said Dinos Andros. "Why don't you prepare a document for us by this time next week, showing which forecasting approach you recommend and why you selected the approach. We must put this baby to bed in a hurry given our planning period is coming up soon. Sound OK, Fay?"

"Our recommendation will be on your desk in one week," Fay said.

After she returned to her office, Fay thought about the meeting and wondered which forecasting approach she would recommend. Many of the managers in the meeting seemed leery of a more mathematical approach to sales forecasting. "Should I just plow ahead with the approach that I think will work, even though it includes regression analysis that seems to scare people, or should I use an approach that is familiar and understandable to management?" she thought.

*Questions*

1. Describe the advantages and disadvantages associated with the old approach to sales forecasting and the new approach to forecasting presented by Fay and her team. Based on your analysis, which approach do you recommend?

2. Run a regression analysis on the database presented in the case. The data can easily be analyzed using a spreadsheet program, like Excel or Lotus 1-2-3.

3. Report and interpret your results. Then test the accuracy of the sales forecast for Andros by plugging in the values for advertising, price, and housing starts for the years 1995 and 1996. How accurate is the regression model? What are forecasted sales if the company decides to spend $1.1 million on advertising, sells its products for an average price of $3,300, and has 36,000 housing starts in 1998?

---

*Case 14-2*

## PRECISION TOOLS, INC.

### Revision of sales forecasting model

"It seems to me that our forecasting system, which we have been so proud of for many years, has sprung a leak. Our forecasts have been right on the money for many years. Now suddenly we missed by 18 percent in 1997 and 22 percent in 1998. Business was better than we thought it would be, so we missed a lot of sales by underplanning production. Something seems to be wrong and it's causing us to lose market share because we don't have enough inventory to supply the demand. What are we doing about it, Pat?" David Haeppner, president of Precision Tools, Inc., of Salt Lake City, Utah, was talking to Pat Michaels, the company's vice president of sales operations.

Precision Tools, Inc., designed, made, and distributed a wide line of specialized machine tools which were used in light manufacturing operations. Most of the firm's products were computer driven; thus the firm was also involved in developing the software needed for operating the machines.

In 1991 the firm's market analyst had developed a relatively simple model for forecasting the demand for the firm's products based on the payroll and employment statistics of the firms included in the SIC categories of the company's target markets. Management became increasingly comfortable with its forecasting model as it provided excellent forecasts for the years of 1992,

1993, 1994, and 1995. However, the model underestimated sales for 1996 by at least 18 percent. It was not known how much more the company could have sold had it been prepared for the unexpected demand.

One sales rep was heard to say, "If this is a recession, let's have more of it." While the firm's customers had reduced their payrolls and employment, their manufacturing activities were increasing. Their increased profits were encouraging their purchase of machine tools. Thus business was good for Precision Tools, contrary to what its forecasting model had predicted.

In response to the president's question, Pat Michaels replied, "I have asked Cori to develop a new forecasting system for us since it has become obvious that the previous relationship between employment and our sales has changed."

"Call her in! I want to know where we now are and where she is in her thinking." David handed the phone to Pat as he dialed Cori's extension.

Cori Newman had joined the company as market analyst in 1996 after working for Microsoft, a software developer in Orem, Utah, for four years in its marketing research group. She had graduated from BYU's MBA program in 1991. She quickly responded to the request for her presence in the executive conference room and took with her the portfolio of work she had already done on the forecasting problem.

After observing the usual courtesies, she began, "As we have suspected, the relationship between employment and machine tool demand has changed. This is a common problem encountered in all forecasting models based on an analysis of historical relationships. Relationships change! We can easily reformulate our existing forecasting equation to determine whatever new relationship evolves between employment and machine

tool demand, but probably that new equation would have to be repeatedly revised.

"I would also like to point out that sales forecasts tend to become self-fulfilling prophecies. If the forecast is low, that is what the company will likely sell. A high forecast likely increases sales through the combined forces of more inventory and more marketing pressure." Cori noted that her audience was receptive so far to her thoughts. She continued, "We have some alternatives. We could ask our customers about their plans for buying our tools the coming year. Academics call it surveying buyers' intentions. We could do it since our total number of customers is not large. Each sales rep would contact each of his or her accounts to find out what they plan to buy for the next budget. Then the reps summarize what they discovered and make a forecast of their sales. We then summarize all of the rep's forecasts to come up with our own. One advantage of this procedure is that we can develop forecasts in more detail, by product lines."

"Then you're recommending that we abandon our mathematical approach to forecasting and go to a survey method. Is that right?" the president asked.

"Not necessarily. I am trying to give you an idea of the different approaches we can use and let you make the decision," Cori replied.

"Whoa! I have trouble with that. You're supposed to be the expert in market analysis, not us. We hired you to tell us what you think we should do. I want a recommendation from you without any equivocation." Pat Michaels firmly told Cori what was expected of her.

Cori was inwardly shaken by his aggressive position but tried to maintain her composure. She replied, "Very well, you'll have my recommendation in writing Monday morning." After exchanging the usual parting words, she returned to her office to begin what would be a hectic weekend.

She mulled over the other forecasting alternative that she had not been allowed to present at the meeting. She had been about to tell her bosses that she could develop another mathematical model based on data other than employment. She would have to do a lot of statistical work to locate and validate such a series of information, but after all that was her job.

Cori wondered if she should recommend continued use of a forecasting method with which management was familiar or if she should recommend switching to the survey of customers' buying intentions system.

**Question:**

What forecasting method should Cori Newman recommend that the company adopt?

---

*Case 14-3*

## THE NEWPORT COSMETICS COMPANY

### Forecasting sales for a new product

"What in the world is going on in there?" asked Marcia Fox, the operations manager for The Newport Cosmetics Company of Newport Beach, California, as she walked into the office on a foggy Monday morning. Her question, addressed to no one in particular, was answered by the accountant.

"They're at it again!"

"What's it all about this time?"

"The sales forecast for the new shaving oil. As usual, they can't agree on it," the accountant added.

"All that noise over coming up with a number that is at best a wild guess. They'll argue over anything," Marcia observed.

"It's not the number they're arguing about; it's how they are going to get the number," the accountant said.

The Newport Cosmetic Company had been founded in 1988 by three young people, Sara Haskell, Kent Graham, and Jim Porter, who had developed an interest in the cosmetic uses for various herbs and herbal compounds. After more than a year developing a line of herbal cosmetic products, they introduced it to the market using various di-

rect marketing techniques which included both direct mail and party-plan selling. The company prospered.

While Sara was legally the firm's president with Jim its treasurer and Kent its secretary, the three founders served jointly as the firm's top management, each with an area of special interest. Jim concentrated on marketing; Kent was concerned with controls and finance; Sara spent her time on production and operations.

In its ongoing product development program, a combination of exotic oils such as frankincense, rosemary, and jasmine proved to be a particularly effective shaving preparation to be used instead of the traditional shaving soaps and after-shave lotion. The panel of people who tested the product praised it highly.

Once the product's effectiveness and acceptability had been established, Jim Porter, the founder who was mostly concerned with marketing, had developed a marketing plan for the new shaving oil, yet unnamed. It was thought that the new oil could not be marketed as a man's shaving preparation because of the extreme competition from big advertisers in that market. Instead, after extensive conversation about positioning the oil as a woman's shaving product particularly designed for legs, it was decided to market the new oil as a woman's cosmetic.

Moreover, a consultant suggested that it might be difficult to get men to change their traditional shaving rituals. For centuries men have shaved with soap, not oil. Marketing history deals unkindly with firms that have tried to get people to change such firmly implanted rituals. Thus the consultant suggested that the company begin by selling the oil as a woman's cosmetic item.

While the three founders were good friends and worked well together, sometimes it was not without considerable strife and stress. They were not quiet people. They yelled a lot: at each other, at other people, and often at no one in particular. Their joint defense of their operating behavior was that it was "therapeutic."

On this day, they disagreed about how to develop a sales forecast for the new shaving oil. Jim Porter strongly insisted that all they could do was to use a "must-do" forecast. He maintained that because the product was so new, there was no way to forecast its sales without a test market. "We're trying to penetrate a market so large that even a 1 percent market share would be a tremendous success. We would need a market test to get some data on which to develop a market-based sales forecast," Jim said.

"So let's test it!" Sara shouted.

"And tell the world what we're up to! Get real!" Kent shouted back. He continued, "I shudder to think how difficult it would be to test market the oil, let alone the validity of the results. It costs as much to test it as to go ahead and market it. We've got the product, now go with it."

Sara defended herself, "Look, it costs us nothing to mix up a batch of the stuff and choose an isolated market to test it in. Let's do it!"

"Why bother? We don't need a sales forecast except to pacify management purists who insist that one should be developed. Since when do we do what those people think should be done? Let's figure out how much sales we need the first few years to make the program worthwhile to us, what sales volume we must have for us to come out all right on the venture." Jim continued his support for his must-do forecast. "I figure that we must sell $500,000 of this stuff the first year to cover our costs. And that's using the marketing program without the heavy advertising campaign! If we use the program that calls for a substantial advertising campaign, we'll have to sell at least $2 million the first year to cover costs."

Kent suddenly threw a different idea onto the table. "There's got to be some other product like this that has been sold in the past. Why don't we do some research and see what we can find out about it and what it sold the first year?"

Both Sara and Jim screamed at him with rude statements about his refusal to make a decision and his bureaucratic inclinations to stall and delay. He tried to defend his thoughts, but to little avail.

Marcia Fox grew weary of listening to the founders' quarrel, particularly because there was much work that was waiting for their attention. She decided to go into the office and tell them what to do. It was not the first time that she had moved things along this way.

*Question:*

What forecasting method should Marcia tell them to use?

# CHAPTER 15

# Sales Territories

Claim jumping can make you awful dead awful fast.
**A U.S. Marshall in the 1880s**

Establishing or revising sales territories and providing for their effective and efficient coverage is a key part of sales management's strategic planning task. Organizing sales territories enables management to bring other aspects of planning—such as sales forecasting and sales budgeting—down to limited geographical areas. Ordinarily, it is not practical to plan, direct, and evaluate salespeople's performances without having sales territories. The total market for most firms is simply too large to be managed efficiently without a territorial structure.

Once such a structure is established, management can then set up a system for covering each territory. This step includes scheduling a rep's territorial coverage—that is, determining which accounts will be called on, in what order, and how frequently. Sometimes this step also involves determining the route that each sales rep will follow in covering his or her territory. Planning territorial coverage has become increasingly important as sales organizations cannot afford to have poorly designed, unbalanced territories.

## ■ NATURE AND BENEFITS OF TERRITORIES

A **sales territory** comprises a number of present and potential customers, located within a given geographical area and assigned to a salesperson, branch, or middleman (retailer or wholesaling middleman).

In this definition, the key word is *customer* rather than *geographical.* To understand the concept of a sales territory, we must recognize that a market is made up of people, not places—people with money to spend and the willingness to spend it. A market is measured by people times their purchasing power rather than in square miles.

A company, especially a medium- or large-sized one, can derive several benefits from a carefully designed territorial structure. In contrast, formal territories may not be needed in a small company with a few people selling only in a local market. In this case, management can plan and control sales operations without the aid of territories and still enjoy many benefits of a formal structure.

## Managerial Benefits Derived from Establishing Territories

**Ensures proper coverage of potential market.** Salespeople are likely to cover their market more thoroughly if they are each assigned a specific geographical area rather than if they are allowed to sell in any area.

**Improves customer relations.** A territorial structure can improve the quality of service that salespeople give their customers. Regularity in sales calls is especially important for staple, repeat-order types of products. If the regular salesperson is not there, the order can just as easily be given to a competitor.

**Increases salespeople's morale and effectiveness.** When sales reps have their own territories, they are virtually in business for themselves. They realize that they alone are responsible for the results in their districts. They may route themselves more carefully and plan the frequency of their calls better.

**Aids in control and evaluation of sales force.** Having assigned territories gives management an effective control mechanism. Also, management can measure a rep's actual performance against a territorial potential or quota.

**Reduces selling costs.** When reps are restricted to one area, they probably spend less time and money traveling than if they sell anywhere in the total market. If reps spend less time traveling, their effective selling time should increase.

**Facilitates performance of other sales and marketing activities.** Analyzing sales and cost data can be more meaningful on a territorial basis rather than for the market as a whole. Management can use marketing research more effectively to set realistic quotas and to prepare sales and expense budgets.

Lack of territories may be justified when personal friendships play a large part in the market transaction. This is one reason automobile dealers and commodity and security brokers usually do not district their sales forces. Highly specialized sales engineers also may serve in troubleshooting assignments or be called in anywhere to help close an important sale.

## ■ PROCEDURE FOR DESIGNING TERRITORIES

The ideal goal in territorial design is to have all districts equal in both sales potential and the sales reps' work load. When sales potentials are equal, it is easier to evaluate and compare sales reps' performances. Equal opportunities also reduce disputes between management and the sales force and generally tend to improve workers' morale. To achieve both objectives is an ideal, but usually unattainable, goal. However, this should not deter an executive from constantly striving to reach it.

Changing market conditions put continuing pressure on companies to adjust their territories. Different procedures may be used to design the districts. However, a company's territorial structure is influenced by the potential business in the firm's market and by the workload required or

■ **FIGURE 15-1** **Procedure for designing sales territories**

sales expected of its sales force. One plan for establishing or redesigning territories includes the following six steps, as seen in Figure 15-1.

1. Select a control unit for territorial boundaries.
2. Determine location and potential of customers.
3. Determine basic territories.
4. Assign salespeople to territories.
5. Establish territorial coverage plans for the sales force.
6. Conduct territorial sales and cost studies on a continuing basis. (We discuss this step in Chapters 17 and 18.)

### Determine Basic Control Unit for Territorial Boundaries

When designing territories, the first step is to select a geographical **control unit** as a territorial base. Commonly used units are states, counties, cities, ZIP-code areas, and metropolitan areas (see Figure 15-2). A typical territory may comprise several individual units. One person's district may consist of four metropolitan areas; another's may be three states. The unit should be small for at least two reasons. First, a small unit helps management realize one of the basic values of territories—the geographic pin-

■ **FIGURE 15-2**

**Territorial control units**

```
┌──────────┐                              ┌──────────────┐
│  State   │────────┐           ┌─────────│ ZIP–code area│
└──────────┘        │           │         └──────────────┘
┌──────────┐   ┌─────────────────────┐
│  County  │───│  Sales territory    │
└──────────┘   │  control unit       │
┌──────────┐   └─────────────────────┘    ┌──────────────┐
│   City   │────────┘           └─────────│ Metropolitan │
└──────────┘                              │ statistical  │
                                          │ area         │
                                          └──────────────┘
```

pointing of potential. Second, the use of small control units makes it easier for management to adjust the territories. If an organization wants to add to one person's district and reduce another's, a county unit facilitates the adjustment better than a state unit.

### States

Territorial systems built around states are simple, inexpensive, and convenient. Territories may be built around states if a firm has a small sales force covering a national market and uses a selective distribution policy. A luggage manufacturer on the West Coast who sells directly to a limited number of selected retail accounts, for example, uses the state unit with apparent success.

However, for most companies, states do not serve well as bases for territories because customers often ignore a state line. An Oregon–Washington boundary ignores the fact that many consumers and retailers in southern Washington buy in Portland. Trade from Alton and East St. Louis, Illinois, gravitates to St. Louis, Missouri, rather than to any Illinois city.

### Counties

For companies that prefer to use a political subdivision as a territorial base, the *county* may be the answer. In the United States there are almost 3,100 counties but only 50 states. Smaller control units help management to design territories that are equal in potential and to pinpoint problem areas. Many kinds of statistical market data (population, retail and wholesale sales, income, employment, and manufacturing information) are available on a county basis.

The only serious drawback to the county unit is that it is still too large for some companies. A manufacturer or a wholesaler may want to assign several reps to cover one county because the potential is far too much for one person to handle. This situation may prevail in such counties as Los Angeles, Cook (Chicago), Wayne (Detroit), or Cuyahoga (Cleveland). It then becomes necessary to divide the county into a series of territories, and some smaller control unit is needed.

### Cities and ZIP-Code Areas

In the past, such firms as wholesalers of food, drugs, and tobacco often used a *city* as a control unit, because most of the market lay within urban limits. In fact, in many instances even the city was too large, and firms used several sales reps within a single city. Then some subcity unit was needed, and precincts, wards, or census tracts were used.

Postal ZIP-code areas are one particular subcity unit widely used when an entire city is too large to use as a basic control unit. By using ZIP-code areas, a company works with geographical areas that ordinarily have a high degree of economic, social, and cultural homogeneity. However, it is difficult to get much statistical market data for geographical units smaller than a county or city.

### Metropolitan Statistical Areas

Many companies have found that a significant share of their market has shifted to suburban and satellite cities outside the major central city. These firms have been aided tremendously by the delineation of *Metropolitan Statistical Areas*. The federal government has identified and established the boundaries for about 325 of these areas. A Metropolitan Statistical Area (MSA) is an economically and socially integrated unit with a large population center. An urban area can qualify in one of two ways to be classed officially as a Metropolitan Statistical Area. An MSA is a county or group of contiguous counties that (1) has a central city with a population of at least 50,000 or (2) has a general urban area of 50,000, with a total metropolitan area population of at least 100,000. The bulk of the workers in an MSA must be nonagricultural employees, and an MSA may cross state lines.

Because an MSA is defined in terms of counties, a vast amount of market data is available.[1] Although small in total land area, the MSAs account for 75 percent to 80 percent of the nation's population, effective buying income, and retail sales. Thus MSAs constitute lush, concentrated markets for many consumer and industrial products. Because of this market potential, some firms assign territories that consist of a number of metropolitan areas. They encourage their salespeople to work only in the metropolitan area and to skip the region outside or between the areas.

## Determine the Location and Potential of Customers

Management should determine the location and potential of both present and prospective customers within each selected control unit. Sales records should indicate the location of *present* customers in each control unit. *Prospective* customers can be identified with the aid of company sales reps plus outside sources such as (1) trade directories (e.g., Thomas's Register), (2) publishers of mailing lists (e.g., R. H. Donnelley Corporation), (3) subscription lists from trade journals, (4) trade association offices, (5) classified telephone directories, or (6) credit rating firms (e.g., Dun & Bradstreet, Inc.).

Once the customers are identified, management should assess the potential business it expects from each account. Management then can classify these accounts into several categories based on their potential profitability to the seller. This step furnishes some of the necessary background for determining the basic territories.

## Determine Basic Territories

The third general step in designing sales districts is to establish a fundamental territory based on statistical measures. This can be accomplished by using either the buildup or the breakdown method. Under the **buildup**

**method** territories are formed by combining small geographical areas based on the number of calls a salesperson is expected to make. This method *equalizes the workload* of salespeople.

The **breakdown method** involves division of the whole market into approximately equal segments based on sales potential. Thus this method *equalizes sales potential*. The buildup method is particularly suited for manufacturers of consumer products or for companies that want intensive distribution. The breakdown method is more popular among manufacturers of industrial products or organizations that want selective distribution.

*Buildup Method*

Several variations are possible in establishing territories by building up from the basic control unit. Usually, however, these variations depend on some type of customer analysis and study of the salespeople's **workload capacity.** A suggested procedure is outlined in the following paragraphs (see Figure 15-3).

1.  **Determine optimal call frequencies.** Management should establish optimal **call frequencies** for each account. In other words, management must determine how many times per year an account should be visited. The call frequency is affected by the sales potential, the nature of the product, customer buying habits, the nature of competition, and the cost of calling on a customer. Thus the call frequency is primarily determined by the profitability of the account. The optimal call frequencies can be determined using several different computer models or estimated using managerial judgment. The computer models are discussed later in the chapter. Figure 15-4 is an example of how management might divide its customers into three classes based on profitability. Class A accounts are the most profitable and are

■ **FIGURE 15-3**   **Buildup method of territorial design**

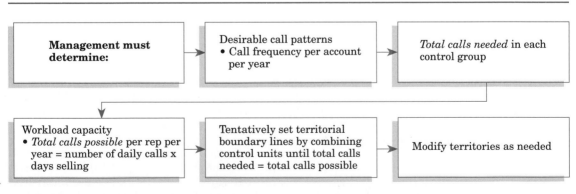

called on twice a month. Class B accounts are visited monthly, and Class C accounts bimonthly.

2. **Determine the total number of calls needed in each control unit.** By multiplying the number of each type of account in the control unit by the number of calls that type of account requires, we can determine the total number of calls needed in each control unit. Assuming that metropolitan areas are the control unit, and using the call frequencies shown in Figure 15-4, it can be seen that control unit (metropolitan area) X requires 630 calls per year and Y requires 660.

3. **Determine workload capacity.** A salesperson's workload capacity is *the average number of calls a salesperson can make in a day times the number of days in a year that the salesperson will make calls.* The number of calls a rep can effectively make in one day depends on several factors. One is the average length of time required for a call. This is influenced by the number of people to be seen on each call and the amount of missionary work to be done. Another factor is the amount of travel time between customers. For example, if a rep works 8 hours per day and the average length of a call is an hour and the average travel time is 15 minutes, then the rep can make six calls per day. If the rep makes calls 250 days per year, the annual total that the rep can make is 1,500 calls.

Continuing with the example in Figure 15-4, a salesperson who can make 1,500 calls per year could call on both area X and area Y and still have time for accounts that require a total of about 210 calls a year (1,500 − [630 + 660] = 210). A salesperson could cover any number of customers who, in total, required 1,500 calls a year.

The box labeled "Salespeople's Workloads" presents a number of factors which influence either the number of calls a salesperson can make or the optimal call frequency.

■ **FIGURE 15-4**    **Example of call frequency for different customer classes**

| Customer Class | Call Frequency | Metropolitan Area X | | Metropolitan Area Y | |
|---|---|---|---|---|---|
| | | No. of Accounts | No. of Calls per Year | No. of Accounts | No. of Calls per Year |
| A | 2 per month | 10 | 240 | 5 | 120 |
| B | 1 per month | 25 | 300 | 15 | 180 |
| C | 1 every 2 months | 15 | 90 | 60 | 360 |
| | | 50 | 630 | 80 | 660 |

## Salespeople's Workloads

Territorial design depends basically on the company's sales potential and the workload of its sales force. Consequently, management should identify and measure the factors influencing these workloads. Two companies, each selling in markets of comparable potential and geographical size, may have quite different territorial structures simply because of a difference in the sales reps' workloads.

**Nature of the job.** A sales rep's call patterns are influenced by the nature of the job. A rep who only sells can make more calls per day than the rep who must do a considerable amount of missionary work along with selling.

**Nature of the product.** The nature of the product can also affect a salesperson's call pattern. A staple convenience good (canned foods) with a rapid turnover rate may require more frequent calls than would an industrial product (conveyor belts) with very limited repeat-sale business. On the other hand, a complex technical product may require longer calls and more presale and postsale calls.

**Stage of market development.** When entering a new market, a company's territories typically are larger than markets where the firm is well entrenched—even though the market potential is comparable in the old and new regions. A large geographical district is needed initially to yield an adequate volume of business.

**Intensity of market coverage.** If a firm wants mass distribution, it will need smaller territories than if it follows a selective or exclusive distribution policy.

**Competition.** No general statement can be made about the net effect competition has on the size of the territory. If management decides to make an all-out effort to meet competition, then territorial borders will probably be contracted. Salespeople will be instructed to intensify their efforts by increasing the frequency of calls and the length of time spent with each account. On the other hand, competition may be so fierce, or the territorial markets so overdeveloped, that the company is not going to make much profit in the district. Therefore, it may decide to expand the geographical limits of the district and have the sales rep call only on selected accounts.

**Ethnic factors.** A company may adjust its territorial boundaries in large cities because of the market concentration of certain racial, national, or religious groups. One part of a city may have a heavy ethnic concentration. Retailers may also be predominantly of the same ethnic group, and use of the group's native (foreign) language may be widespread in the area. A firm selling to these retailers may alter its territorial boundaries so that the particular nationality group comprises one district. In Chicago, a firm may establish separate territories in some parts of the city to cater to the black, Hispanic, Italian, Polish, Jewish, or Vietnamese markets. The person covering each of these districts is from the corresponding ethnic group and often can speak the group's language.

4. **Draw tentative territorial boundary lines.** The final step is to accumulate enough contiguous territorial control units until the yearly number of calls needed in those control units equals the total number of calls a salesperson can make (the workload for one salesperson). A company has a choice of places from which to start this grouping. On a national scale, a firm that groups contiguous metropolitan areas into territories may start in Maine and work south to Florida, then go back to Ohio and again work south to the Gulf of Mexico. Another firm, using county control units, may start each ter-

ritory with a county that includes a major city and then complete a
given territory by fanning out in all directions until the necessary
number of contiguous counties are included. Other organizations
group counties or metropolitan areas around a branch office or plant.

Often, a company is unable to group contiguous control units so
that calls needed equal the calls which one salesperson can make unless it splits a control unit. In our earlier example, metropolitan areas
X and Y together required 1,290 calls. However, no metropolitan area
may be contiguous to X or Y that can be covered with approximately
210 calls, the number needed for a normal load of 1,500 visits per year.

In most cases like this, it is best not to split the control unit.
Rather, the territory can be made a little smaller or bigger than the
rest. However, sometimes this may cause significant inequities among
territories' sales potential. If this is the case, splitting the control unit
may be the best option. This is a matter of managerial judgment.

5. **Modify the tentative territories as needed.** The tentatively
   drawn boundary lines may need to be adjusted due to special considerations with regard to that territory. For example, the competition
   may be particularly strong in one control unit and require more intense effort from the salesperson than other areas. The salesperson in
   this area may need to have a smaller territory so that he or she can
   make more calls on fewer customers.

### Breakdown Method

The breakdown method is often used by firms that want exclusive distribution or that sell some type of industrial products. The steps for this procedure are depicted in Figure 15-5 and are explained below.

1. **Determine sales potential.** The first step is to determine what
   sales volume the company can expect in its entire market. This is
   done using one of the procedures described in Chapter 14.

2. **Determine sales potential in each control unit.** To obtain the
   sales potential in each control unit, a market index (as described in
   Chapter 14) is multiplied by total sales potential to allocate it among
   the various control units.

3. **Determine the sales volume expected from each salesperson.**
   In this step management must estimate how much each sales rep
   must sell to have a profitable business. A study of past sales experience and a cost analysis are often used to determine this information.
   For example, assume that the cost of goods sold and distribution costs
   are estimated to equal 70 percent of sales; direct selling costs are
   $30,000; and management wants to earn a profit of 10 percent of
   sales. Then it can be shown that each salesperson must sell a minimum of $150,000.[2] Of course, based on experience, management may

■ **FIGURE 15-5**    **Breakdown method of territorial design**

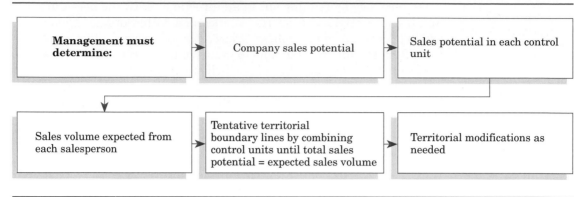

feel that each salesperson can and should sell twice this much. Therefore, expected sales volume is set at $300,000.

4. **Draw tentative territorial boundaries.** The final stage in the statistical phase of the breakdown method is to divide the entire market so that each sales rep has about the same potential. The potential has already been established for each of the basic territorial control units. Therefore, management needs to assign enough contiguous units to each salesperson so that he or she has at least $300,000 of sales potential. In other words, the sales potential of the territory should be equal to or greater than the sales volume expected from each salesperson. The boundaries of each territory should coincide with the borders of the control units.

5. **Modify tentative territories as needed.** As in the buildup method, the tentatively drawn boundary lines may need to be adjusted due to special considerations with regard to that geographic area.

## ■ USING COMPUTERS IN TERRITORY DESIGN

Over the past two decades, sophisticated computer-based mathematical models have been developed to aid in territory design and revision. These models are used to allocate sales effort (calls) across accounts in such a way as to maximize sales or profits for the firm. The procedure consists of two basic steps:

1. **Develop a sales response function for each customer.** A **sales response function** is a mathematical expression of the relationship between number of calls and sales. Figure 15-6 is a graphical representation of a typical sales response function. This function is developed in one of two ways. The first is the *empirical method,* which uses

■ **FIGURE 15-6**

**Customer call frequencies and sales**

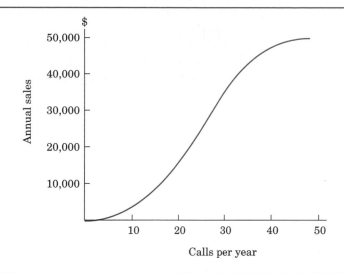

regression analysis to develop an equation that relates past sales to past calls. The second method is a *judgment-based method* whereby salespeople are asked to estimate the sales response to varying numbers of calls. For example, the computer program would ask the reps to estimate how much they would sell in the coming period to a particular customer if they increased their calls by 10 percent, decreased their calls by 10 percent, or made the same number of calls as in the past. From this type of information a sales response function for each customer can be developed.

2. **Allocate calls across accounts based on the sales response functions.** These allocating procedures first evaluate the total level of sales or profits that can be expected from all possible call allocation alternatives. Then the program recommends the specific number of calls to each account which will maximize overall sales for the firm.

Many companies have used these computer models to assist in the design or realignment of territories and report significant increases in sales and/or profit or decreases in costs. Pfizer Pharmaceuticals used a computer mapping program when it wanted to add hundreds of salespeople during a major expansion. As a result, the company realized savings of 10 percent to 15 percent on its travel costs.[3]

## ■ ASSIGN SALESPEOPLE TO TERRITORIES

Once the sales territories have been established, management can assign individual salespeople to each district. Up to this point, we have implicitly assumed that the salespeople have equal selling abilities, and that each person would perform equally well in any territory. Obviously, this is not a realistic assumption.

In any given sales force, the reps may differ in selling effectiveness. They also vary in experience, age, physical condition, initiative, and creativity, as well as selling skills. A sales rep may succeed in one territory and fail in another, even though the sales potential and work load are the same in both districts. For example, in a territory where a high number of the customers are engineers, a salesperson with a technical background may be more effective. Sales performance also may be influenced by differences in local customs, religion, and ethnic background.

Many companies intentionally design some sales territories so that they are *unequal* in size, as measured by the rep's workload or the territorial sales potential. These unequally sized territories accomplish two purposes. One is to accommodate some of the above-noted differences among salespeople. The other is to give executives some flexibility in managing their sales forces. For example, many firms intentionally design a small territory for beginners or sales trainees. Then, as a rep progresses in skill and performance, he or she is moved (or "promoted") to progressively larger and more lucrative territories. Similarly, some companies may initially assign reps to territories out in the hinterland. Then, later, these reps can be "promoted" to better territories closer to their homes or offices.

## ◼ REVISING SALES TERRITORIES

As companies and markets change, territorial structures may become outdated and need revision. Experts recommend that sales managers review their territories at least once a year to see if they need to be realigned.[4] Some sales managers assess and realign territories more frequently. Edward Hu, a manager for AT&T, reviews his salespeople's territories every three months.[5] However, before making any boundary adjustments, management should be certain that the danger signals noted below are the result of poor territorial design, and not of poor administration in other areas. The problem may lie in the compensation plan, inadequate supervision, or a poor quota system.

### Indications of Need for Adjustment

Frequently, sales potential outgrows a territory, and as a result the salesperson skims the district rather than covering it intensively. When out-of-date measures of potential are used, the performance results from a district can be quite misleading. In a fast-growing region, for instance, one salesperson's volume may have increased 100 percent over a four-year period, the largest increase of any rep in the firm. Management praises that person highly as the model of a good sales rep. Actually, that rep may have been doing a very poor job because the territorial potential increased 200 percent or 300 percent during that time. The company really was losing its former share of market because the districts were not small enough to encourage thorough coverage.

Sometimes the selling task changes. Anheuser-Busch found that its customers were demanding more and more value-added services; therefore, the company's salespeople had less time to sell. So the company made the territories smaller and hired new reps, giving each rep more time to sell.[6]

At the other end of the scale, territories may need revising because they are too *small*. They may have been set up that way, or changing market conditions may have caused the situation. Overlapping territories are a structural weakness that should be corrected. This problem generally stems from previous boundary revisions. To illustrate, sales rep Carter originally had as a territory the three West Coast states, California, Oregon, and Washington. As the potential grew in this territory, it was divided into two districts. Carter kept California, and a new rep, McNeil, was assigned Washington and Oregon. However, Carter was also allowed to keep certain preferred accounts in what is now McNeil's territory. The reason for this decision was that Carter had spent much time developing the accounts. The customers liked Carter, and they might switch to a competitor if Carter did not call on them. Therefore, management allowed the overlap to develop in the territories. However, the company planted the seeds for future morale problems because, eventually, McNeil will chafe under the arrangement. Overlapping territories generally result in higher costs and selling inefficiencies.

Territorial adjustments are necessary when claim jumping is practiced. Say that the company has established territories with definite boundaries. However, management has tolerated a person in one district going outside its borders and selling in another's district. If each territory has an adequate potential, and one sales rep jumps another's claim, then the first one obviously is not satisfactorily developing his or her own area. On the other hand, let's assume that one person has done a thorough job in his or her own region and still has the time to go into the next district. Then some adjustment is needed because the first territory is too small. The increasing costs, inefficiencies, and friction among the reps that can develop when one cuts into another's region should be obvious.

## Effect of Revision on Sales Force

Many people dislike change, partially because they cannot predict the consequences. Management may hesitate to make needed adjustments in territorial boundaries for fear of hurting sales force morale. In fact, many territorial problems—overlapping districts, for instance—are a result of management's trying to avoid friction in the past.

*A Day-to-Day Operating Problem*

## MAJESTIC PLASTICS COMPANY (L)

### "Claim jumping" by sales rep formerly in a territory

Clyde Brion, the general sales manager for Majestic Plastics Company, had just finished a telephone call from Lucille Koll, the Majestic sales rep in New Orleans. This was the third call in six months that Brion had received from Koll concerning the same problem. She was upset by what she called "claim jumping" by James Wiggins, the Majestic rep in an adjoining territory. That is, Wiggins was selling to some Majestic customers in Koll's territory. Koll's territory covered the states of Louisiana, Oklahoma, and Arkansas, plus Memphis, Tennessee. Wiggins's territory was the state of Texas, and he was based in Dallas.

Prior to two years ago, both of these territories constituted one large unit that was covered by Wiggins. But the territory had grown too large in potential for one rep to cover. Wiggins was skimming the market, relying on established accounts, rather than intensively developing the growing potential. The territory was split and Wiggins took the new Texas district. Koll was hired to cover the other newly formed territory.

Wiggins had been with the company for 12 years and consistently ranked in the top third of the sales reps, based on total sales volume. His accounts generally spoke well of him, and Brion rarely received any customer complaints about Wiggins. Koll also had done well since she joined Majestic Plastics. She had a good record in opening new accounts and retaining the old accounts that Wiggins had established. Customer feedback reported that she generally did a fine job providing needed services.

Over the past couple of years, however, Wiggins occasionally sold to one of his old accounts in Louisiana or Oklahoma (now Koll's territory). He claimed that an old customer would telephone him to place an order. In a few cases the customer asked Wiggins to drop by on a personal sales call. Wiggins claimed that Majestic Plastics might well lose those accounts if he did not service them. Two of these customers were firms with manufacturing plants in Texas, but the home offices were in Louisiana. Wiggins continued to call on the Texas plants, but he also was in contact with and making sales to the home offices in Louisiana.

It was these incursions into her territory that were infuriating Lucille Koll. She also claimed that Wiggins was undermining her in the eyes of some of his old customers. She told Brion that Wiggins was simply a "claim jumper" and that he was using his "good ole boy" network to take business away from her. She reminded Brion that she was being paid a straight commission, so Wiggins's activities were taking money out of her pocket. She was particularly upset that Brion apparently had done nothing in response to her previous two phone calls about the same issue.

**Question:** How should Clyde Brion respond to Lucille Koll's charges?

Note: See the introduction to this series of problems in Chapter 4 for background information on the company, its market, and its competition.

Morale problems are particularly likely to arise when territories are reduced in size. The reps may suspect that management is trying to curtail their earnings. In addition, the reps are reluctant to lose accounts that they have cultivated over a period of time. It is helpful to get the salespeople's suggestions during the revision process.

A salesperson's attitude toward losing accounts will be influenced by the type of compensation plan. If part or all of a pay plan includes a commission, then a reduction in territory size means the rep's income will initially drop, unless management adjusts the pay plan. If the territory revision has been done properly, the reduced territory ultimately offers a better sales volume opportunity and the chance to cover the area more intensively. Until the sales rep can fully develop the smaller territory, however, that person probably will need some compensation help during the transition period. One procedure is to guarantee the salespeople their previous level of income during a stated adjustment period.

Many firms make no adjustment whatsoever in a person's pay. Instead, management tries to sell the reps on the idea that intensive development of their remaining territory will quickly bring their income to its former level or higher. Understandably, it is usually quite difficult for a rep to accept this line of reasoning.

## TERRITORIAL COVERAGE—MANAGING A SALES REP'S TIME

After designing territories and assigning salespeople to their separate districts, management then should plan how each rep will cover his or her territory. In effect, managing territorial coverage is an exercise in managing the sales reps' time. Time management is becoming increasingly important as companies continue looking for ways to control their field-selling costs.

The management of territorial coverage involves two main tasks—routing salespeople and scheduling their time. Computer technology can be used effectively in both of these activities.

### Routing the Sales Force

**Routing** is the managerial activity that establishes a formal pattern for sales reps to follow as they go through their territories. This pattern is usually indicated on a map or list that shows the order in which each segment of the territory is to be covered. Although routing is referred to as a managerial activity, it is not done only at some executive level. Often a firm asks its salespeople to prepare their own route schedules as part of their job.

#### Reasons for Routing by Management
Managerial routing of the sales force should reduce travel expenses by ensuring an orderly, thorough coverage of the market. Studies indicate that it is not at all unusual for reps to spend one-third of their daily working hours traveling. At that rate, a sales rep is not even inside a customer's office for four months out of a year.

Proponents of management's handling of routing believe the typical salesperson is unable to do the job satisfactorily. They feel that salespeople will look for the easiest, most pleasant way to do their jobs, although this may not be the most effective way. Left to their own routing devices, they will backtrack and crisscross their territory in order to be home several nights a week.

The following diagram illustrates a problem that often occurs when management allows salespeople to route themselves.

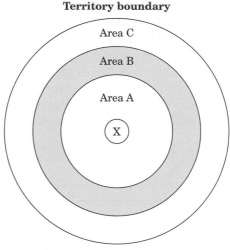

X = rep's home

In area A, the rep can do a full selling job and still easily get home at night. Actual sales in A approximate the area's potential. Sales to accounts in area C also approximate the potential. In this outlying area, a rep is resigned to being away overnight and thus concentrates on doing a creditable selling job. Area B is the problem area where a rep can get home at night only by working less than a full day. Sales there are well below potential.

### Objections to Routing

Many sales executives feel that routing reduces people's initiative and straitjackets them in an inflexible plan of territorial coverage. They believe that a sales rep in the field is in the best position to decide the order in which accounts should be visited. Market conditions often are very fluid. Therefore, it would be a mistake to set up a route plan and prevent a salesperson from making expedient changes to meet some situation. High-caliber reps usually do not need to be routed, and they may resent it if a plan is forced on them.

### Factors Conducive to Routing

Before deciding to route its sales force, management should consider the nature of the product and the job. If the call frequencies are regular and if the job activities are reasonably routine, planning a person's route is easier than if visits are irregular. Salespeople for drug, grocery, tobacco, or hard-

**Some territories are large enough to require frequent air travel.**

ware wholesalers can be routed without serious difficulty. In fact, to attempt an irregular call pattern with a given customer can result in loss of the account. A grocery or hardware retailer, for instance, plans his buying on the basis of a sales rep's call, say, every Tuesday morning. If this retailer cannot depend on the sales rep's regular call, the buyer may seek another supplier.

*Procedure for Establishing a Routing Plan*
In order to establish a routing plan, the present and prospective accounts should be spotted on a map of the territory. Then the daily call rates and the desired call frequency must be determined for each account. This information may have already been determined during the territory design process. With all this information available, the actual establishment of routes is reasonably mechanical. Some of the most commonly used route patterns are circular, straight line, cloverleaf, and hopscotch.[7] When call frequencies differ among the accounts, management may employ a skip-stop routing pattern. On one trip, a salesperson may visit every account, but on the next trip this rep may call on only a third of the accounts—the most profitable third.

Routing salespeople effectively is another sales operational area that is ideal for computer application. A number of computer models have been designed to help management determine the one route through a territory that will minimize either total travel time or travel cost.[8]

## Time Management and Computer Support Systems

Increasingly, companies are setting up computer-based sales support systems to aid in planning, executing, and reporting on sales calls. In many companies, the salespeople have portable laptop computers which they carry as they travel around their territories. The primary objective of these systems is to help salespeople make more efficient use of their time.

Computerized support systems are being used to assist the rep in choosing the most promising prospects, selecting the best approaches, and gaining some knowledge of the prospect's needs before the call.[9]

Many salespeople are now entering and transmitting their call reports on personal computers. Use of a well-designed program can save the salesperson time and produce reports that are generally more thorough, accurate, and timely. For example, the 90 sales managers at Mail Boxes, Etc., the world's largest franchisor of postal service centers, use their laptops to provide daily information on all customer contacts and follow-ups. This information is used to automatically update the centralized database.[10] In *Sales & Marketing Management*'s annual technology survey, 60 percent of the managers surveyed reported that their salespeople use some type of contact management software. Eighty-one percent report that their salespeople use e-mail to communicate with them.[11]

Another area where computerized support systems are gaining wide acceptance is in the entering, checking, and scheduling of orders. Use of computers in submitting orders significantly improves the accuracy of the orders and decreases the order processing time. W. W. Grainger, an Illinois distributor of maintenance and operating supplies, uses the Internet to provide its customers with information about Grainger's inventories, estimated delivery times, and new product information. Grainger's reps report that because their customers are more knowledgeable about Grainger's products, their sales calls are quicker and more meaningful.[12]

This sales support technology also can be used *during* sales calls. Salespeople can telephone (via computer) for up-to-the-minute information on inventory and delivery conditions. Price quotations can be made, and altered if necessary, during a sales call. As described in Chapter 3, computer graphics can also be used in sales presentations.

# ■ SUMMARY

A sales territory is comprised of a number of present and potential customers located within a geographical area. This area is assigned to a salesperson or to a middleman. There are several benefits to be derived from establishing sales territories. However, formal territories may not be needed in a small company with a few salespeople selling in a local market.

Different procedures are available for designing sales territories, and some of these approaches involve sophisticated mathematical models. Basically, however, a company's territorial structure depends on (1) the potential business in the company's market and (2) the work load required from the sales force. The plan we proposed includes three broad steps.

The first step is to select a geographical control unit to serve as a territorial base. Commonly used control units are states, counties, cities, ZIP-code areas, and Metropolitan Statistical Areas.

The next step is to determine the location and potential of each customer. The third step is to determine the basic territories, which can be accomplished by using either the buildup or the breakdown method.

Using the *buildup* method, management determines the desirable call frequencies for each customer and the daily call rate for the sales rep. Contiguous control units are then combined until the total annual calls needed in the control unit equal the total number of calls the rep can make in a year.

Under the *breakdown* method, we start with sales forecasted for the total market and allocate it to the control units based on some type of market index. Then the sales volume expected from each salesperson is determined. With this input, management can set its basic territories by combining control units until the total potential in those units at least equals the expected sales from each rep.

Using either the buildup or breakdown method, the territories' boundaries may have to be modified to account for special circumstances in that geographic area.

After the territories have been established, management must assign individual salespeople to each district. As companies and markets change over time, the territorial structures may become outdated and need revision. Revising boundaries is usually a very difficult job. A key principle that management should follow is to avoid overlapping territories.

Once sales territories are designed and reps are assigned to them, management should turn its attention to planning how each rep will cover his or her territory. The management of territorial coverage involves two main tasks—routing the salespeople and managing their time.

## Key Terms

Breakdown method

Buildup method

Call frequencies

Control unit

Routing

Sales response function

Sales territory

Workload capacity

 ## QUESTIONS AND PROBLEMS

1. What control unit would you recommend in establishing sales territories for the following companies? Support your recommendation.

   *a.* Manufacturer of laptops.

   *b.* Food broker.

   *c.* Appliance wholesaler.

   *d.* Manufacturer of textile machinery.

   *e.* Manufacturer of outboard motors.

   *f.* Lumber wholesaler.

2. The text discussed several qualitative factors that may affect a territory's sales potential and thus necessitate a change in the statistically determined boundaries. How can variations in competition or ability of the sales force be reflected in square miles, trading areas, or other geographical measurements of territories?

3. Is it discriminatory to consider ethnic factors when assigning sales reps to territories?

4. Since it is impossible to equate territories perfectly, should the manager use them to provide promotions for good people? For example, should the best reps be given the choice areas?

5. What are some of the signals indicating that a company's territorial structure may need revising?

6. Assume that a territory's potential has increased to the point where the district should be realigned to form two territories. Properly developed, each of the two new units should bring an income equal to what was previously earned in the one large district. Should management assign the same salesperson, who formerly had the combined territory, to one of the new districts? Or should the rep be transferred to an entirely different area before the division is attempted?

7. Salespeople normally are prohibited from going outside their territorial boundaries in search of business. Sometimes, however, a customer located in one district will voluntarily seek out a sales rep or branch office located in another district. Perhaps this customer can realize a price advantage by buying outside his home area. What should be the position of the seller in these situations? Should it reject such business? Should it insist the order be placed in the territory where the customer is located? If the order is placed in the foreign territory, should the salesperson in the customer's home territory be given any commission or other credit?

8. If a company has several branches and insists that each of its suppliers send the same salesperson to all branches, what problems are involved? What course of action do you recommend for firms that sell to the company in question?

9. In the process of redistricting, many firms do not allow a salesperson to keep any former accounts if they are outside his or her new district. One hardware wholesaler realigned its territories. Then the company found that it faced the loss of some good customers because they said they would do business only with the wholesaler's sales rep who had been calling on them for years. Should the wholesaler make an exception and allow this rep to keep these accounts outside the new district, and thus have overlapping territories? Is the loss of these good accounts the only other alternative?

10. "Routing is a managerial device for planning and controlling the activities of the sales force." Explain the function of routing in relation to each of these concepts.

11. Under what conditions is a firm most likely to establish route plans for its sales force?

12. Under what circumstance should a customer be allowed to access the supplier's internal database?

## ◼ EXPERIENTIAL EXERCISES

A. Assuming that Hallmark has 150 U.S. sales reps, provide your recommendations for the allocation of these reps across sales territories. Be sure to base your recommendation on a relevant market factor or factors.

B. Call 10 companies and ask the sales manager (1) when the company last revised its sales territories and (2) what the catalyst or reasons were for the action.

# ■ REFERENCES

1. For a wealth of market information on MSAs, see "Survey of Buying Power," *Sales & Marketing Management,* published annually in August.

2. The equation is as follows: Sales − Cost of goods sold − Direct costs = Profit. Algebraically it is:

$1X - 0.7X - \$30,000 = 0.1X,$ which is solved as $X = \$150,000.$

3. Melanie Berger, "Take a Right at the Light and . . .," *Sales & Marketing Management,* September 1997, pp. 90–96.

4. Erika Rasmussen, "Protecting Your Turf," *Sales & Marketing Management,* March 1998, p. 90.

5. Ibid.

6. Sarah Lorge, "Marking Their Time," *Sales & Marketing Management,* September 1997, p. 105.

7. In a hopscotch pattern, a sales rep starts one trip at the farthest point, say north, of his home and works back toward home. Then on the next trip, he goes to the most distant point in another direction and works toward home.

8. *The DCI-SFA Show Preview Guide,* a supplement to *Sales & Marketing Management,* March 1998, pp. 1–41.

9. Ibid.

10. Ester Shein, "Answering Machines," *Sales & Marketing Management,* March 1998, pp. 74–78.

11. Andy Cohen, "Out of the Loop," *Sales & Marketing Management,* December 1997, pp. 79–83.

12. Ibid.

---

*Case 15-1*

## ATHENIAN PRESS, INC.
### Redesigning sales territories

Steve Womble, the sales manager for the Athenian papers, was reviewing the quarterly summary for advertising sales and was very concerned by the results, which show a slight decrease from the previous quarter. More important, ad revenues for the past two years have shown a disturbing trend. Not only had the company not made its targeted growth of 2 percent; sales were down over the past two years by 7 percent. While Steve felt that a small part of this trend might be attributed to more intense competition in recent years, he felt that most of the decrease in sales was due to the need for change in the sales organization. The market had been changing in terms of both rapid growth and increased customer expectations. Steve, who had recently been promoted to his current position, felt that Athenian Press had not responded to these changes.

Athenian Press, Inc., founded in 1945, publishes a daily newspaper and a Sunday paper, which serve the community of Athens, Tennessee, home of its main office. The target market contains the central Tennessee counties of McMinn and Meigs plus major portions of Monroe and Hamilton counties. These counties comprise a market of more than 300,000 people.

The *Athenian Daily* has a circulation of 49,582 newspapers. In the average day, over

60 percent of the adults in the area read this paper. *The Athenian Sunday Journal* has a circulation of 83,621, and it is read by approximately 89 percent of the market adults at least once per month.

As with most newspaper publishers, a major source of revenue is the amount of advertising sold. Generally, advertisements comprise more than 60 percent of any newspaper, and the size of any newspaper is determined by the number of advertisements that are included. Most of these advertisements are purchased by retail store merchants to increase customer awareness and to advertise special promotions. The *Athenian* has 800 active accounts. Athenian Press employs eight retail salespeople to call on these merchants. The salespeople report directly to the sales manager. Each salesperson is assigned to a specific territory. Within their territories, salespeople are given a great deal of independence and freedom. Athenian also employs three inside salespeople who are responsible for serving those people who place ads in the classified section. They also report to the sales manager.

Competition for retail advertisements is strong in this area. The Athenian papers compete with several other papers for the advertisements. The *Knoxville Journal* currently holds about 8 percent of the market, while the *Chattanooga Free Press* has 4 percent, and the *Tennessean,* published in Nashville, has 2 percent. The paper also competes against local radio and television stations for the ads of the retail stores. However, its greatest competitor is ADCO Mailing. ADCO is a company which produces advertising fliers that are distributed by mail. To compete with these fliers, the *Athenian* prints a weekly newspaper insert that contains coupons from the local merchants.

A salesperson for the *Athenian* has three main responsibilities. The first and most important is to meet with the customers on a regular basis to solicit their advertising. Each salesperson is expected to make 10 to 15 calls a day ranging from 30 to 60 minutes per call. For the very active accounts (approximately 50 percent of their accounts), the salespeople are supposed to schedule regular weekly meeting times to discuss the weekly order. For the less active accounts, the salespeople are expected to stay in regular contact by making appointments once or twice per month. Each salesperson is responsible for approximately 100 of these active accounts. For those accounts which advertise only infrequently, salespeople are directed to make unscheduled calls when they have time available. The second responsibility is to make all of their customers aware of upcoming promotions. If the newspaper is running a special section on "dining out," the sales force is responsible for contacting all local restaurant owners to suggest that they may want to be included in this special section. The third responsibility is to look for new accounts in their territories. The salespeople must meet with the owners and/or managers of any new stores as soon as they are under construction to inform them of *Athenian*'s services and encourage them to advertise.

Once an order has been taken by a salesperson, the salesperson is in charge of making preliminary sketches of the ad according to the specifications of the customer. These sketches are then sent to the art department, which develops the final copy. The business department is responsible for all billing and accounting; but if a problem arises with bill collection, the salesperson contacts the customer to try to resolve the issue.

The compensation for the salespeople consists of salary and commission plus a yearly bonus based on performance. Salary makes up 60 percent of their total income and commissions account for the remaining 40 percent; the bonuses are added to this base. The average compensation of $32,000 is considered competitive for this size newspaper, and the salespeople are relatively satisfied with their compensation levels. Sales trainees are paid a straight salary. New reps are given a brief indoctrination to the company, then they are assigned to "shadow" an experienced sales rep for two weeks. After this period of observing an experienced rep, they are assigned to a territory.

Steve Womble establishes yearly quotas for the salespeople and conducts their annual evaluations. On a continuing basis, he monitors their call reports and meets with each salesperson at least once a month to discuss his or her progress. Each week, the entire sales force has a breakfast where they share problems and ideas.

Recently Steve had completed a careful analysis of the salespeople's current activities. He concluded that the sales force was not spending enough time with its customers. First of all, each salesperson can spend only about 60 percent of his or her time in the field because of their responsibility of creating the preliminary sketches of the ads. Second, because of the number of accounts salespeople must service, they are not spending as much time as they should with each customer. Additionally, the 15 or 20 minutes it takes to travel between each account also limits the amount of time they can spend with each customer. As a result, most customer calls were brief and less frequent than they should be, and very little time was devoted to calling on new accounts.

Convinced of the need for change, Steve had come up with several options which he discussed with his boss, Linda Gruhn, and with his salespeople. One alternative was to assign the task of creating preliminary sketches to someone other than the salesperson, thus freeing up a significant amount of the salesperson's time. Specifically, art department personnel could perform this task. However, the salespeople felt strongly that the sketches were often needed to "close the sale," and they wanted to keep that part of the sale under their control. They also worried about the necessity for increased coordination between themselves and the artists. Finally, as one rep said to Steve, "I really enjoy that part of my job because it requires creativity and imagination. Take that away and it won't be as much fun."

Another possibility is to hire additional salespeople and realign the territories so that each salesperson would be responsible for fewer accounts. The salespeople's reaction to this option was not too surprising. They all felt that this was a threat to their sales volumes and thus to their commissions as well. Additionally, Linda Gruhn told him that he must be able to justify hiring any additional salespeople before she would approve it.

A final possibility is for Steve to take over selling to several of the largest accounts, thus giving the salespeople more time with the remaining accounts. This would decrease the time Steve spent on his managerial duties, but he felt he could handle 8 to 10 of these accounts and still provide the salespeople with an adequate amount of supervision. Needless to say, the reps were not in favor of this option, which they saw as a threat to their commissions.

**Question:**

What action should Steve take? Be sure to support the decision you recommend with the appropriate analysis.

*Case 15-2*

## NEPTUNE PLUMBING COMPANY*
### A conflict involving sales territories

"I sure don't want to lose Hank, but at the same time, I don't want Nick to get ticked off. Life sure would be simpler if each of our customers could keep all of its branches in one of our territories. Either that or those guys in Chicago should do a better job of setting our territorial boundaries!" Jack Gibson, the regional sales manager for the Neptune Plumbing Company, was speaking to one of the other executives in the company's regional office in Denver, Colorado.

The other executive smiled and replied, "You know, Jack, settling territorial disputes is just one of the jobs you're paid to do as a sales manager."

The Neptune Plumbing Company, with headquarters in Chicago, was a large manufacturer of bathroom plumbing fixtures and fittings. Sales volume in 1994 was $366 million. The line of bath fixtures included bathtubs, toilets, and wash basins (lavatories). The line of fittings included faucets, pipes, and decorative accessories. Neptune also produced bathroom fixtures and fittings for many segments of the industrial market.

Traditionally, Neptune had sold only to plumbing and heating wholesalers and large contractors. In recent years, however, Neptune had expanded its distribution channel system to reach the do-it-yourself consumer remodeling market. In the do-it-yourself market, Neptune appealed both to the ultimate consumers and to intermediaries such as small contractors, firms specializing in remodeling, and retailers who serve these people. During the 1980s, this remodeling market became especially attractive as

new-housing starts fluctuated in an unpredictable fashion. Also, as Jack Gibson commented, people tended to go for luxurious bathroom fixtures and fittings when remodeling.

Through the years, Neptune's main competition had come from large firms such as American Standard, Kohler, Crane, Eljer, and Masco (in faucets). In recent years, additional competition, especially in the remodeling market for faucets and other fixtures, came from low-priced Asian imports.

As sales manager for Neptune's Rocky Mountain region, Jack Gibson directed a regional sales force of seven reps. Jack had started with Neptune as a sales rep and, after several years of being one of the outstanding salespeople in the company, was promoted to his current position two years ago. His entire sales force operated out of the Denver regional office. Each salesperson had a separate territory. Because of the low population density generally throughout the Rocky Mountain region, each territory tended to be large. The reps thus spent quite a bit of time on the road servicing their accounts.

The compensation plan for the sales force consisted of a salary plus a bonus. The salary ranged from $30,000 to $60,000 depending on the rep's experience, time with the company, and overall performance rating. The bonus was related to the percentage of sales volume quotas achieved by a rep. These quotas were determined by the head office in Chicago and could not be adjusted by regional sales managers. The quotas were set and bonuses were paid on a quarterly basis. Separate quotas (and thus bonuses) were established for the fixtures

---
*Adapted from a case written by John P. Corrigan, under the direction of Prof. William J. Stanton.

line and the fittings line. A bonus was paid only when a rep's sales exceeded quota. The following table summarizes the quota-bonus plan:

**Quarterly quota-bonus structure**

| | Bonus paid* | |
|---|---|---|
| **Percent of Quota** | **Fixtures** | **Fittings** |
| 100–109.9 | $200 | $ 325 |
| 110–119.9 | 350 | 600 |
| 120 and over | 500 | 1,000 |

*A rep receives an additional $1,000 if sales exceed 120 percent of quota in both product categories.

As the table shows, a rep could earn a maximum quarterly bonus of $2,500—$500 for fixtures, $1,000 for fittings, and $1,000 for reaching 120 percent of quota in both categories.

Neptune's territories also were established by the home office. The territorial control unit was a state, and thus state boundaries served as territorial boundaries. The states of Colorado and Wyoming each constituted separate territories. In both of these territories, Neptune's main customers were wholesale plumbing distributors and large plumbing contractors.

Nick Costa was Neptune's sales rep in Colorado. He had worked for Neptune for 25 years, most of that time as a sales rep. He had been very successful and currently was selling at 125 percent of quota. The salesperson in Wyoming for the past two years was Henry "Hank" Day, who had been with the company for eight years. During the past two years, Hank Day had barely met his sales quotas and recently was selling at about 25 percent below quota. Hank said he had anticipated some problems in Wyoming because of the slowdown in new-home starts, but he never expected to be so far below quota. During the past few quota periods, Hank said he felt that his quota was unfairly high.

The problem Jack Gibson was worrying about revolved around Columbine Distributors Company. Columbine was a large plumbing and heating wholesale firm in Denver that had been one of Nick Costa's accounts for the past 10 years. It was a big account and Costa had served it well. In fact, Columbine depended on Nick for a monthly review of its inventory of Neptune's products to determine its order requirements.

Columbine was planning to open a branch distributorship, with a complete inventory, in Cheyenne, Wyoming. Hank Day looked forward to the opportunity to sell to Columbine. He estimated that sales to this new Wyoming office could account for 10 percent of his current quota. Hank also knew that many of his current small-contractor accounts were planning to use the new Columbine distributorship because of its close proximity to Interstate 25. Unfortunately for Hank, Costa had other ideas. About a week earlier Nick approached Hank in the Denver office. He asked for a list of Hank's Wyoming contractors who would be using the new Columbine wholesale house in Cheyenne. Costa said that any contractor accounts that bought from Columbine in Wyoming would now be his (Costa's) responsibility.

Hank Day was amazed and stunned by this request, and he refused to turn over the customer list that Nick wanted. Day reported the incident to Jack Gibson and asked that some policy guidelines be set to cover situations where customers have offices in more than one of Neptune's territories. Hank also said that he would leave the company if Costa were given the Columbine Wyoming account and his (Hank's) territory remained otherwise the same.

As Hank left the office, Gibson realized he had a problem on his hands. He did not want to lose Hank Day. He knew that Day was doing a good job in a tough territory. Gibson wished he could revise Day's quota, but company policy prohibited any quota adjustments by regional managers. At the same time, Gibson did not want to antagonize Costa—one of Neptune's finest reps— by splitting the Columbine account. Jack Gibson knew he had to do something and do it soon.

### Question:

What course of action should Jack Gibson take in this territorial dispute involving Nick Costa and Hank Day?

# CHAPTER 16

# Sales Budgets and Quotas

Salespeople underestimate how much they spend and overestimate how much they sell.

**Andy Cohen, *Sales & Marketing Management*,**
**October 1996**

The budgetary process and its offspring, the budget, are the very core of the planning-control structure of most large companies. At the end of each year, top management of most firms requires the organization to prepare a plan for operations during the coming year. Such operational plans are developed by each operating unit (marketing, sales, production, finance, research, etc.) according to the basic sales and profit targets for the year given them by top management. Each department head then develops a detailed plan of what the unit must do to achieve these goals. The plan also includes a detailed itemization of the costs of doing those things—the projected costs. The projected costs ultimately are the basis for the budgets discussed. The budgetary process is a lengthy, time-consuming managerial task. It is not much fun. But it must be done!

The sales forecast provides the basis for developing company operating plans. Everything is keyed to the level of expected sales activity. The budgets are essentially based on the sales forecast. If the forecast is wrong, the resulting budgets will have to be revised often to reflect actual sales results.

A *budget* is simply a tool, a financial plan, that an administrator uses to plan for profits by anticipating revenues and expenditures. By using various planning procedures, management hopes to guide operations to a given level of profit on a certain volume of operations.

## ■ BUDGETING AND STRATEGIC PLANNING

Just how does budgeting fit into strategic and operational planning? The answer is that the budget reflects the dollar manifestation of the plan. It is quite difficult to put dollar costs to those plans and make them all result in a profit. The budget is the planner's governor. It forces a reality on the planner that is mandatory for profitable operation. Ultimately all plans must be quantified into dollars and checked against reality.

451

# ◨ PURPOSES OF BUDGETING

The budget is very important for the successful operation of the sales force. It serves several purposes including planning, coordination, and evaluation, each of which is discussed in this section.

## Planning

Companies formulate marketing and sales objectives. The budget determines how these objectives will be met. The budget is both a *plan of action* and a *standard of performance* for the various departments. Once the budget is established, the department can begin organizing to realize that plan. This is especially important to salespeople. It is through a detailed breakdown of the sales budget among products, territories, and customers that sales reps learn what management expects of them.

## Coordination

Maintaining the desired relationship between expenditures and revenues is important in operating a business. The objective of a business is to buy revenues at a reasonable cost, and a budget establishes what this cost should be. If sales of $5 million are forecast, management can establish how much it can afford to pay for that revenue. If the company wants a profit of 10 percent on sales, then $4.5 million can be paid to "buy" the $5 million in revenue. Part of the $4.5 million would go to the production and administrative departments, and another portion would be available to operate the sales department. Thus the budget enables sales executives to coordinate expenses with sales and with the budgets of the other departments. The budget also restricts the sales executives from spending more than their share of the funds available for the purchase of revenues. Hence the budget helps to prevent expenses from getting out of control.

## Evaluation

Any goal, once established, becomes a tool for evaluation of performance. If the organization meets its goals, management can consider the performance successful. Hence the sales department budgets become tools to evaluate the department's performance. By meeting the sales and cost goals set forth in the budget, a sales manager is presenting strong evidence of his or her success as an executive. The manager who is unable to meet budgetary requirements is usually less well regarded.

# ◨ DETERMINING THE SALES BUDGET

Determining expenditure levels for each category of selling expense is very difficult. Two methods for determining budget levels are discussed below.

## Budgeting by Percentage of Sales Method

Many business people plan and control their enterprises by percentages. Using this method, the manager multiplies the sales forecast by various percentages for each category of expense. The resultant product then becomes the dollar amount budgeted for each of the respective categories.

The percentages used for each category may be based on the manager's experience and/or feelings about what portion of the sales dollar can or must be spent on each business function to achieve the desired profit. The percentages might also be based on published industry averages for expense categories. These published averages should be used only as guidelines which must be adjusted to reflect the unique aspects of the particular organization. These percentages are then used in controlling sales and their costs.

Of course there are no guarantees that setting the budgets using these percentages will lead to optimal performance. In fact the expense allocations, using this method, will follow the direction of change in sales. For example, if sales are forecasted to decline, then the budget allocations for all expense categories will decrease as well. This may or may not be the optimal allocation to counter the sales decline. Additionally, the effectiveness of this method is dependent on the firm having accurate sales forecasts. Despite the limitations, the manager knows that if expenses are kept within their percentage budgets, final operations will come out as planned.

## Budgeting by the Objective and Task Method

In the objective and task method, the manager starts with the sales objectives, which are specified in the sales forecast. Then the manager determines the task that must be accomplished in order to achieve the objectives and estimates the costs of performing those tasks. These costs will be reviewed in light of the company's overall profit objective. If the costs are too high, the manager may be asked to find a different way of achieving the objective or some adjustment may be made to the original objective. This iterative process continues until management is satisfied with both the objectives and the means of achieving them. Many firms use some variation of the objective and task method.

The American Marketing Association, a nonprofit association of marketing professionals and academics, uses an objective and task method to develop its budget. Its budgeting process starts with forecasts of membership revenue and publication sales. Then the senior managers estimate the costs of the programs designed to achieve the forecasted revenues. If the projected expenses exceed revenues, adjustments in costs, programs, and revenues are made until the budget is balanced.

# ▌ BUDGETS FOR SALES DEPARTMENT ACTIVITIES

Sales executives are responsible for formulating three basic budgets: the sales, selling-expense, and sales department administrative budgets.

## The Sales Budget

The **sales budget** is the revenue or unit volume anticipated from sales of the firm's products. This is the key budget. It is the basis of all operating activities in the sales department and in the production and finance areas. The validity of the entire budgetary process depends on the accuracy of this one sales budget. If it is in error, all others will also be in error.

The sales budget is based on the sales forecast, which was discussed in the previous chapter; but the sales budget calls for extreme detail. Every single product sold by the firm must be accounted for. It does little good to tell production planners that $100,000 worth of small parts will be needed. They must be told specifically what small parts will be sold, in what quantities, and when.

Management estimates the sales of each product, and often makes separate forecasts for each class of customer and each territorial division. Budgets for territories and classes of customers usually are of interest only to sales executives. Other departments normally need only the sales budget for product divisions.

To some extent a sales budget can become a self-fulfilling prophecy. You predict that 100 units of Model 101 will be sold in January, so 100 units are produced to be sold in January. While sales of that item may fall short of the goal, they cannot exceed it, for that's all there is to sell. Moreover, there is considerable pressure to make the planned sales figure a reality. Thus, once the sales budget is set, management digs in to make it become fact.

## The Selling-Expense Budget

The **selling-expense budget** anticipates the various expenditures for personal-selling activities. These are the salaries, commissions, and expenses for the sales force. This is not a difficult budget to develop. If the salespeople are on a straight commission, the amount of the revenue allotted for compensation expense will be determined by the commission rate. Experience clearly indicates how much money must be set aside for expenses. If sales reps are paid a salary, the process merely requires compiling the amounts, taking into consideration any raises or promotions to be made during the coming period. Any plans for sales force expansion also should be anticipated in this budget.

The selling-expense budget must be closely coordinated with the sales budget. Suppose the sales budget calls for the introduction of a new product line that requires considerable retraining of the sales force and the addition of a new service department. The expense budgets must reflect those needs. What will it cost to accomplish each line in the sales budget? That is essentially the question the sales manager must answer in preparing the selling-expense budgets that will accompany the sales budget.

## The Administrative Budget

In addition to having direct control over management of the sales force, the typical sales executive is also an office manager. Ordinarily, the staff includes sales department secretaries and office workers; the total staff can be large. There may be several assistant sales managers, sales supervisors, and sales trainers under the sales manager. Budgetary provisions must be made for their salaries and their staffs. Management must also budget for such sales office operating expenses as supplies, rent, heat, power and light, office equipment, and general overhead. These costs constitute the **administrative budget.**

# ■ The Budgeting Process for the Firm

Everything starts with the sales budget, described earlier. From it, data flow in five directions. Figure 16-1 shows the flow of information from one budget to another. The sales budget provides the basis for the various sales department budgets, such as advertising, selling expenses, and sales office expenses. Sales budget figures also flow directly to the production department. Here the total production budget is established, and from that the various materials and labor budgets are determined. The financial officer also uses anticipated sales figures from the sales budget to prepare the cash and the profit and loss budgets. The cash budget is a tool used to determine how many dollars will flow into and out of the firm each month. This budget is necessary because of the time lag between expenditure and receipt of funds. It is necessary to lay out money for materials, labor, advertising, and selling expenses many months prior to selling the merchandise. Then, after sales of the goods, it may be several months before the firm receives cash. The financial officer must ensure that the firm has sufficient cash to enable it to finance the lag between the expenditure and receipt of funds.

The financial officer also uses the anticipated net sales figure as the beginning of the profit and loss budget. The budgets for sales department expenses, production, and general administrative expenses all flow into the profit and loss and cash budgets to determine the expected costs of operation. Thus all budgets are summarized in the profit and loss and cash budgets. Errors in the sales department budgets have a twofold effect on the financial plan. First, the revenues will not be correct. Second, expenses will be out of line because the sales budget determines the production and administrative expenses.

■ **FIGURE 16-1**    **Flow of information from sales budget to other budgets**

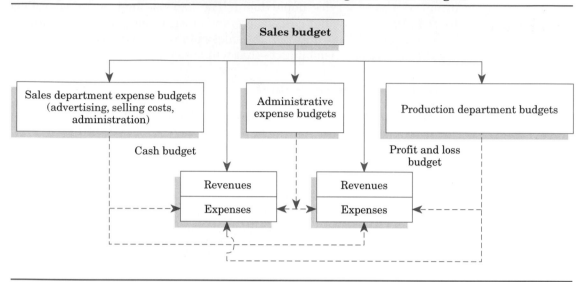

# ■ BUDGET PERIODS

Budgets are commonly created for yearly, semiannual, and quarterly periods. Some firms prepare budgets for all three periods; others prefer to operate on an annual basis, thereby reducing the amount of paperwork required.

The quarterly budget forces a reappraisal of the firm's position four times a year, thereby decreasing the likelihood that operations will get out of control. Many companies find a quarterly system advisable because that is roughly their operations conversion cycle. Garment makers usually have four conversion cycles per year. That is, they put out four different lines of goods, one for each season, and find it convenient to budget for each selling season. The main advantage of a short planning period is that it is more likely to be accurate. The shorter the forecasting period, the less likelihood there is that the estimate will be disturbed by unforeseen developments. In deciding which period to use, a firm must balance the degree of control with the costs of compiling the budgets.

# ■ THE BUDGET-MAKING PROCEDURE

The first step in the budgetary process is to translate the sales forecasts into the work that must be done to achieve the forecasts. This is no easy task. The firm may want to introduce a new line of whoozits, since widgets are now obsolete. What does that mean in terms of the people needed (staff

**Sales managers often get input from their reps when they set quotas.**

requirements)? What will it do to office expenses, field-selling costs, trade show commitments, and so on?

Each administrative unit must determine how much money it will need to meet the performance goals set for it. This is usually done by (1) surveying each of the activities the unit must perform, (2) determining how many people will be required to accomplish the job, and (3) figuring what materials and supplies will be needed for them to do the job properly.

Many sales managers use the previous year's budget as a starting point. Then they take into account any changes in sales strategies and what those will cost to implement. They also get as much information as possible from their salespeople about changes in their territories which may necessitate changes in the budgets.[1] Once the sales department budgets are compiled into one major budget, it is forwarded to the financial executive, who disseminates the information to the other departments.

The due dates on various budgets must be staggered if the budgeting program is to be a success. The sales department budget must be in the hands of the financial officer before final preparation of the production budget, since the production budget is completely dependent on the sales budget. Compiling all the budgets into the overall cash and profit and loss budgets can be done only after all other work on the plans of the organization has been completed.

Meetings, compromises, and much hand-wringing are all part of the budgeting process. This "give and take" process can be seen in the comments of the sales manager for American Paging in Minnesota: "Our senior corporate managers meet for an entire week to hammer out our budget. Generally, we'll fight for what's necessary and they deliver the objectives they expect."[2]

Administrative heads tend to be overly generous in their estimates of funds they will need for the coming year. Few managers relish working on tight budgets, yet in well-managed organizations all budgets are tight. As noted by Bill Thorne, president of Morris Paper Company, "If you have a limited budget, it forces you to pay closer attention to the value of your dollar and the quality you expect in return."[3]

Every aspect of this process has become more efficient with the use of computers. With computer spreadsheets, it is possible to make changes in one part of the budget and see the impact of those changes on all other parts of the budget immediately.

Sound planning procedures dictate that each administrative head sign off on all plans and budgets. That is, they agree that they will make it happen.

## MANAGING WITH BUDGETS

Once prepared and in operation, the budget becomes one of the manager's regularly used tools. The previous month's actual sales and expenses come back from the accounting department by the middle of the present month. All figures that are over budget are marked for attention. Some of the accounts that are over budget are understandable; the manager knows the reason and either accepts it or knows that the matter will be corrected in the near future. If there are others which are significantly over budget and the manager does not know why, he will investigate the overage and take corrective action if necessary.

## SALES QUOTAS

Up to this point in our sales planning activities, we have prepared a sales forecast and a sales budget. We also have established the sales territories. Now it is time to translate the results of these planning activities into work assignments in the form of sales quotas for our sales force or other marketing units.

A **sales quota** is a performance goal assigned to a marketing unit for a specific period of time. The marketing unit may be a salesperson, a branch office, a district or region, or a dealer or distributor. For example, each sales rep might be assigned a sales volume goal or a gross-margin goal for the coming three-month period. This quota goal may be stated in dollars, product units, or selling activities. The specified time period usually is a month, a quarter, six months, or a year; but it may be for as short a period as a week. A marketing unit's quotas may also be established for individual products and/or types of customers. When salespeople achieve their quotas, they often receive some sort of reward for their performance.

### Relation to Sales Potential, Sales Forecast, and Budget

A sales quota—especially a *sales volume quota*—is related to both the sales potential and sales forecast. The sales potential influences the sales forecast, and the forecast helps to shape the quotas. However, a sales quota is *not* the same as *either* of these planning tools. Recall from Chapter 14 that a sales potential is the share of total industry sales that a company expects to sell. But often certain territorial conditions or the characteristics of the sales rep—experience, physical condition, and the like—are such that a particular territory cannot reach its full sales potential. Consequently, in that territory the sales volume quota may very well be *less* than the district's sales potential.

Management usually sets sales quotas so that their total equals the sales budget. Thus if all the reps reached their quotas, the sales budget would be met. This is *management by the numbers;* if everyone reaches "their numbers," the "company's numbers" fall nicely into place, fulfilling the operational plan for marketing.

## SALES QUOTAS AND STRATEGIC MANAGEMENT

Sales quotas help in planning and evaluating sales force activities. When setting sales quotas, the sales managers should consider the goals and strategies developed in the marketing planning. If the marketing goal is to increase market share, then a sales *volume* quota may be appropriate. However, if the goal is to increase a company's return on investment or net profit as a percentage of sales, then a sales *volume* quota probably is *not* appropriate. Instead, some form of quota based on gross margin, or even an expense quota, is more in line with a profit-oriented goal. Thus good sales quotas can help effectively implement the strategic plans.

Additionally, sales quotas can also help guide the sales reps' activities. For example, quotas that are too high can cause sales reps to high-pressure and overload the customers. Quotas that are too low will not serve to motivate the reps.

Finally, sales quotas are a widely used basis for evaluating sales force performance. Salespeople who meet their quotas are judged to be performing adequately in the activity the quota concerns. Thus quotas can have a big impact on a salesperson's morale. Because of these strategic and behavioral considerations, it is important that management do the best job possible when setting quotas.

## PURPOSES OF SALES QUOTAS

Sales quotas serve several useful purposes, as shown in Figure 16-2 and discussed below.

**To indicate strong or weak spots in the selling structure.** When accurate quotas are established for each territory, management can

■ **FIGURE 16-2**  **Purposes of sales quotas**

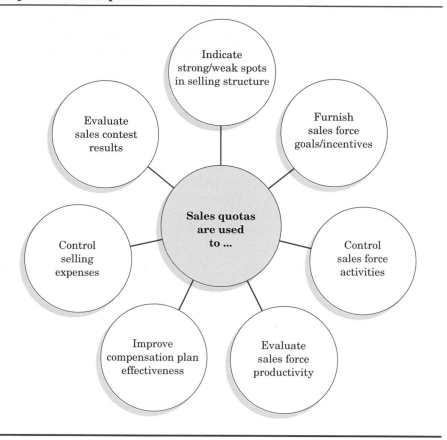

determine the extent of territorial development by whether or not the quota is being reached. If the sales total significantly exceeds the predetermined standards, management should analyze the reasons for this variance. If the sales in a district fail to meet the quota, this failure tells management that something has gone wrong. Of course, it does not tell *why* the failure occurred. It may be that competition is stronger than expected, the salespeople have not done a good selling job, or the potential was overestimated.

**To furnish goals and incentives for the sales force.** In business, as in any other walk of life, individuals usually perform better if their activities are guided by standards and goals. It is not enough to say to a salesperson, "We expect you to do a good selling job." It is much more meaningful to express this expectation in a specific quota consisting of a given dollar sales volume or number of new accounts to be acquired during the next month. Without a standard of measurement, sales reps cannot be certain their performance is satisfactory. A recent survey found that *sales relative to quota* is the most widely used performance criterion by which salespeople are judged.[4]

**To control salespeople's activities.** A corollary to the preceding point is that quotas enable management to direct the activities of the sales force more effectively than would otherwise be possible. Through the use of the appropriate type of quota, executives can encourage a given activity such as selling high-margin items or getting orders from new customers. The sales reps are not likely to know which area of activity should be stressed unless management tells them. Swissotel North America wanted their salespeople to spend a greater percentage of their time with customers, so management instituted a quota of six quality sales calls per day for each rep.[5]

**To evaluate productivity of salespeople.** Quotas provide a yardstick for measuring the general effectiveness of sales representatives. By comparing a rep's actual results with his or her quota, management can evaluate that person's performance. Quota performance also provides guidance for field supervisors by indicating areas of activity where the sales force needs help. Decisions on whether to give salespeople promotions or raises are often based largely on their performance in relation to their quotas.

**To improve effectiveness of compensation plans.** A quota structure can play a significant role in a sales compensation system. Quotas can furnish incentives to salespeople who are paid straight salary. A sales rep knows, too, that a creditable performance in meeting assigned quotas reflects favorably on him or her when it is time for a salary review.

In some cases, salespeople receive a bonus if they achieve a certain quota or they may receive a commission on all sales above some preset level (or quota) of sales. At Disney, for example, the reps earn commissions if they exceed ambitious quotas set by the company for the number of hotel rooms booked.[6]

Inequities in territorial potential may cause inequities in compensation unless a firm establishes a quota system. In one territory, a person may get a $1,500 monthly salary plus a 5 percent commission on sales over a quota of $10,000. In a district that presents low potential and a more difficult selling job, the sales rep may have the same arrangement, except that the commission starts when the rep reaches a quota of only $7,000 each month.

**To control selling expense.** Management can often encourage expense control by the use of expense quotas alone, without tying them to the compensation plan. Some companies gear payments for the salespeople's expenses to a quota. For instance, a business may pay all the expenses of a sales rep up to 8 percent of sales. Other companies may set an expense quota and let the salespeople know their effectiveness is being judged in part by how well they meet it.

**To evaluate sales contest results.** Sales quotas are used frequently in conjunction with sales contests. Salespeople rarely have equal opportunities in a contest unless management makes some adjustment to compensate for variation in territorial potentials and workloads. Using the common denominator of a quota, management can ensure each participant a reasonably equal chance of winning, provided the quota has been set accurately.

## TYPES OF QUOTAS

The most frequently used types of sales quotas, as outlined in Figure 16-3, are those based on:

- Sales volume
- Gross margin or net profit
- Some combination of the four
- Activities
- Expenses

The type of quota that management selects depends on several factors, including the nature of the product and the market. Let's assume a company wants to correct an unbalanced inventory. Then a volume quota set by product lines may be used to move the surplus stocks of the items. If management wants to develop a new territory, it should probably set an activity quota in preference to a volume or expense quota.

### Sales Volume Quotas

Undoubtedly the most widely used type of sales quota is one based on sales volume. A **volume quota** may be established for a geographical area, a product line, a customer, a time period, or any combination of these

**■ FIGURE 16-3**

**Types of sales quotas**

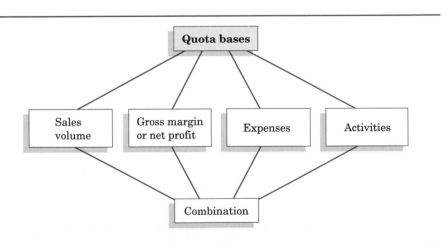

bases. Ordinarily, it is more effective to set a monthly or quarterly quota than an annual one. Some high-performance sales organizations even set daily sales quotas.

Even when a company sells a large number of products, it may be feasible to group them into a few broad lines and then set unit quotas for each line. For example, an appliance wholesaler may set unit goals for small appliances in one group, white goods (refrigerators, ranges, washers) as a second group, and electronic products (radios, stereos, televisions) as a third line.

Management uses volume goals because they are simple to understand and easy to calculate. Many sales managers still regard sales volume as the only real measure of a rep's worth to the company. However, sales volume alone does not tell the full story of a rep's productivity and effectiveness. It does not indicate the profit generated by the person's efforts. Nor does it measure the extent to which the rep has done a fully balanced sales job. In fact, volume quotas discourage balanced activities by the sales force because they stress volume to the detriment of nonselling activities.

## Profit Quotas

Many companies set quotas based on gross margin or net profit. These goals may be established on many of the same bases as a volume quota. For instance, a gross margin quota may be set for a salesperson, a branch, or a group of products. The preference some companies show for profit instead of volume quotas reflects management's recognition of the importance of profit as compared with volume.

High-volume operators are not necessarily the best sales reps for company interests. Easy-to-sell items may be low-margin items. Unless the firm controls these reps, they may decrease company profits every time they increase their volume. They may be emphasizing the sales of unprofitable items or sales to unprofitable customers.

One significant drawback to gross margin or net profit quotas is the possibility that friction may arise between management and the reps. The salespeople may not understand how their quotas were calculated, and the reps may not be able to measure their progress during the quota period. Another limitation—especially of a net profit quota—is that the rep has no control over some of the factors on which the quota is based. For example, unexpectedly high production costs may leave the company with little or no profit on a certain product.

A compromise approach is to base the quota on a rep's contribution to profit. Contribution to profit, or *contribution margin,* is the amount left after deducting a salesperson's direct expenses (the ones the rep can control) from his or her gross margin. The remainder is the amount the rep is contributing to cover the overhead (fixed) costs.

## Expense Quotas

Some companies attempt to encourage a profit consciousness by establishing a quota based on the rep's travel and other expenses. Often, the expense quota is related to sales volume or to the compensation plan. A sales rep may be given an expense quota equal to 4 percent of sales. That is, direct expenses, such as travel, entertainment, food, and lodging, must not exceed 4 percent of net sales volume.

Expense quotas probably encourage a salesperson to be more aware of costs and profits than volume goals. Nevertheless, it seems that an expense quota is a negative approach to the problem. A rep's attention may be devoted more to cutting expenses than to boosting the sales of profitable products.

## Activity Quotas

One way to decrease the overemphasis on sales volume is to establish a quota based on activities. Management may select from such tasks as (1) daily calls, (2) new customers called on, (3) orders from new accounts, (4) product demonstrations made, and (5) displays built. An activity quota properly established and controlled can do much to stimulate a fully balanced sales job. This type of quota is particularly valuable for use with missionary salespeople. Probably the principal difficulties in administering an activity quota are, first, to determine whether the activity actually was performed and, second, to find out how effectively it was done.

The logic is sound. Sales result from doing a lot of things right—making many calls on the right people, giving demonstrations, opening new accounts, suggesting new or additional products. Thus, if the manager wants to build the sales volume, a way must be found to encourage reps to do the basic things that result in sales.

## Combination Quotas

Companies that are not satisfied with any single type of quota may combine two or more types. As an example, a firm may want to establish a quota based on three activities, plus gross margin on the products sold. The results for one rep may come out as follows for the January–March quarter:

|  | Quota | Actual | Percent of Quota Attained |
|---|---|---|---|
| Gross margin, all products | $30,000 | $25,000 | 83 |
| Product demonstrations made | 120 | 135 | 117 |
| Orders from new accounts | 15 | 17 | 113 |
| Window displays obtained | 20 | 19 | 95 |
|  |  |  | Average = 102% |

The salesperson in this example reached a little over 103 percent of her combined quota. The four components were weighted equally, but management may want to assign more value to some elements than others.

A combination quota seeks to use the strong points of several types of quotas, but frequently such a plan is limited by its complexity. In many cases, combination quota structures are so complicated that they are not easily understood by the reps: Then the quota becomes a source of dissatisfaction rather than an incentive.[7] Also, a sales rep may overemphasize one element in the quota plan. In this illustration, for example, the rep may reach 200 percent of the quota for product demonstrations and do virtually nothing to secure orders from new accounts.

# ■ BASES FOR SETTING A SALES VOLUME QUOTA

The sales volume quota illustrates quota-setting procedures well because it is the most commonly used type. However, the same procedure can be used for the other types. Fundamentally, two general approaches may be used to set volume quotas:

- Quotas are set in conjunction with territorial sales potentials.
- Quotas are set on the basis of considerations other than sales potentials, such as past sales, executive judgment, salesperson determination, or compensation design.

## Quotas Based on Sales Potential

One common practice in quota setting is to relate quotas directly to the territorial sales potentials. These potentials are the share of the estimated total industry sales that the company expects to realize in a given territory. The company-wide sales forecast for many firms is often built by piecing together estimates calculated for each territory.

Thus if the territorial sales potentials or forecasts have already been determined and the quotas are to be related to these measures, the job of quota setting is largely completed. For instance, let's assume that the sales potential in territory A is $300,000, or 4 percent of the total company potential. Then management may assign this amount as a quota for the salesperson who covers that territory. The total of all territorial quotas then would equal the company sales potential.

### Adjustments to Potential-Based Quotas
In some cases management chooses to use the estimate of potential as the starting point in determining the quota. These potentials are then adjusted for one or more of the factors discussed below.

*Human Factors.*    A quota may have to be adjusted downward because an older salesperson is covering the district. The rep may have done a fine job for the company for years but is now approaching retirement age and slowing down because of physical limitations. It would not be good human relations—or ethical—to discharge or force the person into early retirement. Nor would it help the rep's morale to be assigned an unreachable quota. Sometimes such reps are given smaller territories with correspondingly lower quotas. Likewise sometimes new reps are given lower quotas for the first few years until they reach a greater level of competence. Giving younger reps more attainable quotas will help build their confidence and keep their morale high.

*Psychological Factors.*    Management understands that it is human nature to relax after a goal has been reached. Therefore, some sales executives set their quotas a little higher than the expected potential, just in case some reps can do better than expected. On the other hand, management must not set the goal unrealistically high. A quota that is too far above potential can discourage the sales force. The ideal psychological quota is one that is a bit above the potential but can still be met and even exceeded by working effectively.

*Compensation.*    Some companies relate their quotas basically to the sales potential, but adjust them to allow for the compensation plan. In such a case the company is really using both the quota and the compensation systems to stimulate the sales force. As an example, one organization may set its quotas at 90 percent of potential. It pays one bonus if the quota is met and an additional bonus if the sales reach 100 percent of the potential.

## Quotas Based on Factors Other Than Potential

A company that does not wish to set its sales quotas in relation to territorial potentials has these alternatives:

- Quotas may be set strictly on the basis of past sales.
- Quotas may be determined by executive judgment alone.
- Quotas may be related to the compensation plan.
- The salespeople may set their own quotas.

### Past Sales Alone

In some organizations, the byword is "Beat last year's figures." As a result, sales volume quotas are based strictly on the preceding year's sales or on an average of sales over a period of several years. Management sets each salesperson's quota at an arbitrary percentage increase over sales in some past period. About the only merits in this method of quota setting are computational simplicity and low-cost administration. If a firm follows this procedure, it should at least use an average sales figure for the past several years as a base, not just the previous year's sales. Random or irregular events would greatly affect a sales index based on only one year.

However, a quota-setting method based on past performance *alone* is subject to severe limitations. This method ignores possible changes in a territory's sales potential. General business conditions this year may be depressed in a district, thus cutting the sales potential. Or promising new customers may have moved into the district, thus boosting the potential volume.

Basing quotas on previous years' sales may not uncover poor performance in a given territory. A person may have had sales of $100,000 last year, and the quota is increased 5 percent for this year. The rep may even reach the goal of $105,000. However, the potential in the district may be $200,000. This salesperson may perform poorly for years without management recognizing that a problem exists. Quotas set on past sales also ignore the percentage of sales potential already achieved. Assume the sales potential in each of two territories is $200,000 and rep A's volume was $150,000 last year while rep B's was $210,000. It may not be realistic to expect each to increase sales the same percentage over last year's figures.

Moreover, "chase your tail" quotas—in which the more the reps sell, the more they are supposed to sell—destroy morale and ultimately cause top producers to leave the company. Consider the case of Leana Grandy, one of Xerox's top sales reps. She sold the Xerox line to the Los Angeles School District. As she kept exceeding her quotas by huge margins, the company kept increasing her quotas, which in turn lowered her pay. She said, "It finally dawned on me that they weren't going to let me earn more than a certain amount."

### Executive Judgment

In setting quotas for sales reps, some companies rely entirely on what they refer to as executive judgment, which is more precisely called guesswork. Executive judgment is usually an indispensable ingredient in a sound procedure for setting quotas, but to use it *alone* is certainly not recommended. Even though the administrator may be very experienced, too many risks are involved in relying solely on this factor without referring to quantitative market measures.

Sometimes management sets "must-do" quotas. One realtor tells her agents, "Sell $3 million or hit the road. You're wasting my time, money, and space." The Keith Landberg Paper Company sets "must-do" quotas for its reps: Make $150,000 a year in commissions or look elsewhere for employment.

### Quotas Related to Compensation Design

Earlier in this chapter we discussed the idea of relating compensation to volume quotas based on potential. Quotas may also be used in compensation plans without any relation to potential. As a case in point, a company may prefer to pay its sales representatives by straight commission. However, management realizes that the reps prefer a salary-plus-commission plan. Therefore, the company adopts a combination plan, with a salary of

$1,200 per month and a commission of 6 percent on all sales over $20,000 a month. By using the quota, management in effect achieves its preference for a straight commission because no commission is paid until the salary is recouped (6 percent of $20,000 equals $1,200).

### Salespeople Set Their Own Quotas

Some companies place the quota problem in the laps of the sales representatives by letting them set their own performance goals. The rationale for this move is that the salespeople are closer to their territories than management and thus can do a better job. Also, setting their own quotas allows the reps to reflect their individual abilities. Finally, if sales reps make the decisions about their own goals, they will have higher morale and strive more to attain the quota.

From a practical standpoint, however, this method leaves much to be desired. Salespeople do not have access to the necessary information. Also, salespeople often tend to be optimistic about their capabilities and the opportunities in their districts. Therefore, they may set unrealistically high quotas. Then as the period goes on and it becomes evident that they cannot reach the goal, a serious morale problem may develop.

## ADMINISTRATION OF SALES QUOTAS

Usually the sales department is responsible for establishing the sales quota, and no approval of a higher executive is needed. Within the sales organization, the task may rest with any of several executives. The chief sales executive may be responsible for setting the total company quota. But the individual breakdown may be delegated down through the regional and district managers. Or territorial sales potentials may be given to the district managers, and they set the salespeople's quotas. Many attributes found in good compensation plans, territorial designs, and other aspects of sales management are also found in good quota plans, as seen in Figure 16-4.

### Typical Administrative Weaknesses

Companies that do not use sales quotas may justify their position by citing various limitations in a sales quota system. Generally speaking, however, these limitations are not *inherent* in the system. Instead they are *administrative* weaknesses that reflect management's failure to utilize the characteristics of a good quota plan.

Probably the major criticism of quotas is that it is difficult or even impossible to set them accurately. This point may be justified in some cases. Perhaps a company sells a new product for which very little marketing information is available. Or a firm sells a product that requires several quota periods to elapse before the sale is consummated. However, just because a company cannot set a goal that is 100 percent statistically correct is no reason for management to abandon the entire project.

■ **FIGURE 16-4**

| | |
|---|---|
| **Characteristics of a good quota plan** | ■ **Realistic attainability.** If a quota is to spur the sales force to maximum effort, the goal must be realistically attainable. If it is too far out of reach, the salespeople will lose their incentive. |
| | ■ **Objective accuracy.** Regardless of what type of quota management uses, it should be related to potentials. Executive judgment is also required, but it should not be the sole factor in the decision. |
| | ■ **Ease of understanding and administering.** A quota must be easy for both management and the sales force to understand. Also, the system should be economical to administer. |
| | ■ **Flexibility.** All quota systems need adequate flexibility. Particularly if the quota period is as long as a year, management may have to make adjustments because of changes in market conditions. |
| | ■ **Fairness.** A good quota plan is perceived as fair to the people involved. The workload imposed by quotas should be the same for all sales reps. However, this does not mean that quotas must be equal. Differences in potential, competition, and reps' abilities do exist. |

In other instances, quotas are not used because management claims they lead to high-pressure selling and generally emphasize some activities at the expense of others. These criticisms may well be justified if a sales volume quota is used alone. Or the compensation and quota plans may be linked to encourage a high volume of sales, irrespective of the gross margin. A quota also may overstress a given selling or nonselling activity. However, these are indications of planning or operating weaknesses. They are not inherent disadvantages of quotas.

## Gaining Sales Force Acceptance of a Quota Plan

A final essential ingredient in a well-planned and well-operated quota system is its wholehearted acceptance by the sales force. Salespeople often are suspicious of quotas, either because the purposes are not apparent or because there are questions about the factors underlying the plan. The purposes of the quota, the bases on which the quota are set, and the methods used in the process should be explained to the reps. When the quota is ready for formal installation, the sales force will probably be more inclined to accept it if they have had a hand in its development. Management also stands to gain by soliciting ideas from salespeople, who may introduce considerations that escaped management's notice.

Sales reps should be kept informed about their progress toward meeting the performance goal. Conferences and correspondence with the reps

**?**

## AN ETHICAL DILEMMA

Many companies have a sales force compensation plan that is a salary plus a bonus for reaching a sales volume quota. Other firms employ a performance evaluation system that rates salespeople based on their ability to reach their sales quotas. In order to reach his or her quota—whether it be for compensation, performance evaluation, or some other purpose—sometimes a rep will predate or postdate some orders.

To illustrate, let's assume that the reps in our company are assigned quarterly (three-month) sales volume quotas. One salesperson has done well during the first quarter, reaching his quota by mid-March. That rep then generates additional orders during the last half of March. But he arranges with the customers to delay delivery until early April, or he simply dates the orders as of early April.

Or he may tell the customers that the company is temporarily out of stock in late March and the product will be available in early April. In any event, these postdated orders show up on his sales record in April. So he gets a running start on meeting his quota for the second quarter.

In another situation, predating orders may occur when a rep is having difficulty meeting her quota, say for the first quarter. In this case, she knows she is going to get some orders from regular customers in early April. So she arranges with the customers to have these orders placed or dated in late March, but for April delivery. Thus these orders are counted toward her January–March quota period.

Is it ethical for sales reps to predate or postdate their orders so they can meet their quotas for a certain period?

often are necessary. The sales force also needs some incentive to reach the goal. This may come from a bonus for achieving the quota or from some other direct link with the compensation plan. Management should make it clear that quota performance is reflected in periodic merit ratings, salary reviews, or considerations for promotion.

## ◼ SUMMARY

The budget is a financial plan that the manager uses to plan for profits by anticipating revenues and expenditures. Budgeting serves several purposes: planning, coordination and control, and evaluation. There are primarily two methods of budgeting. The first is budgeting by percentages, whereby expenses are estimated as a percentage of sales. The other method is objective and task, where the manager determines the tasks necessary to achieve the objectives and then estimates the costs of performing these tasks. Both methods rely on developing an accurate sales forecast.

There are three basic budgets for the sales department. These are the sales budget, the selling-expense budget, and the administrative budget.

The budgetary process begins in the sales department with the formulation of a sales forecast. From that figure, a detailed sales budget is developed that contains the expected sales of each item in the product line. The production budgets and the selling-expense budgets are developed from the sales budget.

Once the sales forecast and budgets are developed, they become the standard by which the manager judges performance.

A sales quota is a sales performance goal. It serves such purposes as (1) indicating strong and weak spots in a company's selling structure; (2) furnishing a goal and an incentive for the sales force; (3) improving the effectiveness of compensation plans; (4) controlling selling expenses; and (5) evaluating sales contest results.

Sales volume (in dollars and in product units) is the most frequently used basis for setting sales quotas. Other commonly used bases are gross margin or net profit, selling expenses, selling activities, or some combination of these elements.

Basically, two general approaches may be used to set sales volume quotas. In the first situation, quotas are based on territorial potentials. Sometimes they are adjusted in light of human factors, psychological factors, or compensation design considerations.

In the second situation, quotas are set independently of any consideration of sales potentials. For example, the quota may be based strictly on past sales. Or it may be determined by executive judgment alone. In some firms, the salespeople set their own quotas.

Management should recognize the characteristics of a good quota plan. They must also make sure that their salespeople understand the bases on which quotas are set and the process which is used to set them.

## Key Terms

| | | |
|---|---|---|
| Activity quota | Profit quota | Selling-expense budget |
| Administrative budget | Sales budget | Volume quota |
| Expense quota | Sales quota | |

## ◼ QUESTIONS AND PROBLEMS

1. How can a manager build flexibility into the budgeting process to provide for unexpected events?

2. How can an executive avoid having subordinates ask for more funds than are needed?

3. Can budgets be developed without an accurate sales forecast?

4. If total expenses must be reduced by 10 percent, should an across-the-board cut or a selective reduction be used? If selective, how should the selection be made?

5. You feel your sales reps are underpaid. You requested a large increase in the budget for them but it was denied in a conference with the other vice presidents, who all wanted pay increases for their people. You still feel strongly that more money is needed if the sales force is to be kept effective. What would you do about the situation?

6. Your CEO demands that you sign off on an operational plan and budget that you feel is totally unrealistic. What would you do?

7. Cite some specific instances when management may have good reasons for not using sales quotas. What are the reasons in each case?

8. Should quotas be used in each of the following cases? If so, what type do you recommend, and what should be the length of the quota period?

 *a.* Missionary or promotional sales rep for a manufacturer of candy bars.

 *b.* Salesperson for manufacturer of industrial central heating and air-conditioning units.

 *c.* Salesperson for manufacturer of room air conditioners for home or industry.

 *d.* In-home selling of cosmetics.

9. A luggage manufacturer uses volume quotas for its sales force.

 *a.* What effective measures may this firm take to encourage its salespeople to do nonselling tasks such as prospecting for new accounts or setting up dealer displays?

 *b.* How can the customers be protected against overstocking, high-pressure selling, and other similar activities by this manufacturer's sales force?

10. One apparel manufacturer established volume quotas for its sales representatives. The 1995 quota was 20 percent higher than the quota for 1994. The sales force seemed perfectly happy with the new quota and generally was meeting it. Reps were paid a straight commission of 5 percent on net sales. Under what conditions would this type of quota work?

## ■ EXPERIENTIAL EXERCISES

**A.** Estimate the sales budget (using *Sales & Marketing Management's* "Survey of Selling Costs") for a sales force of 10, located in the midwestern states of Ohio, Illinois, Michigan, and Indiana, who spend two nights a week out of town.

**B.** Interview sales managers from five different companies to find out how they establish sales quotas.

## ■ REFERENCES

1. Andy Cohen, "Can You Prepare a Budget?" *Sales & Marketing Management,* October 1996, p. 44.

2. Kenny Rottenberger, "How Do You Balance the Sales Budget?" *Sales & Marketing Management,* September 1992, pp. 24–26.

3. Ibid.

4. René Y. Darmon, "Selecting Appropriate Sales Quota Plan Structures and Quota Setting Procedures," *Journal of Personal Selling & Sales Management,* Winter 1997, pp. 1–16.

5. Andy Cohen, "Movin' Out," *Sales & Marketing Management,* January 1996, pp. 24–25.

6. John F. Yarbrough, "Walt Disney Company," in Geoffrey Brewer and Christine Galea, "The Top 25," *Sales & Marketing Management,* November 1996, p. 48.

7. Darmon, "Selecting Appropriate Sales Quota Plan Structures," p. 11.

*Case 16-1*

## AEROSPACE SYSTEMS, INC.

### Budget reduction policy

As Ted Sowinski, the chief executive officer of Aerospace Systems, Inc., stood before the fax machine, his face noticeably hardened as he read the message from NASA being emitted from the contraption's innards. The room fell silent as everyone was aware of the subject of the incoming message. They knew from Ted's face that the news was bad. Their contract for building a new space probe vehicle had been canceled, a victim of the budget cutbacks by the federal government.

This serious setback to the company's future was not unexpected. The board of directors had discussed the matter thoroughly at its last meeting and had directed management to institute immediate budget reductions throughout the company that would offset the revenues that would be lost because of the potential contract cancellation. Management was ordered to submit to the board its plan for those budget reductions at the next board meeting, which was to be held the first Wednesday of the following month, 22 days away.

As Sowinski took the message from the machine, he directed his assistant to assemble all of the company's divisional vice presidents for a meeting the next morning. The sole agenda was to be the execution of the budget reductions.

Bill Rooney, vice president of the company's electronics division, returned to his office after the budget meeting with the president and the other vice presidents. He had been firmly directed to reduce the budgets for his division by approximately 20 percent despite his highly emotional protest. He contended that it was totally irrational to cut the budgets of the company's one division that was still profitable and whose revenues were growing. The other executives were in no mood to hear his case. Some even told him that he could cut costs without hurting revenues. It struck Bill that everyone in the room seemed to think that they knew more about his division than he did. Nevertheless, he was stuck with the order and knew that any appeal to higher echelons would not only be ineffective but would be career suicide.

Bill directed his assistant to call a meeting of all the division's department heads; the agenda: cutting their budgets.

Michiko Takanaga, manager of sales operations for small consumer electronics, returned from the meeting furious. She had been ordered to reduce costs for her department by $12 million. The method by which she was to do it was left largely to her.

Most of the meeting had been devoted to how best to accomplish the reductions while doing as little damage as possible to ongoing profitable operations. Some of the department heads thought that they would concentrate on getting rid of marginal workers. Everyone agreed that the key to meeting the budget mandates was cutting payroll costs and the resultant lowering of the costs of the benefit package, payroll taxes, and workers' compensation insurance. The total benefit package offered by the company to all employees amounted to 32 percent of payroll. FICA taxes plus workers' compensation cost 17 percent of payroll. The department generated revenue of $85 million in 1993, with a total budget of $76 million. Total payroll was $18 million. The department had 331 employees, 91 of whom were sales reps. The sales reps' average compensation was $76,000 a year. Field-selling expenses for

1993 were $2.9 million, of which travel, lodging, and meals accounted for about $2 million, with the rest going for entertaining customers.

Michiko decided to confer with her assistants about how the budget reductions should be done. On one hand, she could just slice everything 20 percent across the board, but that seemed irresponsible to her. She believed that it was her job as manager to make some difficult decisions and this was certainly going to fall into that classification.

She had thought of little else but how she could make the budget reduction since being ordered to do it. She realized that just about all of the reductions would have to come out of payroll and the resulting savings in the benefit and tax package. Previous budget squeezes had reduced administrative overhead items to bare bones.

One alternative she was contemplating was terminating enough sales reps so that the entire $12 million reduction would be from payroll costs and benefit packages. Naturally, she thought of trying to keep the best producers and letting the marginal ones go, but she suspected that she would be cutting into some reps who were good, solid performers even though their records placed them in the lowest quartile of profit producers.

Another alternative was to try to get the sales reps to accept a pay cut sufficient to allow everyone to keep his or her job. She knew that would be a difficult selling job. How could she get a rep who was making $100,000 a year to accept $80,000 just so she wouldn't have to fire anyone? But then she realized that strange things do happen. One offshoot of this thought was to offer to keep the reps who would otherwise be fired if they would accept, say, a 40 percent pay cut. A rep who was making only $60,000 a year might work for $40,000 if it meant keeping his job and benefits package.

The problem weighed so heavily on Michiko's mind that she talked of little else that evening as she dined with a friend who was a sales manager for a large business machines manufacturer in Japan. He was of the opinion that she would have to redesign the entire sales force so that the sales job could be accomplished with the smaller sales force. "You'll have to redesign the territories, replan your call patterns, stop calling on some people, use the telephone a lot more, hire some cheaper help for inside selling, get rid of your expensive sales reps, and hire new ones for a lot less money! You're going to have to work like the devil to find a cheaper way to cover your customers."

Michiko was not sure that her friend's plan could be done. A flat across-the-board reduction of all budgets appealed to her. After all, any damage done could easily be blamed on top management's mandate to cut the budgets.

*Question:*

What advice would you give Michiko on how she should reduce her departmental budgets?

*Case 16-2*

## MASTERS LEAD COMPANY
### How much budget flexibility?

Sue Green had kept quiet for more than three years about the firm's budget system. "Enough is enough!" she told her associate, Mike Driver. "This budget system stinks. It is no system at all. I'm going to have it out with the old man this afternoon. We have a one o'clock tee time at Old Brook. By the turn, I may be looking for work."

Sue Green had been a professional golfer for more than 15 years when a back injury forced her to retire. Since her success on tour had been limited, she began looking for a job. She had met Sam Dodds at a Pro-Am that they had won. Thereafter, Dodds had kept informed about Green's career. When she was injured and could no longer compete professionally, he offered her a job as sales manager.

Masters Lead manufactured a line of products made from lead, and one of the firm's significant lines was lead batteries. These batteries were sold to three markets: golf cart manufacturers, golf cart battery replacements, and private brands for distributive organizations. Green was in charge of selling to the golf cart manufacturers.

During her initial training she inquired about how the budget worked. She was told, "Don't worry about it. If you really need money for something, it will be there for you."

As Green slowly learned how the company's operating system worked, she came to understand that she would be given an overall budget from the accounting office at the first of each year—a budget with no details, just a total amount of money she could spend to do her job. How she spent it was up to her. When the money ran out, as it always did along about the end of summer, she would then go, hat in hand, to Dodds to ask for more money.

Then the games began. Sam would make her justify what had been spent and why she needed more money. Guilt seemed to be the order of the day. Dodds was into management by guilt, and Green hated it. She felt it was demeaning. She had done an excellent job for Masters Lead and did not want to be treated like a little girl asking her daddy for more money.

Green made sure that the bets were large at the golf game that day because she didn't want to go home broke if she was to be out of a job. She knew Dodds's game would come apart once she started talking about money and how he parceled it out. The afternoon developed as Sue anticipated, except she still had her job at the end of the day. Dodds might be a tightwad, but he was no fool.

"How'd it go?" Mike asked Sue the next day.

"I said my piece," Sue replied.

"And?"

"And he said his!"

"Which was?" Mike persisted.

"It's his company and this is the way he wants to run it. He wants to keep tight control over the money and make us defend everything we spend. He wants us to be thinking about having to come before him for more money when we spend the budget. He says that he hasn't hurt anyone yet. Says that it is plain old-fashioned good business to make your people think about how they spend the company's money," Sue reported.

"What did you say?" asked Mike.

"I told him I didn't like it much, and that I thought that the budget must be too small because I keep running out of money too soon when I know I don't waste any money."

"What'd he say to that?"

"Shut up and hit the ball!"

**Questions:**

1. Evaluate Sam Dodds's budget philosophy.
2. What should Sue Green do now?

---

*Case 16-3*

## SOME INCIDENTS IN QUOTA SETTING

### Climb the next mountain

After graduation from a West Coast university, Marcia Hart accepted a job as sales rep for a large business equipment company. Within two years she was the company's leading producer. The following year, during a speech she gave to the students at her alma mater, she mentioned that she was greatly concerned that her financial success was in jeopardy. She had just been told that her sales quota for the coming year had been significantly increased. Since her compensation was based on exceeding her assigned quota, she anticipated that her earnings would suffer next year.

The following year Marcia returned to talk to the class again. She was again the company's leading producer. She had managed to exceed the quota that she had been worried about. However, she related that this year was a repeat of last year. She beat quota, so management increased her quota again, this time even more than last. She again had great doubts about her future earnings. "I'm getting the idea that management is not really too happy with me making all the money I am making. They seem determined to bring me down to earth. I don't know how long I want to play this game. I can understand that my bosses are upset that I am making more than $200,000 a year. And I must confess that I have been putting a lot of money away for the day I may want to do something for myself. But it is tough to keep going out and knocking

yourself out to beat quota only to have the company keep raising it."

The following year she got married, quit her job, and moved to northern California to start her own business.

**Question:**

What, if anything, should the company do about its quota-setting system?

### Pick a number

Mac Carter, sales manager for the Abrams Company, related his quota-setting technique to an associate by saying, "I let them pick their own numbers. That way they can't gripe about unfair quotas." His associate's quizzical look brought forth more information. Mac continued, "We budget 10 percent of sales for sales salaries so the reps are really on a commission even though they are paid salaries. We want to pay them a salary to gain control over them and their non-selling activities. So each December I call each rep into my office and ask him how much money he wants to make the coming year. Suppose the rep says, '$60,000.' Then I say that's fine. Then I say that the quota for the year will be $600,000. Then I break that down by months for the rep. Privately, I have a weekly quota in mind and if the rep falls behind that quota, we'll talk real quick. I'll pull the rep's reports and sales orders and see if I can pinpoint what the problem might be."

The associate asked, "What happens if the rep falls way behind quota?"

"Doesn't happen! The rep is gone before I let that take place. The rep sets the quota. Now before you accuse me of being cold-hearted, understand that I have explained to the rep exactly what is going to happen if quotas aren't met. Then I give the reps an opportunity to lower the quota by modifying their salary demands. They know exactly how I am playing the game."

The associate paused a while to consider her words, then said, "Seems to me that you're missing the point about using quotas. They are supposed to give you some idea of how well the reps are doing in relationship to their market opportunities. Some bozo tells you he is happy with $20,000 a year, so you give him a $200,000 quota that he has no trouble meeting. All the while he is messing up a $500,000 market opportunity. Mac, you're missing the whole point about using quotas."

### Question:

Should Mac change his quota system to one based on market opportunity?

### A serious disagreement

"I don't want to hear about how your market analyst has carefully based our quotas on statistics about our territories. Statistics are history and my territory has changed a lot this past two years. There's no way that I can sell anything close to that quota this year with the way the defense budget has hit my accounts. Now let's talk about some real numbers."

Stan Kolb, sales rep for Precision Castings, was talking to his manager, Norman Holt, evidently to little avail. "Stan, you know I can't do that. All the reps have the same problem you do. Business is down. The analyst has factored that into the quotas. I can't manage a sales force by negotiating quotas with each person. If I did, every rep would be in here and I'd be doing nothing but hassling over quotas."

Stan was having none of it. "Norm, I've been around the block a time or two so don't give me that garbage. There's no way that the analyst could have factored into my quota the impact of the present defense cutbacks. The fact is that there is no way I can meet that quota and we both know it. So there'll be no bonus for Stan this year. That's a cut in pay of 25 percent. Come on! Do you really expect me to sit still for that?"

Norm countered, "These are tough times. At least you have a job. How about all the poor slobs who have lost their jobs at your accounts? At least you have a $60,000 a year salary to fall back on."

Seeing that Norm was visibly upset, Stan offered, "I'll have the analyst review her work carefully to see if an adjustment is due you. Otherwise, you know the policy. The company does not negotiate sales quotas."

Stan left the office with the full expectation that the analyst would hold firm on his quota. "It's time to update my resume," he muttered to himself as the door closed.

### Question:

Is the company's policy on quota renegotiations sound? Can market analysts factor into quota setting such irregular factors as defense cutbacks as they impact any one rep's territory?

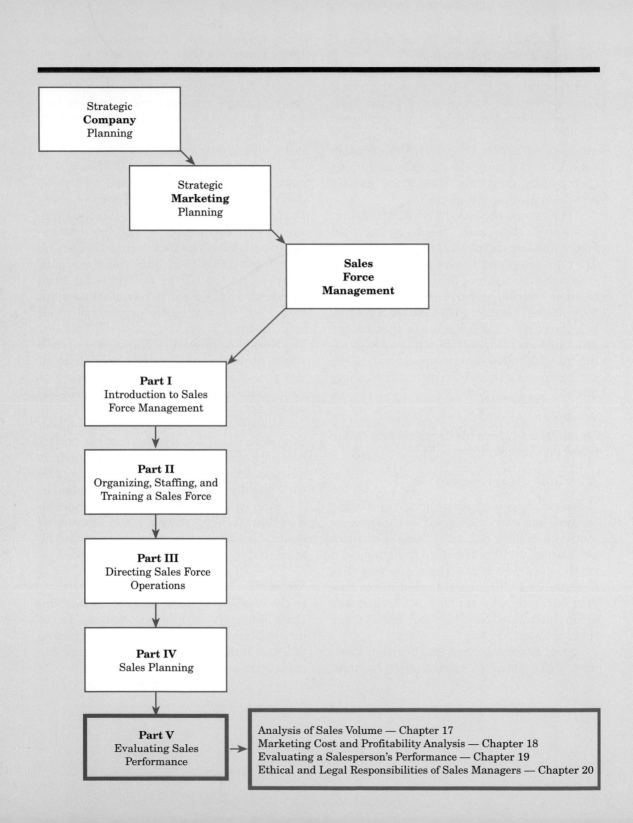

Strategic **Company** Planning

Strategic **Marketing** Planning

**Sales Force Management**

**Part I**
Introduction to Sales Force Management

**Part II**
Organizing, Staffing, and Training a Sales Force

**Part III**
Directing Sales Force Operations

**Part IV**
Sales Planning

**Part V**
Evaluating Sales Performance

Analysis of Sales Volume — Chapter 17
Marketing Cost and Profitability Analysis — Chapter 18
Evaluating a Salesperson's Performance — Chapter 19
Ethical and Legal Responsibilities of Sales Managers — Chapter 20

# PART V

# EVALUATING SALES PERFORMANCE

Up to this point, the major parts of this book (after the introductory section) have been devoted to sales planning and sales operations. Part V deals with the final major stage in the sales management process—evaluating the performance results of the field-selling effort.

Performance evaluation involves both looking backward and looking ahead. In looking backward, management analyzes its operating results in relation to its objectives and strategic plans. These findings can then be used in forward planning for the next operating period. To illustrate, say that upon looking back, management finds that too much sales volume is in low-margin products. This evaluation result can then influence management's future plans for sales force training, supervision, and compensation.

In the first part of Chapter 17, we introduce some general concepts in performance evaluation and misdirected marketing effort. The balance of the chapter is devoted to the analysis of sales volume. Chapter 18 is a survey of marketing cost analysis. Chapters 17 and 18 together constitute a marketing profitability analysis. Evaluating the performance of individual salespeople is discussed in Chapter 19. In the final chapter, Chapter 20, we step back and take a broad look at evaluation as we discuss the ethical and social responsibilities of sales managers.

# CHAPTER 17

# Analysis of Sales Volume

Economic distress will teach men . . . that fact-finding is more effective than fault-finding.

**Carl Becker**

The first stage in the sales force management process is *planning,* followed by *implementing* the plans through sales operations, and ending with an *evaluation* of the sales force performance. These three activities comprising the management process—planning, implementation, and evaluation—are typically conducted in an interrelated, continuous fashion, as shown in Figure 17-1. Plans are made; they are put into operation

■ **FIGURE 17-1**

**Interrelationship of planning, implementation, and evaluation**

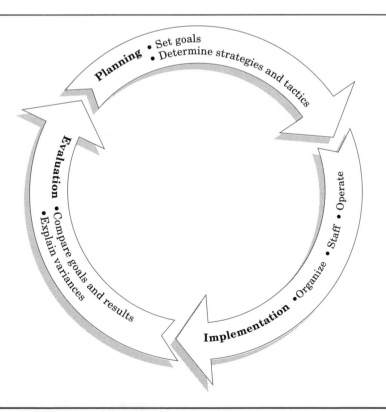

(that is, implemented); and the results are evaluated. Then new plans for the next cycle are prepared, based in part on the preceding evaluation findings.

## STRATEGIC RELATIONSHIP BETWEEN PLANNING AND EVALUATION

Planning and performance evaluation are particularly interdependent activities in the sales force management process. Planning sets forth what *should be* done, and evaluation shows what *really was* done. Either of these activities is virtually worthless without the other. To illustrate, let's assume that an organization has done a good job of strategic sales force planning. But without an effective evaluation, management cannot tell (1) whether its plan has worked, (2) to what degree it has been successful, or (3) what the reasons are for the plan's success or failure. In effect, the lack of adequate evaluation can virtually cancel out the value of strategic planning. It's like deciding to go someplace but never knowing when, or if, you arrived there.

A performance evaluation without prior strategic planning is equally useless, and may even be dangerously misleading. Without planning guidelines, a sales rep may think that she is doing well by stressing the sale of high-margin products. However, management may prefer that she concentrate on opening new accounts or performing more missionary selling activities. If management does not set goals for its salespeople (planning), then what bases can it use for evaluating the reps' performance? Without a "par for the course" (standard of performance), how can management know whether a salesperson is doing a satisfactory job?

Truly, planning and performance evaluation are strategically interrelated and interdependent. Evaluation both follows and precedes planning. Evaluation *follows* the planning and operations of the *current* period of company activity. Actual performance is measured against predetermined standards. Then evaluation *precedes* and influences the planning for the *next* period's operations. To illustrate, let's say that evaluations show the company's gross margin declined because of a heavy sales volume in low-margin products, or there was a decline in the share of total sales coming from new accounts. These evaluation results can influence management when it prepares the next period's plans for sales force training, supervision, and compensation.

### Relation of Performance Evaluation to Sales Control

Many writers and business executives refer to the subject of this chapter as *sales control* or *control of sales operations*. We do not use such a label because we believe it is a misleading and unrealistic use of the term *control*. Control is not an isolated managerial function. It permeates virtually all other managerial activities. For example, management controls its sales force by means of the compensation plan, quota system, territorial structure, and expense-payment plan. Control is also exercised through the training program, sales contests, supervision, and other devices.

# INTRODUCTION TO SALES FORCE PERFORMANCE EVALUATION

Evaluation of sales force performance is a broad term that covers (1) the analysis of sales volume—the topic of this chapter, (2) marketing cost analysis and profitability analysis—the topics of Chapter 18, and (3) various analytical measures used to evaluate an individual salesperson's performance—the topic of Chapter 19.

In 1997 annual average sales volume rose to $1.4 billion. This compares to $1.1 billion in 1994. More important, survey data show that during the 1990s, salespeople have become more effective at retaining existing customers and selling to major accounts.[1] As we move into the 2000s, retaining existing major accounts and developing long-term relationships with those customers will increase in importance. As a result, performance evaluation will take on added importance in the 2000s because of the focus on customer satisfaction, relationship selling, and partnering.

Yes, effective performance evaluations are certainly needed if a company is to remain competitive throughout the 1990s and into the 2000s.

## A Marketing Audit: A Total Evaluation Program

An audit is a review and evaluation of some activity. Therefore, a **marketing audit** is a comprehensive, periodic review and evaluation of the marketing function in an organization—its marketing goals, strategies, and performance. This audit includes an appraisal of the organization, personnel, and tactics employed to implement the strategies and reach the goals.

A complete marketing audit must include *all* the marketing areas referred to in the definition—goals, strategies, performance, organization, personnel, and tactics. A fragmented evaluation of some marketing activities may be useful, but it is not a marketing audit. It is only part of such an audit.

A complete marketing audit is a very extensive project that provides an ideal for management to work toward. It is expensive, time-consuming, and difficult. But the rewards can be great. Management can identify its problem areas in marketing. By reviewing its strategies and tactics, the firm can keep abreast of its changing marketing environment. Any marketing successes should also be analyzed so the company can capitalize on its strong points.

Traditionally, an audit is an after-the-fact review. In marketing, an audit is also used to evaluate the effects of alternatives *before* a decision is reached. Thus the audit becomes an aid in decision making. Further, an audit should anticipate future situations as well as review past ones.

## A Sales Management Audit

A marketing audit covers an organization's entire marketing system. A company can also apply the audit concept to major divisions *within* the marketing system. Thus, for example, a company might conduct a physical distribution audit or an advertising audit. Or, as is pertinent to this book, management can audit the personal selling and sales management activities in a company's marketing system. Thus, like a marketing audit, a **sales management audit** evaluates a firm's *sales* objectives, strategies, and tactics. The *sales* organization and its policies, personnel, and performance are appraised.[2]

## The Evaluation Process

The evaluation process—whether it is a complete marketing audit or only an appraisal of individual components of the marketing program—is essentially a three-stage task, as seen in Figure 17-2. Management's job is to:

1. Find out *what* happened—get the facts by comparing actual results with budgeted goals to determine the variations.
2. Find out *why* it happened—determine what specific factors in the marketing program accounted for the variations.
3. Decide *what to do* about it—plan the next period's activities to improve on unsatisfactory conditions and capitalize on favorable ones.

Much of our discussion in Chapters 17 and 18 is devoted to the first step—that is, explaining the techniques for determining *what* happened. Yet the task in the second step—finding out *why* variances occurred between plans and actual results—is much more difficult and time-consuming. It is relatively easy to discover that sales of product A declined 10 percent last year in the western region when management had forecast a 5 percent increase. The real problem is to identify *why* this variation between actual and forecasted sales occurred. Was the forecast in error? Or does the reason lie in the countless possibilities among the elements of the marketing mix or the myriad aspects of sales planning and operations?

Our reason for devoting significant space to the first step is that you cannot decide *why* something occurred if you first don't know *what* occurred.

■ **FIGURE 17-2**

**The evaluation process—to find out:**

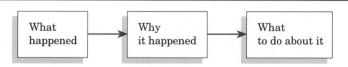

Many companies don't know *what* happened. That is, they have not analyzed their sales and cost performance results in any significant detail. This is surprising because the first step in the evaluation process is actually the easiest, especially with the availability of computer technology and other information-processing equipment.

## Components of Performance Evaluation

Because of the time, cost, and difficulty involved in a full marketing audit, sometimes it is more reasonable to evaluate the separate components of the marketing mix. An evaluation of field-selling efforts involves an appraisal of sales volume results, related marketing expenses, and the performance of individual salespeople. These components are sufficiently independent so that management can conduct one or two evaluations without the need to do all of them. One company may decide to analyze its sales volume, but not its marketing costs. Another firm may study various ratios involving sales force activities without making any detailed sales or cost analyses.

A **sales volume analysis** is a careful study of a company's records as summarized in the net sales section of its profit-and-loss statement. It is a detailed study of the dollar or the unit sales volume by product lines, territories, key accounts, and general classes of customers. A sales volume analysis may be expanded to include a corresponding study of cost of goods sold. The result is an analysis of its gross margin, also broken down into such segments as products or territories. A **marketing cost analysis** continues from the analysis of sales volume. It is a study of the marketing expenses to determine the profitability of various marketing segments in the organization.

In a general sense, the two types of analyses are component parts of a detailed study of a company's operating statement. In effect, a sales volume analysis (SVA) and a marketing cost analysis (MCA) together constitute a marketing profitability analysis (MPA). Or, look at it this way:

$$SVA + MCA = MPA$$

 ## PERFORMANCE EVALUATION AND MISDIRECTED MARKETING EFFORT

A marketing profitability analysis is one step that may be taken to correct the misdirected marketing effort found in many companies today.

### Nature of Misdirected Marketing Effort: The 80–20 Principle

A company does not enjoy the same rate of net profit on every sale. In most firms, a large proportion of the orders (or customers, or territories, or products) accounts for a small share of the profits. This relationship between selling units and profits has been characterized as the 80–20 principle. That is, 80 percent of the orders, customers, territories, or products contributes only

20 percent of the sales volume or profit. Conversely, the other 20 percent of these marketing units accounts for 80 percent of the volume or profit. The 80–20 figure is used to epitomize the misplacement of marketing efforts. Actually, of course, the percentage split varies from one situation to another.

Some companies recognize this problem and adjust their strategies accordingly. Sentrol, which sells security systems, has a customer base of 17,000; yet their 15 salespeople concentrate on only the 2,000 of these customers which are the most profitable.[3] However, many companies are not as focused.

The 80–20 situation stems from the fact that marketing efforts and costs are to some extent related to the *number* of marketing units (territories, products, customers) rather than their *actual* or *potential sales volume and profit*. A firm may have one salesperson and one branch office in each territory, with all the attendant expense, regardless of the volume obtained from these districts. For every order received, the seller must process a purchase order, invoice, and a payment check, whether the order is for $10 or $1,000.

## Reasons for Misdirected Effort

Because they lack sufficiently detailed information, many executives are unaware of the misdirected marketing effort in their firms. They do not know what percentage of total sales and profits comes from a given product line or customer group.

Total sales or costs on an operating statement are often inconclusive and misleading (see Figure 17-3). More than one company has shown satisfactory overall sales and profit figures, but when these totals were subdivided by territory or products, serious weaknesses were discovered. A manufacturer of plastic products showed an overall annual increase of 12 percent in sales and 9 percent in net profit on one of its product lines one year. But when management analyzed these figures, the sales change within each territory ranged from an increase of 19 percent to a decrease of 3 percent. In some territories, profit increased as much as 14 percent; in others it was down 20 percent.

There is a more fundamental reason for misplaced marketing effort. Sales executives must make decisions even though their knowledge of the exact nature of marketing costs is inadequate. In other words, management lacks:

**1.** Knowledge of the disproportionate spread of marketing effort.

**2.** Standards for determining:

    a.  What should have been spent on marketing.

    b.  What results should have been obtained from these expenditures.

As an example, a sales executive really does not know exactly how much to spend on sales training, marketing research, or sales supervision. Even more troublesome is that management has no yardstick to

■ **FIGURE 17-3**

**Total sales figures may hide significant problems**

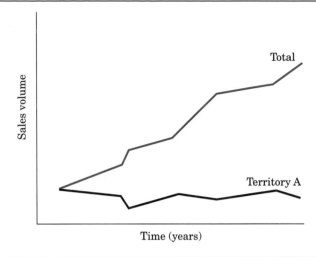

This company may be headed for real trouble. The impressive totals may be hiding some problems that ultimately can destroy the company.

determine whether the results of these expenditures are satisfactory. If a firm adds 10 missionary salespeople or employs field supervisors where none existed before, the executives ordinarily cannot say how much the volume or profit should increase. Nor can they compare the value of two expenditures. Assume that a company spends $200,000 on a contest for the sales force. No one can say how much additional volume this expenditure will bring, as compared with spending the same amount on advertising or on sales training, for example.

## Sales Information Must Be Detailed

Sales administrators who want to analyze sales volume may find they lack detailed data. The sales department works largely with figures supplied by the accounting department. But these records are rarely itemized sufficiently for the sales managers. Before a worthwhile analysis can be made, a system must be established to supply the sales department with the necessary facts.

The possible classifications of sales data and the combinations of these breakdowns have almost no limit. Some widely used subdivisions for reporting and analyzing sales include:

- *Sales territories.*
- *Salespeople.* If each representative has a district, an analysis of sales volume by territory also serves for individual sales reps.

- *Products.* Reports may be in dollars and/or physical units for individual products or lines of products.
- *Customers.* Management may classify the volume by the individual customers, key accounts, industrial groups of customers, or channels of distribution.
- *Size of order.*

# ■ BASES FOR ANALYZING SALES VOLUME

## Total Sales Volume

A reasonable place to begin a sales analysis is with the *total sales volume*—the combined sales of all products in all territories for all customers. This readily available figure gives an overall picture of how the company is faring. However, the *trend* in sales is usually far more important to administrators than the volume for any given year. Two trends—the trend of the company's sales over a period of years and the trend of the company's share of the total industry market—are especially important.

A study of total sales volume is probably the easiest of all types of analyses. The only data needed are (1) the annual sales figures for the company over the past several years and (2) the annual industry sales in the geographic market covered by the firm. From these figures the company's share of the market can be determined.

Figure 17-4 shows the sort of information developed in a total sales volume analysis for the Colorado Ski Company. This concern carries two basic product lines, ski equipment (skis and accessories) and a limited line of ski clothes (ski pants and parkas). The company manufactures some of these items. Others are purchased from outside sources and sold under Colorado Ski's brand. The firm sells to two classes of customers—sporting good stores and specialty ski shops—in some of the major ski markets in the nation. Annual sales in 1998 were $27 million.

An analysis of the company's volume shows that sales have generally increased each year since 1989, with the exception of 1993 and 1995. So far, the picture is encouraging. However, industry figures shed a different light on the situation. The industry's sales also have increased since 1985, but at a more rapid rate than Colorado's volume. As a result, the company's share of the market has steadily declined. Looking at the 10-year picture, management finds that its sales have increased 80 percent, but its share of the market has declined 25 percent.

After management has uncovered the facts as shown in Figure 17-4, the next step is to determine the reasons for the decline in the company's market position. The possible weaknesses in Colorado Ski's operation are almost limitless. Something may be wrong with the product itself, such as styling, construction, or color. Some aspects of the pricing structure may be the problem. The weakness may lie in some phase of advertising, such

■ **FIGURE 17-4**

| Information used in analysis of total sales volume, Colorado Ski Company | Year | Company Volume (in millions) | Industry Volume (in millions) | Company's Share of Market |
|---|---|---|---|---|
| | 1998 | $27.0 | $360 | 7.5% |
| | 1997 | 25.2 | 390 | 6.4 |
| | 1996 | 23.4 | 360 | 6.5 |
| | 1995 | 20.4 | 312 | 7.0 |
| | 1994 | 21.0 | 300 | 8.2 |
| | 1993 | 19.2 | 234 | 8.3 |
| | 1992 | 19.8 | 240 | 8.9 |
| | 1991 | 19.2 | 216 | 8.9 |
| | 1990 | 18.0 | 180 | 10.0 |
| | 1989 | 15.0 | 150 | 10.0 |

as the choice of media or the ads themselves. Then the entire area of sales force management can be examined.

On the other hand, it may be that all of Colorado Ski's operations are as good as ever, but the competitors have made improvements. Possibly there are more competitors. Or some of these firms may have significantly improved their product, distribution, or promotional effectiveness.

### Sales by Territories

Companies usually can do an analysis of *total* sales volume easily and inexpensively. However, its value to management is limited because it tells so little about the details of a firm's marketing progress. Only the aggregate picture emerges and the separate parts remain submerged. One step toward uncovering these parts is the common practice of analyzing sales by territories. Management wants to identify which territories are strong and which are weak in relation to potential. A company must find out *which* territories are weak before it can determine *why* they are weak.

One reasonably simple, inexpensive procedure for analyzing sales volume by territories involves the following four steps:

1. Select a market index that indicates with reasonable accuracy what percentage of total sales should be obtained from each sales territory. For example, one firm may use retail sales as an index. If 10 percent of the total national retail sales were in the midwestern district, then 10 percent of the company's sales should also come from that district. Or, if the firm sells in only eight southeastern states, then the total retail sales in the eight-state area would be equated to 100 percent. If 22 percent of retail sales in the eight states were tallied in Alabama, then 22 percent of the sales in the company should also come from Al-

■ **FIGURE 17-5**     **Analysis of territorial sales volume in five-territory western division, Colorado Ski Company, 1998**

| Territory | Market Index (percent) | Sales Goals ($000) | Actual Sales ($000) | Performance Percentage | Dollar Variation ($000) |
|-----------|-----------------------|--------------------|---------------------|------------------------|-------------------------|
| A | 27% | $ 3,645 | $ 2,700 | 74 | $−945 |
| B | 22 | 2,970 | 3,690 | 124 | +720 |
| C | 15 | 2,025 | 2,484 | 123 | +459 |
| D | 20 | 2,700 | 2,556 | 95 | −144 |
| E | 16 | 2,160 | 2,070 | 96 | −90 |
| Total | 100% | $13,500 | $13,500 | | |

abama. (Market indexes and their use in determining territorial sales and market potentials were explained in Chapter 14.)

2. Determine the company's actual total sales in dollars or units during the period being studied.

3. Multiply the territorial index by the total sales figure to determine the goal in each district.

4. Compare actual regional sales with the regional goals to see how much variation has occurred.

An example of this procedure is developed in Figure 17-5. The five territories in the western division of the Colorado Ski Company are being analyzed. Colorado Ski's total sales in the western division were $13.5 million distributed among five territories, as shown in the column headed Actual Sales. Sales were $2,700,000 in territory A, $3,690,000 in territory B, and so forth. Next we apply a pertinent market index to the western division's total sales. We find that 27 percent, or $3,645,000 of the total sales in the five-territory market, *should* have been made in territory A. The goal in territory B was 22 percent, or $2,970,000, and so on.

A performance percentage is computed by dividing actual sales by the territorial goal. A rating of 100 percent in the district means that the area turned in its predetermined share of the company's business. Figure 17-5 shows that territories B and C did much better than expected. Districts E and D were a shade below par, and A fell considerably short of expectations.

It is not enough to study the *percentage* by which an area's sales are over or under the goals. The more important measure is usually the *dollar volume*. It is possible that the district may be only a few percentage points under par. However, because the territorial potential is very large, these few percentage points may represent a significant sum of money.

A market segment that is below par—its actual performance does not reach its goal—may be called a *soft spot*. In sales management, the **soft-spot principle** states that an administrator reaps the largest possible gain by working with the weakest segments of the organization. Thus a sales manager in the Colorado Ski Company should devote the most attention to territory A because it has the greatest need for improvement. By the same token, it is doubtful that even considerable attention could improve B and C very much. Already they are far above their goals. Probably the main benefits from a study of B and C would be to determine (1) why they apparently are so successful and (2) whether this information can be used to improve A.

Once management has identified the strong and weak territories, the next task is to determine the reasons for the relative performances. Territory A may be doing poorly because competition is particularly effective or because some aspects of Colorado Ski's operation are especially weak. Assuming that industry sales volume figures for each territory are obtainable with reasonable effort, then company sales percentages in each district may be compared with industry percentages. A sales manager may find, for example, that 15 percent of the *industry's* sales are made in territory A and 10 percent in B. In comparison, 12 percent of the *company's* sales are in A and 20 percent in B. Thus the company is below average in A, but it is doing far better than the industry average in B.

## Sales by Products

The 80–20 principle applies to products as well as to territories in many companies. Very often, most of the products in a company's line account for a small percentage of total volume or profit. Conversely, a few products may bring most of the volume. There is no relation between volume and profit. Products that account for a large proportion of the volume may or may not contribute a corresponding percentage of the net profits.

**Scanners ensure that sales data are accurate and timely.**

Several types of volume analyses by product lines may be helpful to management. The first is simply a summary of present and past total sales divided into individual products or groups of products. An appliance manufacturer may want to study the sales trend for each individual product. A hardware wholesaler, however, would be content to group thousands of products into divisions such as housewares, plumbing goods, and electrical equipment.

If industry figures are available for each product line, they may provide a yardstick for a company to measure its own sales performance by products. For example, assume that the sales of product A are decreasing in one firm. Its management need not be too concerned if, over the same period, the industry's sales have decreased at about the same rate.

A further refinement is to study the sales of each product line in each territory. In this way, management can determine the geographical market in which each product is strong or weak. Product A's *total* sales may be up 10 percent over last year, but in the southwestern region, A's volume is down 14 percent. Once these facts are known, an administrator can try to determine the reasons for the variations and then make the necessary corrections.

An analysis of sales by product lines can also be used to refine the territorial analysis discussed in the preceding section. Figure 17-5 showed that territory A was 26 percent under par. B and C were 24 percent and 23 percent above par, respectively. By investigating the product sales in these districts, management can better isolate the reasons for these variations.

In Figure 17-6, market indexes were applied to Colorado Ski's actual volume of $13.5 million to establish targets for products in the five western territories.* For instance, let's assume that the western division's sales had been distributed in relation to potential. Then sales in territory A would have been $3,645,000 with skis contributing $1,629,000, ski accessories accounting for $270,000, and so on.

In Figure 17-5, we found that the company was short of its sales goal in territory A by $945,000, or 26 percent. However, this shortage was not distributed equally among all four products. Further analysis by product lines showed that the sales of ski pants and parkas were the primary sources of the shortages. The company failed to reach its target by $540,000 and $450,000, respectively, for those two products. Sales of skis actually were $81,000 over the performance standard.

Territory B as a whole was $720,000 over its goal figure. However, sales of parkas fell $90,000 (about 12 percent) short of the goal. Volume in

---

*Ideally, a separate index should be used for each product or line of products. To use the same index on all items means that the percentage share of the national market set as a target in the territory is the same for all products. In Figure 17-5, 27 percent of the company's total western division sales should have been contributed by territory A. If the same index is used for all four products, then 27 percent of the sales of each product should be obtained from territory A. Such situations are unusual. Ordinarily, a company selling many different products should not expect that a given territory would contribute the same percentage of the total sales for each product.

■ **FIGURE 17-6**     **Analysis of product sales performance in two territories, Colorado Ski Company, 1998**

| Product | Territory A ($000) | | | Territory B ($000) | | |
|---|---|---|---|---|---|---|
| | **Goal** | **Actual** | **Variation** | **Goal** | **Actual** | **Variation** |
| Skis | $1,629 | $1,710 | $+81 | $1,263 | $1,620 | $+357 |
| Accessories | 270 | 234 | −36 | 222 | 360 | +138 |
| Pants | 900 | 360 | −540 | 765 | 1,080 | +315 |
| Parkas | 846 | 396 | −450 | 720 | 630 | −90 |
| Total | $3,645 | $2,700 | $−945 | $2,970 | $3,690 | $+720 |

skis, accessories, and ski pants was above the target figure in each of these product categories.

As part of its sales volume analysis by products, management must decide what to do about low-volume products and products that did not meet their sales goals. Based on Figure 17-6, ski pants and parkas in territory A and parkas in B seem to be soft spots in terms of sales goals. Thus these products seem to provide the best opportunity for improvement.

Management's initial thought may be to drop low-volume products. But before taking such a drastic step, other considerations should be taken into account. A cost analysis will aid in these decisions. If the product is a losing proposition for the company, this would be a strong point in favor of dropping the item. In some cases, however, a low-volume product must be kept whether or not it is profitable. It may be needed to round out a line, and customers may expect the company to carry the item.

## Sales by Customer Classifications

A company is even more likely to find the 80–20 principle in operation when sales are analyzed by customer groups. It is not unusual to find that a small percentage of customers accounts for a major share of total volume. Typically, a firm sells to many accounts on a marginal or even unprofitable basis.

A firm can analyze its volume by customer groups in several ways. It may classify accounts on an industry basis. An oil company may group its customers into *industry divisions,* such as service stations or marine, farm, transportation, industrial, and governmental agencies. Another basis of classification is by *channels of distribution.* A sporting goods manufacturer may group its accounts by sporting goods wholesalers, department stores, and discount houses. A third classification is on the basis of *accounts,* or just the key accounts. Any of these three groups may be cross-classified. An oil company may want to analyze its sales to key accounts in the service-station industry group, for example.

Any of these customer classifications usually should be analyzed for each territory and for each line of products. In one company, it may be that sales to wholesalers are satisfactory on an overall basis, although sales to wholesalers may be particularly poor in one territory. An oil company may assume that a given industry market that accounts for 10 percent of total sales also contributes about 10 percent of the volume of each product line. However, an analysis may disclose that this industry accounts for 18 percent of the volume in product A, but only 5 percent in product B.

### Sales Volume Analysis Is Usually Insufficient

A sales volume analysis alone usually does not furnish enough information to the sales department. Furthermore, the data produced may be misleading. A study may show, for example, that the dollar *volume* of product A is 20 percent greater than the sales of product B. Yet, if the company were to determine the gross margin or net profit of the two products, management would find that B's dollar *profit* is 10 percent higher than A's. Granted that a full-scale sales and cost study—a marketing profitability analysis—is ideal, a good marketing cost analysis is usually difficult and costly. Further, while an analysis of volume alone has its limitations, it is far better than no analysis at all. In spite of the acknowledged value of a marketing cost and profitability analysis, the most widely used measure of sales performance continues to be sales volume.

A compromise between a volume analysis and a full-scale marketing cost study is to expand the volume analysis to include the cost of the merchandise sold. Thus management ends up with a gross margin analysis by territories, products, or customer groups with relatively little additional expense.

## ■ USE OF COMPUTERS IN SALES ANALYSIS

One of the most significant applications of computers in sales force management is in the area of sales analysis.[4] Detailed sales analyses are needed as a basis for planning, operating, and evaluating. Marketing effort is likely to be misdirected if management is unaware of the sales performance of specific product lines or individual territories in relation to potentials. A computer can process the masses of data used in a sales analysis swiftly and economically. As a marketing executive in the Sperry-Rand Corporation put it, "You no longer have to wait for the present to become past history to learn from its lessons. With the computer, you're on to your mistakes much faster."

## ■ SUMMARY

A particularly interdependent strategic relationship exists between planning and performance evaluation in the sales force management process. In this management process, a marketing audit ideally should play a key role. A marketing audit is a *total* evaluation program. As such, it is a comprehensive periodic review and evaluation of the marketing system in an organization. A sales management audit evaluates sales objectives, strategies, and tactics.

The evaluation process is essentially a three-stage task. First, find out *what* happened—actual results are compared with budgeted goals. Second, find out *why* it happened—what factors accounted for the variation between goals and results. Third, decide *what to do* about the situation—that is, plan next period's activities.

Because of the time and cost needed for a full-scale marketing audit, many companies evaluate only the major components of their marketing programs. One such performance evaluation includes an analysis of (1) sales volume, (2) marketing costs, and (3) salespeople's performance. A sales volume analysis combined with a marketing cost analysis constitutes a marketing profitability analysis.

Performance evaluation is a key tool in reducing the misdirected marketing effort in an organization. Misdirected marketing effort means that a company is expending much effort, but getting relatively few results. The 80–20 principle illustrates misdirected marketing effort. That is, marketing efforts (costs) are related to the *number* of marketing units (territories, products, customers), rather than the *sales volume* or *profit* derived from these marketing units.

The basic reasons for misdirected marketing efforts are that management lacks (1) knowledge of the disproportionate spread of marketing effort and (2) reliable standards for determining (*a*) what should be spent on marketing and (*b*) what results should be derived from these expenditures.

A sales volume analysis is a study of a company's actual sales volume compared with the budgeted sales goals. This volume analysis should be done in great detail. That is, the company's sales should be analyzed in total and also by territory, products, customer groups, salespeople, and order size. In each of these subdivisions, the company's performance should be compared with industry figures. In this way, management can measure its performance against the competition.

Detailed sales performance analysis has been improved immeasurably by the use of computers and other electronic data processing equipment.

### Key Terms

Marketing audit
Marketing cost analysis
Sales management audit
Sales volume analysis
Soft-spot principle

## QUESTIONS AND PROBLEMS

1. Explain the relationship between planning and evaluation in the management process.

2. Explain the concept of a marketing profitability analysis.

3. What does the 80–20 principle mean?

4. If a firm's volume is increasing each year by a satisfactory percentage, is there any reason for the firm to go to the expense of a volume analysis?

5. As a result of sales volume analysis, many firms have eliminated some of their products or customers. Yet in several of these cases the sales volume has *increased* after the market cutback. How do you account for this result?

6. A territorial volume analysis indicated that a firm's sales had increased at about a 10 percent rate for the past three years in a given district. Is this conclusive evidence that the company's performance is satisfactory as far as sales volume is concerned in the given territory?

7. A company with 15 territories found that product A accounted for 40 percent to 50 percent of the sales in 13 of the districts. But this product brought in only about 20 percent of the volume in the remaining two territories. What factors might account for the relatively low standing of product A in the two territories?

8. Is it possible for a product, territory, or class of customer to be far below par, but still not deserve much executive attention? Give examples.

9. Should salespeople be furnished with complete statistics, not only on their own performances but on the performance of other salespeople as well?

10. If a company made a *territorial* volume analysis and found some subpar territories, how might these facts affect the following activities relating to salespeople?
    *a.* Supervision.
    *b.* Compensation.
    *c.* Training.

11. If a firm analyzed its sales volume by *customer classes,* how might the results affect the supervision, compensation, and training of the sales force?

## EXPERIENTIAL EXERCISES

**A.** Ask a local store manager to discuss with you (and possibly show you) the reports which he or she uses to track the store's performance as well as the performance of various product categories and salespeople.

**B.** Contact a field sales representative and discuss the product and customer data reports which he or she uses to plan selling strategies and evaluate performance effectiveness.

## ◼ REFERENCES

1. Christian B. Heide, *Dartnell's 29th Sales Force Compensation Survey, 1996–1997* (Chicago: Dartnell Press, 1996), pp. 156–61.

2. For an excellent explanation of a sales management audit, including a detailed outline of its elements, see Alan J. Dubinsky and Richard W. Hansen, "The Sales Force Man-

agement Audit," *California Management Review,* Winter 1981, pp. 86–95.

3. Geoffrey Brewer, "Targeting Top Customers," *Sales & Marketing Management,* February 1998, p. 114.

4. "Mine Your Own Business," *Midrange Systems,* May 10, 1996, pp. 44–47.

---

*Case 17-1*

## SEAL RITE ENVELOPE COMPANY (A)

### Analysis of sales volume

"You're drowning in data. Haven't you anything better to do around here than reading those reports? You're wasting so much paper the next thing I know the environmentalists will be picketing the place," exclaimed Max Chernak, the company's new president. He had stopped by the office of Rose Douglas, the firm's sales manager for the past seven years, to visit with her. His opening remarks were a reaction to the two-foot-high stack of computer printouts spread out in front of Douglas on her desk. She stopped scanning them and looked up as Chernak walked in.

While he was smiling as he commented on the pile of paper before her, she had been warned previously by an acquaintance who had worked for Chernak in another company that he was not a big believer in paperwork. She recalled the words, "He likes to keep things simple. He doesn't spend much time in his office. He always seems to be around. Delegation is not one of his favorite concepts."

The Seal Rite Envelope Company of St. Louis, Missouri, manufactured and distributed a wide line of paper envelopes of all weights, sizes, and paper stock. Its sales force sold to printers, paper wholesalers,

and to large organizations with their own operations throughout the midwest states.

Douglas was rather proud of the sales analysis system she had developed. All sales orders were classified by the stock numbers of the products bought, who bought them, who sold them, when they were bought, and how much gross margin was realized from the order. The data were for the previous week and previous month, all compared with sales for the same periods the previous year. Any significant changes in performance were automatically highlighted for her attention by the program. A printout of each week's sales orders and shipments was delivered to her home each Sunday morning so she could study it in preparation for the Monday morning sales meeting. The reports were generated on Saturday by Sharon in accounting in response to Douglas's demand for them. The additional costs ($250) incurred for the reports came from Douglas's budget.

Douglas felt obliged to defend her system for analyzing sales. "I find it helpful to have the facts about what has happened before I go into my weekly sales meeting every Monday morning. I know who is selling and who isn't. I know what is selling and what isn't. And I know how much we're making on everything we sell and on every order."

"I see. Knowledge is power. Is that it?" Chernak asked.

Douglas nodded slightly; she understood she was under attack. Had she been too aggressive in defending her system, considering that she hardly knew Chernak, she wondered.

The new president was not a person who avoided confrontation. He rose to the challenge. "OK! I see that something is highlighted on that page you're looking at. What is it?"

"Well, it seems that the sales of item number 2510 are down significantly for the month compared to last year. We sold hardly any of it last week. Let's see, 2510 is our heavy duty, brown, 12 inch by 18 inch mailing envelope," Douglas said as she read from the reports.

"So what?"

"What do you mean, so what?"

Chernak said, "I mean, So what? So what is the significance of that information? So what are you going to do about it?"

Douglas knew she was in a bit of trouble but she could not back down. "I'll make inquiries of the sales force to see if any of them has an explanation. Is something wrong with our product or its pricing? Is it just a random event? Does it reflect a change in market requirements? I'll keep my eye on it to see if anything develops that warrants taking some action."

Chernak replied, "That's what I call micromanagement. How many of such items are there in that report that will require you to do something? Don't answer that! I'm afraid of the answer. We seem to be on different wavelengths. I only want to know a few things, such as our gross margins by broad product lines and sales rep. And, of course, I want to know total dollar sales, gross margins, and expenses. But I would lose all perspective if I had to deal with that volume of information you are processing each week. And what about the costs? Are they worth it? Well, as long as the profit performance of your operation keeps doing as well as it has, you can stare at that paper as long as you like if that's the way you get your kicks."

As Chernak left Douglas's office, she was a bit upset by the president's attitude toward her sales analysis system. She had been taught that if she took care of the details, the totals would take care of themselves. She had found that by having good, recent information about all aspects of sales, she gained power in the organization. Her people had learned not to challenge her since she could always pull out data to support her position. She wanted people to know that she was on top of her job.

Douglas decided to think about the matter for a while and ask some other people about her system before doing anything about it. As she looked at the stack of paper in front of her, a troubling thought crossed her mind. Was she spending too much time on these, analyzing sales? Was it all worth it?

### Questions:

1. How should Rose Douglas evaluate the effectiveness of her sales analysis system?

2. What would you recommend she do in response to the situation in which her boss obviously disagrees with her attitudes toward information systems?

# CHAPTER 18

# Marketing Cost and Profitability Analysis

*Business prophets tell us what* should *happen—but business profits tell us what* did *happen.*

**Earl Wilson**

While an analysis of sales volume is useful, it tells us nothing about the *profitability* of territories, products, or customer groups. To determine the profitability of any of these sales control units, we need a marketing cost analysis. Sales executives are particularly interested in a marketing cost analysis because this information can significantly affect the management of a sales force. The discovery of an unprofitable territory may necessitate a shift in territorial boundaries or a different call schedule. The discovery of unprofitable products may lead to a change in the commission rate paid for sales of those items.

## NATURE AND SCOPE OF MARKETING COST ANALYSIS

A **marketing cost analysis** is a detailed study of a firm's marketing costs. It is used to discover unprofitable segments and inefficiently performed functions of the company's marketing program. It goes beyond a sales volume analysis to determine the profitability of various aspects of the marketing operation. Thus it becomes an important part of an overall sales performance analysis.

Various sales department budgets are frequently an integral part of cost analyses. Management often wants to establish a standard of performance (a budget) for some selling expense, and then try to determine the causes of variation between the actual and budgeted expense.

### Marketing Cost Analysis and the Accounting System

Marketing cost analysis differs somewhat in purpose and scope from the usual accounting system in a firm. Accounting seeks to maintain a complete *historical* record of company events that in any way have a financial flavor. Thus the system provides management with the story of merchandise sales, materials purchased, equipment depreciation, salaries paid, and all other activities relating to finances. Marketing cost analysis is a managerial tool designed more for use in the planning and control of a firm's *future* operations. Of course, an analysis of past financial events often serves as a guide for future operations.

A marketing cost study is *not* usually a part of a company's regular accounting system. It takes up where the accounting system stops. A study of costs is largely analytical and statistical in nature. It is not concerned with the routine accounting practices. The regular accounting system, however, provides virtually all the data necessary to conduct a marketing cost analysis. Therefore, to do an effective cost analysis, it is imperative that there be a detailed system of account classification. For instance, one account for sales commissions is not at all sufficient to analyze the commissions paid (1) on sales of a given product (2) to selected customers (3) in a certain territory.

## Marketing Cost Analysis Compared with Production Cost Accounting

Marketing cost analysis and production cost accounting help to control costs in their respective areas. Beyond this general similarity, however, the two concepts are markedly different, as the comparison in Figure 18-1 shows.

To summarize this comparison, sales executives want to know the marketing costs by product in addition to the costs for other marketing units. Moreover, these costs are incurred by salespeople who are not under direct supervision and whose job is not totally routine, in contrast to production workers and their machines. Finally, production managers usually know the exact cost-volume relationship between an increase in output and a decrease in cost. A sales manager, on the other hand, wants to know what the effect on volume will be if a given cost is changed. For

■ **FIGURE 18-1**  **A comparison of marketing cost analysis and production cost accounting**

| Comparison Factors | Marketing Cost Analysis | Production Cost Accounting |
|---|---|---|
| Bases for computing costs | Marketing unit: territory, customer group, order size, as well as product | Unit of product |
| | *More complex*←——→*Relatively simple* | |
| Source of cost incurred | Salespeople in the field | Machines and closely supervised workers |
| | *Less exact*←——→*More precise* | |
| Cost-volume relationship | Volume is a function of cost $V = (f)C$ | Cost is a function of volume $C = f(V)$ |
| | *Difficult to measure*←——→*Relatively easy to measure* | |

example, what change in volume would occur if two salespeople were added to the eight now operating in the Dallas district? Sales executives typically cannot determine answers to these questions with nearly the degree of accuracy that production managers can.

# ■ TYPES OF MARKETING COST ANALYSIS

A company's marketing costs may be analyzed in three ways:

- As they appear in the ledger accounts and on the income and expense statement.
- After they are grouped into functional (also called activity) categories.
- After they have been allocated to territories, products, or other marketing units.

## Analysis of Ledger Expenses

The simplest and least expensive marketing cost analysis is based on studying object-of-expenditure costs as they are recorded in the company's accounting ledgers. The procedure is simply to take the totals for each cost item (sales force salaries, branch office rent, office supplies) from the ledger accounts and then analyze these figures in some detail. Totals for this period can be compared with similar figures for past periods to determine trends. Management can compare actual expenses with budgeted expense goals. When trade associations disseminate cost information, a company can compare its figures with the industry's averages.

An analysis of ledger-cost items is of limited value because it provides only general information. A study may show, for instance, that sales compensation costs are 4.7 percent of sales, whereas the industry's average for firms of similar size is 6.1 percent. Findings of this nature are of some help in guiding management and controlling the sales force. However, a more detailed analysis is needed to pinpoint the reasons for the trends observed in the company's costs and the variations from industry norms.

In the preceding chapter we introduced the Colorado Ski Company, as part of our discussion of sales volume analysis. At this point, in Figure 18-2, we show that firm's 1998 income and expense statement, sometimes called an *operating statement* or a *profit-and-loss statement*. This statement includes the company's operating expenses as drawn from the firm's ledger accounts.

## Analysis of Activity Expenses

In typical accounting records, expenses are classified according to the immediate object of the expenditure. Thus ledger accounts may be found for such marketing expenses as sales salaries, branch office rent, and adver-

■ **FIGURE 18-2**

**Income and expense statement, 1998, Colorado Ski Company ($000)**

| | | |
|---|---:|---:|
| Net sales | | $27,000 |
| Less cost of goods sold | | 18,900 |
| Gross margin | | 8,100 |
| Less operating expenses: | | |
| Sales salaries and commissions | $3,240 | |
| Sales force travel | 372 | |
| Supplies and telephone | 178 | |
| Media space | 870 | |
| Advertising salaries | 218 | |
| Property taxes | 120 | |
| Heat and light | 168 | |
| Insurance | 84 | |
| Administrative salaries | 930 | |
| Other expenses | 120 | |
| Total operating expenses | | 6,300 |
| Net profit | | $ 1,800 |

tising costs. However, for a more effective marketing cost analysis, sales executives usually regroup these ledger expenses into various activity classifications. All the expenses related to a given marketing function, such as warehousing or advertising, are grouped together.[1]

An activity-related expense analysis is a two-step procedure. The first step involves selecting the appropriate activity categories. Each firm should list the major activities that are relevant to its own marketing program. A retail chain, for instance, ordinarily performs activities different from those of a manufacturer of electric generators. A typical list, however, usually includes many of the following expense categories:

■ Personal selling expenses: sales force compensation and travel expenses as well as all costs connected with branch sales offices.

■ Advertising and sales promotion expenses.

■ Warehousing and shipping expenses.

■ Order processing expenses: costs of processing sales and purchase orders, billing, and receiving payments.

■ Administration expenses: all costs of sales offices, including executives' salaries and travel expenses; marketing's share of company's general administration expenses.

In the second step of an activity-expense analysis, we take each ledger expense and allocate it among the various activity categories. Many of the ledger expenses listed in accounting records cut across several activity groups. Consequently, management must *allocate* a given ledger expense among the appropriate activities. For instance, the ledger account for office supplies must be allocated to each activity group (such as personal selling, advertising, and warehousing) that incurs this expense. A useful tool here is an expense distribution sheet such as the one pictured in Figure 18-3. All the ledger costs are listed vertically in the left-hand column. (Note that these ledger expenses are the same ones shown in Figure 18-2, the company's income and expense statement.) The activity categories are listed at the top of the columns across the sheet.

Some ledger expenses are easy to apportion because they are direct expenses. That is, the entire amount can be allocated to one activity. In Figure 18–3, advertising salaries of $218,000 were apportioned entirely to the advertising activity. Sales force travel expenses of $372,000 were apportioned entirely to the personal-selling category.

Other expenses are indirect. Thus they must be apportioned among several activity groups. The main problem in dealing with each indirect expense is to select a basis for its allocation. For example, property taxes may be distributed on the basis of square feet used for each activity. In the Colorado Ski Company example, about 55 percent of the total floor space was in the warehousing and shipping department. Consequently, $66,000 of the property tax expense (55 percent of $120,000) was allocated to this physical distribution activity.

After all individual ledger expenses are allocated, the columns are totaled, and the resultant figures are the activity expenses. In Figure 18-3 the expenses totaled $6.3 million. The total for personal selling alone was $3,847,000. From this type of analysis, the total cost of each activity can be determined accurately. Moreover, a study of an expense distribution sheet each year shows not only which *ledger* costs have increased or decreased, but also the *activities* responsible for these changes. An analysis of activity expenses also provides an excellent starting point for analyzing marketing costs by territories, products, or other marketing units.

## Analysis of Activity Costs by Market Segments

The third and most beneficial type of marketing cost analysis is a study of the costs and profitability of each segment of the market. The most common practice in this type of analysis is to divide the market by territories, products, customer groups, or order sizes. A cost analysis by market segment enables management to pinpoint trouble spots or areas of satisfactory performance much more effectively than with an analysis of either ledger expenses or total activity costs.

By combining a sales volume analysis with a marketing cost analysis, a profit-and-loss statement may be prepared for each of the products or market segments. These individual income and expense statements then can be analyzed to determine the effectiveness of the marketing program in each of those segments.

**FIGURE 18-3**    Expense distribution sheet, Colorado Ski Company, 1998 (showing allocation of ledger expense items to activity categories)

| | | | | Activity Cost Categories | | |
|---|---|---|---|---|---|---|
| Ledger expenses | Totals | Personal Selling | Advertising | Warehousing and Shipping | Order Processing | Administration |
| Sales salaries and commissions | $3,240,000 | $3,240,000 | — | — | — | — |
| Sales force travel | 372,000 | 372,000 | | | | |
| Supplies and telephone | 178,000 | 43,200 | 22,200 | 40,900 | 43,500 | 28,200 |
| Media space | 870,000 | — | 870,000 | — | — | |
| Advertising salaries | 218,000 | — | 218,000 | — | — | |
| Property taxes | 120,000 | 10,000 | 14,500 | 66,000 | 14,000 | 15,500 |
| Heat and light | 168,000 | 15,300 | 17,400 | 100,500 | 16,200 | 18,600 |
| Insurance | 84,000 | 12,000 | 4,200 | 46,300 | 14,000 | 7,500 |
| Administrative salaries | 930,000 | 144,000 | 62,000 | 168,000 | 126,000 | 430,000 |
| Other expenses | 120,000 | 10,500 | 11,700 | 58,300 | 26,300 | 13,200 |
| Totals | $6,300,000 | 3,847,000 | 1,220,000 | 480,000 | 240,000 | 513,000 |

A complete marketing cost analysis by sales territories or some other marketing unit involves the same three-step evaluation procedure outlined in the preceding chapter. That is, we determine what happened, why it happened, and what we are going to do about the situation.

To determine *what* happened, the procedure in a cost analysis by market segments is quite similar to the method used to analyze activity expenses. The total of each activity cost (the bottom line in Figure 18-3) is prorated on some basis among each product or market segment being studied. Let's walk through an example of a marketing cost analysis in the three geographic sales regions of the Colorado Ski Company, as shown in Figures 18-4 and 18-5. First, for each of the five Colorado Ski activities, we select an allocation basis for distributing the cost of that activity among the three regions. These bases are shown in the top part of Figure 18-4. Then we determine the number of allocation "units" that make up each activity cost, and we find the cost per unit. This completes the allocation scheme which tells us how to allocate costs to the three regions. To illustrate further:

■ **FIGURE 18-4**   **Allocation of activity costs to sales regions, Colorado Ski Company, 1998**

| Activity | Personal Selling | Advertising | Warehousing and Shipping | Order Processing | Administration |
|---|---|---|---|---|---|
| | | **Allocation Scheme** | | | |
| Allocation basis | Direct expense to each region | Number of pages of advertising | Number of orders shipped | Number of invoice lines | Equally among regions |
| Total activity cost | $3,847,000 | $1,220,00 | $480,000 | $240,000 | $513,000 |
| Number of allocation units | — | 61 pages | 9,600 orders | 120,000 lines | 3 regions |
| Cost per allocation unit | — | $20,000 per page | $50 per order | $2 per line | $171,000 per region |
| **Region** | | | **Allocation of Costs** | | |
| Eastern units | — | 21 pages | 3,800 orders | 39,500 lines | one |
| cost | $1,070,000 | $420,000 | $190,000 | $79,000 | $171,000 |
| Midwestern units | — | 11 pages | 2,500 orders | 28,000 lines | one |
| cost | $747,000 | $220,000 | $125,000 | $56,000 | $171,000 |
| Western units | — | 29 pages | 3,300 orders | 52,500 lines | one |
| cost | $2,030,000 | $580,000 | $165,000 | $105,000 | $171,000 |

- Personal-selling activity expenses pose no problem because they are direct expenses, chargeable entirely to the region in which they were incurred.
- Advertising expenses are allocated on the basis of the number of pages of advertising run in each region. The ski company purchased the equivalent of 61 pages of advertising during the year at an average cost of $20,000 per page ($1,220,000/61).
- Warehousing and shipping expenses are allocated on the basis of the number of orders shipped. Since 9,600 orders were shipped during the year at a total activity cost of $480,000, the cost per order was $50. Order-processing expenses are allocated according to the number of invoice lines typed during the year. Since there were 120,000 invoice lines processed on the computer, the cost per line was $2 (120,000 × $2 = $240,000 total cost).
- The administration expense of $513,000—a totally indirect cost—is arbitrarily divided equally among the three regions, at a cost of $171,000 per region.

The final step is to calculate the amount of each activity expense that is to be allocated to each region. The results appear in the bottom part of Figure 18-4. We see that $1,070,000 of *personal-selling* expenses were incurred in the eastern region, $747,000 was charged to the midwestern region, and $2,030,000 to the western region. In the case of *advertising*, 21 pages of advertising were run in the eastern region, so that region was charged with $420,000 (21 pages at $20,000 per page). In similar calculations, the midwestern region was charged $220,000 for

■ **FIGURE 18-5**    **Income and expense statement, by sales region, Colorado Ski Company, 1998 (in $000)**

|                                        | Total    | Eastern | Midwestern | Western  |
|----------------------------------------|----------|---------|------------|----------|
| Net sales                              | $27,000  | $9,000  | $4,500     | $13,500  |
| Less cost of goods sold                | 18,900   | 6,300   | 3,150      | 9,450    |
| Gross margin                           | 8,100    | 2,700   | 1,350      | 4,050    |
| Less operating expenses:               |          |         |            |          |
|   Personal selling           | 3,847    | 1,070   | 802        | 1,975    |
|   Advertising                | 1,220    | 420     | 220        | 580      |
|   Warehousing/shipping       | 480      | 190     | 125        | 165      |
|   Order processing           | 240      | 79      | 56         | 105      |
|   Administration             | 513      | 171     | 171        | 171      |
| Total operating expenses               | 6,300    | 1,930   | 1,374      | 2,996    |
| Net profit (loss)                      | $ 1,800  | $  770  | ($24)      | $ 1,054  |
| Net profit (loss) as percentage of sales | 6.7%   | 8.6%    | (0.53%)    | 7.8%     |

advertising, and the charge to the western region was $580,000. Regarding *warehousing and shipping* expenses, 3,800 orders were shipped to customers in the eastern region. At a unit allocation cost of $50, eastern's total allocated cost was $190,000. Midwestern's allocated shipping cost was $125,000, and the western region was charged $165,000. For *order-processing* expenses, management found that 39,500 invoice lines went to customers in the eastern region. At $2 a line, this expense came to $79,000. In the case of the *administration* expenses of $513,000, each region was charged $171,000. After the five activity expenses have been allocated among the three sales regions, we can prepare a profit-and-loss statement for each region, as shown in Figure 18-5. The sales volume for each region was determined in our volume analysis in the preceding chapter. The cost of goods sold and the gross margin for each region were determined by assuming that the companywide gross margin of 30 percent ($8,100,000/$27,000,000) was maintained in each region.

In summary, Figure 18-5 shows the operating results for each region in the same way that Figure 18-2 reported the income and expense picture for the company as a whole. For example, we see that the eastern region's net profit was 8.6 percent of sales ($770,000/$9,000,000). In sharp contrast, the midwestern region did rather poorly, actually losing $24,000, or 0.53 percent of sales ($24,000/$4,500,000 = 0.53%).

At this point in our performance evaluation, we have completed the *what* happened stage. The next step is to determine *why* the results are as shown in Figure 18-5. As mentioned earlier, it is extremely difficult to answer this question. In the midwestern region, for example, the sales force obtained only about two-thirds as many orders as in the eastern region (2,500 versus 3,800). Was this because we did about half as much advertising in the Midwest as in the East? Or does the reason lie in poor sell-

**This sales manager is analyzing the sales and cost data from his salespeople to make sure that they are achieving their targets.**

ing ability or poor sales training in the Midwest? Or is competition simply much stronger in the Midwest?

After a profitability analysis has determined *why* the regional results came out as they did, management can move to the third stage in its performance evaluation process. That final stage is to determine *what should management do* about the situation? We shall discuss this third stage briefly after we have reviewed some major problem areas in marketing cost analysis.

## ▪ PROBLEMS IN MARKETING COST ANALYSIS

Marketing cost analyses can be expensive in time, money, and personnel. Today, however, the use of computerized information systems enables management to generate data that are more current, detailed, and lower in cost than was true in the past. But even the computers so far have not overcome the problems related to cost allocation and the contribution-margin versus full-cost controversy.

### Allocating Costs

As a foundation for our discussion of cost allocation, let's first distinguish between direct and indirect expenses.

#### Direct versus Indirect Expenses
**Direct costs** are incurred in connection with a single unit of sales operations. Therefore, they can readily be allocated in total to a specific marketing unit, whether it is a territory, product, or customer group. If the company dropped a given territory or product, all direct expenses tied to that marketing unit would be eliminated. These are expenses which can be separated from other costs. **Indirect costs** are those shared by more than one market segment. In general, most marketing costs are totally or partially indirect.

Whether a given cost is classed as common or separable depends on the market segment being analyzed. The cost never remains permanently in one or the other category. Assume that each salesperson in a company has a separate territory, is paid a straight salary, and sells the entire line of products. Sales force salaries would be a *direct* expense if the cost analysis were being made by territories. But the salary expense would be an *indirect* cost if the cost were being studied for each product. They cannot be separated by product. Sales force travel expenses would be a *direct* territorial cost, but an *indirect* product cost.

The term **overhead costs** is frequently used to describe a body of expenses that cannot be identified solely with individual product lines, territories, or other market segments. Sometimes, overhead costs are referred to as *fixed costs*. However, it is preferable to think of these items as *indirect* rather than fixed expenses. They are fixed only in the sense that they are not *directly* allocable among territories, product lines, or some other group of market segments. The point is that these costs cannot be attached solely to individual market units.

### Difficulty of Allocating Costs

A major problem in a marketing cost analysis is that of allocating marketing costs to individual territories, products, or whatever segment of the market is being studied. Actually, the problem of prorating arises at two levels: (1) when accounting ledger expenses are being allocated to activity groups and (2) when the resultant activity costs are apportioned to the separate territories, products, or markets.

A *direct* cost can be allocated in its entirety to the market segment being analyzed. This phase of allocation is reasonably simple. For example, assume that a territorial cost analysis is being made and each salesperson has a territory. Then all of a given rep's expenses—salary, commission, travel, supplies, and so on—can be prorated directly to that rep's territory. Some of the advertising expense, such as the cost of ads in local newspapers and the expense of point-of-purchase advertising materials, can also be charged directly to a given territory.

However, the majority of costs are *common (indirect)* rather than separable, and real allocation problems occur with these expenses. For some costs, the basis of allocation may be the same regardless of the type of analysis made. Billing expenses are often allocated on the basis of number of "invoice lines," whether the cost analysis is by territory, product, or customer group. An invoice line is one item (6 dozen widgets, model 1412, for example) listed on the bill (invoice) sent to a customer. Assume that 22 percent of all invoice lines last year related to orders billed to customers in territory A. Then 22 percent of total billing costs would be allocated to that territory. A cost analysis by product line or customer group would use this same allocation basis—number of invoice lines—when apportioning billing costs.

For other costs, however, the basis of allocation would vary according to whether a firm analyzes its costs by territory, product, or customer group. Consider sales force salaries as an example. In a territorial cost study, these salaries may be allocated directly to the district where the people work. In a product cost analysis, the expense probably is prorated on the proportionate amount of working hours a rep spends with each product. In a cost analysis by customer classes, the salaries may be apportioned in relation to the number of sales calls on each customer group.

### Allocating Totally Indirect Costs

The last big allocation problem discussed here concerns costs that are *totally* indirect. Within the broad category of indirect expenses, some costs are *partially* indirect, and some are *totally* indirect. Many expenses do carry some degree of direct relationship to the territory or other marketing unit being analyzed. Order-filling and shipping expenses, for example, are partially indirect costs. They would *decrease* to some extent if a territory or product were eliminated. They would *increase* if new products or territories were added.

However, other cost items, such as sales administrative or general administrative expenses, are *totally* indirect costs. The cost of maintaining the chief sales executive (salary, staff, and office) remains about the same, whether or not the number of territories or products changes.

Many administrators question whether it is reasonably possible to allocate totally indirect costs. Consider, for example, the problem of allocating general sales manager Cruz's expense to territories. Part of the year Cruz travels in these districts. The costs of transportation, food, and lodging on the road probably can be allocated directly to the territory involved. However, how should Cruz's salary and office expenses be apportioned among sales districts? If Cruz spends a month in territory A and two months in B, then presumably one-twelfth of these expenses may be allocated to A and one-sixth to B. At the same time, this method may be unfair to territory A. During the month's stay in A, Cruz spent much time on the telephone discussing unforeseen difficulties in territory F. Moreover, how would the company apportion the expenses incurred while Cruz is in the home office and not dealing with the affairs of any one particular territory?

Three methods frequently used to allocate indirect costs are shown in Figure 18-6. Each method reflects a different philosophy and each has obvious drawbacks.

■ **FIGURE 18-6**    **Methods used to allocate indirect costs**

| Method | Evaluation |
| --- | --- |
| Divide cost equally among territories or whatever market segments are being analyzed. | Easy to do, but inaccurate and usually unfair to some market segments. |
| Allocate costs in proportion to sales volume obtained from each territory (or product or customer group). | Underlying philosophy: apply cost burden where it can best be borne. That is, charge a high-volume market segment with a large share of the indirect cost. This method is simple and easy to do, but may be very inaccurate. Tells very little about a segment's profitability, and may even be misleading. |
| Allocate indirect costs in same proportion as the total direct costs. Thus if product A accounted for 25 percent of the total *direct* costs, then A would also be charged with 25 percent of the *indirect* expenses. | Again, easy to do but can be inaccurate and misleading. Falsely assumes a close relationship between direct and indirect expenses. |

## The Contribution-Margin versus Full-Cost Controversy

In a marketing cost analysis, two ways of handling the allocation of indirect expenses are the contribution-margin (also called contribution-to-overhead) method and the full-cost method. A real controversy exists regarding which of these two approaches is the best for managerial control purposes.

In the **contribution-margin method,** only the direct expenses are allocated to each marketing unit (territory, product) being analyzed. These are the costs that presumably would be eliminated if the corresponding marketing unit were eliminated. After deducting these direct costs from the gross margin, the remainder is the amount that unit is contributing to cover total overhead (indirect expenses).

In the **full-cost method,** all expenses—direct and indirect—are allocated among the marketing units under study. By allocating all costs, management is trying to determine the net profit of each territory, product, or other marketing unit.

For any given marketing unit, these two methods may be summarized as follows:

| | **Contribution-Margin Method** | | **Full-Cost Method** |
|---|---|---|---|
| | $ Sales | | $ Sales |
| *less* | Cost of goods sold | *less* | Cost of goods sold |
| *equals* | Gross margin | *equals* | Gross margin |
| *less* | Direct expenses | *less* | Direct expenses |
| *equals* | Contribution-margin (the amount available to cover overhead expenses plus a profit) | *less* | Indirect expenses |
| | | *equals* | Net profit |

An example of the contribution-margin method is shown in Figure 18-7. The net sales, cost of goods sold, and gross margin are shown for each of the three geographic regions in the Colorado Ski Company. The direct operating costs of the company are allocated among the three regions. These expenses are then deducted from the region's gross margin. The result is each region's contribution to the remaining $2,196,000 of indirect (overhead) costs. The midwestern region, for instance, incurred $794,000 in direct costs and contributed $556,000 to the overhead expenses and net profit. If the company eliminated the midwestern region, presumably management would save $794,000 in direct expenses. However, the region's $556,000 contribution to overhead would then have to be absorbed by the remaining two regions, assuming the indirect costs still totaled $2,196,000. Figure 18-5 illustrated the full-cost approach to cost allocation. Note the situation the Colorado Ski Company faced in its midwestern region. That region showed a contribution margin of $556,000. But using the full-cost method, the region reported a net loss of $24,000, after the indirect expenses were allocated.

**?** **AN ETHICAL DILEMMA**

One of the problems typically encountered in a marketing cost analysis is the difficulty of allocating total indirect cost. These costs include such items as the salaries and office expense of the top sales executives in a firm. In a figure in the text, we noted some commonly used methods for allocating these expenses.

One such method is to allocate indirect expenses in proportion to the sales volume or gross margin generated in each territory. Assume that a midwestern territory generated $1 million in sales last year and an eastern district's sales were $2 million. Then the eastern territory's allocation of indirect expenses would be twice that of the midwestern unit. The underlying rationale for this expense-allocation basis is that the cost burden should be placed where it can best be borne. That is, the biggest volume (or gross margin) territories should absorb the largest share of indirect costs.

The salespeople and sales managers in these big territories understandably object to this cost-allocation system. The objections increase especially when the reps' or the district managers' compensation includes a profit-sharing element. Those people also object when their performance evaluations include a review of the district's net profitability.

Is it ethical to allocate indirect expenses to territories on the basis of where these costs can best be carried?

There is considerable argument over the relative merits of the contribution-margin and full-cost methods. *Proponents of the full-cost method* contend that the purpose of a marketing cost study is to determine the net profitability of the units being studied. They feel that the contribution-margin approach does not fulfill this purpose. Furthermore, full-cost advocates believe that a contribution-margin analysis may be misleading. A given territory or product may show a contribution to overhead; yet, after the indirect costs are allocated, this product or territory may actually have a net loss (as seen in the midwestern region of the Colorado Ski Company).

*Contribution-margin supporters* contend that it is not possible to accurately apportion the indirect costs among market segments. Furthermore, items such as administrative costs are not related at all to any single territory or product. Therefore, the unit should not bear any of these costs. These advocates also point out that a full-cost analysis may show that a product or territory has a net loss, whereas this unit may be contributing something to overhead (again, the situation in the midwestern region). Some executives might recommend that the losing region be eliminated. But they overlook the fact that the unit's contribution to overhead would then have to be borne by other units. Under the contribution-margin approach, the company would keep this unit, at least until a better alternative could be found.

Actually, both approaches have a place in marketing cost analysis. The full-cost method is especially suited for the systematic reporting of historical costs as a basis for future marketing planning. A full-cost analysis is useful when making long-range studies of the profitability of various

■ **FIGURE 18-7** **Income and expense statement by sales region, Colorado Ski Company, 1998, in $000, *using contribution-margin approach***

|  | Total | Eastern | Midwestern | Western |
|---|---|---|---|---|
| Net sales | $27,000 | $9,000 | $4,500 | $13,500 |
| Less cost of goods sold | 18,900 | 6,300 | 3,150 | 9,450 |
| Gross margin | 8,100 | 2,700 | 1,350 | 4,050 |
| Less *direct* operating expenses: |  |  |  |  |
|   Personal selling | 3,082 | 845 | 595 | 1,642 |
|   Advertising | 732 | 254 | 127 | 351 |
|   Warehousing/shipping | 160 | 64 | 42 | 54 |
|   Order processing | 130 | 43 | 30 | 57 |
| Total *direct* expenses | 4,104 | 1,206 | 794 | 2,104 |
| Contribution margin | $ 3,996 | $1,494 | $ 556 | $1,946 |
| Less *indirect* operating expenses: |  |  |  |  |
|   Personal selling | 765 |  |  |  |
|   Advertising | 488 |  |  |  |
|   Warehousing/shipping | 320 |  |  |  |
|   Order processing | 110 |  |  |  |
|   Administration | 513 |  |  |  |
| Total *indirect* expenses | $2,196 |  |  |  |
| Net profit | $1,800 |  |  |  |

market segments. This type of analysis can also be helpful when establishing *long-range* policies on product lines, distribution channels, pricing structures, or promotional programs.

The contribution-margin approach is especially useful as an aid to decision making in *short-run* marketing situations. Also, when cost responsibility is directly assignable to particular market segments, management has an effective tool for controlling and evaluating the sales force.

# ◾ USE OF FINDINGS FROM PROFITABILITY ANALYSIS

So far in our discussion of marketing cost analysis, we have dealt generally with the first stage in the evaluation process. That is, we have been finding out *what happened*. Now let's look at some examples of how management might use the combined findings from both sales volume and marketing cost analyses—the profitability analysis.

## Territorial Decisions

Once management has completed its volume and cost analyses, it may decide to adjust territorial boundaries to match their current potential. Possibly the district is too small. That is, the potential volume is not adequate to support the expense of covering the territory. Or it may be too large, forcing the salesperson to spend too much time and expense in traveling.

Management may also consider a change in selling methods or channels in an unprofitable area. Possibly mail or telephone selling should be used instead of incurring the expense of personal-selling visits. A company that sells directly to retailers or industrial users may consider using wholesaling middlemen instead.

A weak territory sometimes can be made profitable by an increase in advertising and sales promotion. Possibly, the salespeople are not getting adequate support. Or competition may have grown so strong that management must be resigned to a smaller market share than formerly.

The problems in poor territories may lie with the activities of the salespeople. They may need closer supervision, or perhaps too large a percentage of their sales comes from low-margin items. They also may simply be poor sales reps.

As a last resort, it may be necessary to abandon a territory entirely, not even using the facilities provided by mail, telephone, or middlemen. Possibly the potential once present no longer exists. However, before dropping a territory from its market, a company should consider the cost repercussions. The territory presumably has carried some share of indirect, inescapable expenses, such as marketing and general administrative costs. If the district is abandoned, these expenses must be absorbed by the remaining areas.

## Products

When a cost analysis by products shows significant differences in the profitability of the product line, the executives should determine the reasons for the differences. It may be that these profit variations stem from factors (typical order size or packaging requirements, for example) that are firmly set. That is, management has very little opportunity for profit improvement. On the other hand, many low-profit items often do present opportunities for administrative action. A firm may simplify its line by eliminating some models or colors for which there is little demand. Also, simplification allows the sales force to concentrate on fewer items and probably increases the sales of the remaining products.

Sometimes a product's profitability can be increased by redesigning or repackaging the item. Packaging the product in multiple rather than single units may increase the average order size. This will cut the unit costs of order filling, shipping, and packaging. Another possibility is to alter (increase or decrease) the amount of advertising and other promotional help appropriated for the product. Possibly, a change in sales force compensation is needed (1) to increase the sales of profitable items or (2) to discourage the sales of low-margin goods.

A low-volume item cannot always be dropped from the line. Nor can a company always drop an item even though it shows an irreducible net loss. The product may be necessary to round out a line, and the customers may expect the seller to carry it.

## Size of Order

Management should also consider a cost analysis by **order size.** A common situation plaguing many companies is the **small-order problem.** That is, often orders are so small that they result in a loss to the company. Many costs such as direct selling or billing are often the same for each order, whether it is for $10 or $10,000. A cost analysis by customer groups is closely related to an analysis by order size. Frequently, a customer class that generates a below-average profit also presents a small-order problem. Sometimes large-volume purchasers build up their volume by giving the seller many small individual orders. Management should review both their customer and order-size analyses before making policy decisions in these areas.

At first, it might seem that customers who are sold at a loss should be eliminated, and orders below the break-even point should not be accepted. However, this is a hasty conclusion. Management first should determine *why* the accounts are unprofitable and *why* the average orders are small, and then consider ways to improve these situations. Several reasons may account for a customer's small orders or unprofitableness. For instance:

- An account buys a large amount in total over a period of a year, but the customer buys in small amounts from several suppliers.
- A company buys a large amount in total and all from one supplier. But this customer purchases frequently, so the average order is small. The increasingly popular "just-in-time" (JIT) inventory control systems typically involve the frequent delivery of small orders. However, a JIT delivery system is usually a part of a profitable, long-term purchasing commitment. Consequently, both the buyer and seller can benefit from a just-in-time inventory control strategy.
- An account is small but growing, and a seller caters to it in hope of future benefits.
- A customer is small and, as far as can be projected into the future, will remain small.

There are many practical suggestions for increasing the average size of an order or for reducing the marketing costs of small orders. See Figure 18-8 for examples.

■ **FIGURE 18-8**

**Ways to increase order size and reduce small-order marketing costs**

- Educate customers who buy from several different suppliers. Stress the advantages of purchasing from one supplier.

- For customers who purchase large total quantities in frequent small orders, stress the advantages of ordering once a month instead of once a week. Point out that the buyer eliminates all handling, billing, and accounting expenses connected with three of the four orders. Note further that the buyer writes only one check and one purchase order. In addition, stress that there will be only one bill to process and one shipment to put into inventory instead of three or four.

- Educate the sales force as well as customers. In fact, it may be necessary to change the compensation plan to discourage acceptance of smaller orders.

- Substitute direct mail or telephone selling for sales calls on unprofitable or small-order accounts. Or continue to call on these accounts, but less frequently.

- Shift an account to a wholesaler or some other type of middleman rather than dealing directly, even by mail or telephone.

- Drop a mass-distribution policy and adopt a selective one. This new policy may actually increase sales because sales reps can spend more time with profitable accounts.

- Establish a minimum order size.

- Establish a minimum charge or a service charge to combat small orders.

## ■ RETURN ON INVESTMENT—AN EVALUATION TOOL

The concept of **return on investment (ROI)** is another useful managerial aid in evaluating sales performance and in making marketing decisions. The following formula can be used to calculate return on investment:

$$\text{ROI} = \frac{\text{Net profit}}{\text{Sales}} \times \frac{\text{Sales}}{\text{Investment}}$$

The first fraction expresses the rate of profit on sales. The second fraction indicates the number of times the total investment (assets employed) was turned over. By multiplying the investment turnover by the rate of profit on sales, the ROI is determined.

Two questions may quickly come to mind. First, what do we mean by "investment"? Second, why do we need two fractions? It would seem that the sales component in each fraction would cancel out, leaving net profit divided by investment as the meaningful ratio.

To answer the first query, consider a firm whose operating statement shows annual sales of $1 million and a net profit of $50,000. At the end of the year, the balance sheet reports

| Assets | $600,000 | Liabilities | | $200,000 |
|---|---|---|---|---|
| | | Capital stock | $300,000 | |
| | | Retained earnings | 100,000 | 400,000 |
| | | | $400,000 | $600,000 |

Now, is the investment $400,000 or $600,000? Certainly the ROI will depend on which figure we use. The answer depends on whether we are talking to the stockholders or to the company executives. The stockholders are more interested in the return on what they have invested—in this case, $400,000. The ROI calculation then is

$$\text{ROI} = \frac{\text{Net profit } \$50,000}{\text{Sales } \$1,000,000} \times \frac{\text{Sales } \$1,000,000}{\text{Investment } \$400,000} = 12.5\%$$

Management, on the other hand, is more concerned with the total investment, as represented by the total assets ($600,000). This is the amount that the executives must manage, regardless of whether the assets were acquired by stockholders' investment, retained earnings, or loans from outside sources. Within this context, the ROI computation becomes:

$$\text{ROI} = \frac{\text{Net profit } \$50,000}{\text{Sales } \$1,000,000} \times \frac{\text{Sales } \$1,000,000}{\text{Investment } \$600,000} = 8.33\%$$

Regarding the second question, we use two fractions because we are dealing with two separate elements—the rate of profit on sales and the rate of capital turnover. Management really should determine each rate separately and then multiply the two. The rate of profit on sales is influenced by marketing considerations—sales volume, price, product mix, advertising effort. The capital turnover is a financial consideration not directly involved with costs or profit—only with sales volume and assets managed.

To illustrate, assume that our company's profit doubled with the same sales volume and investment because management operated an excellent marketing program this year. In effect, we doubled our profit rate with the same capital turnover:

$$\text{ROI} = \frac{\text{Net profit } \$100,000}{\text{Sales } \$1,000,000} \times \frac{\text{Sales } \$1,000,000}{\text{Investment } \$600,000} = 16.66\%$$

$$10\% \quad \times \quad 1.67 \quad = 16.66\%$$

As expected, this 16.66 percent is twice the ROI calculated earlier.

Now assume that we earned our original profit of $50,000 but that we did it with an investment reduced to $500,000. We cut the size of our average inventory and closed some branch offices. By increasing our capital turnover from 1.67 to 2, we raise the ROI from 8 percent to 10 percent, even though sales volume and profits remain unchanged:

$$\text{ROI} = \frac{\$50,000}{\$1,000,000} \times \frac{\$1,000,000}{\$500,000} = 10\%$$

$$5\% \quad \times \quad 2 \quad = 10\%$$

Assume now that we increase our sales volume—let us say we double it—but do not increase our profit or investment. That is, the cost-profit squeeze is bringing us profitless prosperity. The following interesting results occur:

$$\frac{\$50,000}{\$2,000,000} \times \frac{\$2,000,000}{\$600,000} = 8\%$$

$$5\% \quad \times \quad 3.3 \quad = 8\%$$

The profit rate was cut in half, but this was offset by a doubling of the capital-turnover rate, leaving the ROI unchanged.

## Use of Return on Assets Managed to Evaluate Field Sales Managers

A variation of the ROI concept is the concept of **ROAM—return on assets managed.** The ROAM concept is particularly useful for evaluating the performance of district sales managers, branch managers, or other managerial segments of a field sales organization. ROAM modifies the factors in the traditional ROI equation to make them appropriate for the organizational segment being analyzed. If management is evaluating sales district performance, for instance, presumably the sales volume in each district is readily available. For the profit figure in the equation, management can determine the contribution margin in each district. That is, from a given district's sales, we deduct the cost of goods sold and all operating expenses directly chargeable to a district. In the "investment" section of the ROI equation, we substitute the assets employed—that is, the "assets managed"—hence the acronym ROAM instead of ROI. In a sales district, the assets managed consist of the average accounts receivable and the inventory carried to serve that district. The net result of these changes is the following equation:

$$\text{ROAM} = \frac{\text{Contribution margin}}{\text{District sales volume}} \times \frac{\text{District sales volume}}{\text{Average accounts receivable} + \text{Inventory}}$$

The usefulness of the ROAM concept as an executive evaluation tool depends on whether the assets in the equation are controllable by the executive being evaluated. If a district sales manager has little or no control over the assets employed in a district, it is not valid to hold the executive accountable for the return earned on those assets. The lack of asset control by individual salespeople is a reason that ROAM should *not* be used to measure the performance of individual reps.

With asset control, however, district sales executives and other field sales managers can improve their ROAM percentage by influencing sales volume, contribution margin, or district asset investment. Thus field sales managers can use the ROAM concept when considering the addition of new customers or products in their districts. In effect, return on assets managed is an analytical tool that facilitates the delegation of profit responsibility to territorial sales managers.[2]

## ◼ SUMMARY

A marketing cost analysis is a detailed study of a company's distribution costs. It is undertaken to discover which segments (territories, products, customers) of the company's marketing program are profitable and which are not. A marketing cost analysis is a part of a company's evaluation of its marketing performance.

In marketing cost analysis, we need to understand the differences between accounting-ledger costs and activity-category costs. Another useful distinction is the one between direct and indirect expenses. In a marketing cost analysis, one of the major problems is the difficulty of allocating costs. Management must allocate ledger accounts into activity categories. Then each total activity cost must be allocated to the marketing segment (territory, product, customer group) being analyzed. Cost allocation is especially difficult in the case of indirect expenses.

The difficulty of allocating indirect costs leads to the contribution-margin versus full-cost controversy. In the contribution-margin approach to marketing cost analysis, only the direct costs incurred by the marketing unit (territory or product, for example) are allocated to that unit. The unit's gross margin minus its direct costs equals the amount the unit contributes to pay the company's overhead (indirect expense). In the full-cost approach, all costs (direct and indirect) are allocated to the various marketing units being studied. In this way, management tries to determine the unit's net profit.

The company's marketing costs can be analyzed in three ways. One way is to analyze the costs as they appear in the accounting ledgers and on the company's income and expense (profit and loss) statement. A second approach is to analyze the marketing costs after they have been allocated to activity categories. The third type occurs after each activity cost has been allocated to the sales territories, products, or other marketing units being studied.

The types of analyses we have summarized tell management *what* happened. Then the executives must try to determine *why* these results occurred. Finally, management must decide *what changes* are needed in the marketing program to correct the misdirected effort.

A marketing cost analysis can be especially useful in identifying and remedying the small-order problem that occurs in so many firms.

Return on investment (ROI) is another tool that management can use in evaluating sales performance and in making marketing decisions. A variation of the ROI concept is ROAM, return on assets managed. The ROAM concept is especially useful for evaluating the performance of field sales managers.

## Key Terms

Contribution-margin
  method
Direct costs
Full-cost method

Indirect costs
Marketing cost analysis
Order size
Overhead costs

Return on assets managed
  (ROAM)
Return on investment (ROI)
Small-order problem

## ■ QUESTIONS AND PROBLEMS

1. Explain the similarities and differences between marketing cost analysis and production cost accounting.

2. Is an analysis of expenses as recorded in a company's accounting ledgers better than no cost analysis at all? What specific policies or operating plans may stem from an analysis of ledger expenses alone?

3. A national manufacturer of roofing and siding materials has 40 salespeople. Each has his or her own territory and sells all three of the firm's product lines. They sell primarily to wholesalers and large retailers in the lumber and building materials field. The company wants to make a *territorial analysis* of marketing costs. What bases do you recommend it should use to allocate among the territories each of the following costs?

  *a.* Sales force salaries.

  *b.* Sales force travel expenses.

  *c.* Sales force commissions paid on gross margin.

  *d.* Salaries and expenses of three regional sales managers.

  *e.* Sales training expenses.

  *f.* Television advertising (local and national).

  *g.* Newspaper advertising.

  *h.* Billing.

  *i.* Shipping from three regional factories.

  *j.* Marketing research.

  *k.* General sales manager's salary and office expenses.

  *l.* Advertising overhead.

4. The company in the preceding problem wants to analyze its marketing cost by *product lines*. Suggest appropriate bases for allocating the above-listed cost items to the three product groups.

5. What supporting points could be brought out by the proponents of each side in the full-cost versus contribution-margin controversy over allocation of indirect marketing costs? Which of the two concepts do you advocate? Why?

6. In an analysis of expenses grouped by activities, a manufacturer noted that last year the firm's direct selling expenses (sales force compensation, travel expenses, branch office expenses, and so on) increased significantly over the preceding year. Is this trend necessarily an indication of weaknesses in the management of the sales force?

7. Each of the following firms made a territorial cost analysis and discovered it had some districts that were showing a net loss. What actions involving the sales force do you recommend each company take to improve its situation?

   a. Hardware wholesaler, covering six southeastern states.

   b. Paint and varnish manufacturer.

   c. National business machines manufacturer.

8. What actions involving its sales force can each of the following firms take if they discover unprofitable products in their lines?

   a. Distributor of electrical goods.

   b. Flower seed producer.

   c. Manufacturer of small power tools.

9. "Large-annual-volume customers never present a small-order problem, while low-annual-volume customers always create small-order problems." Do you agree?

10. To determine return on investment, we multiply two fractions: net profit/sales and sales/investment. Why can't we cancel out the sales factor in each fraction and simply divide net profit by investment?

11. Explain how the ROAM concept may be used to evaluate the profit performance of a territorial sales manager.

## EXPERIENTIAL EXERCISES

**A.** Call sales managers from 10 different companies. Ask them how the performance of their sales districts are evaluated; that is, what measures—such as total sales, gross profit margin, ROI, or ROAM—are used.

**B.** Call sales managers from three companies to determine the process by which they develop their sales budget (sales and selling expenses).

## REFERENCES

1. For an excellent report on the usefulness and effectiveness of analyzing expenses by activity groupings, see Thomas H. Stevenson, Frank C. Barnes, and Sharon A. Stevenson, "Activity-Based Costing: An Emerging Tool for Industrial Marketing Decision Makers," *Journal of Business & Industrial Marketing* 8, no. 2 (1993), pp. 40–52.

2. For a discussion of the limitations of the ROAM concept that may influence its applicability and a proposal for an alternative evaluation tool, see William L. Cron and Michael Levy, "Sales Management Performance Evaluation: A Residual Income Perspective," *Journal of Personal Selling & Sales Management,* August 1987, pp. 57–66.

*Case 18-1*

## SEAL RITE ENVELOPE COMPANY (B)
### Profitability analysis

As Rose Douglas, the company's sales manager, scanned a computer printout of a profitability analysis of the company's customers, she had in mind that a previous analysis had indicated that the firm's direct selling costs per call were $110 for the company's $22 million sales volume in 1998. Since the firm's average gross margin was about 25 percent, the sales reps had to get an average order of $440 for each sales call they made. Even then, a $440 average order just covered the direct selling expenses. That still left the overhead expenses uncovered. She could quickly see from the data in front of her that she had some problems.

Wanting more data on the profitability of customers by their size, she turned to the computer on her desk and extracted the information shown in Exhibit 18-A from the firm's customer database. She did not like what she saw. She recalled a lecture in college given by an old marketing professor who loved to talk about misdirected marketing efforts. At the time she thought that he was hopelessly out of date. No firm in modern times could possibly allow such situations to develop. Now she wished she had paid more attention to the lecture, for she suspected that she had a problem with just such misdirected marketing efforts.

*Questions:*

1. What problems are indicated from the data in Exhibit 18-A?

2. What should Rose Douglas do about those problems?

■ **EXHIBIT 18-A**    **Seal Rite Envelope Company, 1998**

| Annual Customer Volume ($000) | Number of Accounts | Number of Calls | Sales (% of total) | Gross Profit (% of sales) | Selling Expense (% of sales) | Operating Profit (% of sales) |
|---|---|---|---|---|---|---|
| >$200 | 4 | 256 | 10.9 | 15.9 | 4.0 | 11.9 |
| $100–$200 | 4 | 274 | 2.9 | 23.6 | 9.5 | 14.1 |
| $50–$99.9 | 32 | 1,344 | 11.7 | 19.8 | 10.2 | 9.6 |
| $40–$49.9 | 24 | 1,011 | 5.4 | 18.4 | 10.2 | 8.2 |
| $30–$39.9 | 25 | 1,158 | 4.0 | 21.8 | 9.6 | 12.2 |
| $20–$29.9 | 63 | 3,114 | 8.5 | 22.8 | 10.9 | 11.9 |
| $10–$19.9 | 157 | 4,725 | 13.2 | 23.9 | 13.4 | 10.5 |
| $5–$9.9 | 349 | 7,021 | 15.7 | 25.9 | 16.8 | 9.1 |
| $4–$4.9 | 235 | 2,639 | 5.0 | 2.9 | 19.3 | 10.3 |
| $3–$3.9 | 309 | 3,233 | 5.2 | 31.6 | 21.9 | 9.7 |
| $2–$2.9 | 569 | 4,212 | 7.1 | 31.2 | 25.3 | 5.9 |
| $1–$1.9 | 842 | 6,360 | 6.9 | 30.4 | 34.3 | -3.6 |
| <$1 | 871 | 6,345 | 3.5 | 30.9 | 75.3 | -44.4 |
| No sales | 688 | 2,001 | 0.0 | 0.0 | 0.0 | 0.0 |
| Total or Average | 4,172 | 43,693 | 100 | 25.0 | 18.6 | 6.4 |

# CHAPTER 19

# Evaluating a Salesperson's Performance

You are only as good as you think you are.
**Anonymous**

When beginning salespeople are hired, the most important and most difficult task of a sales manager is to guide their development. As these salespeople progress through their careers, the sales manager has the additional responsibility of making sure that they are working up to their potential. These responsibilities involve putting into practice many of the processes that we have discussed in various chapters of this book, such as training, motivation, and supervision.

To improve salespeople's performance through training, motivation, and supervision, it is critical that the sales manager evaluate the strengths and weaknesses of each individual salesperson. Sales managers frequently make evaluations which are too general and too subjective. They may be based on personal observation, managers' attitudes, or a global measure of performance, such as total sales. These measures do not enable sales managers to pinpoint salespeople's strengths and weaknesses so that they may help them improve their performance.

This chapter presents the methods and measures that sales managers should use to systematically and objectively assess the performance of their individual salespeople. After examining the nature and purposes of this managerial activity, we outline a complete program for evaluating sales performance. The last section of the chapter is a case example of how one sales manager interpreted the performance data he assembled.

## ■ NATURE AND IMPORTANCE OF PERFORMANCE EVALUATION

Appraising a salesperson's performance is a part of the managerial function of evaluation. It is part of a marketing audit. Management compares the results of a person's efforts with the goals set for that person. The purpose is to determine what happened in the past and to use this information to improve performance in the future either by taking corrective actions or by rewarding good performance. The evaluation system also is one of the means by which managers *direct* the activities of their salespeople.

## Concept of Evaluation and Development

Evaluation has an added dimension when viewed from the perspective of evaluation and *development* of individual salespeople. Within this wider context, management engages in a counseling activity rather than in a cold statistical analysis. Certainly management wants to measure past performance against standards to identify strengths and weaknesses in the firm's marketing system, particularly as a basis for future planning. But this activity is optimized only if it is also brought to the personal level of the salesperson. It should serve as a basis for the person's self-development and as a basis for a sound company program to guide and develop the personnel.

## Concept of Evaluation and Direction

If salespeople are aware of the criteria by which they will be evaluated, they will try to do things to improve their performance on these criteria. For example, if one of the goals of the company's strategy is to improve customer satisfaction, then this goal should be included in the evaluation process. This will serve to *direct* the efforts of the reps toward this goal. If the reps are aware that customer satisfaction will be an important dimension of their evaluation, then they will try to improve their customers' satisfaction.

## Importance of Performance Evaluation

A good performance review can be a major aid in other sales force management tasks. Promotions and pay increases can be based on objective performance data rather than on favoritism, subjective observations, or opinions. Weaknesses in field-selling efforts, once identified, may be forestalled by incorporating corrective measures in training programs. On the other hand, management can identify the sales techniques of the outstanding performers with an eye toward having other salespeople adopt them. Performance evaluations may also uncover the need for improvements in the compensation plan. For instance, the existing plan may focus too much effort on low-margin items or too little attention on nonselling (missionary) activities.

Performance analysis especially helps in sales supervision. It is difficult to effectively supervise someone without knowing what the person is doing correctly or incorrectly, and why. If a rep's sales volume is unsatisfactory, for instance, a performance review will show it. Moreover, the evaluation may help identify the cause—whether the rep has a low daily call rate, does not work enough days per month, calls on the wrong prospects, has trouble with the sales presentation, and so on.

An effective procedure for appraising the work of an individual can also help morale. Any person who knows what he or she is expected to do and has some benchmarks for measuring accomplishments feels more secure. A performance evaluation should ensure that reps who deserve favorable recognition receive it, and those who deserve criticism are handled appropriately. The salesperson with the highest sales volume is not necessarily the best one and may not even be doing a good all-around job. To reward this person on the basis of sales volume alone can hurt the morale of others in the sales force. Similarly, morale suffers if management criticizes a rep for low volume when the contributing factor was low territorial potential or unusually stiff competition. A performance-appraisal system should forestall and help correct such situations.

By evaluating the salespeople's achievements, management helps them discover their own strengths and weaknesses. This should motivate them to raise their levels of performance. Like most people, salespeople seldom can make an effective self-evaluation. A sales rep may know he is doing something wrong if his output is low. But the rep may be unable to determine the reasons for this poor productivity.

## Difficulties Involved in Evaluating Performance

Many duties assigned to salespeople cannot be measured objectively, and some tasks are difficult to evaluate even on a subjective basis. A manufacturer's representative is supposed to service the firm's accounts; a wholesaler's sales rep is told to avoid high-pressure selling; all salespeople are supposed to build goodwill with customers. Even with close field supervision of the sales force, these tasks can be evaluated only subjectively. And, if management does not closely supervise the salespeople in the field, it may be virtually impossible to measure results from some of these duties.

By the same token, however, many tasks of a seemingly subjective nature can actually be quantified. A salesperson's tendency to pressure or oversell customers, for instance, might be measured by tallying her canceled orders, the number of lost accounts, and the rate of reorders.

The wide variety of conditions sales reps work under makes it difficult for management to compare their productivity. There is no satisfactory method for equating territorial differences in potential, competition, or working conditions. It is difficult to compare the performance of city salespeople with rural salespeople, for example. Even if the districts are equal in potential, they are not comparable in other ways.

Sometimes performance evaluation is difficult because the results of a salesperson's efforts may not be evident for some time. A district's improved position may show up only after a rep has been working there for a year or more. Furthermore, when two or more people are involved in making a sale or in servicing a customer, it usually is difficult to give individual credit for results.

### Importance of a Good Job Description

In the task of sales force evaluation, as we have seen for so many other sales force management activities, a good job description is critical. Evaluators must work from the reference point of a statement about *what* a salesperson is supposed to do. Otherwise, they are not in a good position to determine *whether* or *how effectively* the job was done.

## ■ PROGRAM FOR EVALUATING PERFORMANCE

This section suggests a five-step procedural system for evaluating sales force performance (see Figure 19-1). The program is complete, but it is also expensive and time-consuming.

### Establish Some Basic Policies

**Step 1:** Preliminary to the actual evaluation, management should set some ground rules. One question that calls for a decision is: Who will participate in the evaluation? Several executives normally are involved. One of the most likely is the salesperson's immediate superior—perhaps a field supervisor, a district manager, or a branch manager. The boss of the immediate supervisor is also likely to be involved. Today many companies, such as Chrysler, Bell Atlantic, and G. D. Searle, are using an employee assessment known as 360-degree feedback. This involves getting feedback from an employee's peers, subordinates, and clients, as well as superiors.[1]

Certainly, the salesperson being evaluated should participate actively, usually with some form of self-evaluation. Involving salespeople in the development of their objectives creates a greater sense of responsibility and commitment on the part of the salespeople. In some firms, the manager and salesperson identify and negotiate specific goals for the upcoming period. Then the rep and manager sign a performance agreement which specifies these goals as the performance standards. This ensures that there will be no misunderstandings about what is expected. This process is often called **management by objectives.**

Another policy decision concerns the frequency of evaluation. While many companies conduct complete performance evaluations only once a year, most employees prefer that evaluations take place more frequently—

■ **FIGURE 19-1**     **Procedure for evaluating salespeople**

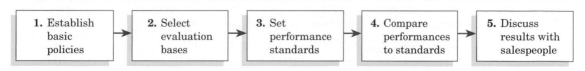

1. Establish basic policies → 2. Select evaluation bases → 3. Set performance standards → 4. Compare performances to standards → 5. Discuss results with salespeople

**Frequent evaluations are an important part of improving performance.**

every six months or even quarterly.[2] Although the time and costs required to conduct more frequent evaluations must be balanced against the benefits, the improvements in performance generally outweigh the costs.

## Select Bases for Evaluation

**Step 2:** One key to a successful evaluation program is to appraise a sales rep's performance on as many different bases as possible. To do otherwise is to run the risk of being misled. Let's assume that we are rating a sales rep (Ryan) on the basis of the ratio of selling expenses to sales volume. If this percentage is very low compared to the average for the entire sales force, Ryan probably will be commended. Yet Ryan actually may have achieved that low ratio by failing to prospect for new accounts or by otherwise covering the territory inadequately. Knowing the average number of daily calls Ryan made, even in relation to the average call rate for the entire sales force, does not help us very much. By measuring Ryan's ratio of orders per call (batting average) we learn a little more, but we still can be misled. Each additional piece of information—sales volume, plus average order size, plus presentation quality, and so on—helps to give a clearer picture of Ryan's performance.

When selecting the bases upon which to evaluate salespeople, it is important to remember that the evaluation serves two purposes. One is to recognize and reward people for a job well done; the other is to develop a clear understanding of the person's performance in order to help him or her improve performance. To get a clear understanding of a person's performance, it is important to look at both output and input measures.

### Output Measures
These are the measures of the salesperson's results—sales volume, gross margin, number of orders, and so on. A list of some output factors ordi-

■ **FIGURE 19-2**

**Output factors used as evaluation bases**

- Sales volume
  In dollars and in units
  By products and customers (or customer groups)
  By mail, telephone, and personal sales calls
- Sales volume as a percentage of:
  Quota
  Market potential (i.e., market share)
- Gross margin by product line, customer group, and order size
- Orders
  Number of orders
  Average size (dollar volume) of order
  Batting average (orders ÷ calls)
  Number of canceled orders
- Accounts
  Percentage of accounts sold
  Number of new accounts
  Number of lost accounts
  Number of accounts with overdue payment

narily used as evaluation bases is shown in Figure 19-2. These measures are often used to make some meaningful comparisons. For example, one rep may be compared to another, performance this year may be compared to performance for last year, performance may be compared to a goal or target, or the rep's share of the market may be compared to that of competitors.

Each of these measures can be further broken down by type of product, customer type, or channel of distribution, and similar comparisons can be made. Breaking the information down by various subcategories may provide some insights into the rep's performance which would otherwise be overlooked. If the salesperson's performance is below average, it may be that the problem can be isolated to one type of selling situation or to one category of product. If a manager can pinpoint the cause of a performance problem, it becomes much easier to find a solution to alleviate that problem.

All of the output bases are *quantitative* measures. To a large extent, the use of these quantitative measures minimizes the subjectivity and biases of the evaluator. Quantitative properties are also relatively easy to measure. However, since they consider results *only,* these measures may not provide an equitable base upon which to compare the performance of one salesperson to another.

### Problem of Data Comparability

Ideally, a salesperson should be judged only on factors he or she can control. Management should identify the uncontrollable factors and take them into consideration when appraising an individual's performance.

The sales potential in a territory, especially in relation to size and number of customers, is a good example of an uncontrollable factor. The greater sales potential in one territory versus another may make it easier for the rep in the first territory to reach his or her goals while the rep in the second territory struggles to meet the same goals. Differences in competitive activity or physical conditions among territories must also be considered when comparing performances. Usually, there are territorial variations in the amount of advertising, sales promotional support, or home-office technical service available to customers. These and several other factors make it difficult to compare performance data. This is one of the reasons for considering information on inputs or efforts as well as results.

### Input Measures

Two types of input measure are used in the evaluation process. The *quantitative* measures focus on the salesperson's efforts or activities. The number of calls a salesperson makes in a day and the number of letters written to prospects are examples of quantitative input measures. Figure 19-3 lists the more commonly used factors; tracking these factors is considered so important by Bell South Cellular that 25 percent of their sales managers' quarterly bonus is based on how closely they monitor their reps' activities.[3]

■ **FIGURE 19-3**

| **Input factors used as evaluation bases** | ■ Calls per day (call rate) |
| :--- | :--- |
| | ■ Days worked |
| | ■ Selling time versus nonselling time |
| | ■ Direct selling expense<br>In total<br>As percentage of sales volume<br>As percentage of quota |
| | ■ Nonselling activities<br>Advertising displays set up<br>Letters written to prospects<br>Telephone calls made to prospects<br>Number of meetings held with dealers and/or distributors<br>Number of service calls made<br>Collections made<br>Number of customer complaints received |

The second group of input measures are the *qualitative* factors. These factors measure such things as the quality of the sales rep's presentation, product knowledge, customer relations, and the salesperson's attitude. Figure 19-4 lists other qualitative factors which are often used in the evaluation process.

Both the quantitative and the qualitative input factors are based on behaviors which are usually under the salesperson's control. Therefore, they are less subject to criticisms concerning inequities among the reps. But the most important value in using these measures is that they are usually critical in locating trouble spots. Assume a salesperson's output performance (average order size, gross margin, and so on) is unsatisfactory. Very often the cause lies in the certain behaviors over which the rep has control.

Research has demonstrated that an evaluation system which emphasizes behaviors more than outcomes has a number of positive effects on the salesperson's overall performance.[4] For example, the more behavior-based the evaluation system, the more the salesperson is willing to cooperate as part of the sales team and the more the salesperson is committed to the organization. With such a system, the salesperson places a greater emphasis on implementing adaptive strategies. However, it has also been shown that evaluation systems which measure both inputs and outputs lead to higher sales and profits.[5]

■ **FIGURE 19-4**

| | |
|---|---|
| **Qualitative factors used as evaluation bases** | ■ Personal efforts of the sales reps<br>Management of their time<br>Planning and preparation for calls<br>Quality of sales presentations<br>Ability to handle objections and to close sales<br><br>■ Knowledge<br>Product<br>Company and company policies<br>Competitor's products and strategies<br>Customers<br><br>■ Customer relations<br><br>■ Personal appearance and health<br><br>■ Personality and attitudinal factors<br>Cooperativeness<br>Resourcefulness<br>Acceptance of responsibility<br>Ability to analyze logically and make decisions |

*Ratio Measures*

Most of the quantitative measures discussed above can be combined to create ratios which can be used for evaluative and comparative purposes. Orders/calls, expenses/sales, and sales/orders are some of the more common ratios that are used by managers to evaluate and compare the performance of salespeople.

A quantitative evaluation of a sales rep's performance can involve the following equations:

$$\text{Sales} = \text{Days worked} \times \frac{\text{Calls}}{\text{Days worked}} \times \frac{\text{Orders}}{\text{Calls}} \times \frac{\text{Sales}}{\text{Orders}}$$

$$\text{Sales} = \text{Days worked} \times \text{Call rate} \times \text{Batting average} \times \text{Average order}$$

If the sales volume for a representative is unsatisfactory, the basic cause must rest in one or more of these four factors. An analysis (such as that done in Figure 19-6 on pages 540–541) can help focus the manager's attention on the trouble spot so additional detailed investigation can pinpoint the rep's exact difficulties.

*Sources of Information*

When choosing factors to use as bases for a performance evaluation, management should select only those for which data are available at a reasonable cost. The four main sources of information are company records, the sales reps themselves, field sales managers, and customers.

Company records are the main source for data on most of the quantitative *output* factors. By studying sales invoices, customers' orders, and accounting records, management can discover much about a sales rep's volume, gross margin, average order size, and so on. Most firms fail to make optimum use of their records for evaluation purposes. In the past, the information often was not recorded in usable form for a performance evaluation. Firms found it was too expensive and time-consuming to tabulate and present the data in usable form. However, most companies today use computers in collecting, analyzing, and reporting data in a form useful for evaluation.

Reports submitted by the sales force are an important source of information, particularly for performance *input* factors. The regular use of call reports, activity reports, and expense reports can provide the necessary data on the salespeople's work. The Achilles' heel in using sales reps' reports for evaluation is that the information is only as good as the accuracy, completeness, and punctuality of the reps' reporting efforts. This is often a serious problem.

As a rule, sales supervisors and other sales executives regularly travel with the sales reps in the field. The managers observe the reps during sales calls on customers. This allows executives to make a firsthand appraisal of a salesperson's performance with customers.

Customers can be used as a source of evaluation information in one of two ways. The more common method is to gather information submitted

## AN INTERNATIONAL PERSPECTIVE

Building effective sales teams in international locations is to a large extent a function of the evaluation systems which are used by multinational corporations. These systems, which provide direction and control of the salesperson's activities and efforts, vary across cultures.

In many parts of the world, the emphasis on profits is much less than in the United States. For example, in Japan firms are more concerned with providing stable employment opportunities for their workers than in generating as much profit as possible. As a result, a typical Japanese firm focuses its evaluation system more on overall qualitative measures than on quantitative measures. Firms in Hong Kong, Singapore, Malaysia, the Philippines,

Thailand, and Mexico report infrequent use of quantitative measures for evaluating salespeople. Rather, most firms in these countries prefer to use more subjective measures.

The competitive environment also has an impact on the type of evaluation used. For example, in most developing countries where the potential sales for many products are great and the competition is small, many companies are able to do well without investing in complex evaluation and control systems. Many managers in these countries rely on their own subjective, informal appraisal of whether the salesperson is performing at acceptable levels.

Source: John S. Hill and Arthur W. Allaway, "How U.S.-Based Companies Manage Sales in Foreign Countries," *Industrial Marketing Management* 22 (1993), pp. 7–16.

by customers on a voluntary, informal basis. Unfortunately, this usually takes the form of complaints, because customers rarely report commendatory performance by sales reps. Increasingly companies are actively soliciting opinions from customers on a regular basis. Some companies ask their customers such questions as *How well does the salesperson analyze your needs?* and *How well does the salesperson build trust?* The customer is certainly in the best position to answer these kinds of questions.[6] However, some firms don't use customers as a source of data. They feel that customers often give excessively good reviews to protect salespeople whom they like.[7]

## Set Performance Standards

**Step 3:** Setting standards is one of the most difficult phases of performance evaluation. The standards serve as a benchmark or a par for the course, against which a sales rep's performance can be measured. Also, standards let a salesperson know what is expected, and they serve as a guide in planning work. Standards must be equitable and reasonable or salespeople may lose interest in their work and confidence in management, and morale may decline. If the standards are too high or too low, using them to evaluate performance will be worthless or even harmful.

Standards for many of the output (results) factors can be tied to company goals for territories, product lines, or customer groups. Such performance measures as sales volume, gross margin, or market share probably have already been set.

It is more difficult to set performance standards for the effort (input) factors. A careful time-and-duty analysis of sales jobs should give management some basis for determining satisfactory performance for daily call rates, displays arranged, and other factors. Another approach is to use executive judgment based on the personal observations of those who work with the salespeople in the field.

To measure the efficiency of a company's selling effort, management must balance the output against the input. Consequently, a firm should develop standards for such output/input ratios as sales volume/calls, orders/calls, gross margin/order, and sales volume/expenses.

Once the standards have been set, it is critical that these standards be communicated to the salespeople. Even if the salespeople were involved in establishing the standards, they should be formally communicated to the rep. This ensures that there are no misunderstandings about the benchmarks against which the rep's performance will be judged.

## Compare Performance with Standards

**Step 4:** The accumulated information must be interpreted. This step involves comparing an individual's performance—both efforts and results—with the predetermined standards.

### Interpreting Quantitative Data

Some factors ordinarily used as bases for performance appraisal were shown in Figures 19-2 and 19-3. The following discussion shows how these factors can be used with the performance standards in step 3 to evaluate a rep's performance.

*Sales Volume and Market Share*     The first criterion most sales managers use to judge the relative performance of salespeople is their sales volume. Some executives believe that the rep who sells the most merchandise is the best salesperson, regardless of other considerations. Unfortunately, sales volume alone may be a poor indicator of a rep's worth. Total volume alone tells the firm nothing about the rep's contribution to profit or customer relations.

Sales volume can be a useful indicator of performance, however, if it is analyzed in sufficient detail and with discretion. For evaluation purposes, a rep's total volume may be studied by product line, by some form of customer grouping, or by order size. Even then, the volume figures are not very meaningful unless they can be related to some predetermined standard of acceptable performance, volume quota for each product line or customer group, for example.

Another important evaluation factor is the share of market each salesperson obtains. Firms compute this figure by dividing the rep's sales volume by the territorial market potential. Here again the data are more useful if share of market can be determined for each product line or customer group.

*A Day-to-Day Operating Problem*

## MAJESTIC PLASTICS COMPANY (N)

### A sales rep objects to her evaluation

In December each year Clyde Brion compiled information from the firm's sales analysis files on each sales rep, added to it qualitative or subjective information he had about the person's performance, and wrote a letter to each rep summarizing how well the rep had done during the year and what that rep should endeavor to do during the coming year.

It was not one of Brion's favorite jobs, but the company's top management was committed to formal evaluation programs. He knew there would be repercussions from his letter to Margaret Badger, a Los Angeles area sales rep. Neither her numbers nor Brion's observation of her performance would allow her much praise. He was considering how to replace her but was constrained because of company policies.

About 32 seconds after opening Brion's evaluation letter, Margaret Badger phoned him angrily.

"This is a bunch of garbage you cooked up to justify getting rid of me. If you want to fire me, then do it, but don't insult my intelligence by expecting me to buy this rubbish!" Badger challenged.

"I rather expected that you would be coming in to see me. Let's sit down and go over the items you disagree with one by one. We do have excellent records and statistics on what you have done and sold in comparison with the other sales reps," Brion said calmly.

"I'm not talking numbers. I know the numbers stink and I'm not happy about them either. I am talking about comparing noncomparables. It is patently unfair to compare me with the other sales reps. Being the new kid on the block, I was handed a bad territory. Why was it open? The guy in it before me told me why he quit, and I am fighting the same lack of potential and competitive conditions," Badger said.

Brion was well aware that one particular competitor was extremely aggressive because its plant was located there. Stalling for time, he asked, "What do you want me to do?"

"I want some understanding of my situation and consideration in my treatment. This evaluation in my file is the kiss of death for any future here. It says I stink. It says I can't plan my work or penetrate the market. It says I can't sell. And that isn't so!" Badger fumed.

**Questions:** 1. What should Clyde Brion say and/or do in response to Margaret Badger's request? 2. What changes in the evaluation procedure might help?

Note: See the introduction to this series of problems in Chapter 4 for the necessary background on the company, its market, and its competition.

Management must be cautious when comparing market-share performance of one person with another. Sales rep A may get 20 percent of the market in his district, while sales rep B captures only 10 percent of her market. Yet B may be doing a better job. Competition may be far more severe in B's district. Or the company may be giving A considerably more advertising support.

*Gross Profit*   In most firms, a sales manager is (or should be) more concerned with the amount of gross profit the salespeople generate than with their dollar sales volume. Gross margin in dollars is a much better measure of a salesperson's effectiveness because it gives some indication of the rep's ability to sell high-margin items. Since the prime objective of most businesses is to earn a targeted return on investment, a person's direct contribution to profit is a logical yardstick for evaluating performance.

Management can reflect its gross margin goals by setting volume quotas for each product line. In this way, the company can motivate the sales force to achieve a desirable balance of sales among the various lines. Then, even though the reps are later evaluated on the basis of sales volume, this evaluation will automatically include gross margin considerations.

As an evaluative yardstick, gross margin has some limitations, however. When management ignores selling expenses, there is no way of knowing how much it costs to generate gross margin. Thus sales rep A may have a higher dollar gross margin than sales rep B. But A's selling expenses may be proportionately so much higher than B's that A actually shows a lower contribution margin. Furthermore, a salesperson does not fully control the product mix represented in his or her total sales volume. Territorial market potential and intensity of competition vary from one district to another, and these factors can influence the sales of the various product lines.

*Number and Size of Orders*   Another performance measure is the number and average size of orders obtained by each sales rep. The average sale is computed by dividing a rep's total number of orders into his total sales volume. This calculation may be made for each class of customer to determine how the rep's average order varies among them. This analysis discloses which reps are getting too many small, unprofitable orders, even though their total volume appears satisfactory because of a few large orders. The analysis also may show that some reps find it difficult to obtain orders from certain classes of customers, but make up for this deficiency by superior performance with their other accounts.

*Calls per Day—Call Rate*   A key factor in sales performance is the number of calls made. A salesperson ordinarily cannot sell merchandise without calling on customers; generally, the more calls, the more sales. Sales rep A makes three calls a day, but the company average is four for sales reps who work under reasonably comparable conditions. If management can raise A's call rate up to the company average of four, her sales should increase about 33 percent.

For evaluation purposes, a salesperson's daily (or weekly) call rate can be measured against the company average or some other predetermined standard. Discretion must be exercised in interpreting a rep's call rate, however. Call rates are influenced by the number of miles reps must travel and by the number of customers per square mile in the territory.

Usually, in a given business a certain desired call rate yields the best results. If the rep falls below this rate, sales decline because the rep is not seeing enough prospects. If the rep calls on too many prospects, sales may also decline, since he or she probably does not spend sufficient time with each one to get the job done.

*Batting Average*   A salesperson's batting average is calculated by dividing the number of orders received by the number of calls made ($O/C$). The number of calls made is equivalent to times at bat; the number of orders written is equivalent to the hits made. As a performance index, the batting average discloses ability to locate and call on good prospects and ability to close a sale. A salesperson's batting average should be computed for each class of customers called on. Often, a rep varies in ability to close a sale with different types of customers.

Analysis of the call rate in relation to the order rate can be quite meaningful. If the call rate is above average but the number of orders is below normal, perhaps the rep does not spend enough time with each customer. Or suppose the call rate and batting average are both above standard but the average order is small. Then a field supervisor may work with the salesperson to show the rep how to make fewer but more productive calls. The idea here is to raise the size of the average order by spending more time and talking about more products with each account.

*Direct-Selling Expenses*   Direct-selling expense is the sum of travel expenses, other business expenses, and compensation (salary, commission, bonus) for each salesperson. These total expenses may be expressed as a percentage of sales. Also, the expense-to-sales ratios for the various salespeople can be compared. Or management can compute the cost per call for each salesperson by dividing total expenses by the number of calls made.

In a performance evaluation, these various cost indexes may indicate the relative efficiency of the salespeople in the field. However, management must interpret these ratios carefully and in detail. An expense-to-sales ratio, for instance, may be above average because the salesperson (1) is doing a poor job; (2) is working in a marginal territory; (3) is working in a new territory doing a lot of prospecting and building a solid base for the future; or (4) is working a territory that covers far more square miles than the average district. A rep with a low batting average usually has a high cost per order. Similarly, the one who makes few calls per day has a high ratio of costs per call.

*Routing Efficiency*   Dividing the miles traveled by the number of calls made gives the average miles per call. This figure either indicates the density of the sales rep's territory or measures routing efficiency. If a group of salespeople all have approximately the same size and density of territories, then miles per call is a significant figure for indicating each one's routing efficiency. Suppose five salespeople selling for an office machines firm in a metropolitan area vary considerably in the number of miles traveled per call. Then the sales manager may have reason to control the routing of those who are out of line.

### Evaluating Qualitative Factors

Lack of objectivity in evaluations is largely minimized when quantitative factors are used as bases in a performance evaluation. However, when the evaluation is based on qualitative factors, the personal, subjective element comes into full play. The evaluator assumes a key role at this point. In fact, recent studies have shown that managers often give considerable weight to factors such as citizenship behaviors—civic virtue, sportsmanship, or altruism, for example—which are not part of the formal evaluation process.[8] The success of a qualitative evaluation depends largely on the evaluator's ability to be as objective and impartial as possible.

Merit-rating forms are a helpful tool in evaluating qualitative factors. These forms permit several evaluators' judgments to appear in a generally standardized manner. Such uniformity aids in comparing one person with another. Rating forms also provide a written report for company records. More important, however, they make an evaluator more thorough because the appraisals will be on record.

There is an almost limitless variety of evaluation forms. Often each manager develops whatever form seems appropriate for the situation. Most such subjective forms suffer from three major defects.

First is the **halo effect.** Evaluators may be biased by a generalized overall impression or image of the person they are evaluating. If the manager does not like the way a rep dresses, that attitude may bias all aspects of the manager's evaluation. Similarly, the manager who is impressed with a person's sales ability is also likely to rate other aspects of the person's performance highly.

Second, some rating forms generally overvalue inconsequential factors and undervalue truly important ones. The sales manager should be interested in the salesperson's ability to make money for the firm, not whether the individual is socially adept or impressively dressed. In evaluations, it is essential for the manager to keep in mind what is important and what is not. Often when a former employee files a legal case involving discrimination in hiring, firing, and promotion, the key point is that the manager based evaluations on unimportant factors.

Third, most subjective evaluation forms force the evaluator to make judgments on some factors without a valid basis for doing so. Lacking valid information on the factor, the evaluator allows the halo effect to take over.

In addition, firms face two even more serious problems. First, many raters refuse to give poor ratings to reps who deserve them because of fear of reprisal. As one executive put it, "Who knows what the future holds? The person I downgrade today may be my boss tomorrow." Such managers fail to see any personal advantage in giving accurate ratings. Yet, in any good management evaluation program, a manager's ability and willingness to accurately appraise people is a key factor in that executive's rise in management. A second serious problem is that some people just don't get along. In these cases, evaluators have difficulty being fair.

Management writers have extolled the virtues of behaviorally anchored rating scales (BARS) as superior instruments for subjectively evaluating people. A BARS instrument contains detailed descriptions of the subject's behavior to guide the evaluator's numerical rating of that

■ **FIGURE 19-5**   **A behaviorally anchored rating scale for evaluating team participation**

| Rating Description | Numeric Rating | Behaviors |
|---|---|---|
| Outstanding | 10 | Can be expected to go beyond what is normally expected to help the team achieve its goals |
| Above average | 8 | Can be expected always to cooperate and contribute to the team objectives. Tries hard to help make the team successful. |
| Average | 5 | Usually willing to cooperate and participate in team efforts. |
| Below average | 2 | Can be expected to participate in team efforts only to the extent required. Shows no initiative with regard to team efforts. |
| Poor | 0 | Unwilling to participate. At times may work against team goals. |

person. A sample of one question is shown in Figure 19-5. It is important to remember, however, that no amount of instrument sophistication can overcome the basic weaknesses inherent in subjective rating systems.

### Discuss the Evaluation with the Salesperson

**Step 5:** Once the salesperson's performance has been evaluated, the results should be reviewed in a conference with the sales manager. This discussion should be viewed as a counseling interview, in which the manager explains the person's achievements on each evaluation factor and points out how the results compared with the standards. Then, the manager and the salesperson together may try to determine the reasons for the performance variations above or below the standards. It is essential to discuss the manager's ratings on the qualitative factors and to compare them with the salesperson's self-evaluation on these points. Based on their review of all evaluation factors, the manager and the salesperson can then establish goals and an operating plan for the coming period.

The performance-evaluation interview can be a very sensitive occasion. It is not easy to point out a person's shortcomings face-to-face. People dislike being criticized and may become quite defensive in this situation. Some sales executives resist evaluation interviews because they feel these discussions can only injure morale. The concern is real and valid. They reason, "Why stir up trouble when you are basically happy with the person's performance?" Unperceptive managers often lose sight of subordinates' virtues and strengths and criticize unimportant factors. One key factor in management is learning to use people's virtues to the best advantage, while not allowing their weaknesses to hurt the firm.

# ■ Using Evaluation Data: An Example

The case example in this section illustrates the computations, interpretation, and use of several quantitative evaluation factors, both input (efforts) and output (results).

The Colorado Ski Company distributes four lines of products nationally—skis, ski accessories, and a limited line of ski pants and parkas. The firm sells to two basic classes of customers—sporting goods stores and specialty ski shops. The company uses its own sales force to reach these customers directly. Salespeople are paid travel expenses plus a straight commission of 5 percent on sales volume.

For purposes of a performance evaluation, the sales manager of the Colorado Ski Company has divided the products into two basic lines: skis and ski accessories (equipment) and ski pants and parkas (clothing). The retailers' usual initial markup on these products is 50 percent of the retail selling price. There are no significant variations among products in the gross margin percentages realized by the Colorado Ski Company.

The sales manager is especially interested in the performance of three of the sales reps: Joe, who sells in the Rocky Mountain region (a huge territory); Gus, selling in the Pacific Northwest; and Paula, who covers the New England market. Much of the quantitative performance data for these three sales reps is summarized in Figure 19-6. Based on an analysis of these data, the sales manager is trying to decide (1) which of the three did the best job and (2) which particular points should be discussed with each person to improve performance.

If the sales manager of the Colorado Ski Company looked just at the sales production of these three people, he would have to conclude that Joe was best by far. He might even consider replacing Paula, since her volume looks weak in comparison. However, after comparing each rep's volume against the market potential, it is evident that Paula sold a larger share of her market than did either Joe or Gus.

## Joe's Sales Performance

The sales manager could see that Joe had worked the fewest number of days (220), made the fewest calls (700), and took the fewest orders (500). He also spent more money than the others ($48,000) and traveled far more miles (60,000). The sales manager can make some allowance for this because Joe's territory, the Rocky Mountain region, is more sparsely settled than either Gus's or Paula's territory.

Joe's batting average (0.714) is certainly adequate, and his average order ($2,400) is more than satisfactory. In fact, it is astonishingly high in comparison with the others ($1,133 and $612). The sales manager can justify this. The tremendous market potential ($6 million) in Joe's territory, in comparison with the number of customers evidently located there, would naturally result in a high average sale. Joe evidently has done a satisfactory job of covering potential prospects. It appears that the market potential per dealer in the Rocky Mountain region is far higher than in the other areas in the country. This would explain why he could take such large orders. Joe makes a little over three calls per day, which is relatively low in comparison to the others (3.75 and 4.8). However, it is not sufficiently out of line to cause any action to be taken, in light of his territory. The large number of miles per call is again indicative of the territory.

Considering expense per sales dollar, it *appears* that Joe is the most efficient sales rep, since he spends only 4 percent of sales for expenses. The reps are paid a straight commission of 5 percent of sales, which brings Joe's total cost of selling to 9 percent. However, the sales manager can see that this low expense ratio is simply a function of his abnormally high sales, which, in turn, are a result of his large market potential.

Joe's cost per call ($68.57) and cost per order ($96) seemed exceedingly high in comparison with those for the other reps. He worked 20 fewer days than Gus and 10 fewer than Paula. Granted that he traveled 15,000 miles more than Gus, the cost of those miles at 26 cents a mile would be about $3,900, which leaves something to be explained. The sales manager probably should investigate Joe's expense accounts. Expenses are usually related to the number of days worked and miles traveled. They are not related directly to sales volume; it costs as much to take an order for $100 as one for $600. A large market potential that results in large sales can cause the expense-to-sales ratio to be misleading. Thus Joe's high sales volume caused his expense ratio to appear low, when in reality he was spending too much money making calls.

Let's analyze Joe's selling effort with regard to products and customers. He has a more difficult time getting orders from a sporting goods store (0.500) than from a ski shop (0.875) even though his average sale to sporting goods stores ($5,087) is fantastically high. The sales manager may wonder if this is part of Joe's batting average problem. Possibly in attempting to sell sporting goods stores so much merchandise he simply scares some of them away. However, the sales manager should be cautious here. In total, it is better that Joe continue to sell a high average order to sporting goods stores and settle for fewer orders than to bring both figures to average.

The sales manager may want to investigate Joe's high average order to sporting goods stores. It may be that a few large discount sporting goods stores in the territory are placing huge orders with Joe. This may be no reflection at all on his ability to build up an order. Therefore, if his batting average could be raised in the sporting goods field, possibly no loss would occur at all to the average order. Then the result would be higher sales volume. It is something to investigate.

■ **FIGURE 19-6**    **Evaluation of sales representatives' performance**

| Product Line: | Joe Jackson | | | Gus Dean | | |
|---|---|---|---|---|---|---|
| | Equipment | Clothing | Total | Equipment | Clothing | Total |
| Total sales (000) | $ 480 | $ 720 | $ 1,200 | $ 220 | $ 460 | $    680 |
|   Sporting goods stores | 320 | 440 | 760 | 160 | 320 | 480 |
|   Ski shops | 160 | 280 | 440 | 60 | 140 | 200 |
| Total calls made | | | 700 | | | 900 |
|   Sporting goods stores | | | 300 | | | 500 |
|   Ski shops | | | 400 | | | 400 |
| Total orders taken | | | 500 | | | 600 |
|   Sporting goods stores | | | 150 | | | 450 |
|   Ski shops | | | 350 | | | 150 |
| Days worked | | | 220 | | | 240 |
| Expenses | | | $48,000 | | | $40,000 |
| Miles traveled | | | 60,000 | | | 45,000 |
| Total market potential (millions) | $2.00 | $4.00 | $6.00 | $1.20 | $2.40 | $    3.60 |
|   Sporting goods stores | 1.60 | 2.40 | 4.00 | 0.80 | 1.60 | 2.40 |
|   Ski shops | 0.40 | 1.60 | 2.00 | 0.40 | 0.80 | 1.20 |

| | Sporting Goods Stores | Ski Shops | Total | Sporting Goods Stores | Ski Shops | Total |
|---|---|---|---|---|---|---|
| Average order | $5,087 | $1,257 | $2,400 | $1,067 | $1,333 | $1,133 |
| Batting average | 0.500 | 0.875 | 0.714 | 0.900 | 0.375 | 0.666 |
| Calls per day | | | 3.18 | | | 3.75 |
| Miles per call | | | 86 | | | 50 |
| Expense per sales dollar | | | 4.0% | | | 5.9% |
| Cost per call, excluding commission | | | $68.57 | | | $44.44 |
| Cost per order, excluding commission | | | $96.00 | | | $66.67 |

| | Equipment | Clothing | Total | Equipment | Clothing | Total |
|---|---|---|---|---|---|---|
| Total percent of market | 24.0% | 18.0% | 20.0% | 18.3% | 19.0% | 19.0% |
|   Sporting goods stores | 20.0% | 18.0% | 19.0% | 20.0% | 20.0% | 20.0% |
|   Ski shops | 40.0% | 17.5% | 22.0% | 15.0% | 17.5% | 16.7% |

Another thing the sales manager may notice: Joe seems able to sell equipment (24 percent of potential) better than he sells clothing (18 percent of potential). He is well above average in his ability to sell skis, particularly to ski specialty shops (40 percent of potential), but he is below average in attention to clothing (17.5 percent). This may be just a reflection

■ **FIGURE 19-6** *(concluded)*

| Product Line: | Paula Burns | | | Total | | |
|---|---|---|---|---|---|---|
| | Equipment | Clothing | Total | Equipment | Clothing | Total |
| Total sales (000) | $ 240 | $ 280 | $ 520 | $ 940 | $1,460 | $ 2,400 |
| Sporting goods stores | 100 | 160 | 260 | 580 | 920 | 1,500 |
| Ski shops | 140 | 120 | 260 | 360 | 540 | 900 |
| Total calls made | | | 1,100 | | | 2,700 |
| Sporting goods stores | | | 500 | | | 1,300 |
| Ski shops | | | 600 | | | 1,400 |
| Total orders taken | | 850 | | | 1,950 | |
| Sporting goods stores | | 400 | | | 1,000 | |
| Ski shops | | | 450 | | | 950 |
| Days worked | | | 230 | | | 690 |
| Expenses | | | $36,000 | | | $124,000 |
| Miles traveled | | | 35,000 | | | 140,000 |
| Total market potential (millions) | $1.20 | $1.20 | $ 2.40 | $4.40 | $ 7.60 | $ 12.00 |
| Sporting goods stores | 0.72 | 0.64 | 1.36 | 3.12 | 4.64 | 7.76 |
| Ski shops | 0.48 | 0.56 | 1.04 | 1.28 | 2.96 | 4.24 |

| | Sporting Goods Stores | Ski Shops | Total | Sporting Goods Stores | Ski Shops | Total |
|---|---|---|---|---|---|---|
| Average order | $ 650 | $ 578 | $ 612 | $1,500.00 | $947.00 | $1,231.00 |
| Batting average | 0.800 | 0.750 | 0.773 | 0.679 | 0.769 | 0.722 |
| Calls per day | | | 4.8 | | | 3.90 |
| Miles per call | | | 32 | | | 52.00 |
| Expense per sales dollar | | | 6.9% | | | 5.2% |
| Cost per call, excluding commission | | | $32.72 | | | $ 45.92 |
| Cost per order, excluding commission | | | $42.23 | | | $ 63.59 |

| | Equipment | Clothing | Total | Equipment | Clothing | Total |
|---|---|---|---|---|---|---|
| Total percent of market | 20.0% | 23.3% | 21.7% | 21.4% | 19.2% | 20.0% |
| Sporting goods stores | 13.9% | 25.0% | 19.1% | 18.6% | 19.8% | 19.3% |
| Ski shops | 29.2% | 21.4% | 25.0% | 28.1% | 18.2% | 21.2% |

of his basic interest. He may prefer to talk about skis, bindings, and poles rather than about pants and parkas. The sales manager should mention to Joe that he should be doing a bit better in his sales of clothing. However, Joe is not sufficiently below par in any category for the sales manager to be unduly concerned.

## Gus's Sales Performance

Probably the first thing the sales manager would note about Gus's sales performance is his apparent inability to sell to ski shops. He is closing only 37.5 percent of these calls, whereas the company average is 76.9 percent. On the other hand, he has an extremely high batting average in getting orders from sporting goods stores (90 percent). The sales manager may conclude that Gus speaks the language of the nonskiing owner of a sporting goods store but does not communicate well with a ski expert. The sales manager may consider a conference with Gus to talk over the needs or problems of the ski shop owner and how they differ from those of the sports shop. Gus may not be sufficiently trained in the technical aspects of skiing to answer the questions and gain the confidence of the ski professional. Gus's expenses seem to be in line with the company average, and his calls per day are satisfactory. While Gus is not achieving par as far as market share is concerned, the deviation is not significant enough to warrant any conference on the matter.

## Paula's Sales Performance

Paula seems to do fairly well in getting orders from both sporting goods stores and ski shops. But her average order ($612) is significantly below the company average ($1,231). This indicates a problem area. The sales manager probably wants to determine first if these low average orders are a function of the size of Paula's customers or whether this truly reflects her inability to sell merchandise. The fact that Paula made 1,100 calls with the smallest market potential indicates that her average customer is considerably smaller than those of the other reps. The sales manager may become alarmed at Paula's relatively high expense of sales. However, he should realize that this is caused by the limited sales potential. Paula's cost per call and cost per order are the lowest of the three reps, indicating that her expense accounts are not out of line with her efforts.

It should be obvious to the sales manager that Paula works hard; she makes almost five calls per day. This factor helps to explain several of the others. Her high call rate probably explains her low cost per call and the relatively large number of calls she makes. It also may explain why she does not sell much per order. Perhaps she does not spend sufficient time with each customer. On the other hand, the number of miles per call (32) indicates that her territory is relatively dense, and this alone may be the reason she can make almost five calls per day. She spends less time traveling between calls than the other two reps.

While a sales manager might at first consider discharging Paula, a detailed analysis shows that she is doing as well as, if not better than, the other two reps. Her costs for efforts undertaken are lower. Also, she achieves a larger percentage of the business available to her. Her only problem seems to be that her territory has limited market potential.

## The Sales Manager's Decisions

In conclusion, the sales manager probably will undertake several different projects. First, he may try to get Joe to work a few more days in the year. It is understandable that this rep is tempted to do a little loafing. He has an annual income of $60,000 and leads the sales force in sales. However, Joe's territory has a tremendous sales potential. If he does not want to service it properly, the company can cut it in half, giving each rep a $3 million potential to work with. This would still result in two territories of larger potential than that worked by Paula. Also, the sales manager may investigate why Joe does not sell to more sporting goods stores.

With Gus, the sales manager probably will focus his entire attention on why ski shops are such an obstacle. He probably needs additional instruction on the technical aspects of skiing.

The sales manager may want to ask Paula why she does not sell more skis to sporting goods stores. That is about her only real weakness, outside of her low average order. Certainly, the sales manager should investigate the reasons for Paula's low average order. However, as previously noted, this may not be the result of poor selling ability.

## ■ SUMMARY

A fair and accurate evaluation of the company's sales force is a critical and difficult task. The manager's appraisal of the salespeople is important not only because pay and promotions should be based on such rating, but also because good supervision and training should be based on an objective evaluation of the sales rep's performance. However, the task is difficult. Subjective methods leave much to be desired, as managerial biases may distort the ratings.

The factors affecting a person's performance are many and varied. Moreover, many of those factors are beyond the person's control. It is critical that a person be evaluated only on factors over which he or she has control.

First, management should set some basic policies on the evaluation of the sales personnel. It should establish who will do the rating, when and how often it will be done, how the results will be used, and on what bases people will be rated. Both output and input factors should be measured in the process. Output factors include measures such as sales, orders taken, gross margins realized, new accounts, and lost accounts. They are all quantitative. The input factors are both quantitative and qualitative.

Calls per day and days worked are examples of quantitative measures. Sales presentation quality, product knowledge, and customer relations are examples of qualitative factors.

By comparing the quantitative input and output measures, various efficiency ratings can be developed. The basic performance equation is

Sales = Days worked × Call rate ×
Batting average × Average order

By factoring each element in the equation, the sales manager can obtain a good picture of what each rep is doing and why he or she is successful or unsuccessful. Company records are the basic source of information needed for such evaluations.

The qualitative factors are more difficult to measure. The evaluator's subjective biases may influence his or her ratings of these factors. The use of a well-designed merit rating form can help in the measurement of these factors.

Next, some standards must be developed. Relative standards such as what other groups are doing are widely used. However, there is a place for some absolute standards such as total selling costs and days worked.

Then performance must be compared with the standards and the evaluation must be discussed with the salesperson.

## Key Terms

| | | |
|---|---|---|
| Batting average | Input measures | Ratio measures |
| Call rate | Management by objectives | Routing efficiency |
| Direct-selling expense | Market share | Sales volume |
| Gross profit | Number of orders | Size of orders |
| Halo effect | Output measures | |

## QUESTIONS AND PROBLEMS

1. How can a sales manager determine the accuracy of salespeople's reports?

2. How can a sales manager determine the differences the reps encounter in the severity of competition in each territory?

3. How should a manager decide what weights to place on the quantitative versus the qualitative factors in an evaluation?

4. What are some of the indexes a sales manager can use to evaluate the degree to which each salesperson is covering the assigned territory?

5. As sales manager for a baby food concern, you want to evaluate the ability of your reps to attain good shelf space in grocery stores. How would you do this?

6. How can a sales executive determine the ability of each rep to regain lost customers?

7. An owner-manager of a medium-sized apparel manufacturing company proclaimed, "Don't bother me with all that evaluation hogwash. Just give me sales volume and a good bottom line and I'm as happy as a horse in clover. I am making so much money now that I can't spend it all. So why should I waste my time and effort massaging such numbers?" How would you reply to this owner?

8. How can an evaluation system be used to direct the efforts of salespeople?

9. The importance of sales force evaluation increases with the size of the sales force and management's distance from it. Comment.

10. Should citizenship behaviors play a role in the evaluation of salespeople? If so, how much?

## EXPERIENTIAL EXERCISES

**A.** Ask the sales managers from three different companies how they evaluate the performance of their salespeople. Copy any forms that they use. Compare the procedures and provide your evaluation of which sales manager is doing the best job of evaluation.

**B.** Contact salespeople from three different companies. Ask them to explain how their performance is evaluated and whether these evaluations are tied to their compensation. Also ask them whether they think that their evaluations help them improve their performance and whether or not they think the evaluations are fair.

**Note:** If both A and B are undertaken, you may contact sales managers and salespeople from the same three companies.

## REFERENCES

1. Jack Snader, "How Sales Reps Make a 360-Degree Turnaround," *Marketing News,* February 17, 1997, p. 11.

2. Minda Zetlin, "Up for Review," *Sales & Marketing Management,* December 1994, pp. 82–86.

3. Michele Marchetti, "Board Games," *Sales & Marketing Management,* January 1996, pp. 43–46.

4. Richard L. Oliver and Erin Anderson, "Behavior- and Outcome-Based Sales Control Systems: Evidence and Consequences of Pure-Form and Hybrid Governance," *Journal of Personal Selling & Sales Management,* Fall 1995, pp. 1–16.

5. Ibid.

6. "What the Numbers May Not Tell You," *Nation's Business,* January 1996.

7. "Customers Rating Salespeople Is an Idea That Comes and Goes," *The Wall Street Journal,* May 6, 1997.

8. Scott B. Mackenzie, Philip M. Podsakoff, and Richard Fetter, "The Impact of Organizational Citizenship Behavior on Evaluations of Salesperson Performance," *Journal of Marketing,* January 1993, pp. 70–80.

*Case 19-1*

## LORRIE FOODS, INC.
### Designing an evaluation system

Lorrie Foods, Inc., is a privately owned wholesale food distributor serving the Gainesville, Florida, market since 1943. It commands a 60 percent share of the Gainesville market with annual sales of $6 million and profits of approximately $1 million. It is a small, loosely structured firm which employs 20 people. Top management consists of the general manager, Tom Adair, a marketing manager, Jennifer Walters, and a sales manager, Warren Gottlieb. Recently the company changed ownership. Both Tom Adair and Jennifer Walters were new to the firm. Warren had been with the firm for 17 years and remained under the new management as the top-ranking sales executive.

Lorrie Foods has three main product lines, food, paper, and chemicals. Food products include packaged goods, canned foods, and drinks. They represent 70 percent of Lorrie's business. Paper products, which include disposable items such as paper plates, cups, and napkins, account for 25 percent of sales. The remaining 5 percent comes from sales of chemicals such as floor cleaning solutions and kitchen and bathroom supplies.

At the current time, Lorrie has approximately 800 active, major accounts. This customer base, which is very stable, consists of institutions such as hospitals and educational facilities, restaurants, churches, fraternities, sororities, and other organizational groups such as the scouts. These accounts are served by six outside salespeople. There are another 200 to 300 accounts which are not considered major accounts. Many of these accounts are offices which purchase only paper products and chemicals. Their business is solicited by six telephone salespeople.

Although Lorrie has significant market share, there is strong competition in the Gainesville market. Most of the competition is based in Jacksonville, but there are several national competitors as well such as Continental Food Services and Kraft. Lorrie is currently the only wholesaler with a warehouse operation in the immediate area. However, soon Lorrie will not be the only local service supplier. The third largest independent food distributor in the nation, Bower Foods, headquartered in Georgia, is planning to enter the market as a full-service warehouse wholesaler. Bower's anticipated entry is the primary driving force behind the reorganization at Lorrie.

Tom Adair, Jennifer Walters, and Warren Gottlieb have worked together to establish a set of strategic objectives for the marketing and sales operations. In order of importance, they are: (1) greater profitability through deeper penetration of the existing market and new product introductions; (2) greater cooperation between the field sales reps and the telemarketing reps; (3) increased market feedback from the reps; and (4) greater nonprice competition. Warren and Jennifer have both been charged with the responsibility of improving the efficiency and effectiveness of the sales force in achieving these goals. At the current time Warren is working to establish an evaluation program for his salespeople.

The field salespeople are responsible for calling on their largest accounts two to five times per week. They are expected to make contact with the remainder of their accounts less frequently; but for those accounts which are seen less, the salesperson is expected to stay in touch through frequent phone contacts. In addition to their established accounts, they must also solicit the business of new accounts. The salespeople are also encouraged to bring customer and competitive information back to the sales manager. The phone salespeople have responsibility for servicing the smaller accounts as well as handling all customer order data entry (their own and that of the outside sales reps) and processing all customer complaints.

The field and phone sales reps are compensated differently. The field reps are given a salary plus a commission, which can amount to as much as 60 percent of their pay. The salary base is the same for all the reps. They can also earn additional incentives in the form of dollars or prizes from Lorrie's suppliers. For example, a supplier may offer four dollars for every carton of its product sold. Lorrie would receive two dollars and the individual rep would receive the remaining two dollars. Other suppliers give points for products sold, which then can be turned into vacations or other merchandise by the rep. Phone sales reps are paid a flat salary with no incentives based on sales.

Currently, the evaluation of salespeople is done by Warren on a rather informal basis. Each representative has monthly activity reports indicating the level of sales and profits for their territories. In addition, Warren has recently instituted a monthly chart of personal goals for each rep, which can be compared to actual performance. Warren believes in management by objectives. He counsels his people to set realistic goals and then helps the rep attain them.

Warren and Jennifer both realized that the current evaluation policies were inadequate. They agreed there was a need to establish specific time periods for the evaluations and that these should be tied to an annual review of performance as well as salary. However, Warren and Jennifer were at odds with one another when it came to deciding what criteria should be used in evaluating the outside salespeople.

As Warren told Jennifer, "The primary goal should be to tie our reporting of sales and profits into a formal evaluation of the rep. This would become the primary input for considering raises." Warren believed that the salespeople should be evaluated primarily on the basis of sales and profit contribution because that is what drives the company's bottom line. "We just need to formalize what I've been doing all along."

Jennifer felt that Warren was wrong. In fact she felt that the salespeople's sales and profit should play a minor role in their evaluations and reward. Rather, she felt that greater weight should be placed on their behaviors. For example, she wanted to include criteria such as the degree to which the rep provides frequent, high-quality customer feedback, cooperates with the phone sales rep, performs the administrative aspects of the job in a timely fashion, and is customer oriented. She argued, "The large percentage of commission pay encourages and rewards them for sales. They don't need any more incentive to sell, but they do need to be motivated to do the more complete selling job. It is these nonselling activities which will help us maintain our position in the marketplace."

Warren didn't buy it. He felt, first, that these criteria were not necessarily related to good sales performance, and, second, that the evaluation of these "behaviors" would be too subjective. More important, he also knew that the administration of such a program would be very costly in terms of both time and money.

**Question:**

Who is right, Warren or Jennifer? If you were designing the new evaluation program for Lorrie's sales force, what specific criteria would be used to evaluate the performance of the salespeople?

*Case 19-2*

## SEAL RITE ENVELOPE COMPANY (C)
### Evaluation of telemarketing reps

After several weeks of considerable discussion with top management about the company's misdirected marketing efforts, Rose Douglas, the company's sales manager, had been given permission to begin a telemarketing program to lower the costs of covering smaller customers. It had been disclosed by an analysis of customer sales volume in relationship to the company's costs of selling to them that the company was spending too much money covering a large number of small accounts while not giving enough attention to the highly profitable large customers.

Seal Rite Envelope Company made and marketed a wide line of envelopes. It sold directly to printers, to wholesalers, and to corporations with printing facilities. The availability of relatively low-cost printing equipment combined with computer-generated copy had resulted in many companies maintaining in-house printing operations which often were quite large.

Douglas classified the firm's customers into four categories: (1) printers, (2) paper wholesalers, (3) companies buying envelopes for routine mailing purposes, and (4) companies buying envelopes for sales promotional purposes. Companies in the last category required considerable attention, for their needs were diverse and continually changing. A decision had been made to increase the coverage of the larger customers in the last category and make fewer calls on smaller firms in other categories. However, to replace the direct field calls that were being redirected, and to give better support to the entire sales effort, Douglas had been given permission to develop a telemarketing group to handle both outbound and inbound sales programs.

To that end, she had hired six people who were being trained by a telemarketing consultant experienced in such programs. Initially, three of the telephone salespeople would be assigned to handle inbound calls from customers on the company's 800 number line. Such calls would vary from requests to have a sales rep call immediately to deal with some pressing need of the customer to a reorder of some envelope the firm was using. The outbound sales calls would be to customers that had frequent needs for envelopes and to smaller customers with infrequent needs.

A callback dating system had been developed. Each customer's usage rate was studied by the sales rep covering that account so that the customer could be contacted a short time before it needed to reorder envelopes.

Douglas was trying to figure out how she was going to evaluate these new telephone sales reps. Could all the reps be evaluated as a group with no distinction between the inbound and outbound telemarketers? Or would she have to evaluate the three inbound people against each other and do the same with the outbound sales reps? She wondered in what way these new telemarketers could be evaluated against the outside sales reps. Would it be a case of trying to compare oranges and apples?

Her boss, Max Chernak, the president, had asked for a complete report on the telemarketing program when Douglas finalized her plans for it. He had specifically mentioned that he was eager to learn how she intended to evaluate the program.

At the company's 1993 Christmas party, Rose Douglas had an opportunity to talk with Steve Hunter, the firm's top sales rep, about the telemarketing program that was to be online by March 1. She chose to sound him out on some of the questions she was pondering. She asked him, "How often do you think the telemarketers should be evaluated?"

He smiled and answered, "How about hourly?"

She retorted, "Seriously, I've got to make some decisions."

"I was serious. It seems to me that one of the real advantages of an inside telephone selling program is that you can continually monitor and evaluate how each person is doing. You can look at each day's efforts and production," Steve observed.

"I could do that on you guys, too. But when you get too close, random events distort the evaluation. One tough problem during the day could totally ruin a rep's evaluation data. I've got to look over a large enough span of time that I can get a valid reading of the person's performance. I was thinking about monthly evaluations. What do you think?"

"I told you what I think. I'd be evaluating each day's work. A lot of bad things can happen in a month," Steve said as he left to say hello to Max Chernak.

Rose wandered over to the corner where the company's controller was trying to look inconspicuous. Somehow the ensuing conversation turned to evaluation programs. They spent some time talking about the different bases on which the new people could be evaluated, such as time on the telephone, calls attempted, calls completed, orders taken, size of orders, total volume, and errors made. Rose was somewhat bothered by

the controller's emphasis on making many short calls. She was more concerned with what she called meaningful calls—-that is, that the person talk long enough to the customer to get the job done. It had been her experience as a sales rep that if she kept the customer talking long enough, she received additional orders as the customer thought of other things that were needed. Her experience was that some customers just liked to talk with her. She was reminded of a lecture she once heard about the social aspects of the sales call. The professor had maintained that a sales call was partly a social event at which social amenities should be observed. He had maintained that the sales rep should leave neither too soon nor too late. Rose wondered if all of this would be changed in telephone selling: Would the customers want to talk or would efficiency be the order of the day? Should she acquire some mechanical means of measuring the number and length of the telephone calls?

Howie Masters, a foreman in the cutting room, strolled up to Rose to make idle conversation, but she had other ideas. She knew that Howie was a nut about computers and electronics. She told him about the telemarketing program being developed and asked, "Would it be difficult to record each telephone call so we can tell how they are doing and help them improve?"

Howie quickly responded, "No problem at all. All sorts of equipment is available to do the job. You want me to set it up for you?"

"Let me think about it and get back to you. Thanks for offering," Rose responded as she wondered if any problems would arise if the phone calls were recorded. She knew that there were some laws governing such things. She speculated that there had to be some way around any legal or ethical problems involved with recording the calls. She had read that other firms did it.

Suddenly, Rose became somewhat angry with herself, thinking that she was spending too much time contemplating relatively minor matters when she was not certain what she wanted to measure. She admonished herself to focus more on the content of the evaluation program and less on its format.

As Rose drove home from the party, she put together in her mind everything she wanted to put in her report to Mr. Chernak. She would write it the next day.

*Questions:*

1. How often should the telemarketers be evaluated?

2. Should the calls be recorded?

3. On what bases should the telemarketers be evaluated?

4. Should the telemarketers be evaluated against the field sales reps? Against each other?

# CHAPTER 20

# Ethical and Legal Responsibilities of Sales Managers

The likelihood of unethical behavior is directly proportionate to the size of the carrot.

**Michele Marchetti**

Open a newspaper or a business trade journal today and you are likely to find a story about some firm or administrator in trouble with the authorities. Accusations of improprieties are everywhere. The actions of business executives and public officials are now scrutinized as never before. Even if a businessperson is innocent of breaking any law, charges of unethical behavior are hurled, careers are ruined, and family lives are drastically altered. Years of wise leadership and superior performance can be nullified by one unwise decision that leads to a legal or ethical hassle.

An actual case history will show that these words of warning are not merely moralistic hyperbole. The incident concerns a former student of one of your authors. This student, upon graduation, accepted a job as sales representative with a large, well-known corporation to sell certain large equipment to governmental units. He was informed that it was not unknown for sales reps to "share" some of their commissions with the public officials who controlled these purchases. And so the graduate became quite proficient at "sharing" his good fortunes with certain customers, and he prospered.

Unfortunately, one of the public officials got into trouble with the Internal Revenue Service. It seems that the official "forgot" to report his "share" of the commissions. He had also forgotten many other such "shares." The affair was widely publicized in the local papers, forcing state officials to take action, for most people looked upon the "shares" as bribes—a violation of state law. When the dust settled, the only person punished was our graduate—who got three years in the state penitentiary. The elected official settled with the IRS and somehow escaped jail. Company executives said, "We had no idea that was going on!" Our graduate's career and life were ruined. When he went to college, instructors didn't talk or write about such things. Well, now we do.

## ◼ BUSINESS ETHICS AND SALES MANAGEMENT

*Webster's New Collegiate Dictionary* defines **ethics** as the science of moral duty or the science of ideal human character. Ethics are moral principles or practices. They are professional standards of conduct. Thus, to act in an ethical fashion is to conform to some standard of moral behavior.

Sales managers have important ethical responsibilities with regard to their own actions as well as the actions of their salespeople. Sales managers are often faced with ethical dilemmas in hiring, setting quotas, evaluating, and many other aspects of their managements tasks. They are also responsible for establishing, communicating, and enforcing the ethical standards which they expect their salespeople to follow.

Salespeople are exposed to greater ethical pressures than individuals in many other jobs. They work in relatively unsupervised settings; they are primarily responsible for generating the firm's revenues, which at times can be very stressful; they are continually faced with problems that require unique solutions, which is also stressful; and they are often evaluated on the basis of short-term objectives. Being evaluated on the basis of short-term objectives can cause salespeople to promote short-term solutions to customers' problems, which may not be in the customers' best interests. A recent survey of sales managers revealed that 49 percent of the managers say their reps have lied on a sales call and 22 percent say their reps have sold products their customers didn't need.[1]

### The Legal-Ethical Confusion

One often reads in the trade press or hears of such matters as price discrimination, bribes, kickbacks, insider trading, or conflicts of interest. These practices are considered evidence of management's deficient ethical code.

While these practices may be unethical, they are—more important— illegal! It is illegal to take or give bribes. It is illegal to participate in insider trading on the securities exchanges. It is even illegal to pad an expense account—it's called *embezzlement.* Indeed, a large portion of the so-called ethical issues raised by critics of business are not really ethical problems at all. They are law enforcement problems.

In the United States, Americans have standardized a partial common code of ethics based on our complex federal, state, and city statutes—the law. Indeed, there are people for whom the law is their code of ethics: if it is legal, it is ethical. To others, just because something is illegal does not make it unethical. Most speeders, for example, see nothing unethical about their driving habits.

However, most people understand that the law cannot possibly cover and regulate all aspects of life—nor should it attempt to do so. They understand the need for a personal code of ethics beyond that covered by the law.

In this chapter, we focus first on ethical questions and then on legal issues. Nevertheless, understand clearly that the line between ethics and law is murky. Our discussion will jump over it continually. For example, many laws governing business practices are seldom enforced. One can violate them rather safely to great personal advantage. It is an unfair business practice—and illegal—to knowingly lie to a customer about a competitor's situation. It is illegal to discriminate in price in violation of the Robinson-Patman Act. Yet these practices are widespread. Now one's ethical code comes into play. Will you do something that is illegal but to your advantage if you think it is safe to do so? Bear in mind, for example, that insider trading has been widespread for decades, but the law was not enforced until recently. Many practices which at one time were legal are now illegal. The trend is clearly toward higher and more ethical business standards.

An example of the dilemma faced by businesspeople is the case of an outstanding securities sales manager who was hired as president of a highly publicized small investment company. This firm specialized in over-the-counter and penny stocks. The manager came home at noon of his first day at work and told his family, "I quit! It's a scam. These people are crooks." He bailed out. The hundreds of others in the firm were not so foresighted, nor were they fortunate when the Securities and Exchange Commission and the FBI closed in. As one vice president of sales told a class, "It's not a whole lot of fun to be hauled off to jail in the middle of the night in front of your family." The one sales manager's future was saved by a personal code of ethics that would not allow him to become involved with a firm that was doing what he knew was wrong.

## The Pressure to Compromise Personal Ethics

Most of us have our own personal codes of ethics—what we will and will not do. Often we would prefer not to do certain things, but if pressed sufficiently hard our ethical codes may bend. A person's true ethical code surfaces when tested under difficult conditions. It is easy to be ethical when no hardship is involved—when one is winning and life is going well. The test comes when things are not going so well—when the competitive pressures build up. The pressure brought on by quotas, pay plans, and a fierce competitive environment breeds unethical behavior.

Some business executives believe that in order to advance in an organization, a person must occasionally do something that he or she would prefer not to do. In a recent survey of sales agents, nearly half of the respondents admitted to taking part in some illegal or unethical activity, such as deceiving customers, as a result of pressure. The largest number of offenders were from computer and software companies—high growth, highly competitive industries.[2]

This is not to say that individuals involved in such deceptive practices get away with them. Prudential Insurance Company recently agreed to

pay a minimum of $425 million to settle a class action suit for selling prac-
tices which deceived their customers. Archer Daniels Midland, the United
States' largest miller of corn, soybeans, and wheat, paid a $100 million
fine for price-fixing. One of its executives pleaded guilty to theft, money
laundering, conspiracy, and tax evasion.[3]

For executives who ignore the unethical activities of their reps, the
consequences are serious—lawsuits, fines, careers ended, and imprisonment. So, regardless of the pressure to compromise personal standards, all
of the recent evidence suggests that it is not in the best interests of salespeople and sales managers to do so.

## The Problem of Determining Ethical Standards

As individuals, sales managers usually have their own standards of ethical conduct. And they usually abide by these standards in managing their
sales forces. Most of us believe we act ethically by our own standards.
However, ethical standards are set by a group—by society—and not by the
individual. Thus the group evaluates what you as an individual think is
ethical.

The problem is that the group (society) lacks commonly accepted standards of behavior. What is considered ethical conduct varies from one
country to another (see "An International Perspective," page 562), from
one industry to another, and from one situation to another. Looking to the
law or corporate policy for guidance often leads only to more gray areas
rather than to clearly defined, specific guidelines.

The moral-ethical-legal framework presents special problems for
sales executives, more than for most other managers. Entertaining customers in a gambling house, for example, may be either moral or immoral
from an individual's point of view. This entertainment may be considered
acceptable (ethical) or not depending on the industry's practice. And it
may be legal or illegal, depending on whether it happened in Nevada or
California.

In some of the situations discussed in the following sections, it is apparent that, at times, it will be difficult for the manager to decide whether
a particular action is ethical or not.

## Ethical Situations Facing Salespeople and Sales Executives

Ethical questions are involved in many of the relationships that sales
managers have with their salespeople, their companies, and their customers. A few of these situations are discussed here.

### Relations with the Sales Force
A substantial portion of sales managers' ethical problems relates to their
dealings with the sales force. Assume, for instance, that a salesperson has
built a territory into a highly profitable district. The rep may even have

This sales manager makes the point with his reps from Denmark and Hong Kong that they must always adhere to the company's code of ethics.

worked under a straight commission compensation plan and paid his or her own expenses. An executive who sees this salesperson's relatively high earnings may decide there is too much territory and split it. Is this ethical? On the other hand, is it sound management not to split the district if the sales executive believes there is inadequate coverage of an overly large district?

In some companies, management takes over the very large, profitable accounts as *house accounts*. (These customers are sold directly by some executive and the salesperson in that district usually receives no commission on the account.) Is this ethical, particularly if the salesperson spent much time and effort in developing the account to a profitable level? Yet management may feel that the account is now so important that an executive should handle it.

Ethical questions often arise in connection with promotions, termination, and references. If there is no likelihood that a sales representative will be promoted to a managerial position, should the rep be told? If the sales manager knows that the rep is working in expectation of such a promotion, to tell him means to lose him. In another instance, when a managerial position opens up in another region, a sales manager may keep a star sales rep in her present territory despite the rep's qualifications and desire for promotion. And what is management's responsibility in giving references for a former salesperson? To what extent is a manager ethically bound to tell the truth or give details about former employees?

### Relations with the Company

Changing jobs and handling expense accounts illustrate the ethical problems involved in sales executives' relations with companies. When changing positions, a manager may want to take key customers to the new employer. Ethical and legal questions may arise if this executive tries to move those customers to the new firm.

Many times a sale manager possesses information that could be highly useful to a competitor. Naturally, it is difficult to control the information a manager gives to a new employer. But beyond certain limits, such behavior is clearly unethical.

Ethical questions may arise in the interpretation of expense account policies. Suppose that top management states it will pay only 26 cents a mile to sales reps or sales managers who use their personal cars for company business. Yet a sales manager, knowing that actual expenses are 30 to 35 cents a mile at the minimum, may be tempted to pad mileage and then encourage the reps to do so too to make up the difference. The manager may justify this action on the basis that the money is really being spent for business purposes, and the spirit of the expense account is not being violated. Ethical questions include the following: Should sales personnel manipulate expense accounts to protect themselves from the stingy policies of top management? In so doing, they only recover money honestly spent in the solicitation of business for the firm. Or should they attempt to get policies changed? Or, failing that, should they change employers rather than commit what they believe are unethical acts?

### Relations with Customers

Perhaps the most critical set of ethical questions facing sales managers is associated with customer relations. The major problem areas involve information, gifts, and entertainment.

*Information.*    It is important that salespeople provide their customers with *all* of the information that enables them to make informed decisions. Sometimes salespeople make recommendations that are not in the best interests of their customers. For example, they may neglect to give the customers complete information. To cite one example, a group of insurance reps were trying to sell new policies to their current policyholders. In doing so the reps failed to tell their customers that the new policies seemed less expensive than they really were because they were paid for in part by using up the cash value of the older policies.[4]

Sometimes salespeople knowingly sell a higher priced product when a lower priced product would have fulfilled the customer's need just as well. The *Journal of the American Medical Association* claims that pharmaceutical sales representatives are pushing higher priced calcium channel blockers for high blood pressure when cheaper diuretics and beta blockers are just as effective.[5]

*Gifts.*    The practice of giving gifts to customers, especially at the holiday season, is time-honored in American business. But today, perhaps more than ever before, the moral and ethical climate of giving gifts to customers is under careful scrutiny. The practice is being reviewed by both the givers and the receivers of gifts. Some firms put dollar limits on the business gifts they allow their employees to give or receive. The Internal Revenue Service places a limit of $25 a year on the amount that may be deducted for business gifts to any one person. Other firms have stopped the practice of giving Christmas gifts to customers. Instead, some of these firms offer to contribute (in amounts equal to their usual gifts) to their customers' favorite charities.

It is unfortunate that gift giving to customers has become so complicated and so suspect. A reasonably priced, tastefully selected gift can express appreciation for a customer's business. Today the problem lies largely in deciding what constitutes "reasonably priced" and "tastefully selected." The following examples illustrate this problem:

- A box of golf balls may be a reasonable Christmas gift to give a $5,000-a-year customer. But is a $3,000 personal computer a gift or a bribe when given to a million-dollar customer?
- It is customary for appliance manufacturers to reward their distributor-customers with an all-expense-paid incentive trip to the Bahamas. But is it acceptable for a pharmaceutical company to invite its doctor-"customers" to Jamaica for an all-expense-paid seminar?
- It is a legal and acceptable practice for a manufacturer to give a department store's sales clerks "push money" to promote the manufacturer's brand. But can this manufacturer rightfully give the head buyer a little something extra for first getting the product into the store?

Fortunately, sales executives have some time-tested guidelines to help them avoid gift giving that is unethical or in bad taste.

- A gift should never be given before a customer does business with the firm.
- Do not give gifts to customers' spouses.
- The value of gifts should be kept low to avoid the appearance of undue influence on future purchase decisions.[6]

*Entertainment.*    Business entertainment is definitely a part of sales work, and a large portion of the expense money is often devoted to it. Reps who spend this money unwisely on accounts with little potential waste time, and their selling costs will be out of line. Indeed, a contributing factor in salespeople's success may be their ability to know the right person to entertain and the nature of the entertainment called for.

Over the years, some useful generalizations have been developed for customer entertainment:

- Entertain to develop long-term business relationships, not one order.
- Keep the entertainment appropriate to the customer and the size of the account.
- Be sensitive to customer attitudes toward types of entertainment.
- Do not rely on entertainment as one of the foundations of the selling strategy—use it only to complement the strategy.

## Setting Ethical Guidelines

It is not realistic for a sales manager to construct a two-column list of practices, one headed "ethical" and the other labeled "unethical." A better approach is to depend on time and conscious examples to point out the difference between acceptable and nonacceptable standards of performance. Cite the philosophy followed in the writing and subsequent administration of Section 5 of the Federal Trade Commission Act. The act outlaws unfair competition, but it does not state what that term means. The legislators wisely left the task of definition to the commission and the courts. Thus through the years examples have accumulated as the law has been administered case by case.

### Take a Long-Run Point of View

Sales executives should understand that ethical behavior not only is morally right but, over the long run, realistically sound. Too many sales administrators are shortsighted. They do not see the possible repercussions from their activities and attitudes. Whether or not the buyer was deceived or pressured may seem unimportant so long as the sale is consummated. Management often does not recognize that such practices can lose customers or invite public regulation. The brushmark of one immediate sale is unimportant when the entire canvas is examined. Figure 20-1 provides some questions that may help a sales executive evaluate the ethical status of proposed actions.

---

■ **FIGURE 20-1**

---

**Evaluating the ethical status of a business decision**

1. Is this sound from a long-run point of view?
2. Would I do this to a friend?
3. Would I be willing to have this done to me? (The Golden Rule)
4. Would I want this action publicized in national media?
5. Would I tell others about it?
6. Who is damaged by the action?

---

### Put Guidelines in Writing

In the mid-1970s, spurred by revelations of bribery at home and in foreign business dealings, many U.S. companies developed **codes of ethics,** which are written ethical guidelines to be followed by all employees. A recent survey by the Ethics Resource Center showed that 84 percent of the companies surveyed have codes of conduct and 45 percent of them have ethics offices.[7] Figure 20-2 presents the main points of the Code of Ethics which has been adopted by the American Marketing Association, the largest association of professional marketers in the world.

Writing a code of ethical conduct is no easy task. Critics claim that such a statement usually is public relations window dressing that covers up a bad situation and corrects nothing. Nevertheless, there is growing

■ **FIGURE 20-2**

| | |
|---|---|
| **Code of Ethics— American Marketing Association** | **Marketers' Professional Conduct must be guided by:**<br><br>1. The basic rule of professional ethics: not knowingly to do harm;<br>2. The adherence to all applicable laws and regulations;<br>3. The accurate representation of their education, training and experience; and<br>4. The active support, practice and promotion of this Code of Ethics.<br><br>**Honesty and Fairness:**<br>*Marketers shall uphold and advance the integrity, honor and dignity of the marketing profession by:*<br><br>1. Being honest in serving consumers, clients, employees, suppliers, distributors and the public;<br>2. Not knowingly participating in conflict of interest without prior notice to all parties involved; and<br>3. Establishing equitable fee schedules including the payment or receipt of usual, customary and/or legal compensation for marketing exchanges.<br><br>**Rights and Duties of Parties in the Marketing Exchange Process:**<br>*Participants in the marketing exchange process should be able to expect that:*<br><br>1. Products and services offered are safe and fit for their intended uses;<br>2. Communications about offered products and services are not deceptive;<br>3. All parties intend to discharge their obligations, financial and otherwise, in good faith; and<br>4. Appropriate internal methods exist for equitable adjustment and/or redress of grievances concerning purchases. |

agreement that these formal written statements are desirable. They lessen the chance that executives will knowingly or unknowingly get into trouble. They strengthen the company's hand in dealing with customers and government officials who invite bribes and other unethical actions. They strengthen the position of lower-level executives in resisting pressures to compromise their personal ethics in order to get along in the firm.

In addition to providing guidelines for ethical decision making, a code of ethics can contribute to the general ethical climate of an organization if it is endorsed and enforced by top management. If an organization has a code of ethics, it is a concrete sign that the organization cares about whether or not its employees behave in an ethical manner. Reps who violate the code should be reprimanded; if they don't cease their unethical behavior, they should be fired. In other words, a code of ethics becomes an effective means of guiding behavior only if it is enforced; otherwise it is meaningless.

### Provide a Role Model

Top management must serve as an ethical role model for employees. They must not only verbally endorse ethical behavior, they must practice it. Clearly salespeople are not going to take any code of ethics seriously if they see their immediate managers and other executives behaving unethically.

## PUBLIC REGULATION AND SALES MANAGERS

Public regulation at any level of government—federal, state, or local—touches a company's marketing department more than any other phase of its operations. This does not imply that regulation of nonselling activities is unimportant. The Securities and Exchange Commission affects corporate financing; minimum wage legislation influences several aspects of personnel and labor relations; various measures establish safety regulations for offices and factories; local zoning laws affect plant location, and so on. However, the various regulatory measures that affect areas of marketing, such as pricing, advertising, and personal selling, generally have a greater impact on a company's success.

There are four areas where sales executives are affected by government regulation of business. They include price discrimination, unfair competition, the Green River type of municipal ordinance, and cooling-off laws.

### Price Discrimination

The Clayton Antitrust Act (1914) and its Robinson-Patman Amendment (1936) are federal laws that generally restrict **price discrimination.** Sales administrators, for example, cannot allow members of their sales force to indiscriminately grant price concessions. Some customers may demand larger discounts than are normally allowed and threaten to take their business elsewhere if their demands are not met. If the seller grants the unusual discount, assuming no corresponding cost differential to justify the transaction, he (and the buyer) may be violating the Robinson-Patman Act.

In another situation, in order to make a sale it may be necessary for a seller to absorb some or all of the freight ordinarily paid by the buyer. Care must be taken to ensure that the move is made in good faith to meet an equally low price of a competitor. Firms normally cannot make price guarantees to some customers without making the same guarantees to other competing customers. Let's assume that a firm wants to grant allowances to customers for such things as cooperative advertising or demonstrators. Then these attractions must be offered to all competing customers on a proportionately equal basis.

## Unfair Competition

Unfair trade practices that may injure a competitor or the consumer are generally illegal under the Federal Trade Commission Act and its Wheeler-Lea Amendment. No specific examples of **unfair competition** are spelled out in these laws. However, a large body of illustrations has built up through the years as the Federal Trade Commission administered these legislative acts. Bribery and providing misleading information to customers have been the focus of many FTC legal actions against firms and their employees.

### Bribes

Using **bribes**—the payment of money or gifts to gain or retain a customer—is illegal. Using bribes to gain information about competitors is also illegal. Bribery in selling is an unpleasant fact of life that apparently has existed, in varying degrees, since time immemorial. Blatant bribes, payoffs, or kickbacks may be easy to spot—and they are patently wrong. Unfortunately, today much bribery is done in a more sophisticated manner and is less easy to identify. Sometimes the lines are blurred between a bribe, a gift to show appreciation, and a reasonable commission for services rendered.

In sales, the bribe offer may be initiated by the salesperson, or the request may come from the buyer. Usually the buyer's request is stated in a veiled fashion, and it takes a perceptive sales rep to understand what is going on.

Undoubtedly bribery will continue to put sales managers and salespeople to the ethical test. If nothing else, sales executives should realize that the idea "Everyone else is doing it" is not a valid excuse. The penalties can be stiff for those found guilty of taking or giving bribes.

### Misleading Information

It is illegal to make false, deceptive, or misleading claims about a product or about the services that accompany that product. If a salesperson makes exaggerated claims about a product and those claims lead to misuse of the product, the seller may also be sued for any property damages or personal

## AN INTERNATIONAL PERSPECTIVE

Bribery is found in many (perhaps all) cultures and political systems. In fact, in many foreign countries there is no way a company can hope to make sales without paying fees or commissions (translate that as bribes) to agents in those countries. Bribery is so implanted in many cultures that various languages have slang words to designate it. In Latin America it is called the *mordida* (small bite). It is *dash* in West Africa and *baksheesh* in the Middle East. The French call it *pot de vin* (jug of wine). In Italy there is *la bustarella* (the little envelope) left on a bureaucrat's desk to cut the red tape.

However, under the Foreign Corrupt Practices Act of 1977, it is illegal for U.S. companies to offer bribes to foreign officials or candidates. This law was amended by the Omnibus Trade and Competitiveness Act of 1988. In this amendment a distinction is made between **subordination** and a **facilitation payment.** Subordination involves payment of large sums of money, for which there is not proper accounting, to entice an official to commit an illegal act. This is considered illegal under U.S. law. A facilitation payment, on the other hand, involves the payment of relatively small sums of cash to low-ranking officials, where not prohibited by law, to facilitate or expedite the normal, lawful performance of a duty.

It is important to remember that all employees of every U.S. company are subject to the laws of the United States regardless of the country in which they are conducting business. Furthermore, sales managers are held responsible for not only their own actions, but also the actions of their internationally based employees. So any subordination payments made by U.S. companies doing business in any foreign country would be considered illegal and punishable under U.S. law.

injuries arising out of a customer's misuse of the product. In one unusual situation, a group of salespeople from Pacific Bell, which was taken over by Southwestern Bell, filed a complaint with the California Public Utilities Commission. They charged that since the takeover, their company is forcing them to use deceptive selling practices.[8]

Making false, deceptive, or disparaging statements about a competitor or its products is also illegal. Yet this practice is very prevalent.[9] The lies may run from fibs about the competitor's financial stability to personal attacks on their salespeople. Regardless of their nature, these actions all have the same purpose of discrediting the competitor. This is illegal and can lead to prosecution, fines, and imprisonment.

The following guidelines help salespeople minimize the probability of legal proceedings and increase their chances of defending themselves if a legal complaint is brought against them.[10]

- Always make accurate, understandable, and verifiable statements about the product.
- Ensure that customers have the necessary knowledge and skills needed to use the product in the proper manner.
- Caution (in writing) customers who intend to use the product in an improper manner.

*A Day-to-Day Operating Problem*

## MAJESTIC PLASTICS COMPANY (O)

### Sales rep accused of passing confidential information

In their visits to customers' plants, Majestic sales reps were sometimes given confidential information by the customers' personnel about new products, advertising plans, or forthcoming price changes. They also had opportunities to overhear private conversations or to read interoffice correspondence left exposed.

In March, Clyde Brion received a long-distance call from Detroit. Beryl Heckman, president of Northern Foods Company, a packer of fruits and juices, told him angrily: "It *has* to be your salesman who did it! My buyer, Al Resor, assures me that there was no one else in his office but that fellow, Jenner, on the day that Al had my memorandum about our surprise carload sale coming up on April 1! In fact, Al remembered that Jenner walked out with the memo. He brought it back an hour later with the lame excuse it had got caught under a paper clip behind some of *his* papers! Now, of course, it's plain that Orchard Industries, down the street, got the word. They are running the very same offer, two weeks ahead of our jumpoff date! We checked, and we know for sure that Jenner called on the buyer at Orchard that same day, right after he left here! And then, to top it all off, Al tells me he knows that Jenner has a criminal record! Did you know that?"

Brion knew that his Detroit sales rep was an ex-convict. Brion had rehired Jenner on the recommendation of Ohio penal officials as a rehabilitation measure. Jenner had been grateful for the chance and had worked hard. His sales record was better than it had been before his conviction, but there was no spectacular upswing. His wife's health had also improved, but Jenner continued to have personal financial problems.

Brion promised Heckman that he would make a thorough investigation. Brion then telephoned Jenner in Detroit and told him of the accusation against him by Northern Foods Company. Jenner readily admitted knowledge of the planned carload sale. He said that Resor had shown him the interoffice memorandum containing prices and dates. He said that Resor had used this forthcoming sale as a reason for Jenner to expedite a shipment of bottles. Jenner said he even took down some notes from the memo but denied having given any information to Orchard.

Northern Foods was the largest firm of its industry in the Detroit territory and was growing. However, it had never been a large buyer from Majestic.

**Question:** What further action should Clyde Brion take in this situation?

Note: See the introduction to this series of problems in Chapter 4 for the necessary background on the company, its market, and its competition.

---

- Customers should be reminded to read warning labels.
- Be able to verify any statements made about competitors.

Sales managers must ensure that their salespeople are aware of their legal responsibilities. To do this, they must provide training with regard to their legal responsibilities and routinely provide updates concerning the most recent legislation and court decisions.

If a manager believes that the behavior of a particular salesperson may lead to legal problems, the sales manager should take action immediately to make the rep cease the questionable behavior.

## Green River Ordinances

Many cities have ordinances, called **Green River Ordinances,** restricting the activities of salespeople who represent firms located outside the city. These representatives may sell door-to-door (in-home), or they may call on retailers or other business establishments. Ostensibly, most of these laws were passed to protect local consumers and businesses from the fraudulent, high-pressure, and otherwise unethical selling practices of outlanders. Actually such measures not only serve this purpose, but they also tend to insulate local firms from external competition. Generally, these ordinances require salespeople to have a local license to do business in the town. But it often is difficult for representatives from some types of outside firms to get the necessary license. While the constitutionality of these laws is highly questionable, they do serve as a deterrent to unethical sales activity.

## Cooling-Off Laws

Legislation at the federal, state, and local levels protects consumers against the sales activities—sometimes unethical—of door-to-door salespeople. Much of the state legislation and FTC administrative rulings are of the "cooling-off" type. That is, the regulations provide for a cooling-off period (usually three days) during which the buyer in a door-to-door (in-home) sale may cancel the contract, return any merchandise, and obtain a full refund.

The Federal Trade Commission rulings (1972) apply to all sales of $25 or more. They require the salesperson to inform the customer orally and in writing about the opportunity to "say no to the company even after you have said yes to the salesperson." By 1973, nearly 40 states, as well as several cities, had passed some type of **cooling-off law.** This poses real problems of compliance for national direct-selling companies, who must deal with many different laws and sales contracts.

## Current Problems

The advent and rapid growth of direct-response marketing, telemarketing, and Internet marketing have given rise to some new problems that many people feel have certain ethical overtones. Is it ethical to bother people at home over the telephone, particularly at night? Or is it right to send unsolicited promotional material to prospects over their own fax machines or via e-mail? Some legislation about these practices is pending.

The securities industry is plagued with so-called boiler room operations that use telemarketing techniques to sell financial schemes to people the seller will never know or see. The SEC is doing its best to regulate such operations, but it is not an easy task.

# ■ SUMMARY

Ethics may be defined as moral standards of behavior. Sales managers and salespeople face many different ethical dilemmas. In the United States, many ethical decisions are actually legal questions. Our system of laws standardizes our interpretation of many ethical situations by making them illegal. However, there are still many situations which are not covered by the law—where ethics becomes an important factor.

It is easy to be ethical when it does not cost you anything—when you are winning. The test comes when things are *not* going well. Then there may be real pressure to compromise your personal ethics. There is an increasing awareness and concern over ethics in selling. Adherence to ethical standards is becoming increasingly important.

The problem is to determine what the ethical standards are. Society lacks commonly accepted standards of behavior. Ethical considerations are involved in many of the relationships sales executives have with their sales forces, their companies, and their customers. Customer relations, especially involving information, gifts, and entertainment, can have serious ethical overtones.

When setting ethical standards, it is important to take a long-run perspective. One good ethical guideline to follow is to do what you would feel comfortable explaining to your family, your friends, or even to the public at large on television. A company may help establish an ethical climate by taking a long-run perspective on business decisions, by developing a written code of ethics which managers are expected to enforce, and by managers providing ethical role models through their words and actions.

Public regulation touches a company's marketing department more than any other phase of its operations. History tells us that government regulation of business has occurred because either (1) business has not acted in a socially responsible manner or (2) special-interest groups lobbied for the regulations. Government regulation has occurred in several areas which affect sales: price discrimination, unfair competition, Green River ordinances, and cooling-off laws.

## Key Terms

| | | |
|---|---|---|
| Bribes | Ethics | Price discrimination |
| Codes of ethics | Facilitation payment | Subordination |
| Cooling-off laws | Green River Ordinances | Unfair competition |

# ■ QUESTIONS AND PROBLEMS

1. "We always use a manufacturer's rep to open up a new territory; but once that territory is generating enough revenue to support a company rep, we take it away from the rep and put one of our own salespeople in the territory." Is this an ethical policy?

2. "Let's face it. Our product is no different than that of 20 other competitors. It sells for the same price and for the same terms. We all give the same service. It really doesn't matter to the buyer which of us gets the order. So the only way we can get an edge is through our aggres-

sive entertainment and gift program. We work hard at making our buyers happy with us. They enjoy doing business with us." Do you see any ethical problems involved here?

3. You have managed to hire a particularly qualified person to be your assistant sales manager in Los Angeles. The young man moves his wife, who yearns for a singing career, to Los Angeles. The new assistant sales manager is paid a salary that seemed attractive in his former Kansas City area. Economic and culture shock quickly take their toll as the couple learns the economic facts of life in Los Angeles. They find that their $100,000 Kansas City home sells for $500,000 in West Los Angeles. Moreover, the new assistant's job performance is most unsatisfactory. You are thinking of firing him. What are the ethical considerations involved in this situation?

4. "Come on now, if I didn't sell my sales jobs to our recruits I'd never be able to hire any of them. I have dirty jobs to fill. I need people. So they all quit inside a month or two. Still they manage to sell our products to a few of their relatives and friends before they quit. We make money on it." What ethical considerations do you see in this situation?

5. "Sure we promote our product to fax owners by sending them flyers over their own machines. Why not? We sell fax supplies at great values. If they don't like it, why do they buy so much from us? We're doing great with the program. So a few people complain. So what? Some people will complain if the sun shines while others complain if it

doesn't. We're not in business to make everybody happy. Besides, there is no better way to do it." Evaluate the sales manager's statement. Is there any way she could head off such complaints?

6. As sales manager, you have been asked to recommend someone for a job as sales manager with another, noncompetitive firm. You have several salespeople who would be excellent for the position, but you don't want to lose them. The other position would be a definite improvement for them. They will never be able to do so well within your own firm. Would you tell them about the opening? Would you recommend them to the other firm?

7. Loyalty is a trait highly prized by most top executives. They expect their subordinates to be loyal to them and to the company. When might those loyalties conflict? How much loyalty does an employee owe to a superior? To the company?

8. As an American citizen managing a large corporation owned by a large foreign trading company, you have been ordered to do some things that you feel are clearly detrimental to the welfare of the U.S. economy. What concerns, if any, would you have in following those orders?

9. You are a salesperson and you happen to oversee your manager's expense report for a time period during which he was making calls with you. Clearly he has reported some expenses which are fictitious. He has been with the company for a long time and is a respected manager. What should you do about this?

## EXPERIENTIAL EXERCISES

**A.** You are a sales manager of a firm that makes printed electronic circuits. You have been requested to write down your policies on entertaining customers, giving gifts, and handling bribery. State your policies in clear, specific terms so that all people concerned know exactly how you will handle each situation.

**B.** Speak with a sales representative about an ethical issue that he or she faced as part of the job and ask how she or he dealt with the problem. Would you have handled the situation any differently?

## REFERENCES

**1.** Michele Marchetti, "Whatever It Takes," *Sales & Marketing Management,* December 1997, pp. 29–38.

**2.** Ibid.

**3.** Ibid.

**4.** Ibid.

**5.** Catherine Arnst, "Is Good Marketing Bad Medicine?" *Business Week,* http://www. businessweek.com, April 13, 1998.

**6.** I. Fredrick Trawick, John E. Swan, and David R. Rink, "Industrial Buyer Evaluation of the Ethics of Gift Giving: Value of the Gift and Customer vs. Prospect Status," *Journal of Personal Selling & Sales Management,* Summer 1989, pp. 31–37.

**7.** Marchetti, "Whatever It Takes."

**8.** "Sales Force Complains about PacBell," Yahoo! News UPI Story, http://dailynews.yahoo.com/headlin. . . . and_regional_news/ capacbell_1.html, April 7, 1998.

**9.** Melinda Jensen Ligos, "Dirty Rotten Scoundrels," *Sales & Marketing Management,* August 1997, pp. 90–96.

**10.** Karl A. Boedecker, Fred W. Morgan, and Jeffrey J. Stoltman, "Legal Dimensions of Salespersons' Statements: A Review and Managerial Suggestions," *Journal of Marketing,* January 1991, pp. 70–80.

---

*Case 20-1*

### NATIONAL PUBLISHING COMPANY
#### An entrepreneurially inclined sales manager

"It's not as if we didn't have fair warning that this might happen. He's done it before. When we hired him, we were told by some of his previous employers that Jim liked to do his own deals on the side." Derek Newman, vice president of marketing, was talking to Linda Alverez, executive vice president, about an unsigned letter that she had received in the morning's mail. Purportedly, it was from one of the firm's sales representatives. It concerned Jim Power, the company's field sales manager, who was the rep's boss.

In the letter the rep claimed that Jim Power was also involved in a newly established computer software company located in Salt Lake City. The rep thought that management should be aware of Mr. Power's outside interests.

National Publishing Company, with headquarters in San Francisco, published college textbooks. Its 24-person sales force called on college professors throughout the country seeking adoptions for the company's books as well as searching for manuscripts worthy of publication.

Jim Power had been promoted to sales manager in 1992 after spending five years with the firm in various sales and editorial positions. After graduation from Northwestern Mr. Power had spent his working life in the publishing industry, holding sales and editorial jobs for many of the largest publishers. While his record for productivity was outstanding, his advancement in most firms had been hindered by his lack of social skills. One story that circulated about Jim's difficulties with top management concerned a time when the president of a large publishing company ordered Jim, as the firm's editor-in-chief, to publish 300 new books for the coming year. Jim had replied, "But there aren't 300 good books out there."

To which the president had replied, "Nobody said that they had to be good books." Neither the president nor the firm lasted long, but Jim's departure from the company had been even quicker.

National Publishing Company had hired Jim because it was in a severe bind for someone who knew how to sell college textbooks and would do the traveling and hard work necessary for the job. Jim was known to be a hard worker and would travel. Moreover, his salary demands were reasonable. The company's president knew of Jim's past entrepreneurial ventures. He had spent 10 years with his own company publishing some high school educational materials but, tired of the battle for cash flow, he accepted National's job offer. He wanted some security and a benefits package for his old age. At the time of hiring, Jim said that he was not involved in any other business activities.

Alverez asked Newman, "How's Jim doing?"

"Fine. Sales are up. We're now making money. He knows what he is doing. He's out there fighting all the battles." Newman continued, "I hate this unsigned letter business. This rep's got to be a gutless creep trying to even up some score with Jim. Looks like a hatchet job to me. I don't like it."

Alverez responded, "I don't either, but now that I have the information I've got to follow up on it. I can't ignore it. So find out what is going on and get back to me by next week."

Newman had his orders. After a few calls, he found Jim driving a rental car somewhere between Manhattan and Emporia, Kansas. "Didn't I see on the morning news that they're having a blizzard somewhere near you?"

"Near me isn't quite accurate. Around me would describe my plight right now. It's awful! I've got to get to the next town and hole up until this blows through. Hope you didn't call me just to chat about the weather," Jim said.

"No, I need some quick answers to give the boss lady. She was told that you have some business interests in a software firm in Utah and she is worried about the possible conflicts of interest it might pose. What can you tell me?"

"I invested in my son's new business. His concept is to develop educational materials on CD-ROM disks for distribution through college bookstores," Jim replied.

"Are you working for him?"

"No!" was Jim's succinct and definite answer.

Newman thought for an instant and then took the opportunity to talk about some other company business.

Newman reported his information back to Alverez, who responded, "I think it would be naive to believe for an instant that Jim is not helping his son in every possible way he can. It must be conflicting with his position with us. Find out more about it. How much of the company does he own? How much money has he invested? How much contact does he have with his son and what does he do to help him?"

Newman thought for a while, carefully selecting his words before saying, "I think you might want to think about this situation a bit more. Are there any potential problems here? The company hasn't asked me about any of my investments and how much I talk to my children. Could Jim claim discrimination? To what extent are we free to investigate an employee's life outside the company? Keep in mind that Jim has been doing what he was hired to do."

Alverez did not like what she thought she was being told. "I hear you saying that maybe it isn't any of our business what Jim does with his money and outside time. Just close our eyes to it. Is that it? I hardly think

that the man can be working with reps in college towns on our time and money without doing some business for his son at the same time. Mark my words, if he is in a bookstore, he will try to sell some of his own product."

Newman looked for directions. "What do you want me to do? Talk to him? Fire him? It's your call."

"No, it's not. He works for you. He's your problem," Alverez stated firmly as she indicated the meeting was over.

Newman thought to himself that he knew that all along. He wondered what he should do about the matter.

### Questions:

1. Evaluate both the ethics involved in Jim's interest in his son's enterprise and the company's interest in Jim's investments in other firms.

2. What should Newman now do about the situation?

---

*Case 20-2*

## AEROSPACE SYSTEMS (B)

### Disclosure of planned terminations

More than 10,000 employees of Aerospace Systems had already been terminated as a result of the defense contract cutbacks being experienced by all firms in the defense industry. The company's plight was well reported in the news media.

One of the company's divisions was involved in developing computer networking systems. While its work was not being discontinued, it was being reduced to a level that could be sustained by its nondefense business. Consequently, its sales staff of 56 people had been reduced to 35 sales reps in early 1993. Mark Simpson, the divisional vice president, was meeting with Simon

West, the sales manager, about future plans for the sales force. Simpson informed West, "You'll have to let 10 more of your sales reps go on January 1. Give them two weeks notice and the usual severance package. Try to get rid of the highly paid ones first. Some of your older sales reps are making over $100,000 a year, while most of the younger people are making 50 to 60 thou."

West detested what he was being told. He disagreed with the company policies. His silent response to Simpson's orders were, "Yeah, they're being paid a lot more than the young ones and for good reason. They make us a lot more money." But Simon West kept his thoughts to himself because he had no place else to work and he enjoyed his $130,000 a year salary plus benefits. He did ask, "Can't we give them more than two weeks notice?"

Simpson stared coldly at West and said, "You know better than that. Don't you dare tell anyone about our plans. The minute you tell someone they're history, they quit working for you and start working for themselves. Our obligation is to the company, not its former employees. We are trying to save this company. It's been good to us. A lot of people are depending on us to do what must be done if the company is to survive. Now if you don't want to do the job, just say so and. . . ."

Simpson did not have a chance to finish his statement before West cut him off, "No, no, I'll do it. I'll have to work out a lot of details about maintaining the coverage of accounts." He said no more and left Simpson's office.

Upon returning to his office, he was met by Bob Lilly, the company's leading sales rep who also serviced the company's most important commercial account.

After the customary greetings, Bob said, "I just got off the phone with Mike Markings, who is now president of Spacetech. He wants me to be his sales manager. The pay is about the same as I am making here and you know that I like it here. I have 20 years of my life invested here so I don't want to leave. However, the jungle tom-toms have been sending out some messages that there are going to be some more cutbacks coming up in the sales department. If that's true, me and my big salary could be a tempting target. So if I am going to be history around here, then I'll have to leave now to take the Spacetech job. We've been buddies for over 10 years, Simon. Tell me, is it time to move on? You owe me that much!"

Simon West knew he had to give Bob Lilly an immediate answer. If he didn't, that in itself would be the answer.

*Question:*

What should Simon West say to Bob Lilly?

---

*Case 20-3*

## FAIRFAX FILTER FABRICATORS*
### A question of ethics in selling

"I realize I'm the new kid on the block, and I may be unduly influenced by my background at Wheelabrator where our sales policies were highly structured. In that company we really followed the book. Even so, I don't see how Fairfax Filters can continue with the freewheeling selling tactics that some of our guys are using." The speaker was Elsa Brock, the newly hired sales manager for the Fairfax Filter Fabricators Com-

pany. Brock was especially concerned about the selling technique employed by Bernard Nally, one of Fairfax Filter's top salespeople.

Fairfax Filter Fabricators was a Louisiana-based company that produced dust-collector bags—a replaceable part of the equipment used to clean polluted air discharged from smokestacks. These dust-collector bags typically were long, cylindrically shaped pieces of fabric with a closed end. They were produced in a variety of diameters and lengths, depending on the design specified by the filter equipment manufac-

---

*Adapted from a case prepared by George W. Kyle, under the direction of Prof. William J. Stanton.

turers. The bags were available in several fabrics. The particular fabric selected depended on the size of the particulates being filtered, the heat of the discharged air, and how much shock the bags would receive. The most widely used bags were heavy-duty units made from a synthetic felt material with a plastic coating.

Most filter equipment periodically shook the bags or reversed the air flow in order to clean the particulates from the bag so it could be reused. Nevertheless, these bags had to be regularly replaced. The bags were rather simply made and the start-up equipment to manufacture dust-collector bags was relatively inexpensive.

But the market for these bags was big and growing, with all the attention being devoted to reducing air pollution in the United States. Fairfax's annual sales were about $20 million. Its main market was the Louisiana–Texas Gulf Coast, where there was a concentration of petrochemical and other industrial manufacturing plants. In that geographical market, Fairfax was a major supplier of dust-collector bags. In terms of nationwide business, however, Fairfax was not classed as a major firm. Nationally, the big firms were a division of Albany International Company (which in turn was a division of the Carborundum Company), Menardi-Southern Corporation, and P & S Textiles Company.

The bag-replacement industry was very competitive because there was little difference among the products of the various manufacturers. Most firms had experienced sales reps calling on engineers and purchasing agents at the customers' plants. Most of them knew each other from occasional chance meetings at the customers' locations. All reps were familiar with the others' products and selling methods. However, the people at Fairfax believed they had one competitive differential advantage in their primary target market—the Louisiana–Texas Gulf Coast region. In that market Fairfax was the only bag manufacturer that was not a division of a large national company that assigned profit requirements to its bag-replacement division. Fairfax executives felt that this feature allowed them to respond quickly and flexibly to their customers' requirements and requests.

In the past, all the usual activities of a sales manager had been handled by Fairfax's president, Edward Jurgens. Typically he had hired male sales reps who had selling experience, but not necessarily in the air-filter industry. Currently the sales force consisted of eight men who averaged four years each with Fairfax. They were paid under a straight-commission compensation plan. Each rep was assigned a sales volume quota based on the sales forecast for his territory. The reps were paid a commission of 3 percent on sales up to their quota and 4 percent for all sales over the quota. The additional 1 percent was calculated at the end of the year and added to the last month's commission check. The average annual pay for the salespeople was $80,000, which was above the industry average.

As Fairfax's market continued to grow, Ed Jurgens realized he could not, and should not, continue to wear two hats—company president and sales manager. Consequently, he established a separate position of sales manager. For that position Jurgens wanted someone with some technical knowledge of original filter equipment. He hired Elsa Brock, who had been a top-performing sales rep at Wheelabrator-Frye, a major producer of filter equipment. Brock had a bachelor's degree in engineering and an MBA from Louisiana State University. Jurgens felt that Brock knew the petrochemical industry and other industries that constituted Fairfax's primary market. Jurgen's only concern was whether his all-male sales force would work as effectively for Elsa Brock as they had for him.

Fairfax's top rep in terms of sales volume was Bernard Nally, an ex–All American football player from one of the football powers of the Southeastern Conference. Nally's territory included primarily chemical plants and oil companies located along the Mississippi River from Baton Rouge, Louisiana, down to the Gulf of Mexico, plus some firms along the Gulf Coast near the mouth of the Mississippi River.

Nally had a reputation of doing whatever was necessary to get an order. He had been able to operate in this manner because Ed Jurgens had been too busy running the company to establish any policies for sales rep relationships with customers. Elsa Brock, on the other hand, came from a highly structured multinational organization with very strict policies covering sales force–customer relations. Consequently, when she arrived at Fairfax, Brock felt that policies in the rep-customer area needed to be established, put in writing, and enforced.

Brock was especially concerned about one relationship that Bernie Nally had established with several of his customers. Nally had what was called "the last look" at competitive bids submitted. Nally, along with competitors' sales reps, submitted a bid on a filter-bag order being placed by a chemical company. After all the bids were in, the purchasing agent for the chemical company gave Nally a "last look" at all the bids. Then Nally could revise the Fairfax bid to come in with a lower price and consequently get the order. Nally had established this last-look relationship with several customers, and this was a major factor accounting for his high sales volume. Nally had been able to develop these relationships by a mix of (1) his image as a winner, (2) a pleasant personality, (3) entertainment that included football tickets and golf outings, and (4) the fact that his customers liked the idea of associating with a former All-American who was a conference legend.

Elsa Brock then discussed several sales policy situations with Ed Jurgens without spotlighting Bernard Nally's last-look bidding system. Jurgens reminded Brock that she had been hired to run the sales force. He told her to do whatever she thought was necessary as far as sales policies were concerned. He went on to say that he had complete confidence in her decisions. He also agreed that Fairfax was now large enough to need established policies regarding sales tactics and techniques.

Back in her own office, Brock realized that the Nally problem had no really good solution. Any decision she made could easily result in a loss of business, a loss of Fairfax's best sales rep, or a compromise in her belief that Nally's technique was unethical.

Brock decided to have a talk with Nally, and she believed it would be better if this meeting were held some place outside their offices. She thus used the occasion of a joint sales call with Nally on a new account. After the call, they went to a restaurant for lunch and Brock took that opportunity to discuss the idea of establishing policies to cover various selling situations.

She explained to Nally that she felt the company should have a firm policy to the effect that only one bid would be offered on potential orders. She went on to explain that the company's bid should be based on a predetermined profit margin. She pointed out that even though Nally was the rep with the highest sales volume and dollar profits, his percentage profit margin was the lowest among the entire sales force.

Bernie Nally was very upset with Brock's proposed change in his method of doing business. He told her that his margins were lower than those of other reps because most of his customers placed orders that were very large and did not allow for a larger margin. He also reminded her that many of his orders were contracts for annual supply for multiplant usage. He reminded her that he had built up his business over several years of hard work and that Ed Jurgens was aware of his practices. Nally went on to say that it would not be fair to the reps to change the rules since the sales force was being paid on a straight commission.

Nally implied that Elsa was not qualified to make such sweeping changes. He also suggested that if he lost business because of her policy changes, he could always go with a competitor and take the business with him. Since filter replacement bags were fairly generic in nature, Brock knew that if Nally went, it could have a very negative effect on Fairfax's sales volume.

Brock decided not to press the situation in the restaurant and told Nally she would decide by the next sales meeting what changes would be made. Brock began to doubt her decision to leave Wheelabrator-Frye. She wondered if being a woman had any bearing on the situation involving Nally. She knew that whatever she decided to do in this situation, it must be done soon, and with an appearance of confident firmness.

*Questions:*

1. What sales policy, if any, should Elsa Brock introduce regarding the bidding practices used by the Fairfax salespeople?
2. Is Bernard Nally's "last-look" bidding technique an ethical selling tactic?

# Integrative Cases

**Integrative cases: Case-by-chapter grid***

| | | | | | | | | | | Chapter | | | | | | | | | | |
|---|---|---|---|---|---|---|---|---|---|---|---|---|---|---|---|---|---|---|---|---|
| | 1 | 2 | 3 | 4 | 5 | 6 | 7 | 8 | 9 | 10 | 11 | 12 | 13 | 14 | 15 | 16 | 17 | 18 | 19 | 20 |
| Johnson Drug Company | X | X | X | | X | X | | X | | X | | X | | | | | | | | |
| National Paging, Inc. | | X | | | | | | | | | | | | | | | | X | | X |
| Hanover-Bates Chemical Corp. | | | | | | | | | | | | X | X | | | | X | X | | |
| ChemGrow, Inc. | | | | | | | | | | | | | | | X | | X | X | X | |
| PEP Threads, Inc. (A) | X | X | | X | | | | | | | | | | | | | | | | |
| PEP Threads, Inc. (B) | | | | | X | X | X | X | | X | X | | | | | | | | | X |

*The grid indicates for which chapters each case is an appropriate supplement.

*Case A-1*

## JOHNSON DRUG COMPANY
### Implementing a sales strategy change

Late in 1998, Eric Johnson, president of the Johnson Drug Company, a drug wholesaler, was studying the company's sales force. The industry was shifting from an outmoded "product-loading" philosophy to strategies based on consumer needs and wants. "We used to be able to sell individual products to the pharmacist and take orders on a routine basis," Johnson commented, "but now we should sell a complete system which assists the pharmacist in managing as well as selling." The drug wholesaler is increasingly looked upon as a service wholesaler who provides a sophisticated system of information, recording, analysis, and management consulting. Mr. Johnson believed that a redefinition of sales force responsibilities to align them with corporate objectives was critical to this transition. He recognized a need for closer correspondence between the responsibilities and objectives of the sales force and management's long-term commitment to systems selling.

### Company background

The company began its operations in Peoria, Illinois, in 1875. It is a family-owned business that was handed down from grandfather to father to son. Mr. Johnson has served as the chief operating officer for the past 15 years. He oversees the major departments, which are operations, sales and buying, credit, and accounting. Reporting to him are the vice president of merchandise, the secretary-treasurer, the sales manager, the operations manager, and the credit manager. The sales force consists of 10 salespeople, who call on the independent retailers in the Peoria trading area.

The products which the company has distributed for over a century fall into the following product classes: cosmetics, drugs, narcotics, pharmaceuticals, proprietary products, sundries, and toiletries. The market for these commodities comprises physicians and pharmacists located in the hospitals, clinics, and pharmacy departments of both medical and retail institutions. The Johnson Drug Company has three major competitors in the Peoria area. Each has a dollar volume that does not quite equal Johnson's annual sales of $25 million. In addition, recently such mass merchandisers as Revco, SuperX, and Walgreen have competed with the local independents which the drug wholesalers serve. In describing the structure of the company's accounts, Mr. Johnson indicated that, as in many businesses, 80 percent of the company's profit was attained through 20 percent of its accounts. Many of Johnson's customers, including its larger accounts, are not yet buying the "system." Rather, when the salesperson calls on them, they place periodic orders for the individual product lines. Ideally, Johnson would like to have all of its customers utilizing the "service system."

### The evolution of drug wholesaling

From 1940 to 1970, the drug wholesaling industry experienced a "growth-oriented" era, characterized by a surge in consumer demand and rapid growth in competition. During this period, the Johnson Drug Company stressed the sales function and the company's objectives were stated in terms of increased sales volume. By the early 1970s, American pharmaceutical markets had grown considerably, competition for the consumer dollar was acute, and selection of the appropriate distribution channels was becoming increasingly difficult. Drug wholesalers began to identify and respond to the needs of their customers, the retailers and hospitals. The Johnson Drug Company recognized such additional goals as margin contribution and profit maximization. As part of the effort to satisfy its customers' needs, the Johnson Drug Company, like its competitors, placed more emphasis on services—increased delivery scheduling, acceptance of special emergency orders, credit extensions, shelf stocking, discount pricing, and "free goods," for example. This trend played a major role in the transformation of the wholesale drug industry. In fact, some wholesale houses began to refer to themselves as "service drug wholesalers."

The 1980s were characterized by intense product and service competition. Three consequences of this competition were the standardization of products and services, price/profit erosion, and the demand for free services. Standardization resulted because the innovative services which were offered to the customer by a particular drug wholesaler were copied by all of its competitors. Thus sales personnel were quickly deprived of product/service differentiation as a selling point. Price/profit erosion occurred as retailers "shopped" wholesale competitors for discounts. Under this pressure to offer discounts, the gross profit margins of wholesale drug companies became uncomfortably thin. Also, retailers began to demand more "free services" (e.g., promotion management and business consultation) by employing the same "shopping" strategy. The combination of these three consequences seriously diminished the profitability of drug wholesaling firms for several years.

In the late 1980s, many business observers began to wonder whether the independent pharmacist was a thing of the past. Chain drugstores, supermarkets, and discounters grew steadily. These larger operations utilized their financial clout to negotiate favorable terms with bankers, developers, and manufacturers. Their advertising stressed discount pricing, ample parking, huge stores, and unlimited product variety. Obviously, neighborhood pharmacies were being threatened by competition more powerful than they could combat. The intense competition, reduced market share, higher costs, and lower margins had retailers and their wholesalers searching for ways to avoid possible extinction. Struggling to survive, the druggist found help by taking advantage of the updated and extended services offered by the drug wholesaler. During the 1990s, the pharmaceutical wholesaler systems have extended the competitive life of the independent retailers as well as that of the wholesaler function.

## The drug service system

A pharmaceutical system is a sales-generating package comprised of the various health care commodities, computerized order processing equipment, and related merchandising services. Marketed as a complete system, it has the ability to add value to a firm's total product offering. (The added value is derived from the system's contribution to decreasing the customer's overall costs and increasing its revenues.) The system may contribute to decreasing costs in any of the following areas: order replacement decisions (timing, source, and quantity), labor employment, credit policy formulation, bookkeeping, shelf stocking, inventory decisions, carrying costs, traffic flow, layout structure, financial decision making, and merchandising strategy planning. The system may also contribute to increasing revenues by helping solve problems caused by poor selection of inventory and inconsistent pricing.

The Johnson Drug Company adopted the "system" approach in 1985. Its drug service system offers a complete inventory management system including order entry, price stickers, shelf labeling, microfilm inventory and price files, and annual inventory reports, as well as operating statements, quarterly reports, accounts receivable analysis, and customer billing. As part of the package, Johnson Drug also offers a cooperative promotional program and sponsors centralized group buying from certain manufacturers. (See Exhibit 1 for a more detailed description of these services.)

## The sales force

The field sales manager reports to Mr. Johnson. The 10 salespeople are responsible only to the sales manager. The salesperson's duties include not only selling the system but also selling the individual product lines to those customers who are not on the system, as they have always done. The duties of the sales manager include being a public relations person, a field supervisor of the sales force, a field intelligence person, a troubleshooter, and last but not least, a seller of systems. In his role as an intelligence person, the sales manager serves as a vital link

---

### ■ EXHIBIT 1

**The pharmaceutical drug service system**

1. **Order entry**—a hand-held computer terminal which contains keyed item code numbers. Memory capacity allows for "recall-and-search" on the display. Dialing a special order entry telephone number and placing the terminal into a transmission "cradle" transmits the order to the wholesale house for processing delivery.
2. **Invoicing**—same-day delivery guaranteed by the purchase invoice for merchandise ordered.
3. **Price labeling**—price stickers preprinted and attached to the merchandise ordered.
4. **Shelf labeling**—the wholesale company product display which indicates item location, item number, and inventory.
5. **Quarterly and annual reports**—the wholesale firm provides performance reports which detail item turnover, expenses, revenues, margin analysis, and other pertinent data.
6. **Retailer accounts receivable**—a periodic compilation of a pharmacist's accounts receivable is prepared and mailed after evaluation by either the pharmacist or the wholesaler.

*Systems may also include any combination of the following:*

7. **Accounts payable payroll.**
8. **Operating statements.**
9. **Prescription files**—patient profiling and drug interaction and allergy control checking.
10. **Long- and short-term financing.**
11. **Management counseling.**
12. **Automatic reorder plans.**
13. **Drug inventory and pricing services** (microfilm).
14. **Sales and promotional programs.**
15. **Merchandising and advertising programs**—these programs aim "to accent the neighborhood store's competitiveness in the consumer's mind and to fortify the drugstore's position against so-called discounters."

in the communications chain between the marketplace and top management.

Promotion from within the company has been the major source of sales personnel. In terms of qualifications, there are no set policies. Prior experience in sales or in the wholesale drug industry is, of course, considered a "plus" in a new hiree. The level of education has never been an imperative criterion. The major selection tool is the personal interview. Typically, the credit manager or the operations manager conducts an initial interview. Upon the recommendation of these managers, the field sales manager or Mr. Johnson will conduct a second interview with an applicant. Both of them have the authority to hire the applicant if the sales force has an opening.

Upon selection, each new salesperson is required to work in the warehouse preparing orders until they have been exposed to all of the product areas. This facilitates their understanding of the product groups and the industry language. Second, the salesperson is required to gain a working knowledge of the equipment utilized in the drug service system. The sales manager is responsible for reviewing pertinent company policies with each new recruit. Finally, before being assigned to a territory, the trainee travels with an established salesperson in order to get a "feel" for the job ahead.

As noted earlier, the sales manager is primarily responsible for the field supervision of the salespeople. The manager's only formal sources of information are the monthly sales account reports submitted by each salesperson. The monthly sales account report details the amount of gross profit generated by each account and indicates whether sales were based on a cost-plus discount or the regular price. Sales meetings are held monthly to relay information to the salespeople regarding promotional drives and new products. In terms of

territory design, every attempt is made to divide sales volume evenly among the salespersons.

The salespeople are paid a straight commission, based on the gross profit generated by each territory. This gross profit is based on the amount of delivered goods. "Returns" are deducted from total sales, and this affects the total compensation paid. Newly hired people are paid a salary until they reach a predetermined volume of sales, at which time they are switched to a commission basis. The average annual compensation of the salespeople is between $35,000 and $50,000, which is comparable to that paid by Johnson's competitors.

The salespeople pay for their personal expenses and their gas, hotel, and food bills. They are also responsible for telephone charges incurred by clients placing orders to the Peoria warehouses. There are no general sales quotas, but the salespeople can earn bonuses which are paid by the drug manufacturers. These are offered in conjunction with promotional drives for specific products. A salesperson can earn a 1 percent to 2 percent bonus, depending on the volume of the sales generated by these products.

Mr. Johnson stated that selling the "system" was more than just an efficient method of moving product—it represented a new commitment to the customer. "The Johnson Drug Company," he said, "is committed to the profit improvement of its customers." He recognized that this required a thorough knowledge and evaluation of customers' operations in order to locate costs that the system could affect positively and to identify product groups for which higher levels of sales could be achieved. He also recognized that this commitment changed the Johnson Drug Company's basic relationship with the retailer—it transformed the pharmacist from a customer to a client. In turn, the salesperson was responsible not only for the sale of products but, more important, for the management of the system, and thus for the management of profits at the retail level. Mr. Johnson wondered whether his salespeople were adequately prepared for and committed to systems selling and what actions he should take to help them adjust to and fulfill their new roles and responsibilities. Although some customers had accepted the new system, many had been slow to see its advantages. Recognizing that the company's future was likely to be heavily dependent on the success of the customer service system, Mr. Johnson was trying to formulate a strategy for both improving the system and speeding up its implementation.

**Question:**

What changes in the sales management program would you recommend to Mr. Johnson to improve the implementation of the "system"?

---

*Case A-2*

## NATIONAL PAGING, INC.
### Conducting a sales analysis

"We've been led to believe that National's best asset is its sales force. If we're going to pay for it, then I think we should audit its sales operations. Let's find out what we are buying." Joe Newman, president of International Telecommunications, was talking to his assistant, Patty Baugh, who was in charge of the company's acquisition of National Paging, Inc. She nodded and said, "I'll have someone down in marketing get on it right away."

When Todd Clayton, marketing trainee freshly graduated from a large Midwest university, was given the assignment, he gave silent thanks for the sales management course he had taken. He felt that at least he knew where to start.

From a financial prospectus Todd learned that National Paging, Inc., was a leading provider of one-way wireless messaging services in the United States, with operations concentrated in Florida and in the Mid-Atlantic and Midwest regions. The company had experienced strong growth in the number of pagers in service, increasing from 161,600 at the end of 1994 to 460,900 at year-end 1998, a compound annual growth rate of 30 percent. The number of pagers in service increased 43 percent from the end of 1997 to year-end 1998. The company's net revenues also grew rapidly from $29.3 million in 1994 to $64.4 million in 1998. Net revenues grew 33.9 percent from 1997 to 1998. The company had 578 full-time employees.

The company's business strategy was to provide the highest quality service through one of the industry's most technologically advanced transmission systems, a focus on strong customer service, and a competitive pricing policy. This strategy resulted in above–industry average net customer growth, above–industry average monthly revenue per unit, and below–industry average customer disconnect rates. These factors, combined with strong productivity gains, allowed the company to substantially increase its cash operating margin.

The company's 108 customer service representatives in its 38 sales and service centers provided 24-hour-a-day, 7-day-per-week customer service in all of its markets. The company has improved customer satisfaction and, according to a survey, 93 per-

cent of the company's customers would recommend the company to friends and business associates. Additional evidence of the
company's quality service was a monthly
churn rate (customers lost as a percentage
of total customers) that was below the industry average. The company's average
monthly churn rates for 1996, 1997, and
1998 were 3.2 percent, 2.9 percent, and 2.9
percent, respectively, as compared to the industry average of 3.2 percent and 3.0 percent for 1996 and 1997, respectively.

National marketed its service directly,
through its sales force complemented by
customers' representatives, and indirectly,
through third-party resellers, agents, and
retailers. It employed 216 direct-sales executives. The direct-sales staff was responsible for the development of large-, medium-,
and small-business accounts, individual accounts, and the promotion of nationwide
paging services. The customer service staff
was responsible for sales support, customer
retention, and generation of customer leads.
A performance-based incentive program encouraged each group to exceed new business
growth and turnover reduction goals.

National offered its services to third-
party resellers and retailers under marketing agreements. The firm offered resellers
paging air time in bulk quantities at wholesale rates. Resellers then sold the air time to
end users at a markup. Agents, on the other
hand, refer customers directly to the company's sales organization. Retail outlets sell
the pagers to the customers, who in turn then
purchased the services from National. Re-

sellers and retailers may also sell the products and services of competitive companies.

National's cost of obtaining customer
units through resellers was substantially
less than the cost of obtaining customer
units through direct sales or retail distribution. Resellers incur the cost to acquire
customers as well as service, billing, and
collecting revenues from the customers.
They also assume the cost of the paging
unit for those who rent rather than purchase the unit. The data in the following
table reflect the company's growth in re-
seller units in service. The distribution of
pagers through local retail outlets significantly increased market penetration. By
the end of 1996, more than 1,500 retail outlets were selling pagers and marketing National services.

The company consistently generated an
average retail price per unit above the industry average. During 1997 the average retail
price per unit was $14.93 per month com-
pared to an industry average of $13.27. De-
spite intense competition, National had been
able to increase prices to its existing customers in all of its markets each year without
significant customer disconnections.

Todd Clayton wondered what additional
information he should include in his audit.
He thought about applying for a job with
National to see what he could learn about
the firm's recruiting and selection practices
and skills. He had been told that he could
contact Marion Martin, the firm's public relations officer, who was National's liaison
with International Telecommunications.

**National Pagers unit distribution**

| Channels | 1994 | 1995 | 1996 | 1997 | 1998 |
|---|---|---|---|---|---|
| Direct | 145,448 | 182,468 | 213,139 | 135,285 | 308,803 |
| Resellers | 16,152 | 24,882 | 46,786 | 87,023 | 152,097 |
| Total | 161,600 | 207,350 | 259,925 | 322,308 | 460,900 |

Todd thought about talking with some of National's salespeople. He wondered what could be learned if he should enter the process to become one of National's customers. And what about National's customers? Should he talk to some of them? Todd knew that he needed more information, but he was uncertain of what it was and how to get it.

**Questions**

1. Are there any ethical problems involved in what Todd was thinking about doing?

2. What evidence does Todd now have of National Paging, Inc.'s, sales force competence?

3. What else would Mr. Newman want to know about National's sales operations?

---

*Case A-3*

## HANOVER-BATES CHEMICAL CORPORATION*
### Evaluating district performance

James Sprague, newly appointed northeast district sales manager for Hanover-Bates Chemical Corporation, leaned back in his chair as the door to his office slammed shut. "Great beginning," he thought. "Three days in my new job and the district's most experienced sales representative is threatening to quit."

On the previous night, James Sprague, Hank Carver (the district's most experienced sales representative), and John Follett, another senior member of the district sales staff, had met for dinner at Jim's suggestion. During dinner, Jim had mentioned that one of his top priorities would be to conduct a sales and profit analysis of the district's business in order to identify opportunities to improve the district's performance. Jim had stated that he was confident that the analysis would indicate opportunities to reallocate district sales efforts in a manner that would increase profits. As Jim had indicated during the conversation, "My experience in analyzing district sales performance data for the national sales manager has convinced me that any

district's allocation of sales effort to products and customer categories can be improved." Both Carver and Follett had nodded as Jim discussed his plans.

Hank Carver was waiting when Jim arrived at the district sales office the next morning. It soon became apparent that Carver was very upset by what he perceived as Jim's criticism of how he and the other district sales representatives were doing their jobs—and more particularly, how they were allocating their time in terms of customers and products. As he concluded his heated comments, Carver had said:

> This company has made it darned clear that 34 years of experience don't count for anything . . . and now someone with not much more than two years of selling experience and two years of pushing paper for the national sales manager at corporate headquarters tells me I'm not doing my job . . . Maybe it's time for me to look for a new job . . . and since Trumbull Chemical (Hanover-Bates's major competitor) is hiring, maybe that's where I should start looking . . . and I'm not the only one who feels this way.

---

*This case was prepared by Prof. Robert W. Witt of The University of Texas, Austin. Reproduced by permission.

As Jim reflected on the scene that had just occurred, he wondered what he should do. It had been made clear to him when he had been promoted to manager of the northeast sales district that one of his top priorities should be improvement of the district's performance. As the national sales manager had said, "The northeast sales district may rank third in dollar sales but it's our worst district in terms of profit performance."

Prior to assuming his new position, Jim had assembled the data presented in Exhibits 1 through 7 to assist him in his work. The data had been compiled from records maintained in the national sales manager's office. Although he believed that the data would provide a sound basis for a preliminary analysis of district performance, Jim had recognized that additional data would probably have to be collected when he arrived in the northeast district (District 3). To provide himself with a frame of reference, Jim had also requested data on the north-central sales district (District 7). This district was generally considered to be one of the best, if not the best, in the company. Furthermore, the north-central district sales manager, who was only three years older than Jim, was highly regarded by the national sales manager.

■ **EXHIBIT 1**      **Summary income statements (thousands), 1992 to 1996**

|  | 1992 | 1993 | 1994 | 1995 | 1996 |
|---|---|---|---|---|---|
| Sales | $39,780 | $43,420 | $38,120 | $43,960 | $47,780 |
| Production expenses | 23,868 | 26,994 | 24,396 | 27,224 | 29,126 |
| Gross profit | 15,912 | 16,426 | 13,724 | 16,736 | 18,654 |
| Administrative expenses | 5,212 | 5,774 | 5,584 | 5,850 | 6,212 |
| Selling expenses | 4,048 | 4,482 | 4,268 | 4,548 | 4,798 |
| Pretax profit | 6,652 | 6,170 | 3,872 | 6,338 | 7,644 |
| Taxes | 3,024 | 2,776 | 1,580 | 2,852 | 3,436 |
| New profit | $ 3,628 | $ 3,394 | $ 2,292 | $ 3,486 | $ 4,208 |

■ **EXHIBIT 2**      **District sales and gross profit quota performance (thousands), 1996**

| District | Number of Sales Reps | Sales Quota | Sales Actual | Gross Profit Quota* | Gross Profit Actual |
|---|---|---|---|---|---|
| 1 | 7 | $ 7,661 | $ 7,812 | $ 3,104 | $ 3,178 |
| 2 | 6 | 7,500 | 7,480 | 3,000 | 3,058 |
| 3 | 6 | 7,300 | 6,812 | 2,920 | 2,478 |
| 4 | 6 | 6,740 | 6,636 | 2,696 | 2,590 |
| 5 | 5 | 6,600 | 6,420 | 2,620 | 2,372 |
| 6 | 5 | 6,240 | 6,410 | 2,504 | 2,358 |
| 7 | 5 | 5,440 | 6,210 | 2,176 | 2,260 |
|  |  | $47,600 | $47,780 | $19,040 | $18,654 |

*District gross profit quotas were developed by the national sales manager in consultation with the district managers and took into account price competition in the respective districts.

**■ EXHIBIT 3      District selling expenses, 1996**

| District | Sales Rep Salaries* | Sales Rep Commissions | Sales Rep Expenses | District Office | District Manager's Salary | District Manager's Expenses | Sales Support | Total Selling Expenses |
|---|---|---|---|---|---|---|---|---|
| 1 | $354,200 | $38,852 | $112,560 | $42,300 | $67,000 | $22,920 | $139,000 | $ 776,832 |
| 2 | 286,440 | 37,400 | 101,520 | 42,624 | 68,000 | 24,068 | 142,640 | 702,692 |
| 3 | 314,760 | 34,060 | 108,872 | 44,246 | 70,000† | 24,764 | 140,000 | 736,722 |
| 4 | 300,960 | 33,180 | 98,208 | 44,008 | 65,000 | 22,010 | 132,940 | 696,306 |
| 5 | 251,900 | 32,100 | 85,440 | 42,230 | 66,000 | 22,246 | 153,200 | 653,116 |
| 6 | 249,700 | 32,530 | 83,040 | 41,984 | 67,000 | 22,856 | 134,200 | 631,310 |
| 7 | 229,700 | 35,060 | 89,400 | 44,970 | 63,000 | 23,286 | 117,500 | 602,916 |
| | | | | | | | | $4,797,830 |

*Includes cost of fringe benefit program, which was 10% of base salary.
†Salary of Jim Sprague's predecessor.

■ **EXHIBIT 4**   **District contribution to corporate administrative expense and profit, 1996**

| District | Sales (thousands) | Gross Profit (thousands) | Selling Expenses | Contribution |
|---|---|---|---|---|
| 1 | $ 7,812 | $ 3,178 | $ 776,832 | $ 2,401,168 |
| 2 | 7,480 | 3,058 | 702,692 | 2,355,308 |
| 3 | 6,812 | 2,478 | 737,058 | 1,740,942 |
| 4 | 6,636 | 2,590 | 696,306 | 1,893,694 |
| 5 | 6,420 | 2,372 | 653,116 | 1,718,884 |
| 6 | 6,410 | 2,358 | 630,752 | 1,727,248 |
| 7 | 6,210 | 2,620 | 600,516 | 2,019,484 |
| | $47,780 | $18,654 | $4,797,272 | $13,856,648 |

■ **EXHIBIT 5**   **District sales and gross profit performance by account category, 1996**

| District | A | B | C | Total |
|---|---|---|---|---|
| | Sales by Account Category (thousands) | | | |
| Northeast | $1,830 | $3,362 | $1,620 | $6,812 |
| North-central | 1,502 | 3,404 | 1,304 | 6,210 |
| | Gross Profit by Account Category (thousands) | | | |
| Northeast | $712 | $1,246 | $520 | $2,478 |
| North-central | 660 | 1,450 | 510 | 2,620 |

■ **EXHIBIT 6**   **Potential accounts, active accounts, and account call coverage, 1996**

| District | Potential Accounts | | | Active Accounts | | | Account Coverage (total calls) | | |
|---|---|---|---|---|---|---|---|---|---|
| | A | B | C | A | B | C | A | B | C |
| Northeast | 90 | 381 | 635 | 53 | 210 | 313 | 1,297 | 3,051 | 2,118 |
| North-central | 60 | 286 | 499 | 42 | 182 | 216 | 1,030 | 2,618 | 1,299 |

## The company and the industry

The Hanover-Bates Chemical Corporation was a leading producer of processing chemicals for the chemical plating industry. The company's production process was, in essence, a mixing operation. Chemicals purchased from a broad range of suppliers were mixed according to a variety of user-based formulas. Company sales in 1996 had reached a new high of $47,780,000, up from $43,780,000 in 1995. Net pretax profit in 1996 had been $7,644,000, up from

$6,338,000 in 1995. Hanover-Bates had a strong balance sheet and the company enjoyed a favorable price-earnings ratio on its stock, which was traded on the over-the-counter market.

Although Hanover-Bates did not produce commodity-type chemicals (e.g., sulfuric acid), industry customers tended to perceive minimal quality differences among the products produced by Hanover-Bates and its competitors. Given the lack of a variation in product quality and the industrywide practice of limited advertising expenditures, field sales efforts were of major importance in the marketing programs of all firms in the industry.

Hanover-Bates's market consisted of several thousand job shop and captive (i.e., in-house) plating operations. Chemical platers process a wide variety of materials including industrial fasteners (e.g., screws, rivets, bolts, washers), industrial components (e.g., clamps, casings, couplings), and miscellaneous items (e.g., umbrella frames, eyelets, decorative items). The chemical plating process involves the electrolytic application of metallic coatings such as zinc, cadmium, nickel, and brass.

Regardless of the degree of plating precision involved, quality control is of critical concern to all chemical platers. Extensive variation in the condition of materials received for plating requires a high level of service from the firms supplying chemicals to platers. This service is normally provided by the sales representatives of the firm(s) which supply the plater with processing chemicals.

Hanover-Bates and the majority of the firms in its industry produced the same line of basic processing chemicals for the chemical plating industry. The line consisted of a trisodium phosphate cleaner (SPX), anisic aldehyde brightening agents for zinc plating (ZBX), cadmium plating (CBX), and nickel plating (NBX), a protective postplating chromate dip (CHX), and a protective burnishing compound (BUX). The company's product line is detailed in Exhibit 7.

### Company sales organization

The sales organization consisted of 40 sales representatives operating in seven sales districts. Sales representatives' salaries ranged from $28,000 to $48,000 with fringe-benefit costs amounting to an additional 10 percent of salary. In addition to their salaries, Hanover-Bates's representatives received commissions of 0.5 percent of their dollar sales volume on all sales up to their sales quotas. The commission on sales in excess of quota was 1 percent.

■ **EXHIBIT 7**       **Product-line data**

| Container Product | Size | List Price | Gross Margin | Sales (000) |
|---|---|---|---|---|
| SPX | 400 lb drum | $160 | $56 | $7,128 |
| ZBX | 50 lb drum | 152 | 68 | 8,244 |
| CBX | 50 lb drum | 152 | 68 | 7,576 |
| NBX | 50 lb drum | 160 | 70 | 9,060 |
| CHX | 100 lb drum | 440 | 180 | 8,820 |
| BUX | 400 lb drum | 240 | 88 | 6,952 |

In 1994, the national sales manager of Hanover-Bates had developed a sales program based on selling the full line of Hanover-Bates products. Anticipated benefits included the following: (1) sales volume per account would be greater and selling costs as a percentage of sales would decrease; (2) a Hanover-Bates sales representative could justify spending more time with such an account, thus becoming more knowledgeable about the account's business and better able to provide technical assistance and identify selling opportunities; (3) full-line sales would strengthen Hanover-Bates's competitive position by reducing the likelihood of account loss to other plating chemical suppliers (a problem that existed in multiple-supplier situations).

The national sales manager's 1994 sales program had also included the following account call frequency guidelines: A accounts (major accounts generating $24,000 or more in yearly sales)—two calls per month; B accounts (medium-sized accounts generating $12,000 to $23,999 in yearly sales)—one call per month; C accounts (small accounts generating less than $12,000 yearly in sales)—one call every two months. The account call frequency guidelines were developed by the national sales manager after discussions with the district managers. The national sales manager had been concerned about the optimum allocation of sales efforts to accounts and felt that the guidelines would increase the efficiency of the company's sales force, although not all of the district sales managers agreed with this conclusion.

It was common knowledge in Hanover-Bates's corporate sales office that Jim Sprague's predecessor as northeast district sales manager had not been one of the company's better district sales managers. His attitude toward the sales plans and programs of the national sales manager had been one of reluctant compliance rather than acceptance and support. When the national sales manager succeeded in persuading Jim Sprague's predecessor to take early retirement, he had been faced with the lack of an available qualified replacement.

Although most of the sales representatives had assumed Hank Carver would get the district manager's job, he had been passed over in part because he would be 65 in three years. The national sales manager had not wanted to face the same replacement problem again in three years and had wanted someone in the position who would be more likely to be responsive to the company's sales plans and policies. The appointment of Jim Sprague as district manager had caused considerable talk, not only in the district but also at corporate headquarters. In fact, the national sales manager had warned Jim that "a lot of people are expecting you to fall on your face. They don't think you have the experience to handle the job, in particular, and to manage and motivate a group of sales representatives most of whom are considerably older and more experienced than you." The national sales manager had concluded by saying, "I think you can handle the job, Jim. I think you can manage those sales reps and improve the district's profit performance, and I'm depending on you to do both."

*Questions:*

1. Evaluate the performance of the northeast district in comparison with the other Hanover-Bates sales districts.

2. What are the weak spots in the northeast district's performance?

3. What should management do to improve areas of poor performance in the northeast district?

*Case A-4*

## CHEMGROW, INC.*

### Evaluating sales performance

By September 18, 1998, Mr. John Kee, vice president of agricultural sales, will be presenting his newly conceived Dealer Marketing Plan and Evaluation Program to the president of ChemGrow, Inc., Mr. William Joseph.

### Company history

ChemGrow is one of the largest fertilizer manufacturers in the world. It is basic in phosphate rock and manufactures phosphoric acid, anhydrous ammonia, and other mixed fertilizer products. In the past 10 years, the company's production characteristics have shifted dramatically from a manufacturer of specialized NPK (nitrogen, phosphates, and potassium) materials in over 40 plants to the production of high-analysis fertilizers in a few very large capacity installations.

ChemGrow's major production facilities are in Florida, Louisiana, and Arkansas. They are located on or close to river or ocean transportation, and can therefore take advantage of low-cost barge transportation to large terminal points located to supply the market at the lowest possible cost (Exhibit 1).

During late 1995 and 1996, ChemGrow evaluated future fertilizer demand and found the need to develop a large-scale expansion program. The $250 million project included a new 425,000-ton-a-year anhydrous ammonia plant at Verdigris, Oklahoma (cost: $35 million), expansion of the phosphate rock mining facilities that it bought from Southern Gas at South Pierce,

Florida, and construction of a 400,000-ton phosphoric acid plant near Donaldsonville, Louisiana, as well as sulfuric acid, nitric acid, urea, and granulation facilities, and several formulating facilities.

Much of the ammonia made at Verdigris will start flowing early next year through ChemGrow's own 4,900-mile pipeline that runs from Oklahoma up through the fertilizer-hungry Midwest farm states and into North Dakota, Minnesota, and Ohio. ChemGrow's present expansion activities alone should boost its fertilizer output 50 percent over the 3.7 million tons of products it made in 1996.

The key to capacity growth for ChemGrow has been its control of its raw materials. ChemGrow has enough phosphate rock reserves to maintain its present phosphate production levels for 70 years. For the nitrogen side of its business, ChemGrow signed early last year a 17-year natural gas contract with Oklahoma Natural Gas Company. ChemGrow's expansion program also includes exploration for natural gas in seven offshore Texas and Louisiana tracts.

ChemGrow has been very optimistic about fertilizer growth, but there have been critics of the company—mostly competitors—who believe that ChemGrow's fertilizer expansion is atrociously ill-timed. They feel that after last year's boom, when buyers feared shortages and seized all the fertilizer they could find, the industry may now be on the verge of a worldwide glut, perhaps comparable to the agonizing oversupply of 1972–1974.

### Management team

At the headquarters of ChemGrow, Inc., in Tulsa, Oklahoma, Mr. William Joseph has

---

*This case was developed by William D. Perreault, Jr., of the University of North Carolina at Chapel Hill and Kevin McNeilly of Miami University. This case is copyrighted by the authors and is reprinted here with their permission.

■ **EXHIBIT 1**

**ChemGrow's current major production facilities**

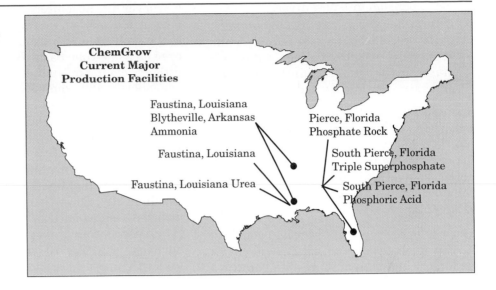

ChemGrow
Current Major
Production Facilities

Faustina, Louisiana
Blytheville, Arkansas
Ammonia

Pierce, Florida
Phosphate Rock

Faustina, Louisiana

South Pierce, Florida
Triple Superphosphate

Faustina, Louisiana Urea

South Pierce, Florida
Phosphoric Acid

built a winning managerial combination for an industrial empire. Mr. Joseph believes that when it comes to executives, the best are the cheapest for the company in the long run and that you don't make money by being a scrooge.

In selecting top people, he has looked for such qualities as initiative and drive; then he provides his people with the tools with which to work and with an incentive. Money is an incentive, but Mr. Joseph also believes they must have a pride in the company. The job of a chief executive includes creating the atmosphere that these people can operate in successfully. Mr. Joseph has built on the managerial philosophy that in order to succeed in any venture, you don't need a team of people, you need the right man to head up the effort and then he'll develop his own team.

Mr. John Kee, one of Mr. Joseph's leaders, is now in the process of reevaluating and developing his own marketing team. His first step was to define a basic outline for the Dealer Marketing Plan and Evalua-

tion Program. Some of the major aspects of the plan are outlined below:

1. *State ChemGrow's marketing philosophy*—include various statements on channel trade goals, major emphasis products, customer classification and qualifications, and price strategy.

2. *Analyze present position*—use historical sales data, customer/product/territory profiles; define major and minor competition's supply network; describe ChemGrow's strengths and weaknesses compared to each competitor.

3. *Project future environment*—by product tons consumed per acreage, industry projections for product mix, favorable and unfavorable trends, and future competitive programs.

4. *Define marketing regions' goals*—develop goals for product tonnage by account manager for the long and short term; plan strategies to attain these goals by increasing customer growth, increasing the market share in the region

by obtaining new customers, and locating expansion into new areas.

5. *Determine support required to obtain goals*—include manpower requirements, supply and distribution requirements, marketing programs, training programs, and extra services needed.

Mr. Kee felt that the overall basic plan for marketing was specific in terms of the company's primary interests for growth but too general for the region managers to put into action, so another outline was developed for the mechanics of the account manager marketing plan:

1. *Prior to customer call*—outline your territory, locate and identify present customers and their trading area, locate yours and competitor's supply points, and identify prospective areas of concentration for new customers.

2. *Steps to be completed with customers*—complete sales forecast, update sales history for each customer, and complete customer profile with prospective customers.

3. *Steps to summarize territory marketing plans*—prepare product profile for present customers, prepare marketing plan worksheet, and prepare sales volume forecast for the territory.

4. *Your territory plans*—make up six-month time allocation schedule, make up a monthly calendar, prepare first call action plan for prospective customers, and get regional approval and support for plans and needed help.

### Current issues

Mr. Kee is pleased with the marketing plans which he has outlined, but he knows that getting the appropriate information to complete and implement the plans may be a problem. In the past, efforts at sales analysis had always been done on a "crisis" basis; whenever he absolutely needed a certain form of information, an analyst was assigned to the problem and the answers were developed on a one-time basis. But there was still little *systematic* evaluation of the sales data available in the company. Mr. Kee knows that this void needs to be filled if adequate information is to be available for decisions concerning sales effort planning and control.

Mr. Kee's general concern about the present quantitative evaluation program has recently been highlighted by an upcoming deadline. He knows that at the end of the month decisions need to be made involving (1) a special bonus plan for the most productive region, (2) a 10-day vacation to Mexico for the most outstanding salesperson in each region, and (3) a list of "most valuable" customers, who will be invited to participate in a luxury Dealer Council meeting. At the beginning of 1997, when Mr. Kee set up the program which offered these sales promotion incentives, he was intentionally vague about how the customers, salespeople, and regions would be evaluated in arriving at the award decisions. He knows that time is running short and that these evaluations must be made soon. Yet he is also sensitive to the fact that the salespeople and customers alike will be irritated if the award decisions do not appear to be fair. He wants whatever decisions are made to be objective and consistent.

Mr. Kee has expressed to several of his aides his frustration that he is in need of sales analysis information and that once again it must be assembled on a crisis basis. He said in his last staff meeting that he is placing high priority on developing a usable, accessible computerized information system so that problems of this sort do not arise in the future, and so that in the future ongoing sales analysis reports can provide systematic inputs for sales force decision making.

In recent years, all quantitative sales analysis has been done manually under the direction of Mr. Kee's assistant, Richard Evans. Richard never enjoyed these jobs in the past, feeling that he was spending his time on what appeared to be work that was clerical in nature or, worse yet, that could have been done more rapidly, accurately, and completely by computer. This time, however, Richard feels a new sense of intellectual challenge in the job. While he knows that he faces the immediate task of identifying the best performing territory overall, the best salesperson in each territory, and the list of key customers, he also sees that he can have inputs to the design of an integrative sales analysis system. He knows that he can work himself out of this recurring drudgery if he does a good job of figuring out what information is needed and in communicating that need to the computer personnel in the firm. In fact, Mr. Kee has told him that he wants a memorandum from Richard outlining his thoughts on what sales analysis reports they can request starting in the immediate future.

### The available information

In preparing for his assignment, Richard has talked with several others on the sales management staff and he has been sensitized to the fact that his problem is not a simple one. For example, he has been reminded that each salesperson sells three different products and that each product has a different gross margin associated with it. Moreover, the sales department is concerned with its sales (and margin) growth over time, so Richard wants to be certain that he does not take a static view in evaluating performance.

Unfortunately, the information which he would like is not currently assembled in one place. From the accounting department he is able to get good estimates of the gross margin per ton of sales for each of the three major products (ammonia, phosphate, and potash) sold in this division. These gross margin figures are summarized in Exhibit 2.

Richard knows that different salespeople tend to sell these products in different proportions, however. In fact, several months ago this was raised as a concern. Mr. Kee felt that some of the salespeople were selling primarily the products that were easy to sell, rather than a complete product line in general and a profitable mix of products in particular. At that time, Richard had done an analysis on that issue, and it occurs to him that it might be useful for him to check his files for the report he prepared then. With the report in hand, Richard is reminded of what he had done. First, he had tabulated for each salesperson what proportion of his total ton sales were in each of the product lines. The summary table from his report is reproduced here as Exhibit 3. He also remembers that he had found the same information across different customers and during different time

---

■ **EXHIBIT 2**     **Dollar gross margin contribution for each product**

| | Gross Margin | | |
|---|---|---|---|
| **Product** | **1994** | **1995** | **1996** |
| Ammonia | $8 | $14 | $20 |
| Phosphates | 12 | 12 | 12 |
| Potash | 16 | 9 | 5 |

■ **EXHIBIT 3**     **Average Percentage of Total Sales for Each Salesperson**

| Region | Salesperson | Ammonia | Phosphates | Potash |
|---|---|---|---|---|
| Eastern | McFee | 60% | 35% | 5% |
| | Collam | 5 | 20 | 75 |
| | Parks | 80 | 10 | 10 |
| | Dow | 100 | 0 | 0 |
| Central | Thums | 80 | 20 | 0 |
| | Cook | 25 | 50 | 25 |
| | Block | 20 | 30 | 50 |
| | Fowler | 75 | 20 | 5 |
| Northwest | Vans | 70 | 20 | 10 |
| | Schiffman | 65 | 20 | 15 |
| | Lukbore | 80 | 10 | 10 |
| | Wilkie | 20 | 10 | 70 |
| Southwest | Goodie | 5 | 5 | 90 |
| | Stubber | 5 | 15 | 80 |
| | Holden | 0 | 0 | 100 |
| | Macke | 10 | 20 | 70 |

periods. Richard puts that report to the side, but makes a mental note that this information can be helpful to him in his current assignment.

Finally, to get sales information on different customers, Richard goes to the accounting department, where he is told, in a pleasant manner, that right now they are in the middle of an audit and will not be able to respond to his requests until after his immediate deadline. However, G. N. Leshades, the head of the accounting department, suggests that the distribution center may have some of the information he needs. At the distribution department, Richard does in fact find some helpful information: an alphabetical computer printout summarizing the total tons of products shipped to each customer in 1994, 1995, and each quarter of 1996.

Back at his office, Richard's secretary volunteers to reorganize the information on the computer printout and to group the different customers according to the salesperson that sells to them and the region in which they are located. The secretary prepares a different summary table for each region, and gives them to Richard. These are summarized here as Exhibits 4 through 7.

Richard knows that more information would be better, but it is not clear that he would be able to get more complete information, even if he had the time to wait. As he sits down to work on his analysis, he focuses on the immediate evaluations that he needs to have completed by the end of the month, but he also writes down his more general thoughts about what computer-generated reports the sales department will want in the future. In fact, he finds that in organizing some of his current analysis he is developing good formats and specifications for the reports that he will suggest in his memorandum to Mr. Kee.

■ **EXHIBIT 4**       **Sales analysis at the ChemGrow Company: Sales to each customer over time—central region**

| Obs | Salesperson | Customer | Sales 94 | Sales 95 | 1st Qtr. 1996 | 2nd Qtr 1996 | 3rd Qtr 1996 | 4th Qtr 1996 |
|-----|-------------|----------|----------|----------|---------------|--------------|--------------|--------------|
| 1 | Collam | EPF | 6,523 | 4,800 | 2,800 | 3,000 | 2,635 | 2,635 |
| 2 | Collam | FEV | 3,010 | 4,550 | 4,740 | 10,000 | 0 | 0 |
| 3 | Collam | FSC | 1,505 | 4,100 | 3,685 | 5,000 | 3,025 | 3,030 |
| 4 | Collam | HFC | 3,261 | 4,350 | 3,000 | 3,000 | 633 | 0 |
| 5 | Collam | M | 8,028 | 13,000 | 5,000 | 15,000 | 3,000 | 584 |
| 6 | Collam | PI | 2,760 | 4,650 | 0 | 2,948 | 0 | 0 |
| 7 | Dow | CSS | 517 | 2,165 | 1,000 | 2,000 | 500 | 0 |
| 8 | Dow | FSC | 3,430 | 5,065 | 1,500 | 1,500 | 0 | 0 |
| 9 | Dow | FSI | 10,756 | 8,400 | 1,050 | 1,000 | 1,000 | 1,000 |
| 10 | Dow | OSS | 7,097 | 5,470 | 800 | 1,200 | 950 | 900 |
| 11 | McFee | CFS | 1,395 | 2,490 | 950 | 1,000 | 723 | 0 |
| 12 | McFee | EGS | 4,161 | 6,410 | 500 | 4,500 | 1,500 | 925 |
| 13 | McFee | FCS | 2,963 | 3,360 | 1,485 | 1,485 | 1,485 | 1,485 |
| 14 | McFee | LAS | 15,694 | 9,030 | 2,500 | 1,500 | 1,500 | 34 |
| 15 | McFee | OI | 10,076 | 7,500 | 1,785 | 1,783 | 1,780 | 1,780 |
| 16 | Parks | JCS | 427 | 2,800 | 500 | 500 | 500 | 35 |
| 17 | Parks | LBC | 1,373 | 7,120 | 1,605 | 2,000 | 500 | 500 |
| 18 | Parks | MFS | 5,628 | 4,395 | 900 | 1,200 | 800 | 170 |
| 19 | Parks | PFF | 12,409 | 0 | 3,000 | 10,000 | 415 | 400 |
| 20 | Parks | SFM | 193 | 3,350 | 0 | 1,535 | 0 | 0 |
| 21 | Parks | VT | 2,878 | 5,700 | 1,640 | 1,500 | 1,500 | 1,500 |
| 22 | Parks | WT | 3,663 | 6,600 | 0 | 0 | 0 | 0 |

■ **EXHIBIT 5** **Sales analysis at the ChemGrow Company: Sales to each customer over time—eastern region**

| Obs | Salesperson | Customer | Sales 94 | Sales 95 | 1st Qtr 1996 | 2nd Qtr 1996 | 3rd Qtr 1996 | 4th Qtr 1996 |
|-----|-------------|----------|----------|----------|--------------|--------------|--------------|--------------|
| 23 | Block | CR | 8,650 | 2,940 | 600 | 700 | 700 | 0 |
| 24 | Block | LFS | 17,350 | 7,549 | 200 | 1,400 | 1,050 | 350 |
| 25 | Block | LSF | 8,750 | 2,526 | 1,920 | 400 | 100 | 80 |
| 26 | Block | TCF | 5,100 | 1,623 | 0 | 0 | 0 | 0 |
| 27 | Block | WDB | 11,400 | 9,167 | 3,500 | 3,000 | 1,500 | 1,500 |
| 28 | Cook | BFH | 2,711 | 3,110 | 1,000 | 1,500 | 1,070 | 1,000 |
| 29 | Cook | FFA | 2,575 | 3,730 | 200 | 4,000 | 1,000 | 284 |
| 30 | Cook | HD | 3,170 | 3,465 | 1,500 | 2,700 | 2,070 | 1,500 |
| 31 | Cook | JC | 2,145 | 6,450 | 5,000 | 5,280 | 0 | 8,000 |
| 32 | Cook | PF | 1,980 | 1,190 | 0 | 456 | 0 | 0 |
| 33 | Cook | RBR | 2,880 | 1,275 | 600 | 675 | 510 | 500 |
| 34 | Cook | TLA | 3,375 | 2,935 | 3,000 | 3,855 | 0 | 0 |
| 35 | Fowler | FGC | 8,429 | 7,493 | 1,020 | 1,020 | 0 | 0 |
| 36 | Fowler | GFS | 9,164 | 5,994 | 450 | 4,245 | 1,005 | 800 |
| 37 | Fowler | MSF | 11,284 | 6,368 | 1,535 | 2,480 | 1,085 | 960 |
| 38 | Fowler | RAP | 3,843 | 12,175 | 0 | 1,610 | 0 | 0 |
| 39 | Thums | FWM | 1,084 | 2,700 | 1,260 | 2,120 | 1,000 | 300 |
| 40 | Thums | WW | 3,458 | 3,100 | 300 | 4,000 | 0 | 1,004 |
| 41 | Thums | WWN | 3,709 | 3,400 | 1,500 | 1,500 | 1,420 | 1,408 |
| 42 | Thums | YF | 15,315 | 8,660 | 4,500 | 9,000 | 1,200 | 588 |

■ **EXHIBIT 6**    **Sales analysis at the ChemGrow Company: Sales to each customer over time—northwest region**

| Obs | Salesperson | Customer | Sales 94 | Sales 95 | 1st Qtr 1996 | 2nd Qtr 1996 | 3rd Qtr 1996 | 4th Qtr 1996 |
|-----|-------------|----------|----------|----------|--------------|--------------|--------------|--------------|
| 43 | Lukbore | BAS | 6,200 | 7,444 | 2,875 | 3,596 | 2,485 | 74 |
| 44 | Lukbore | MVF | 4,800 | 7,603 | 1,650 | 1,550 | 1,550 | 1,710 |
| 45 | Lukbore | SCF | 9,300 | 5,648 | 2,500 | 2,500 | 1,360 | 0 |
| 46 | Lukbore | WFL | 5,500 | 3,555 | 0 | 6,050 | 1,460 | 0 |
| 47 | Sciffman | HF | 11,300 | 6,764 | 3,595 | 3,740 | 2,460 | 605 |
| 48 | Sciffman | JN | 2,100 | 4,194 | 0 | 5,000 | 0 | 380 |
| 49 | Sciffman | LS | 4,200 | 1,044 | 800 | 820 | 840 | 820 |
| 50 | Sciffman | RM | 4,300 | 3,890 | 2,160 | 564 | 2,010 | 66 |
| 51 | Sciffman | VF | 5,500 | 4,747 | 345 | 568 | 327 | 300 |
| 52 | Vans | AGC | 4,600 | 2,200 | 1,550 | 1,550 | 0 | 0 |
| 53 | Vans | CF | 5,900 | 5,400 | 1,875 | 1,875 | 1,875 | 1,875 |
| 54 | Vans | DBI | 2,200 | 2,100 | 1,265 | 864 | 871 | 0 |
| 55 | Vans | ECG | 8,500 | 4,620 | 2,467 | 3,495 | 2,140 | 898 |
| 56 | Vans | OFC | 2,800 | 6,080 | 6,591 | 3,140 | 719 | 100 |
| 57 | Wilkie | ASI | 4,800 | 5,230 | 2,100 | 1,565 | 346 | 1,889 |
| 58 | Wilkie | BG | 1,150 | 1,160 | 3,800 | 3,800 | 4,000 | 3,600 |
| 59 | Wilkie | CF | 4,100 | 3,700 | 0 | 2,600 | 0 | 0 |
| 60 | Wilkie | CI | 4,350 | 15,720 | 4,860 | 10,400 | 5,140 | 0 |
| 61 | Wilkie | F&R | 13,000 | 5,720 | 0 | 2,250 | 0 | 0 |
| 62 | Wilkie | IO | 8,750 | 2,690 | 1,200 | 1,240 | 1,200 | 1,200 |
| 63 | Wilkie | LF | 5,100 | 3,100 | 1,125 | 1,695 | 2,433 | 2,147 |

■ **EXHIBIT A-7** **Sales analysis at the ChemGrow Company: Sales to each customer over time—southwest region**

| Obs | Salesperson | Customer | Sales 94 | Sales 95 | 1st Qtr 1996 | 2nd Qtr 1996 | 3rd Qtr 1996 | 4th Qtr 1996 |
|-----|-------------|----------|----------|----------|--------------|--------------|--------------|--------------|
| 64 | Goodie | BSF | 6,350 | 4,500 | 900 | 700 | 400 | 362 |
| 65 | Goodie | GFF | 6,540 | 8,350 | 2,465 | 1,245 | 1,240 | 2,500 |
| 66 | Goodie | KMA | 0 | 0 | 0 | 904 | 0 | 0 |
| 67 | Goodie | LCS | 3,650 | 3,840 | 1,105 | 1,365 | 750 | 981 |
| 68 | Goodie | PGC | 8,510 | 9,125 | 2,500 | 3,262 | 2,500 | 2,500 |
| 69 | Goodie | RGC | 19,280 | 7,240 | 4,750 | 20,000 | 300 | 671 |
| 70 | Holden | AGS | 2,324 | 2,505 | 1,125 | 3,685 | 1,038 | 662 |
| 71 | Holden | FCS | 3,150 | 5,370 | 0 | 5,500 | 0 | 0 |
| 72 | Holden | GF | 4,195 | 5,190 | 2,531 | 2,530 | 2,400 | 2,664 |
| 73 | Holden | IFS | 5,800 | 3,340 | 4,659 | 3,178 | 993 | 0 |
| 74 | Holden | OFS | 2,811 | 5,935 | 3,418 | 8,650 | 67 | 0 |
| 75 | Macke | CE | 4,600 | 2,505 | 621 | 652 | 262 | 0 |
| 76 | Macke | CF | 3,400 | 8,670 | 12,512 | 3,150 | 1,013 | 200 |
| 77 | Macke | DG | 5,900 | 2,765 | 850 | 855 | 850 | 855 |
| 78 | Macke | FER | 2,200 | 2,495 | 650 | 650 | 610 | 600 |
| 79 | Macke | SCG | 8,500 | 4,620 | 2,350 | 1,240 | 1,175 | 1,180 |
| 80 | Macke | TMN | 2,800 | 3,279 | 0 | 5,525 | 0 | 0 |
| 81 | Stubber | BAC | 4,505 | 4,820 | 1,000 | 1,000 | 1,080 | 1,080 |
| 82 | Stubber | DPC | 2,810 | 2,600 | 1,975 | 1,975 | 0 | 0 |
| 83 | Stubber | GCC | 8,125 | 8,150 | 5,000 | 5,000 | 775 | 0 |
| 84 | Stubber | GSS | 4,015 | 3,050 | 575 | 685 | 834 | 181 |
| 85 | Stubber | HDS | 6,050 | 5,530 | 2,475 | 3,156 | 1,004 | 240 |
| 86 | Stubber | TPS | 8,933 | 6,286 | 365 | 2,010 | 0 | 83 |

*Questions:*

1. What decisions would you make with regard to which is the most productive region, who is the most outstanding salesperson, and who are the most valuable customers?

2. What computer reports should be generated on a regular basis to assist the managers in their evaluations?

*Case A-5*

*Case A-5*

# PEP THREADS, INC. (A)
## Selecting a sales manager

"Your in-basket is overflowing and some of the items require your immediate attention. I've handled everything I could and left only those things that you will have to take care of." Monica Stone, office manager, was addressing her comments to Sally Wood, founder, owner, and general manager of PEP Threads, Inc., who had just returned from a three-day vacation. This company manufactures specialty garments for high school and college support organizations such as cheerleaders, pep squads, and drill teams.

PEP Threads had been formed in 1980 out of Sally's frustrations in trying to attire the 10 cheerleaders for her daughter's high school pep group. Not being able to locate the outfits she wanted, she made them. Her efforts were so well received that she was asked by the parents and administrators of some other high schools to do the same thing for them. Soon Sally found herself in the business of making clothes for high school cheerleaders. As the business grew she kept calling on the members of her family to help out. Her husband took over manufacturing. Mike, the only son, handled all logistical work connected with receiving and shipping goods. Originally Sally had designed all the garments, but in recent years, she had to hire several designer-patternmakers. One of her daughters worked in the field, selling to the southern California territory.

By the summer of 1996, the business had grown so substantially that 78 sales representatives were needed to cover the country for PEP Threads, contacting high school and collegiate pep organizations. The high school market segment across the country is PEP's largest market by far. To date, PEP is the leading supplier in the colleges and universities located within 200 miles of PEP's facilities, but their penetration is not as good in other parts of the country. Sally projects that PEP's growth over the next 10 years will come primarily from college markets. Some parts of the country were not covered; since Sally did not think that the High Plains states such as the Dakotas, Montana, and western Nebraska would have sufficient business to warrant coverage. For example, eastern Nebraska and western Iowa were covered by one rep who was also a woman's basketball coach for a small high school just outside Omaha.

Sally, in addition to her other duties, kept control of the sales organization. She recruited and selected new reps when they were needed, trained them herself, and followed the new reps' progress closely for the first few months. All reps officially reported to her; however, much of their day-to-day correspondence was with Monica in the office. Monica, Sally's administrative assistant and secretary, handled the routine business connected with sales operations.

The reps were paid a 6 percent straight commission on the orders they submitted and they paid their own expenses. Since their workload was highly seasonal, they were permitted to have other jobs as long as these jobs did not interfere with the reps' work for PEP. Each rep was assigned a quota based on the number of high school students in the territory. After the first few months, the reps operated fairly independently.

As PEP's sales volume reached $20 million in 1996, Sally was under pressure from the family to hire a sales manager and stop trying to "do everything." While Mike had been pushing for the sales manager's job, he had made himself "indispensable" in the warehouse by doing a great job managing the firm's logistical problems. "But I want out of that bat cave we call a warehouse. I'm not going to spend my life pushing boxes in and out of the place." Everyone would nod, acceding to Mike's pleas for relief, and then he would be told that they would "work something out soon," but for the time being, he was needed where he was.

As Sally reached for the in-basket on her desk she noted the first letter on top of the pile was from her son, Mike. It was his letter of resignation effective in 30 days. The letter shocked Sally's system. She looked at Monica, who stood nearby. Monica said, "I guess he was serious about wanting to get out of the warehouse."

Sally replied, "OK, that's number one. Let me sleep on it. What's bomb number two?"

### Questions

1. Should Sally hire a sales manager?
2. What should Sally do about Mike's sales management aspirations?

---

*Case A-6*

## PEP THREADS, INC. (B)*
### A possible conflict of interest

In business since 1980, PEP Threads is a leading manufacturer of specialty garments for college and high school support organizations such as cheerleaders, pep squads, and drill teams. It is primarily a family-owned and operated business. Sally Wood is the founder, principal owner, and general manager. Her husband, Jim, is in charge of manufacturing operations and their son, Mike, handles all logistical work connected with receiving and shipping goods.

During the early years, Sally had done most of the selling herself, but as the business grew, she hired sales representatives to call on the support organizations. All of the reps are personally hired by Sally. When PEP has an opening she places an advertisement in the local newspaper for that area. Then she conducts telephone interviews with all of those who respond to the ad and sets up appointments for personal interviews with those who seemed qualified. If she feels that she has found a good candidate for PEP, she first checks the applicant's references; if they are satisfactory, she then extends a job offer.

There are no specific qualifications for the job. Sally feels that the desire to succeed is the most important characteristic and she trusts her instincts in deciding which candidates are highly motivated. Finding salespeople who will stay with the firm for more than a year or two has been difficult over the years. Sally attributes this primarily to the nature of the selling job, which is highly seasonal. Many reps, who hold two jobs to counter the seasonal nature of PEP's sales, often give up their PEP position to pursue the other position full time. Sally acknowledges that recruiting and retaining good reps is a constant challenge.

Currently PEP has 78 sales representatives who cover most of the United States. They are each assigned a quota based on the number of high school students in their territory. They are paid a 6 percent straight commission on all orders they submit and

---

*For additional background on this company, see Case A-5, PEP Threads, Inc. (A).

they pay all of their own expenses. Some of the more experienced reps earn in excess of $50,000, while others earned under $20,000. Any rep whose earnings consistently fall below $10,000 is fired.

The reps receive very little training and supervision. Sally doesn't feel it is necessary. When a new rep is hired he or she spends a week in the home office, learning about PEP's products and procedures. Then Sally spends a week with the new rep, calling on the larger accounts in the territory. After this initial two-week period, the rep is expected to start making calls on his or her own.

Sally had just returned from a badly needed three-day vacation. Monica, her office manager, had given her a stack of correspondence which needed action. Having set aside the first letter to deal with a little later, she noticed that the second letter was from the principal of East Dale High School.

As Sally read the rather lengthy letter, her face became increasingly contorted. It seemed that the company's sales rep covering that school was dating one of the school's teachers, who just happened to be the faculty adviser to the school's large cheering squad. The principal felt that there was a definite conflict of interest involved.

Sally asked Monica, "Do you know anything about this?"

Monica replied, "I called Briggs (the rep) to tell him about the letter and to see what he had to say. He told me that we have been supplying this school for the past five years and only recently has he seen the teacher socially. He thinks the principal himself may be interested in the teacher. He told me he'd handle it."

"Yeah, but I'm not sure I want him to handle it," Sally responded. "Contact Briggs and ask him to come in and see me tomorrow." Sally was not looking forward to tomorrow's meeting. Briggs was one of her best reps and the most fiercely independent.

### Questions

1. Exactly what should Sally do about Briggs, the company's sales rep who is dating one of his customers?

2. How should Sally respond to the principal's letter?

3. Would you suggest any general changes in PEP's sales management policies?

# Careers in Sales Management

This appendix provides some insights into the sales manager's job and some ideas about what to do to be a successful sales manager.

A sales manager of an industrial fasteners manufacturer said:

> I wasn't at all certain that I wanted to be sales manager when it was offered to me. After all, I was making real good money in the field, I liked the freedom and the customer contact. I wasn't all that sure I would like managing, let alone be able to do so. Now, as I look back, I can't understand my reluctance to go into management. Working with these people, building the organization, getting things done—I really get a kick out of it. For instance, take a green kid, turn him into a real producer, and you'll know what accomplishment feels like.

## ◼ THE CHALLENGE

People of ability thrive on challenge. Jobs that do not test their capabilities quickly bore them. A key question to ask about an anticipated career is: "Will it offer sufficient challenge to sustain my interest in doing a continually better job?" A sales manager's job has such challenges.

For example, a consumer products company with $14 million sales volume was foundering. Its 1995 losses exceeded $4 million. The firm hired a proven executive from another consumer products company. His experience was in the brand management side of the business, although he had started his career in sales and was widely known in the industry for his selling skills. He was given control over the firm's 40-rep sales force with the mandate to remake it into a reasonably productive unit. The company's average annual sales per salesperson were $350,000, but it was generally felt that a $600,000 average would be more in line with industry standards.

The new sales manager went into the field to work with each of the reps for one day to evaluate their talents. He found most reps not only lacking sales skills but also lacking the desire and ability to develop them. He spotted 20 people he could use; the others were asked to find other employment. With overhead reduced, he set about molding his new crew into a hard-hitting sales force. They put together a new sales plan, and it worked. As the manager later explained, "I used to think that getting out a new product was a challenge. But it's nothing compared to turning a sick operation into a profitable one while giving 20 people more successful careers. It's the toughest job I've ever had, but it made me grow!"

The sales manager is in the front lines, where performance is easily appraised by peers and superiors. While the abilities or contributions of a bookkeeper, personnel manager, or a design engineer may be difficult to assess, the sales manager's effectiveness is quite evident. Such measurable indexes as sales volume, selling expenses, turnover of the sales force, and percentage of market share are potent arguments either for or against the manager's performance. There is no place to hide.

## ◼ CAREER PATHS IN SALES MANAGEMENT

**Career paths** in sales management vary from company to company as well as from individual to individual within the same company. Different individuals within the same company may take different paths to a top-level executive sales position because they have different professional experiences and education and because they have different preferences.

### Typical Career Paths

Figure B-1 depicts the typical positions that individuals may hold during their careers in sales management. As we noted earlier, the path to the top may vary; most individuals will not serve in all of these positions. Sales careers almost always start with a position in sales.

A sales trainee may progress through several levels of increasing sales responsibility such as **sales representative, senior sales representative,** and possibly **national account manager.**

As discussed in Chapter 1, the entry-level sales management position is often as a **sales supervisor,** providing day-to-day supervision to four or five salespeople. In companies where the team approach to selling has been adopted, the first managerial position would be as a **client team leader.** Also, many companies do not have supervisors; then the first management position is typically **district manager.**

As depicted in Figure B-1 by the shaded boxes, some first-line managers may progress in a straight path through all of the line management positions—**regional sales manager, national sales manager,** and finally **vice president of sales** or **vice president of marketing.** This would be likely in a small or medium-sized company.

In most larger companies, the career paths of most managers include assignments in some staff positions. These staff assignments give individuals the experience they need to manage the entire sales and

■ **FIGURE B-1**

**Typical sales management career paths**

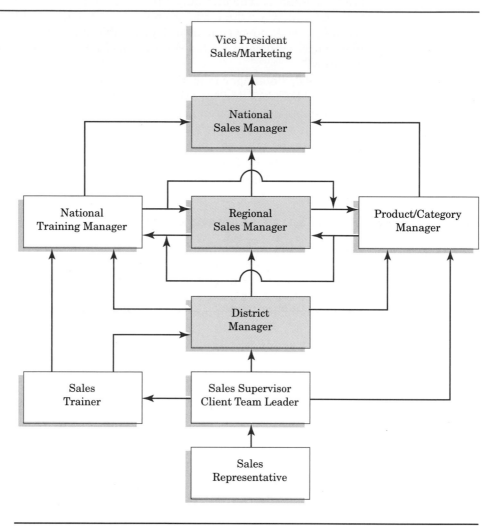

marketing operations. For example, a sales supervisor's next position might be sales trainer. A district manager might move into the position of **national training manager** or a **product** or **category manager,** instead of becoming a **regional manager.** In fact a manager could serve in all three of these positions before moving on to become **national sales manager.**

The following promotion would be into executive management as a **vice president of sales** and/or **marketing.** A survey of Fortune 500 companies indicated that sales and marketing will be the fastest route into upper management at least until 2003.[1]

## Geographic Coverage

The amount of territory the sales manager controls can vary from the whole world to a small city. Prospective sales executives can choose the size of area they prefer. A person who wants to minimize traveling should join an organization whose distribution is limited to a small geographic area. Many such opportunities exist in automobile dealerships, appliance distributorships, business-machine branch organizations, office supply houses, insurance agencies, and local radio, television, and newspaper firms—in general, any retail or wholesale organization that serves a local trading area. Positions with small firms can be as desirable or challenging as those with companies that distribute nationally.

## Geographic Location

Sales management positions are located in every section of the country. Prospective sales executives can determine their living environment by getting a job in the area where they want to live. Of course, this limits their bargaining power and choice of firms. However, most sales management positions are located in larger cities and in the more densely populated areas of the country where corporations have their home offices, branches, and sales offices. This does not suggest that there are no firms with headquarters in small towns. The home offices of Maytag Company, for example, are located in a small town in Iowa.

## Types of Selling Activities

The sales executive can also choose the type of selling to administer. Each type of sales job requires a varying degree of pressure, different personal qualities, and varying efforts. The job of managing a door-to-door sales organization is different from the task of guiding individuals in selling large industrial installations to top executives. The task of managing a group of automobile salesmen is different from that of administering the activities of a manufacturer's sales force.

The sales job in each industry is unique and has its own characteristics and demands. In planning a sales management career, give considerable thought to what you will be happiest selling. Experience indicates that there are great advantages to staying in one industry throughout a sales career. People who stay in the same industry build a valuable base of knowledge and a strong network of contacts.

# ◼ THE REWARDS OF A SALES MANAGEMENT JOB

Reward systems are important in shaping people's behavior. In several direct and many subtle ways, how much people are paid and the compensation methods influence what they do. The rewards awaiting a sales manager are an important consideration in your job choice.

## Direct Monetary Rewards—The Money

According to *Dartnell's 29th Sales Force Compensation Survey,* top sales executives' salaries range from $65,000 to $192,000, with an average of $99,000. The average for a regional sales manager is $85,000 with the highest salaries over $120,000. District sales managers earn an average of $80,000. There is a lot of variability across different-sized companies and industries. In general, smaller companies pay less than larger ones. The electronics industry is relatively high paying, as are health services and office equipment.[2]

## Indirect Monetary Payments

Little is known statistically about the extent of indirect monetary payments for sales managers. These payments include company-paid insurance plans, pension systems, country club memberships, access to company-owned airplanes, and other company-furnished enhancements to a manager's standard of living. However, such indirect payments are important and widely used. At some point in their careers, sales managers may place a high value on deferred compensation, such as stock option plans, pension plans, and insurance policies, which are nontaxable or are tax deferred. A $10,000 country club membership would be worth about $14,000 if it were paid as regular compensation.

These considerations are of particular importance to the sales manager. It is easier to justify to the Internal Revenue Service that the sales manager needs such things as a company-owned airplane or a country club membership than it is to build the same case for the production manager. It is far more likely for the sales executive to be given these benefits than it is for any other executive on the same level in the organization.

## The Life of a Sales Executive

While it is true that each sales manager's job is unique, there are some common elements.

- **Travel.** Some traveling is required for the performance of any sales management job. However, the amount can vary from an occasional convention trip to an extensive amount of field work with the sales branches or with customers. The amount of traveling sales managers do depends somewhat on their attitudes toward traveling. Many enjoy being on the road and seize every opportunity to get out of the office and into the field.

- **Paperwork.** Inherent in modern management is the nuisance called administrative tasks. No one relishes it, but "it goes with the territory," and few people who are lax in handling the paperwork advance very far in management. A manager who neglects the paperwork input to the company's information system places a burden, sometimes a difficult one, on other executives who need the information. What constitutes doing paperwork properly? First, paperwork should be done accurately and completely, not haphazardly. Second, it should be done on time.

- **Conferences and meetings.** Sales managers are involved in many decisions which are made with the input of several people. Often these people meet to discuss the issues at hand. For example, the sales manager might frequently be involved in meetings with the product manager, the design engineers, the marketing manager, the research manager, or vice president of human resources. Sometimes these meetings are face-to-face meetings; sometimes they are teleconference or videoconference calls.

    Sales managers also regularly conduct sales meetings for their salespeople. The purposes of these meetings may vary, but they often include training, new program introduction, or information sharing. A capable administrator learns how to participate effectively in such meetings.

- **Work with people.** If there is one common denominator among sales managers, it is that they must deal with people at all levels. In one day, the sales manager may hold conferences with both the sales force and the board of directors or may contact both top executives and a customer's operating staff.

- **Sales.** Some sales managers continue to sell to certain customers; they may retain key accounts. Others go into the field for important sales. Few sales managers ever get very far away from selling.

**Helping your customers is a very rewarding aspect of the sales job.**

■ **Picking people—talented ones.** We have stressed in this book that the sales manager's most important job is selecting sales personnel. The ability to select individuals who become successful salespeople is critical to the sales manager's own success.

■ **Firefighting.** All sorts of problems continually arise that require immediate attention. A customer calls to voice a complaint; something must be done. Corporate counsel requires a deposition in a lawsuit. A sales rep is injured while skiing and cannot cover the trade for a month. There is no anticipating what is going to happen. However, the sales manager must somehow handle each problem presented.

■ **Market exposure and opportunity.** Since sales managers continually interface with the market and with the buyers in it, they are in an advantageous position to observe and intercept market opportunities. Many entrepreneurs have used sales management as a springboard into their own enterprises. Such opportunities are hidden from the person who is buried in an office or who does not operate in the market.

■ **Above all, they are managers.** Many super salespeople have failed as sales managers because they did not realize that, above all, they were expected to be managers. A manager manages! A manager leads a group of individuals to accomplish its mission. A manager gets and organizes resources and makes things happen. Responsibility is a key concept. The manager is responsible for the productivity of the group—for recruiting, training, and motivating people within the group.

## WHAT IT TAKES TO BE A SUCCESSFUL SALES MANAGER

### Education

Not too many years ago a sales manager needed only successful sales experience to qualify for the job. Today, perusal of the job specifications for a wide range of sales management positions indicates that applicants for these jobs must have college degrees.

### Experience

Sales experience is necessary, but you do not have to be an outstanding sales producer to be promoted into a management position. Nevertheless, you have a brighter future as a sales manager if you have performed successfully in a selling job. Such a background provides several advantages.

First, the sales force will have respect for you. They will know that you have been in the field and recognize the problems they face each day. When you tell them to do something, they will have confidence that you know what you are talking about.

Second, sales experience enables you to be realistic in planning activities and in your supervision and control efforts. You are not likely to expect the impossible of the sales force, but you will be able to recognize a loafer when you see one.

Third, the customer contact provided by selling is valuable for any top policy-making executive. Knowing the problems of the customer is essential in developing sound marketing plans. Having personal acquaintances among the firm's customers is also helpful.

More important than sales experience, however, is managerial experience. To become a high-level sales or marketing executive, you must build a base of experience through several lower levels of management experience. It is through the lower level positions that one learns and demonstrates the requisite leadership and administrative skills necessary for top management positions.

## Leadership Skills

The ability to lead is so important to sales managers that we devoted an entire chapter to the topic earlier in this book. Sales managers must be effective leaders. The only way they can accomplish their goals is through directing the efforts of others. This requires a change of perspective. Salespeople are primarily concerned about their own efforts to sell and service customers. Managers, in contrast, must be focused on developing and coordinating the efforts of others.

Leaders must also have more of a strategic perspective than salespeople. They should understand the strategic mission of the firm and how the sales strategy contributes to the overall objectives of the firm. Finally, as we noted in the chapter on leadership, the most charismatic manager is one who leads by example.

## Administrative Skills

The ability to organize people and activities is a critical dimension of being a successful manager. The best way to learn these skills is to put yourself into positions where you must practice these skills.

For example, a member of the Young Presidents Organization, when questioned about how he had developed his administrative skills, advanced this idea:

> After I got out of college and settled down into my first job, I made it a point to get involved in all sorts of community activities, any group that would take me. Little League, church, neighborhood, you name it and I joined it. I volunteered to do whatever it was that had to be done. I found out that you can learn a great deal about how to get people to do what it is you want them to do—managing them, if you will—in just such activities.

At first I found I was terrible at it. I remember that first year. It was awful. Everything was messed up, nothing flowed right, and I couldn't organize my people. But with experience I learned the ropes. I learned how to organize projects, how to line up things, and how to get things done. I attribute a large part of my success in business to those early years in community activities where I learned to manage people.

That is the way one person developed administrative skills. He learned by doing. He projected himself into situations that required administrative skills and then was perceptive enough to learn them. You can do the same thing while you are still in college by accepting positions of leadership in various campus organizations. Of course you can also seek out such opportunities on the job as well.

The vice president of manufacturing for a large machine tool company used several opportunities on the job to develop administrative skills.

In my first years with the company I seized every opportunity I could to show some management skills. I remember that first year the boss wanted someone to organize the company picnic. I stepped forward and knocked myself out to make sure that was the best-run picnic the company ever had. And it was! The boss never forgot that. For the next ten years he was continually reminding me of the great job I did on that picnic. Then there was the time we had all of the confusion when the workers struck. We were trying to keep the plant open to get out critical orders and run the place on a skeleton staff. I worked round the clock organizing that effort, and I think more than anything else that was responsible for getting me where I am now. The boss was really impressed with how I held things together during that strike.

## Desire

Probably more than anything else, you must *want* to be a successful sales manager if you are to become one. Your desire must be great enough so that you will apply yourself diligently to all the difficult tasks that lie ahead of you. Many otherwise successful salespeople do not become sales managers simply because they have no desire to do so. If you really want to be a sales manager, you probably will have the opportunity at some point in your career.

## YOUR STRATEGIC CAREER PLAN

Throughout this book we have included a section on the role of the chapter topic in the firm's strategic market plan at the beginning of most chapters. Now it is time for you to think strategically. What is your strategic plan for yourself? What are your goals? How do you plan to achieve them? The members of one of the author's classes were asked about their strategic plans. Their puzzled looks disclosed that few of them had given such plans much thought. Guess what the next assignment was!

## The Matter of Goals

It would be folly to suggest that you can now foresee what you will be doing and who you will be at age 50. All evidence clearly shows that fate plays a heavy hand in your career game. Nevertheless, you need goals. You can change goals as you discover new information about yourself and the markets you're dealing in. But you still need ultimate and intermediate goals. Some career specialists suggest that you set goals each year. What do you want to accomplish by this time next year? What do you want to be doing?

One advantage of having goals is that it helps you resist temptations that will lead you into unacceptable situations. For example, assume that you know that you want to end up at age 35 with your own business. Then you might refuse attractive job offers that would provide little opportunity to acquire the skills you need to be your own boss. If one of your goals is to live in the Sun Belt, then you might shun offers from firms whose bases of operation are in the Northeast. Success with such firms might mean living somewhere you don't want to live.

The bottom line is that you should know what you want in life if you want to maximize your chances of getting it.

## What Do You Need to Do to Achieve Your Goals?

We are all imperfect, and our imperfections may block the path to our goals. If you are to achieve your goals, you will have to develop yourself in diverse ways. Identify what you need to learn and what skills you need to acquire to become what you want to be. Then, formulate a plan to remedy your deficiencies. If you see a need for selling skills, go to work for a firm that can give you excellent sales training and sales experience. Think in terms of who knows what you want to know, and then tap that source of knowledge.

Your first few jobs out of school form the base of your credentials for future opportunities. Go where you can acquire the knowledge and skills you'll need to reach your ultimate goals.

## What Is Your Level of Aspiration?

Many of you will want to play in the "Major Leagues"—whatever that may mean to you. It means different things to different people. Others want no part of the fast track. It is best to identify what level of competition you seek early because it is difficult to climb in "class." Coaches wanting to coach in professional football usually do not start out coaching in high schools.

## What Is Your Timetable?

You need to achieve a position by a certain time lest you fall behind your competitors. To a somewhat lesser degree, the same thing is true in business. You can become too old for a job just as you can be too young, at least in the mind of the person making the decision about you.

If you are not making normal progression toward your goals, you need to reassess what you are doing. If your boss likes your work and intends to promote you, you will be given some very tangible evidence of that intention. If nothing good is happening on your job, your firm is sending you a message. Look for tangible rewards.

## Personal Criteria

You need to give considerable thought to your personal criteria for any job you accept. You need answers to such questions as:

- How much must you earn to consider yourself successful?
- Where do you want to live and work?
- What kind of people do you want to work with?
- What kind of lifestyle do you want?
- How much job security do you need?
- How much power do you need?
- What health limitations do you have?
- What family conditions affect your work?

Unless a job meets your personal criteria, you're not likely to be successful in it for long. Get started right! Don't spend years in a job that cannot give you what you ultimately want.

## ◼ A FINAL WORD

One of your authors has been a sales rep and both authors have worked with and socialized with sales reps and their managers for many years. They cannot recall one instance during that time where the person in sales voiced dissatisfaction with his or her career. To the contrary, they have been and remain excited about their careers, their products, and their customers.

## ◼ REFERENCES

1. "Female Execs See Marketing as Fastest Track," *Sales & Marketing Management,* August 1993, p. 10.

2. Christian P. Heide, ed., *Dartnell's 29th Sales Force Compensation Survey* (Chicago: Dartnell Corporation, 1997), pp. 46–48.

# INDEX